MEGA MAN

OFFICIAL COMPLETE WORKS

ロックマン オフィシャルコンプリートワークス

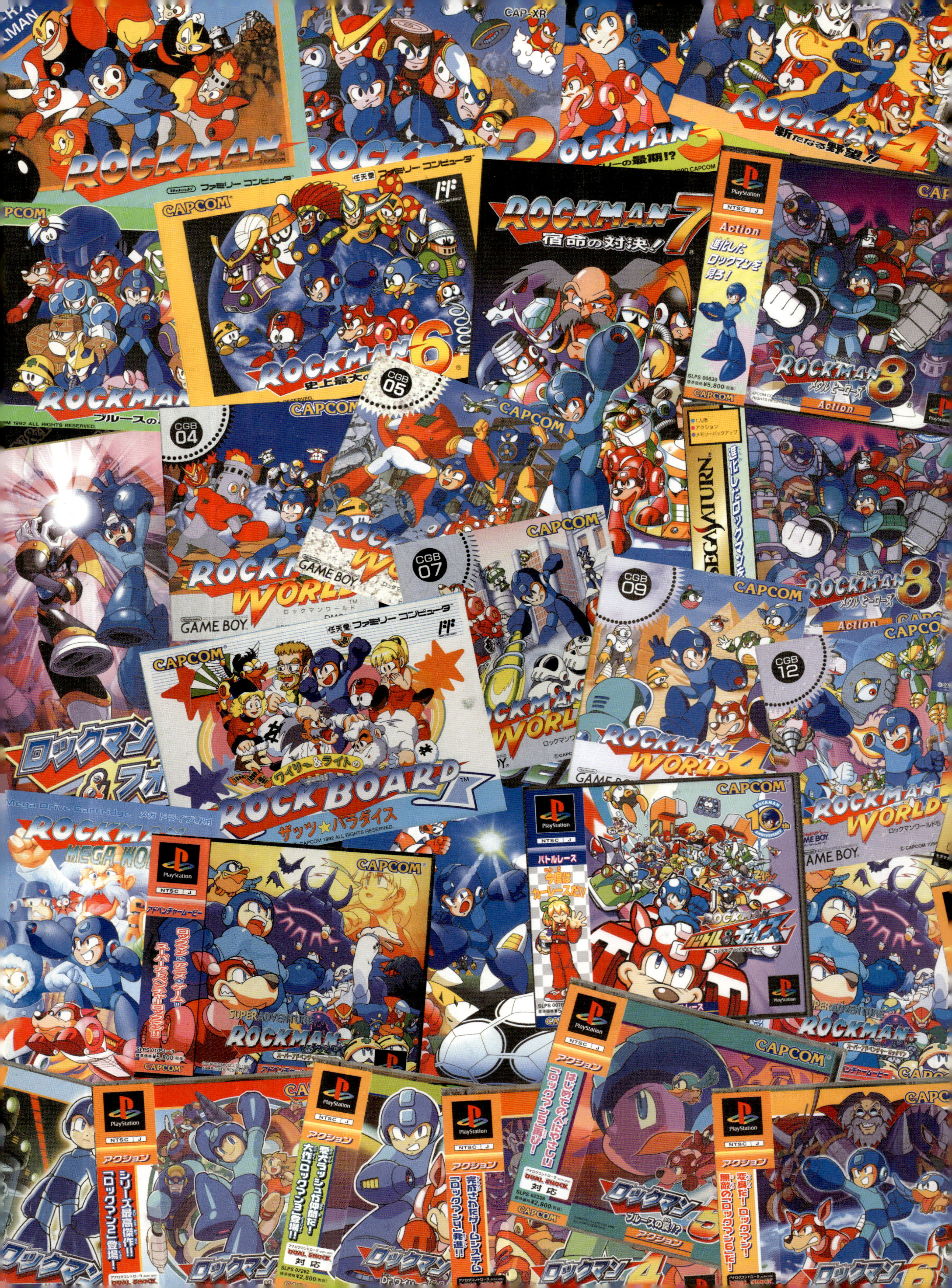

ROCKMAN
ファミリーコンピュータ
CAP-XR
ROCKMAN 4
新たなる野望!!
CAPCOM
ROCKMAN 6
史上最大の
ROCKMAN 7
宿命の対決!
PlayStation
Action
ROCKMAN 8
メタルヒーローズ
CGB 04
CGB 05
CGB 07
CGB 09
CGB 12
GAME BOY
ROCKMAN WORLD
SEGASATURN
ROCKMAN WORLD 4
ワイリー&ライトの
ROCK BOARD
ザッツ★パラダイス
バトルレース
SUPER ADVENTURE ROCKMAN
アクション
ロックマン
ロックマン4
ロックマン6

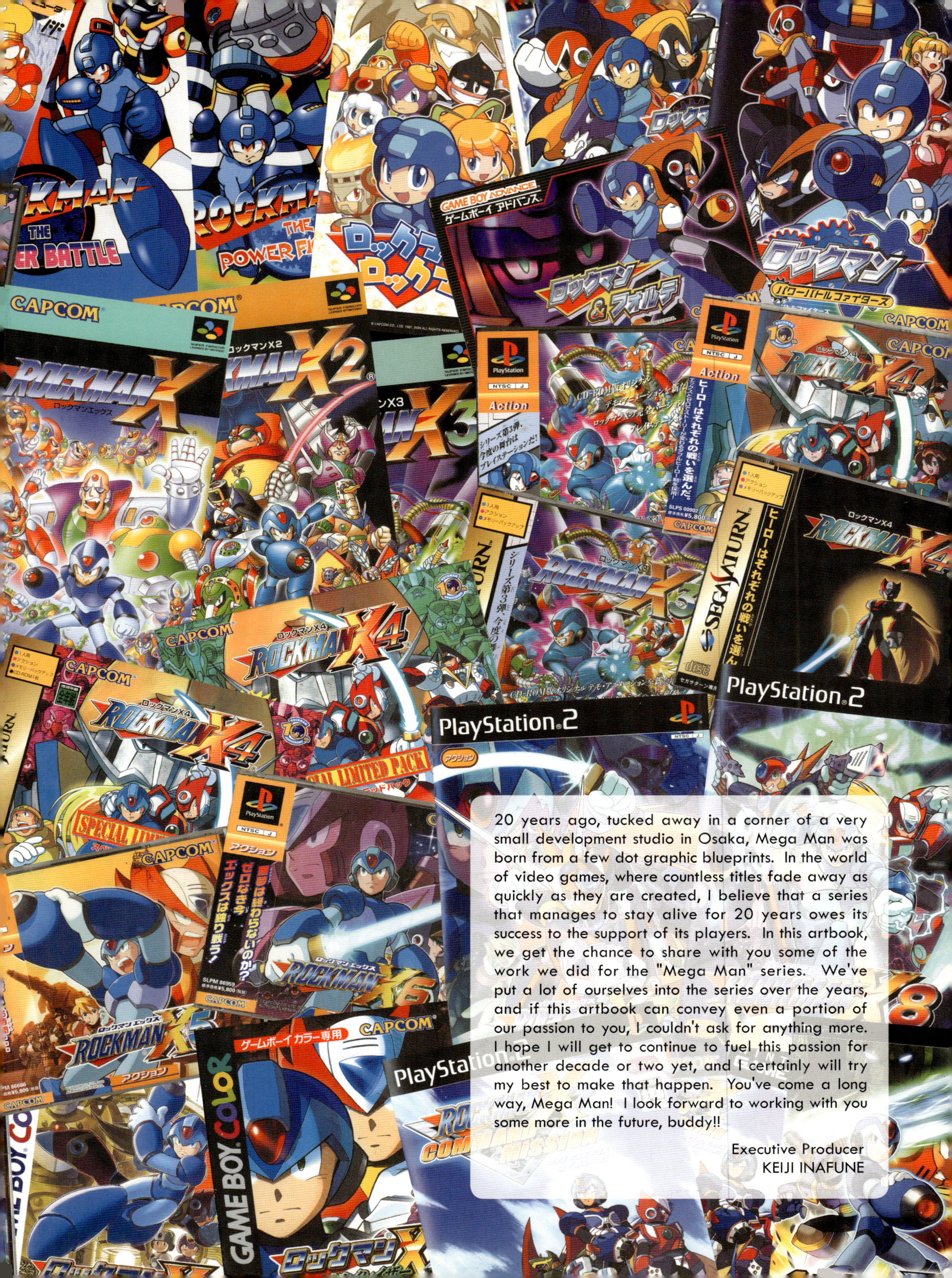

20 years ago, tucked away in a corner of a very small development studio in Osaka, Mega Man was born from a few dot graphic blueprints. In the world of video games, where countless titles fade away as quickly as they are created, I believe that a series that manages to stay alive for 20 years owes its success to the support of its players. In this artbook, we get the chance to share with you some of the work we did for the "Mega Man" series. We've put a lot of ourselves into the series over the years, and if this artbook can convey even a portion of our passion to you, I couldn't ask for anything more. I hope I will get to continue to fuel this passion for another decade or two yet, and I certainly will try my best to make that happen. You've come a long way, Mega Man! I look forward to working with you some more in the future, buddy!!

Executive Producer
KEIJI INAFUNE

MEGA MAN
OFFICIAL COMPLETE WORKS
ロックマン オフィシャルコンプリートワークス

*The various platforms will be denoted by the following abbreviations.

NES = Nintendo Entertainment System	PC = Personal Computer
GB = Game Boy	NGP = NeoGeo Pocket
SG = Sega Genesis	GBA = Game Boy Advance
SNES = Super Nintendo Entertainment System	GBC = Game Boy Color
AC = Arcade	PS2 = PlayStation 2
PS = PlayStation	GC = GameCube
SS = Sega Saturn	PSP = PlayStation Portable

*Please understand that some of the illustrations in this book have been cropped, or are not represented in their original color as a result of the mediums used and/or the passage of time. With the assistance of the Capcom Design Studio, a portion of these old illustrations were digitally reproduced while remaining as faithful to the original works as possible.

*In order to best represent the authenticity of the artwork included in this book, any and all misprints or other unique oddities have not been edited.

*Game logos featured are the original Japanese versions. The official English titles are listed in the blue box usually near the logo. Release dates listed are for the original Japanese games.

MEGA MAN SERIES

A collection of the official illustrations from the original Mega Man series. You'll find Mega Man and the various boss characters in this section, as well as many illustrations of the enemies.

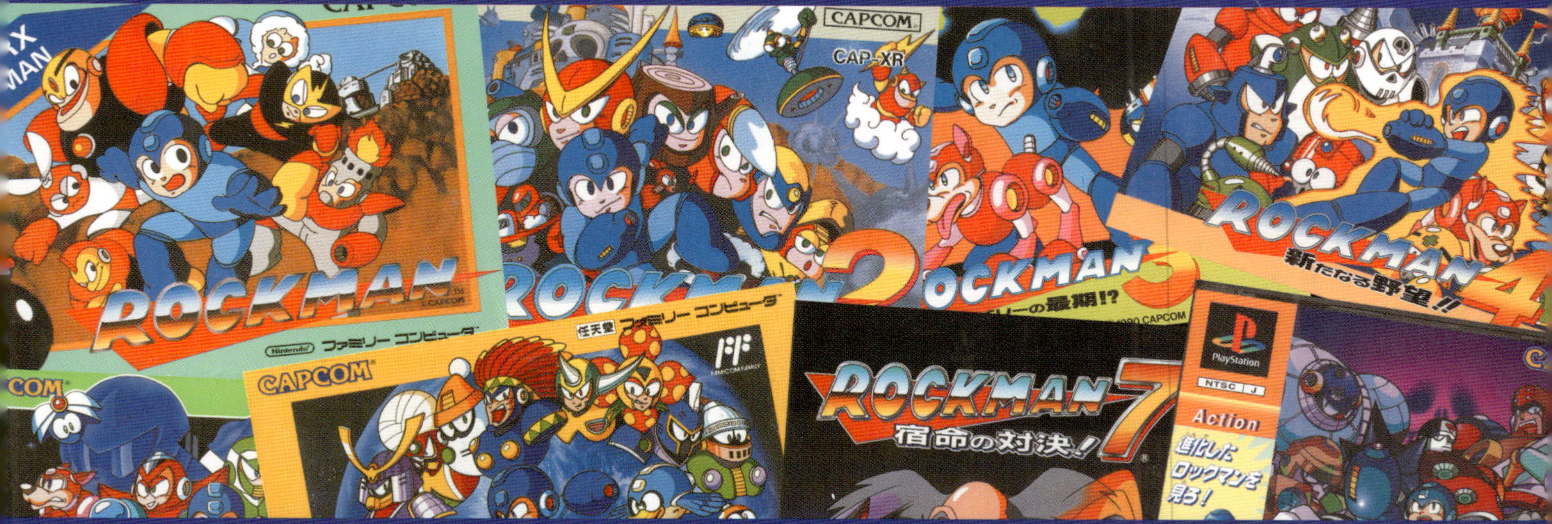

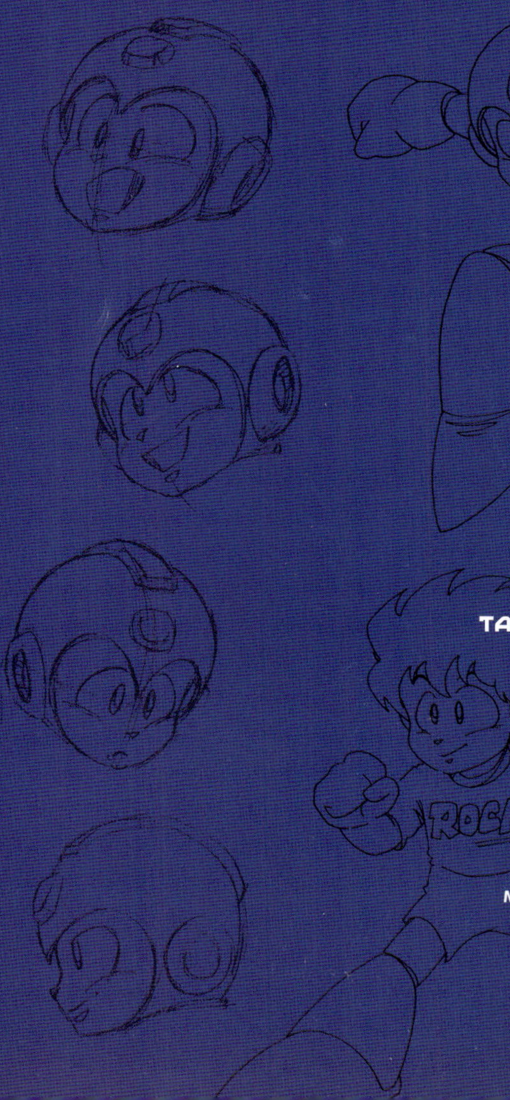

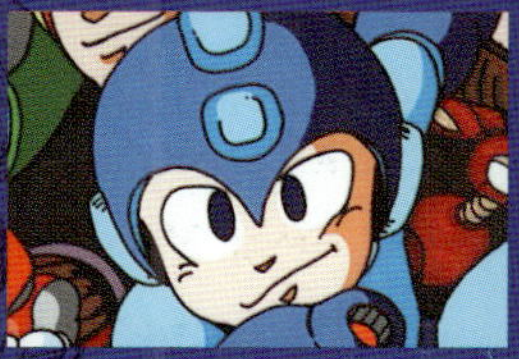

KEIJI INAFUNE
OVERALL SERIES PRODUCER

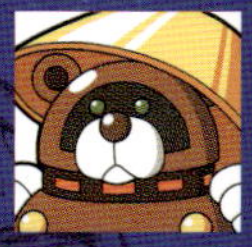

RYUJI HIGURASHI
Relevant Titles
Rockman 1~6 (PS versions)
Rockman Battle & Fighters
Rockman Power Battle Fighters
Mega Man X5/X6
Mega Man X: Command Mission
Mega Man Battle Network series

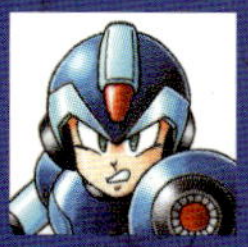

HAYATO KAJI
Relevant Titles
Mega Man 4/5/7/8
Mega Man X1/X3/X4
Mega Man Battle Network

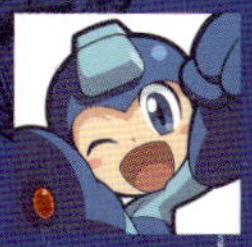

KEISUKE MIZUNO
Relevant Titles
Mega Man: Powered Up
Mega Man: Maverick Hunter X

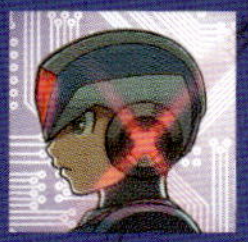

TATSUYA YOSHIKAWA
Relevant Titles
Mega Man 7
Mega Man: Powered Up
Mega Man X1/X3/X7/X8
Mega Man: Maverick Hunter X

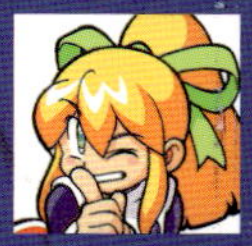

HIDEKI ISHIKAWA
(ILLUSTRATOR)
Relevant Titles
Mega Man 7/8
Mega Man & Bass
Mega Man Battle & Chase
Super Adventure Rockman

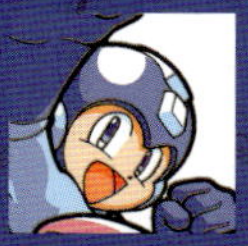

SHINSUKE KOMAKI
Relevant Titles
Mega Man 8
Mega Man Battle & Chase
Mega Man X3/X6
Mega Man Battle Network series
Mega Man Star Force

YOSHIHISA TSUDA
(INTI CREATES CO., LTD.)
Relevant Titles
Mega Man 7
Mega Man X1/X2
Mega Man Zero 1~3

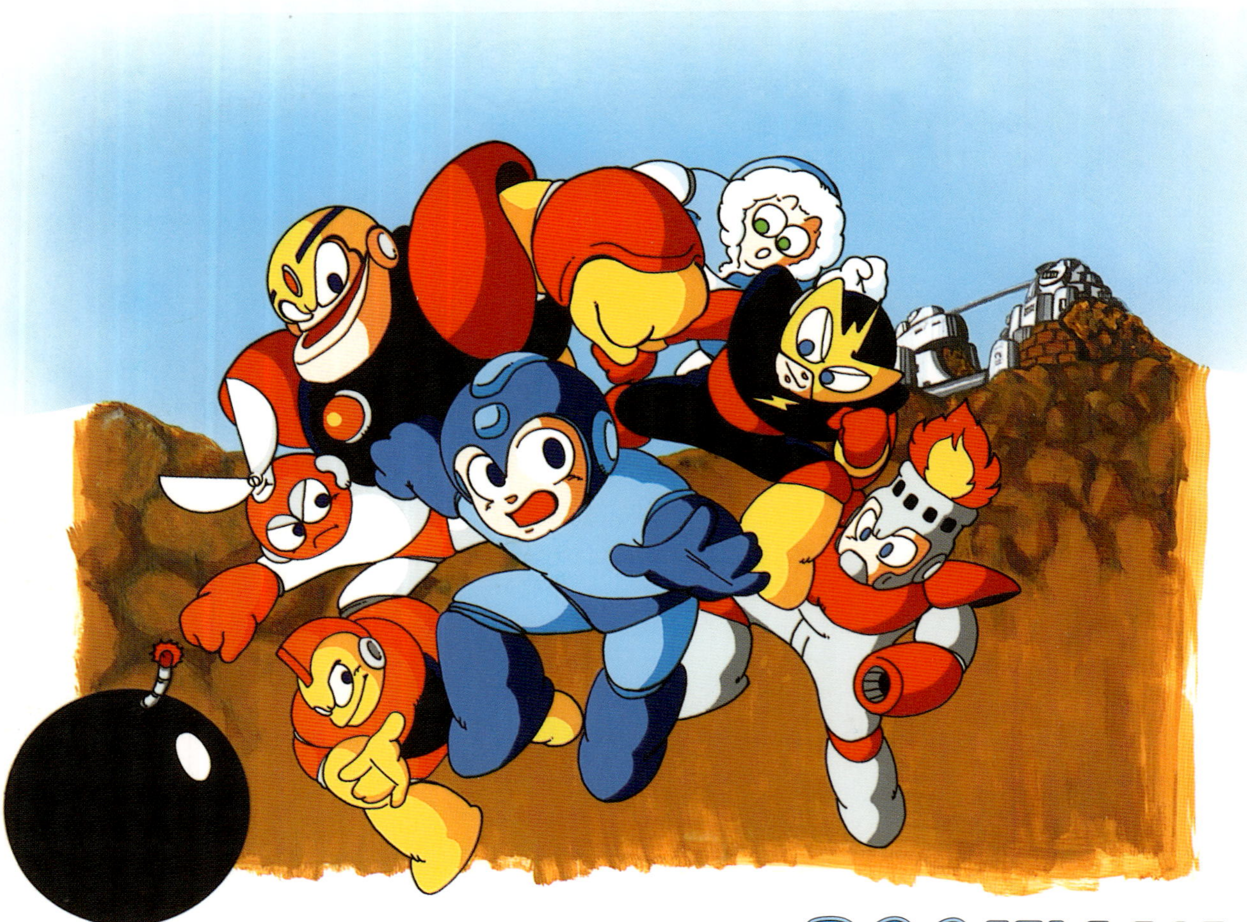

ROCKMAN

Mega Man
NES 12/17/1987

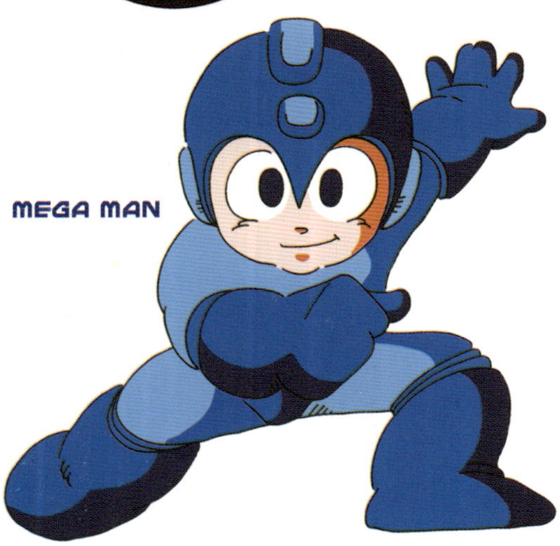

MEGA MAN

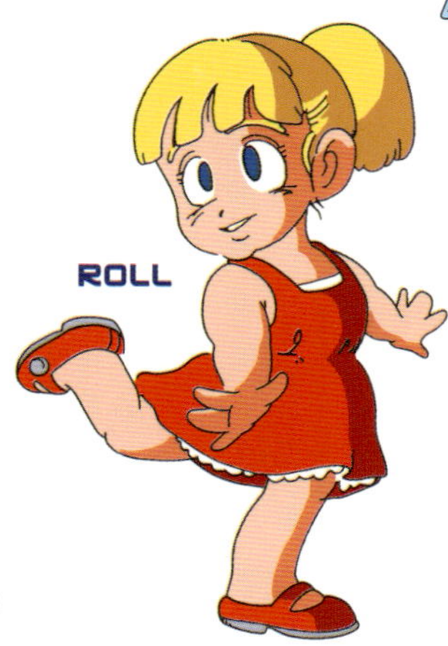

ROLL

In the year 200X, industrial robots suddenly began to run amok. The robots were created by Dr. Light, the leading authority on industrial robots, but were altered by the evil genius Dr. Wily. It was Wily's hope that he would be able to use Light's robots to take over the world. In order to stand against Wily's forces, Dr. Light made the difficult decision to modify Rock, a robot whom he loved like a true son. Rock was thus reborn as Mega Man, the combat-ready robot.

"I knew absolutely nothing about what it takes to create a game when I was thrust into the Mega Man team, in a position where I would be responsible for the characters. In an unfamiliar world surrounded by unknowns, I was finding out all too quickly what would be expected of me. It was really fun, but just insanely hectic. The guy who put this whole project in motion was my mentor. He began his career as a designer, and he was the one who created the original forms of Mega Man, Roll, and Doctor Light as dot graphics. I then took those images and turned them into illustrations, giving them motion and making adjustments to their designs." (Inafune)

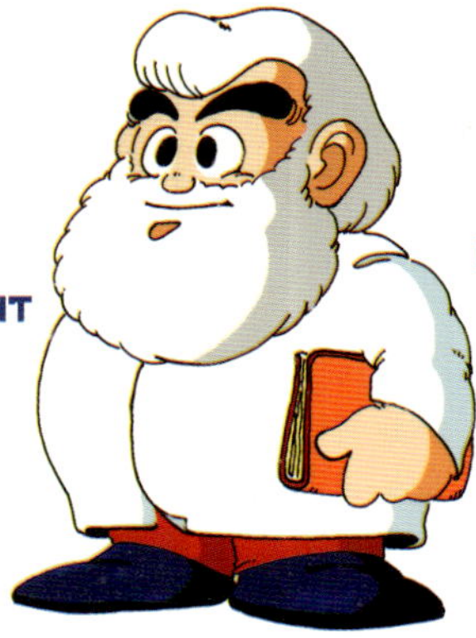

DR. LIGHT

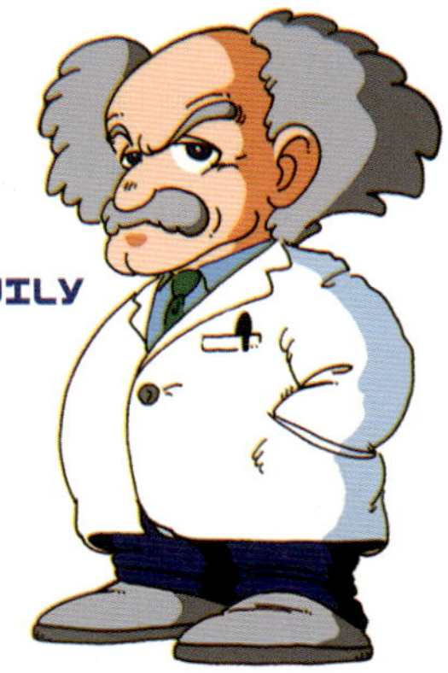

DR. WILY

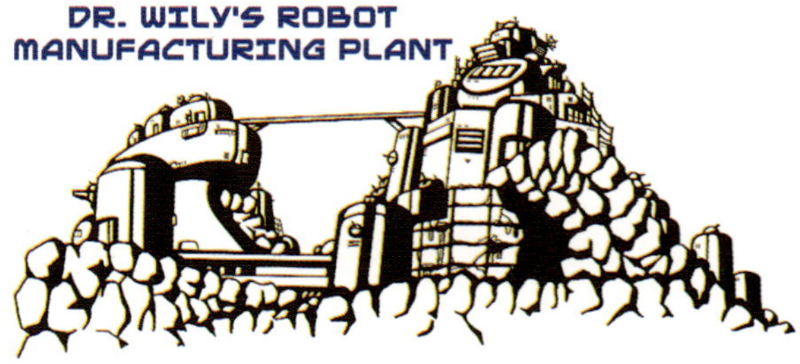

DR. WILY'S ROBOT MANUFACTURING PLANT

"By the time I joined in, Cut Man, Ice Man, Guts Man, and Fire Man were already taking form. Cut Man and Ice Man have basically retained their original designs." (Inafune)

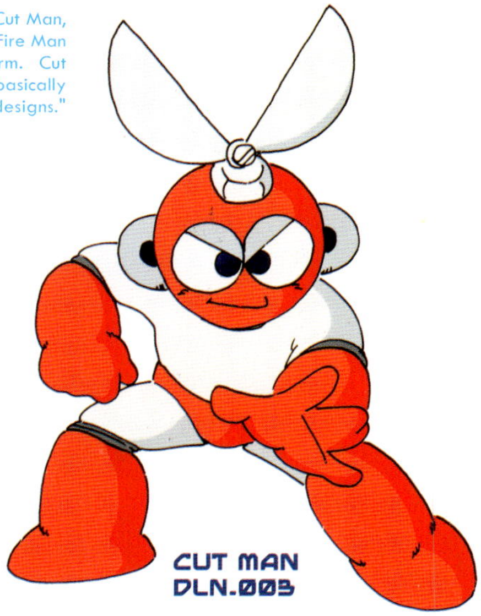

CUT MAN
DLN.003

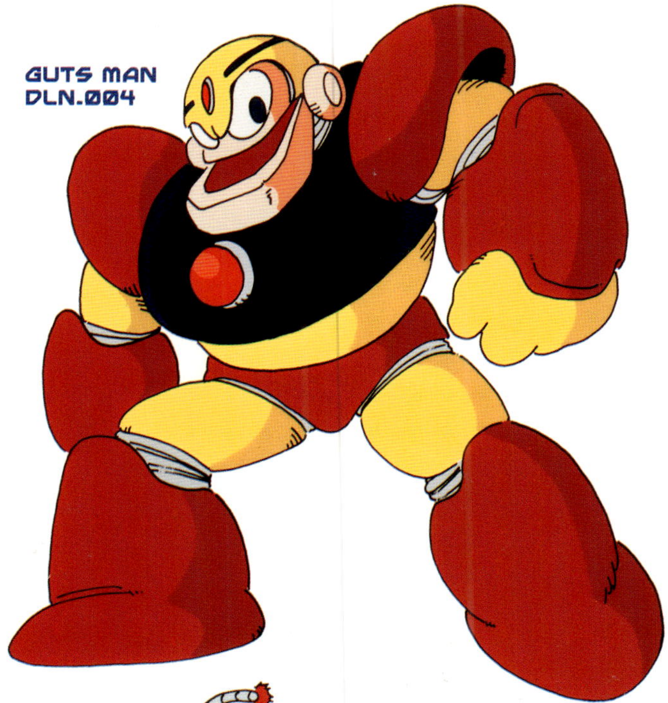

GUTS MAN
DLN.004

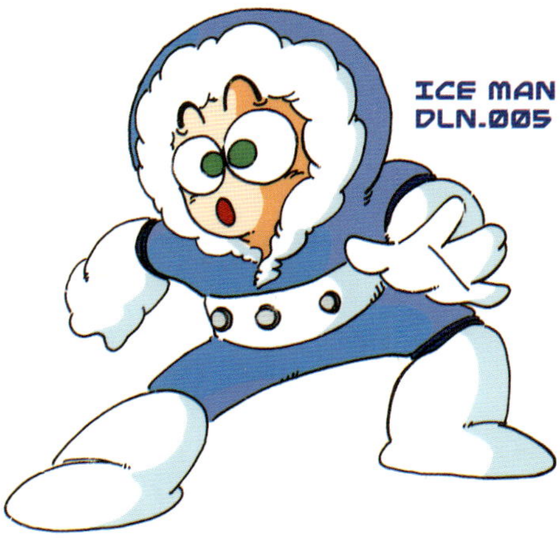

ICE MAN
DLN.005

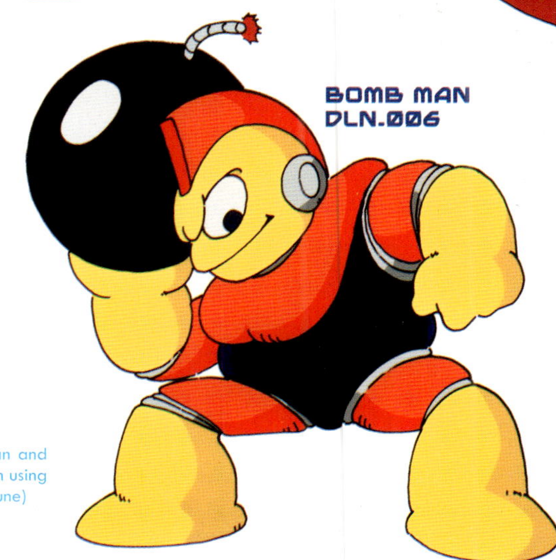

BOMB MAN
DLN.006

"As the new guy, it was my job to create Elec Man and Bomb Man. I was also allowed to participate when using dots to give Guts Man and Fire Man motion." (Inafune)

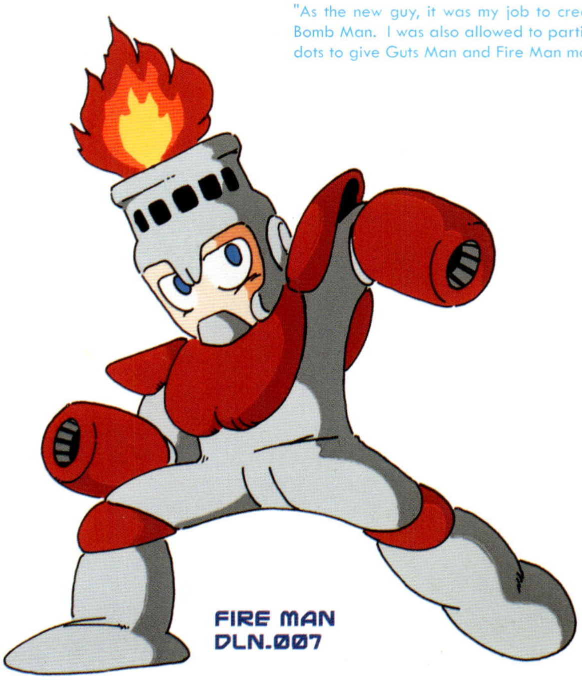

FIRE MAN
DLN.007

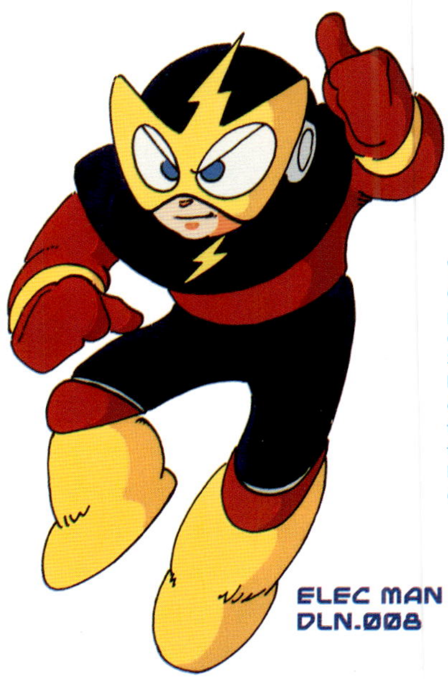

ELEC MAN
DLN.008

"As the first character I designed, Elec Man has plenty of things I really like as well as things I don't like. Sometimes I think about how I could have done things differently, but at the same time I'm tickled by the thought that he was my first character. It's hard to explain how I feel about him. (laughs)" (Inafune)

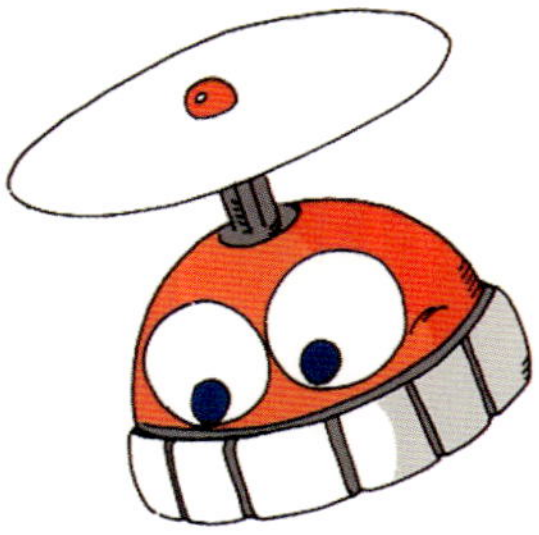

BUNBY HELI

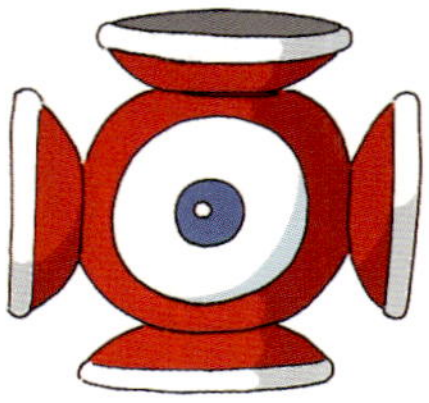

ADHERING SUZY

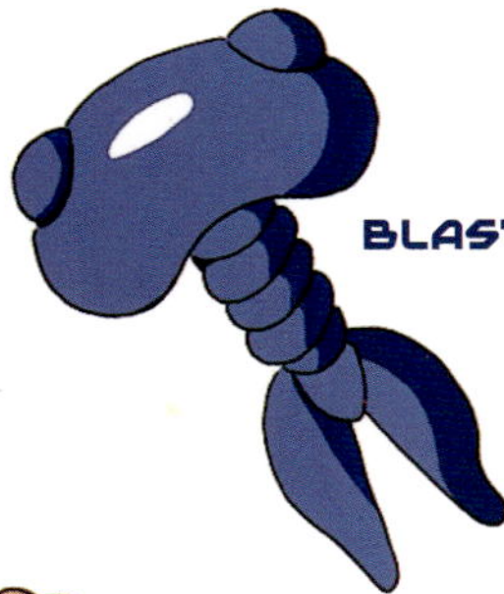

BLASTER

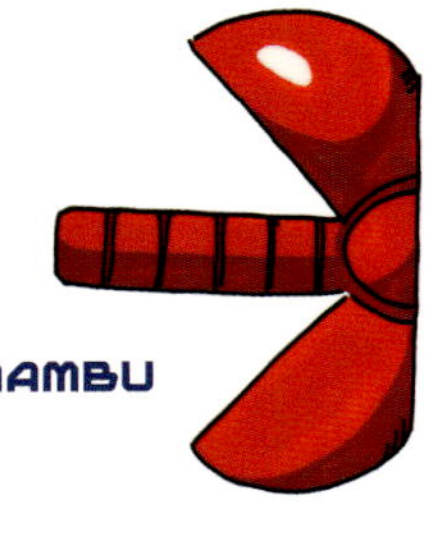

MAMBU

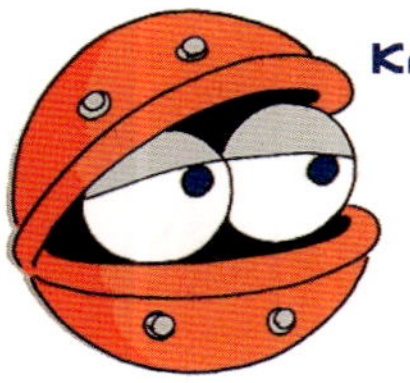

KAMADOMA

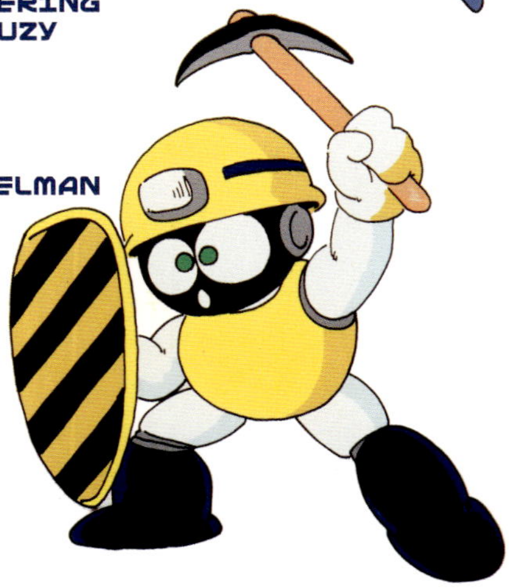

PICKELMAN

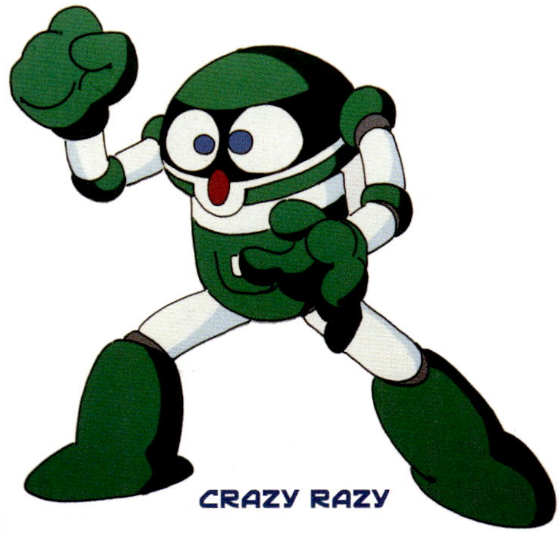

CRAZY RAZY

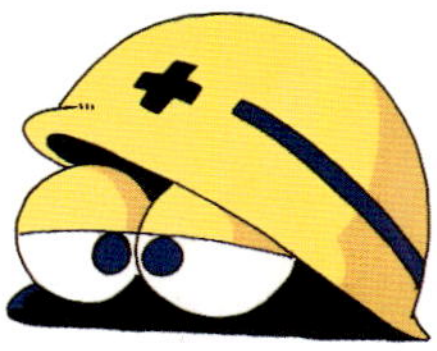

METALL

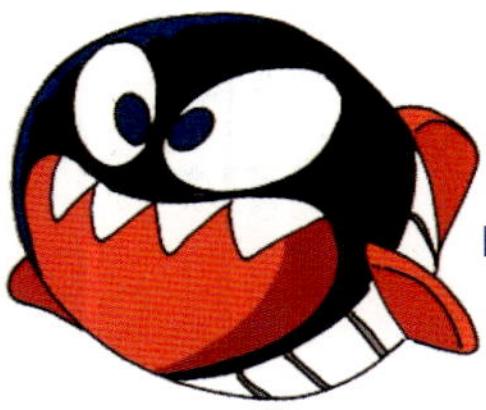

KILLER BOMB

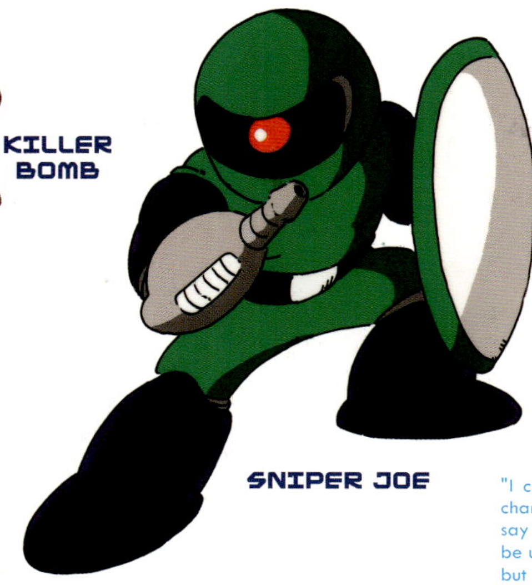

SNIPER JOE

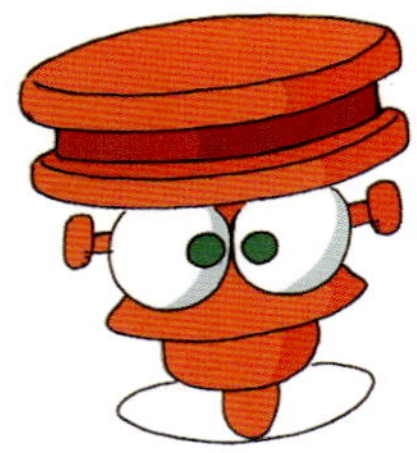

FOOT HOLDER

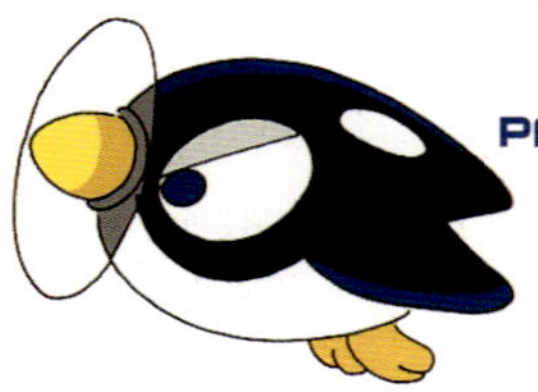

PEPE

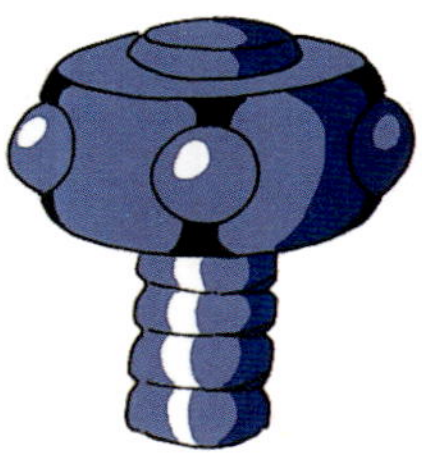

SCREWDRIVER

"I came up with the designs, dot graphics, and names of the minor enemy characters. When they asked me, the new guy, to do all this, I was blown away to say the least. I couldn't wrap my head around the fact that what I produced would be used. I mean, that's obviously what I was hoping for when I joined the company, but I never would have expected to get that kind of responsibility in my first year. It's pretty unthinkable in today's industry. To be honest, I wanted to put a lot more details into my characters, but there were some severe visual restrictions when it came to bringing them to life in the dot matrix of the NES. That was my main dilemma when working on '1'." (Inafune)

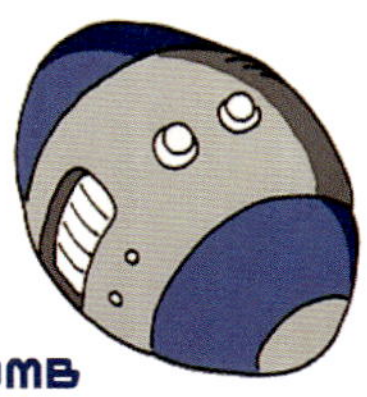

BOMBOMBOMB

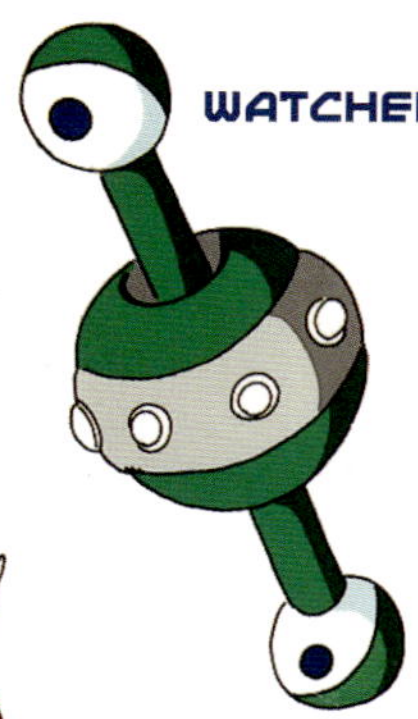

WATCHER

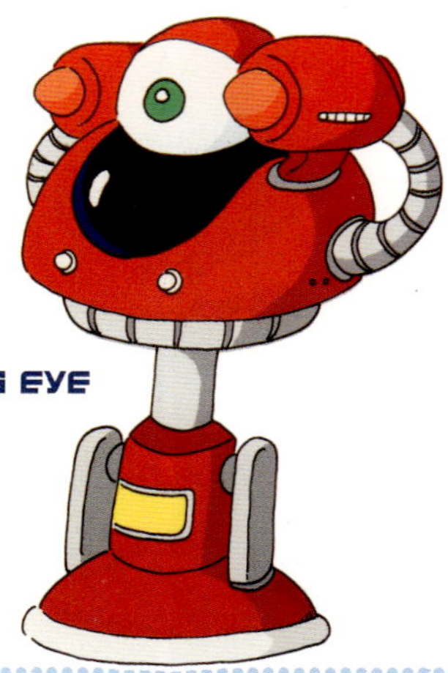

BIG EYE

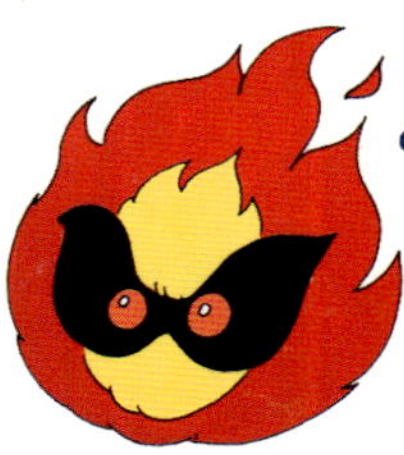

CHANGKEY

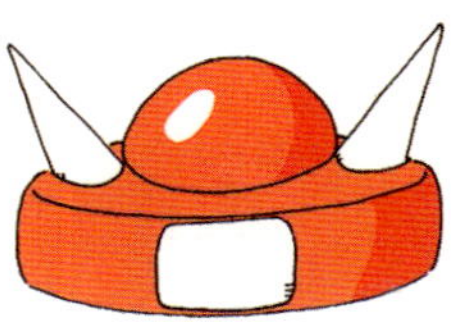

GABYOALL

"The man who set this whole project on its feet is a really strict guy, and at the same he knows exactly what he wants, and is not willing to settle for anything less. Most of what I know about making games, I learned from him. As hardware, the NES can be pretty weak, so we often had to twist our brains to figure out how to do what we wanted. Yellow Devil, for example, was such a physically large character, and we knew it would be too boring if all he had was an expressive background and projectiles as weapons. That's when he would tweak this and that, pulling out every trick in his hat to bring the game up another level. I often found myself saying things like, 'Seriously!? You can do that?' and 'So this is how games are made...' while I watched him work." (Inafune)

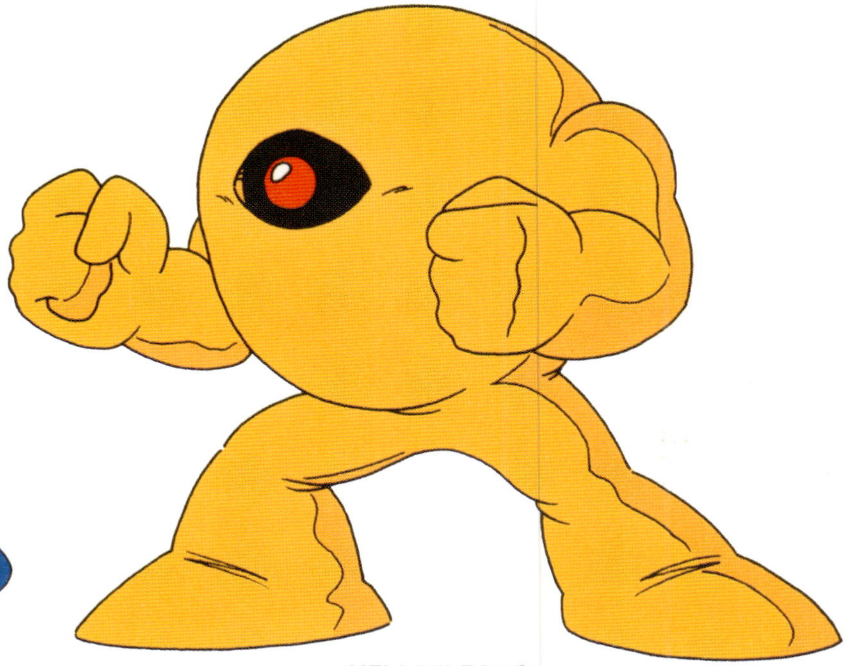

YELLOW DEVIL

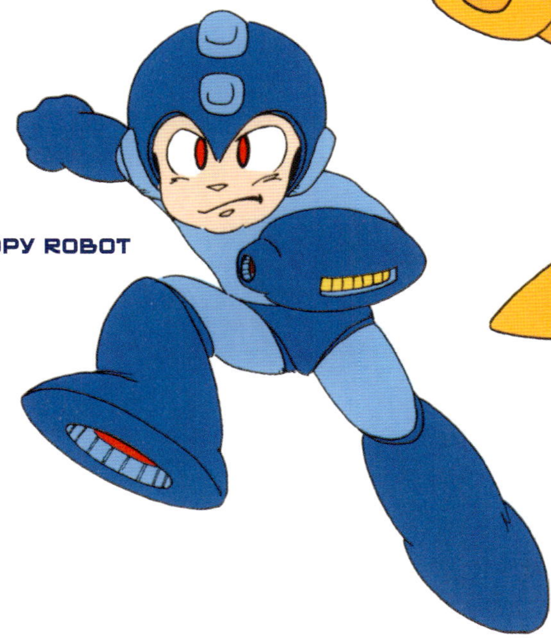

COPY ROBOT

"I often heard people say, 'Mega Man can't crouch,' but we actually had a dot graphic of him crouching while we were working on '1.' Our wise leader, however, wanted a system that 'utilizes simple control yet offers deep gameplay.' On the NES, with only a split second to see the slight height difference, the player wouldn't really be able to differentiate between a projectile that could only be dodged by jumping, and one that could only be dodged by crouching. That was the reason why we decided to go with a jumping-only system for Mega Man 1 and 2, and I think we did a good job refining it." (Inafune)

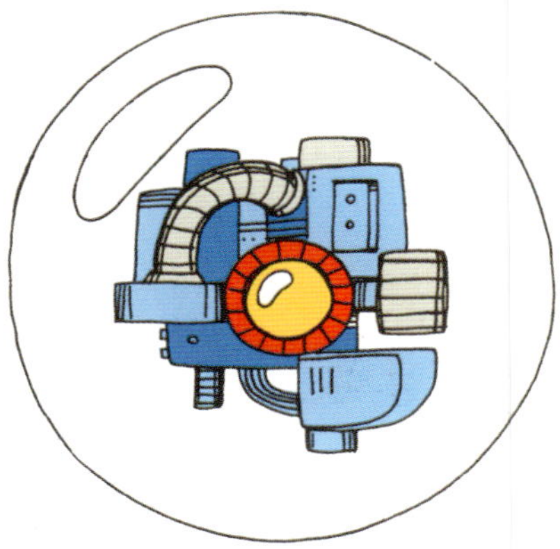

CWU-01P

"Mega Man's world and the characters who live in it existed so clearly in our minds, but with the NES's capacity and expressive limitations being what they are, I sometimes think that the only part that really got across to the players the way it was in our minds was the ending. Still, I think I was very fortunate to have had the opportunity to work on a game like that." (Inafune)

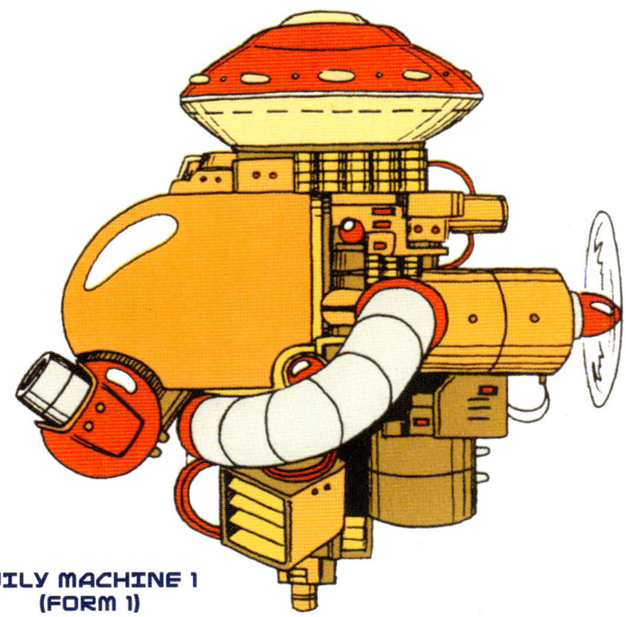

WILY MACHINE 1 (FORM 1)

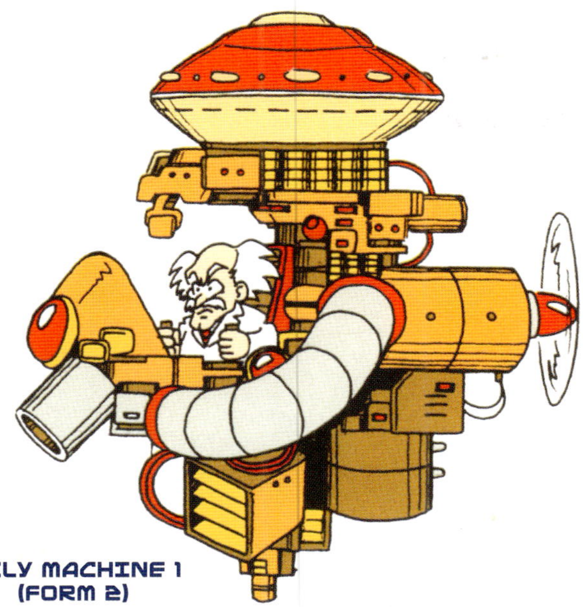

WILY MACHINE 1 (FORM 2)

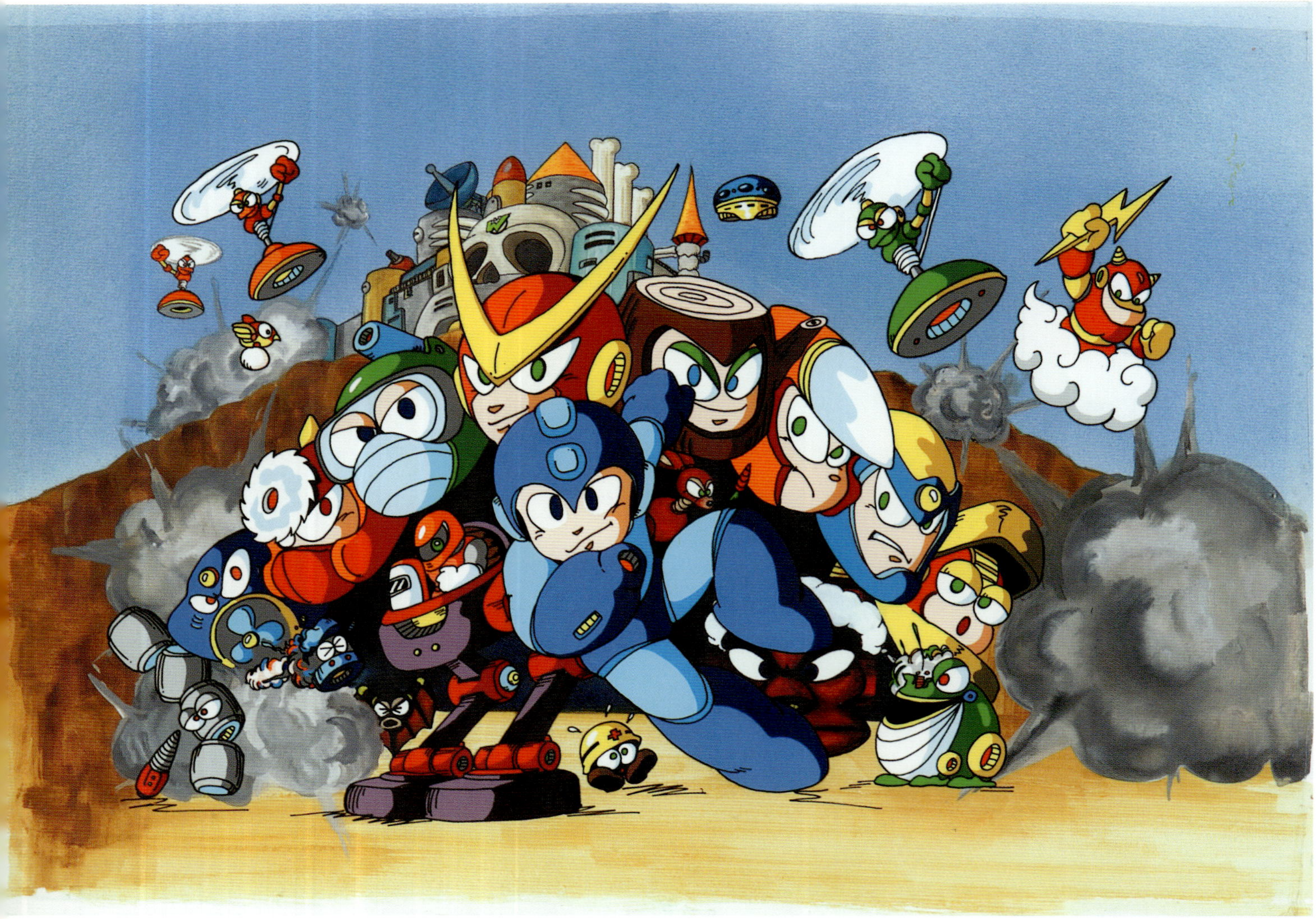

Mega Man 2
NES 12/24/1988
Total number of boss character submissions: 8,370

Dr. Wily's ambitions for world domination had been successfully supressed by Mega Man, the super robot created by Dr. Light. Peace returned to the world once more, but sadly, it did not last very long. Despite his devastating loss, Dr. Wily returned with eight new powerful robots to challenge Mega Man.

WILY CASTLE

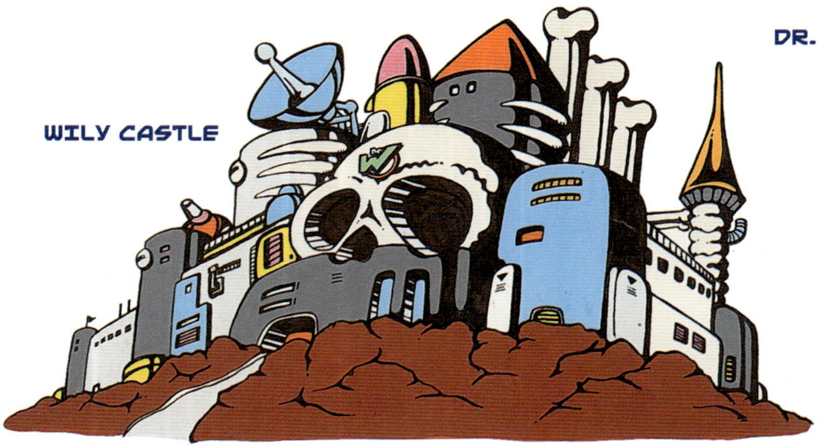

DR. WILY

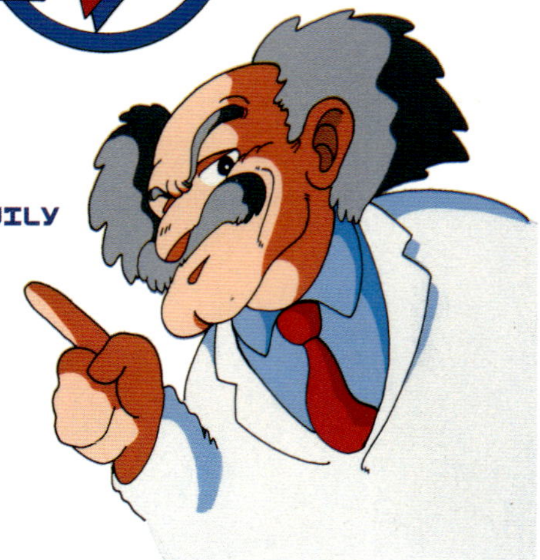

"I designed Dr. Wily all by myself. I was aiming for the archetypical image that everyone would immediately think of when imagining a mad scientist. Personally, I think he turned out quite well." (Inafune)

"I think '2' is the most memorable for me, both in that it was the most fun and the most stress. I was actually working on a different project at the time, but our fearless leader from '1' approached me one day to ask me if I was willing to join them again. Making a sequel wasn't a corporate decision, it was more like the team just kind of saying 'Let's do it!' Seeing as how it would be my first time working on two projects simultaneously, I was rather intrigued. I asked him what timeframe they were aiming for, and his reply was, 'Including the checks? Three months.' I was like, 'Whaaa!?' (laughs) So yeah, that's how '2' began." (Inafune)

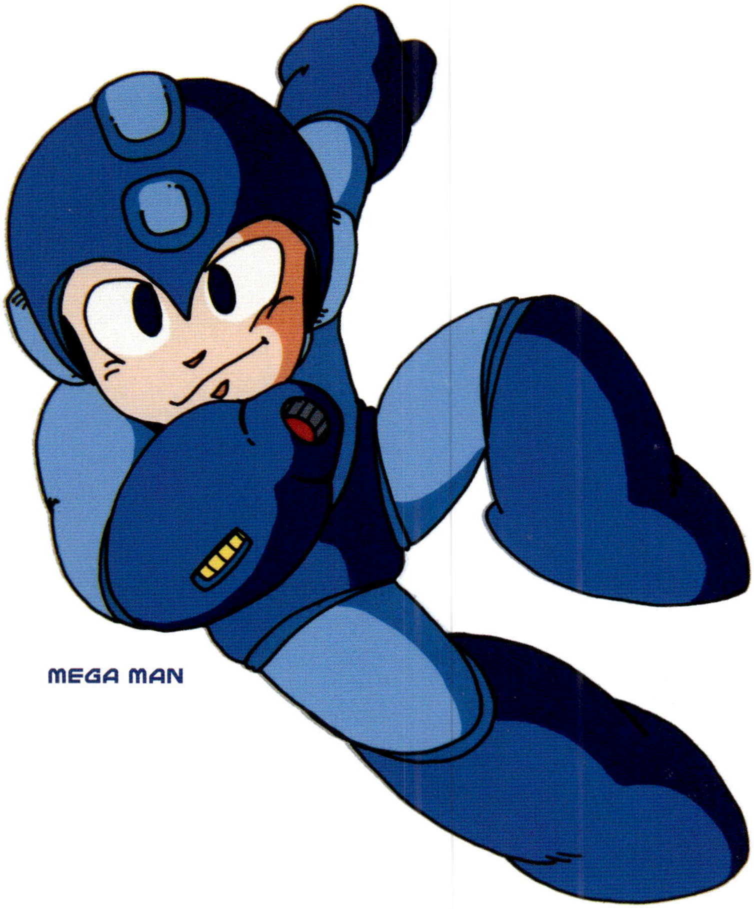

MEGA MAN

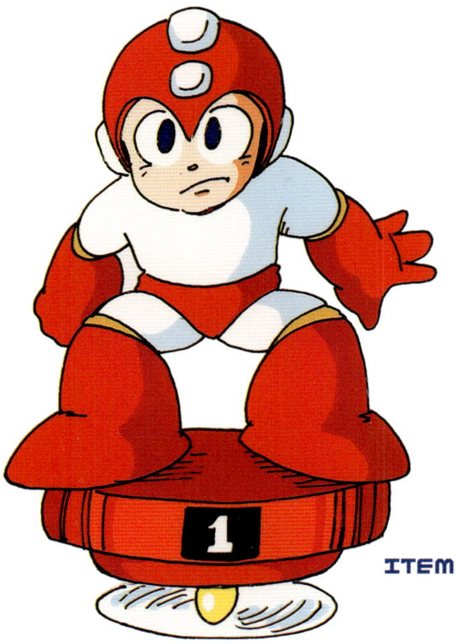

ITEM 1

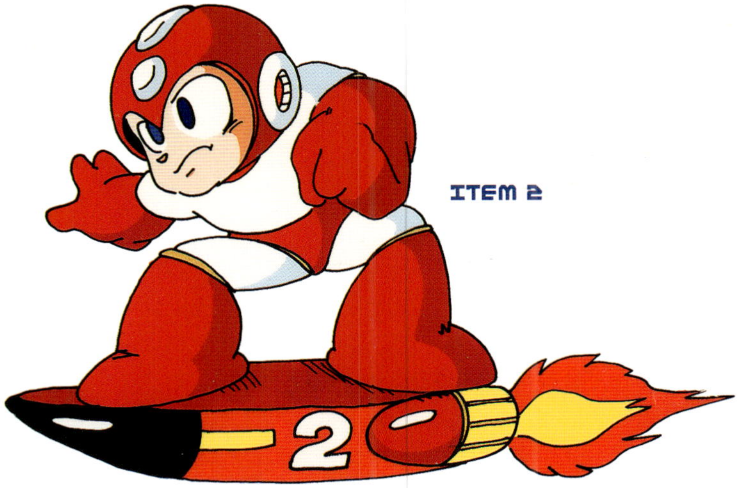

ITEM 2

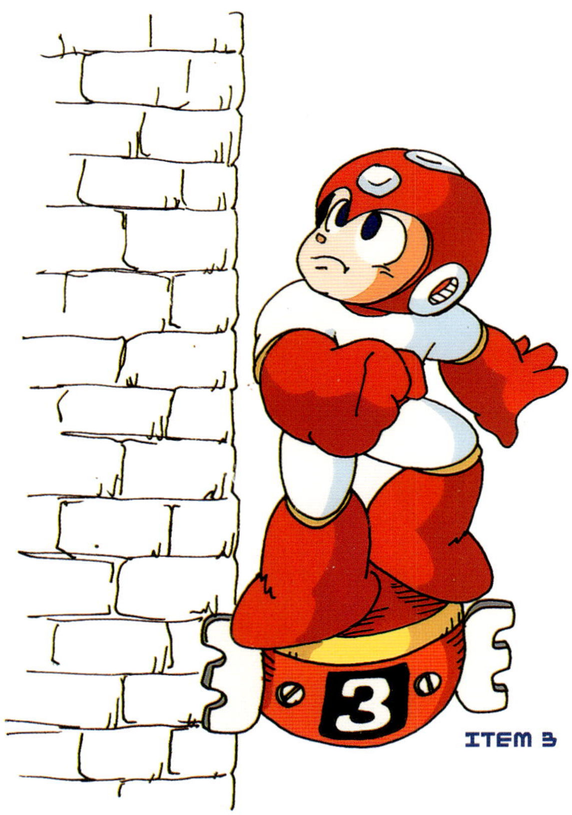

ITEM 3

"In Mega Man 1, the basic actions involved shooting and knocking stuff over, but there were also many traps on the map that players had to navigate. In Mega Man 2, we kept all of the above, but added many more traps. We implemented Items 1, 2, and 3 to assist the players in this respect. We had gotten a lot of feedback for '1' that stated that there were some areas that were 'too difficult.' We even had the marketing department asking us to make things a little more playable. Our leader was especially unsure about the use of Energy Tanks. He wasn't sure that they were really necessary, and even asked me what I thought about them." (Inafune)

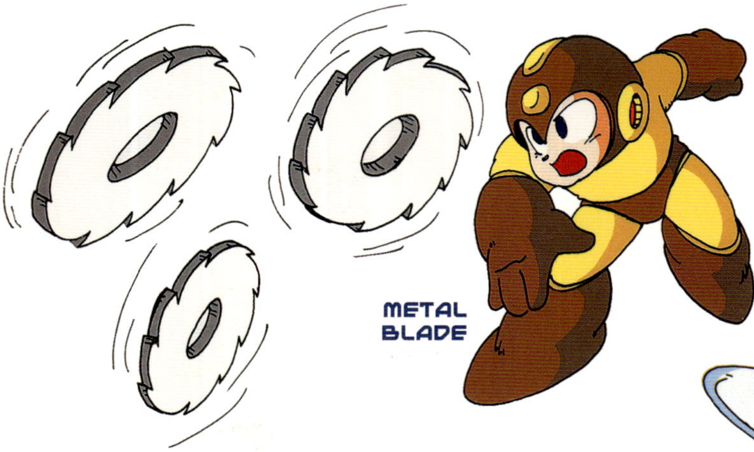

METAL BLADE

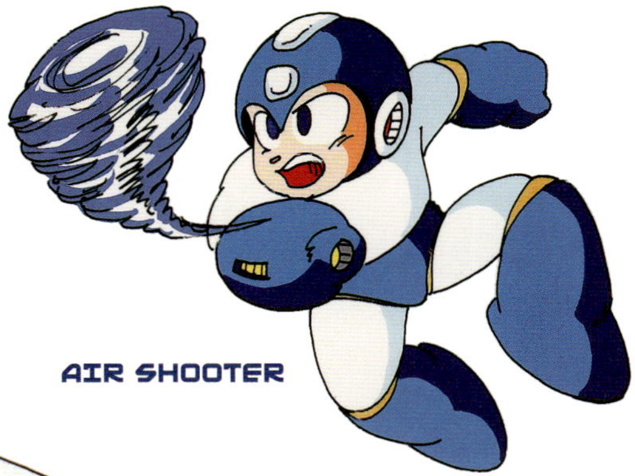

AIR SHOOTER

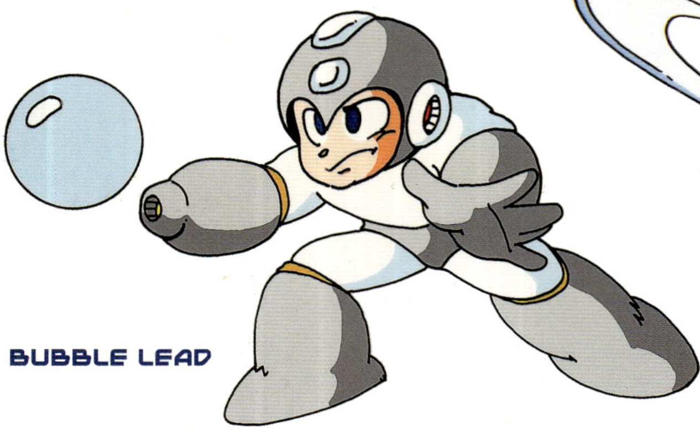

BUBBLE LEAD

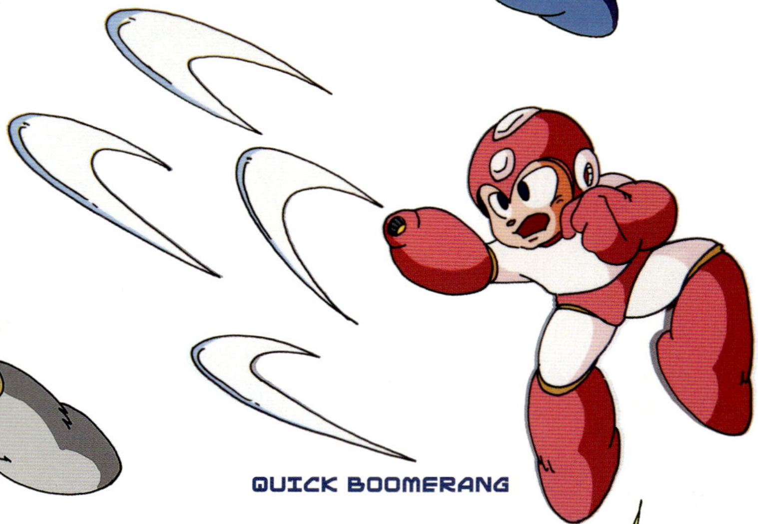

QUICK BOOMERANG

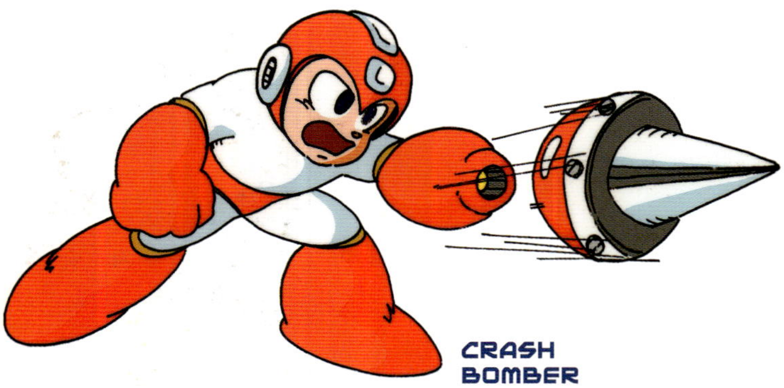

CRASH BOMBER

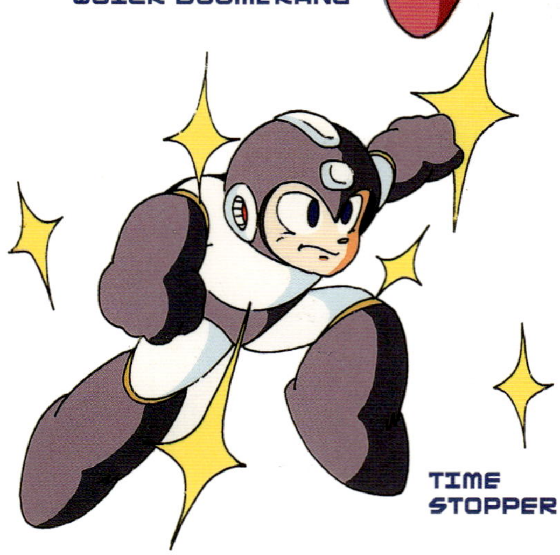

TIME STOPPER

"I was trying to make the art of Mega Man 2 a little more 'anime-ish.' If asked which package illustration I had more time to do, though, I have to admit I hardly had any time at all to do '2.' (laughs) Still, I had a lot of fun doing it. I think I was able to give it a lot of life." (Inafune)

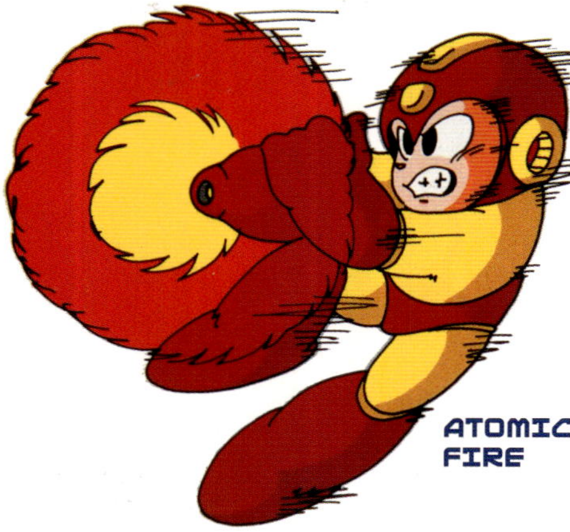

ATOMIC FIRE

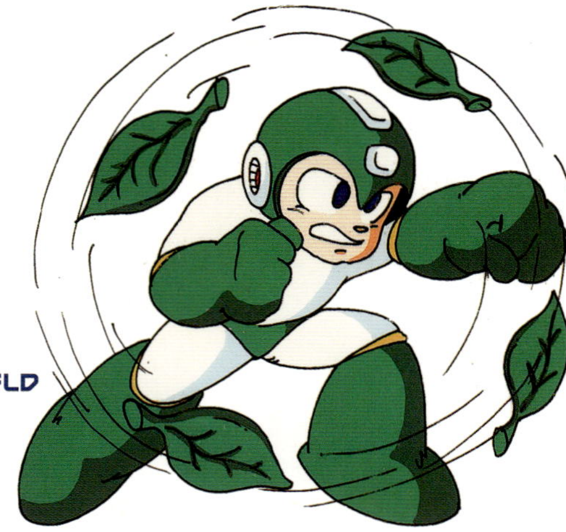

LEAF SHIELD

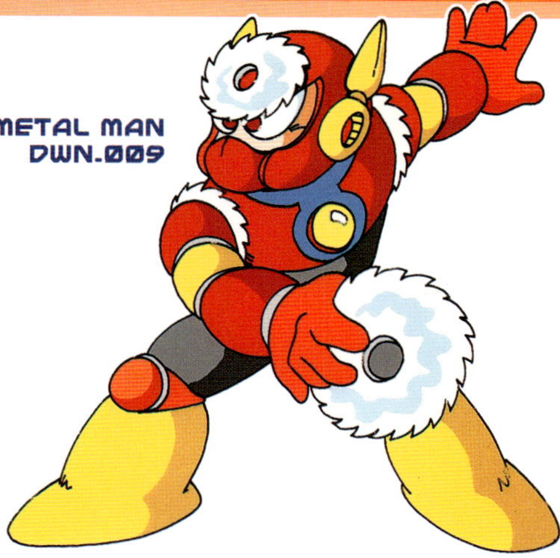

METAL MAN
DWN.009

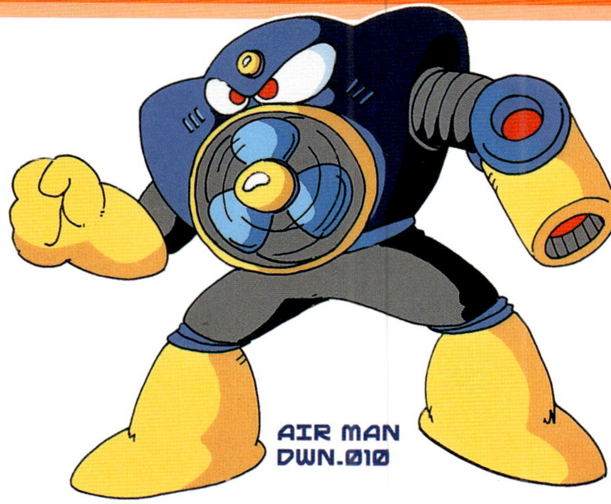

AIR MAN
DWN.010

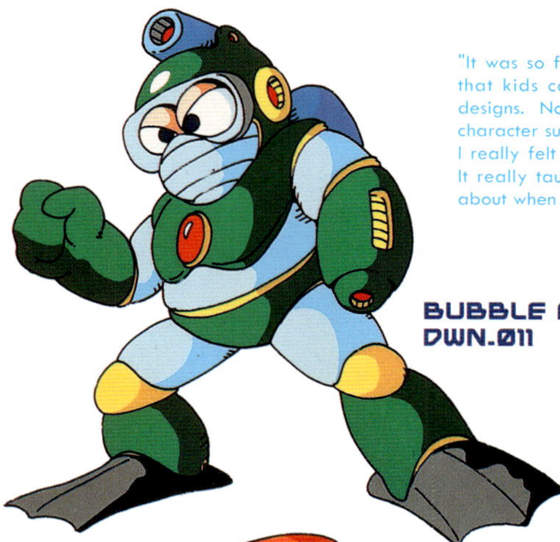

BUBBLE MAN
DWN.011

"It was so fun to take the boss characters that kids came up with and tweak their designs. Now that I think about it, the boss character submission event was the first time I really felt like a 'Producer' in this project. It really taught me what we need to think about when creating games." (Inafune)

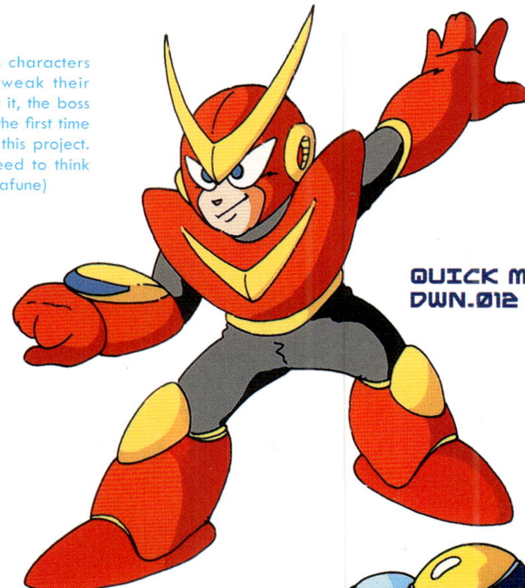

QUICK MAN
DWN.012

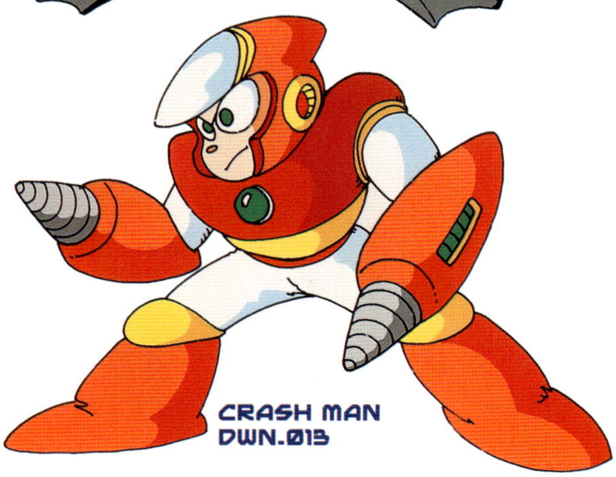

CRASH MAN
DWN.013

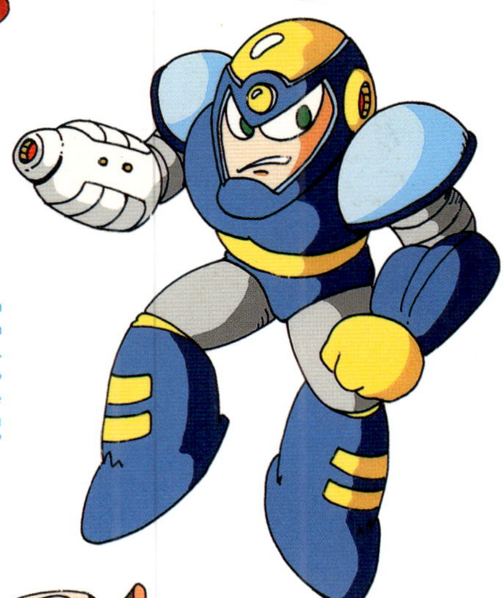

FLASH MAN
DWN.014

"In '2,' I think Heat Man is my favorite. He is such a 'gimmicky' character. (laughs) He's like a Zippo flipping open. None of the other robots really had a gimmick like Heat Man." (Inafune)

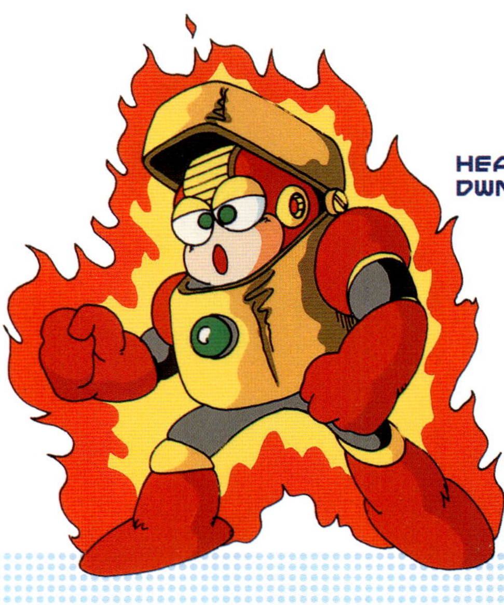

HEAT MAN
DWN.015

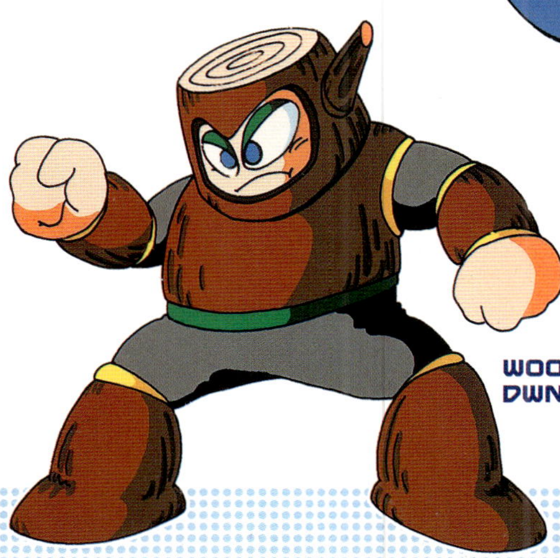

WOOD MAN
DWN.016

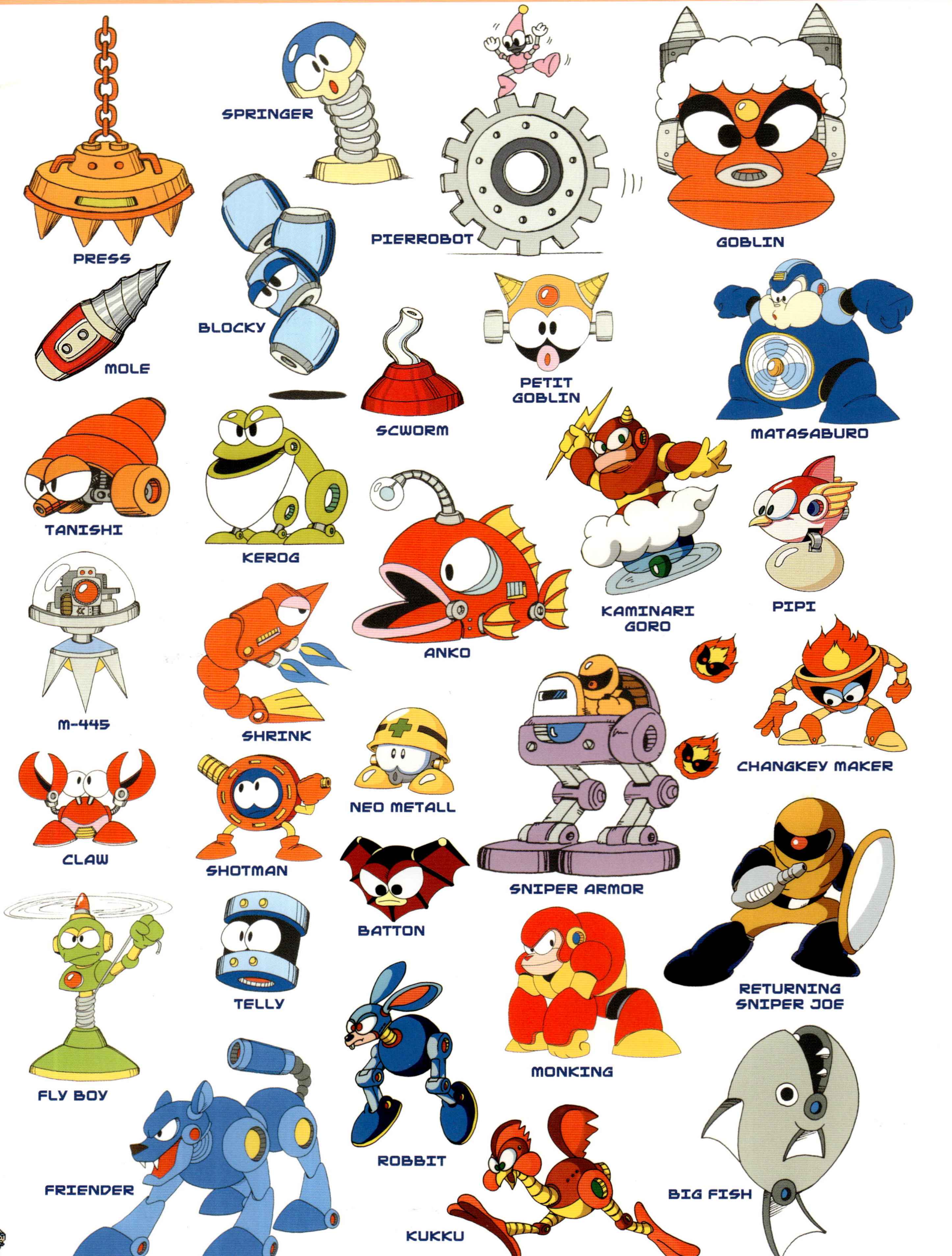
PRESS
SPRINGER
BLOCKY
PIERROBOT
GOBLIN
MOLE
SCWORM
PETIT GOBLIN
MATASABURO
TANISHI
KEROG
ANKO
KAMINARI GORO
PIPI
M-445
SHRINK
NEO METALL
SNIPER ARMOR
CHANGKEY MAKER
CLAW
SHOTMAN
BATTON
RETURNING SNIPER JOE
FLY BOY
TELLY
MONKING
ROBBIT
FRIENDER
KUKKU
BIG FISH

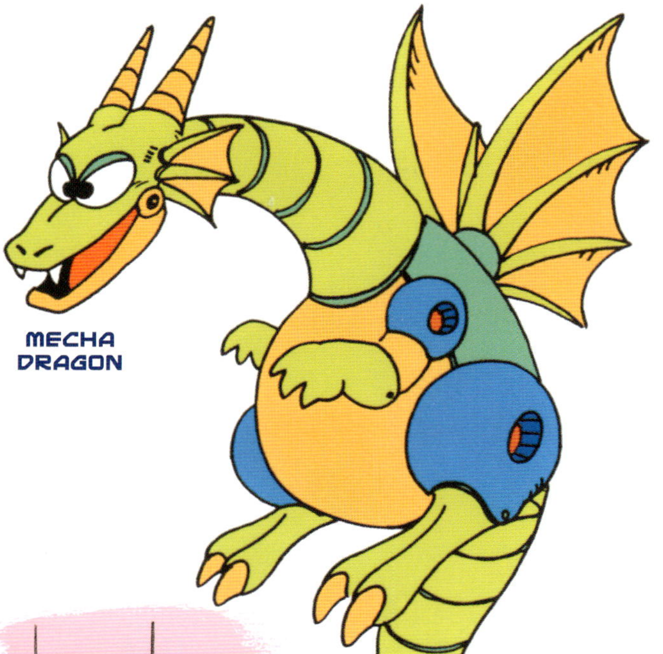

MECHA DRAGON

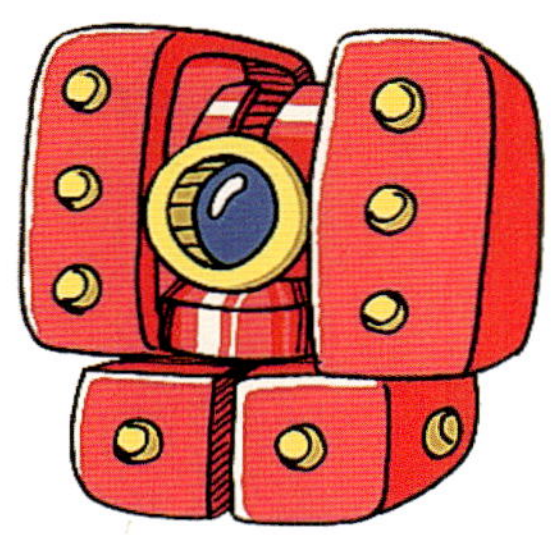

PICOPICO-KUN

"Working on '2' marked my second year at this, and I even got to mentor a 'new kid,' which opened up a whole new world of stress for me. Something that would take me three hours to do would take three days... So I'd show them how it's done, and three days eventually turned into one day, which in turn became eight hours, and so on. Mentoring was definitely fun in its own way." (Inafune)

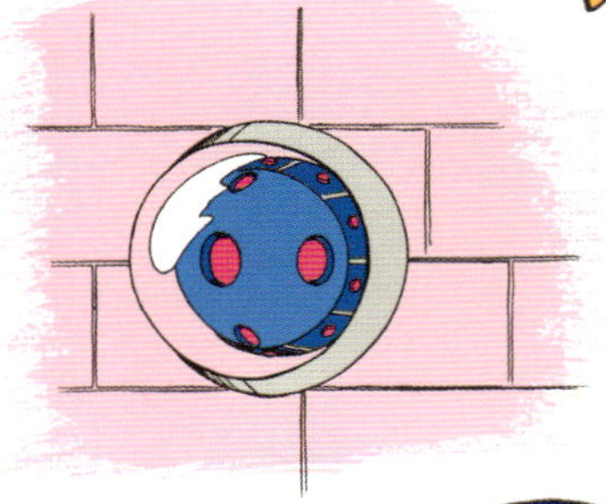

BOOBEAM TRAP

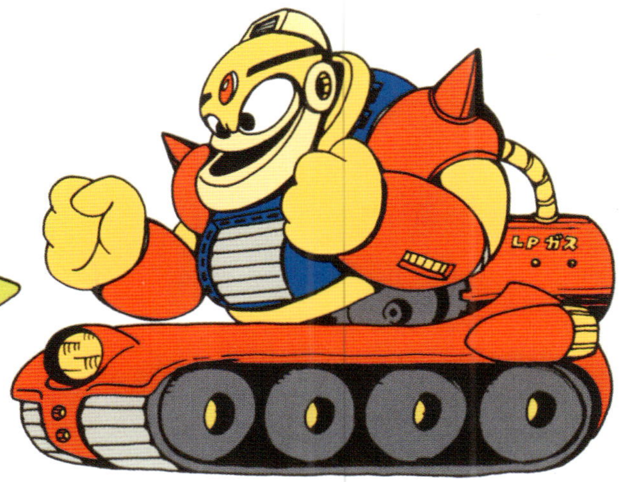

GUTS TANK

"When time gets tight, I help out wherever I can. For Guts Tank, I not only did the dot graphics, but also did most of the planning. Guts Tank's main body is actually part of the background; I had to tweak the visuals to make sure Mega Man's footholds didn't look like they were moving around ." (Inafune)

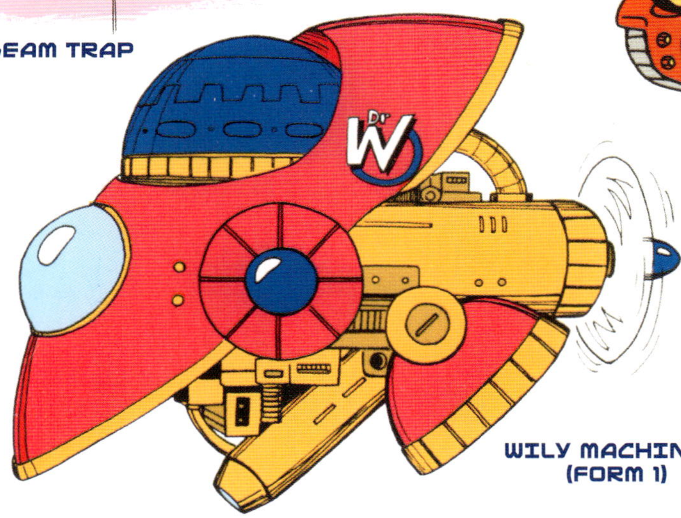

WILY MACHINE 2 (FORM 1)

"Thinking back on it now, working late for this project and even sleeping at the office was lots of fun. There's nothing better than seeing everything gradually coming together every day. The three months I spent on this game showed me how fun making games could really be, and I only have the best of memories about it." (Inafune)

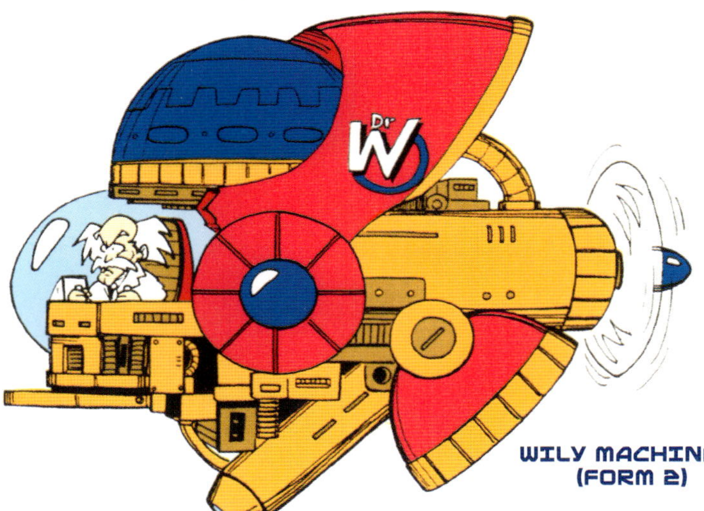

WILY MACHINE 2 (FORM 2)

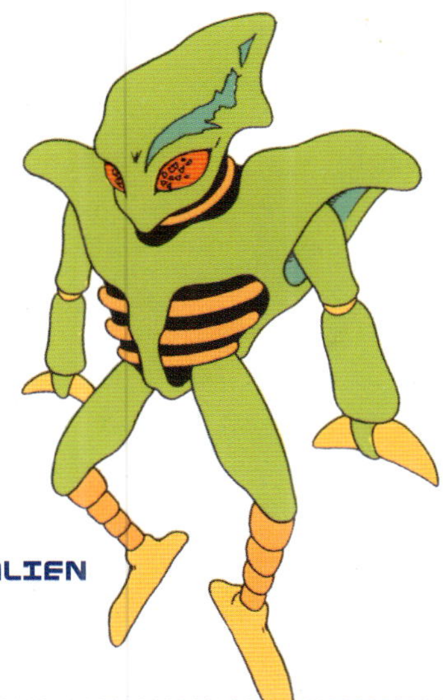

ALIEN

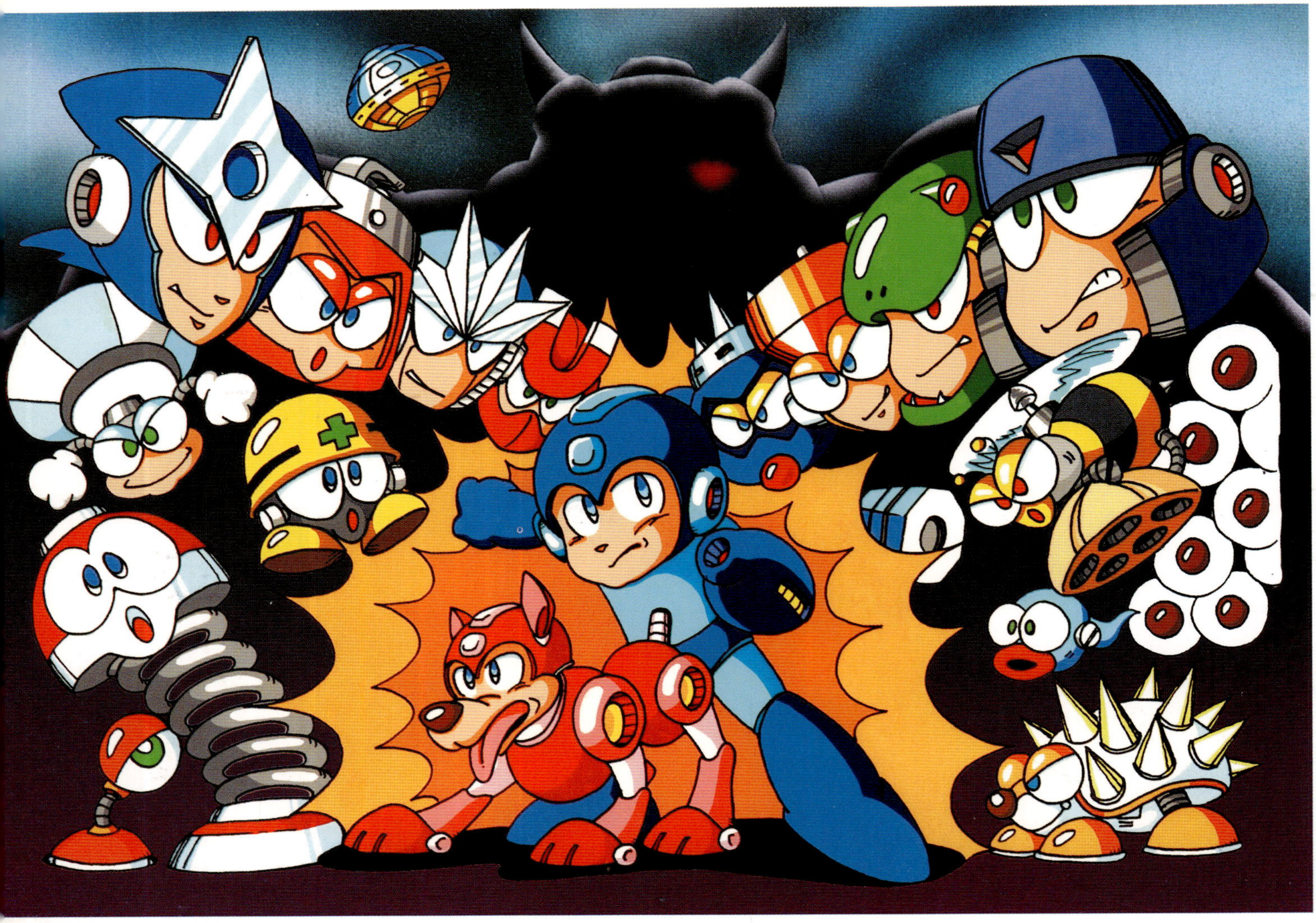

ROCKMAN 3 Dr.ワイリーの最期!?

Mega Man 3
NES 09/28/1990
Total number of boss character submissions: 50,000

Reformed, Dr. Wily began assisting Dr. Light in the creation of the giant robot "Gamma" to serve the purposes of world peace. Just as it seemed that Gamma would be completed, disaster struck. Something was happening to the robots that had been harvesting an energy source for Gamma on a far away planet! Mega Man's newest battle was about to begin!

"Although '2' was a huge success, about a year passed before we started work on '3' simply because our eternal leader quit his job. We got a new leader for '3,' but he didn't really understand Mega Man the way his predecessor did... and that resulted in some headaches. It was especially hard on me because I had learned so much while working on '1' and '2,' which left me with a lot of preset notions about how things should be." (Inafune)

MEGA MAN

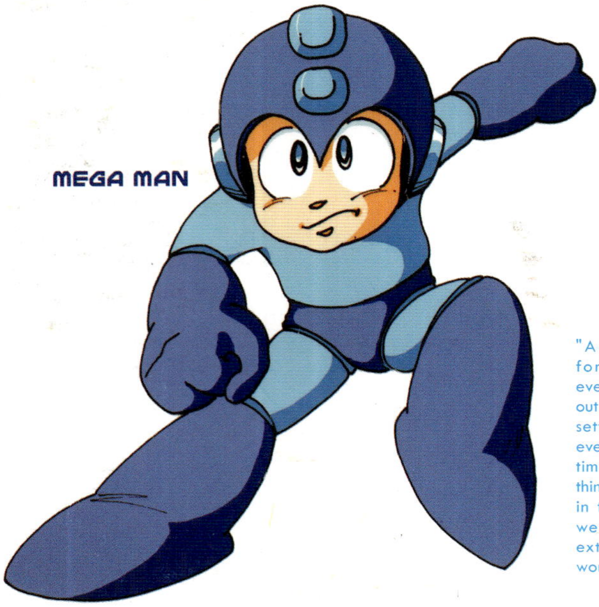

DR. WILY

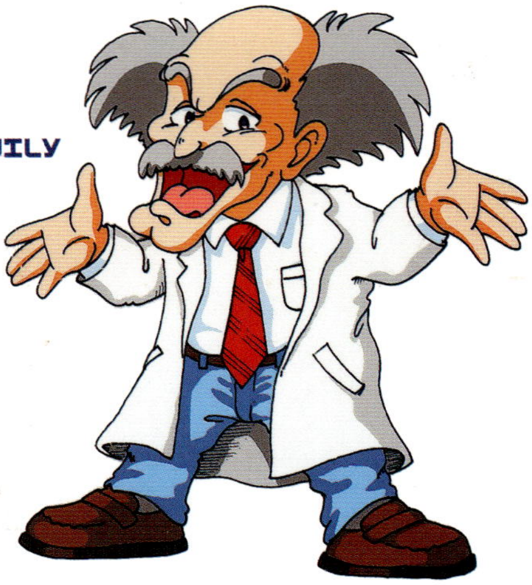

"Again, I was responsible for taking on anything and everything that we were running out of time on. I did the enemy settings, the specifications, and even worked on the maps. By the time I started working on these things, however, we were already in trouble as far as deadlines were concerned, so I got some extra help and divided up the work amongst us." (Inafune)

"Starting in '3,' we added the sliding action. That meant the game controls lost some of their simplicity, but I was just glad we didn't incorporate crouching. If an enemy jumped at you and you were all like 'Oh no!' you could slide under them and get a shot at them from behind. In this way, sliding was an action that had a good balance between being an offensive and defensive tactic." (Inafune)

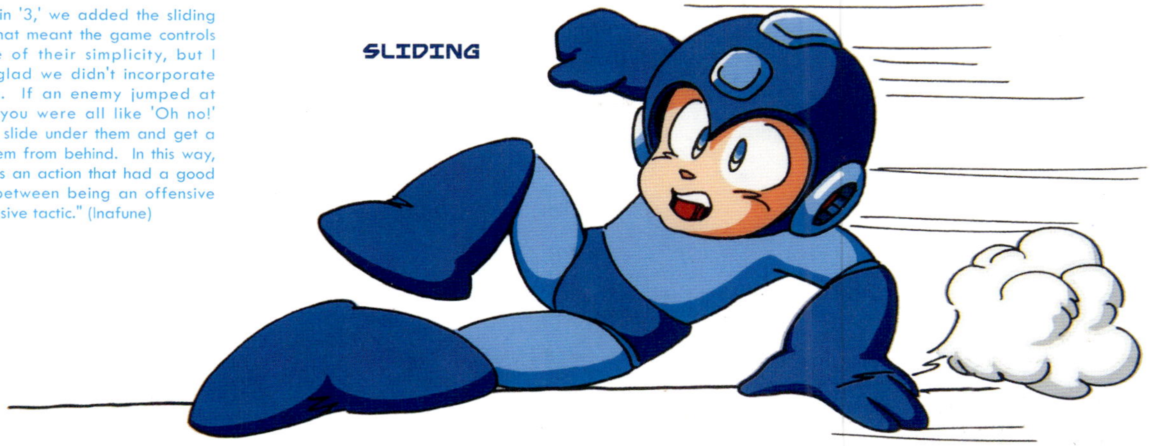

SLIDING

"Items 1, 2, and 3 had some interesting capabilities, but they really had no life to them. So, based on the idea that all good anime heroes had a trusty dog sidekick, we took Mega Man's helmet, and mixed in the color scheme from Items 1, 2, and 3 to come up with Rush." (Inafune)

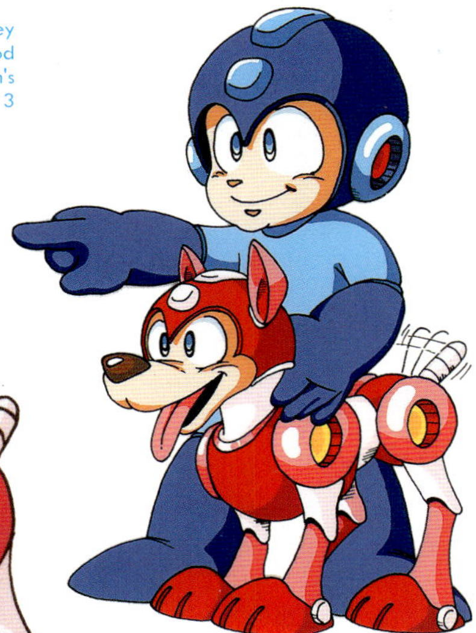

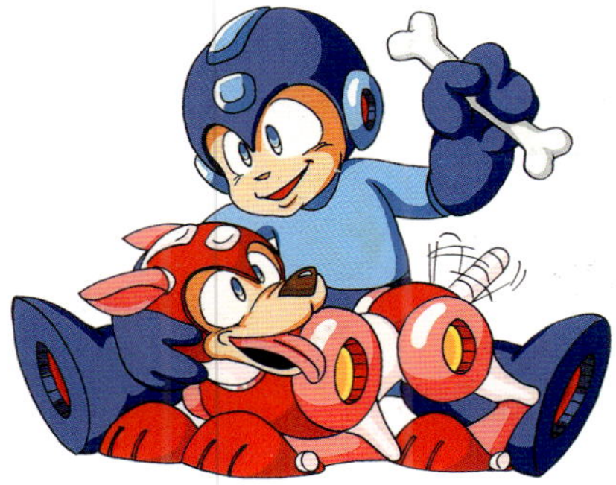

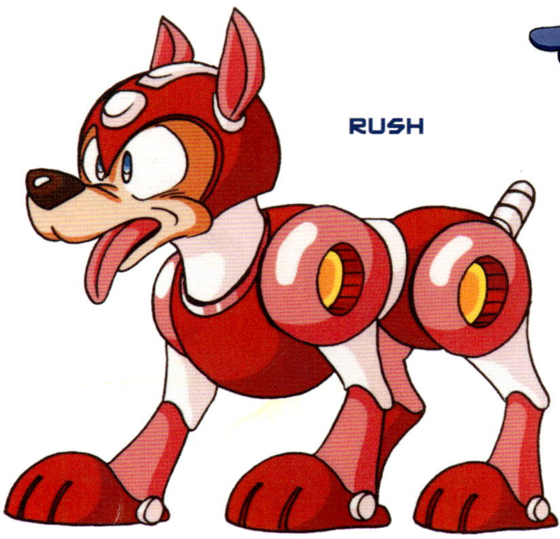

RUSH

"We wanted people to be unsure of whether Proto Man was a friend or foe. On the one hand, he'd seem like a rival to Mega Man, but at the same time he'd seem like a comrade of sorts. There were so many characters like this in the classic animes of my generation, and that's where the idea for this character came from. (laughs) We gave him a scarf to add to his 'cool' factor, and gave him a shield to make him seem tougher than Mega Man." (Inafune)

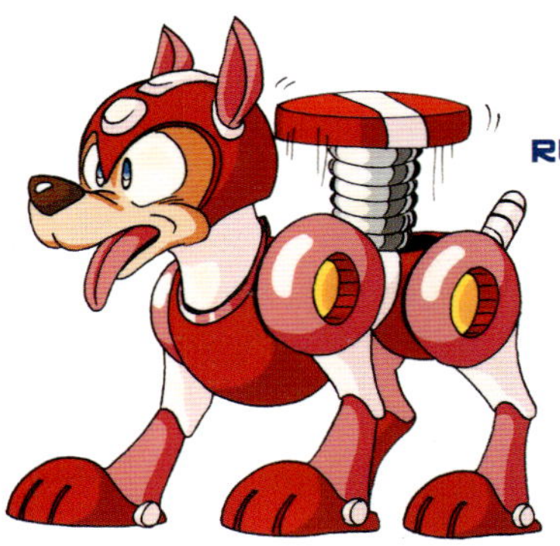

RUSH COIL

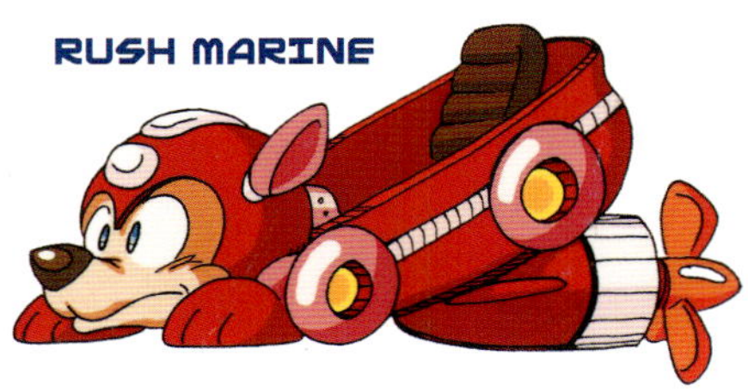

RUSH MARINE

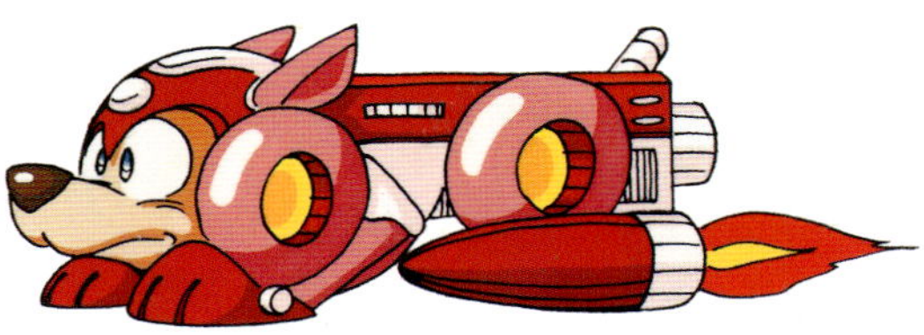

RUSH JET

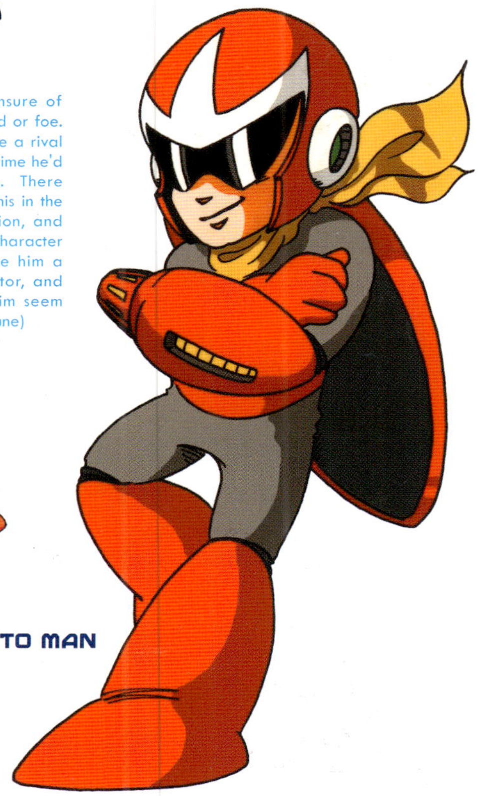

PROTO MAN

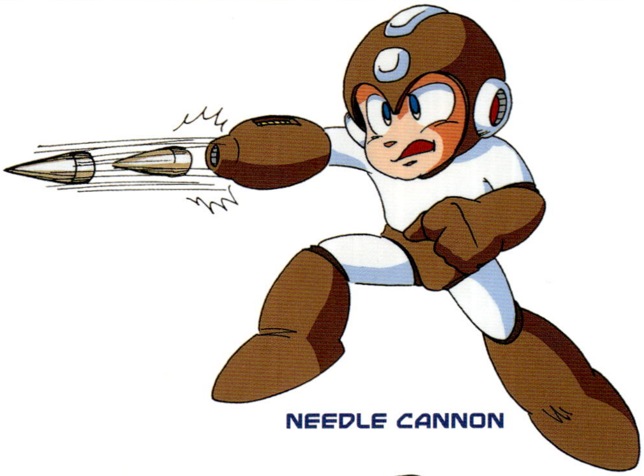

NEEDLE CANNON

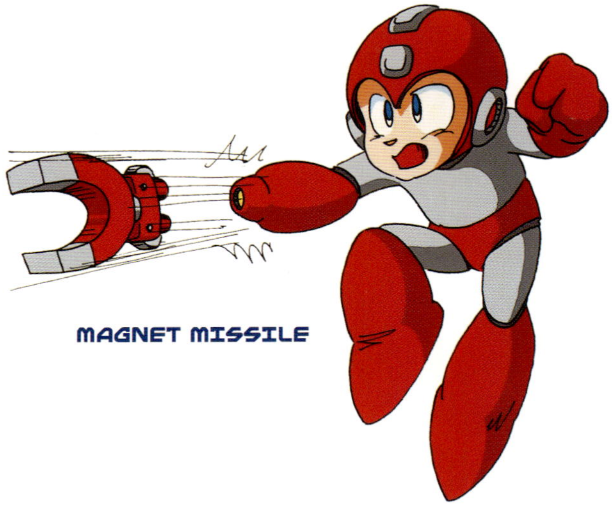

MAGNET MISSILE

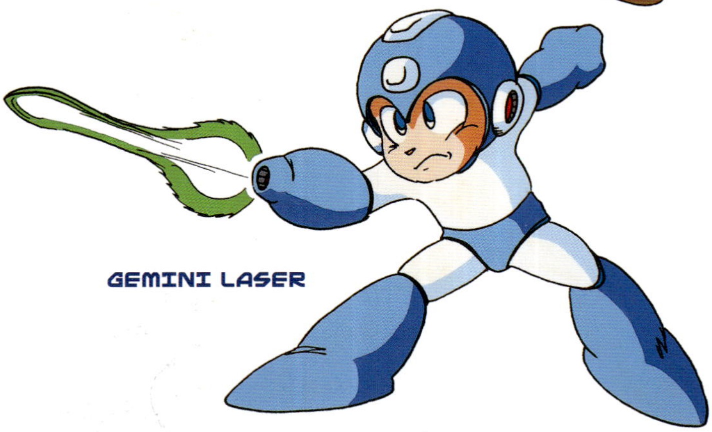

GEMINI LASER

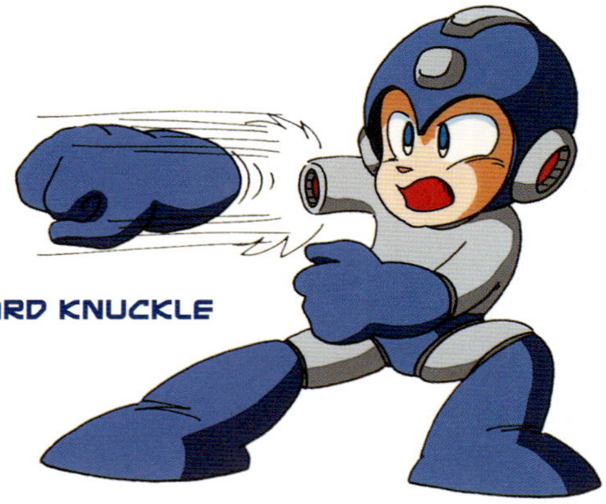

HARD KNUCKLE

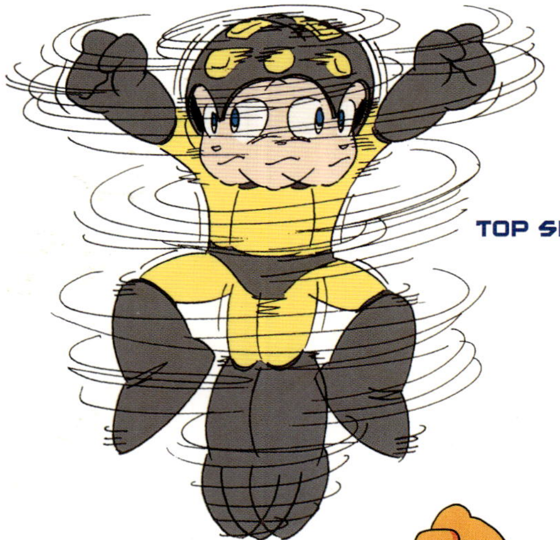

TOP SPIN

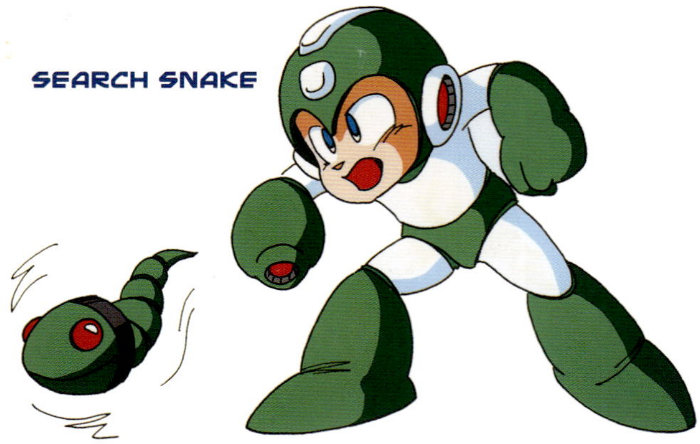

SEARCH SNAKE

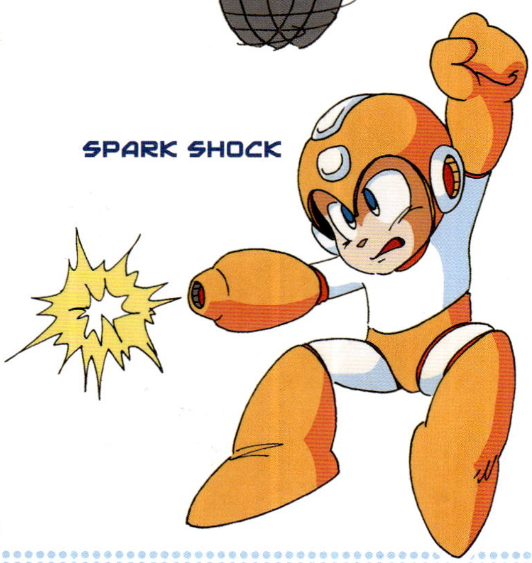

SPARK SHOCK

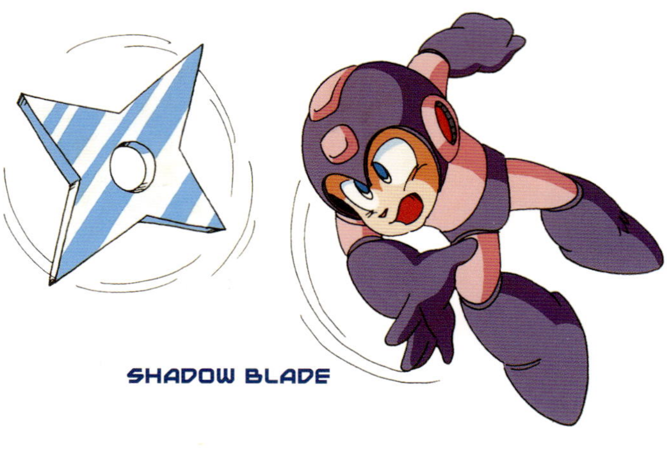

SHADOW BLADE

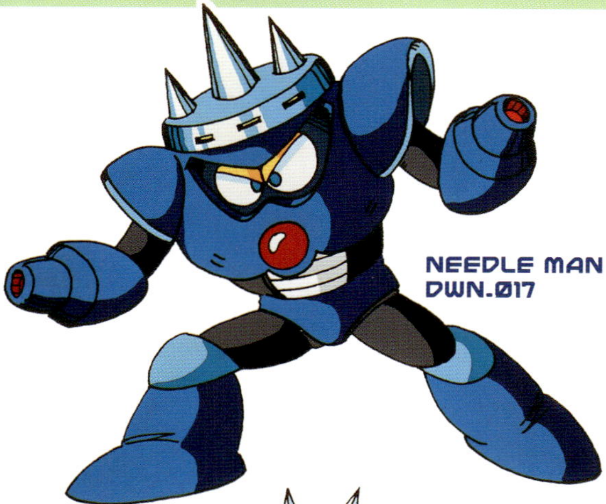

NEEDLE MAN
DWN.017

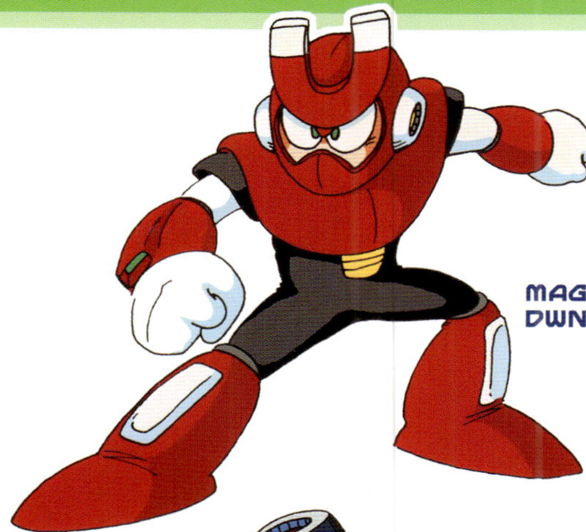

MAGNET MAN
DWN.018

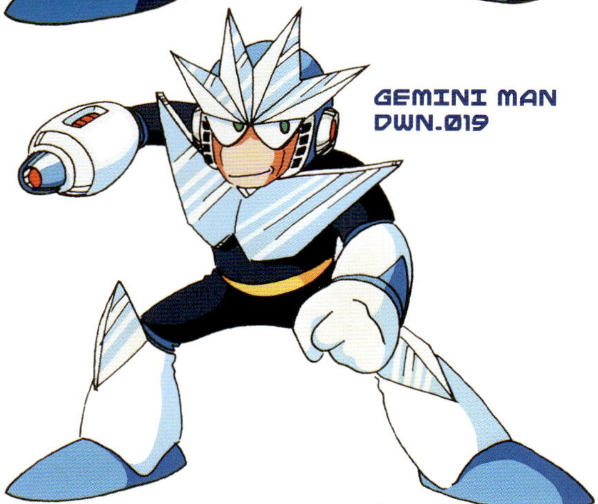

GEMINI MAN
DWN.019

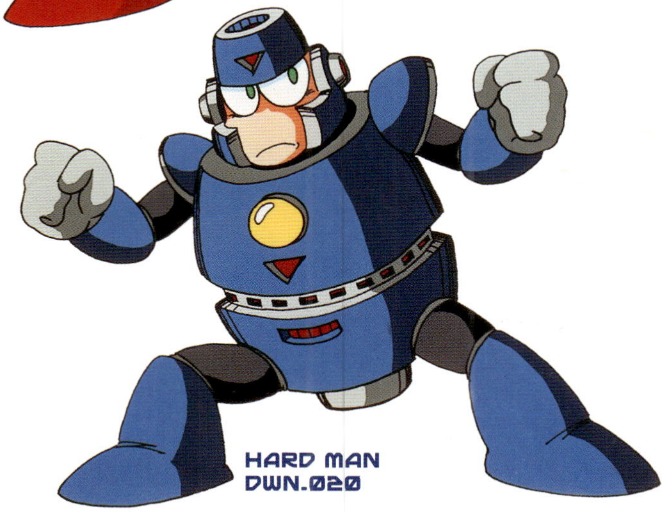

HARD MAN
DWN.020

"I focused entirely on Top Man for an entire week, but lost all of the data in a big [computer] crash when someone tripped over the power cord. I was so devastated, but with everything so fresh in my mind I was able to get back to where I was in about three days. This incident is why I'll never forget Top Man... sometimes I wonder if my first attempt would have made a better Top Man (laughs)." (Inafune)

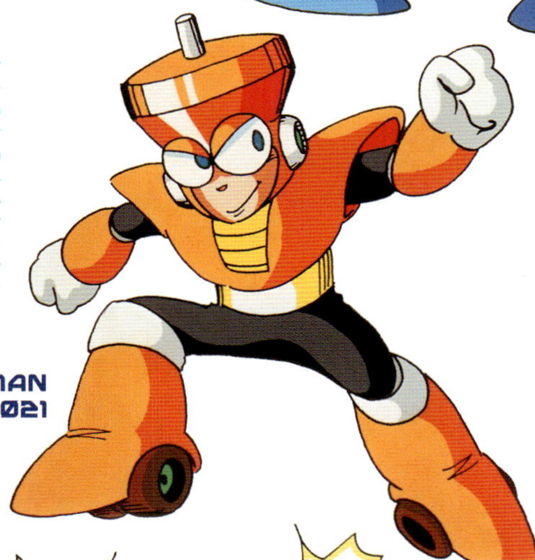

TOP MAN
DWN.021

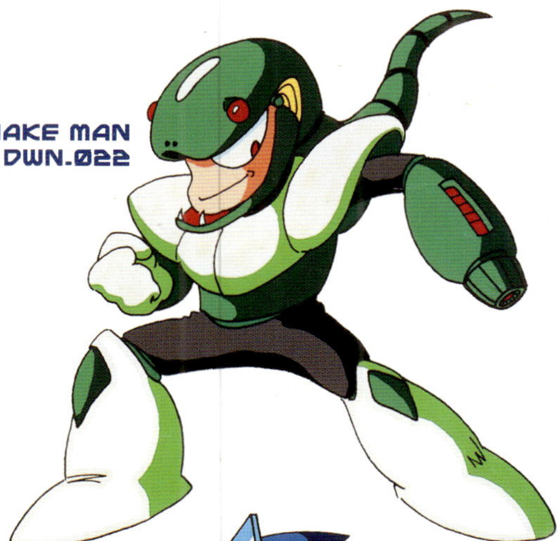

SNAKE MAN
DWN.022

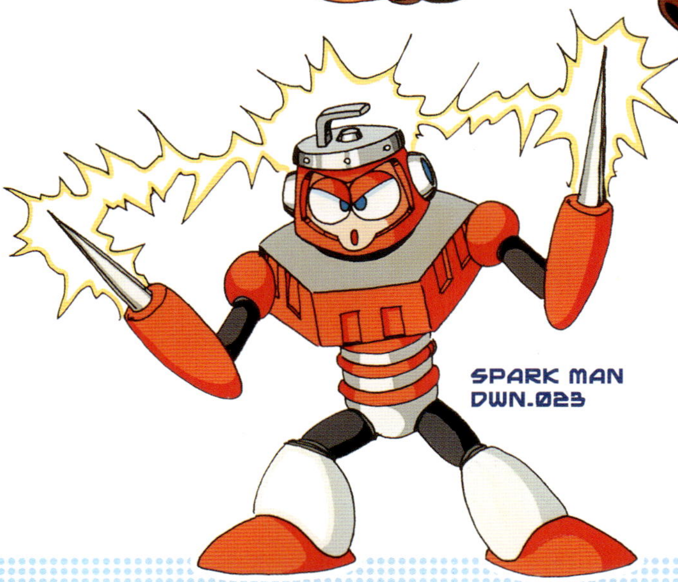

SPARK MAN
DWN.023

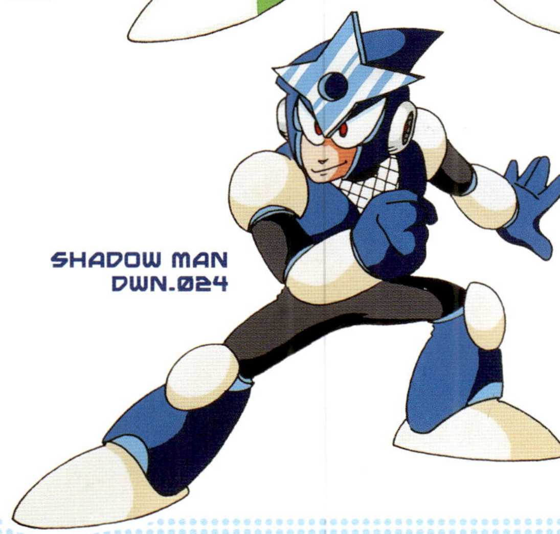

SHADOW MAN
DWN.024

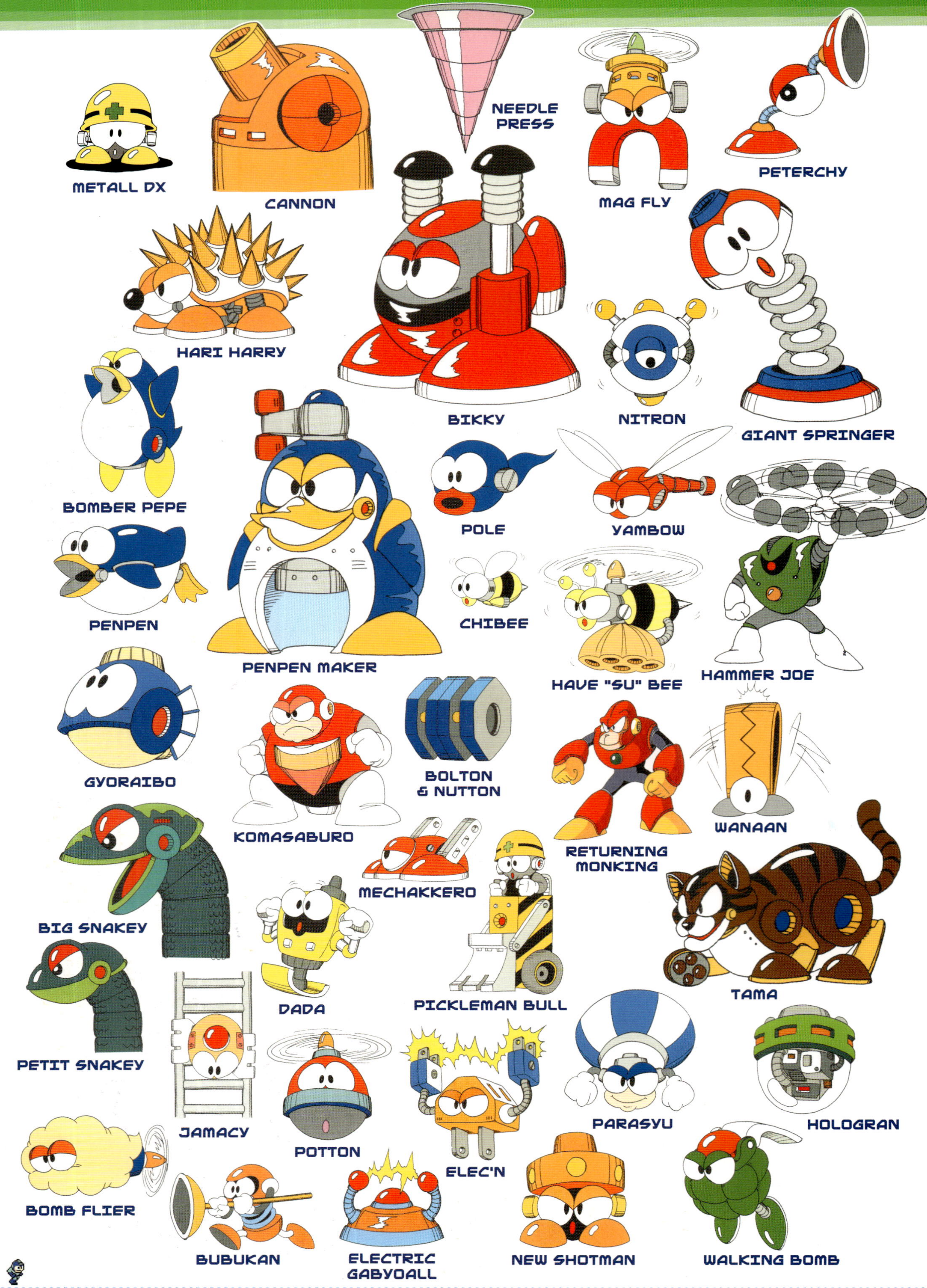
METALL DX
CANNON
NEEDLE PRESS
MAG FLY
PETERCHY
HARI HARRY
BIKKY
NITRON
GIANT SPRINGER
BOMBER PEPE
POLE
YAMBOW
PENPEN
PENPEN MAKER
CHIBEE
HAVE "SU" BEE
HAMMER JOE
GYORAIBO
KOMASABURO
BOLTON & NUTTON
RETURNING MONKING
WANAAN
BIG SNAKEY
MECHAKKERO
DADA
PICKLEMAN BULL
TAMA
PETIT SNAKEY
JAMACY
POTTON
ELEC'N
PARASYU
HOLOGRAN
BOMB FLIER
BUBUKAN
ELECTRIC GABYOALL
NEW SHOTMAN
WALKING BOMB

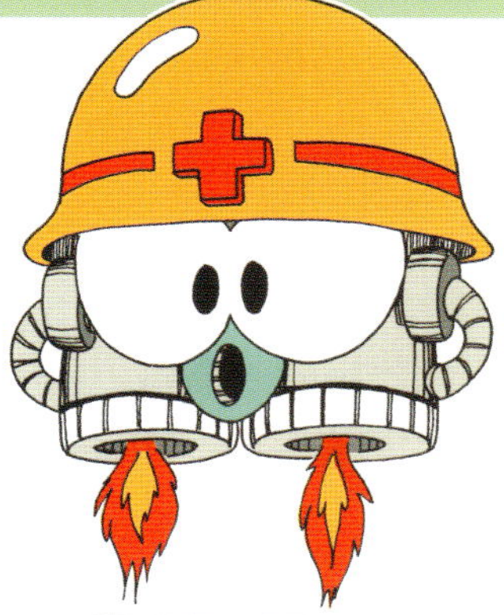

GIANT METALL

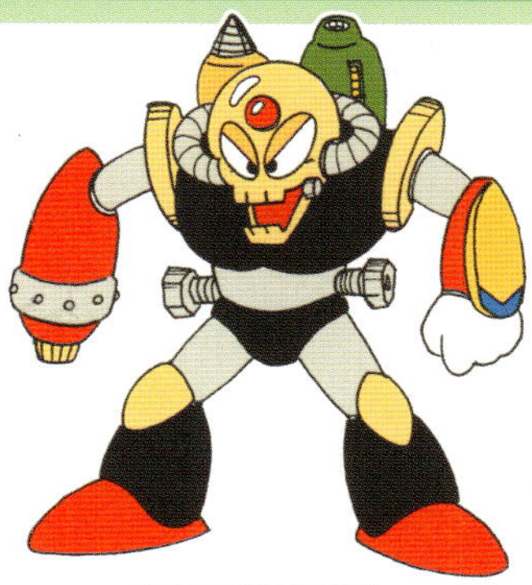

DOC ROBOT
K-176

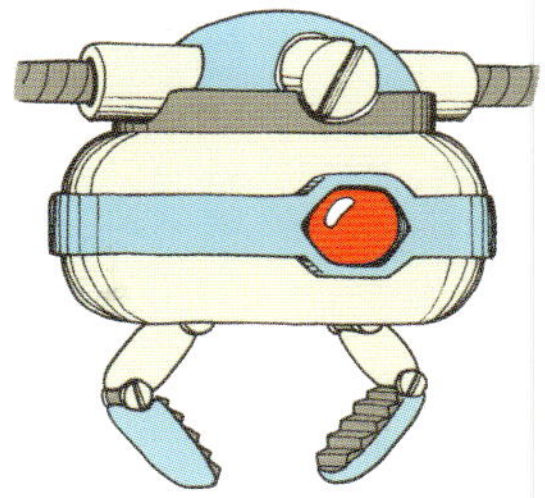

KAMEGORO MAKER

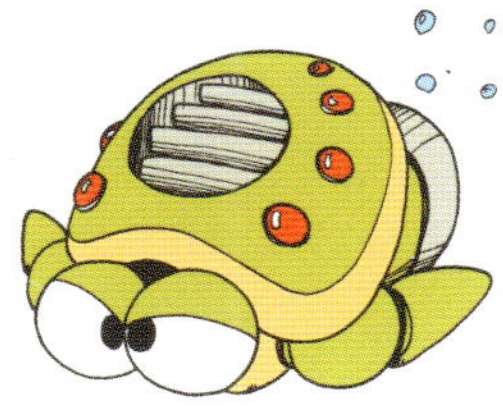

KAMEGORO

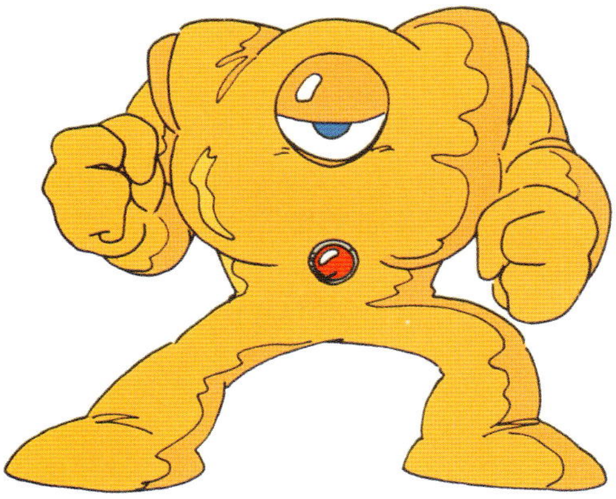

YELLOW DEVIL MK-II

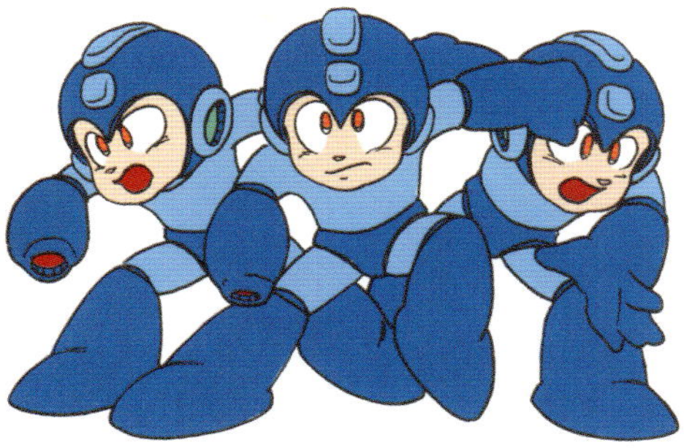

HOLOGRAPH MEGA MANS

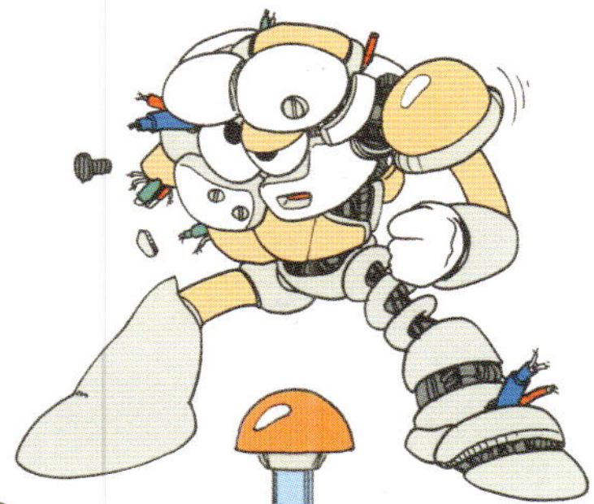

JUNK
GOLEM

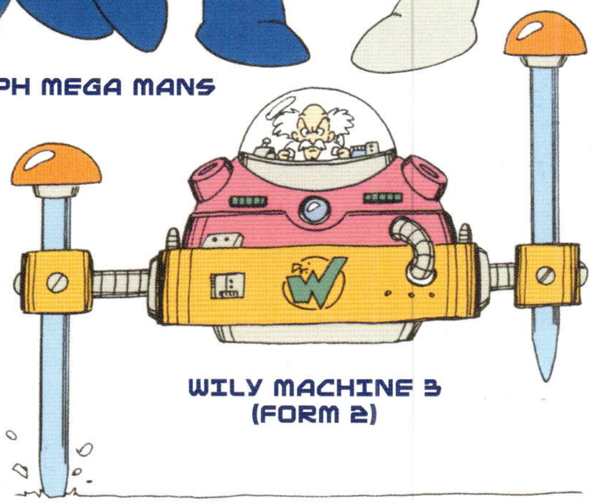

WILY MACHINE 3
(FORM 2)

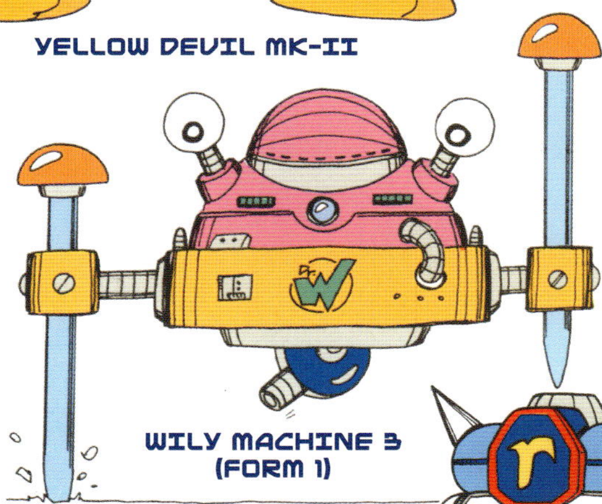

WILY MACHINE 3
(FORM 1)

GAMMA (FORM 2)

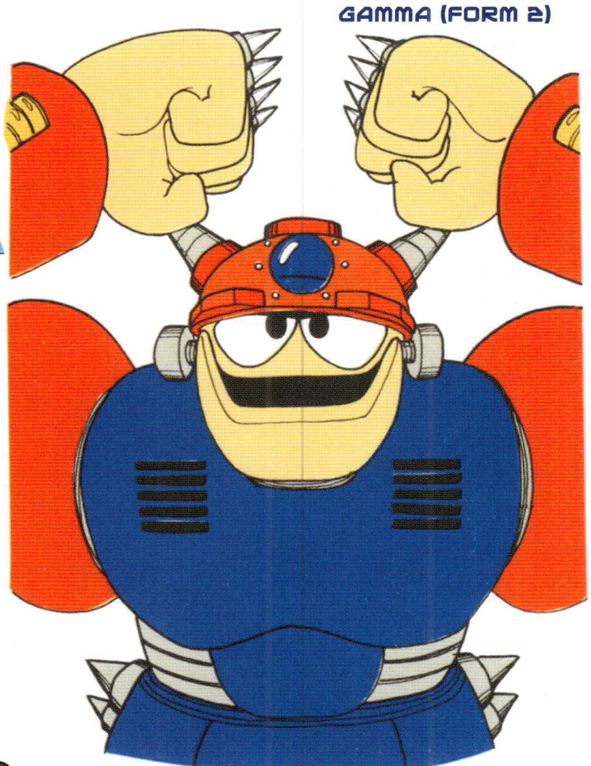

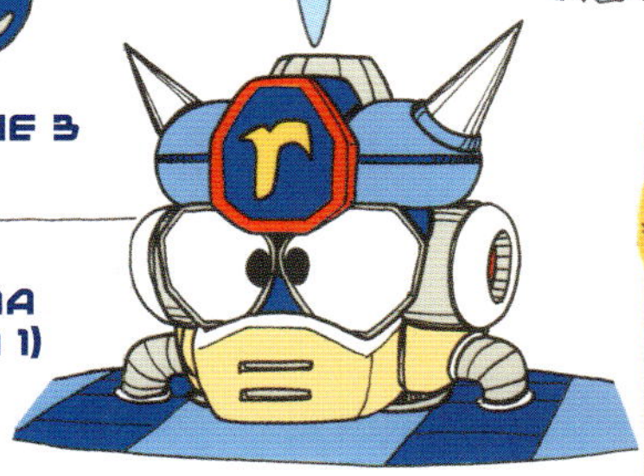

GAMMA
(FORM 1)

"I was stretched well beyond my job description for '3' to say the least. At one point, I even found myself having a discussion with the Sound Lead, although that certainly did not mean I had any less illustration work to do. Suffice to say, I was kept very busy. There are a lot of little things that I'm unhappy with when it comes to '3,' and if I had the chance I would definitely redo most of it." (Inafune)

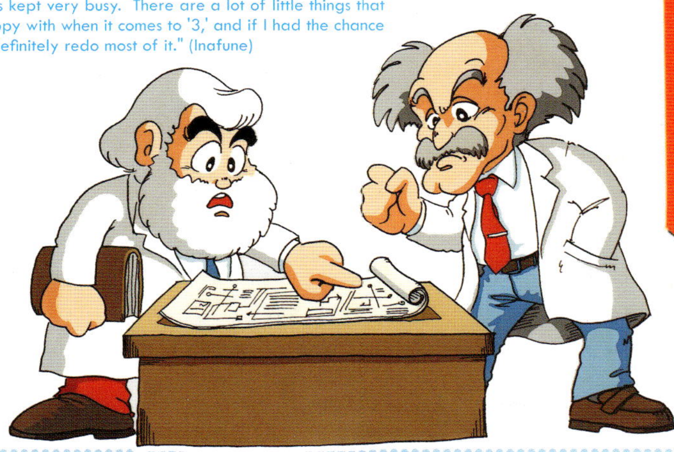

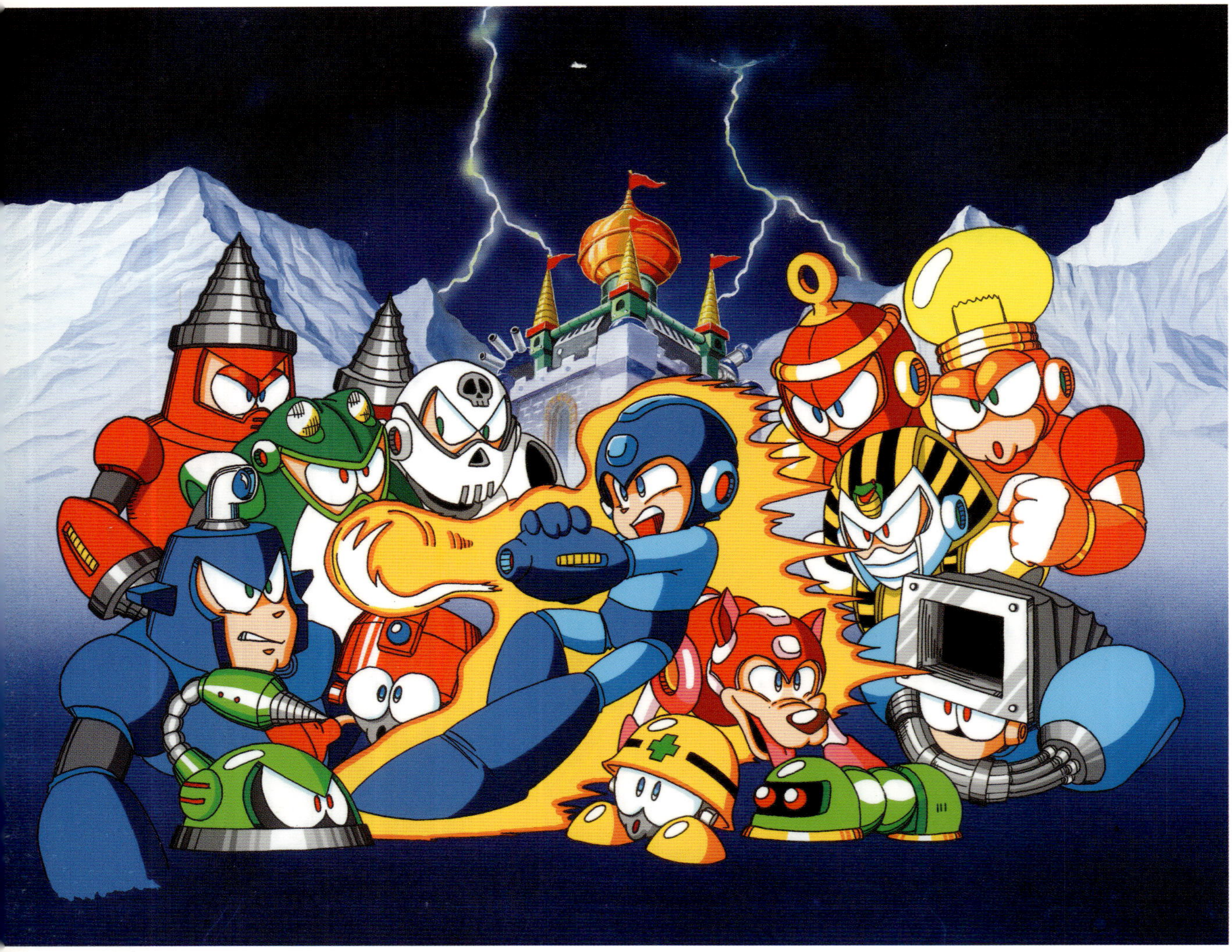

ROCKMAN 4 新たなる野望!!

Mega Man 4
NES 12/06/1991
Total number of boss character submissions: 70,000

A new challenge was presented by the ambitious Dr. Cossack who, like Dr. Wily before him, wanted to take over the world. Outfitted with the new Mega Buster that Dr. Light had secretly been working on, Mega Man set out to return peace to the eight cities that had been seized by Dr. Cossack.

"Since both Light and Wily were elderly, we made Cossack more of a 'young scientific genius.' For some reason, that made me think of American influences, but I really wanted to take it to a completely different country, so I incorporated a lot of flavor from the north." (Inafune)

"Dr. Cossack was initially named Dr. Vice, but we decided we wanted to stay with the music theme and changed it to Cossack instead." (Kaji)

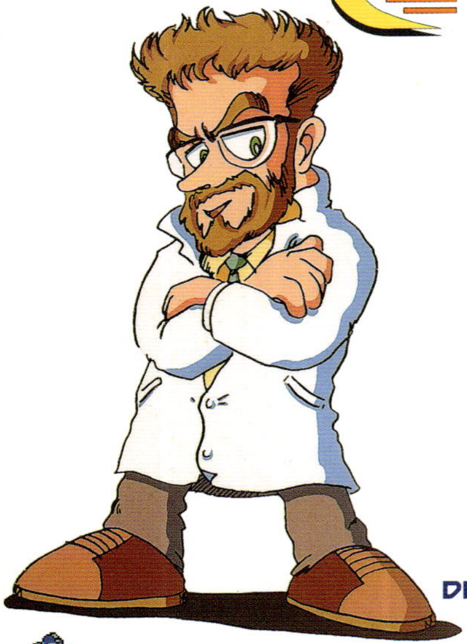

DR. COSSACK

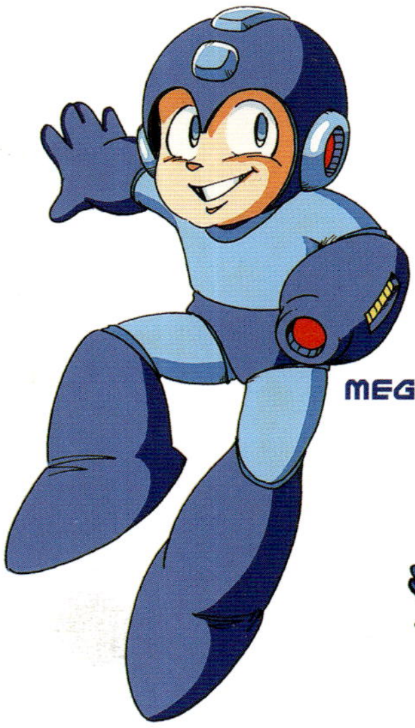

MEGA MAN

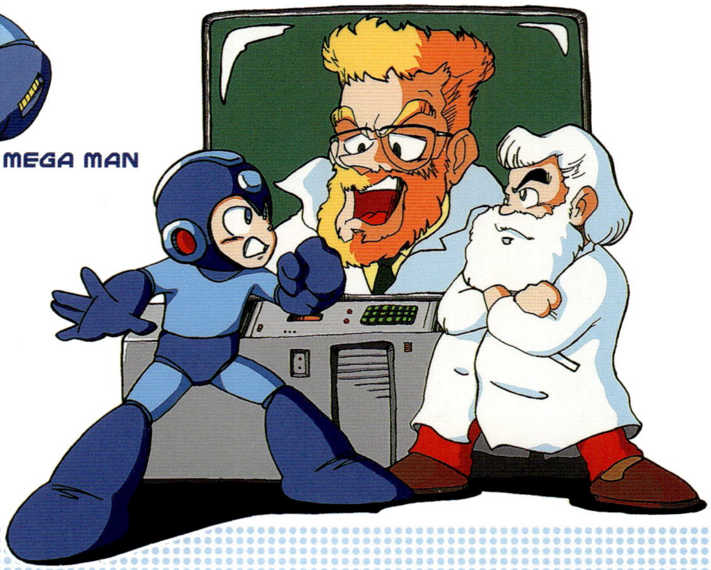

NEW MEGA BLASTER

"The Charge Shot became a staple attack starting with '4,' but we knew adding a two-level or three-level charge would change the whole flavor of the game in some respects, and we were very mindful of that." (Inafune)

"I think I was the one working on the Charge Shot. I had a lot of trouble perfecting it. At one point the shot would disappear if it was right next to you. (laughs)" (Kaji)

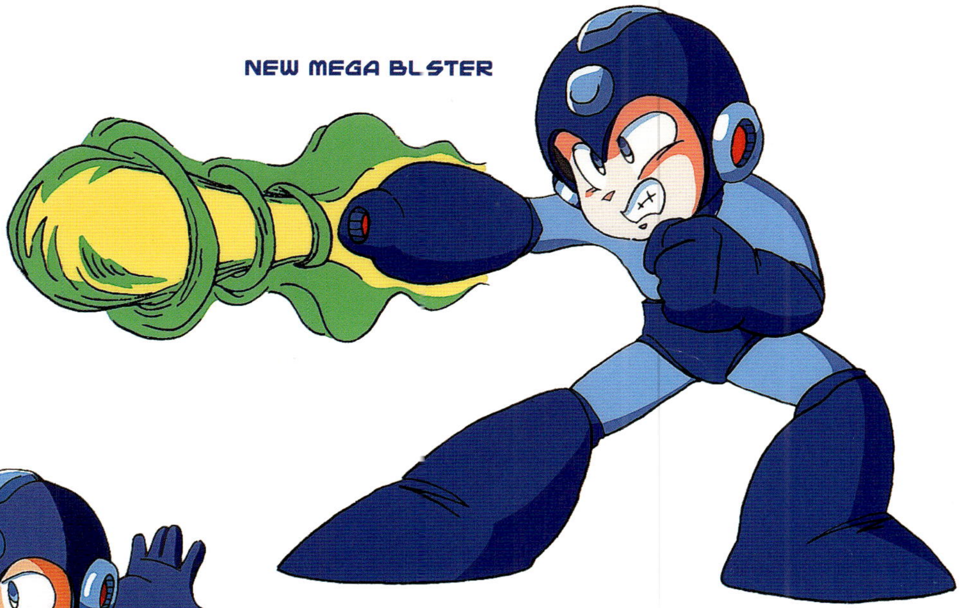

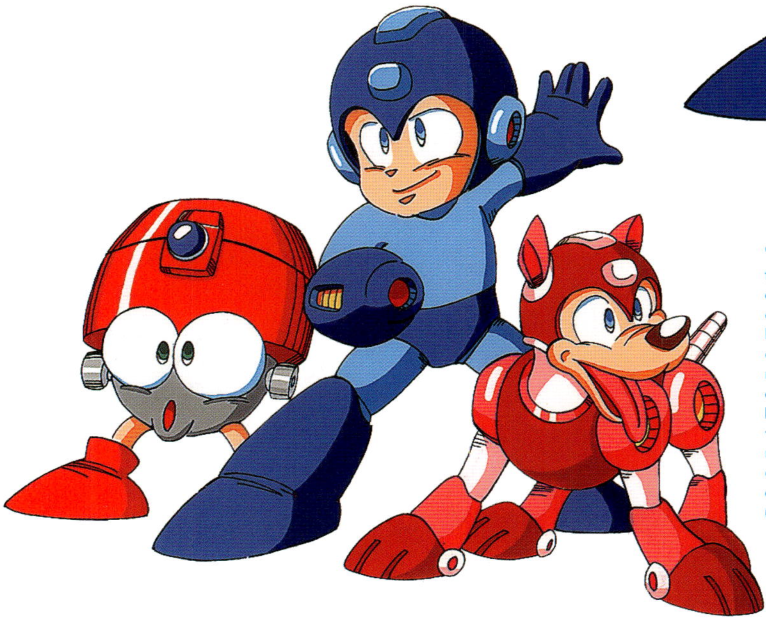

"Eddie was an idea that came to us while we were working on '2.' Instead of just placing an item to be discovered by the player, we wanted a character in a supporting role that would behave kind of like a lottery. You never knew what to expect, and we wanted the player to be really happy or be really disappointed depending on what came out. (laughs)" (Inafune)

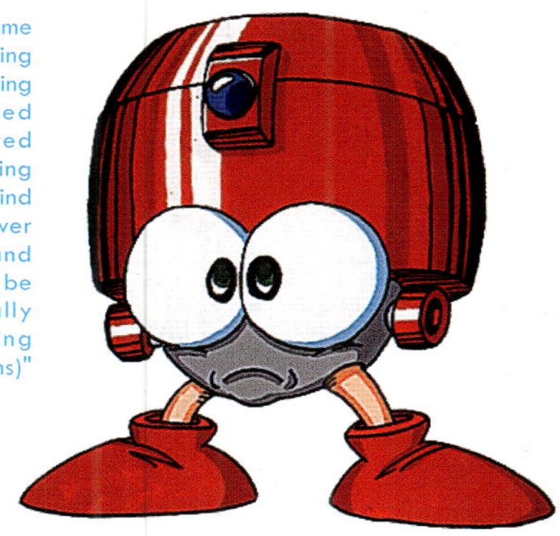

EDDIE

"It was getting pretty stuffy with all of these male characters, so we decided to add a cute new character as well. This is how Kalinka came about. It's not like we were trying to give Roll any competition, but I guess you can't really help but compare the two. I had a lot of fun working on '4,' and I'm very happy with the two new character designs." (Inafune)

"When creating new characters, Inafune really enjoys starting from their story or some other detail like that and expanding out." (Kaji)

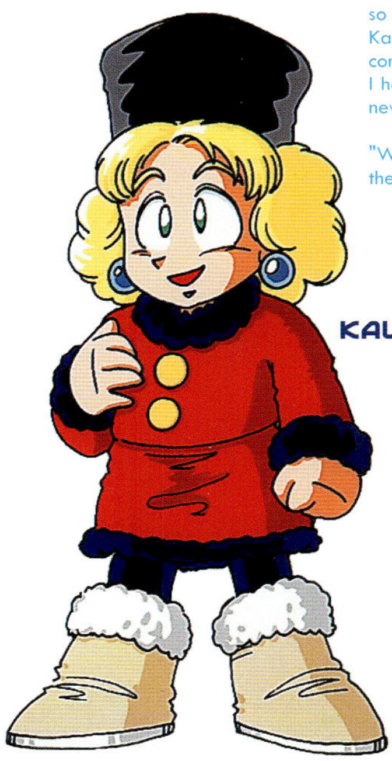

KALINKA

DR. COSSACK'S CITADEL

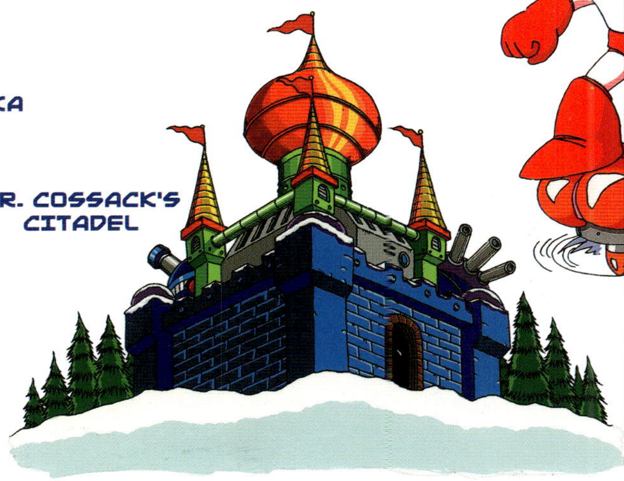

BALLOON ADAPTER

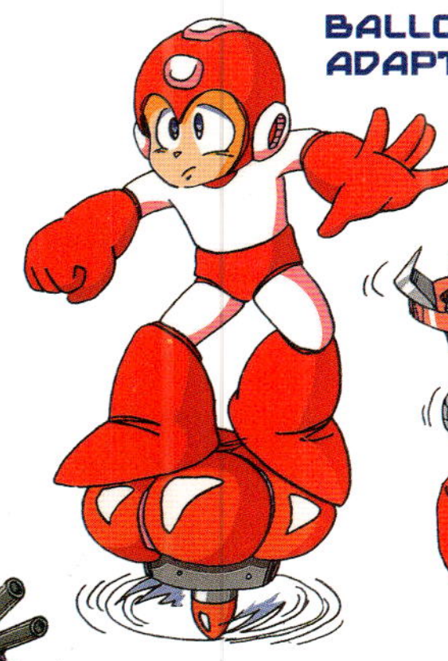

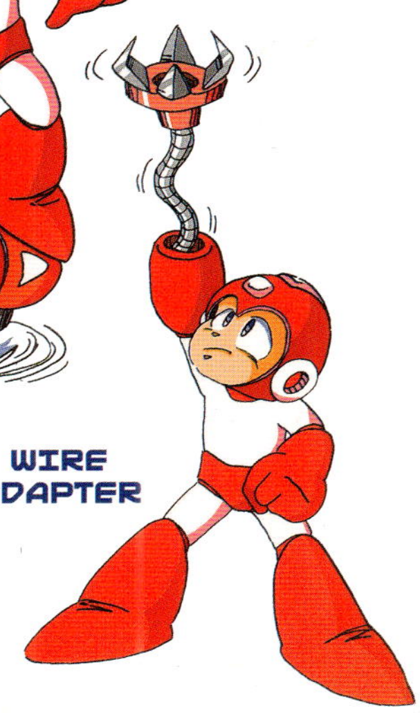

WIRE ADAPTER

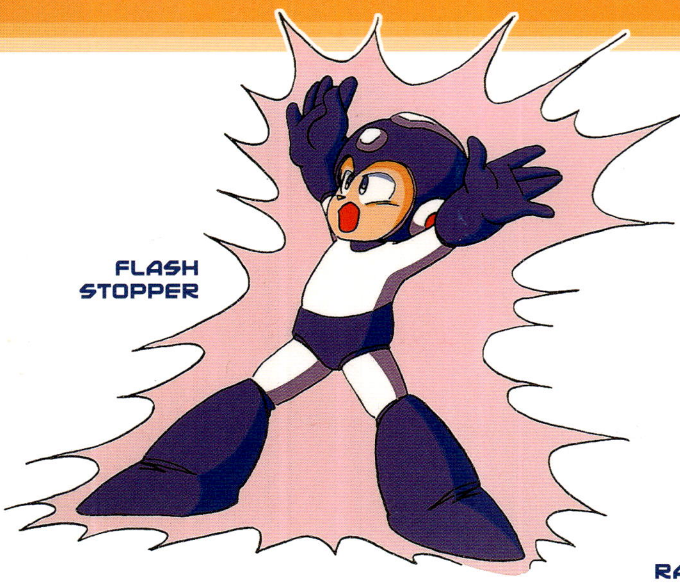

FLASH STOPPER

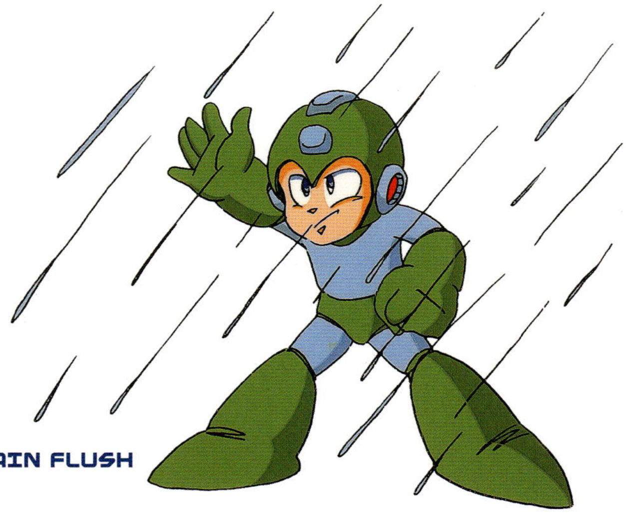

RAIN FLUSH

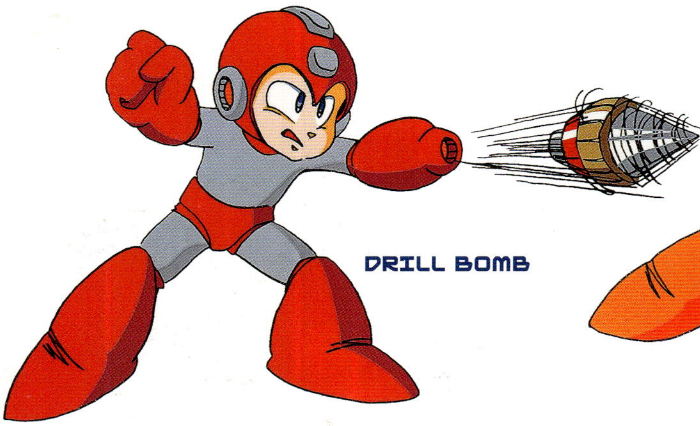

DRILL BOMB

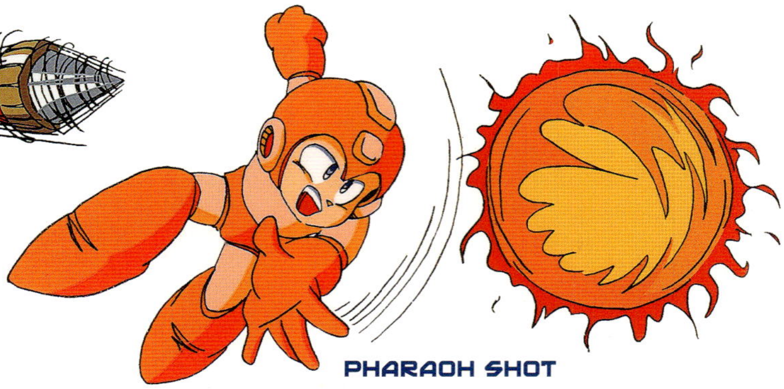

PHARAOH SHOT

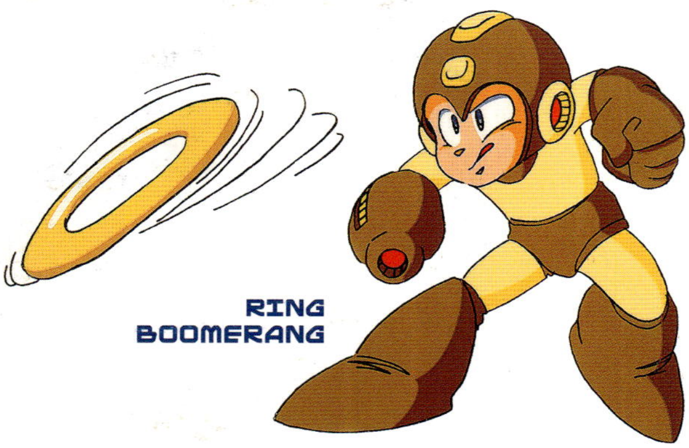

RING BOOMERANG

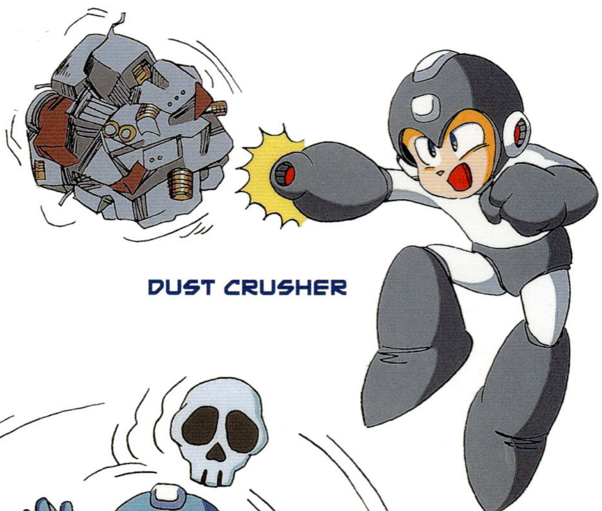

DUST CRUSHER

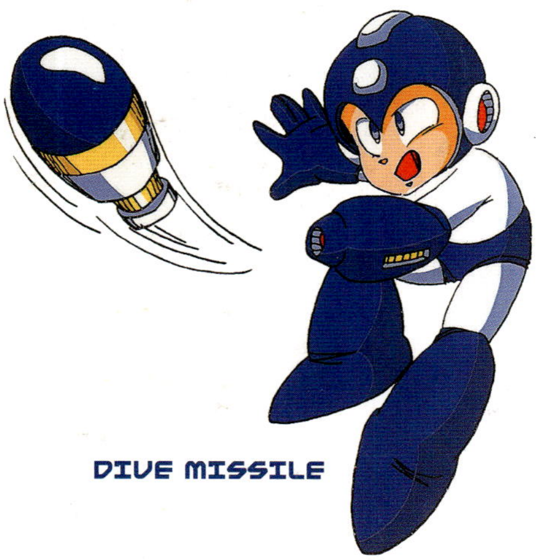

DIVE MISSILE

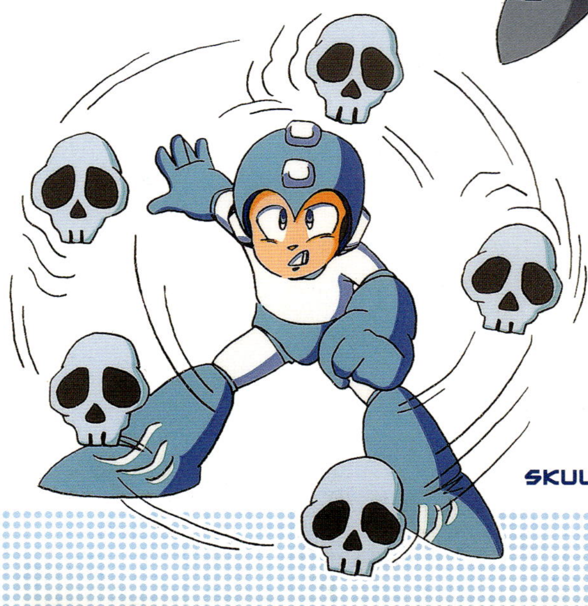

SKULL BARRIER

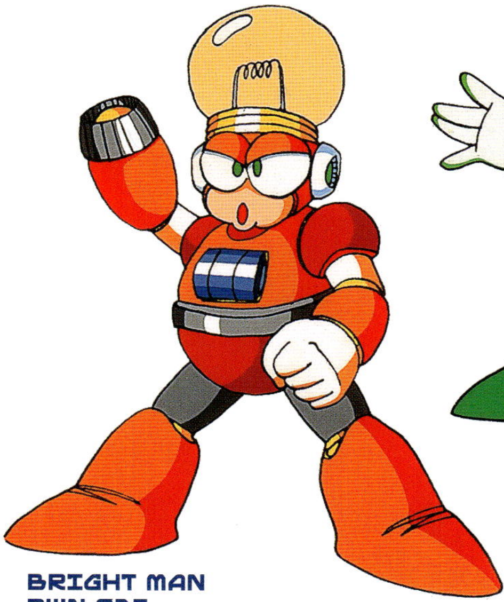

BRIGHT MAN
DWN.025

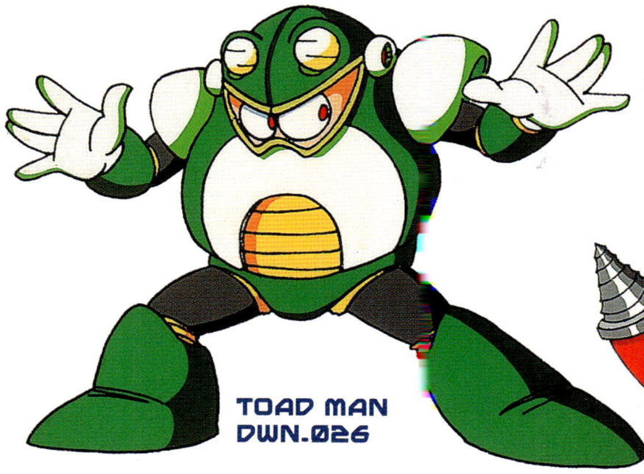

TOAD MAN
DWN.026

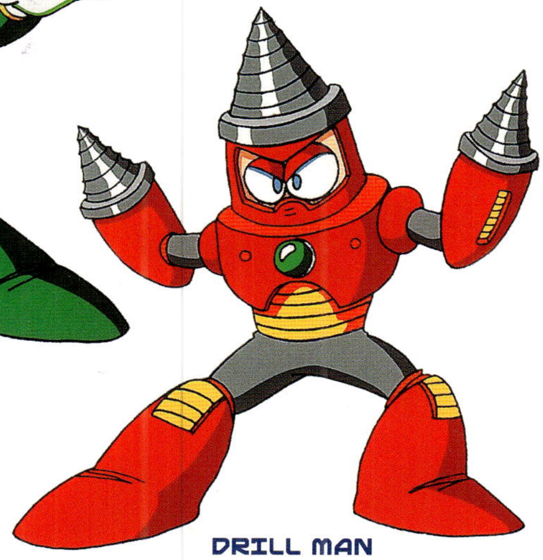

DRILL MAN
DWN.027

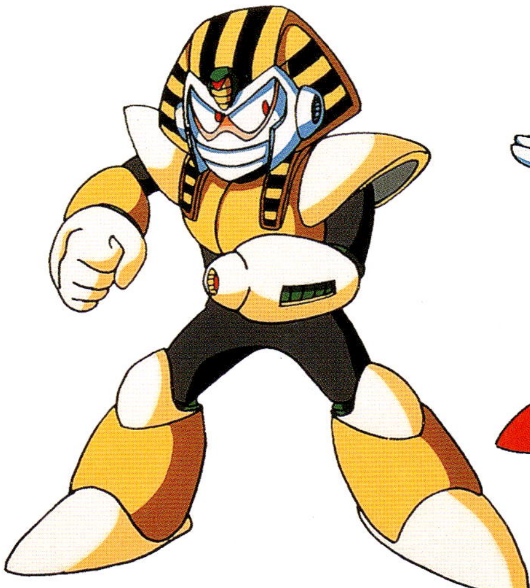

PHARAOH MAN
DWN.028

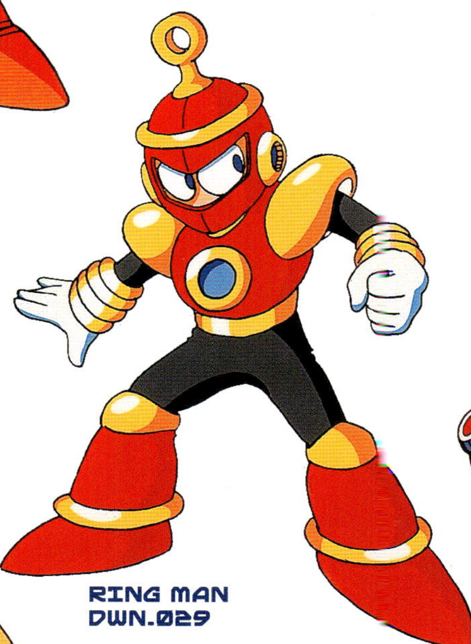

RING MAN
DWN.029

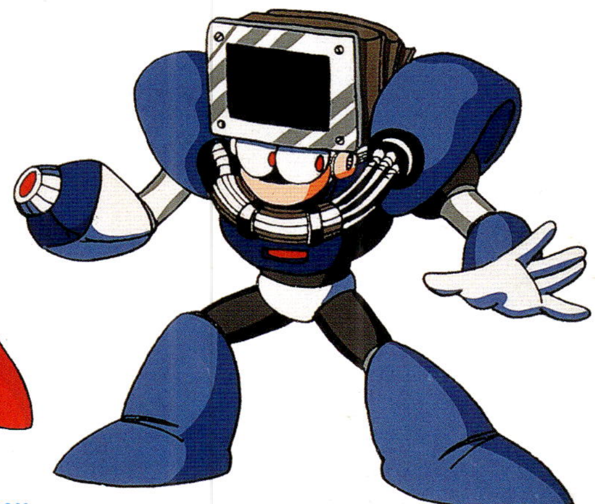

DUST MAN
DWN.030

"We received so many submissions for boss characters that we basically had to camp out when going through the selection process." (Inafune)

"So many of the entries were really good, and you could tell that they really 'got it' as far as Mega Man was concerned. We hardly had to make any adjustments at all once we had selected the winning entries. I remember Skull Man in particular, as we scrapped a whole level that was in progress to recreate it specifically for Skull Man." (Kaji)

"I'm sure a lot of it has to do with the great initial design concepts, but I've got to say I think the designs and selections of boss characters for '4' turned out really well. I really like these characters." (Inafune)

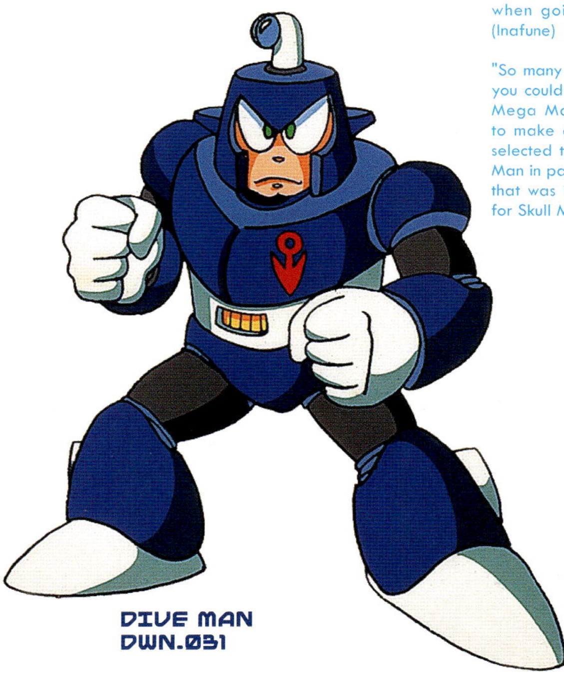

DIVE MAN
DWN.031

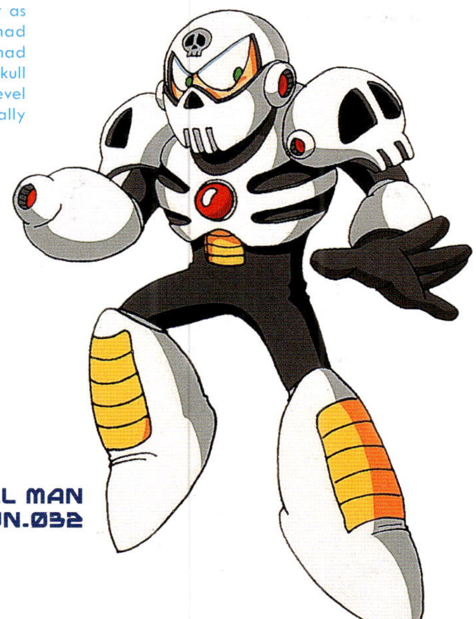

SKULL MAN
DWN.032

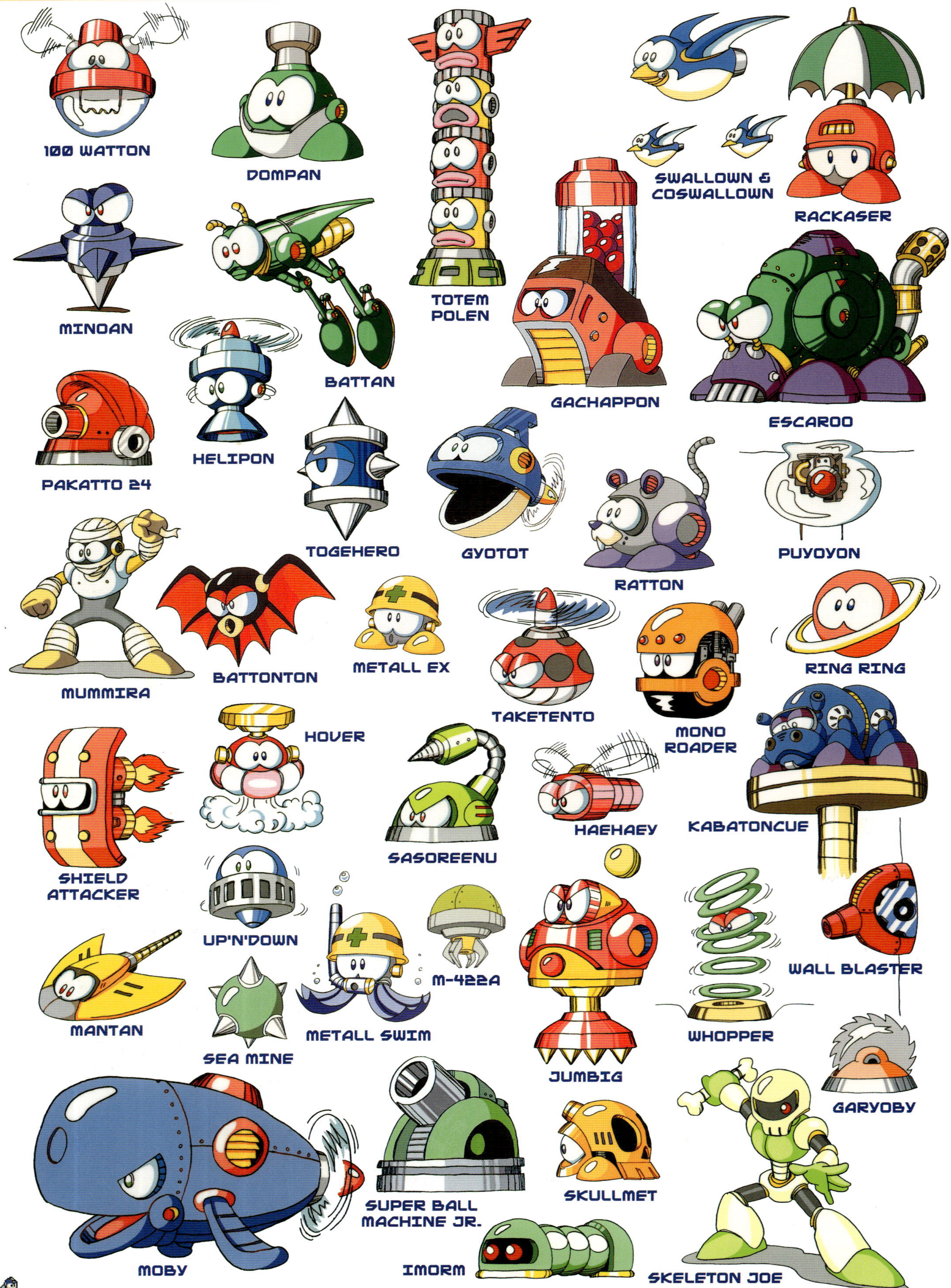
100 WATTON
DOMPAN
TOTEM POLEN
SWALLOWN & COSWALLOWN
RACKASER
MINOAN
BATTAN
GACHAPPON
ESCAROO
PAKATTO 24
HELIPON
TOGEHERO
GYOTOT
RATTON
PUYOYON
MUMMIRA
BATTONTON
METALL EX
TAKETENTO
MONO ROADER
RING RING
SHIELD ATTACKER
HOVER
SASOREENU
HAEHAEY
KABATONCUE
UP'N'DOWN
M-422A
METALL SWIM
JUMBIG
WHOPPER
WALL BLASTER
MANTAN
SEA MINE
GARYOBY
MOBY
SUPER BALL MACHINE JR.
SKULLMET
IMORM
SKELETON JOE

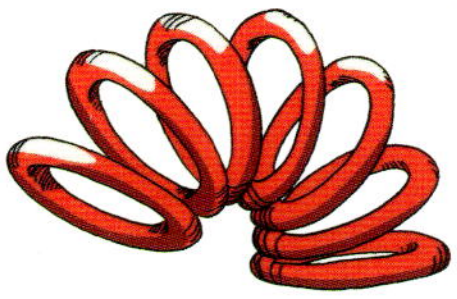

TOM BOY

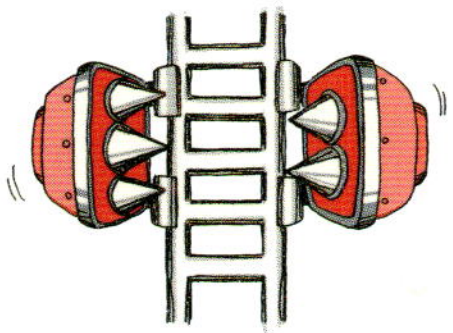

LADDER PRESS

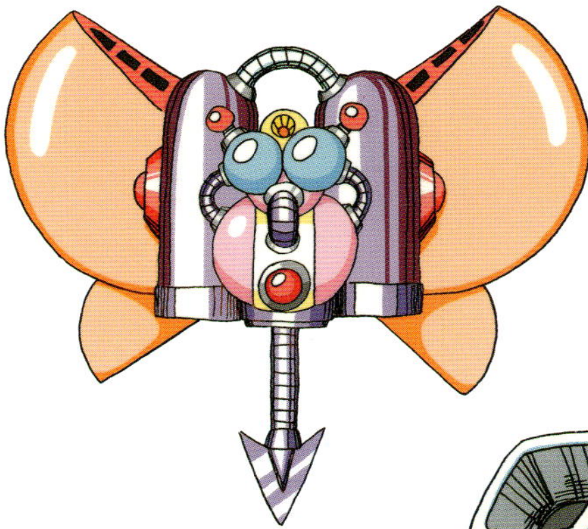

MOTHRAYA

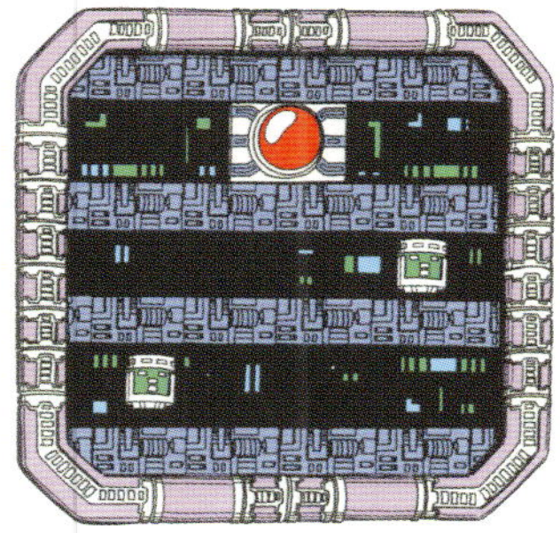

SQUARE MACHINE

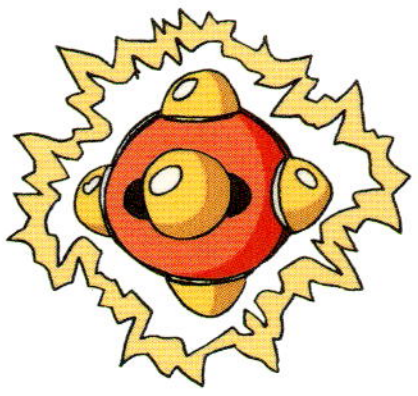

BIREE

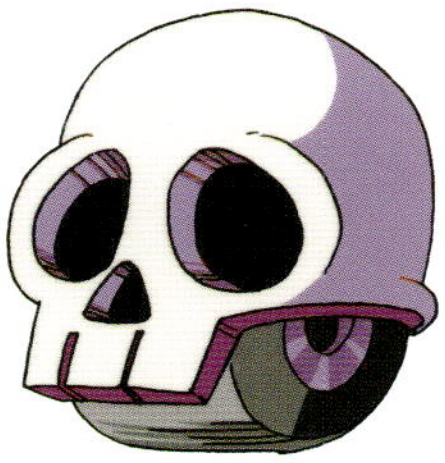

DOCRON

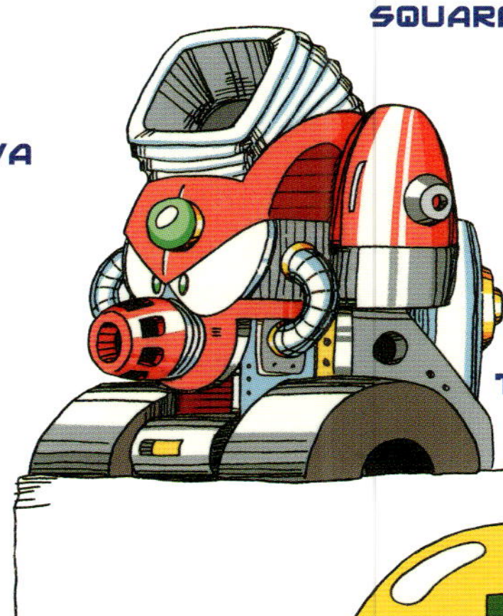

TAKOTRASH

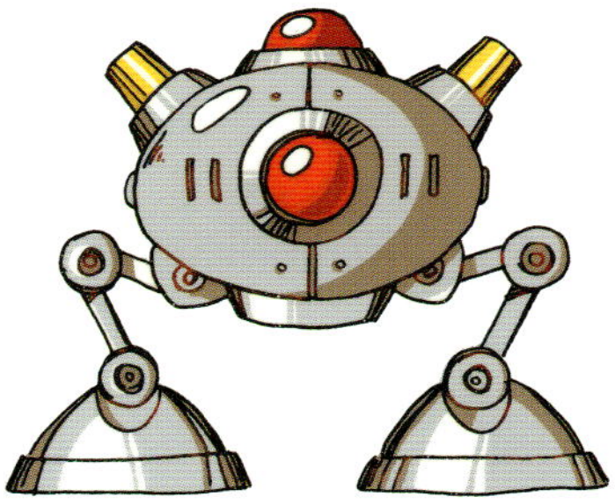

COCKROACH TWIN

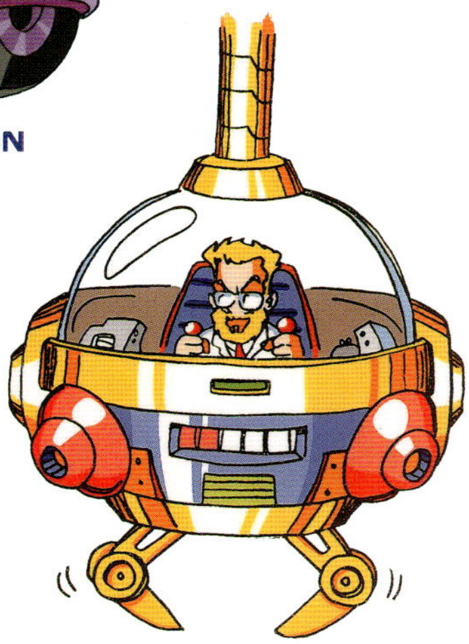

COSSACK CATCHER

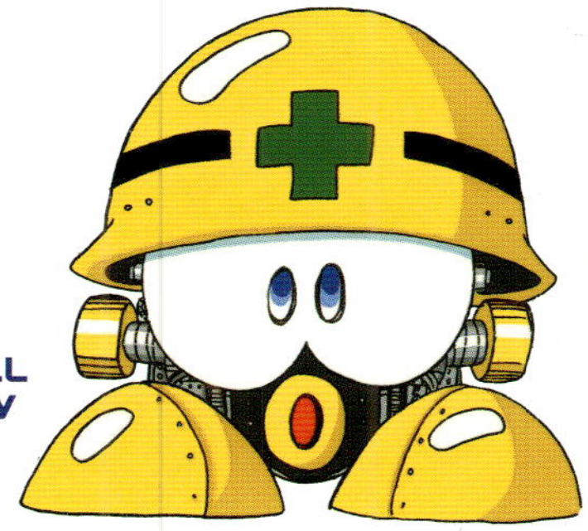

METALL DADDY

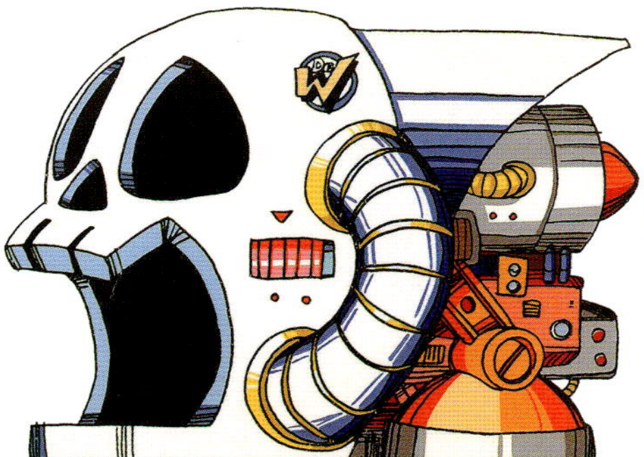

WILY MACHINE 4 (FORM 1)

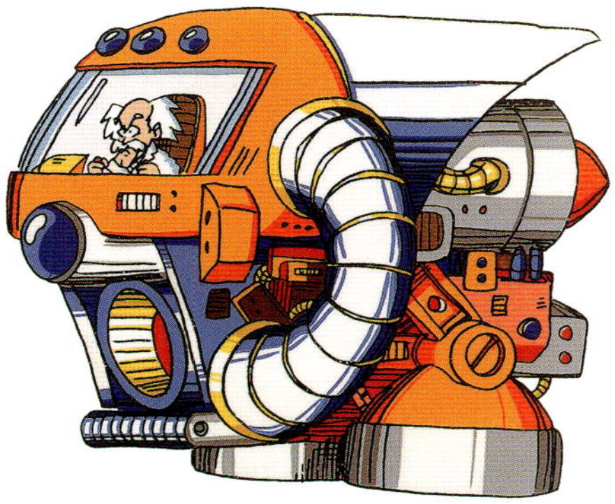

WILY MACHINE 4 (FORM 2)

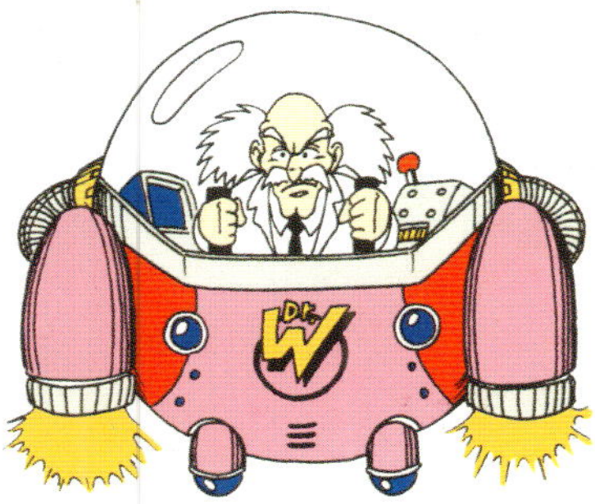

WILY CAPSULE

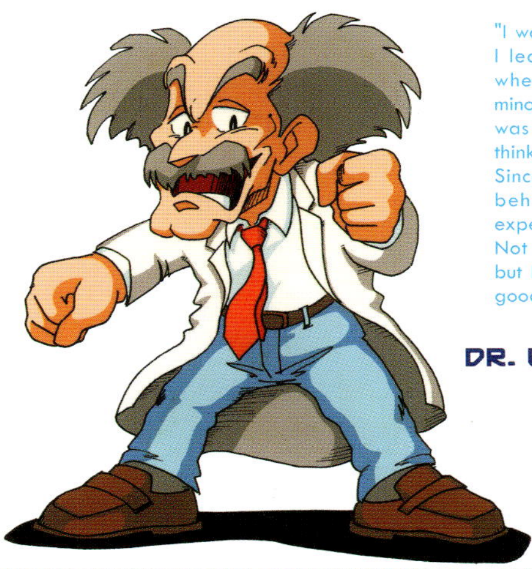

"I was the new guy who came in for '4.' I learned a lot under Inafune's wing, where I got to work on some of the minor enemy characters. Shield Attacker was something that I came up with by thinking from a gameplay perspective. Since you can only land attacks from behind, it kind of forces people to experiment with the new sliding feature. Not to toot my own horn or anything, but I think Shield Attacker was a pretty good idea. (laughs)" (Kaji)

DR. WILY

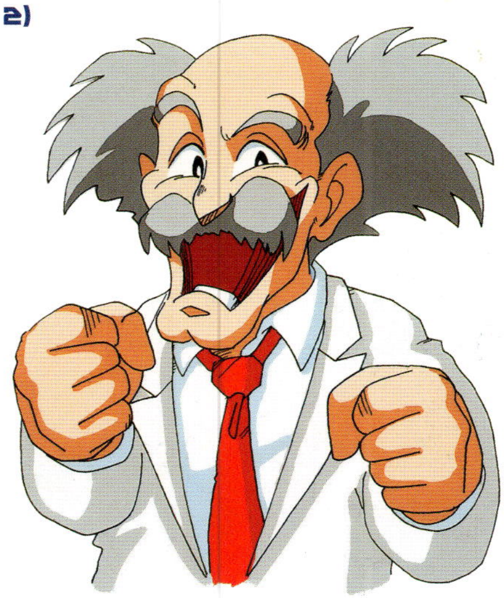

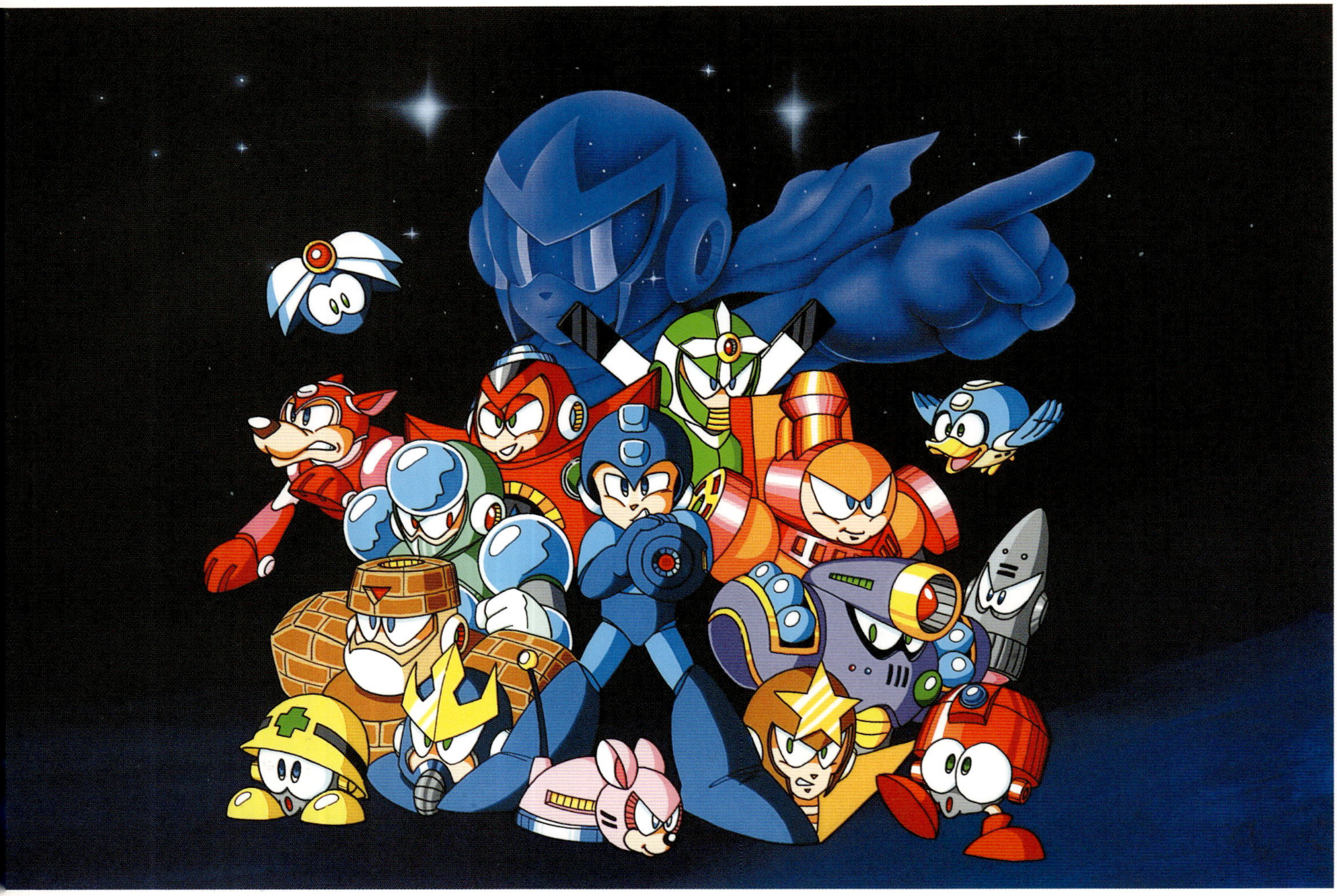

ROCKMAN 5 ブルースの罠!?

Mega Man 5
NES 12/04/1992
Total number of boss character submissions: 130,000

Two months had passed since the last battle, and Mega Man was enjoying his well-deserved break from fighting. Then one day, Proto Man showed up with a whole army of mysterious robots behind him and began laying siege to the city. To make matters worse, Proto Man also kidnapped Dr. Light. Why would he do this!? Surrounded by many unanswered questions, the battle between Proto Man and Mega Man begins!

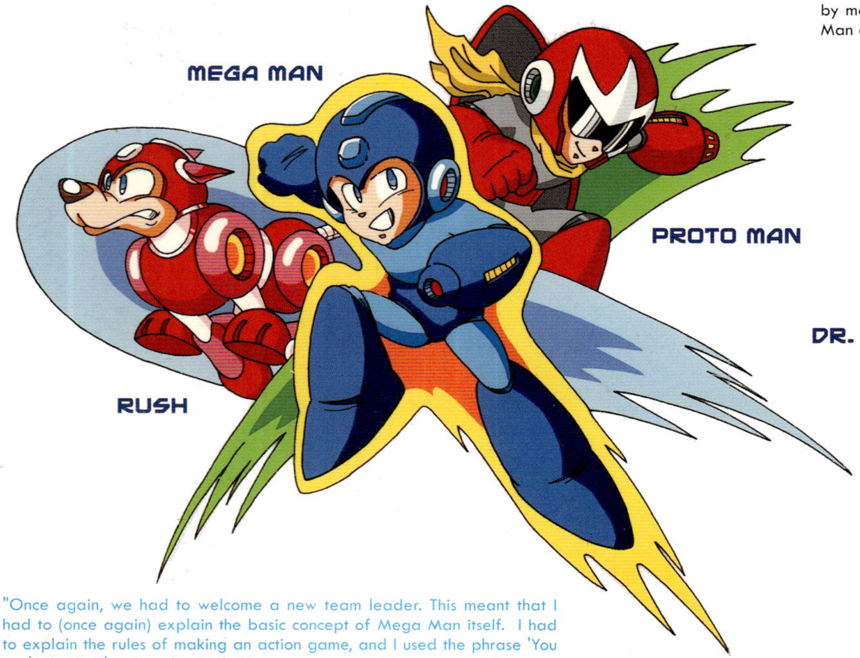

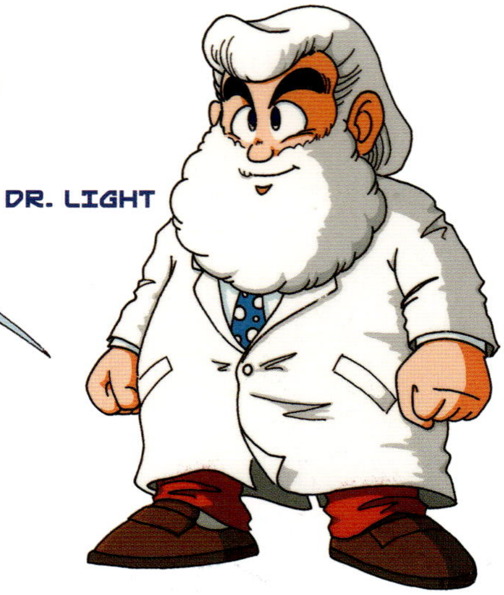

"Once again, we had to welcome a new team leader. This meant that I had to (once again) explain the basic concept of Mega Man itself. I had to explain the rules of making an action game, and I used the phrase 'You can't do that!' quite often. Making an unreasonable game, for instance, would be an affront to the players. I had many such conversations during the development of this game, and I think it may have a lower level of difficulty as a result." (Inafune)

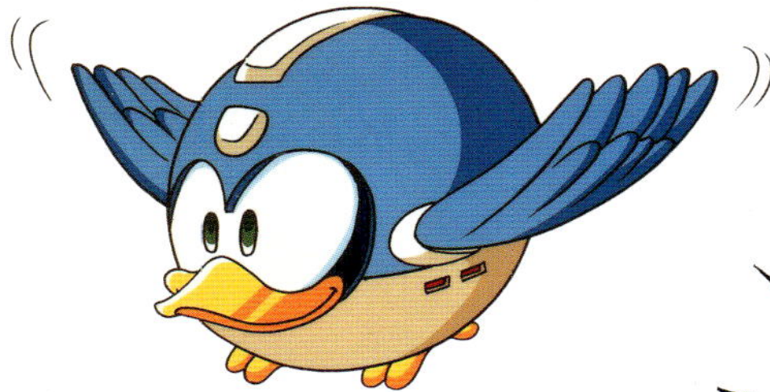

BEAT

"It's a bird... that's a helmet. (laughs) I didn't have a very hard time with the design. I just tried to imagine what a cute bird would look like, and this is what I got. I hadn't had much experience drawing birds, but I got it approved on my first shot." (Inafune)

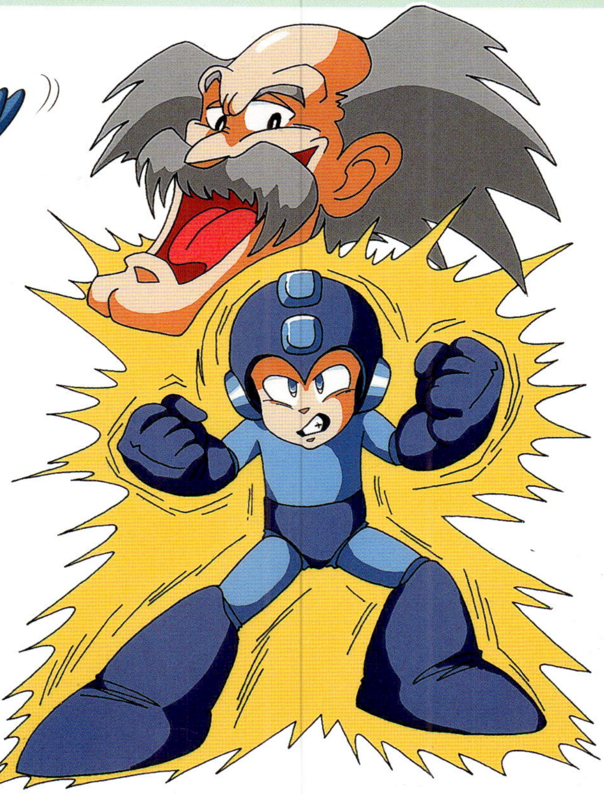

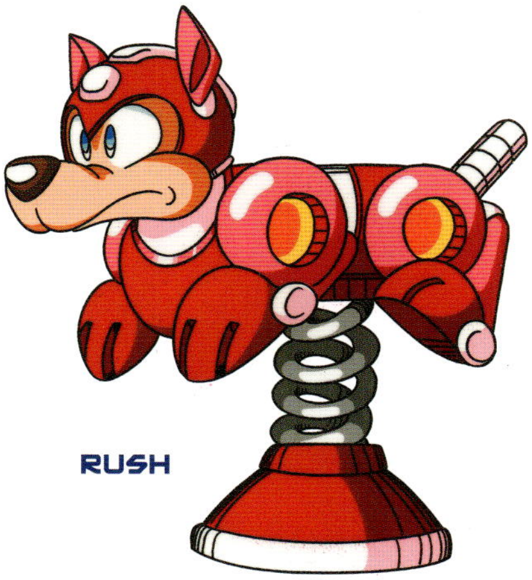

RUSH

"I knew we had to come up with something new, so we powered up the Charge Shot. It felt like everything had already been 'done' in '4,' so all we really had left to do was introduce powered up versions of everything in '5' and '6.'" (Inafune)

"We didn't just make the Charge Shot bigger in '5,' but also added some different colors where we could." (Kaji)

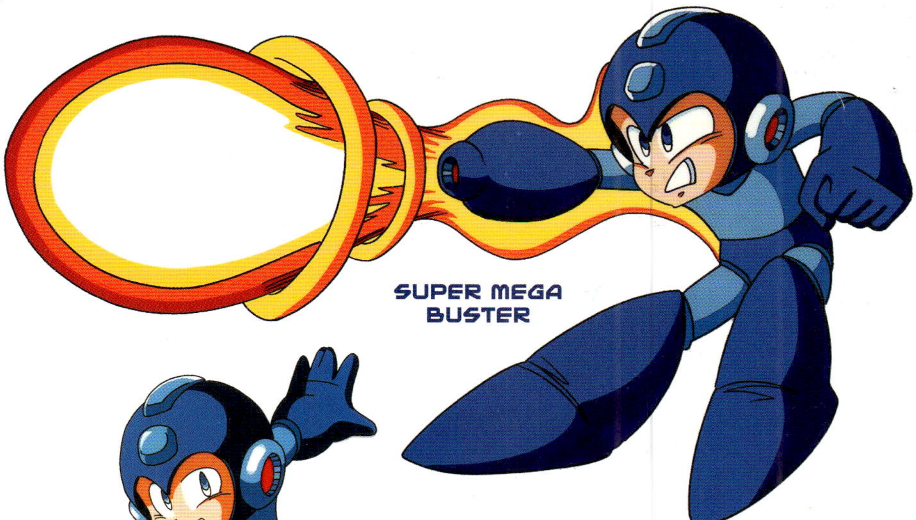

SUPER MEGA BUSTER

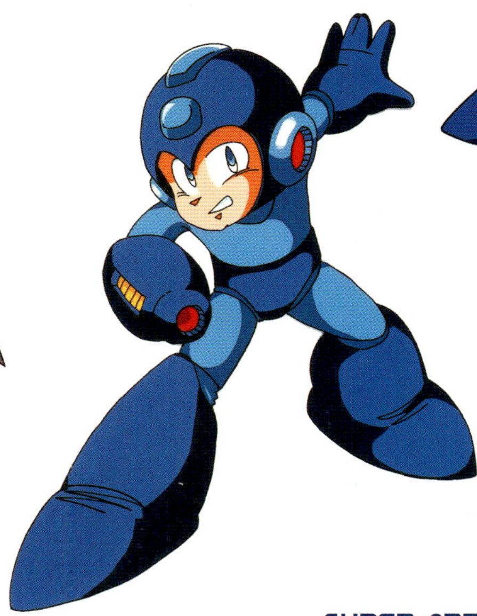

DR. WILY

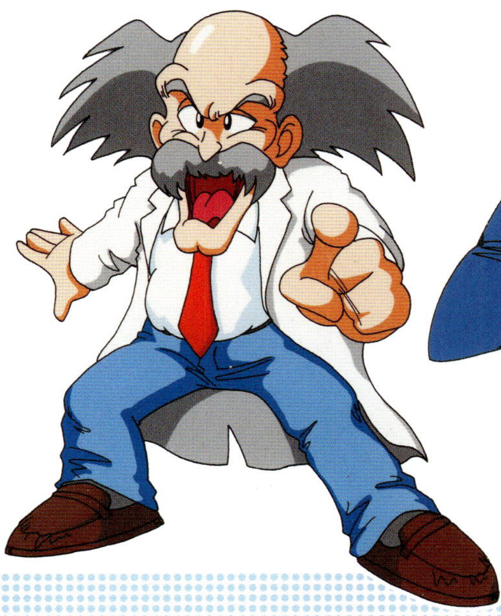

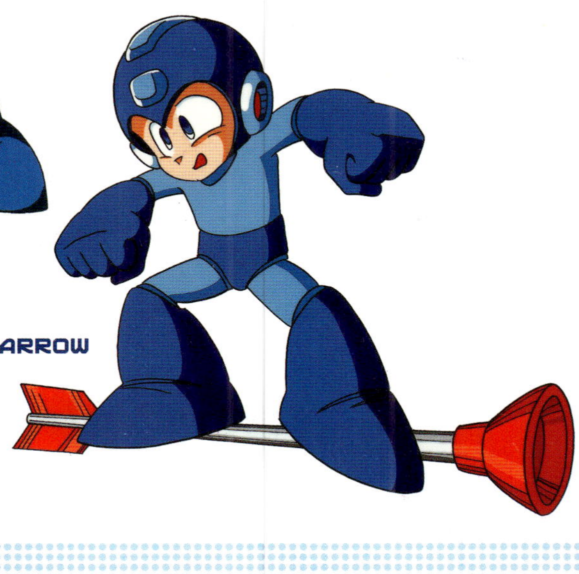

SUPER ARROW

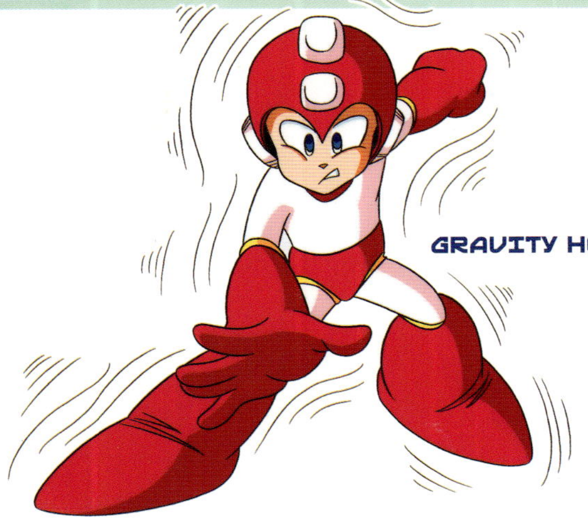

GRAVITY HOLD

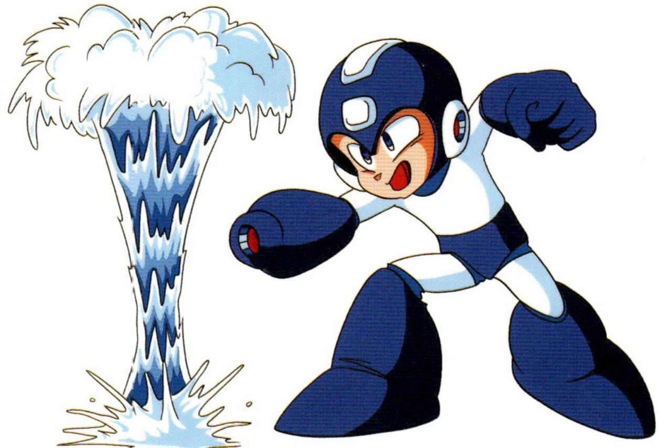

WATER WAVE

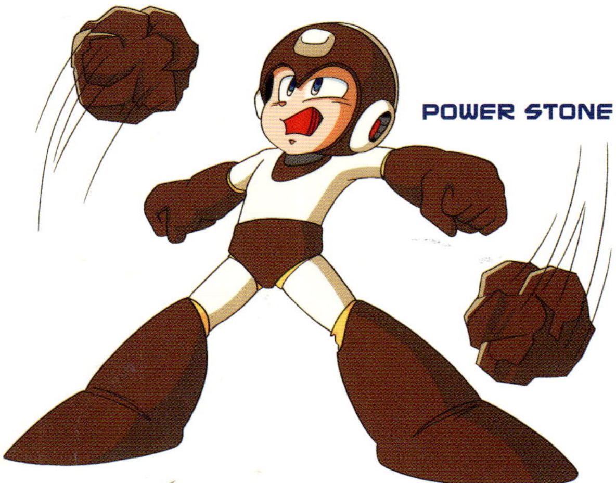

POWER STONE

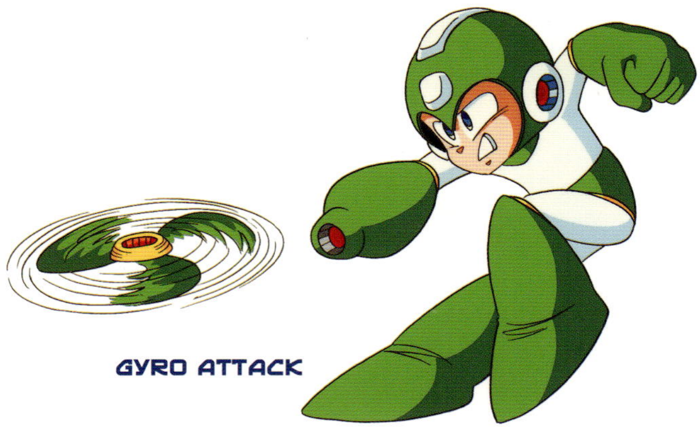

GYRO ATTACK

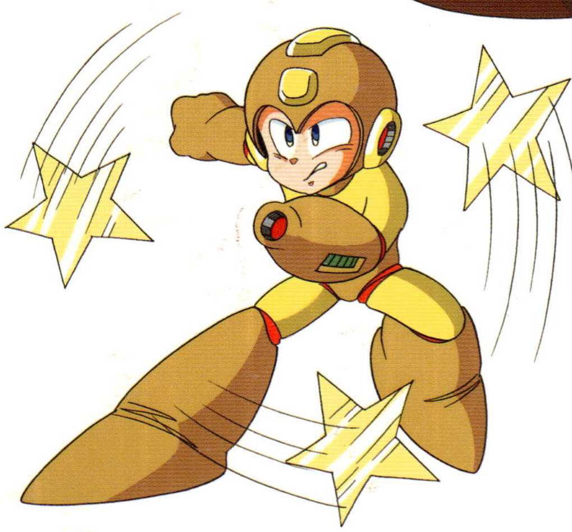

STAR CRASH

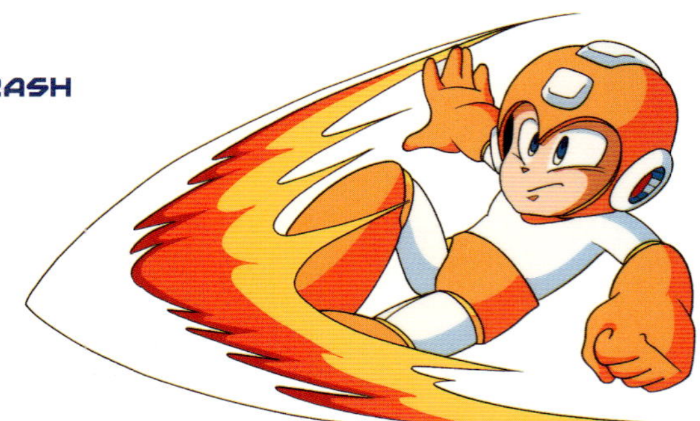

CHARGE KICK

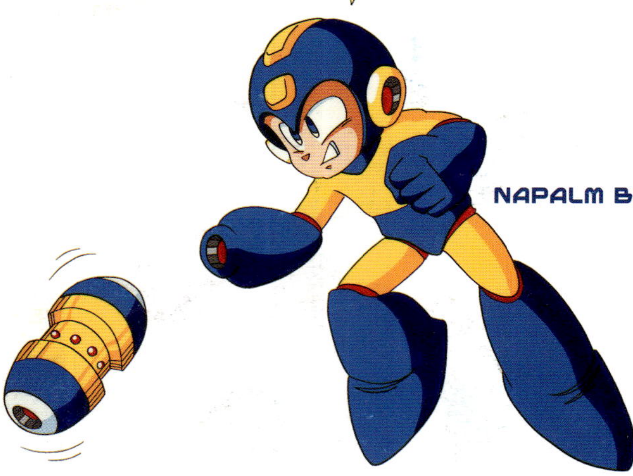

NAPALM BOMB

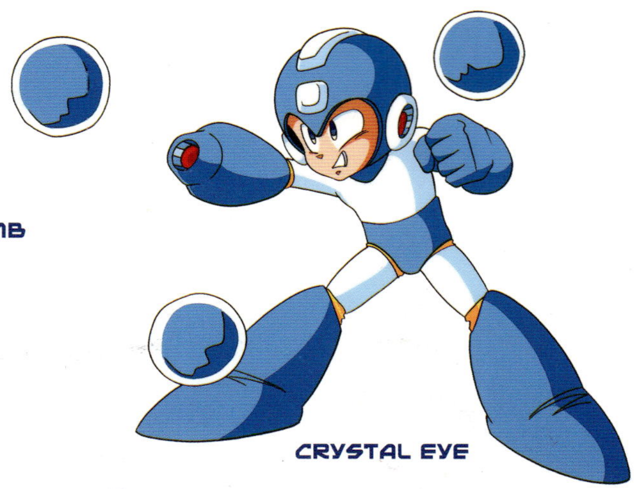

CRYSTAL EYE

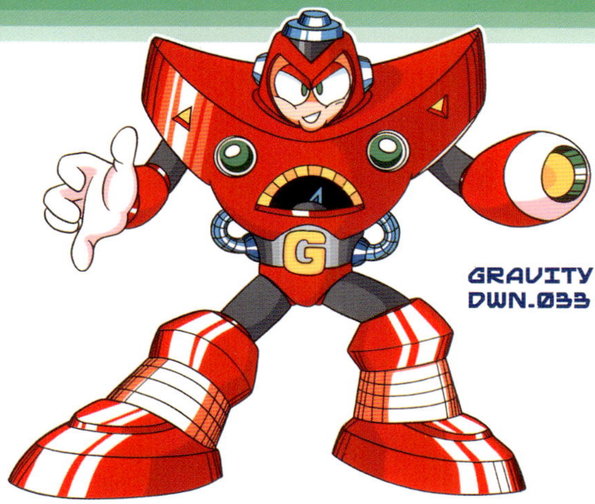

GRAVITY MAN
DWN.033

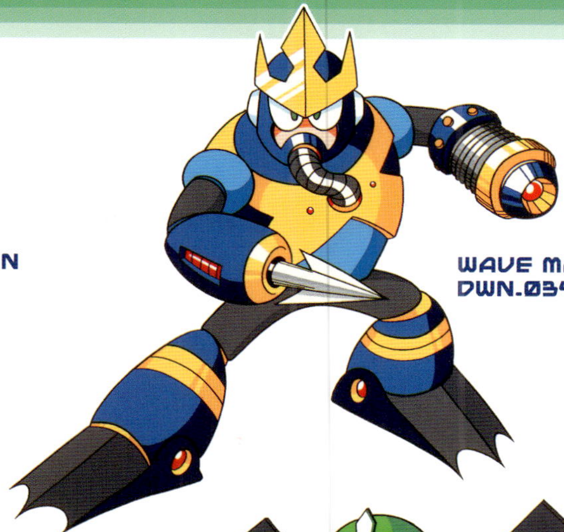

WAVE MAN
DWN.034

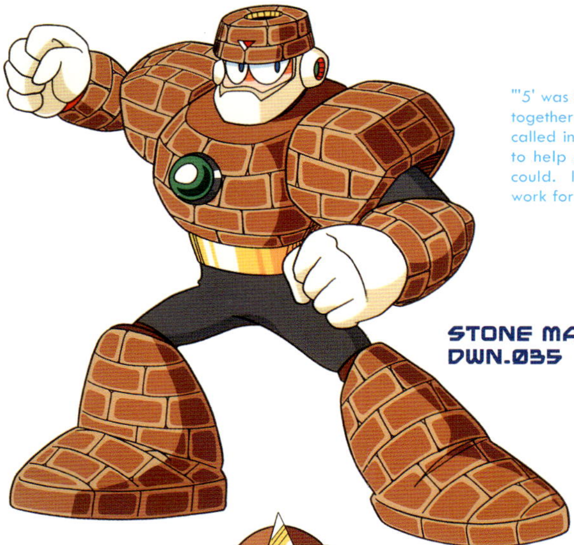

STONE MAN
DWN.035

"'5' was taking a while to come together as a game, and I was called in in the middle of it all to help out in any way that I could. I did some of the dot work for Stone Man." (Kaji)

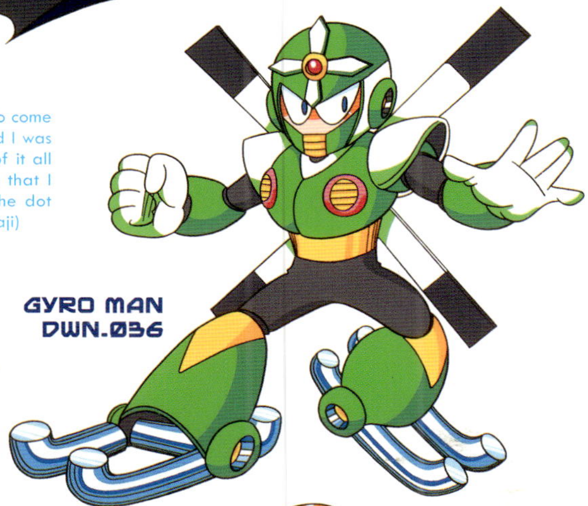

GYRO MAN
DWN.036

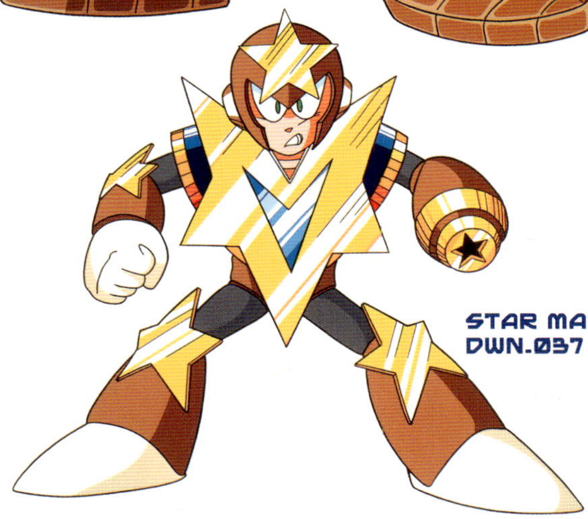

STAR MAN
DWN.037

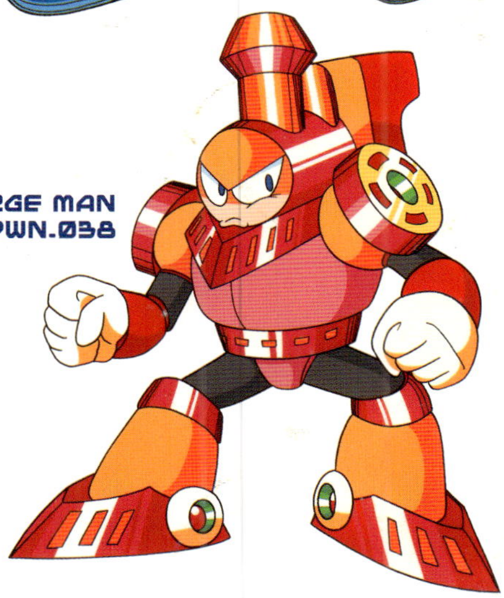

CHARGE MAN
DWN.038

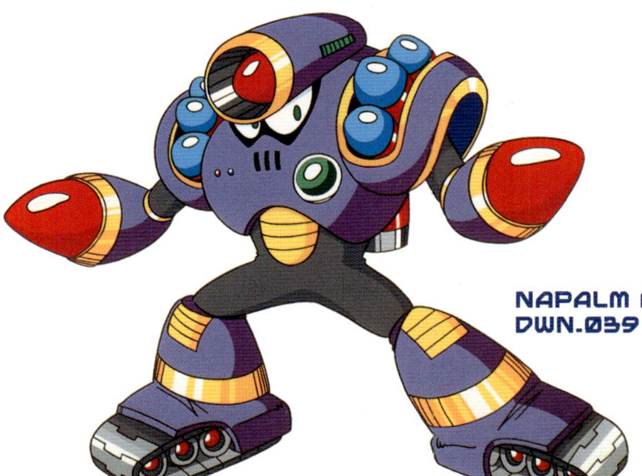

NAPALM MAN
DWN.039

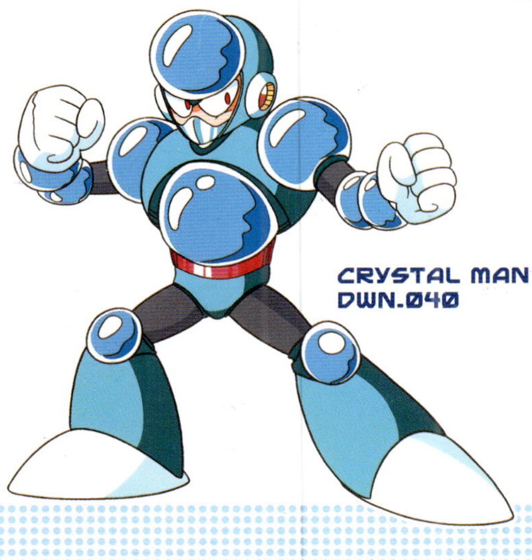

CRYSTAL MAN
DWN.040

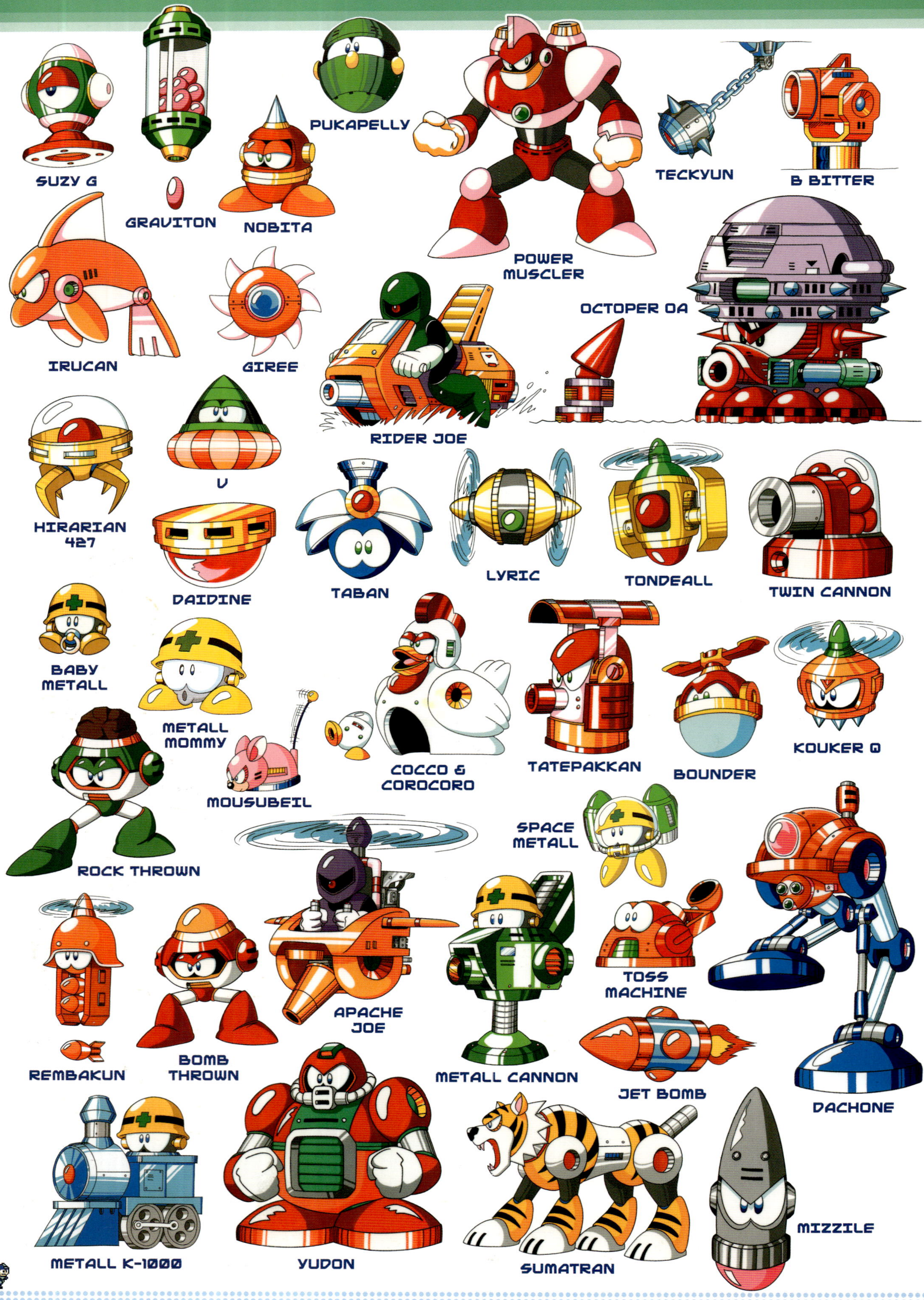
SUZY G
GRAVITON
NOBITA
PUKAPELLY
POWER MUSCLER
TECKYUN
B BITTER
IRUCAN
GIREE
RIDER JOE
OCTOPER OA
HIRARIAN 427
V
DAIDINE
TABAN
LYRIC
TONDEALL
TWIN CANNON
BABY METALL
METALL MOMMY
MOUSUBEIL
COCCO & COROCORO
TATEPAKKAN
BOUNDER
KOUKER Q
ROCK THROWN
SPACE METALL
APACHE JOE
TOSS MACHINE
REMBAKUN
BOMB THROWN
METALL CANNON
JET BOMB
DACHONE
METALL K-1000
YUDON
SUMATRAN
MIZZILE

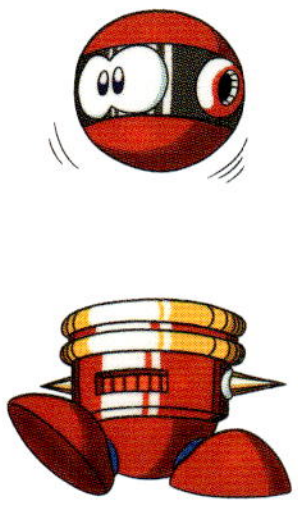

PUKAPUCKER

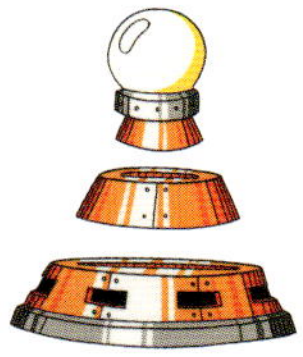

SUBEIL

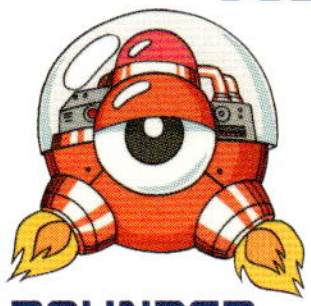

ROUNDER

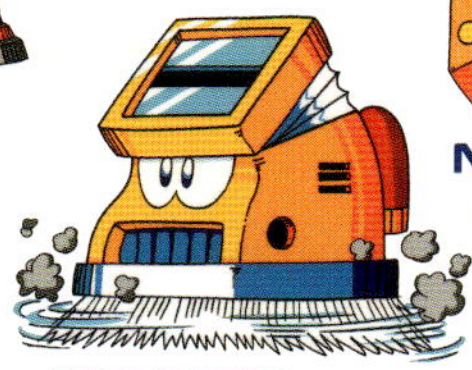

FOOJEEN

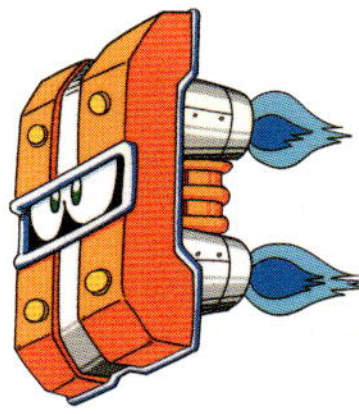

NEW SHIELD ATTACKER

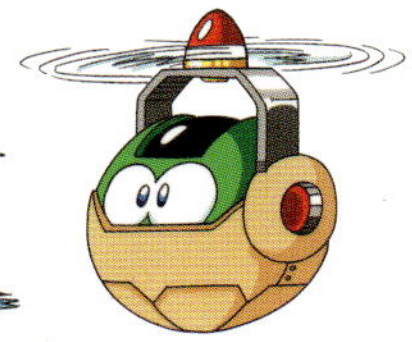

BOMBIER

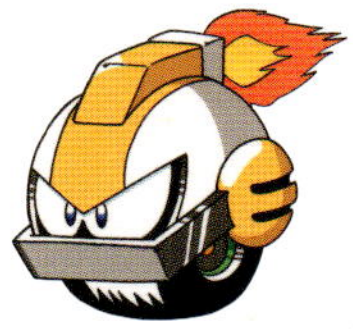

CAMON

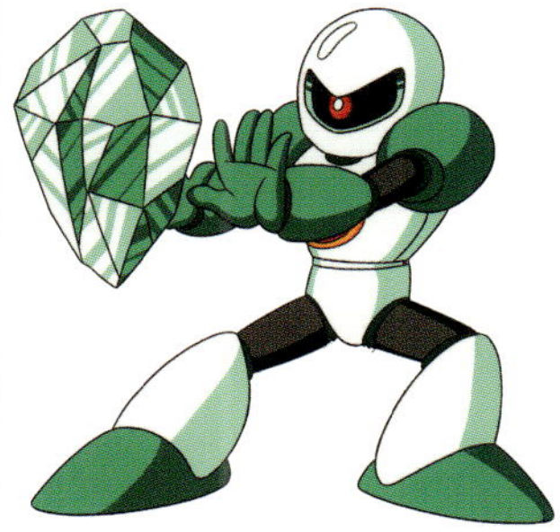

CRYSTAL JOE

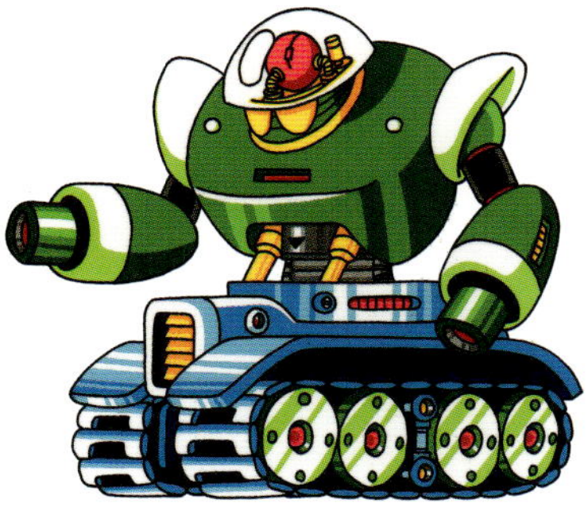

DARK MAN 1

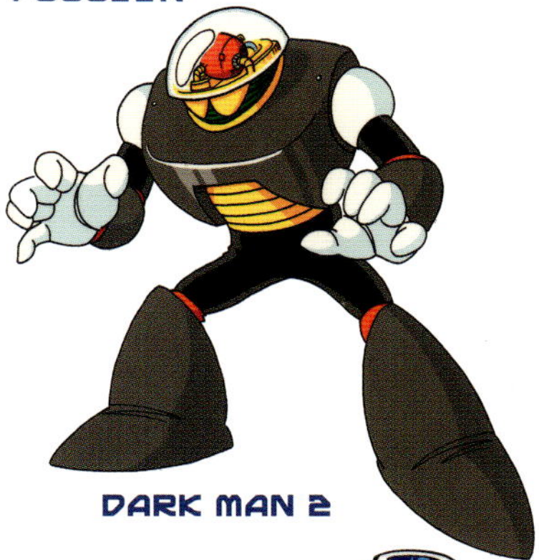

DARK MAN 2

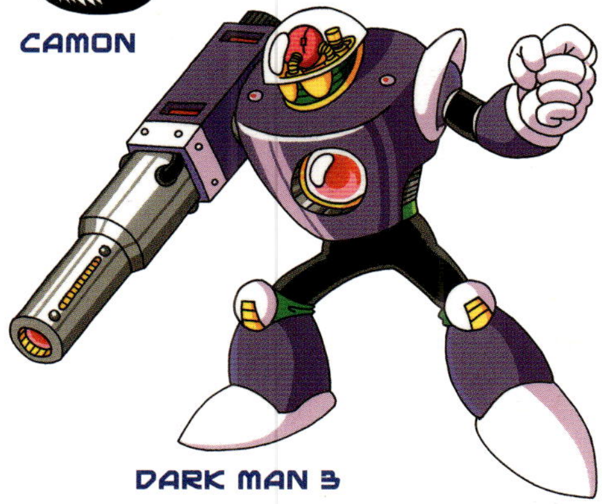

DARK MAN 3

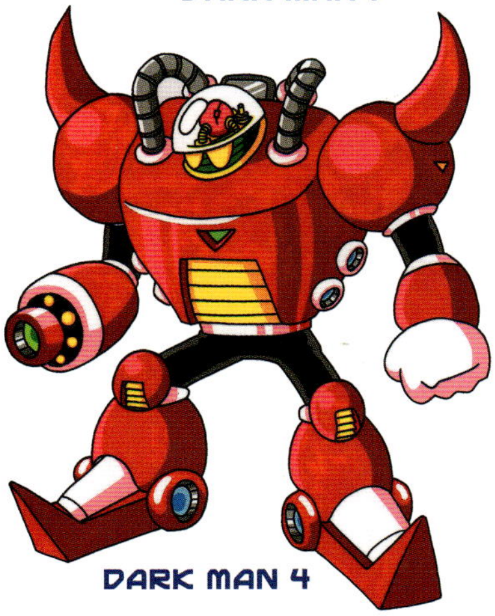

DARK MAN 4

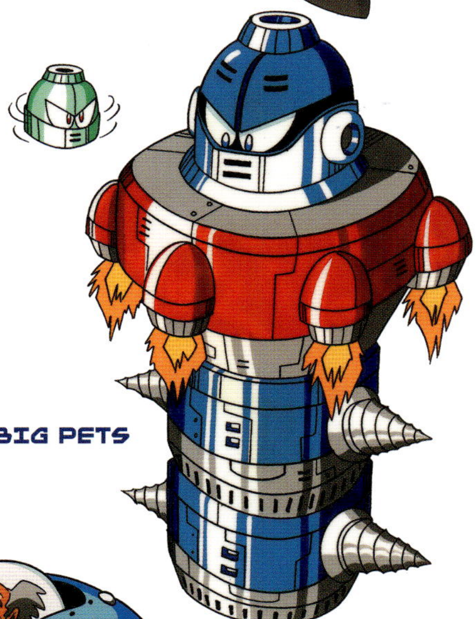

BIG PETS

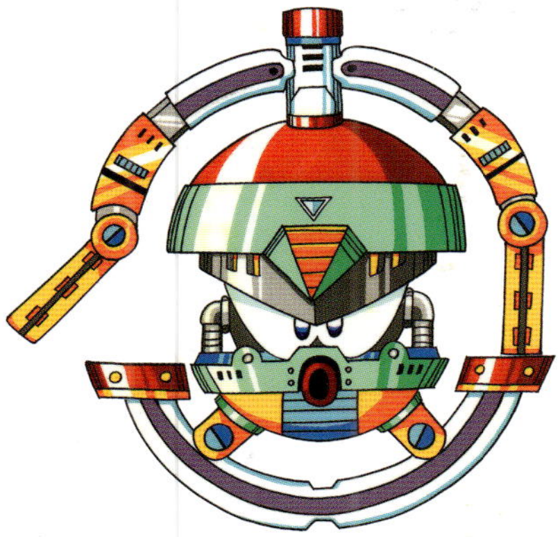

CIRCRING Q9

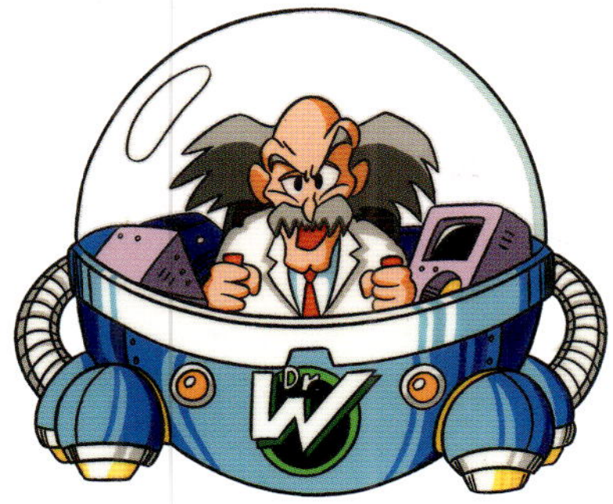

WILY CAPSULE II

"I think '5' was pretty fun to do, but I do remember having a lot of trouble with the designs, the balance, and the colors." (Inafune)

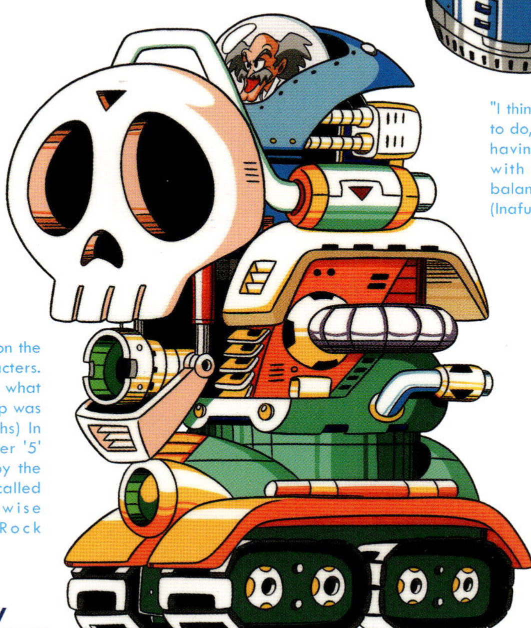

WILY MACHINE 5

"They let me work on the minor enemy characters. With the NES being what it was, lining them up was pretty hard. (laughs) In the end, I remember '5' was put together by the staff that Inafune called together, otherwise known as the Rock Family." (Kaji)

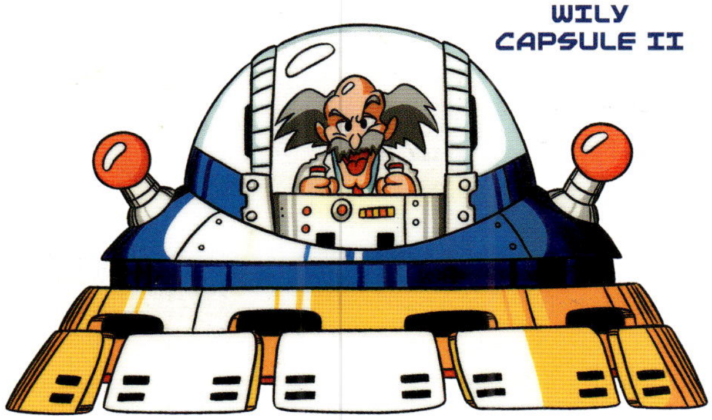

WILY PRESS

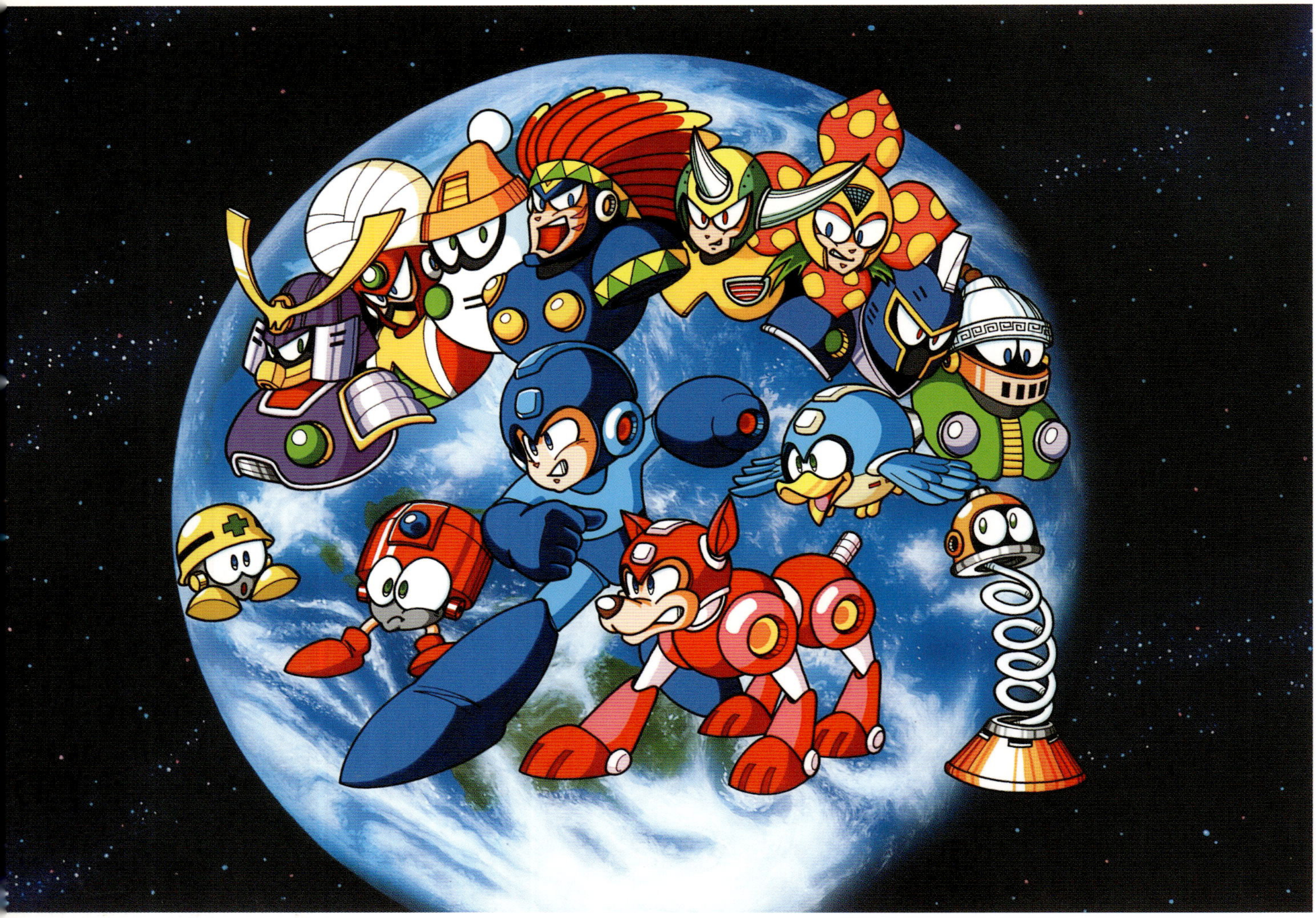

ROCKMAN 6 史上最大の戦い!!

Mega Man 6
NES 11/05/1993
Total number of boss character submissions: 200,000

The year is 20XX. The 'Global Robot Alliance' was formed to battle Dr. Wily's ambitions for world domination. One year later, the very first tournament was held to determine the greatest peace-supporting robot. The event was interrupted when Mr. X, who had been a strong supporter of the Alliance, stole the robots and moved forward with his own plans to take over the world. Will Mega Man be able to stop Mr. X before it's too late!?

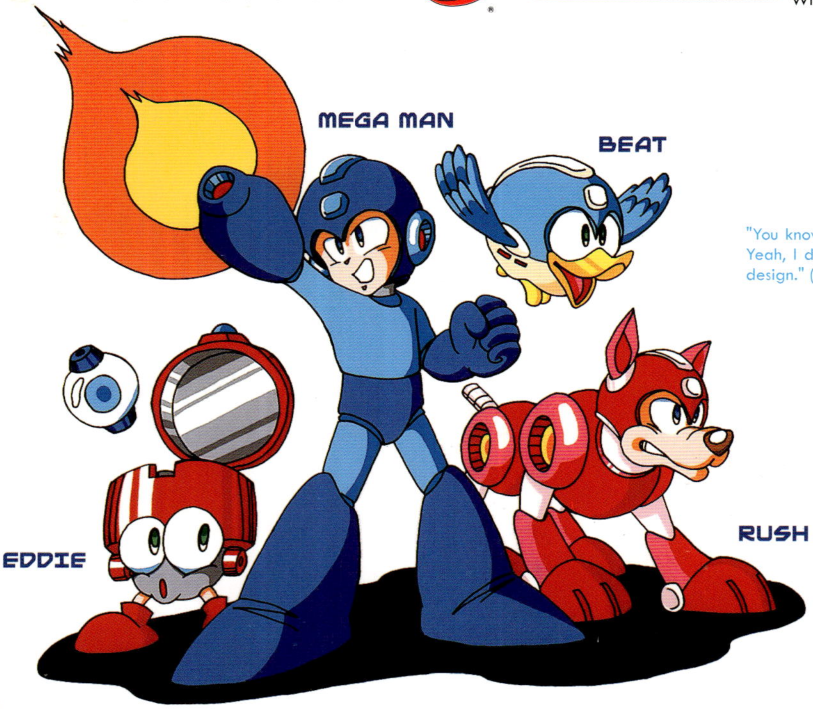

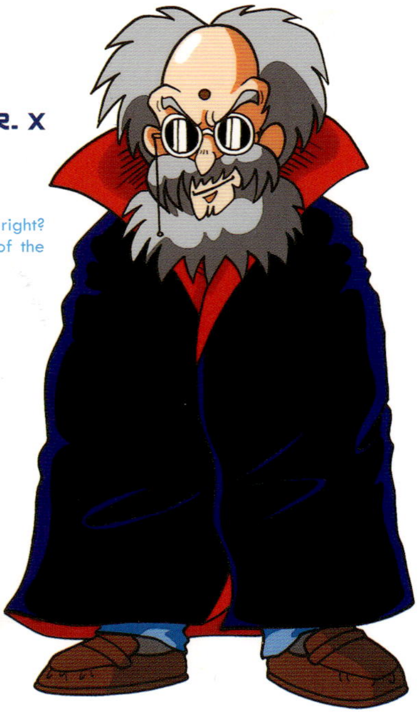

"You know who this is, right? Yeah, I didn't do any of the design." (Inafune)

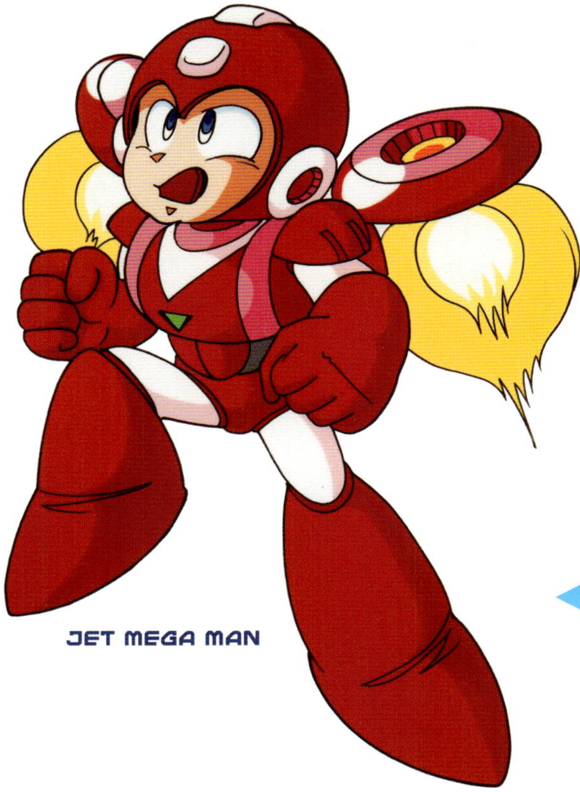

JET MEGA MAN

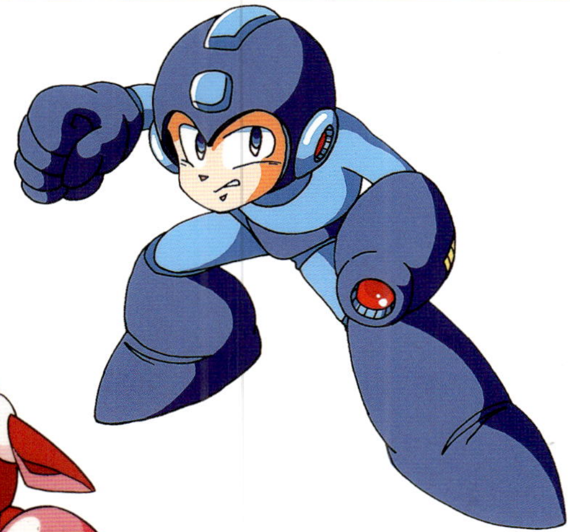

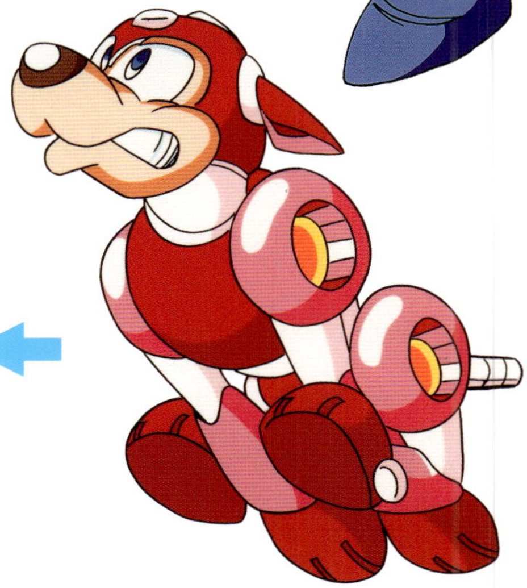

"This was around the time when I was working on 'Mega Man X,' so I think the character illustrations were closer in density to 'X,' the density of the Super NES." (Inafune)

"We were always implementing new ideas, and we finally arrived at the inevitable 'assembling!' (laughs) I really struggled with these designs... If you think about it, they shouldn't be able to combine like this. It would have been a little awkward if parts of Rush like his neck were left over after they combined, so what was I supposed to do? (laughs)" (Inafune)

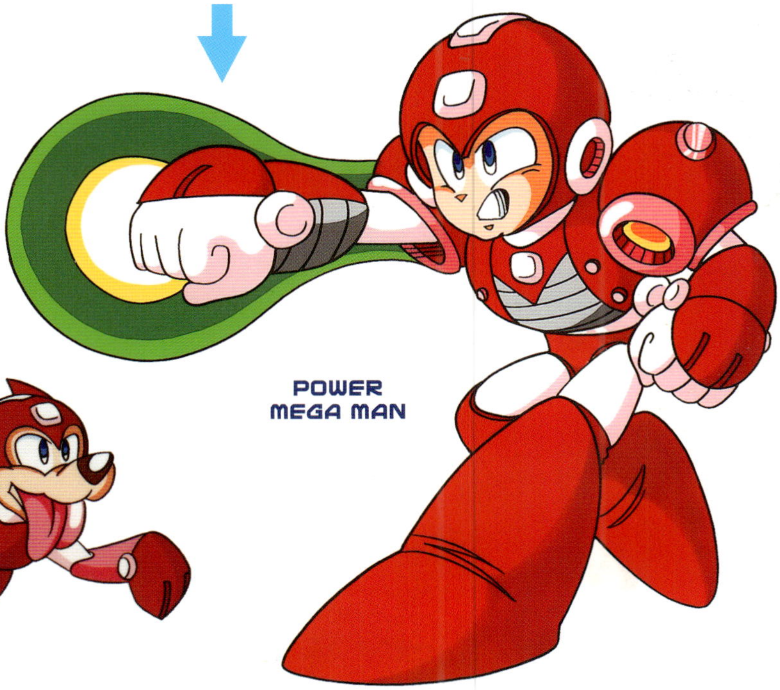

POWER MEGA MAN

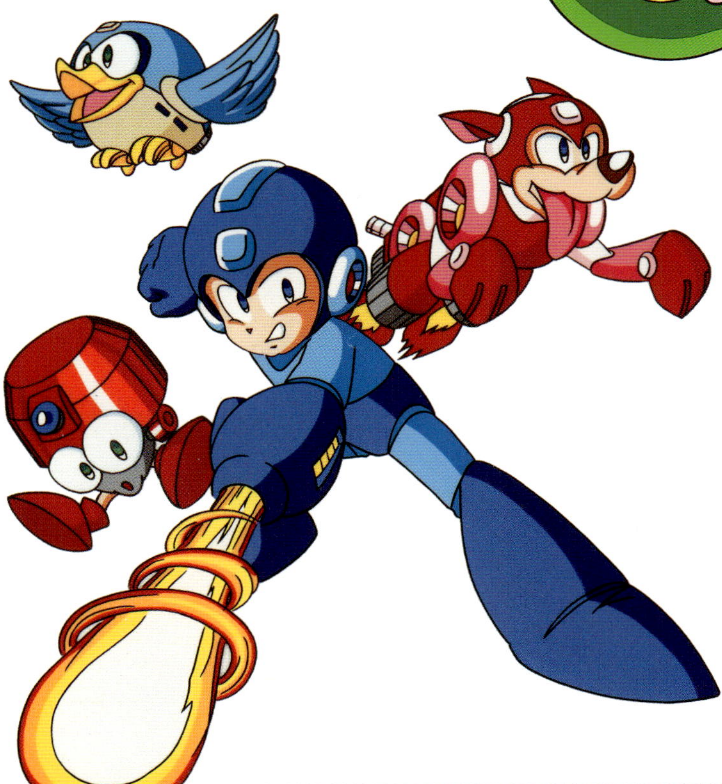

"At the time, series that made it to their sixth title were pretty rare, and one of the pleasant perks of such repeated successes was the fact that some of the things in the games came to be 'expected' by the players." (Inafune)

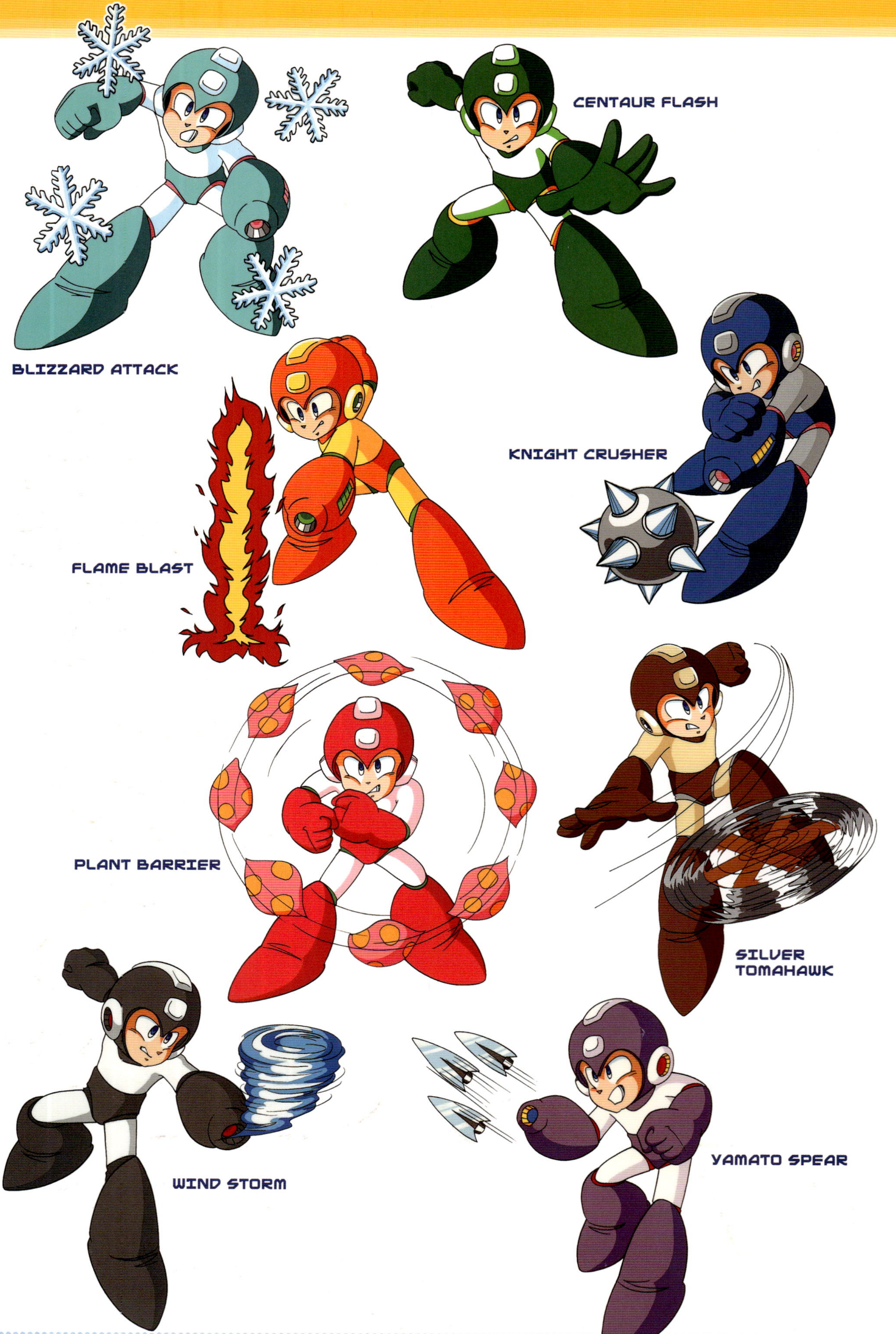
CENTAUR FLASH
BLIZZARD ATTACK
KNIGHT CRUSHER
FLAME BLAST
PLANT BARRIER
SILVER TOMAHAWK
YAMATO SPEAR
WIND STORM

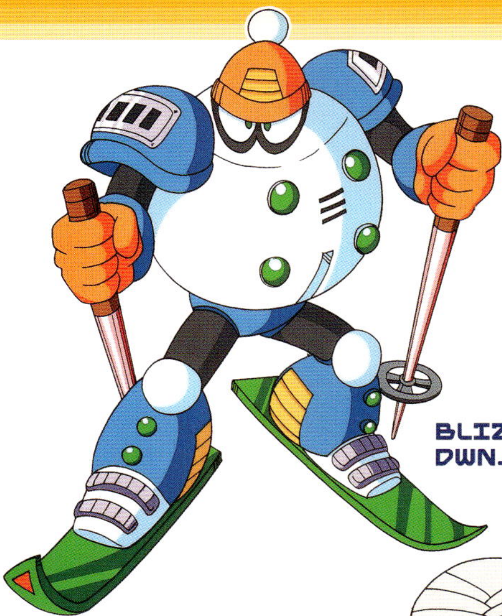

BLIZZARD MAN
DWN.041

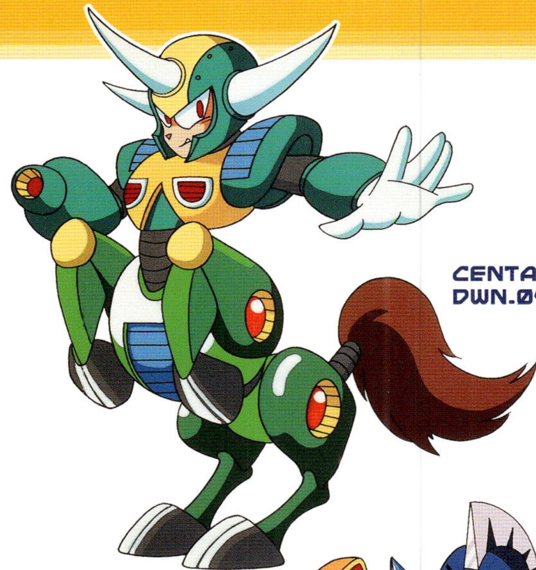

CENTAUR MAN
DWN.042

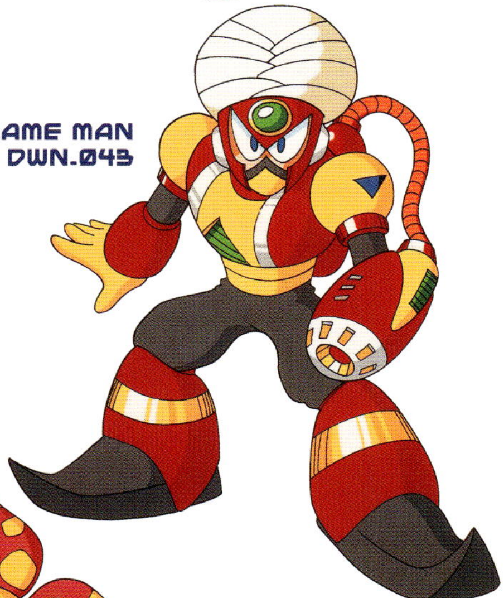

FLAME MAN
DWN.043

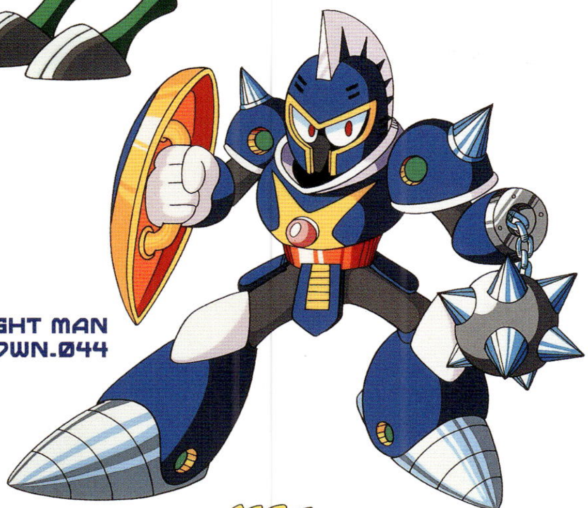

KNIGHT MAN
DWN.044

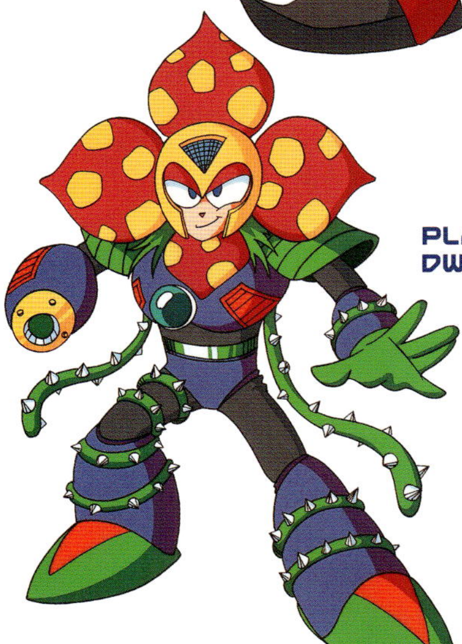

PLANT MAN
DWN.045

"We tried taking boss character submissions from overseas for '6,' and the overall sense of design was so different from ours that it was pretty interesting in and of itself. I admit I was consciously not thinking about the NES's capabilities while doing my illustrations. Sometimes, I'd stop to think about just how we were going to express a certain character in dot graphics, but I would always dismiss that train of thought saying, 'We'll figure something out.' (laughs)" (Inafune)

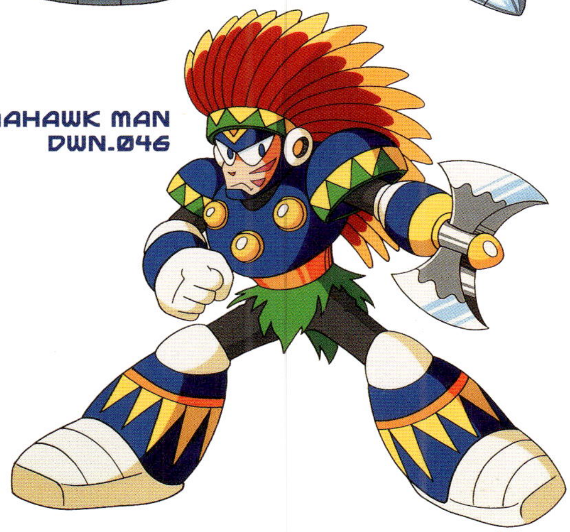

TOMAHAWK MAN
DWN.046

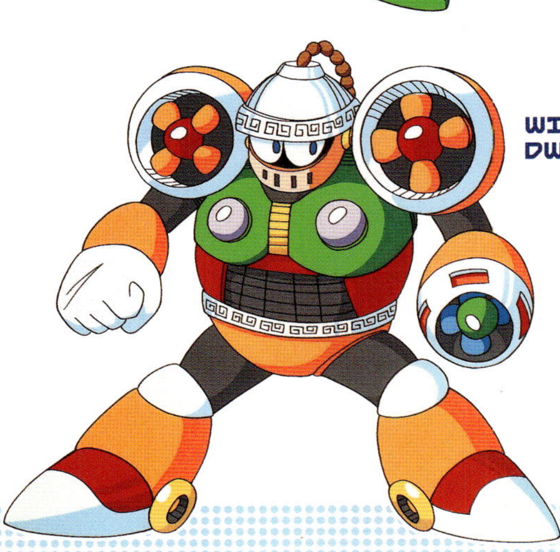

WIND MAN
DWN.047

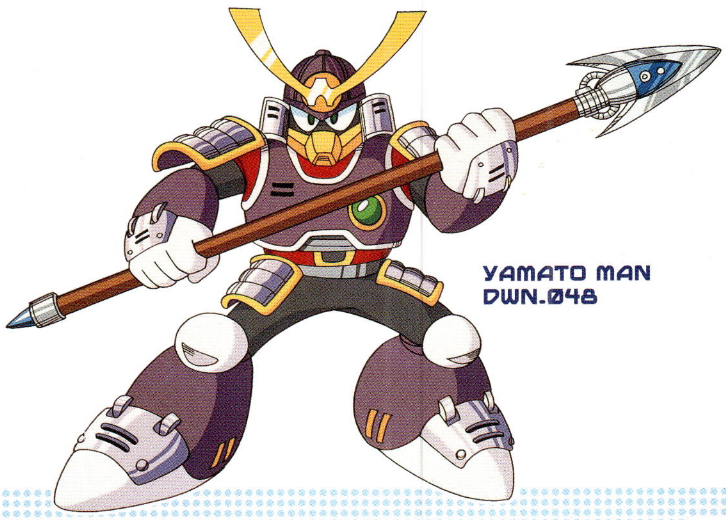

YAMATO MAN
DWN.048

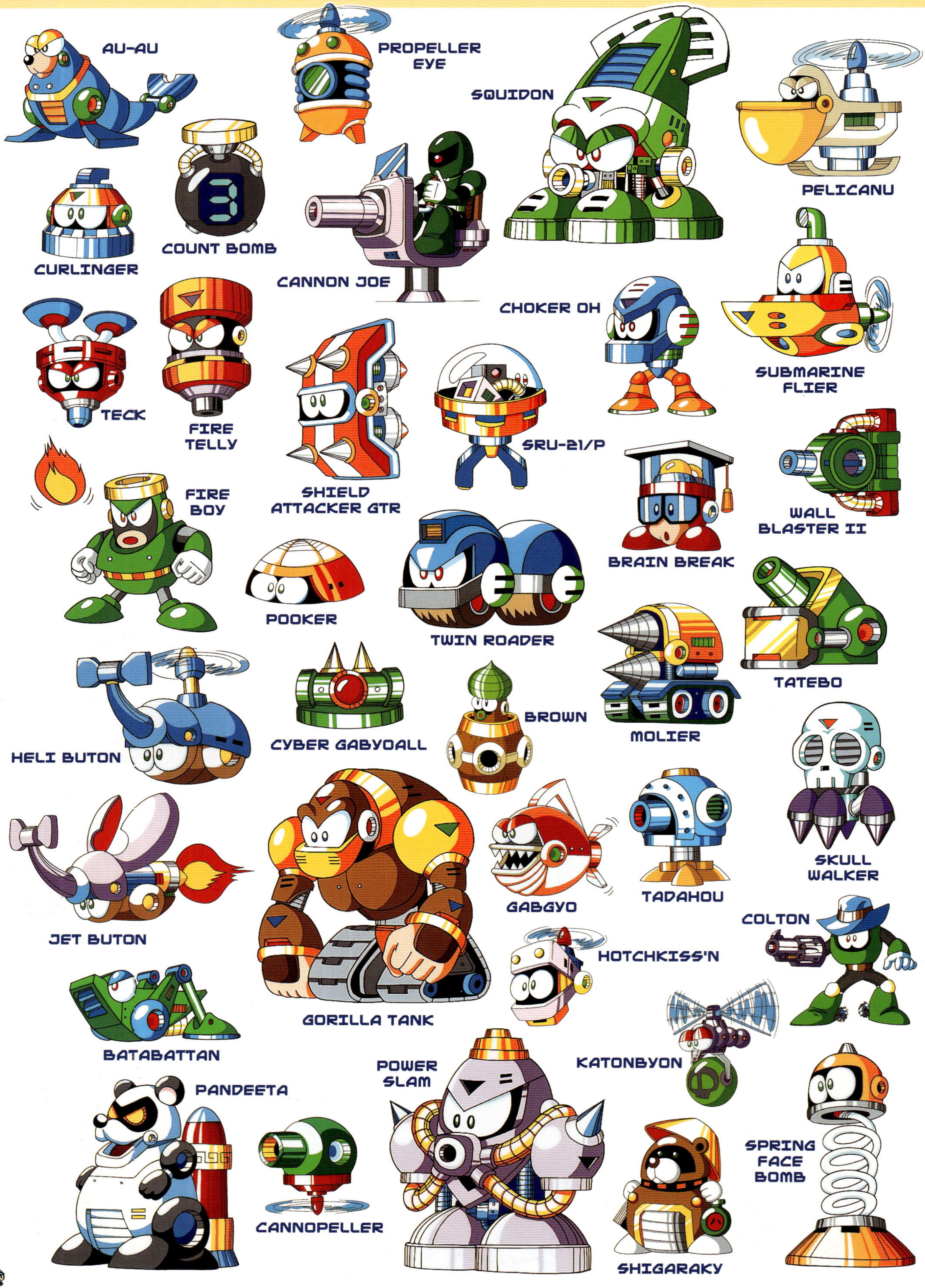
AU-AU
PROPELLER EYE
SQUIDON
PELICANU
CURLINGER
COUNT BOMB
CANNON JOE
CHOKER OH
SUBMARINE FLIER
TECK
FIRE TELLY
SHIELD ATTACKER GTR
SRU-21/P
FIRE BOY
WALL BLASTER II
BRAIN BREAK
POOKER
TWIN ROADER
TATEBO
MOLIER
BROWN
CYBER GABYOALL
HELI BUTON
SKULL WALKER
TADAHOU
GABGYO
JET BUTON
COLTON
HOTCHKISS'N
GORILLA TANK
BATABATTAN
KATONBYON
POWER SLAM
PANDEETA
SPRING FACE BOMB
CANNOPELLER
SHIGARAKY

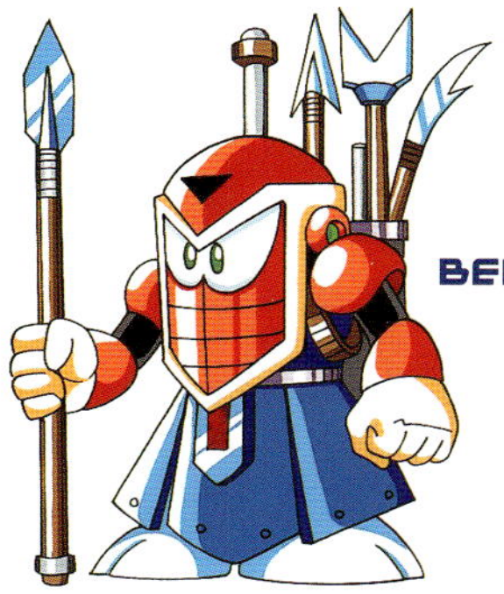

BEN K

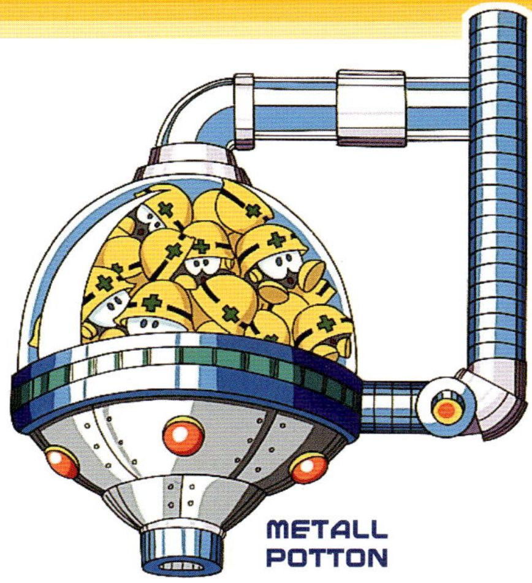

METALL POTTON

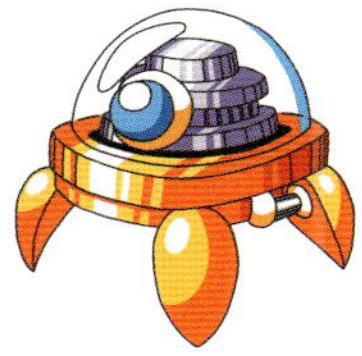

SW-525

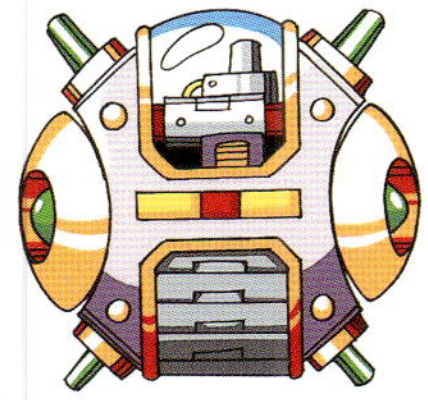

ROUNDER II

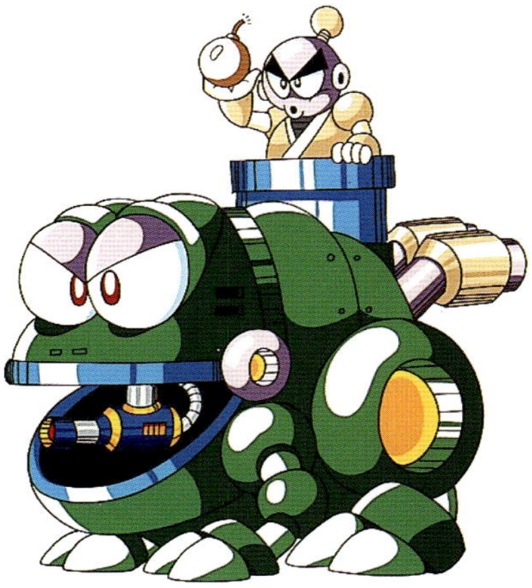

GAMARN & GAMADAYU

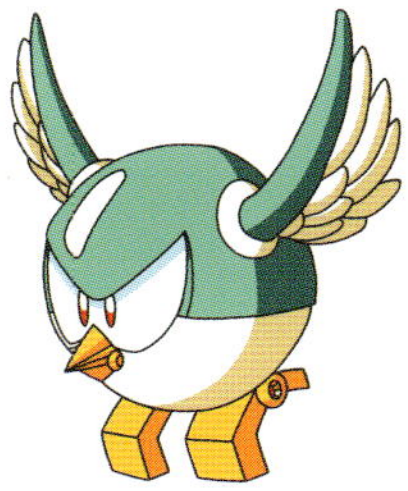

PEAT

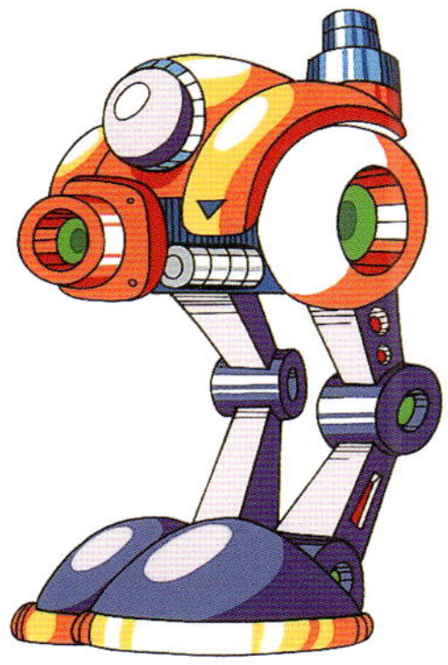

DACHONE LTD. ED.

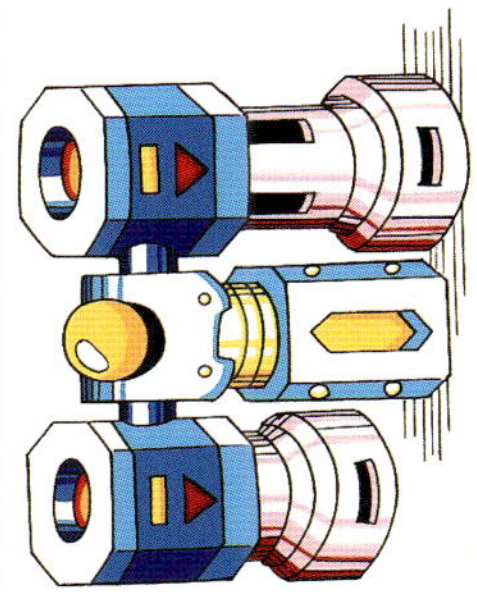

POWER PISTON

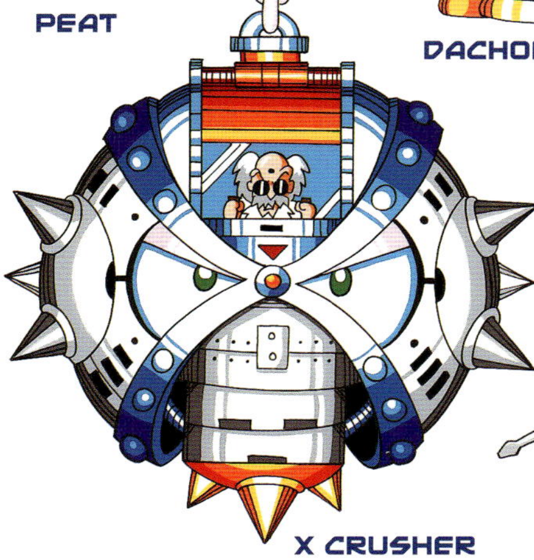

X CRUSHER

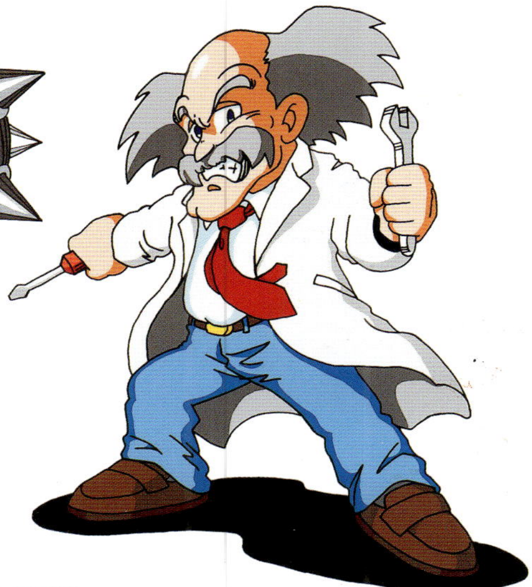

DR. WILY

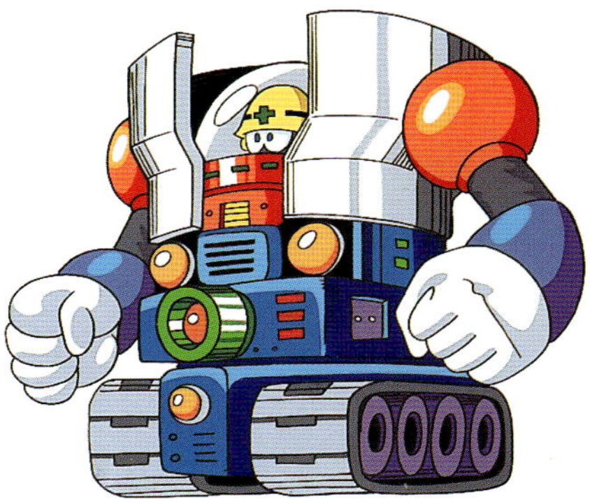

METONGER Z

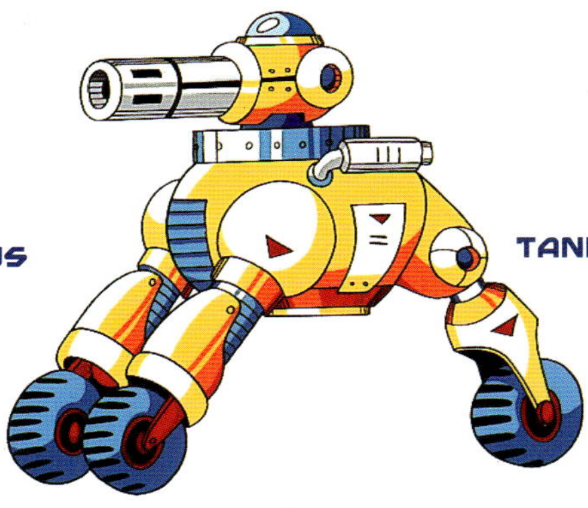

TANK CSII

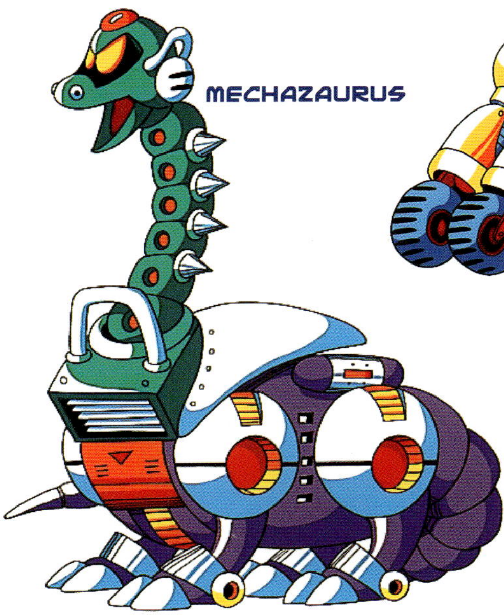

MECHAZAURUS

"For having hit a lot of roadblocks, I feel like we got a lot done for '6.' The theme for our designs was 'The world is our stage,' and I really enjoyed bringing what I felt was the unique flavor of different countries into the game." (Inafune)

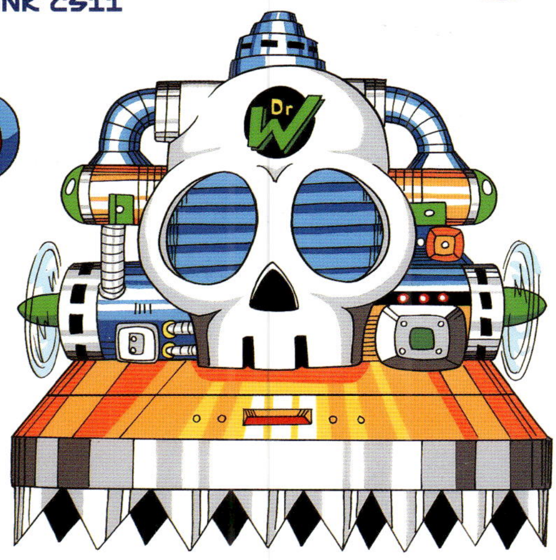

WILY MACHINE 6

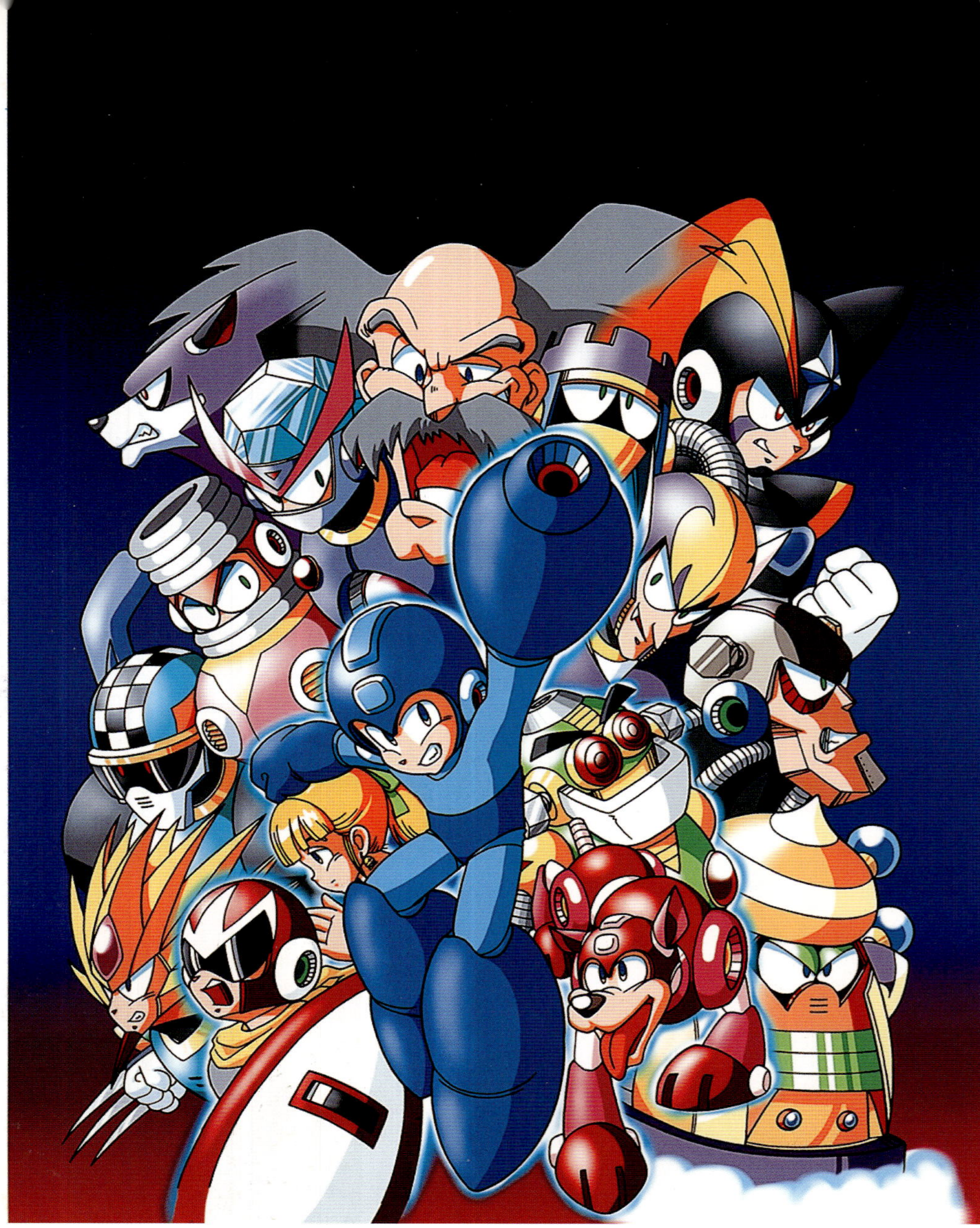

"Moving into the Super NES meant that everything was going to be different, including the way we color things. I always had lots to do besides drawing characters, but I made sure to set aside plenty of time to focus on the character drawings for '7.' This was the last package illustration I did, and in some ways it turned out like a compilation piece." (Inafune)

Mega Man 7
SNES 03/24/1995
Total number of boss character submissions: 220,000

Thanks to Mega Man's efforts, Dr. Wily had finally been arrested, and peace was restored to the world once again. It was only a few months later, however, that an army of Dr. Wily's combat robots stormed the prison where he was being held and proceeded to conquer the surrounding area. Mega Man rushes to the city to find the fugitive Dr. Wily, but...

ROCKMAN 7 宿命の対決!

"Due to the bad timing of certain things coming together at the time, we basically only had three months to make '7.' Fortunately, the members we had working on '7' were highly motivated, and I remember having a lot of fun." (Inafune)

"We were seriously hard pressed for time, but it was like a 'Rock Family' reunion! We even had people from the '2' team come back, and despite the lack of time, they managed to be quite picky about the littlest details. (laughs)" (Kaji)

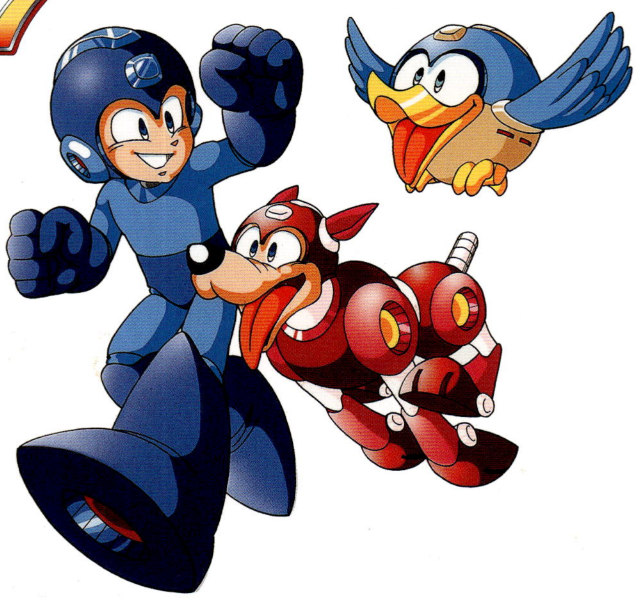

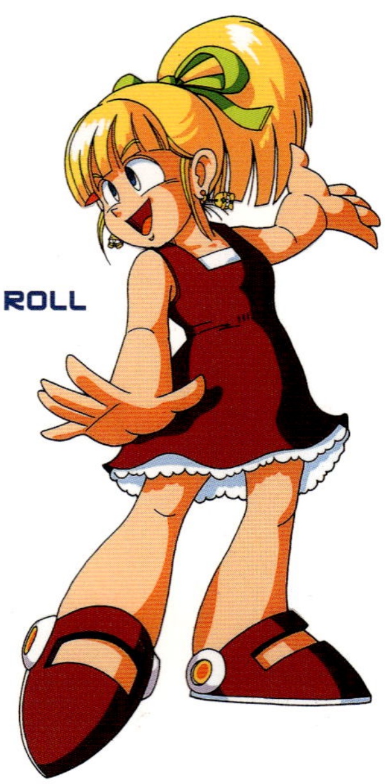

ROLL

ROCKMAN 7 宿命の対決!

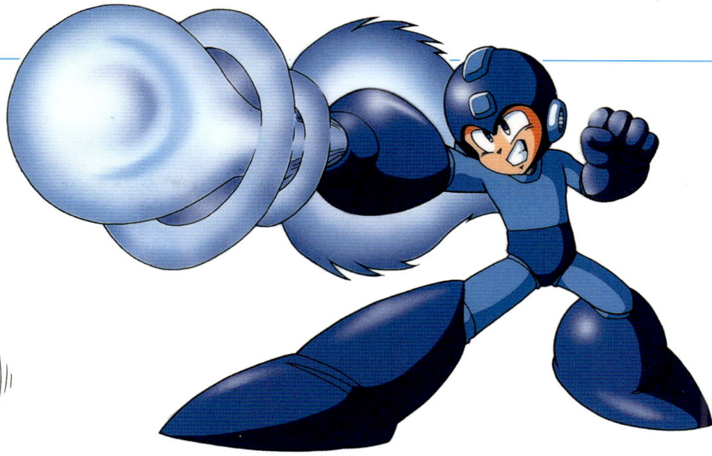

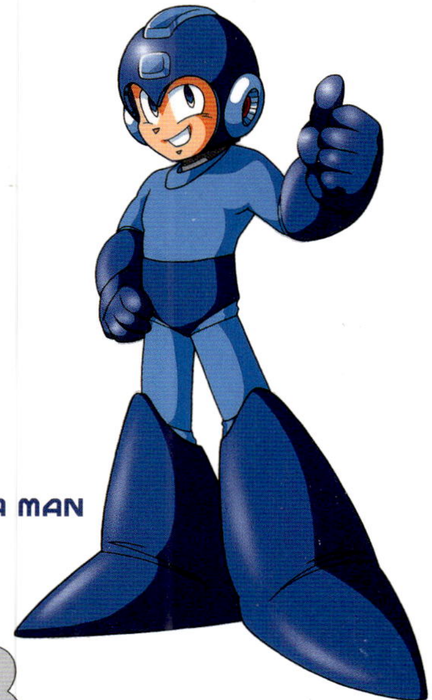

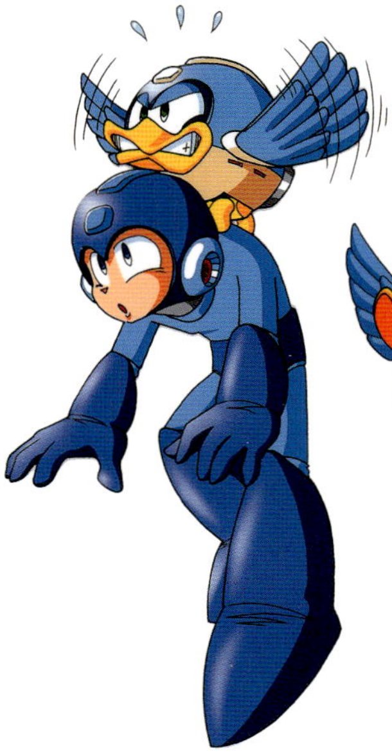

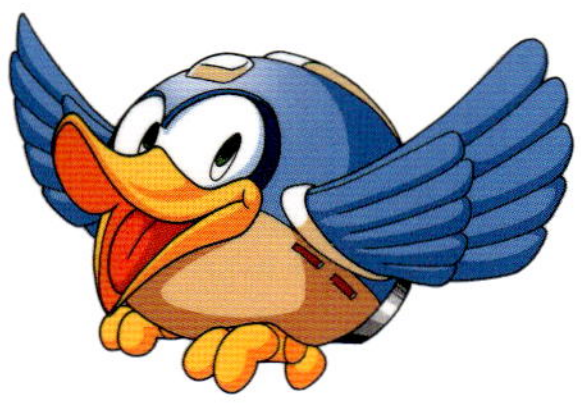

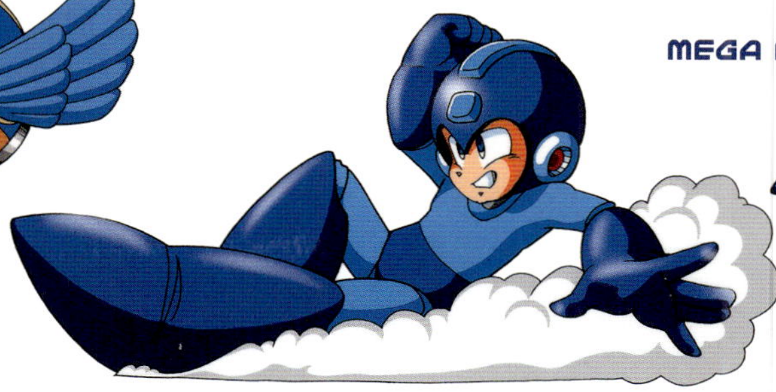

MEGA MAN

BEAT

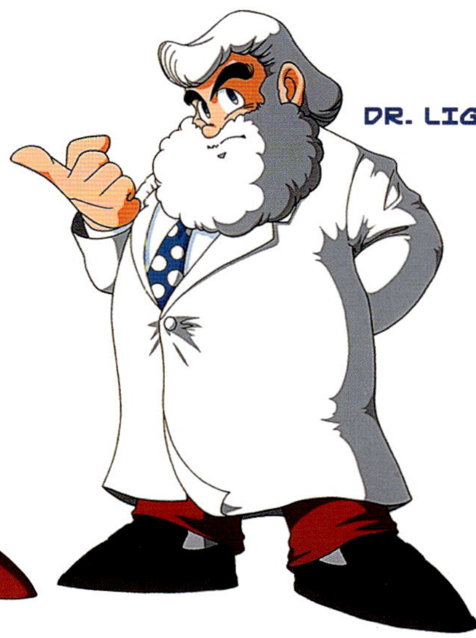

DR. LIGHT

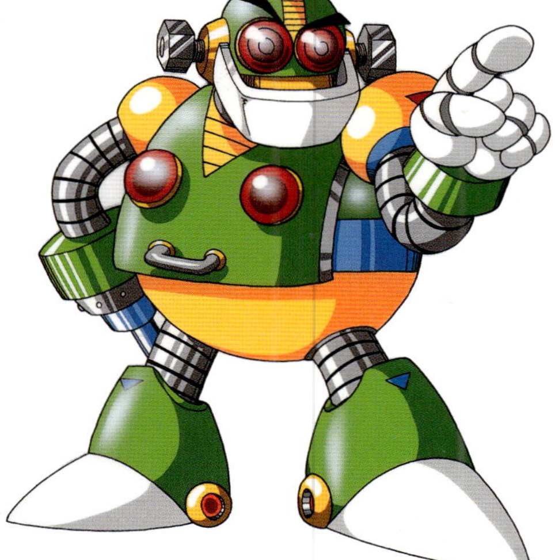

AUTO

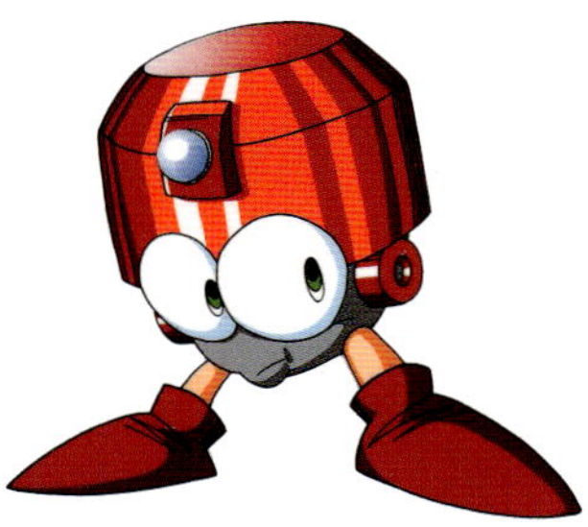

EDDIE

"We had a rough design done for Auto, but Inafune made alterations from the ground up. I recall him being pretty upset about this character, saying things like, 'Why do we even need a guy like this, anyway?' I wonder how he feels about Auto now? (laughs)" (Kaji)

BIG EDDIE

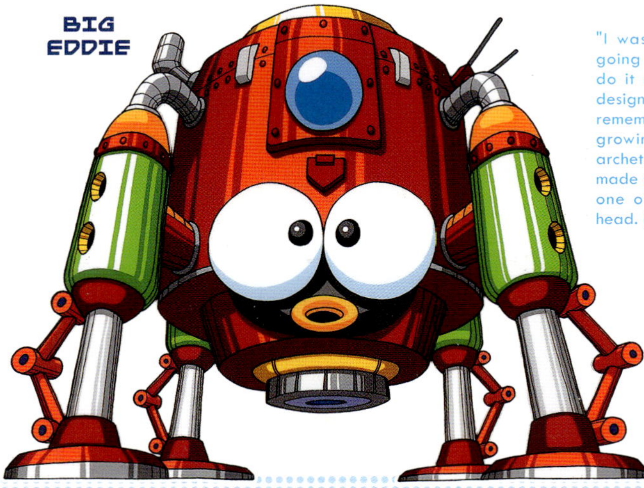

"I was just saying if we're going to do it, we ought to do it right. I based Auto's design on the classic robots I remember seeing while I was growing up... you know, the archetypical 'tin man.' I also made sure that he was missing one of the screws from his head. (laughs)" (Inafune)

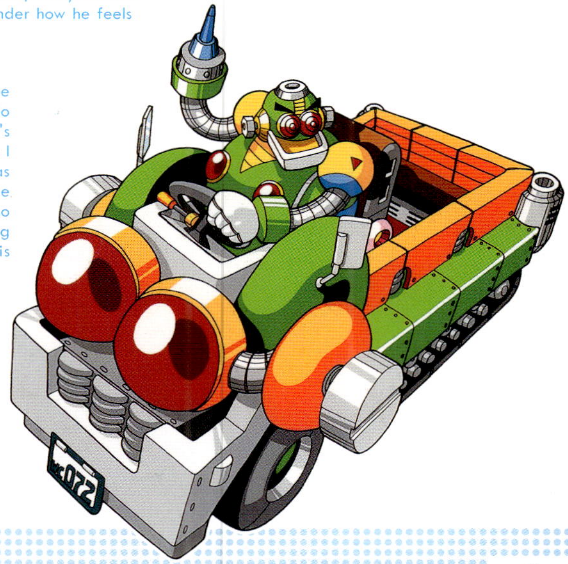

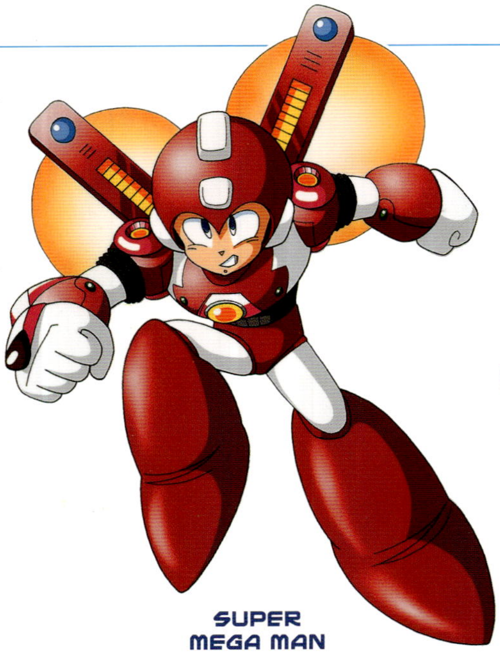

SUPER
MEGA MAN

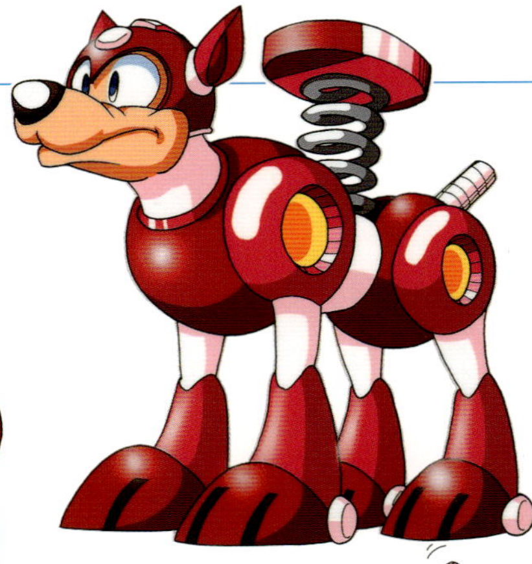

RUSH COIL

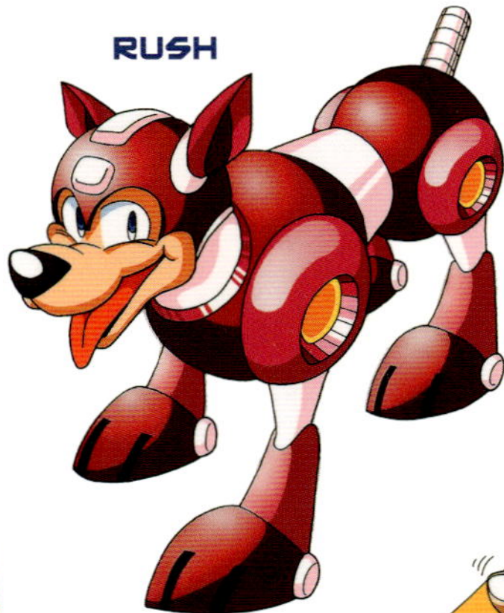

RUSH

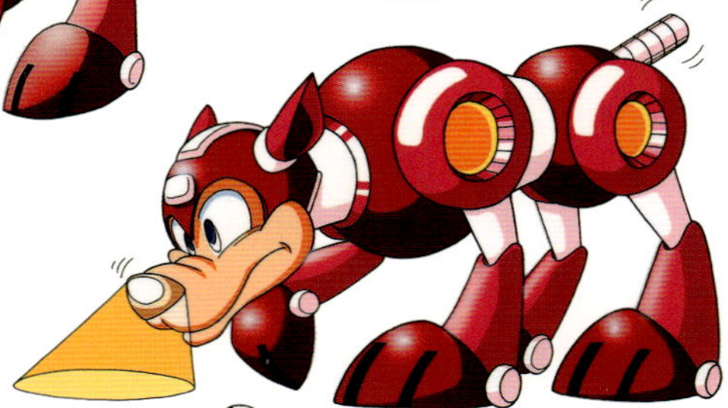

RUSH SEARCH

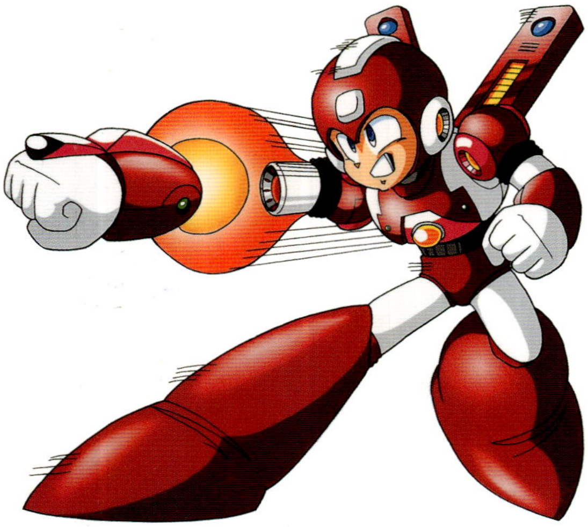

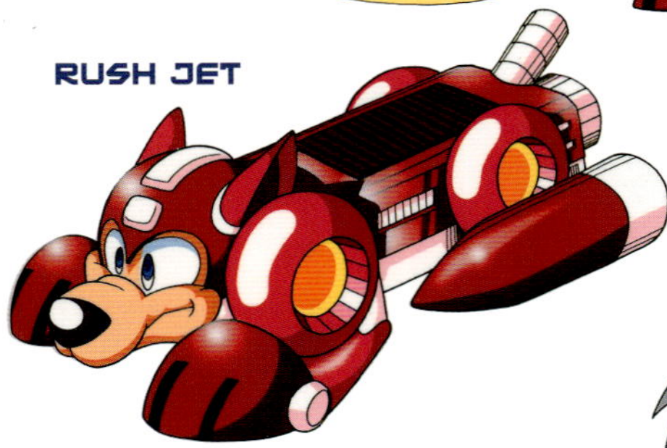

RUSH JET

"From the time we came up with the concepts for Bass and Treble, I knew they were going to be interesting characters. I asked Kaji to do the designs, and I think he did a great job!" (Inafune)

"For Bass, I was also asked to do the dot work. When it came to animating his motions, however, I kept getting confused about his head and how it was supposed to work visually... even though I was the one who designed him. (laughs)" (Kaji)

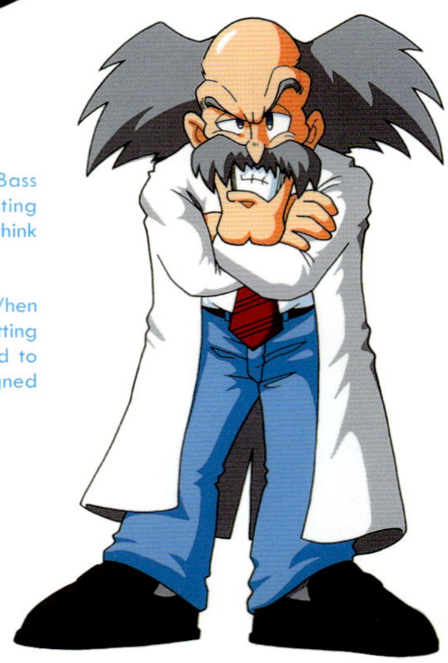

DR. WILY

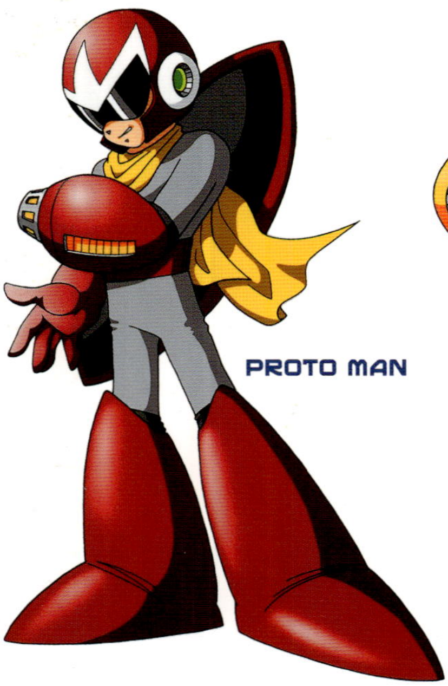

PROTO MAN

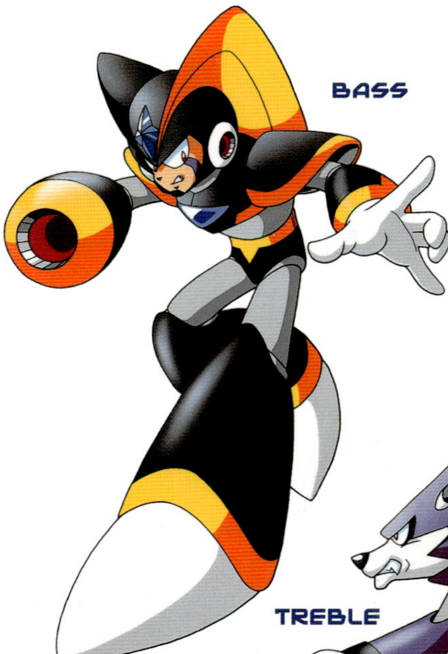

BASS

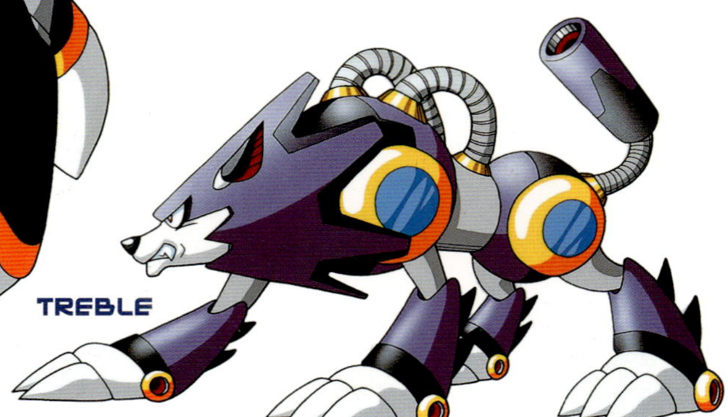

TREBLE

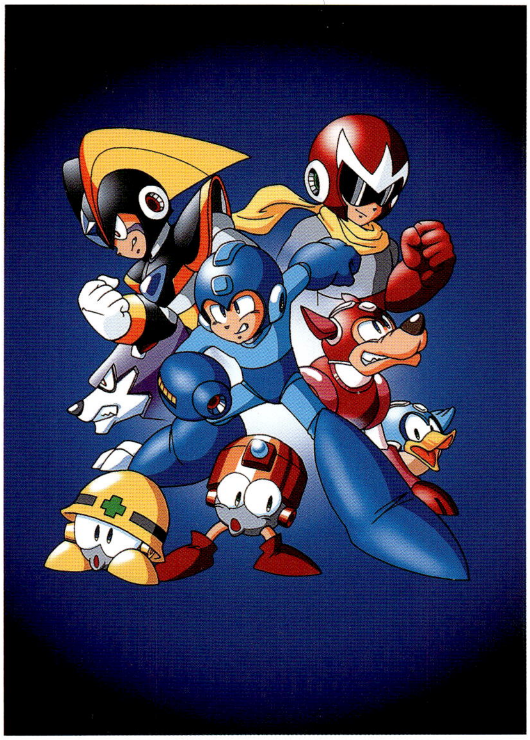

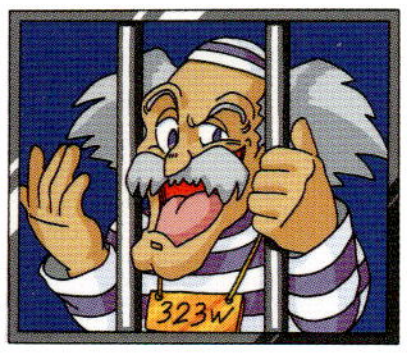

WILY DURING THE BOSS DESIGN CONTEST APPLICATIONS

CONCEPT ART

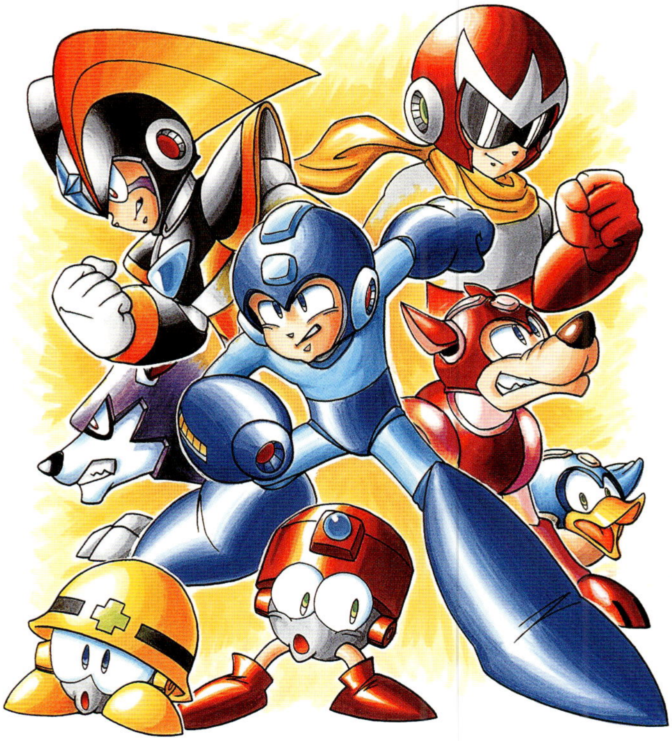

"How nostalgic! I drew the scene below, and I still remember it so well. I also did the cel of Dr. Wily in the top right. I remember I had to redo it because I forgot that I was drawing it from the back, and the numbers on his plate turned out backwards the first time! (laughs)" (Hideki)

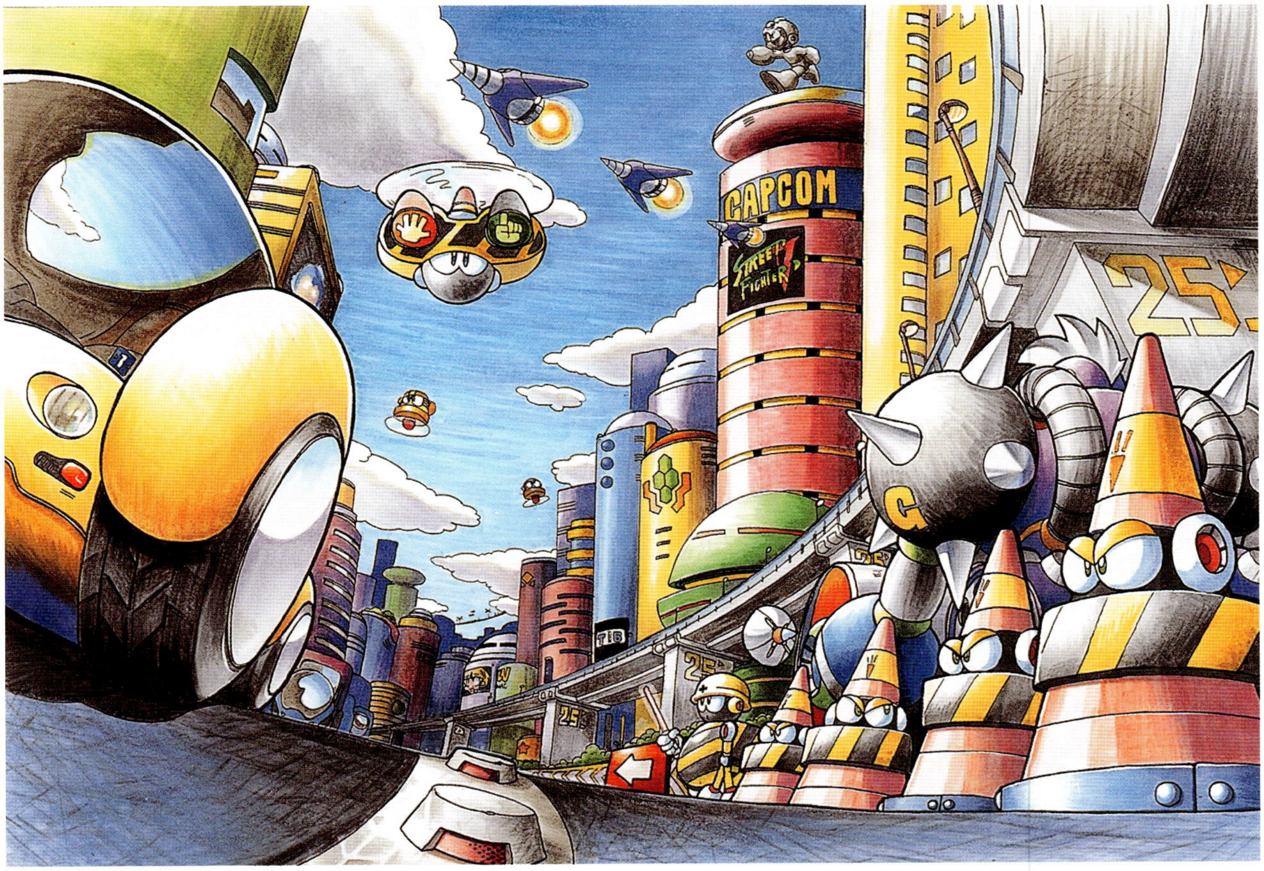

ILLUSTRATION USED IN THE MANUAL

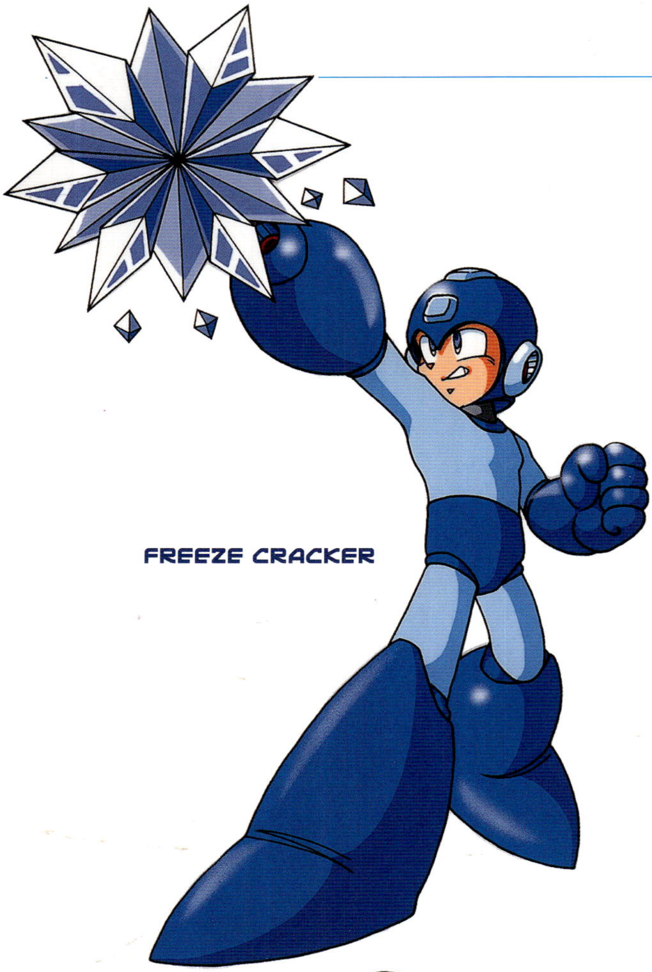

FREEZE CRACKER

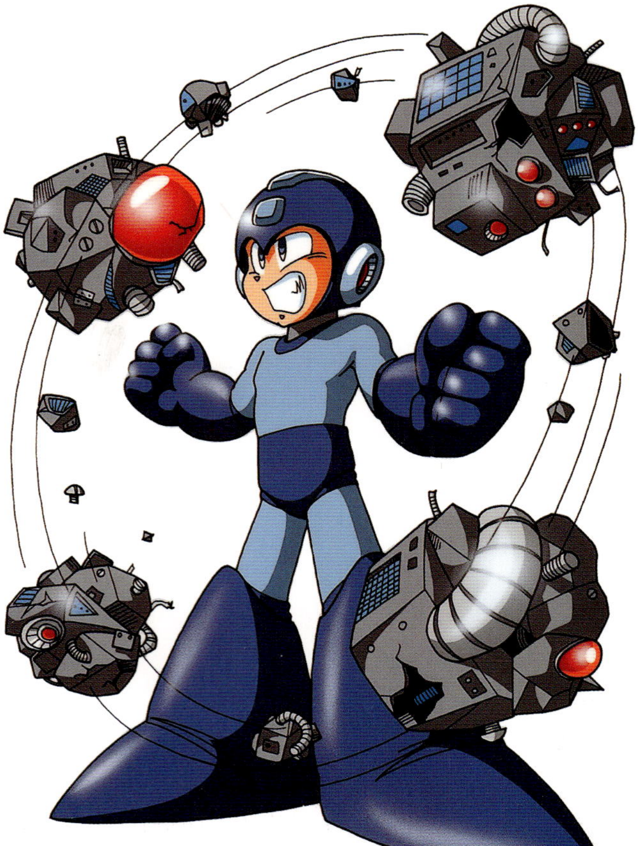

JUNK SHIELD

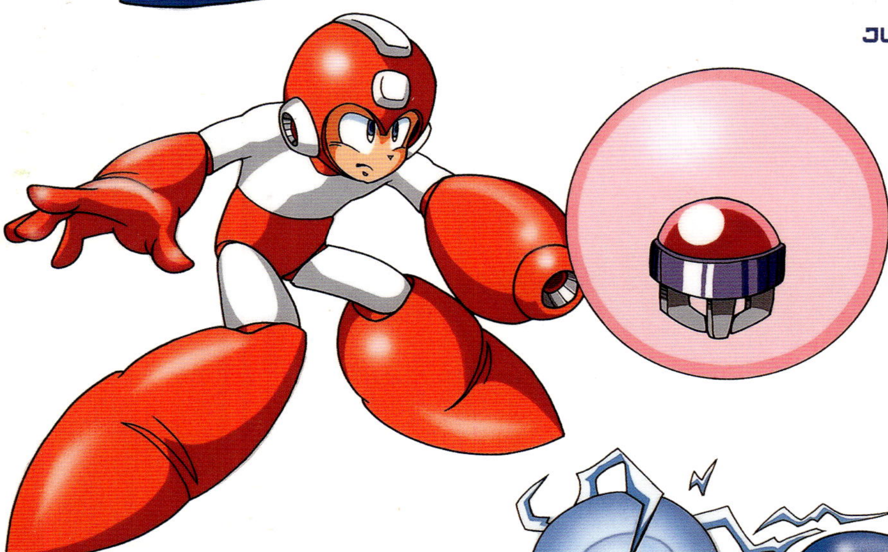

DANGER WRAP

"The counter-weakness weapons were created, in part, to increase the reactions of the special weapons. One of the major concepts for '7' was to 'create lots of places where the player can have fun with the special weapons.'" (Tsuda)

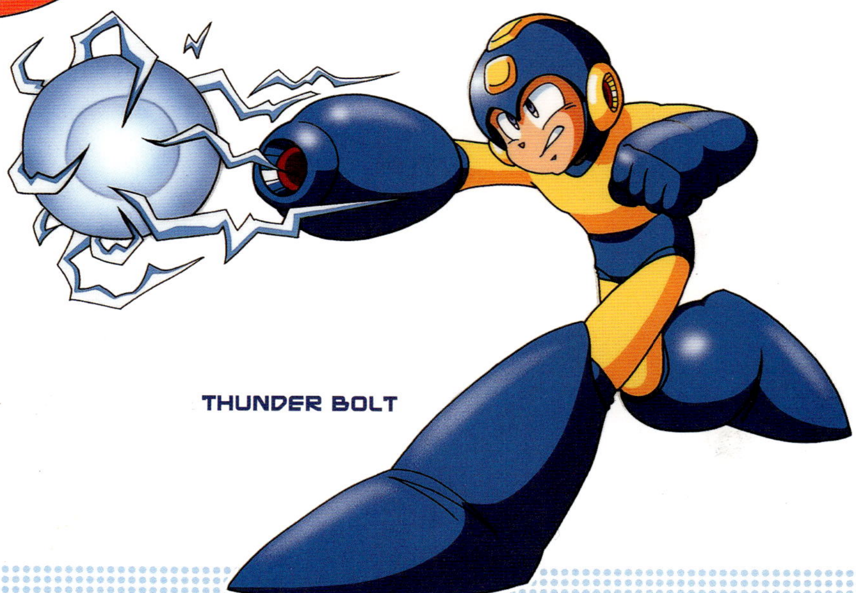

THUNDER BOLT

"It was a lot of fun... but also quite rigorous." (Kaji)

"The team leader and about 15 programmers were basically sealed in a tiny room. When the air quality assessment guy came around, he was like, 'Whoa!' (laughs)" (Inafune)

"Yeah, and the people from the character division would swap out constantly, bringing in fresh data as it became available... which would then be handed off to whoever was closest to finishing whatever they were working on at the time. The atmosphere was pretty much at its climax from the very beginning, and we just sprinted all the way to beta." (Tsuda)

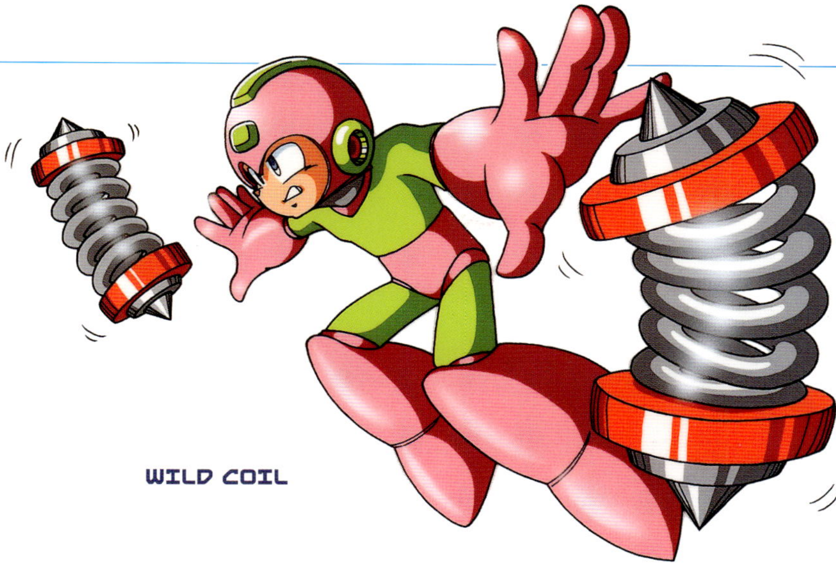

WILD COIL

"It all started with Inafune sneaking around to the character division lead and myself, whispering his idea about a 'hidden boss fight mode' into our ears. Then, just a week before going to beta, it turned into 'Let's do it!!' (laughs) We were able to work out a deal with the programmers that it would only be Mega Man and Bass, and they were able to hammer it out in just two days. We were told that the whole thing would be scrapped if it contained a single bug, so I'm very happy that we were able to make it work.' (Tsuda)

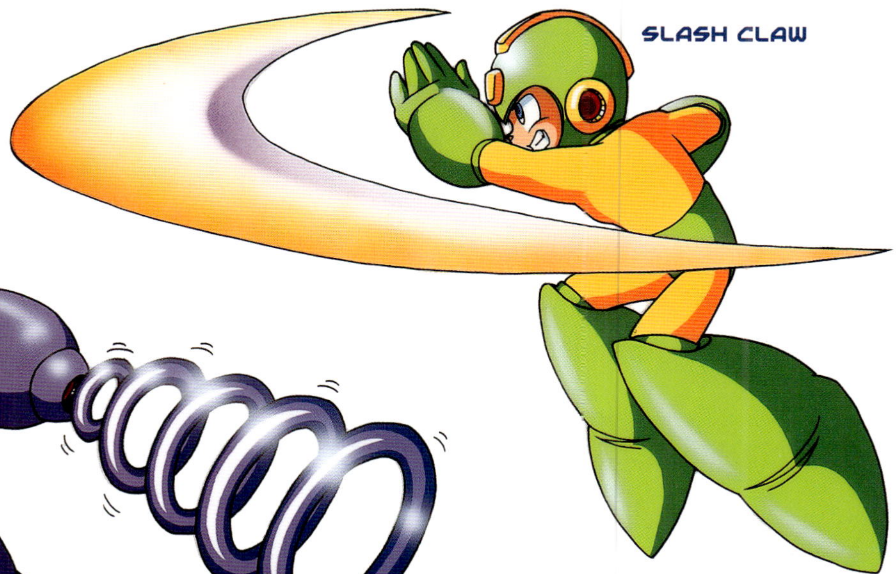

SLASH CLAW

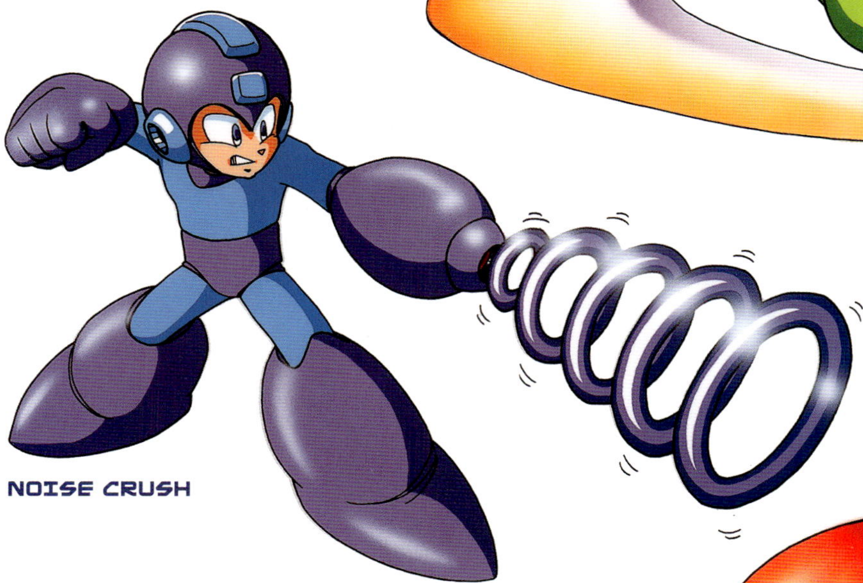

NOISE CRUSH

"The beta for the overseas version happened at the same time. I was still pretty young at the time, and although we had to pull a lot of all-nighters, it didn't really feel like hard work. I remember it being quite fun, like a sports team spirit camp or something. Still, there are so many things about this title that I have regrets about, and even at the time we all found ourselves wishing for another month or so to work on it. Of course, I don't know if I would have survived another month of that lifestyle... but it would have totally been worth it. (laughs)" (Tsuda)

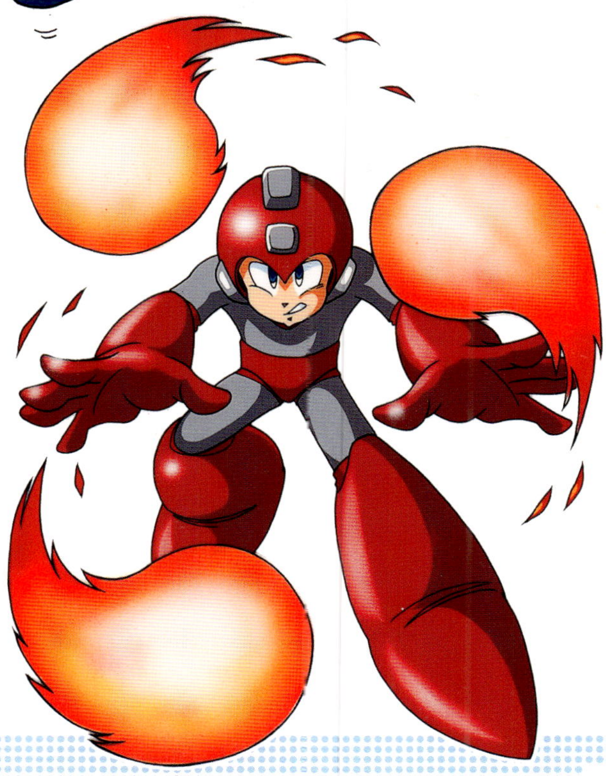

SCORCH WHEEL

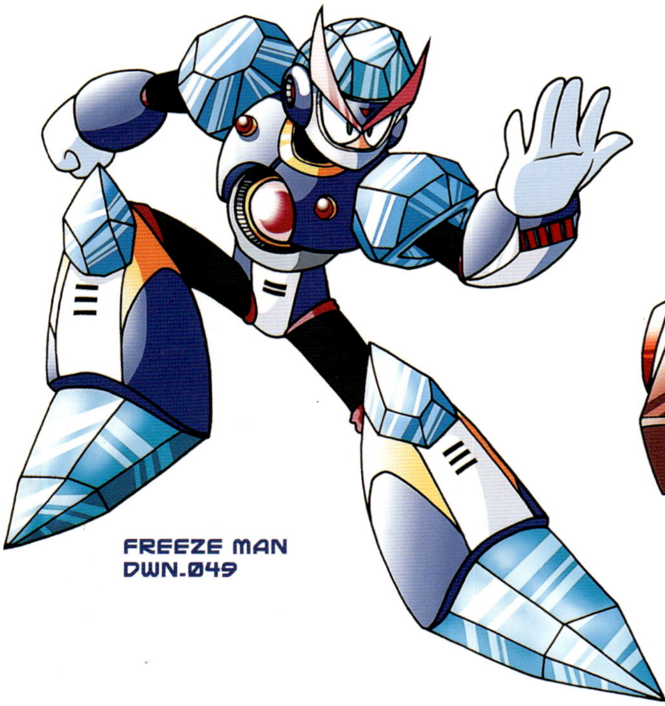

FREEZE MAN
DWN.049

JUNK MAN
DWN.050

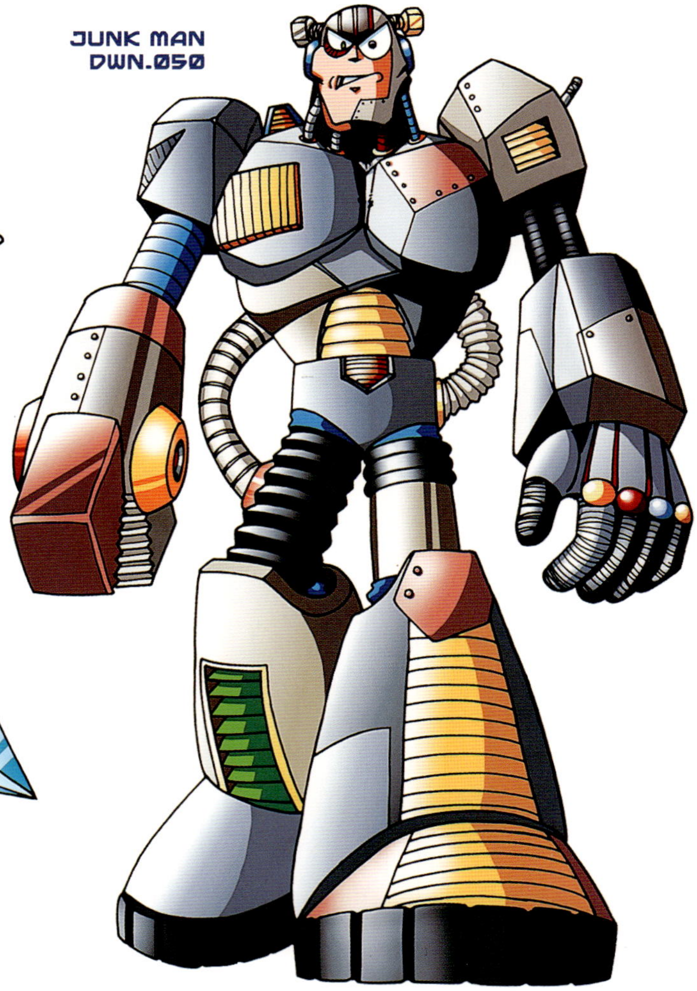

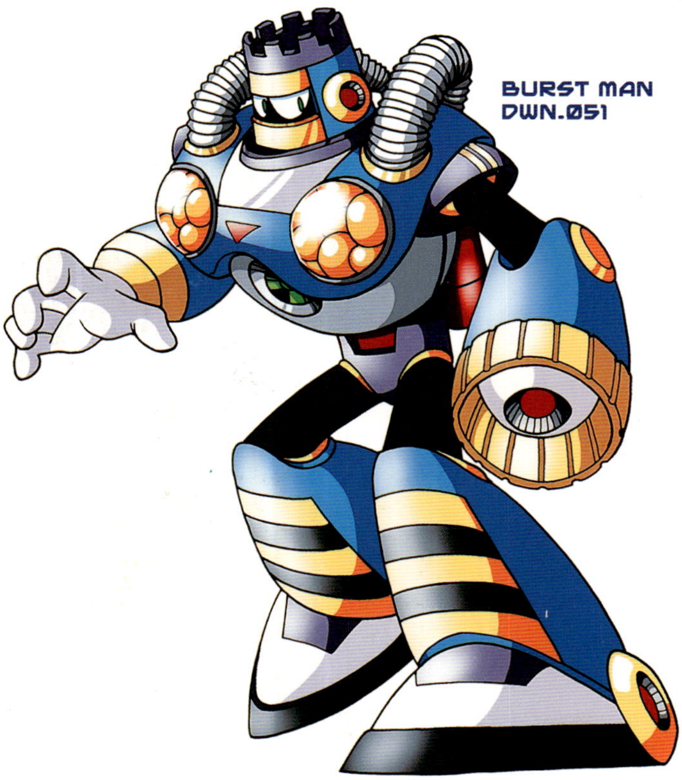

BURST MAN
DWN.051

CLOUD MAN
DWN.052

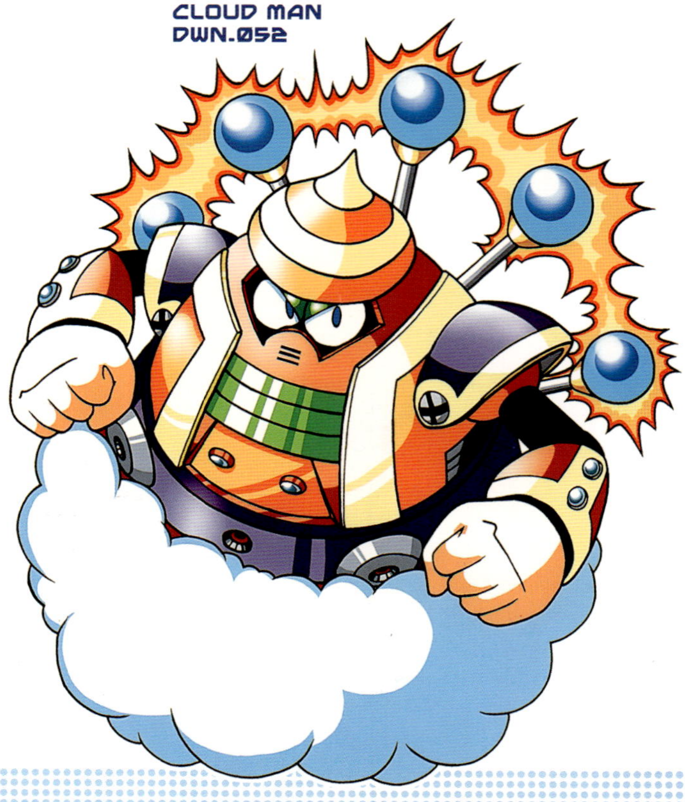

"I did the work on Cloud Man and Slash Man." (Kaji)

"I was called in to help, and I did the images for the boss faces on the stage select screen." (Yoshikawa)

"It could have been because we were so short on time, but I feel like we called in a lot of people for '7.' We had someone who was working on a Disney game do the dot work for Shade Man, and I think that's why his movement is so visually stunning compared to the ones we did. (laughs)" (Kaji)

SPRING MAN
DWN.053

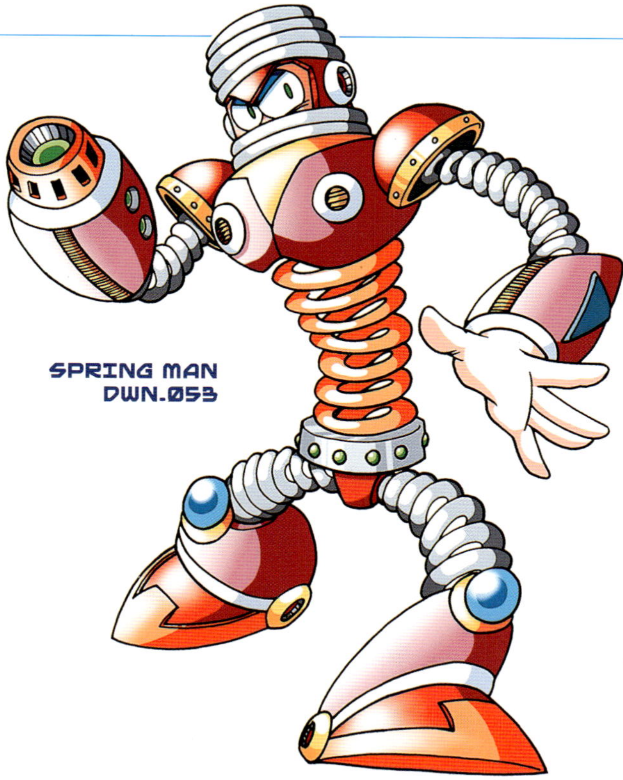

SLASH MAN
DWN.054

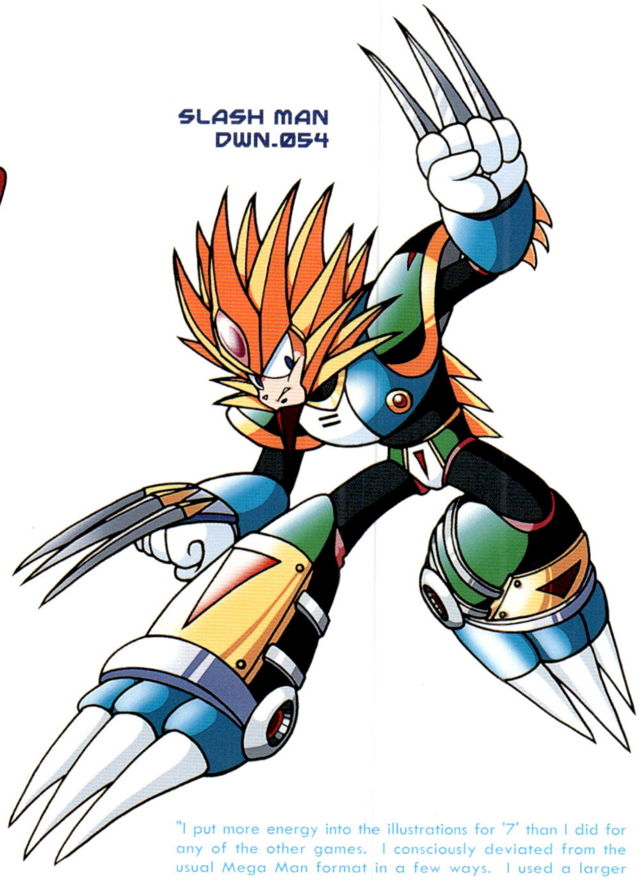

"I put more energy into the illustrations for '7' than I did for any of the other games. I consciously deviated from the usual Mega Man format in a few ways. I used a larger sketchbook than I usually did for my rough sketches, and I changed up the poses for the character illustrations a lot. With Turbo Man and Freeze Man, for instance, you can see that their eyes are not focused on us." (Inafune)

SHADE MAN
DWN.055

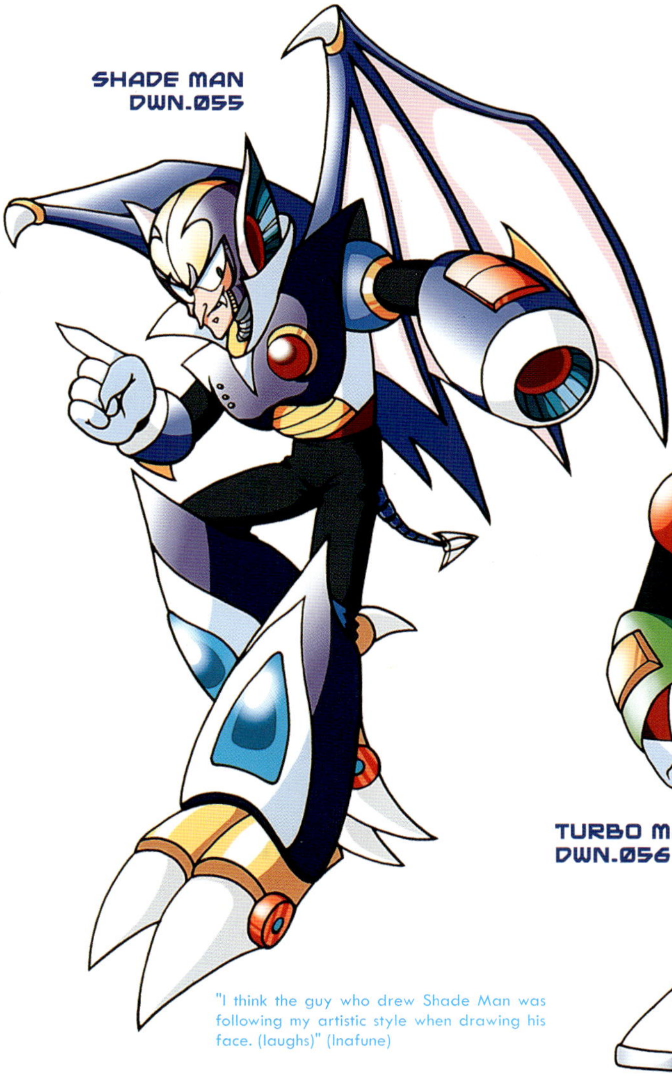

"I think the guy who drew Shade Man was following my artistic style when drawing his face. (laughs)" (Inafune)

TURBO MAN
DWN.056

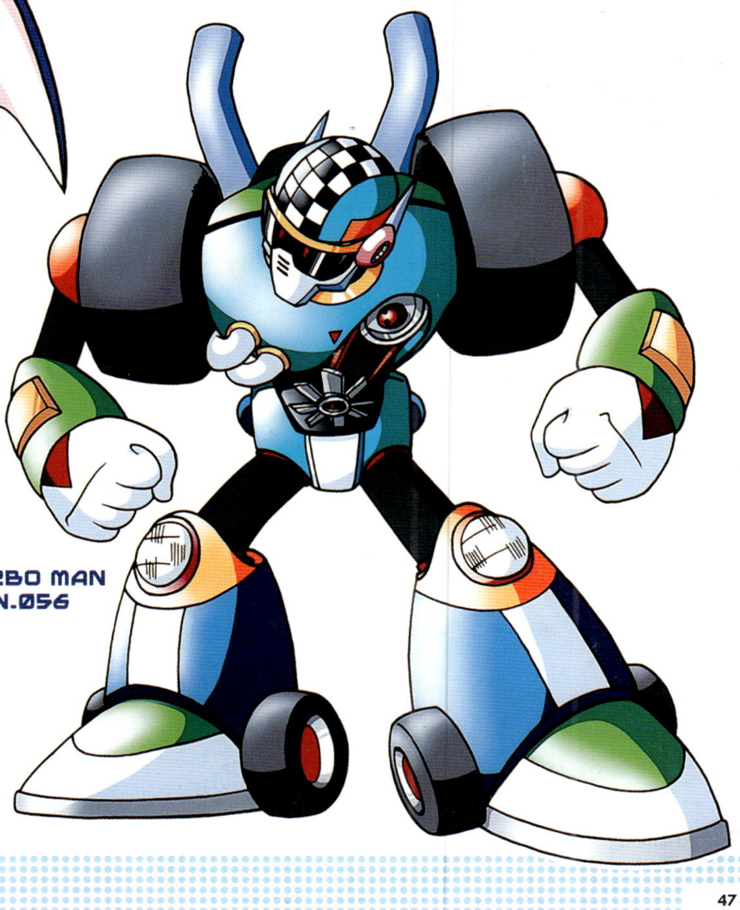

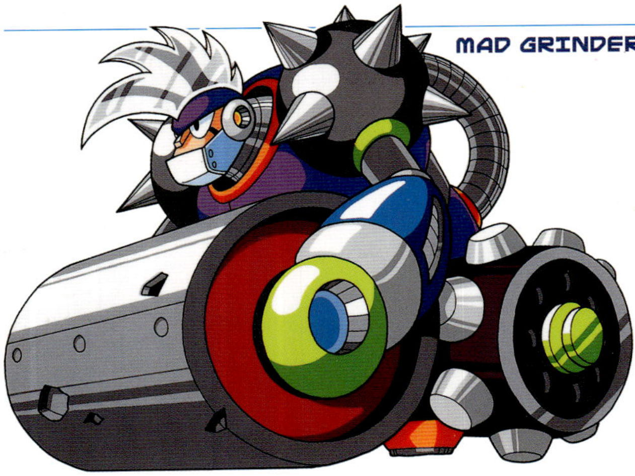
MAD GRINDER

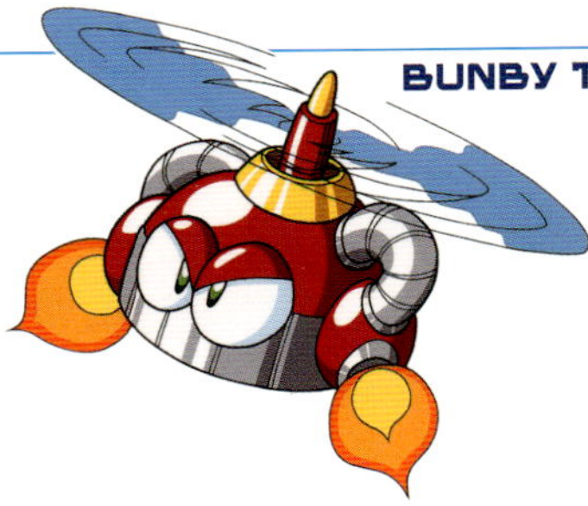
BUNBY TOP

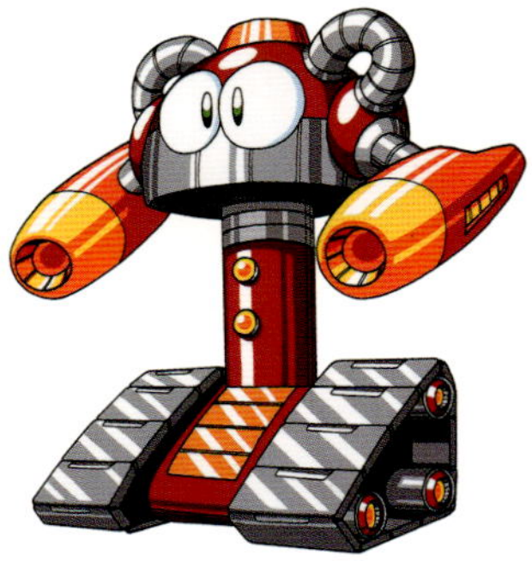
BUNBY TANK

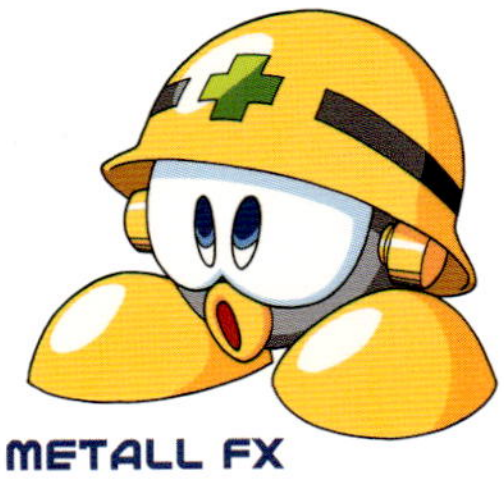
METALL FX

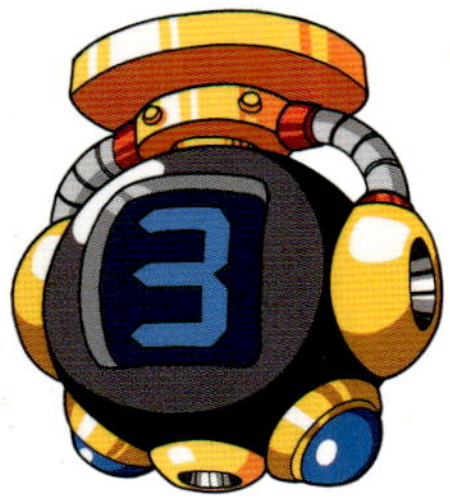
COUNT BOMB NEO

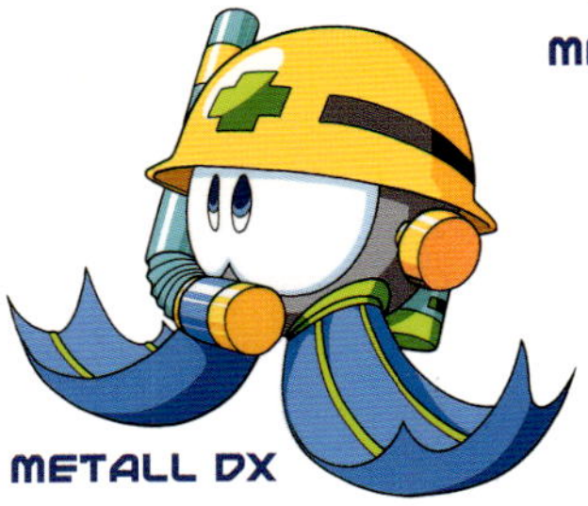
SWIM METALL DX

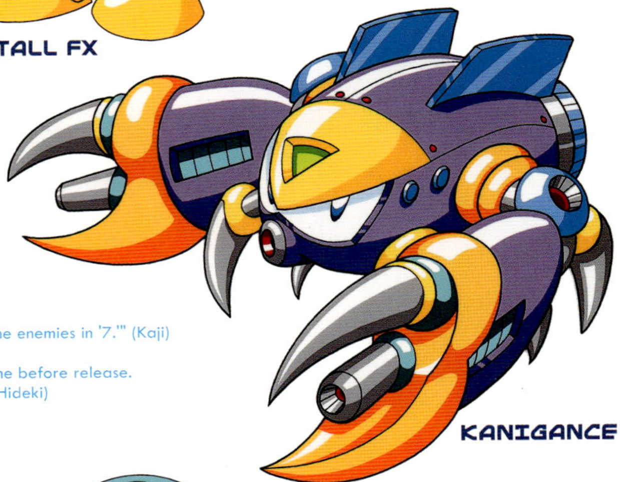
KANIGANCE

"I worked on many of the dot graphics and designs for the enemies in '7.'" (Kaji)

"There were just so many... It was hard to get the cels done before release. At this stage, the minor enemy images weren't CG yet." (Hideki)

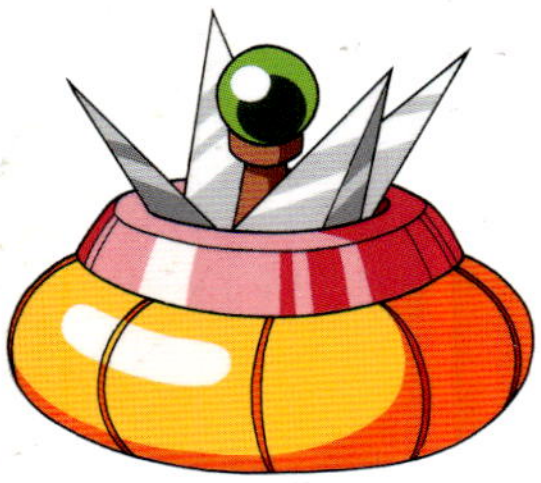
SPIRAL GABYOALL

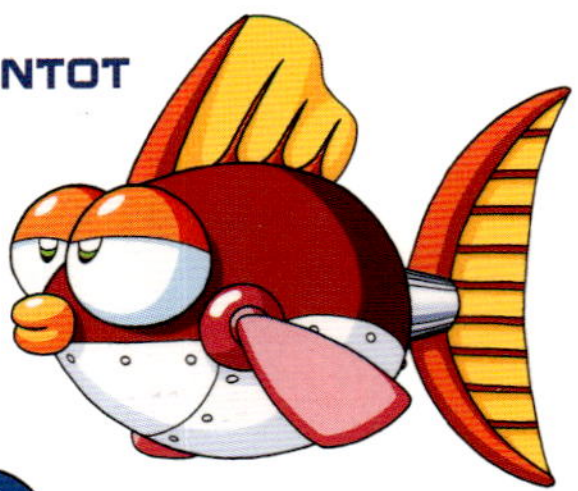
KINTOT

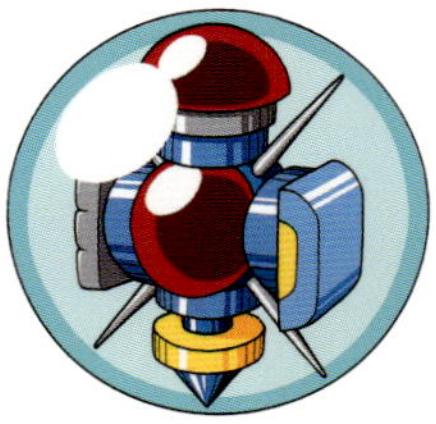
CFN-24

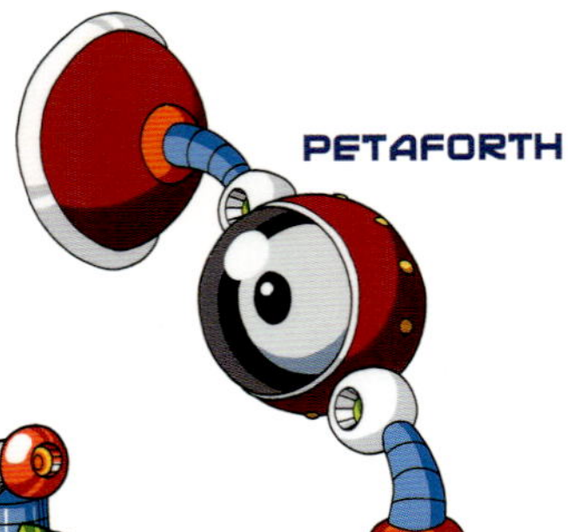
PETAFORTH

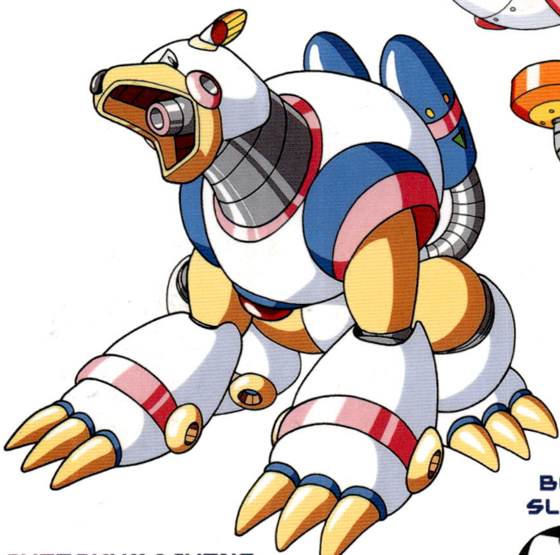
SHIROKUMACHINE GTV

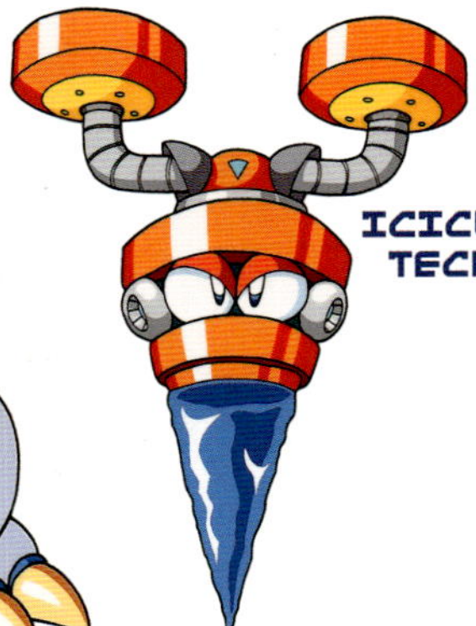
ICICLE TECK

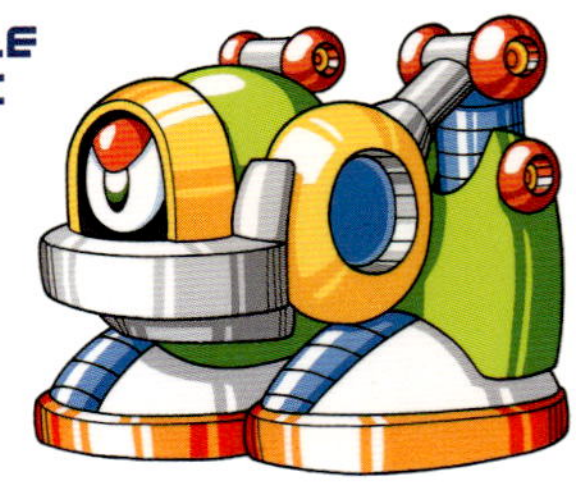
KERONE

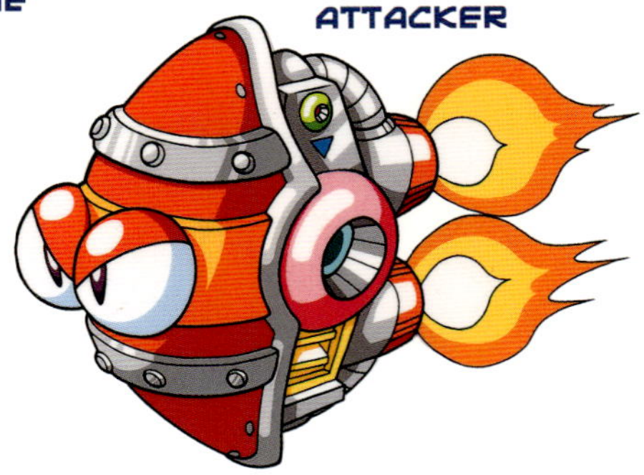
TRUE SHIELD ATTACKER

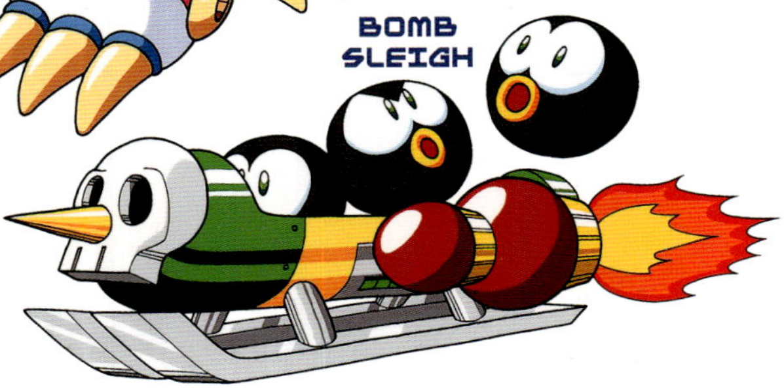
BOMB SLEIGH

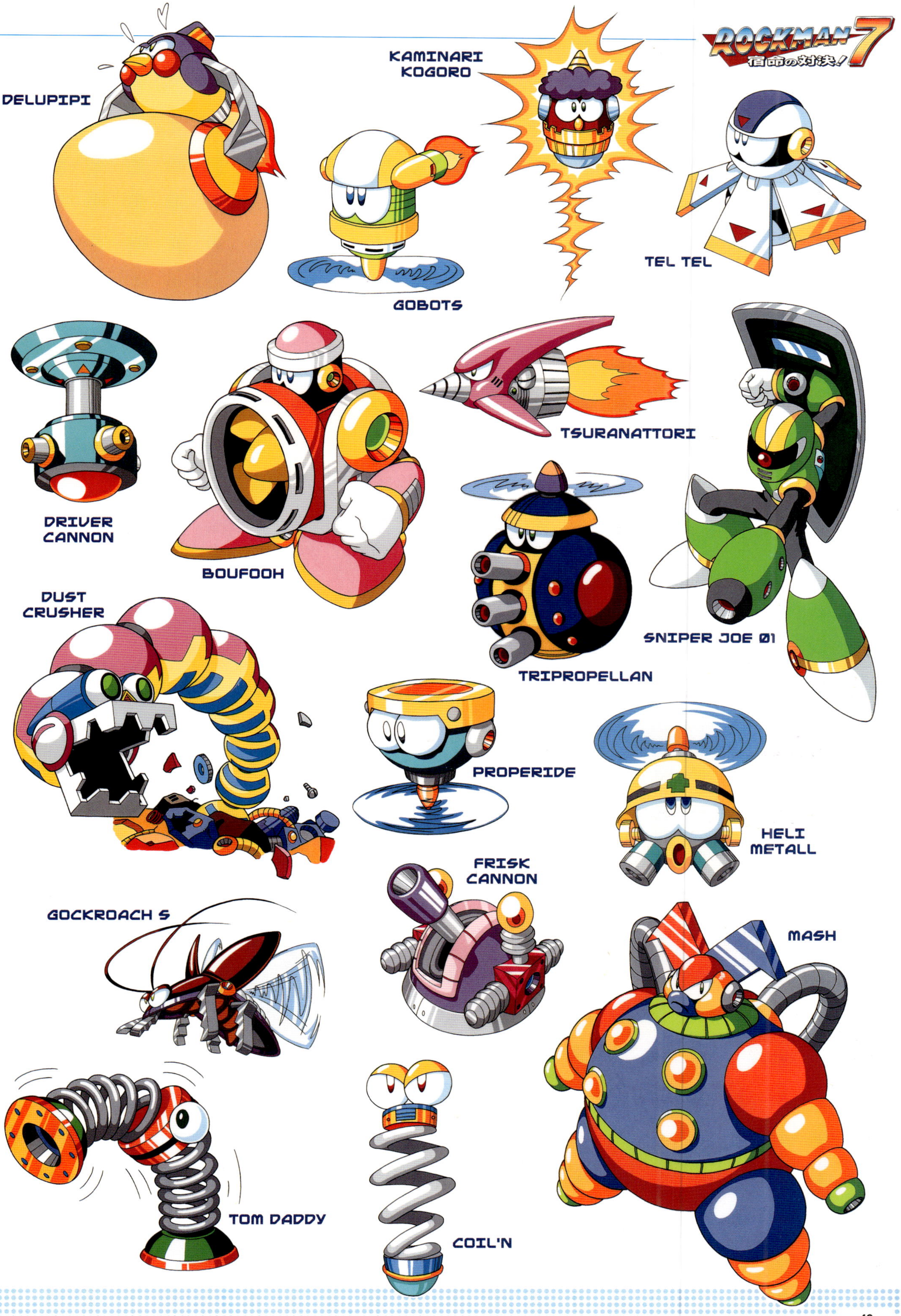
DELUPIPI
KAMINARI KOGORO
GOBOTS
TEL TEL
DRIVER CANNON
BOUFOOH
TSURANATTORI
TRIPROPELLAN
SNIPER JOE 01
DUST CRUSHER
PROPERIDE
HELI METALL
FRISK CANNON
GOCKROACH S
MASH
TOM DADDY
COIL'N

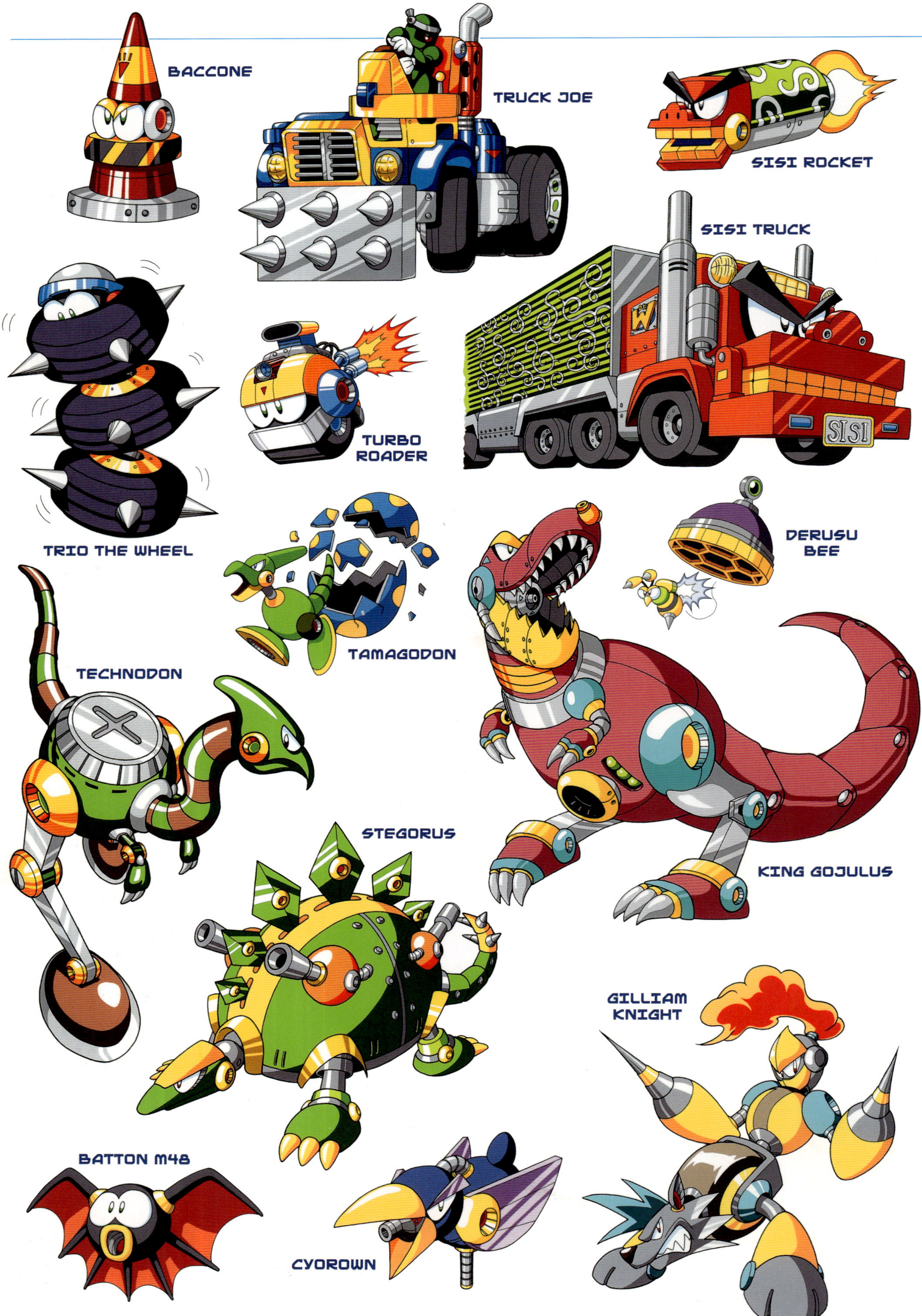
BACCONE
TRUCK JOE
SISI ROCKET
SISI TRUCK
SISI
TRIO THE WHEEL
TURBO ROADER
DERUSU BEE
TAMAGODON
TECHNODON
STEGORUS
KING GOJULUS
GILLIAM KNIGHT
BATTON M48
CYOROWN

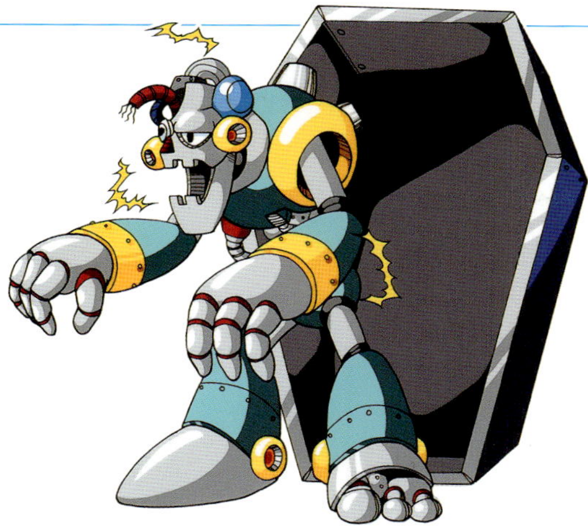
ASTRO ZOMBIEG

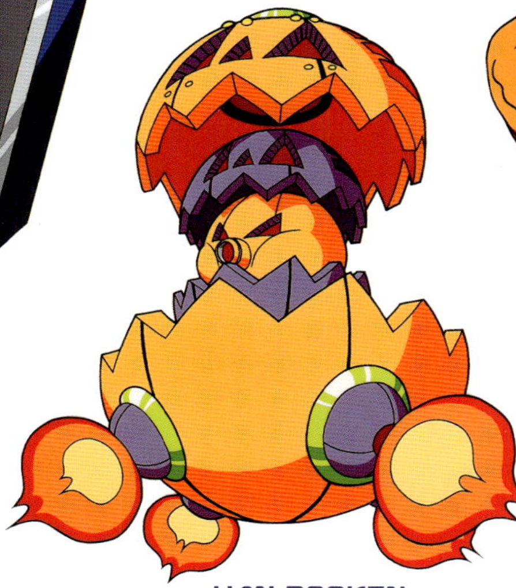
VAN POOKIN

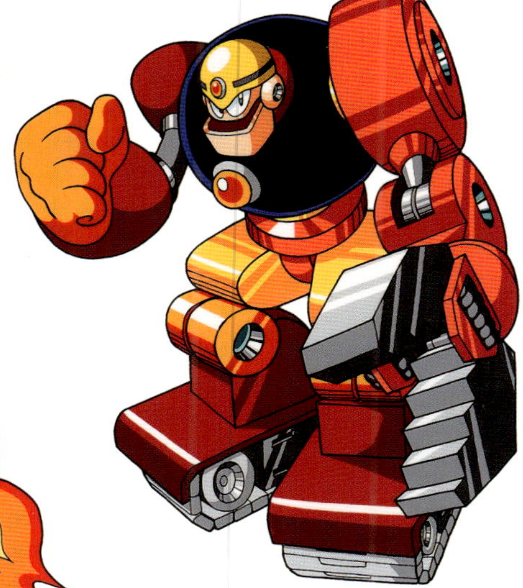
GUTS MAN G

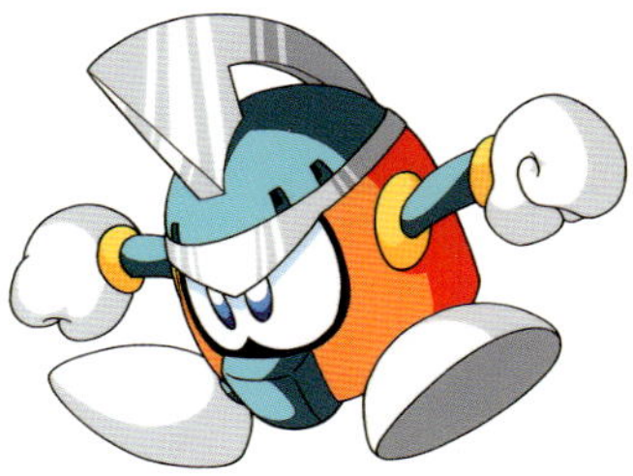
RAGGER

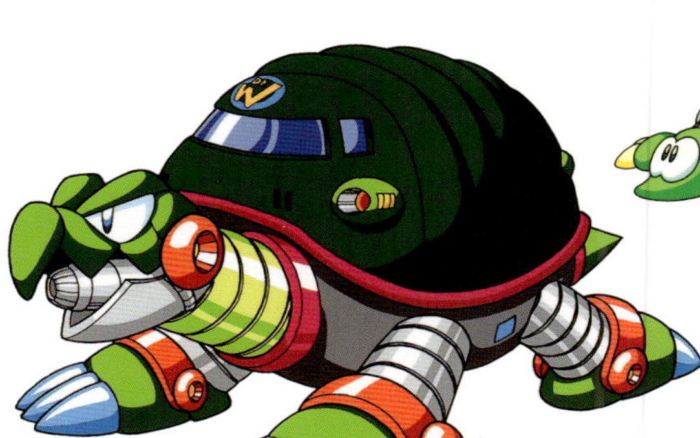
GAMERIZER

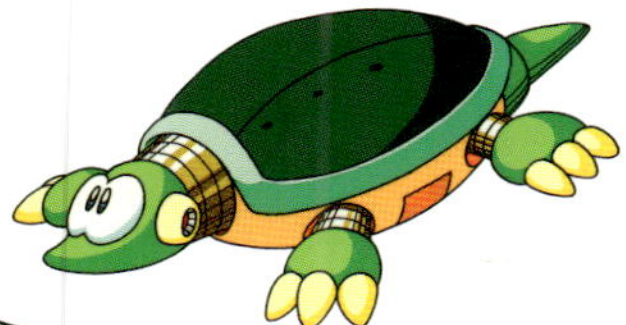
SPOTARO

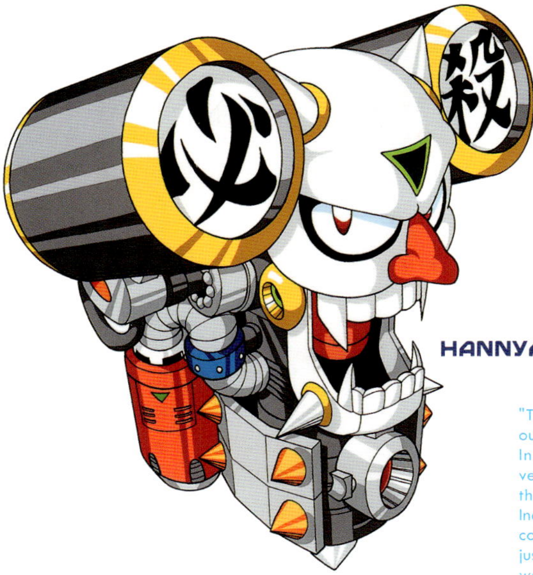
HANNYA NED^2

"The Wily Capsule in '7' turned out as tough as it did because of Inafune saying, 'Let's make the very last fight insanely hard!' At the time, the lead programmer, Inafune, and myself had pooled our collective energy into working on just the Wily Machine. In the end, we created something that cannot be defeated without the use of an Energy Tank. (laughs)" (Tsuda)

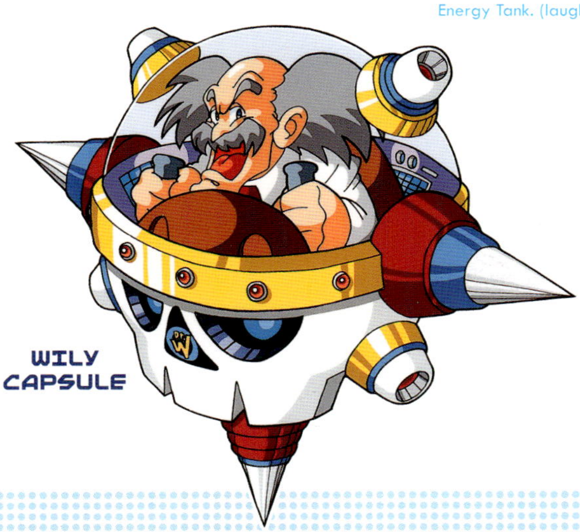
WILY CAPSULE

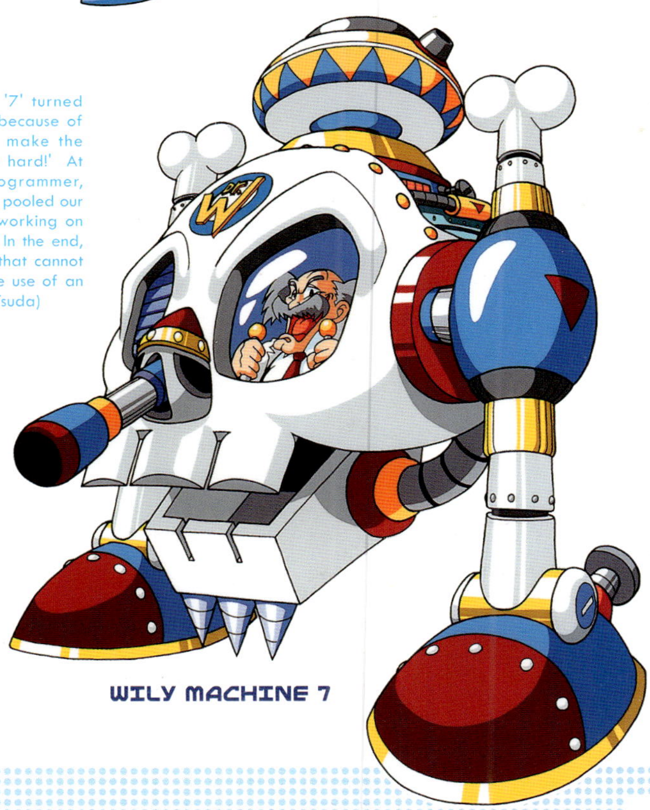
WILY MACHINE 7

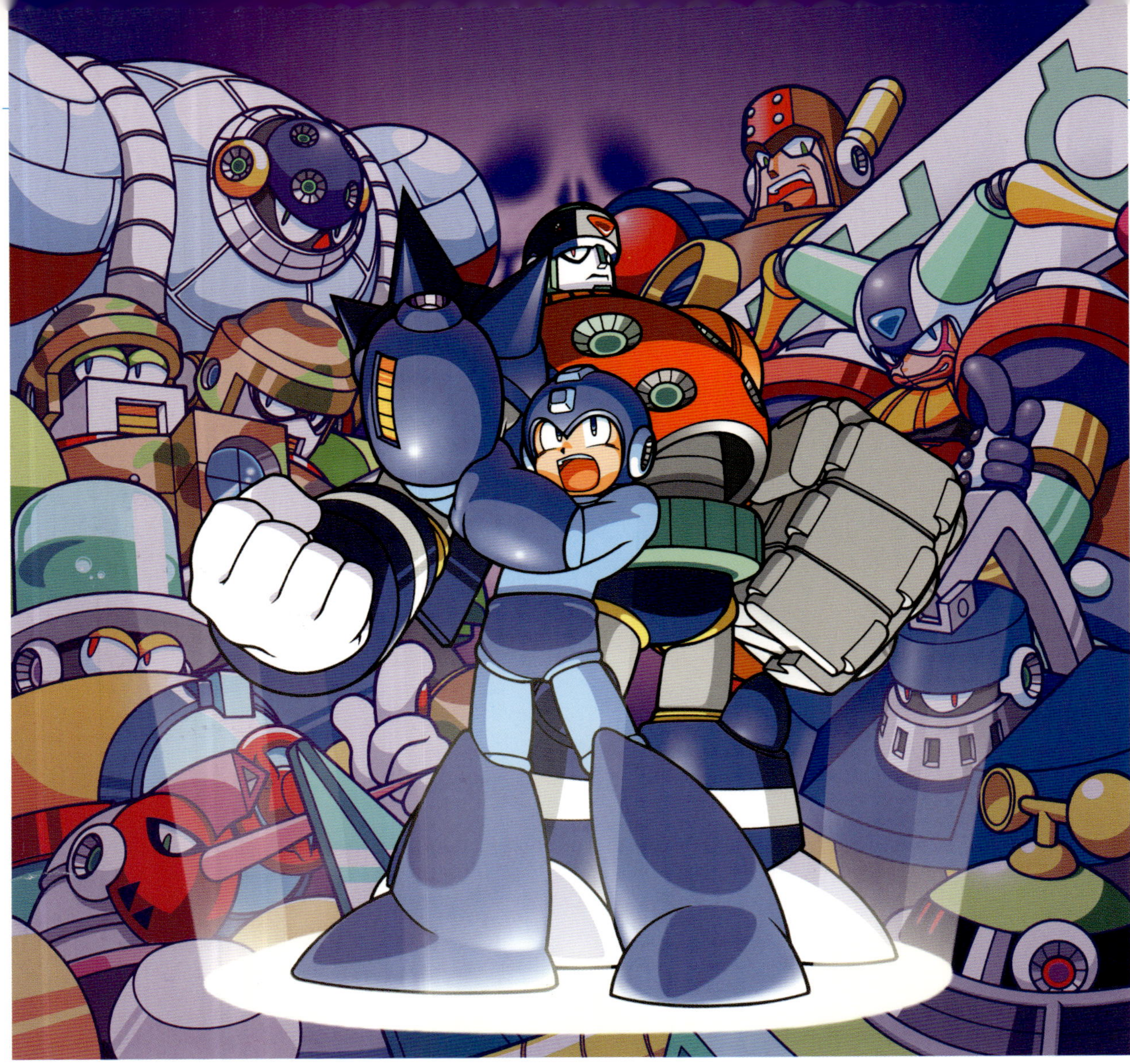

ROCKMAN 8 メタルヒーローズ

Mega Man 8
PS 12/17/1996
SS 01/17/1997
Total number of boss character submissions: 110,000

In an area of space far from Earth, a robot of justice and a robot of evil were locked in a heated battle. The battle finally ended when both combatants simultaneously struck their final blow, and fell to Earth. Dr. Light received readings on what appeared to be a meteor that had crashed into a deserted island, and sent Mega Man to investigate. Upon arriving on the island, Mega Man discovered Wily's secret base...

"With new hardware came new responsibilities. Up to '7,' my main duty was always drawing... but for '8,' I found myself squarely in the role of a producer. I even had to take the train to the studio when we were putting in the animations. (laughs) I'd always wanted to go in the animated direction, ever since '1,' so I had a lot of fun with this opportunity. We brought out so many of the old enemies... This is probably one of my favorites." (Inafune)

"For this title, Kaji was the main designer, and I was put in charge of all the illustrations, including the package art." (Hideki)

RUSH

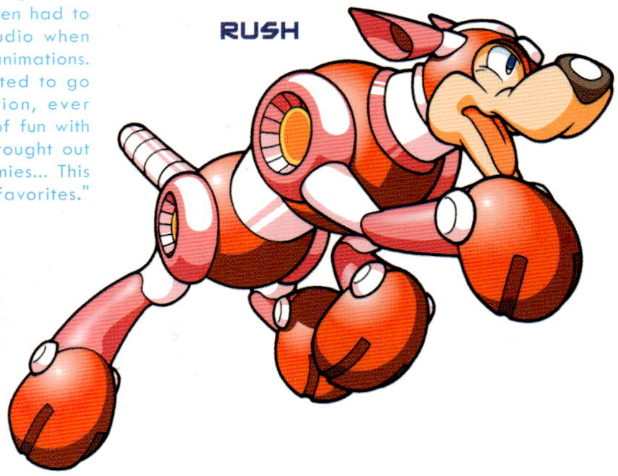

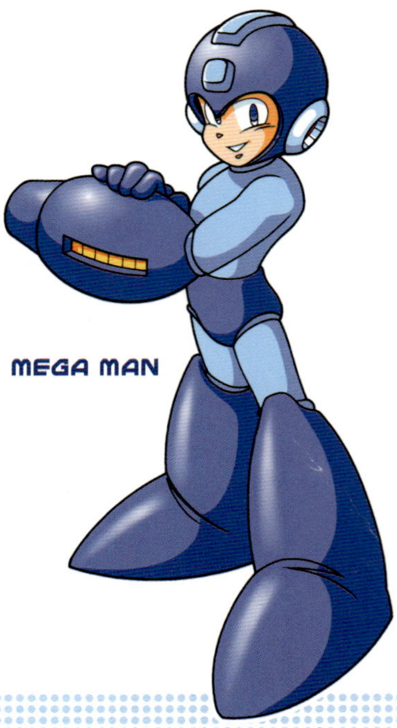

MEGA MAN

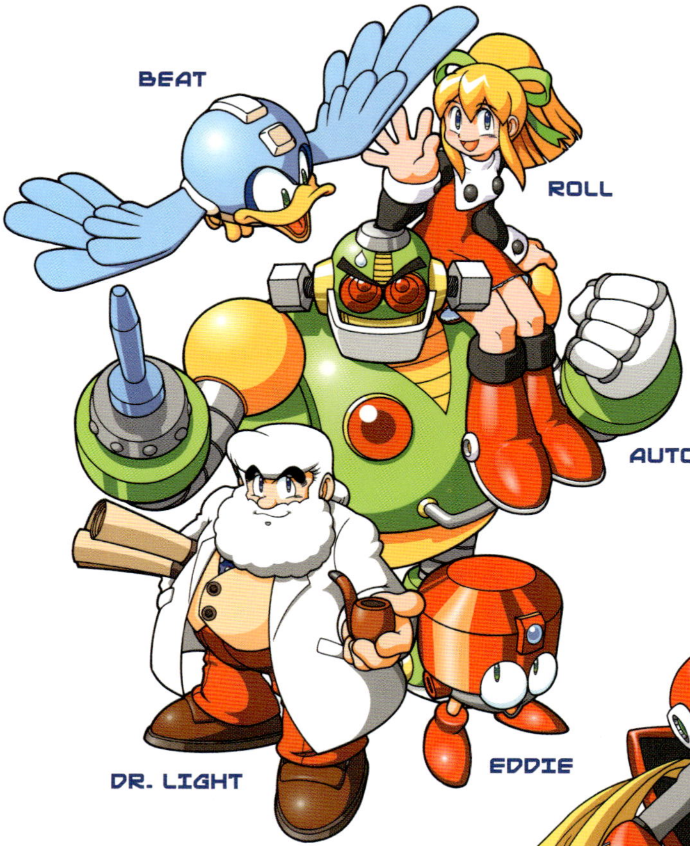

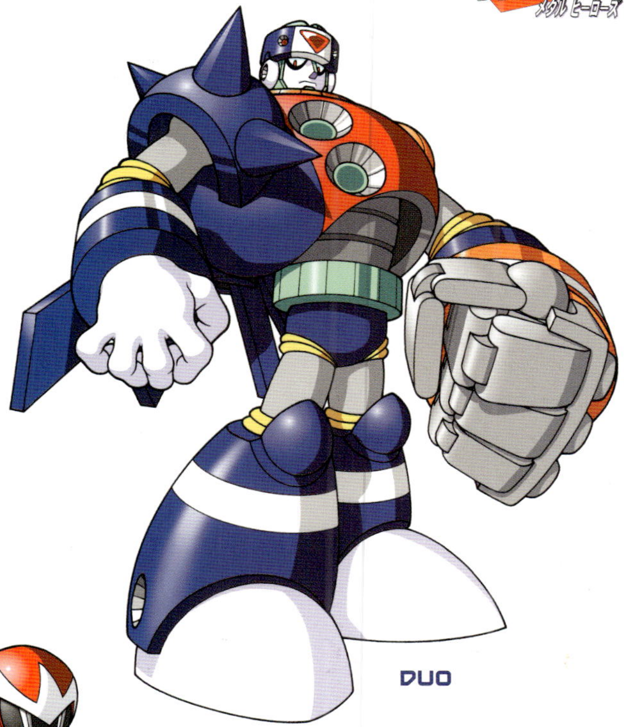

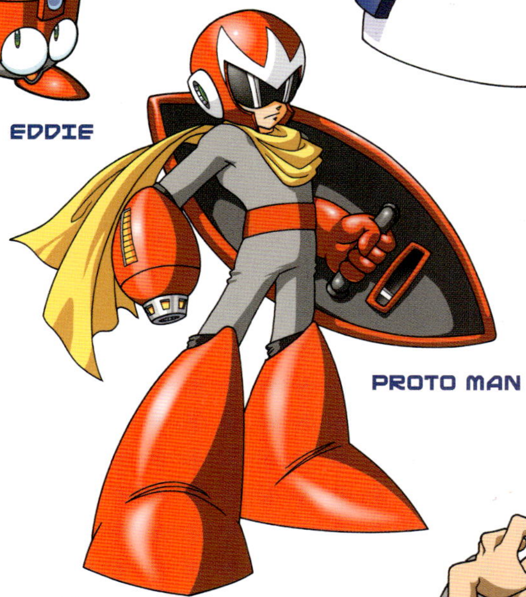

"I did the design for Duo, but he started off as a robot created by Cossack, so there's still a lot of Russian flavor left in him. The shape of his head was supposed to look like a classic Russian hat, and the circles on his chest were meant to look like coat buttons... but then he turned out to be a robot from space. (laughs)" (Kaji)

"I got the idea for 'Good and Evil, falling from space' from one of my favorite movies. (laughs)" (Inafune)

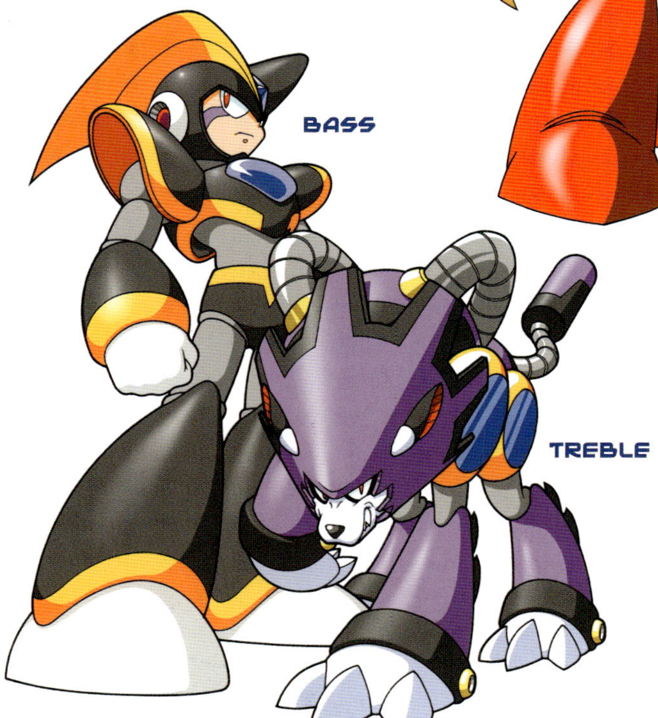

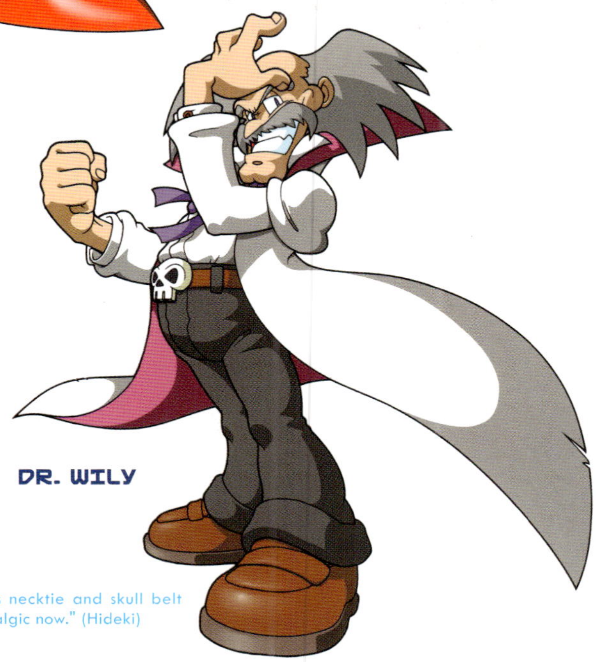

"Kaji designed Wily's necktie and skull belt buckle. It's all so nostalgic now." (Hideki)

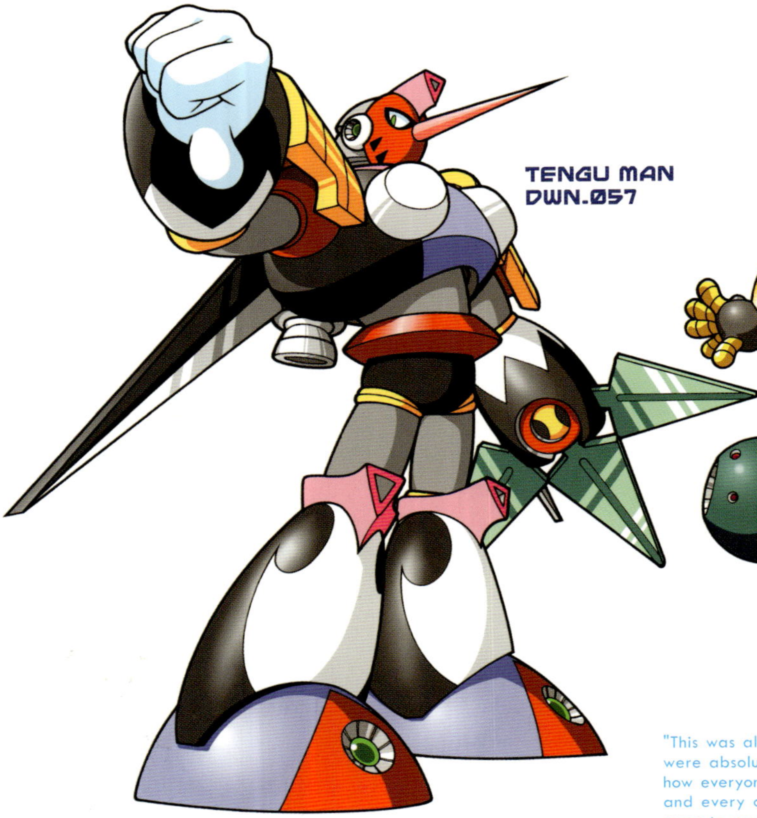

TENGU MAN
DWN.057

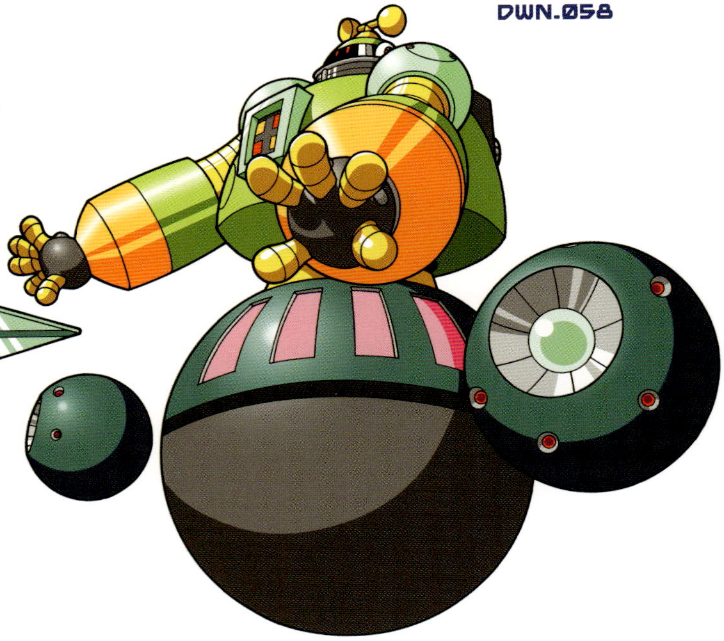

ASTRO MAN
DWN.058

"This was always the fun part. The submissions we'd get for the boss characters were absolutely brimming with the youthful imagination of kids. I still remember how everyone had permanent smiles painted on their faces as we looked at each and every one of the submissions that came through. There were some that we came to expect, though, like 'Black Mega Man' and bosses with terrifying weapons. Poison was pretty popular... like poison weapons that could 'kill Mega Man with just one drop!' Yeah, we got a lot of those. (laughs)" (Hideki)

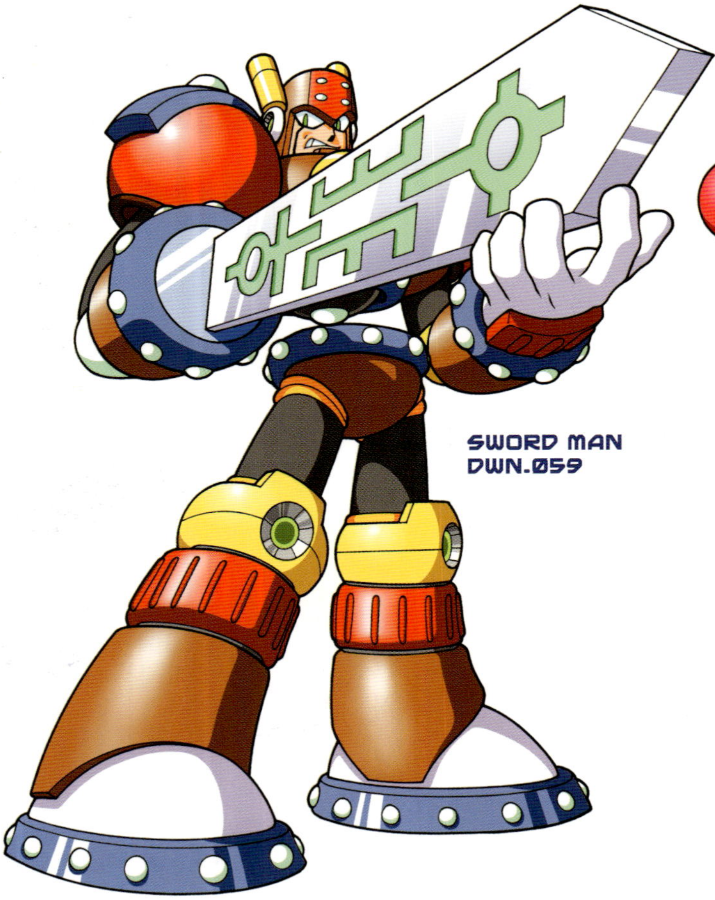

SWORD MAN
DWN.059

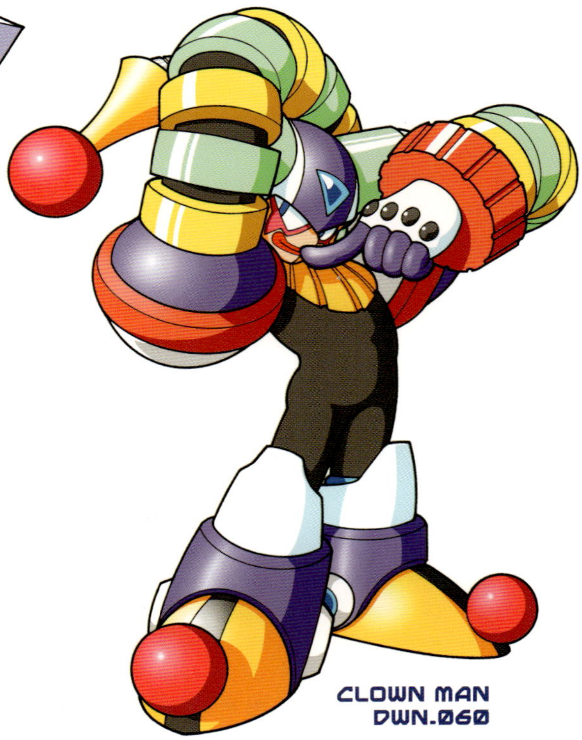

CLOWN MAN
DWN.060

"I did the dots for Grenade Man and Sword Man. Now that we were moving into the PS, with greater hardware capacity, they wanted us to make the most of it by doing more variations and such. Easy for them to say when they're not the ones who have to do the actual work. (laughs)" (Kaji)

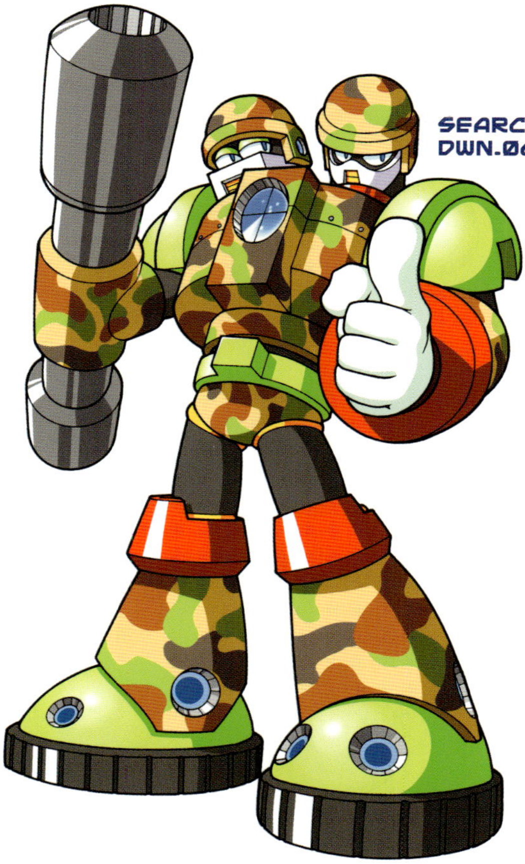

SEARCH MAN
DWN.061

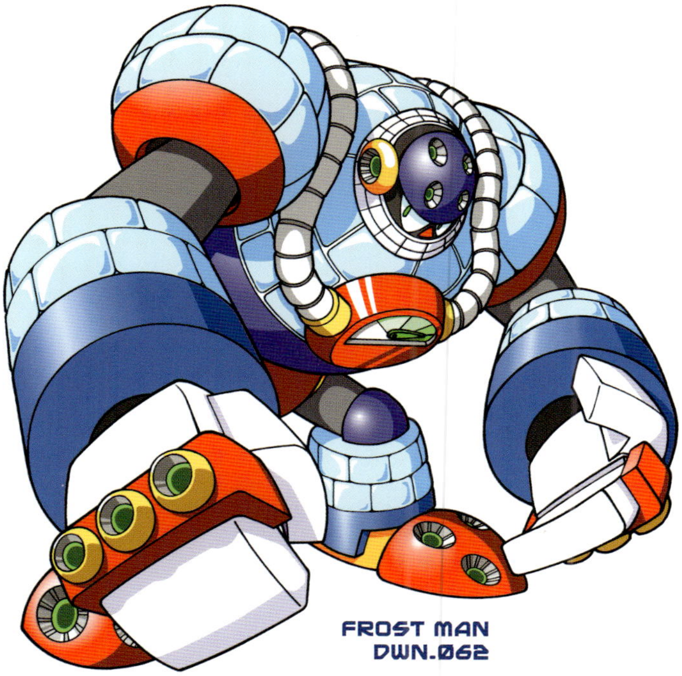

FROST MAN
DWN.062

"I had the honor of working on a few of the illustrations. Ishikawa did most of them, but someone else did Search Man and Grenade Man. I did Clown Man and Frost Man. I remember doing Clown Man specifically, because that was when I really started to get the hang of Ishikawa's style and habits. I actually remember him saying, 'You're finally starting to get it.' (laughs)" (Komaki)

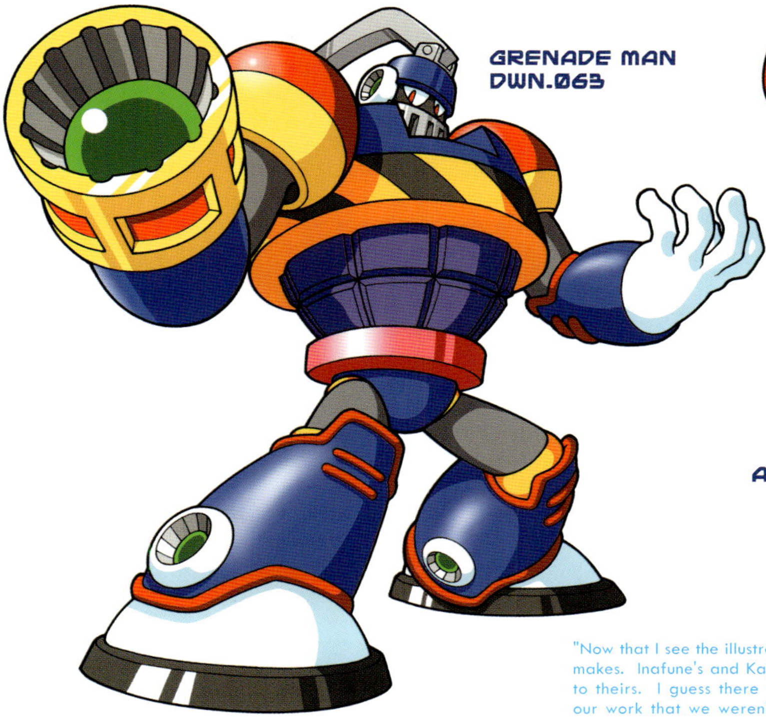

GRENADE MAN
DWN.063

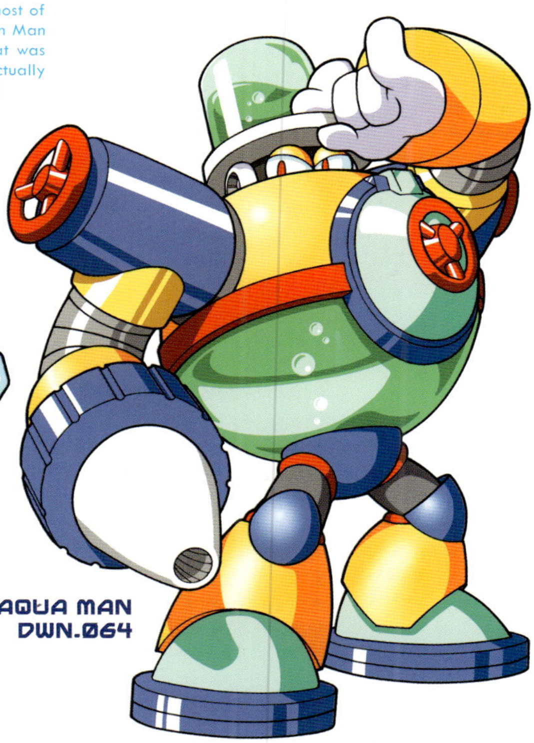

AQUA MAN
DWN.064

"Now that I see the illustrations side by side, I can really see the difference experience makes. Inafune's and Kaji's lines simply exude life. Our lines seem so stiff compared to theirs. I guess there was always a bit of hesitation in the way we approached our work that we weren't able to shake off. I reckon that kind of self-control and understanding are skills that you acquire through years of practice." (Hideki)

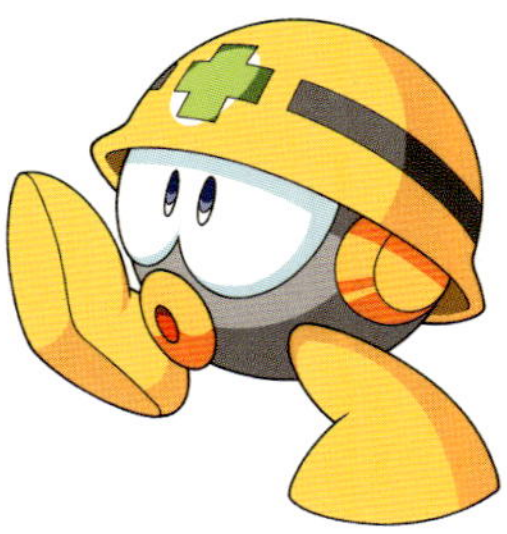

METALL SV

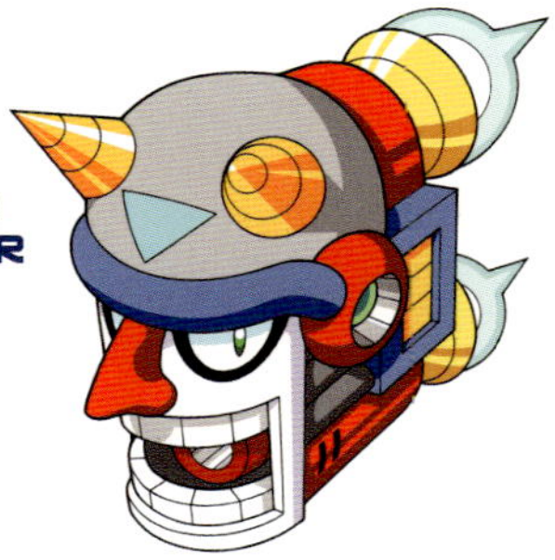

HANNYA ATTACKER

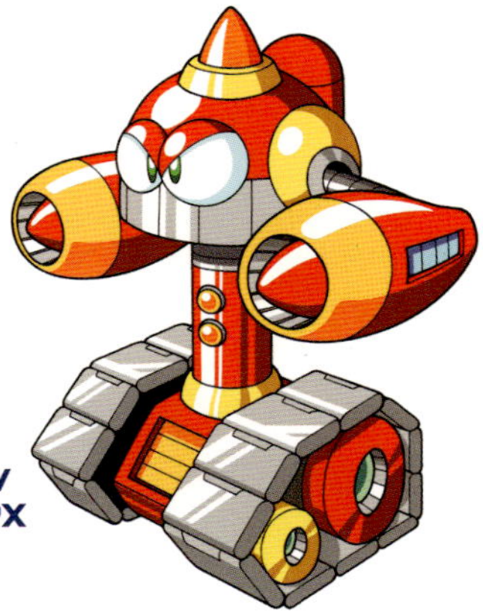

BUNBY TANK DX

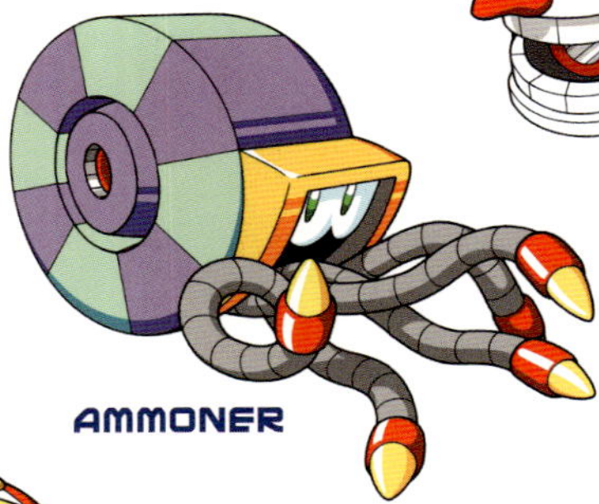

AMMONER

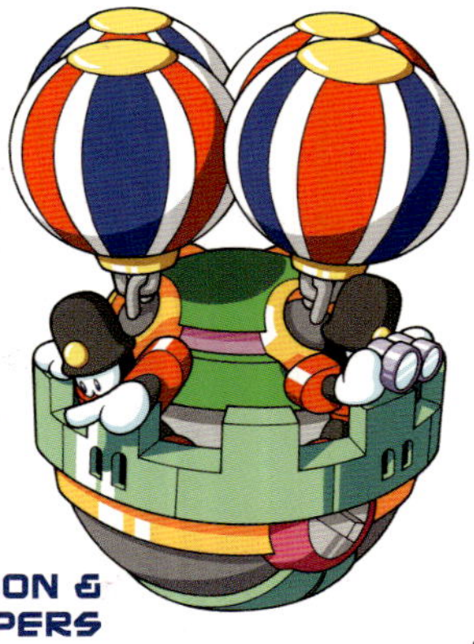

KIKYOON & ROMPERS

"I did all of the illustrations of the minor enemy characters. I wasn't using a Mac yet at the time, and was instead using a program called Hyper Paint." (Komaki)

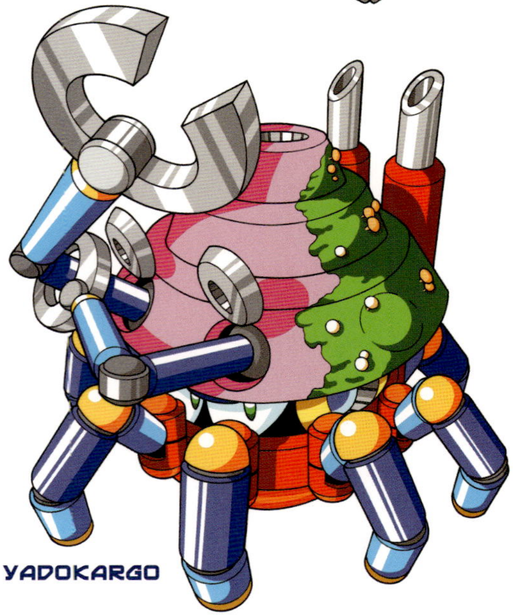

YADOKARGO

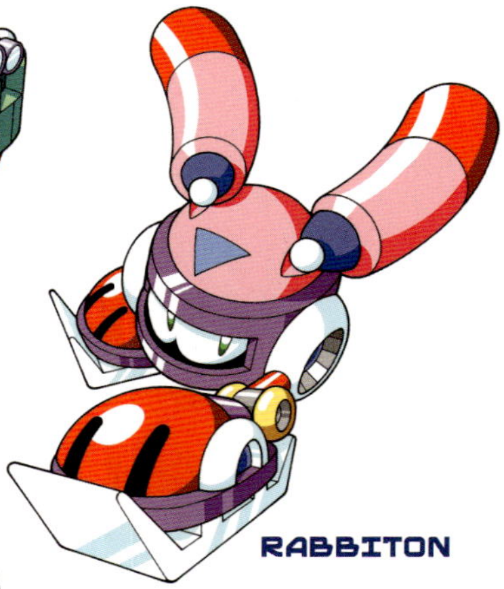

RABBITON

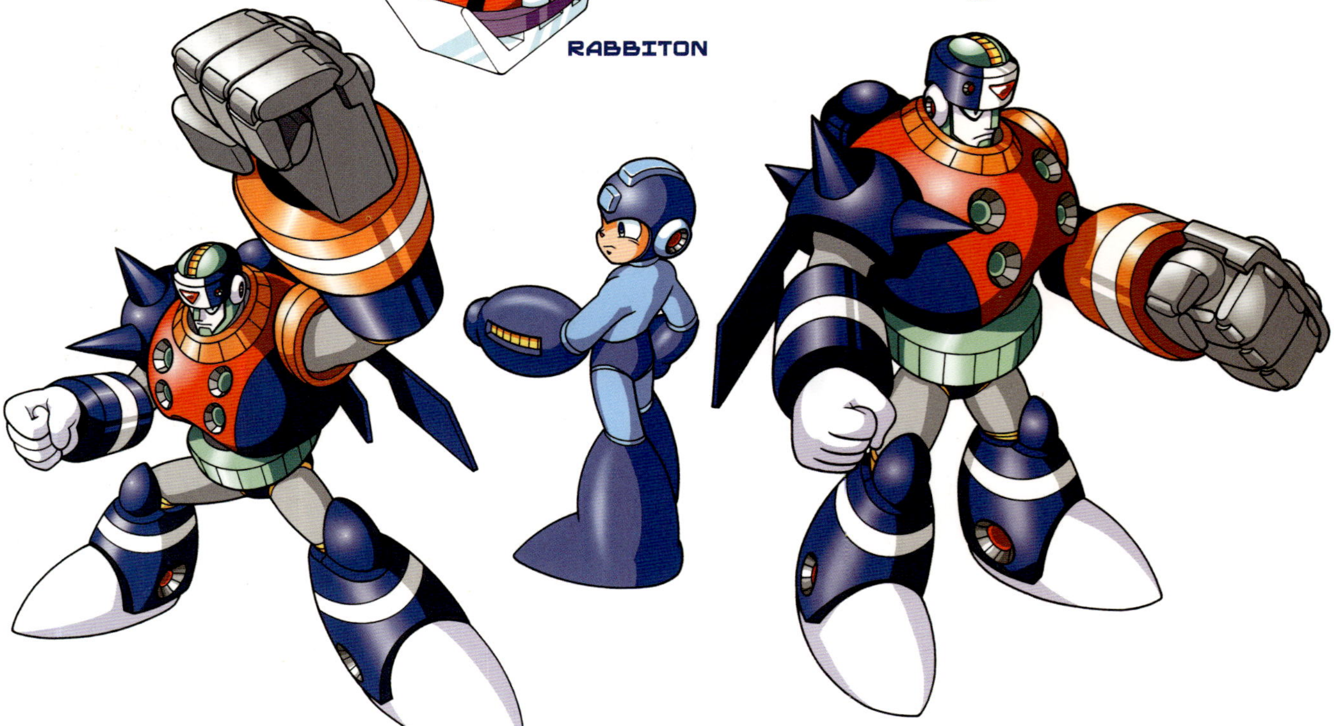

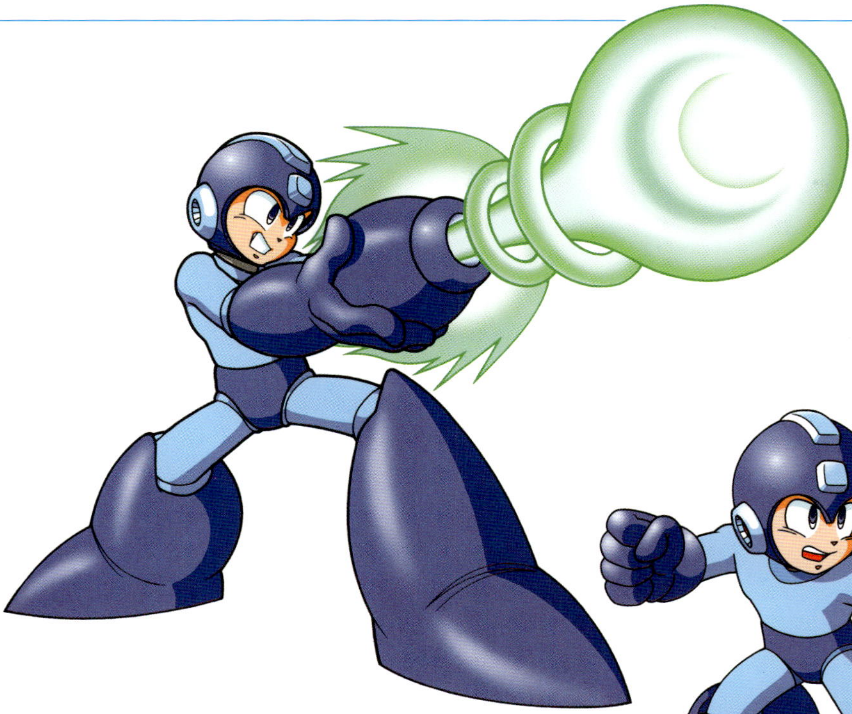

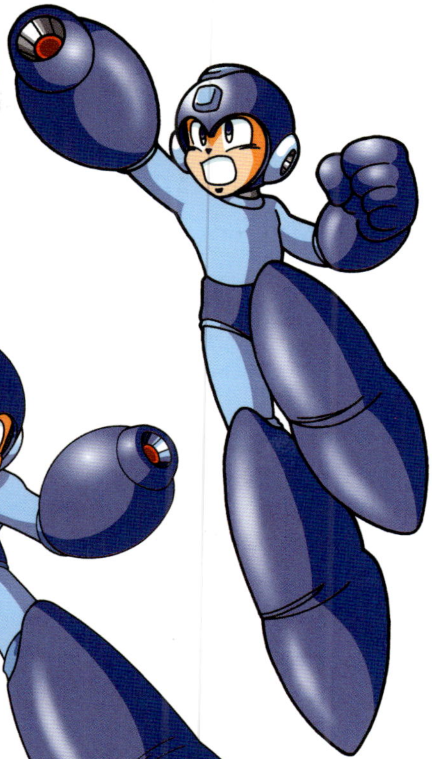

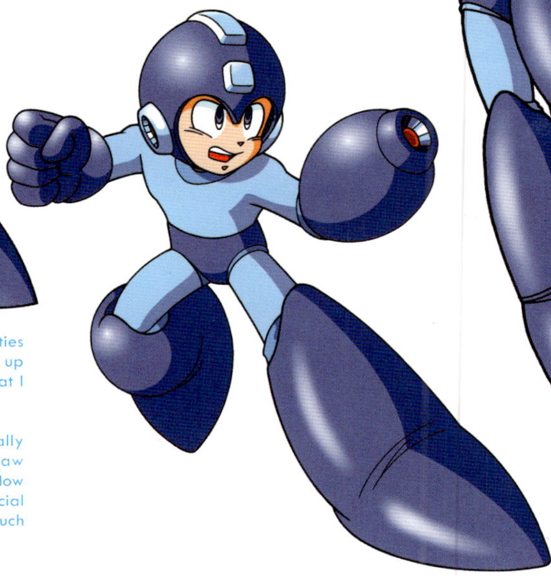

"There are so many different parts to an illustration, and with the duties all divided up it's sometimes hard to tell who drew what. I finished up some of Kaji's illustrations, and I think the illustrations of Proto Man that I touched up were done by Inafune?" (Komaki)

"I'd say this illustration of Proto Man is one of Inafune's. We basically divided up the work. I'd draw Mega Man, and Inafune would draw Proto Man... it was all pretty chaotic, since we weren't working in the flow of a modern day design studio. Up until '7,' Inafune did all of the official artwork. From '8' onward, we were so busy that he'd only draw as much as he had time to." (Kaji)

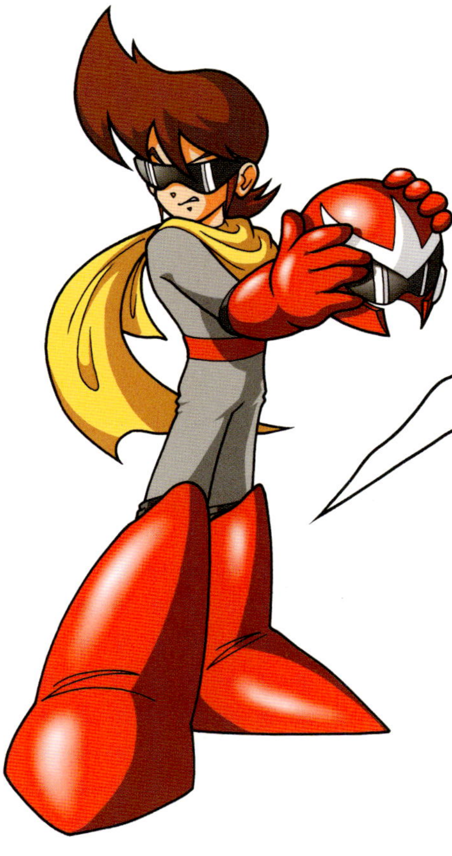

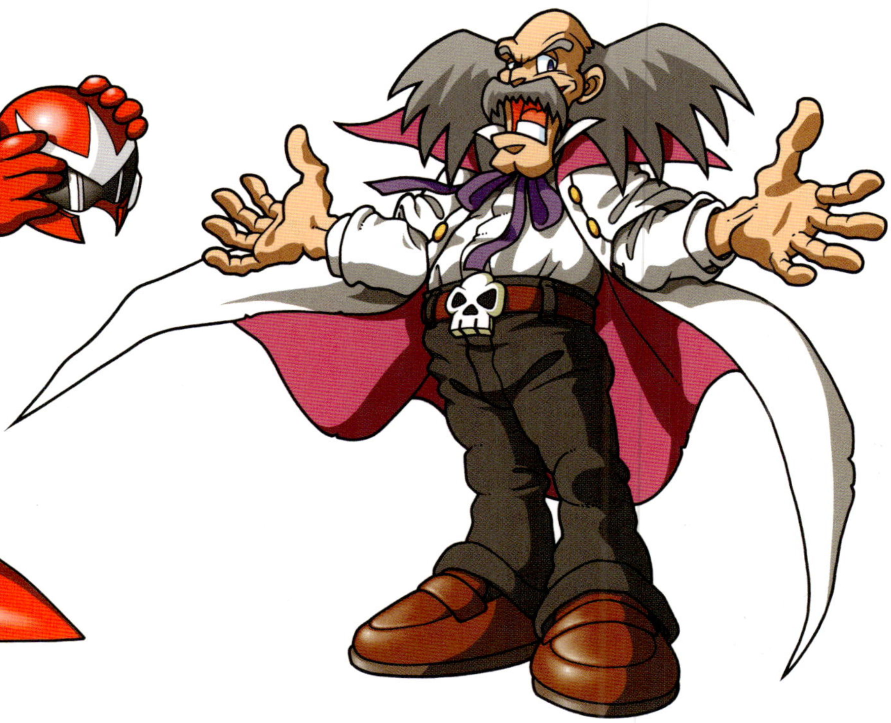

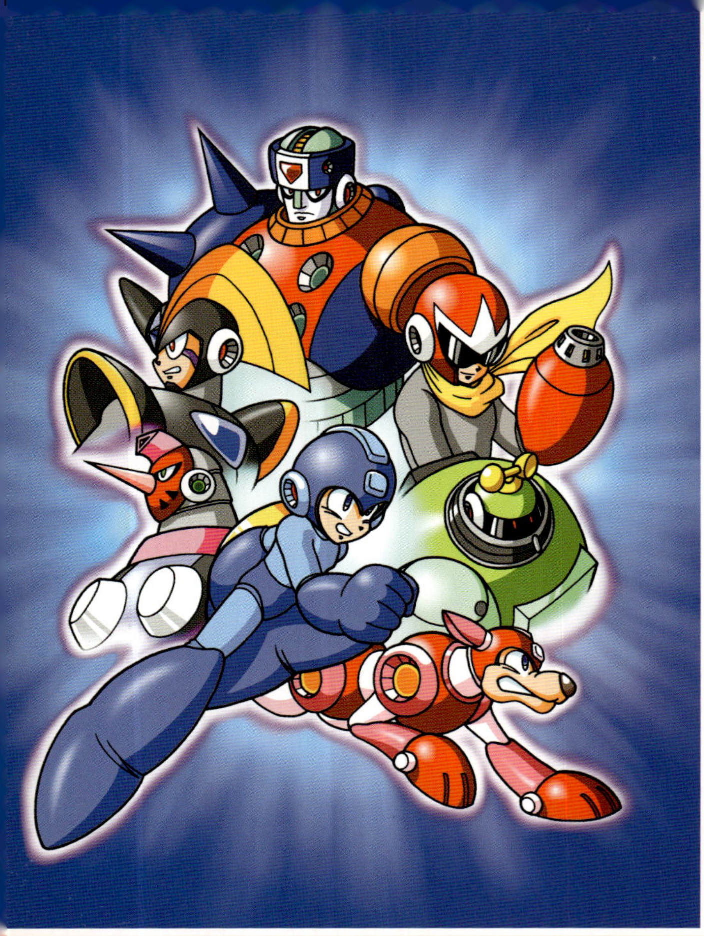

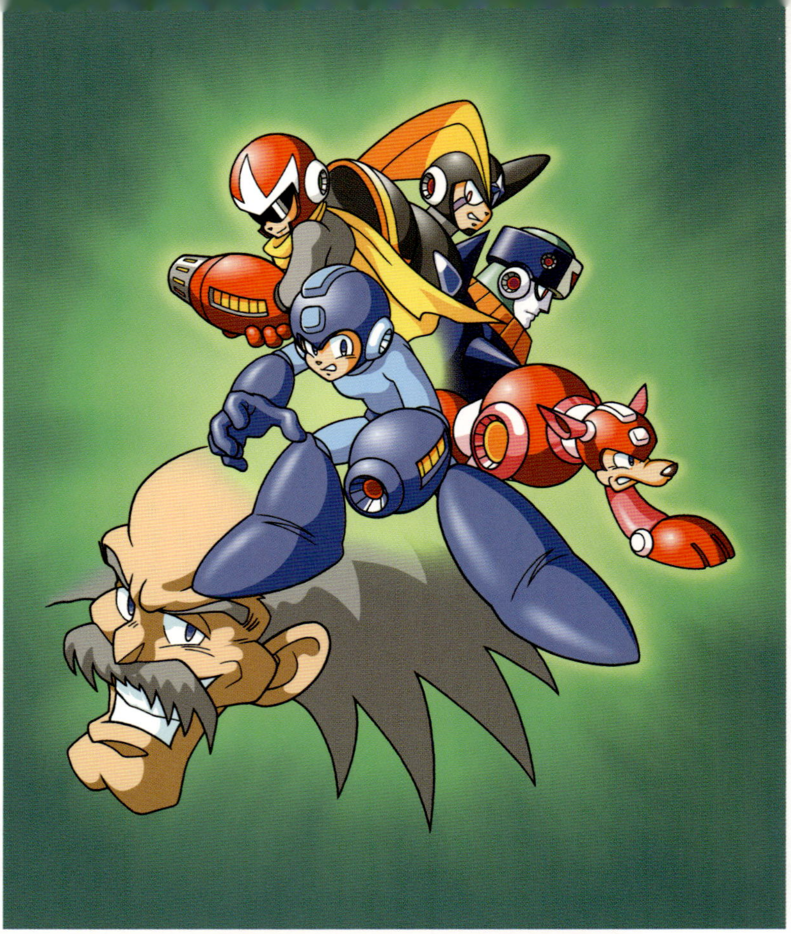

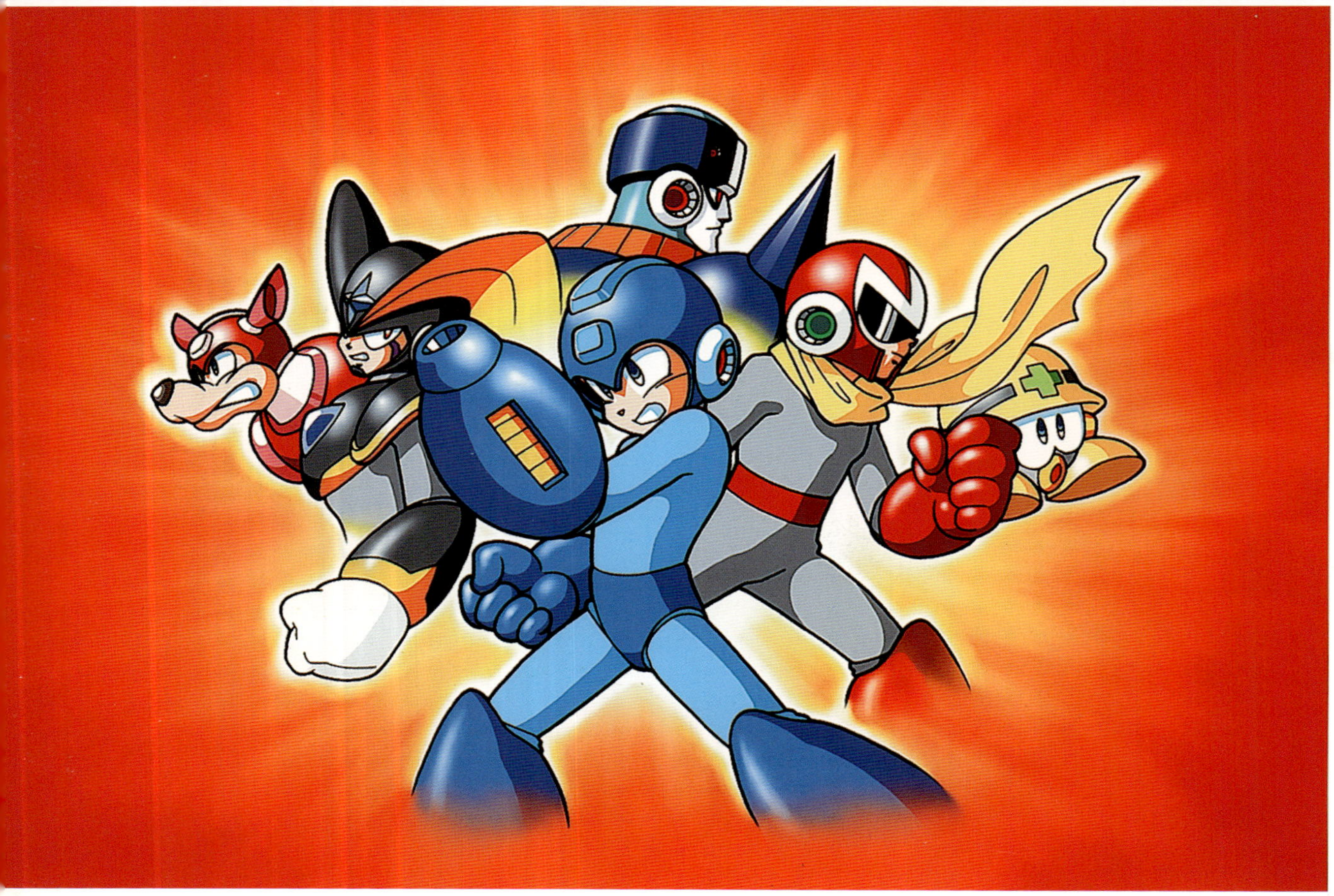

"This is the end of the opening animation, right? I think I remember doing the draft." (Kaji)

"Kaji was at the center of '8.' In other words, my student was finally out there on his own. This allowed me to take a very different approach to creating a Mega Man game. 'Seeing Mega Man from a distance,' I guess you could say." (Inafune)

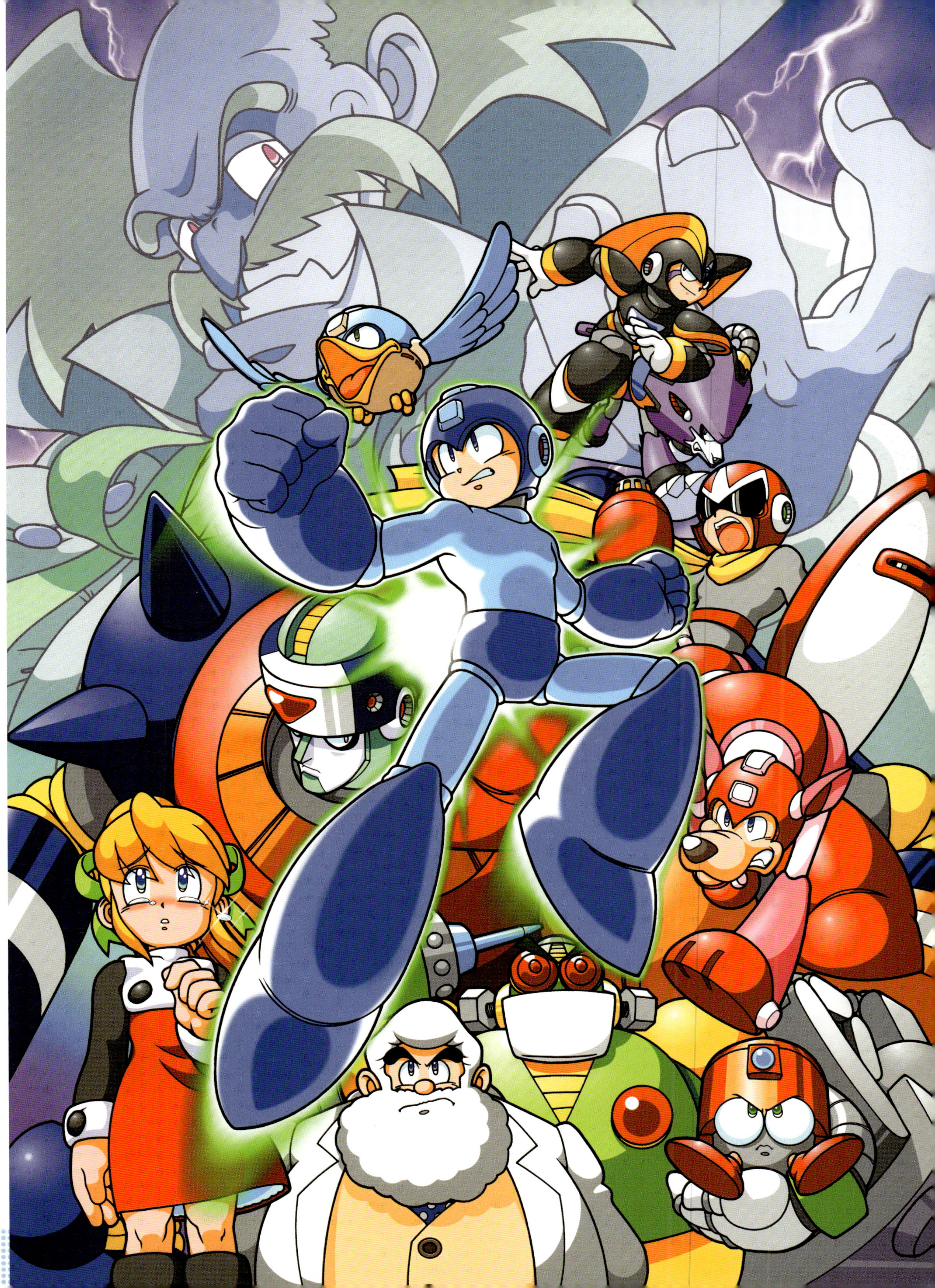

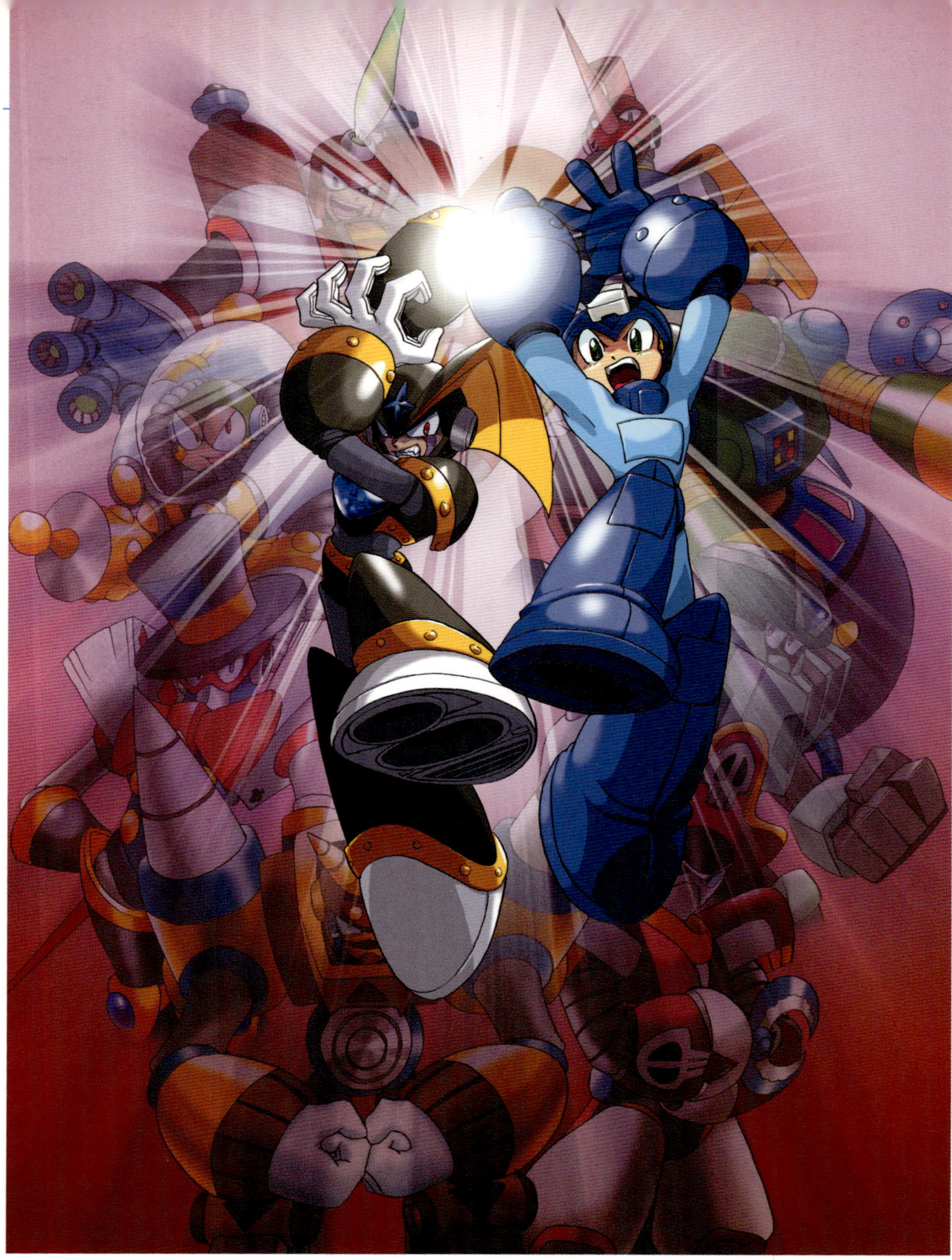

"For me personally, this title is one that I mostly see out of the eyes of a producer. Since it was like a spin-off, I asked Ariga to do the package art, and had manga artists do the boss characters." (Inafune)

"I never would have imagined that I would get the opportunity to do package art for a Mega Man game. I was so very happy and so terribly nervous at the same time. I remember asking Inafune things like 'Should I include all eight bosses in the image?' and he said, 'You can do whatever you like,' which really didn't make it any easier on me. (laughs)" (Ariga)

Rockman & Forte
SNES 04/24/1998

After being defeated by Mega Man, Dr. Wily built himself a castle to aid his attempts at world domination, but soon found his new home occupied by a robot calling himself King. Claiming that the world belongs to robots, who are superior to humans in every way, King stated that he would steal all of the data on past Robot Masters from the museum. Mega Man and Bass depart to see what they can find out about the situation.

ロックマン&フォルテ

"When we made the shift in hardware to the PS and the SS, there were many children who couldn't play '8' because they didn't own either of those consoles. As kids, they didn't have the ability to go out and buy consoles. Even though 'X' had opened its world up on the SNES, the original Mega Man series only went to '7' on that console. That's why we decided to bring out another title for the SNES that was based on '8.' Even though trying to bring out a new title on the SNES was a little backwards at the time, we didn't want to make a half-hearted attempt at it. We decided to reexamine the game from the ground up and make it something that our players could really sink their teeth into." (Inafune)

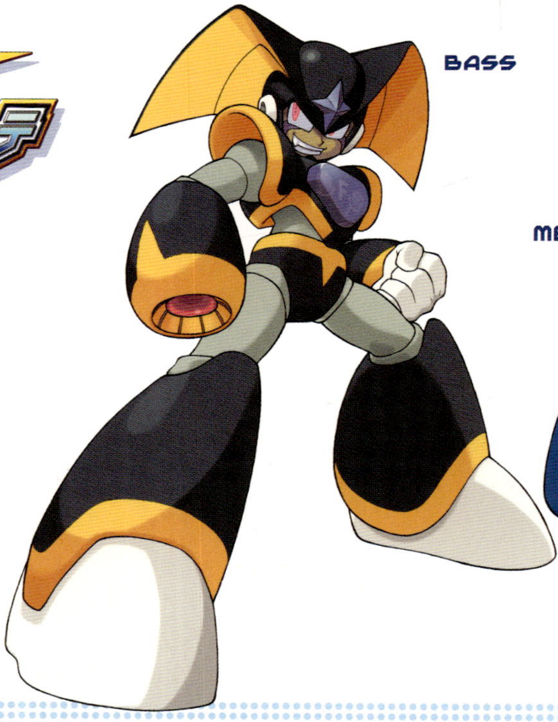

BASS

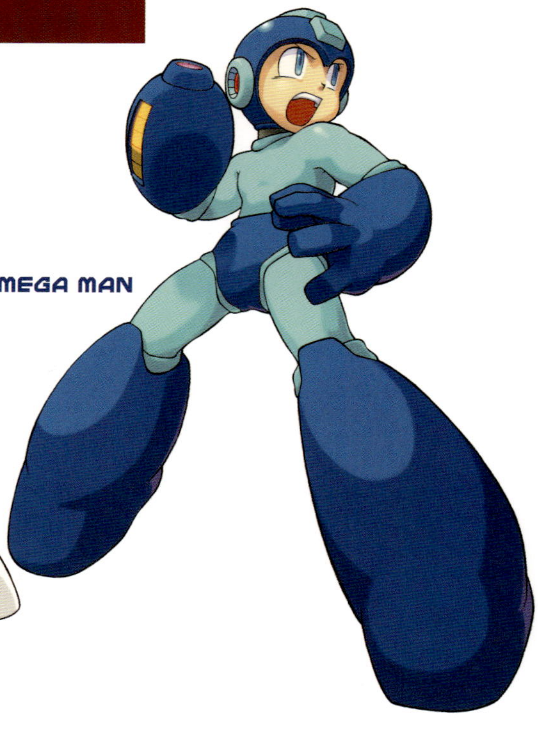

MEGA MAN

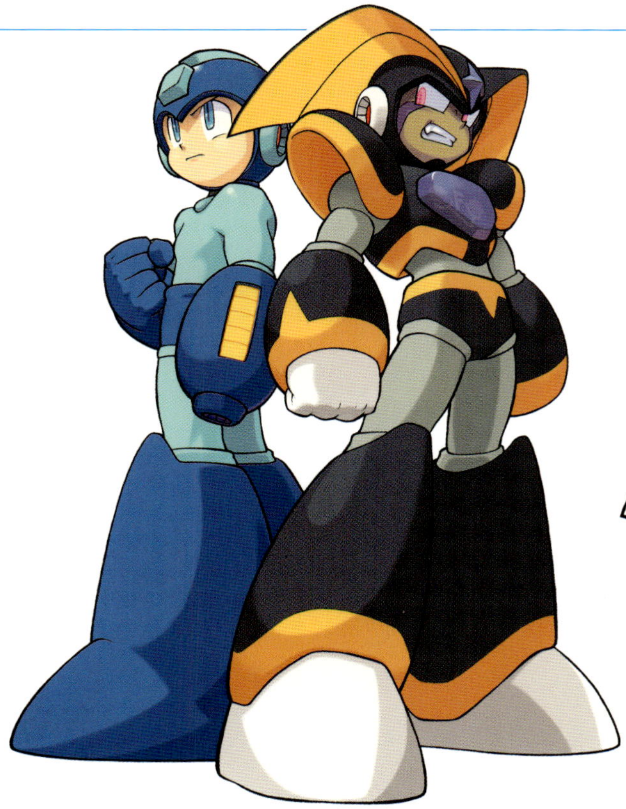

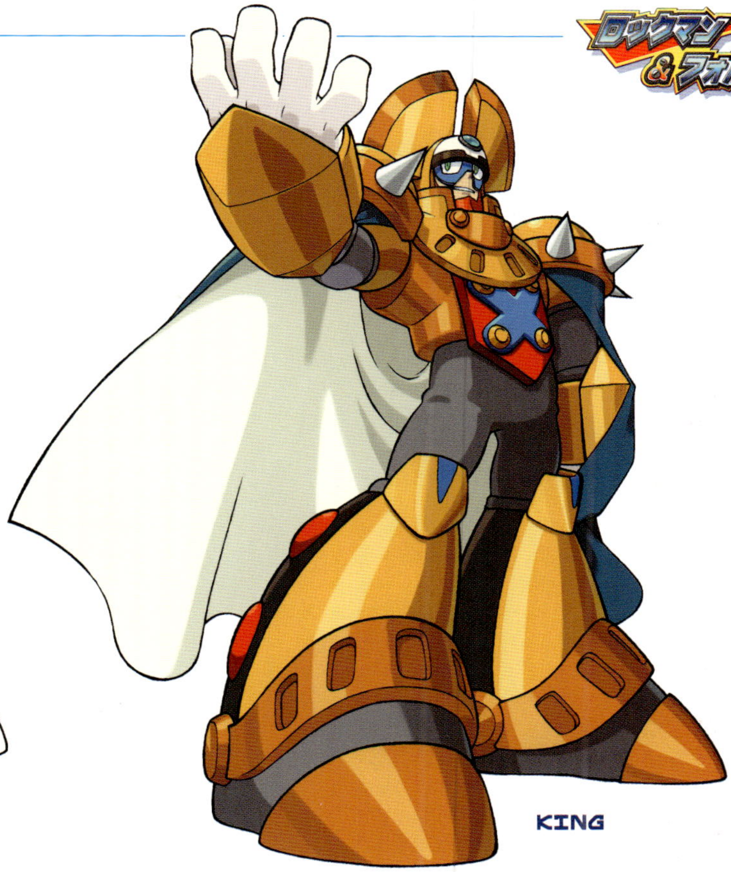

KING

ROLL

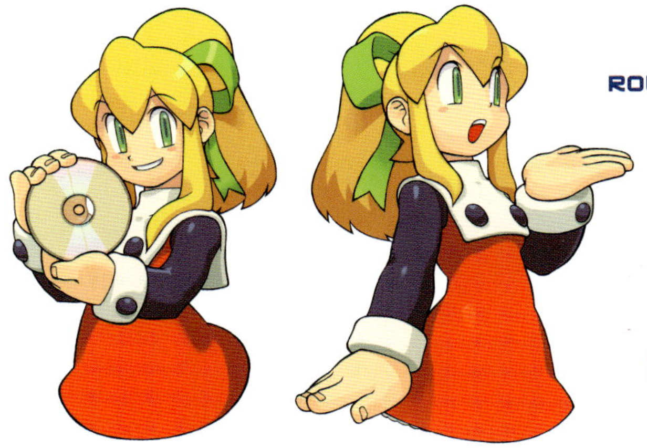

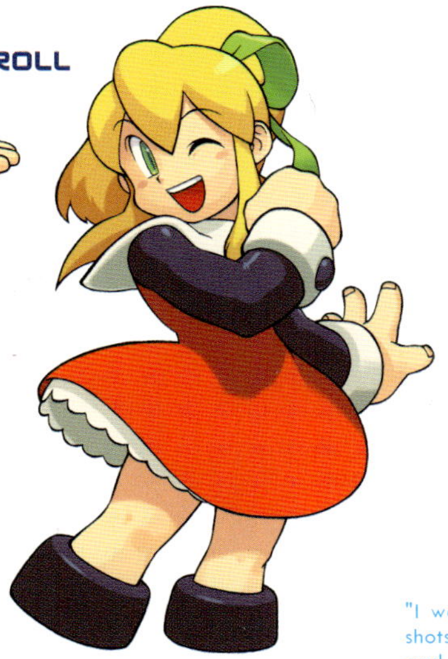

"There were a lot of new people working on the creation of this game, though I did manage to get some of the staff members from the original Mega Man team to form the core of this team. I told them not to compromise, and to make the game as hardcore as possible. 'You're going too easy on them here,' and 'Isn't there something more you can do?' were two phrases that I used a lot during development. (laughs)" (Inafune)

"At around this time, I started moving away from the traditional colors of Mega Man, and began experimenting more with colors and combinations that felt right to me. I wanted to make Bass more visually distinct from Mega Man through reflections and double shading. I also darkened his skintone a bit. Thinking back on it now, though, I do wonder if my personal will weighed in a little too heavily. (laughs)" (Hideki)

"I was told that we would need bust shots of Roll and Auto for the manual, and I remember pushing these out as quickly as I could." (Hideki)

AUTO

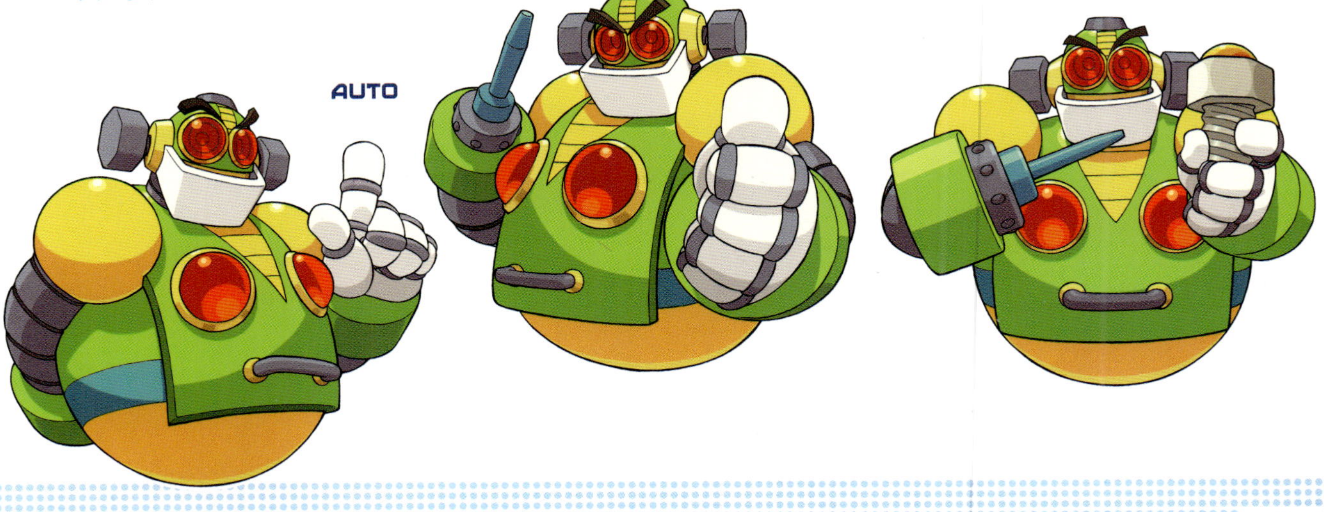

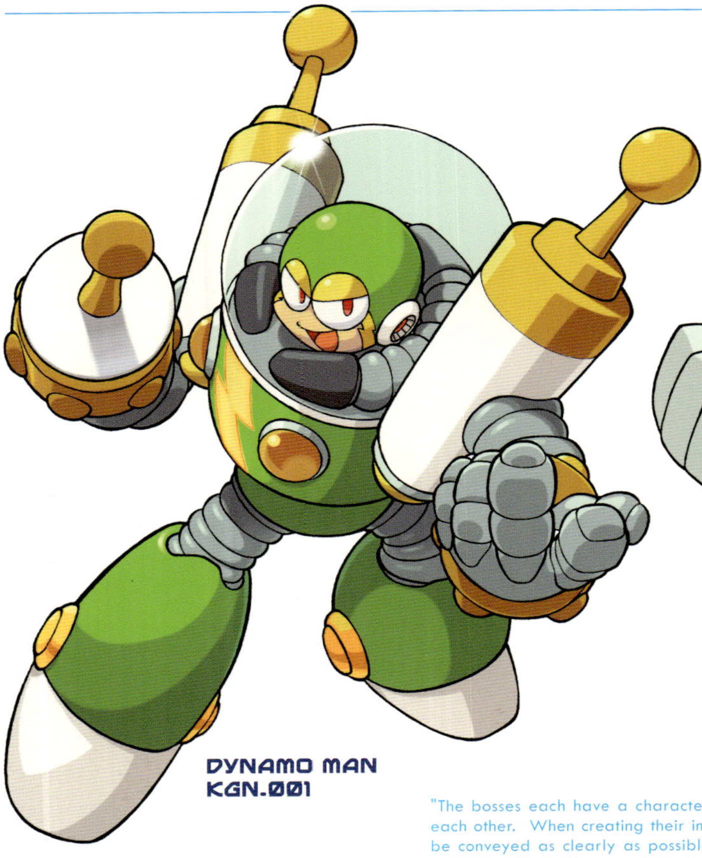

DYNAMO MAN
KGN.001

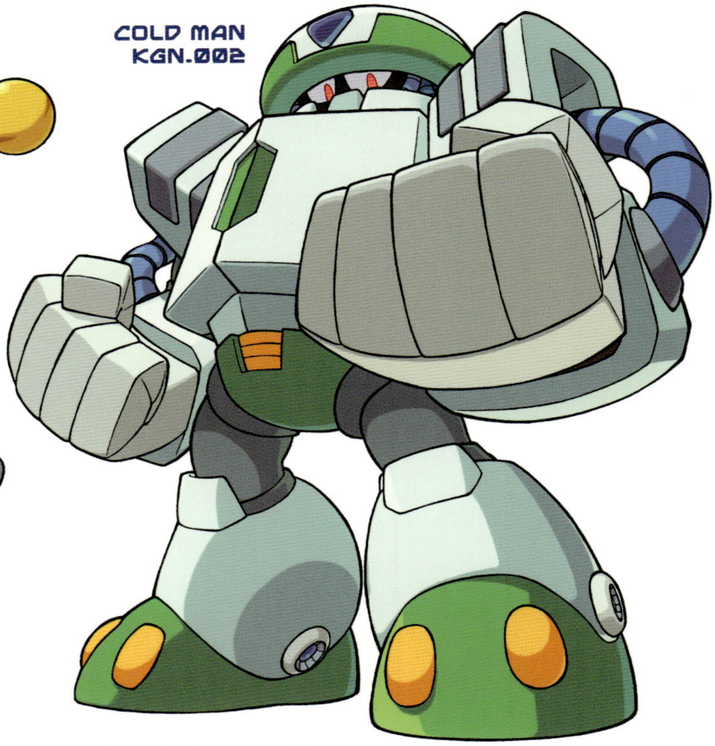

COLD MAN
KGN.002

"The bosses each have a characteristic that makes them unique from each other. When creating their images, these characteristics need to be conveyed as clearly as possible. Ground Man, for example, has multiple drills jutting out of his body. I also took into consideration things like his wild personality, and his 'I'll get him!' attitude. Comical characters, on the other hand, need to appear comical, and honorable guys need to have that characteristic emphasized. Doing this allows players to easily get a sense of each character's personality just by seeing them." (Hideki)

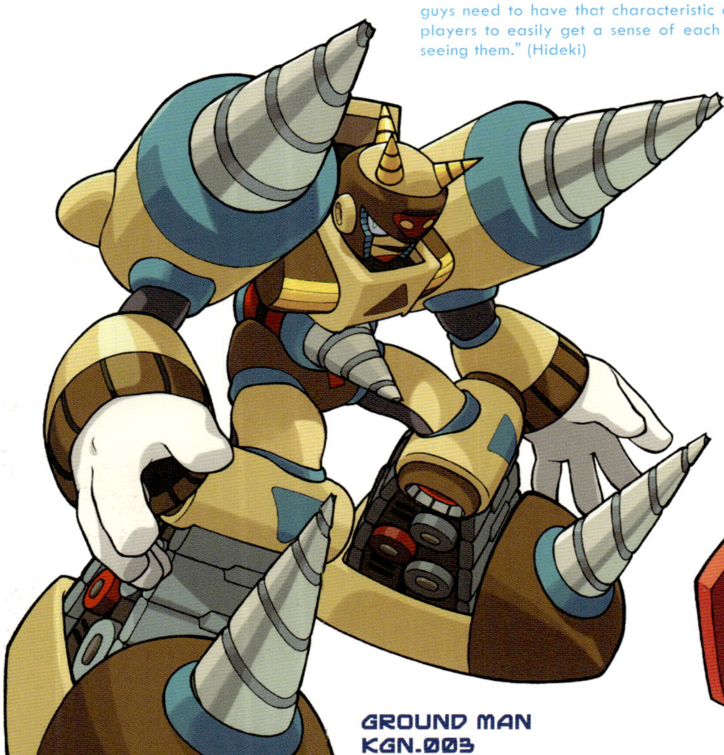

GROUND MAN
KGN.003

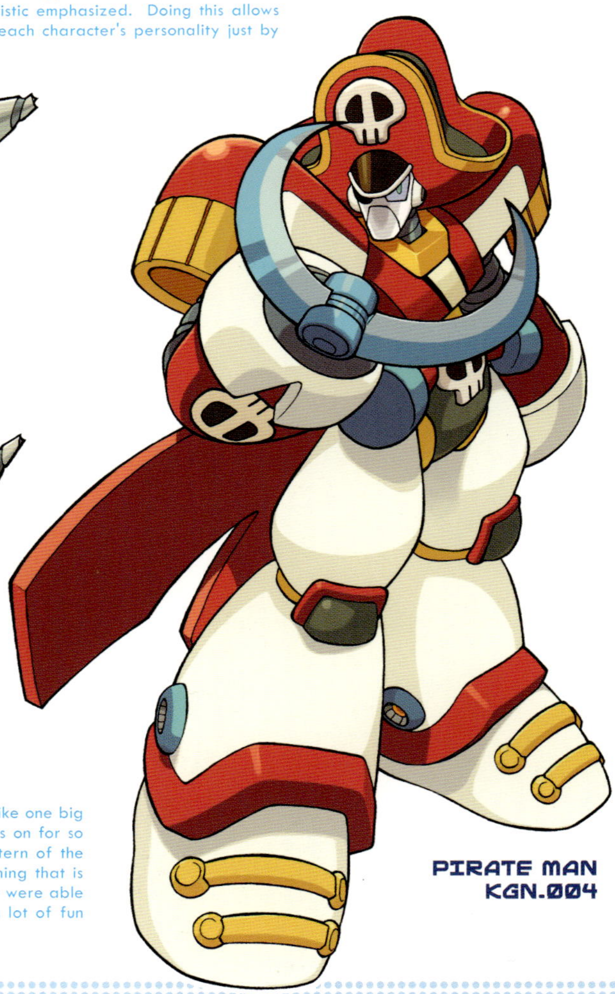

PIRATE MAN
KGN.004

"In some ways, I feel this title was like one big party. When the same series goes on for so long, it's easy to fall into the pattern of the original work and produce something that is 'same old, same old.' I feel like we were able to avoid that pitfall, and I had a lot of fun doing it." (Hideki)

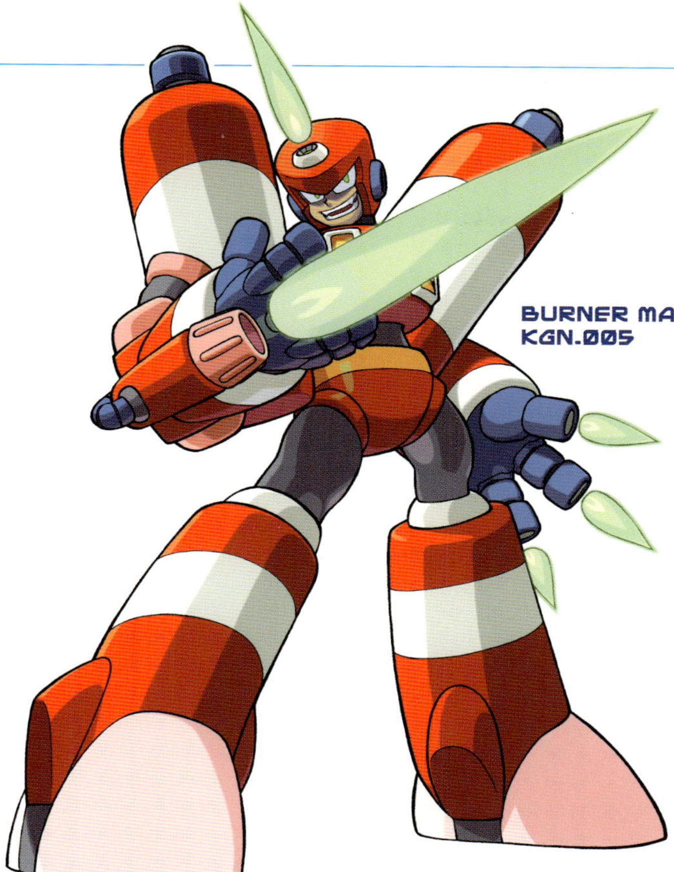

BURNER MAN
KGN.005

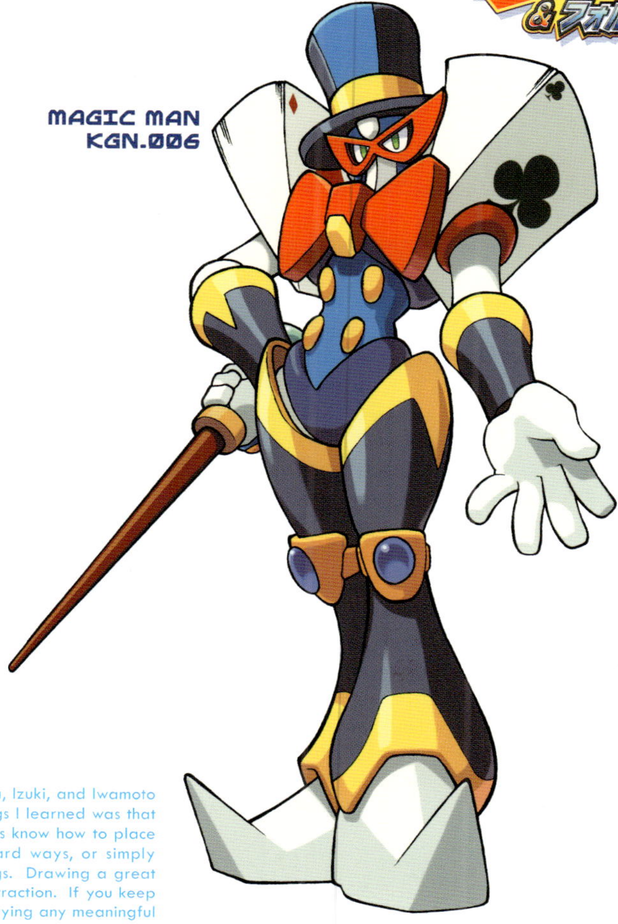

MAGIC MAN
KGN.006

"Getting to see the designs of professionals like Ariga, Izuki, and Iwamoto was both educational and fun. One of the many things I learned was that people who have a lot of experience under their belts know how to place accents properly. They don't place them in awkward ways, or simply add too much, like children often will in their drawings. Drawing a great piece is about the balance between addition and subtraction. If you keep adding and adding to your drawing, you'll end up burying any meaningful accents you put in." (Hideki)

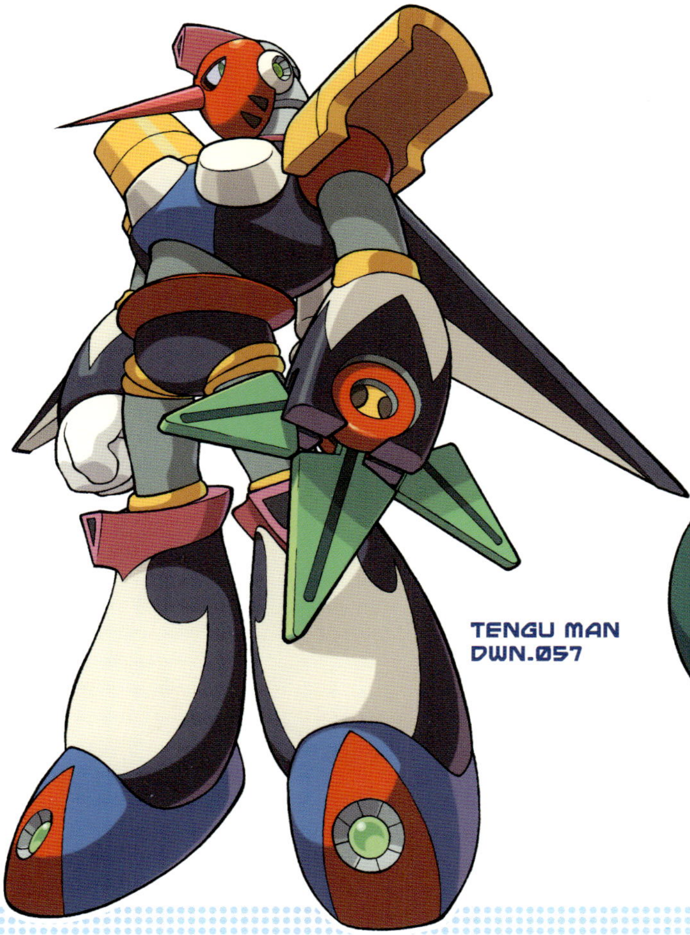

TENGU MAN
DWN.057

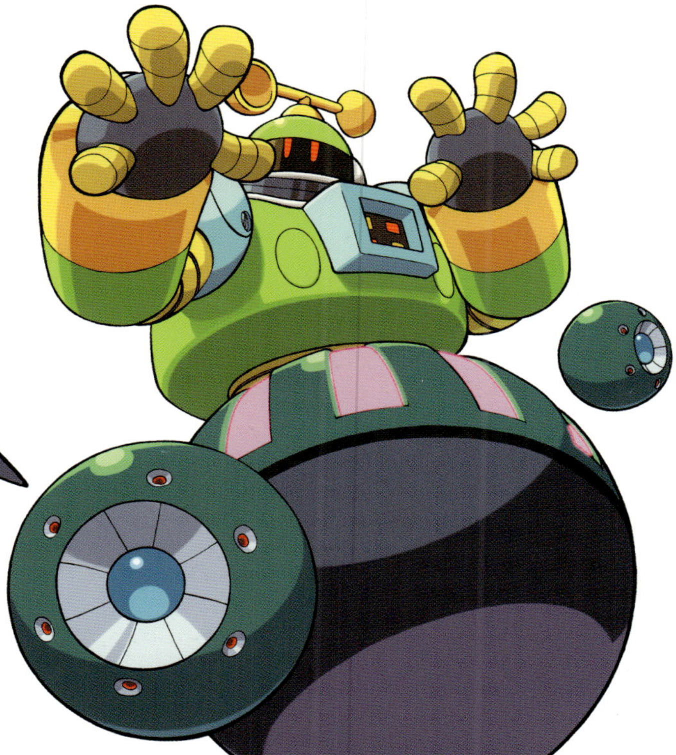

ASTRO MAN
DWN.058

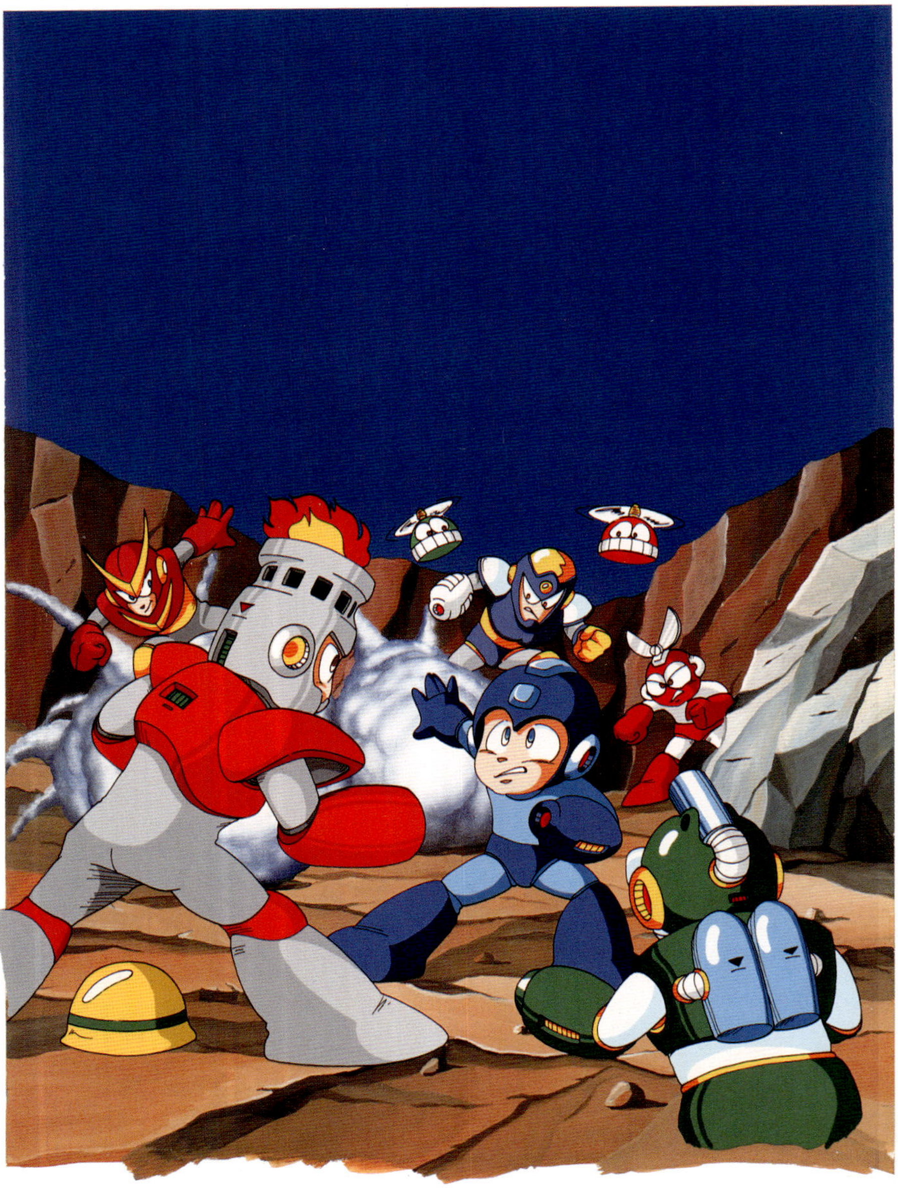

ROCKMAN WORLD
ロックマンワールド

Mega Man: Dr. Wily's Revenge
GB 07/26/1991

Thanks to the efforts of Mega Man, the super robot created by Dr. Light, Dr. Wily's ambitions did not come to fruition. Peace had returned to the world, but Dr. Wily had secretly altered the industrial robots developed by Dr. Light. After everything that had happened, Dr. Wily had not abandoned his desire for world domination. In order to stop Dr. Wily from realizing his dream, Mega Man headed to the city.

"This was the first Mega Man to be outsourced. I was curious about what kind of Mega Man an outsider would create. The team leader of "World 1" was a huge Mega Man fan, and I could see right away that he really 'got it.' In some ways, you might say he understood Mega Man better than some of our own people! (laughs) I think this was the main reason why "World 1" turned out so well." (Inafune)

[Editor's note: The creators often identify the GB Mega Man games as "World 1," "World 2," referring to the series' original Japanese name "Rockman World."]

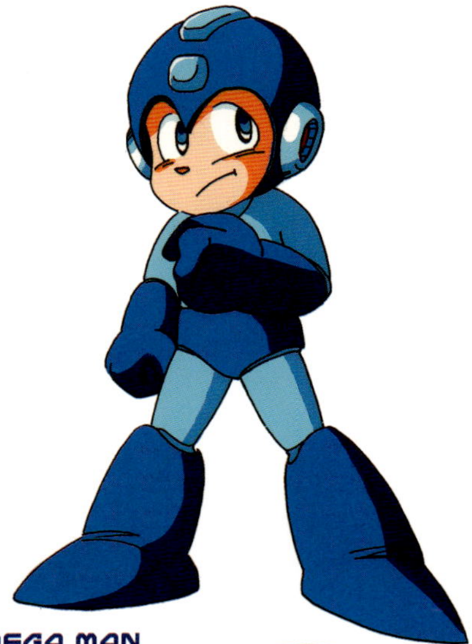

MEGA MAN

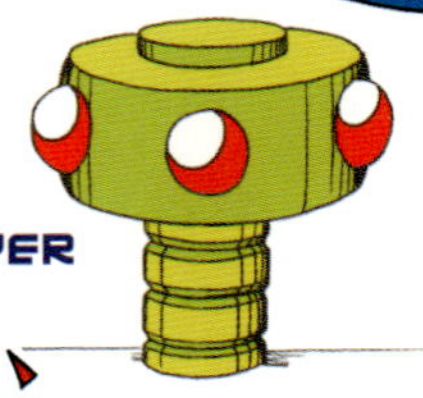

SCREWDRIVER

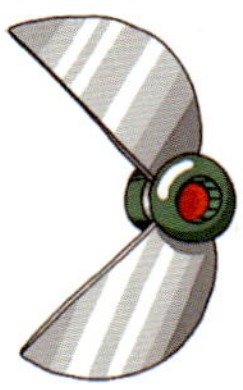

SUPER CUTTER

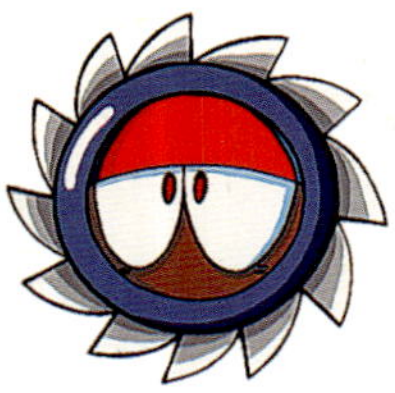

CUTTING WHEEL

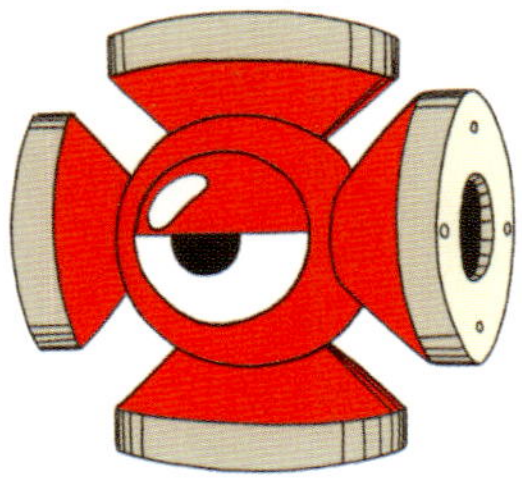

ADHERING SUZY

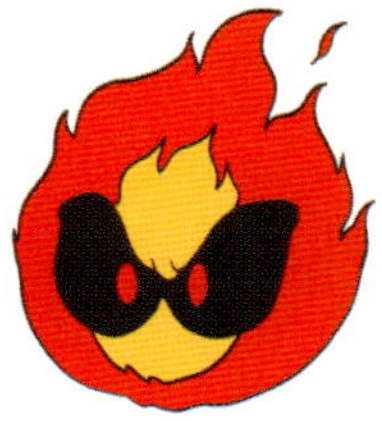

CHANGKEY

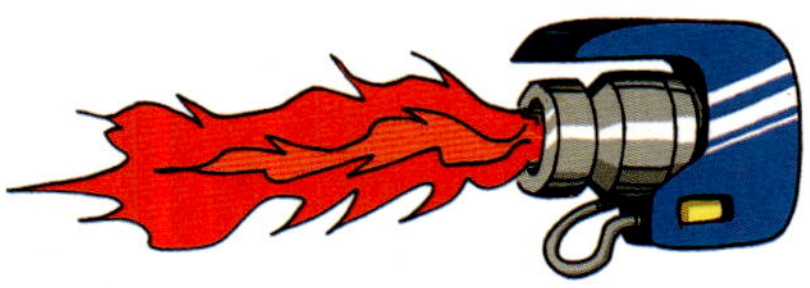

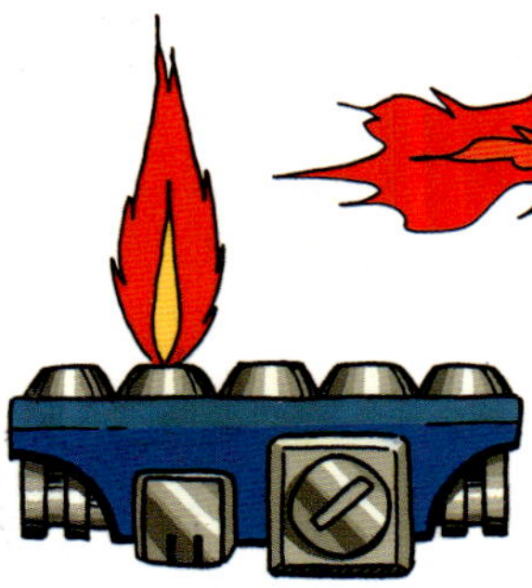

BURNER BLOCK

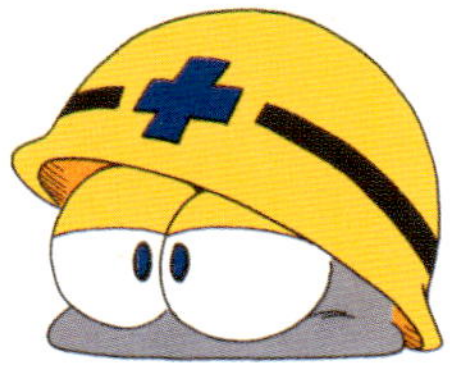

METALL

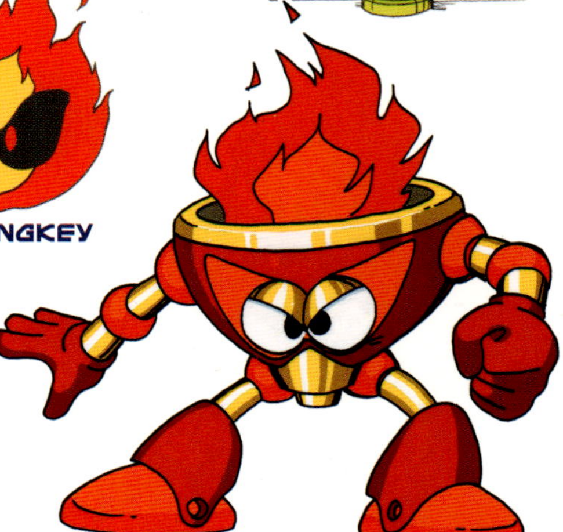

CHANGKEY MAKER

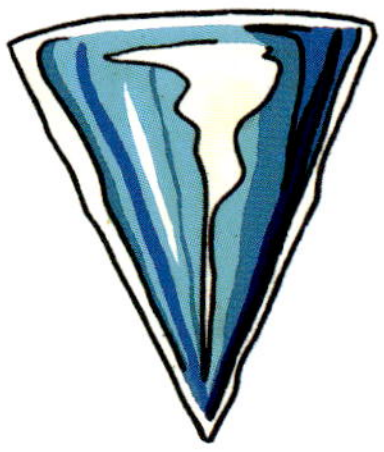

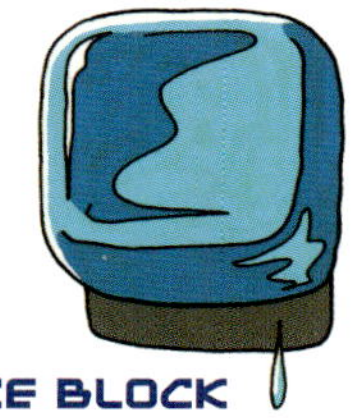

ICE BLOCK

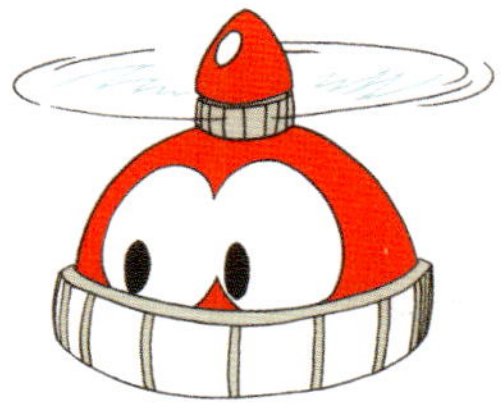

BUNBY HELI

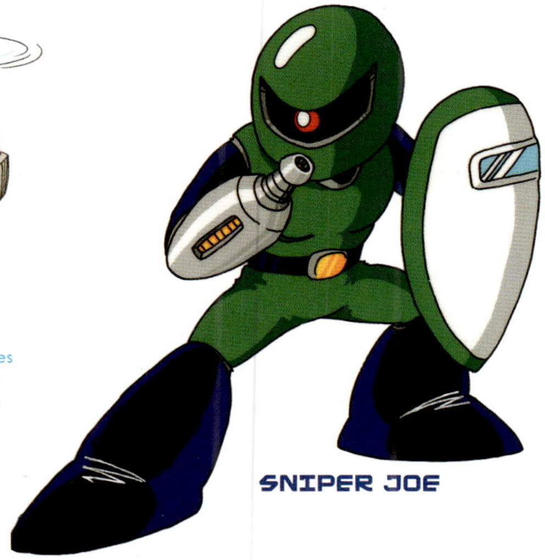

SNIPER JOE

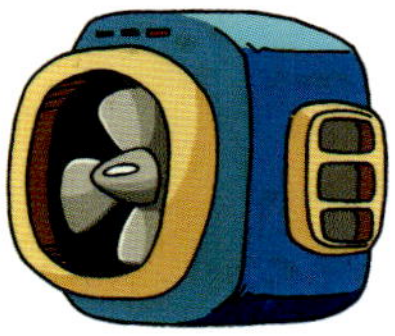

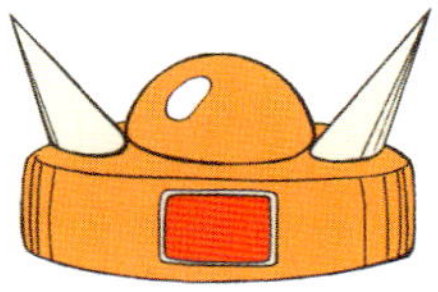

GABYOALL

"I was so happy, I drew a bunch of illustrations. The original pieces from '1' were so old; I wanted to provide newer art of Sniper Joe, for instance." (Inafune)

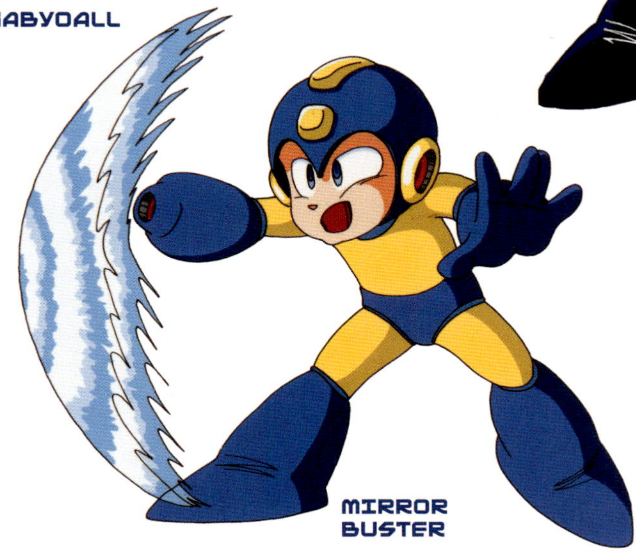

MIRROR BUSTER

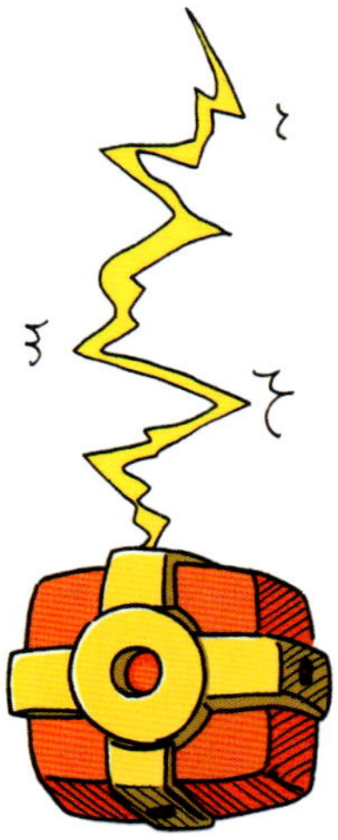

THUNDER BLOCK

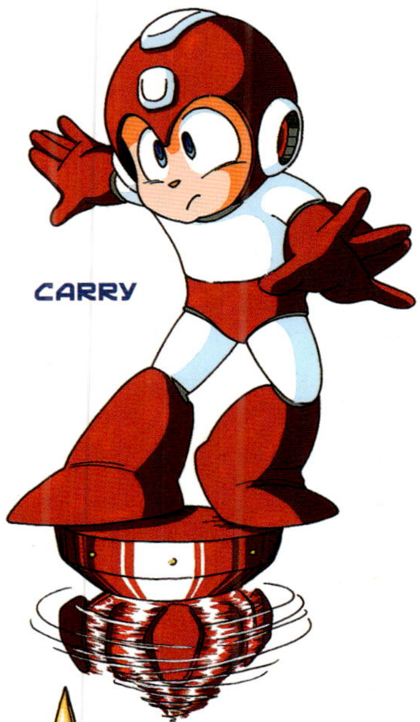

CARRY

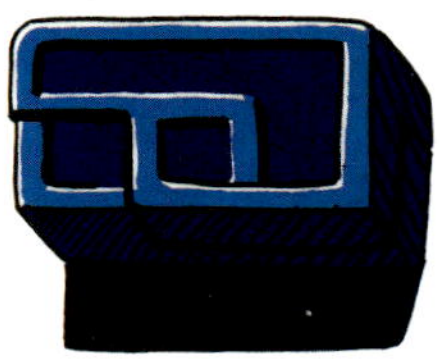

APPEARING BLOCK

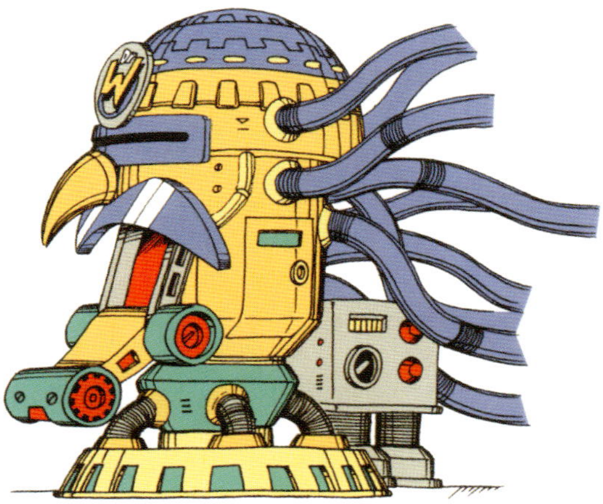

WILY MACHINE I

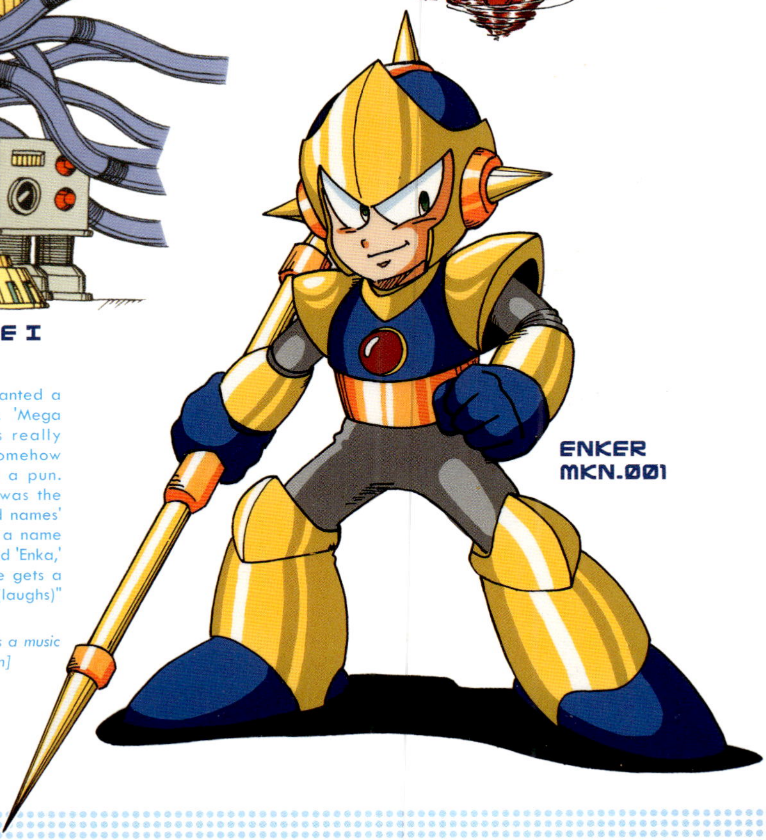

ENKER MKN.001

"We decided we wanted a 'World-specific' boss. 'Mega Man Killer' sounds really cool, right? But somehow we ended up with a pun. (laughs) I guess it was the whole 'music-themed names' thing that led us to a name based off of the word 'Enka,' but I hope everyone gets a giggle out of that. (laughs)" (Inafune)

[Editor's note: 'Enka' is a music genre popular in Japan]

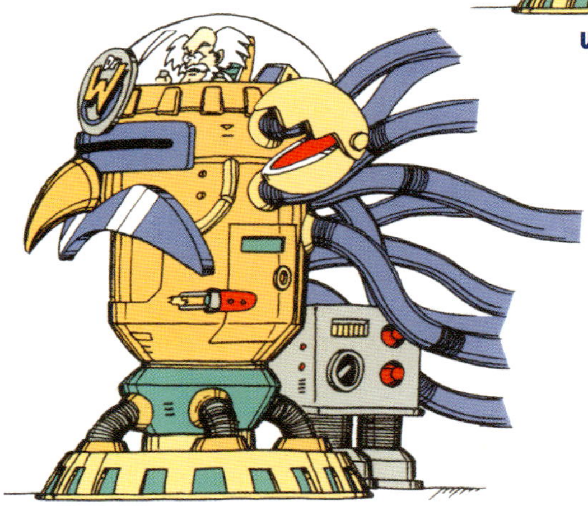

WILY MACHINE I'

ROCKMAN WORLD 2

ロックマンワールド2

Mega Man II
GB 12/20/1991

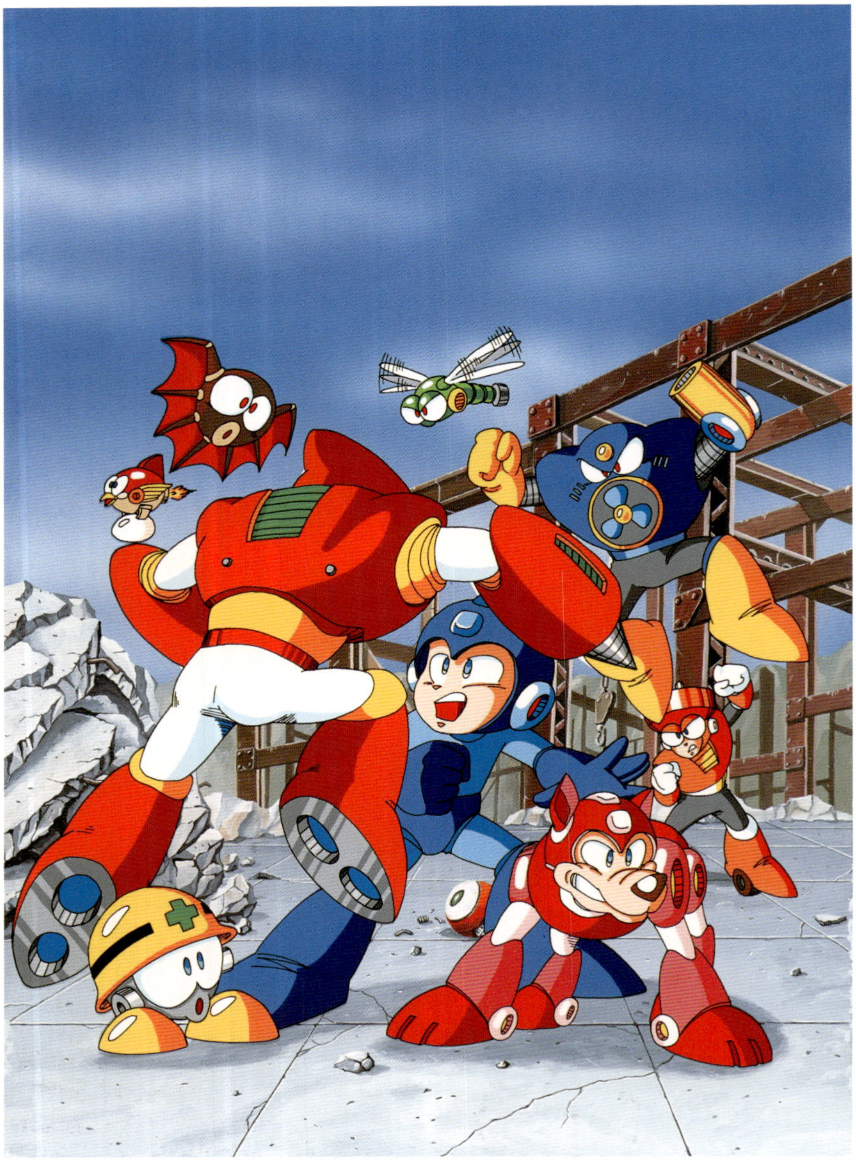

Devastated by his defeat at the hands of Mega Man, Dr. Wily stole the time machine from the Time-Space Research Laboratory and headed to the future. Dr. Wily's new plan involved kidnapping the future Mega Man and bringing him back in time to fight present-day Mega Man. While working in the Time-Space Research Laboratory, Dr. Light was made aware of Dr. Wily's plot thanks to Rush's enhanced sense of smell. Dr. Light immediately sent Mega Man to search for Dr. Wily.

"We hired a different company to do 'World 2,' and that was a total nightmare. They just didn't understand Mega Man like the company that did 'World 1.' This experience really made me realize just how important it is to ensure that the people working on Mega Man are people who really 'get it.' This aspect is reflected in the game itself, so I'm sure the players know what I'm talking about better than anyone." (Inafune)

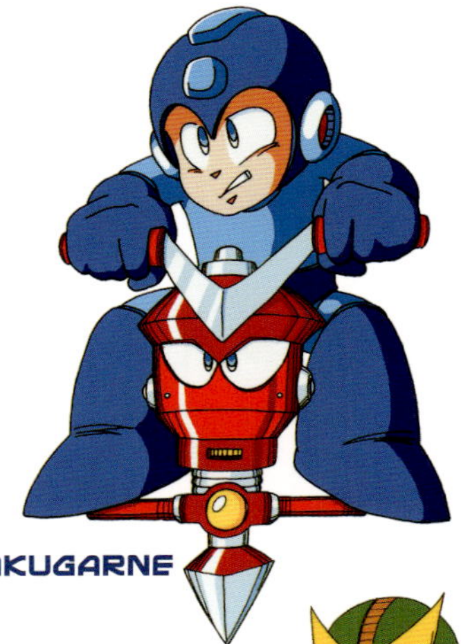

SAKUGARNE

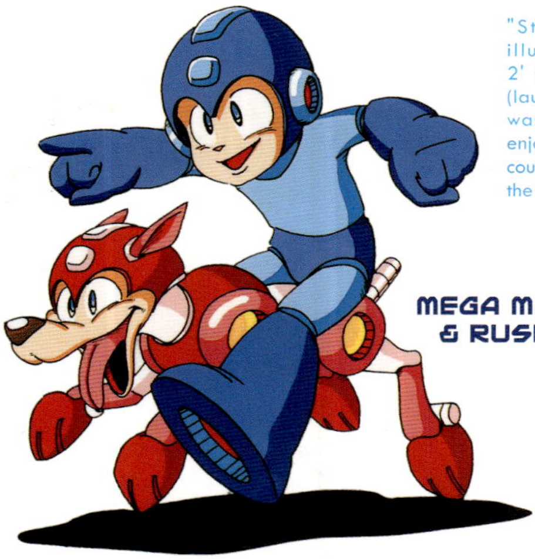

MEGA MAN & RUSH

"Still, I think the main illustrations for 'World 2' turned out quite well. (laughs) The 'World' series was a spin-off, so I could enjoy more freedom than I could with the packages for the NES titles." (Inafune)

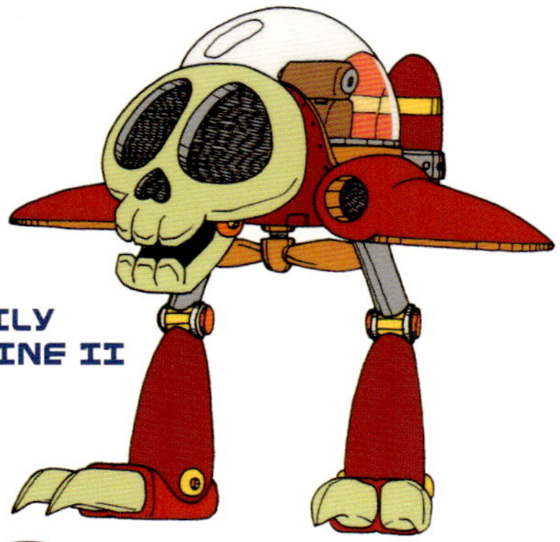

WILY MACHINE II

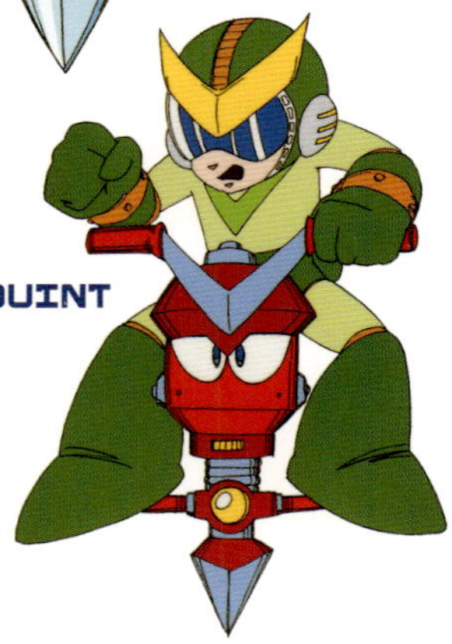

QUINT

"The game was working out so poorly, and I think my very low level of motivation shows through in my design art. I mean, I didn't use shadows properly or anything. I feel that this is something that should never happen, and I would like to offer my sincerest apologies to our players." (Inafune)

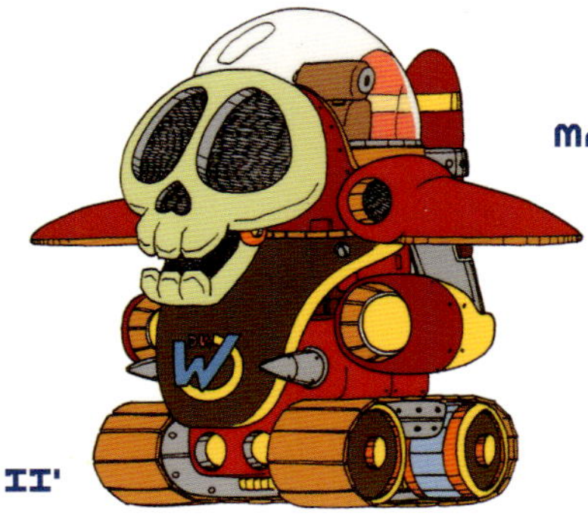

WILY MACHINE II'

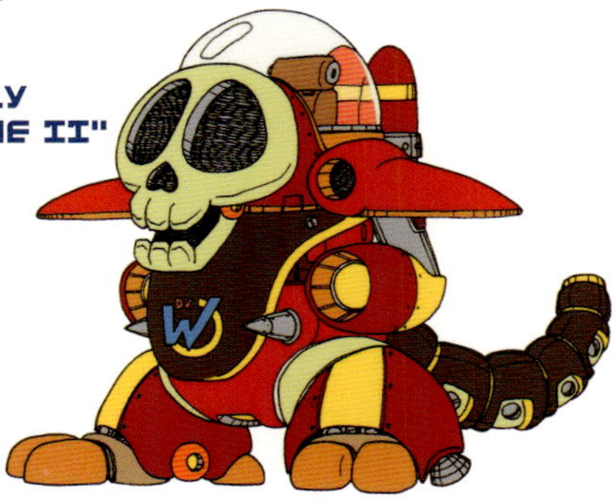

WILY MACHINE II"

ROCKMAN WORLD 3

Mega Man III
GB 12/11/1992

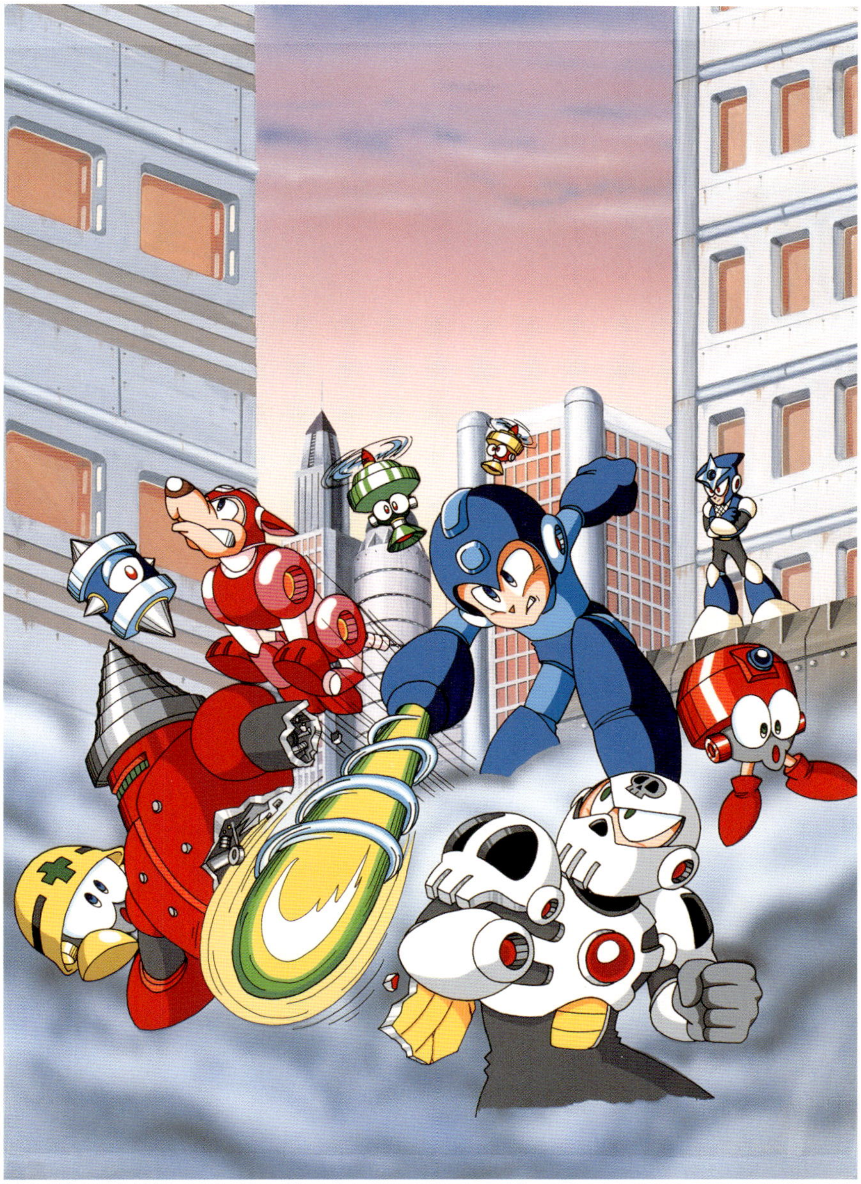

A few months after their difficult struggle with Dr. Wily, some terrible news reached Dr. Light's laboratory. Something strange was happening to the supercomputer that was responsible for managing the details of everyday life. With outrageous weather patterns and a sudden halt in the transportation system, panic consumed the entire city. To make matters worse, armed robots showed up and began wreaking havoc in the streets. In hopes of reclaiming peace, Mega Man headed out to the urban wasteland.

"For some reason, Inafune was set on having background landscapes in the main illustrations for the 'World' series, even though we had never included backgrounds for the NES titles. I did several backgrounds for the 'World' series, but I remember having a hard time getting my work approved. (laughs)" (Kaji)

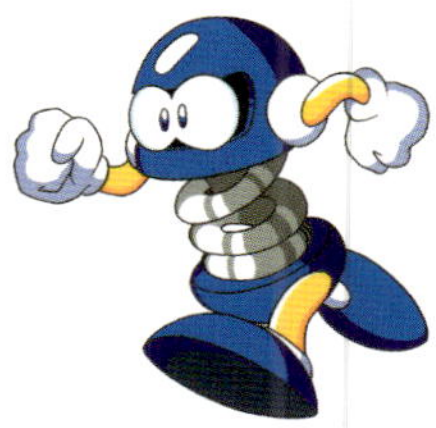

BUBUKAN MK-II

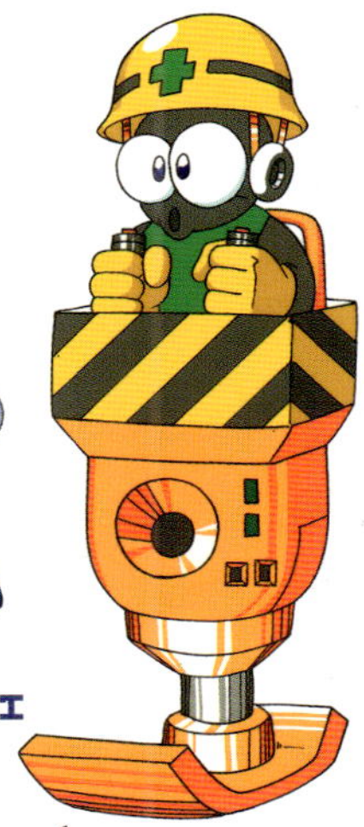

PICKLEMAN DADA

"Learning from our mistakes with 'World 2,' we went back to the same company that did 'World 1' for 'World 3' and onwards. We refused to hire any other company, and pushed out titles at a pace of one game per year." (Inafune)

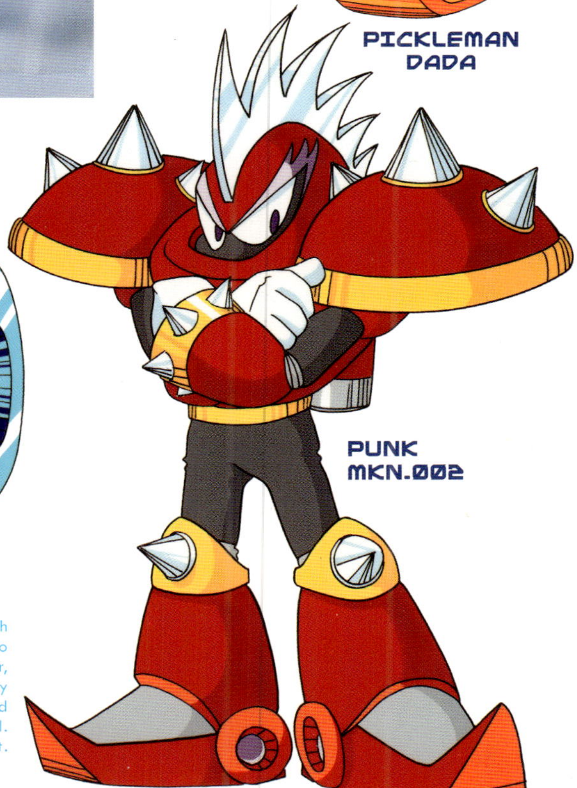

PUNK MKN.002

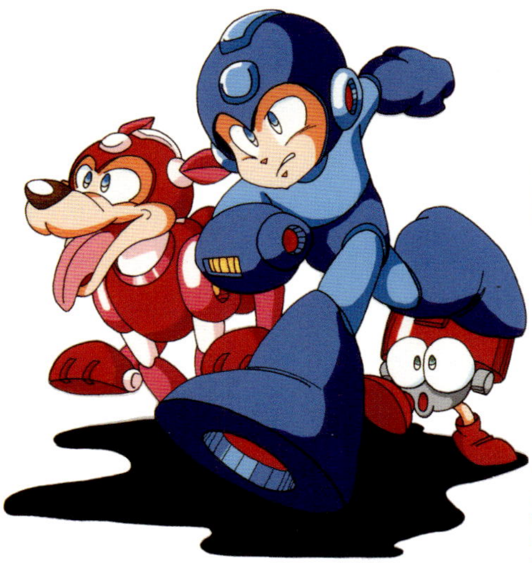

MEGA MAN & RUSH & EDDIE

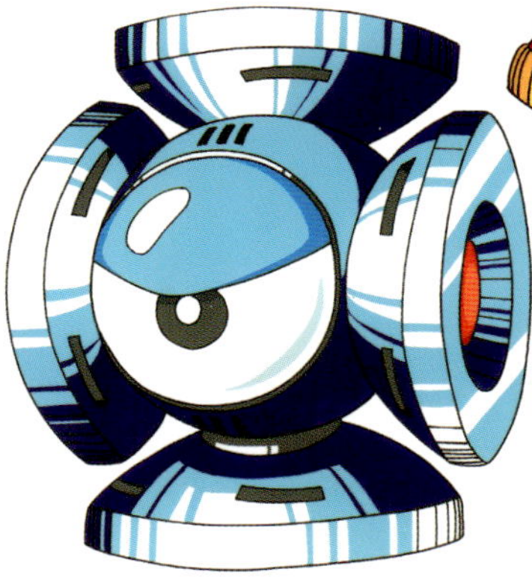

GIANT SUZY

"I decided to look at 'World 3' as a fresh new start, and I remember digging into it with renewed zest. Punk, in particular, was a favorite of mine and I used my sway as the producer to have him included in 'Mega Man Battle Network' as well. Yeah, he gets preferential treatment. (laughs)" (Inafune)

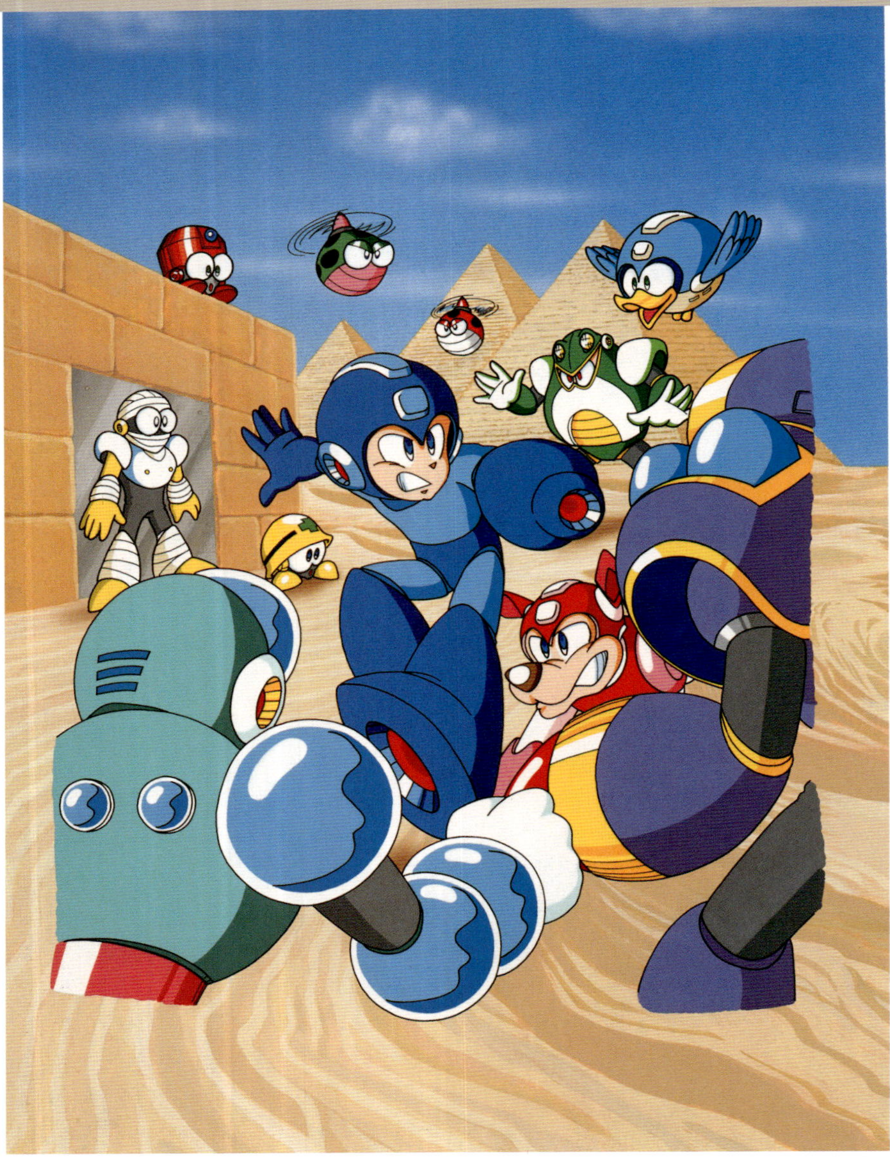

ROCKMAN WORLD 4

Mega Man IV
GB 10/29/1993

Dr. Light was attending the World Robot Exposition, where scientists from all over the world gathered to present their newest robots. Unbeknownst to the others, Dr. Wily also attended the function and released a special electrical pulse into the crowd. All of the robots present went out of control, and proceeded to scatter into different regions. Mega Man, who was able to retain his sense of self due to his Conscience of Justice circuitry, immediately headed out to make things right.

"It all felt like one continuous flow from 'World 3' to 'World 4.' We took two titles from the NES series and added new things to spice them up. We were pretty much hanging ten by this point." (Inafune)

GUNNER JOE

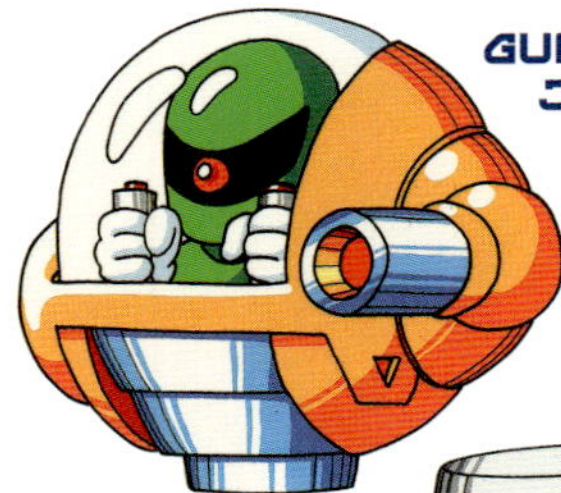

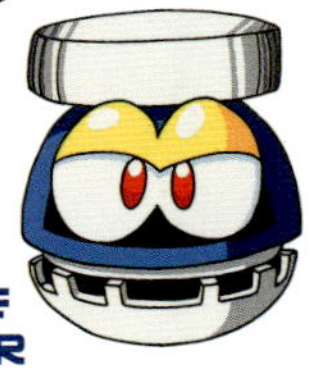

MOVE HOVER

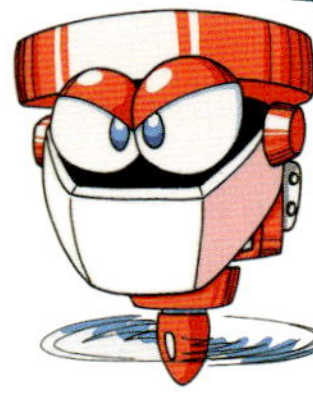

GUTS HOVER

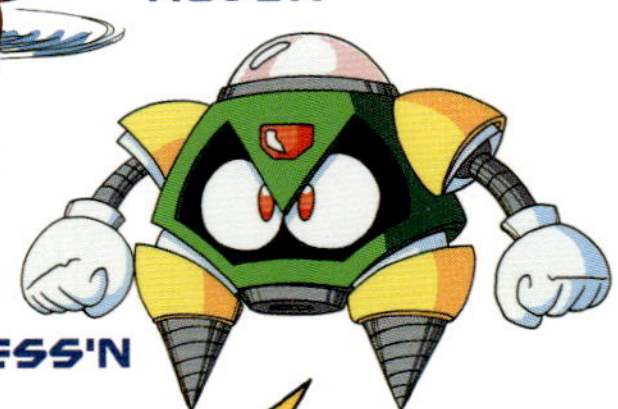

PRESS'N

HUNTER

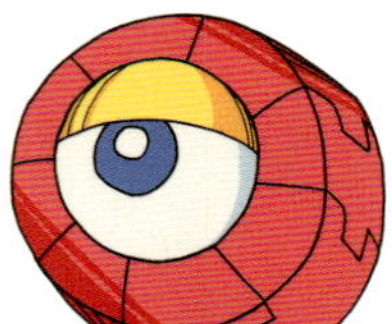

WILY ROBO IRON GOLEM

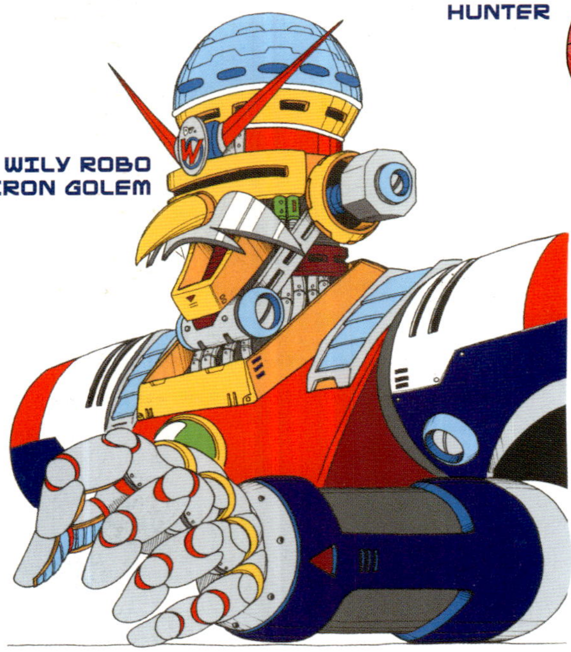

BALLADE MKN.003

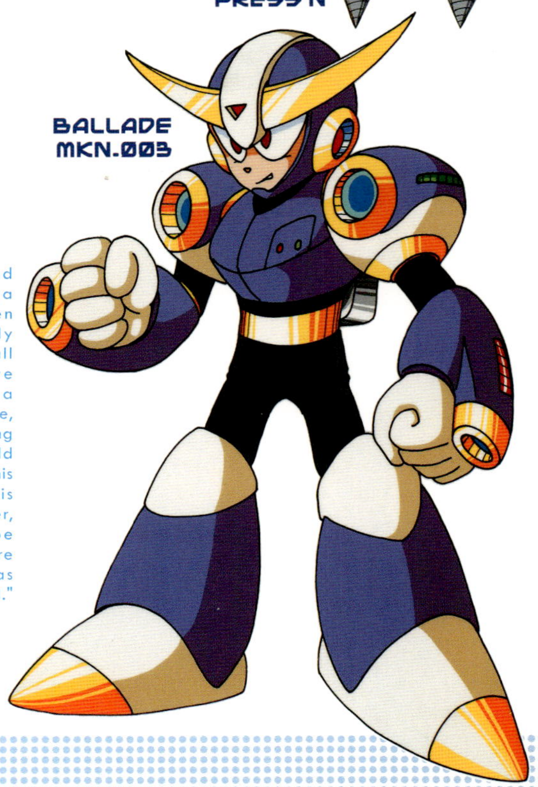

"With Enker, Punk, and Ballade, the 'Mega Man Killers' had been established. I'm really happy with how they all turned out. When we decided to include a second form for Ballade, I had a lot of fun thinking up the changes he would undergo. The horns on his head would turn up, his bombs would get bigger, and his eyes would be covered by shades... there were all kinds of ideas running through my head." (Inafune)

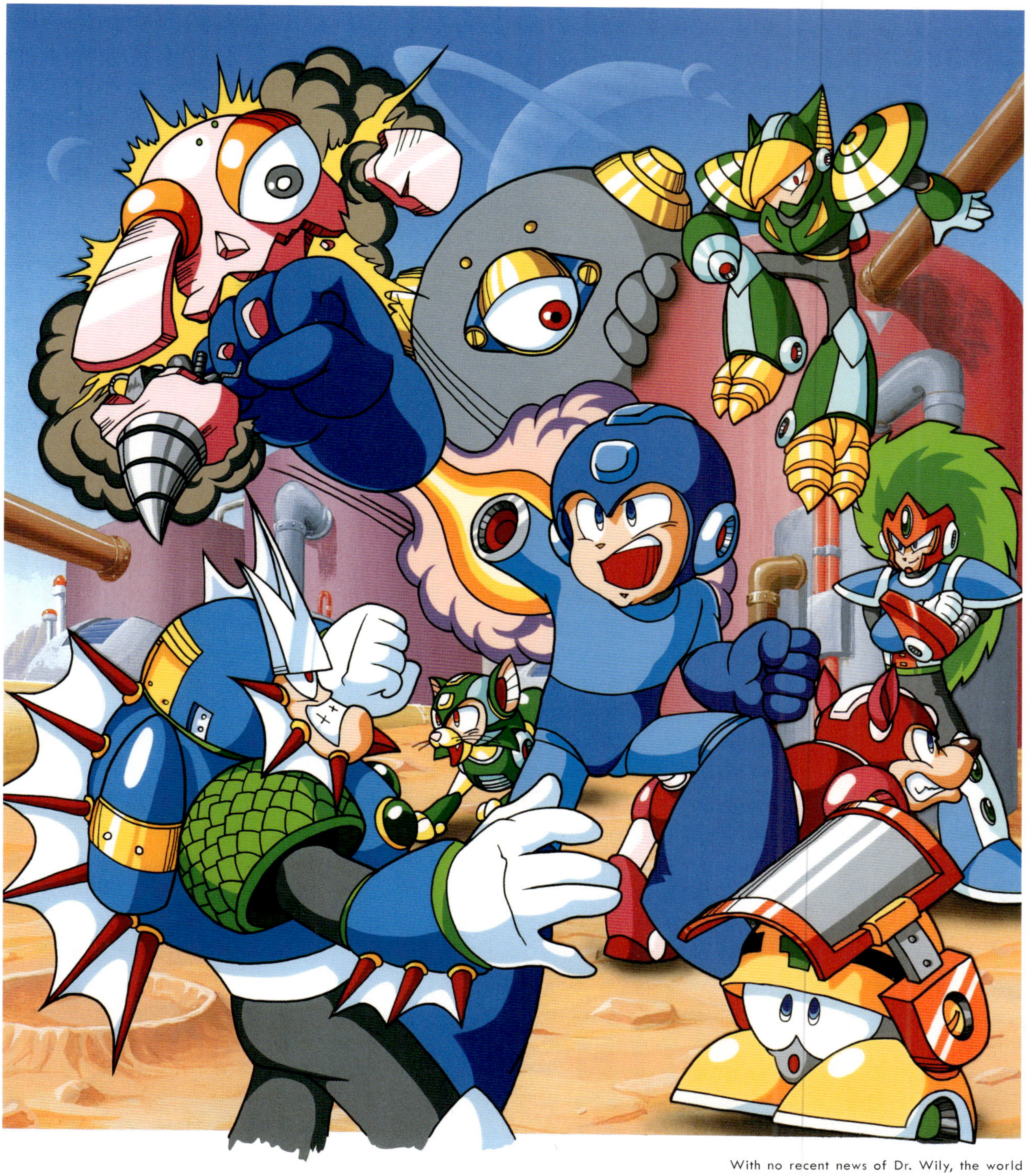

Rockman World 5

Mega Man V
GB 07/22/1994

With no recent news of Dr. Wily, the world was slowly forgetting he ever existed. Then a combat robot called Terra suddenly showed up and defeated Mega Man in battle. It was only a few hours later that cities all over the world were being taken over by a group called the "Stardroids," who claimed to hail from space. Fully restored, Mega Man equipped his new weapon, the Mega Arm, and headed out to meet his newest adversaries.

"We had basically been combining two NES titles each time so far, and at this point we only had '6' left... So we decided to create something new and original. Of all the 'World' titles, I think this one took the most time." (Inafune)

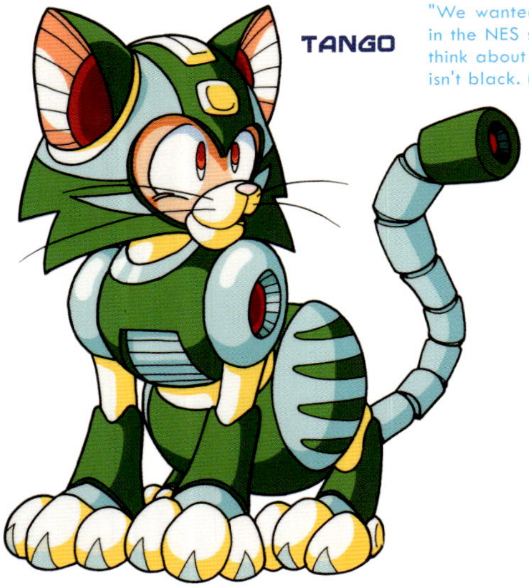

TANGO

"We wanted to introduce a new support character that didn't appear in the NES series, and that's when we came up with Tango. Now that I think about it, Tango is also a music themed name... although this Tango isn't black. (laughs)" (Inafune)

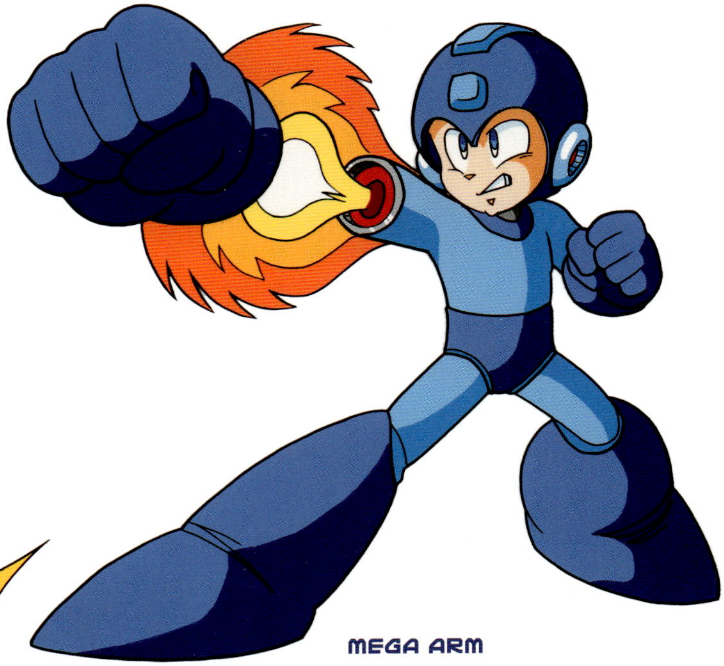

MEGA ARM

"When talks first started about making Mega Man's default attack a rocket punch, I was like, 'A rocket punch!?' (laughs)" (Inafune)

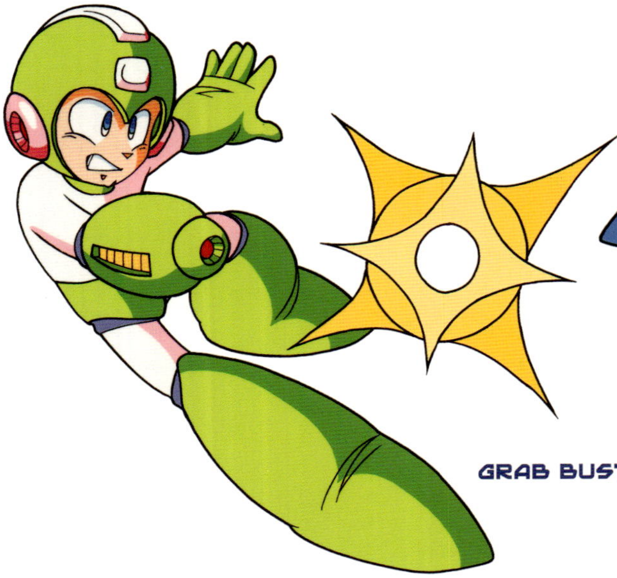

GRAB BUSTER

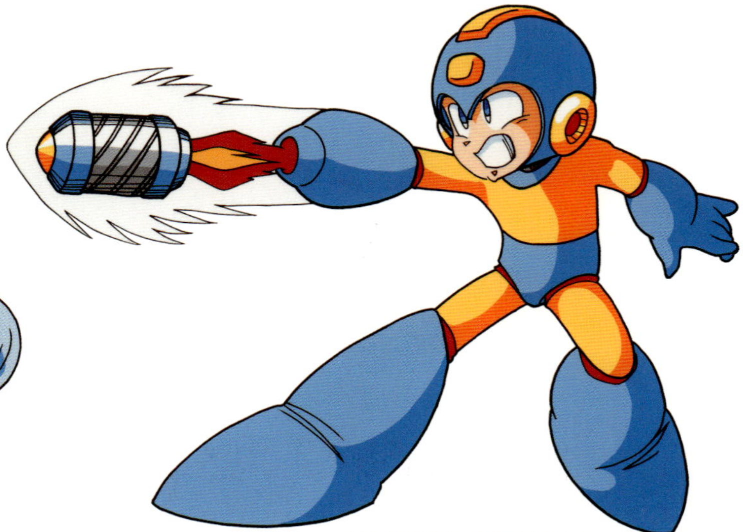

PHOTON MISSILE

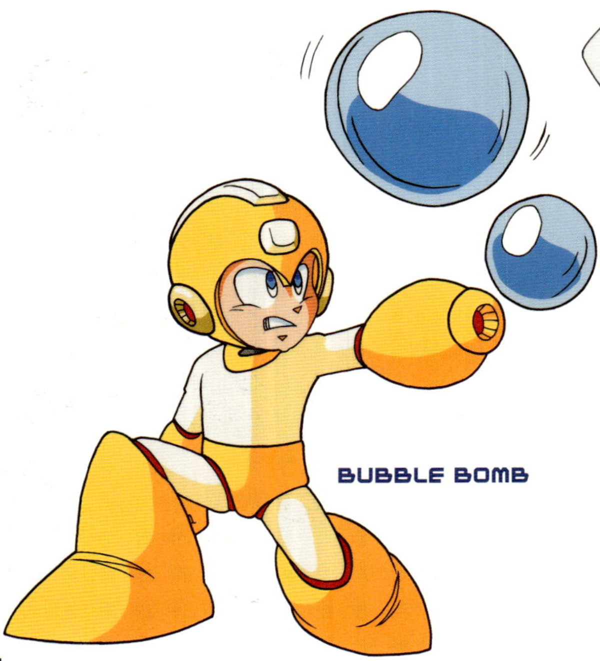

BUBBLE BOMB

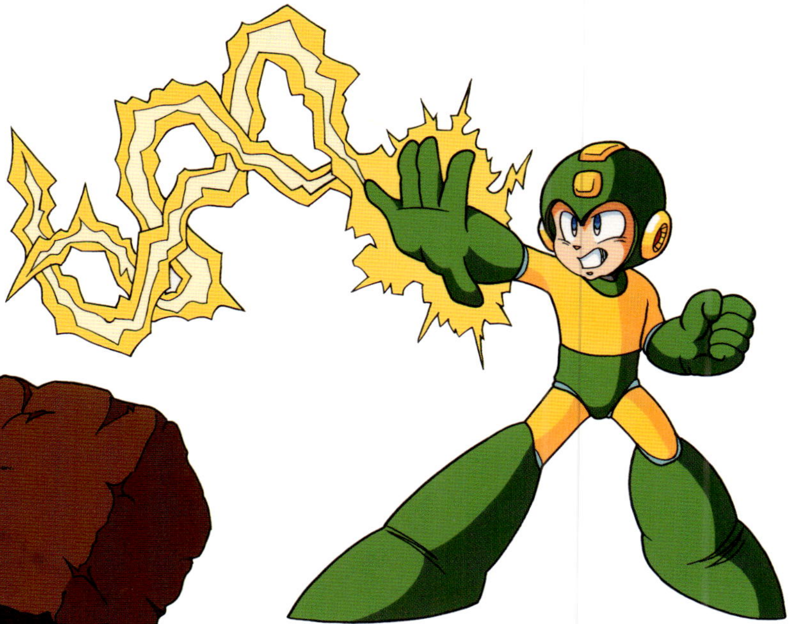

ELECTRIC SHOCK

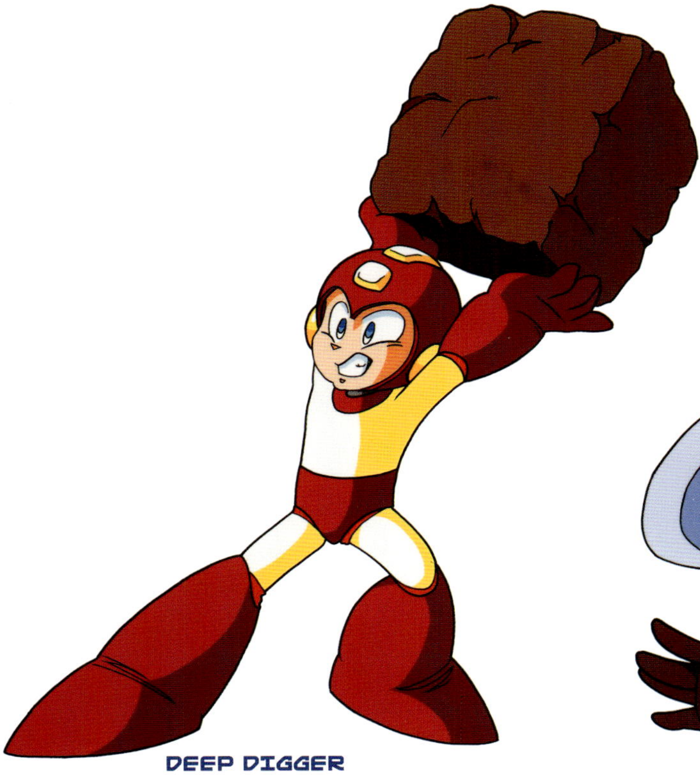

DEEP DIGGER

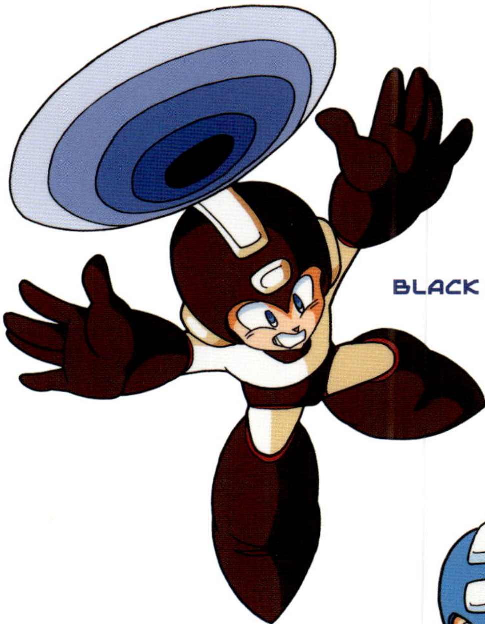

BLACK HOLE

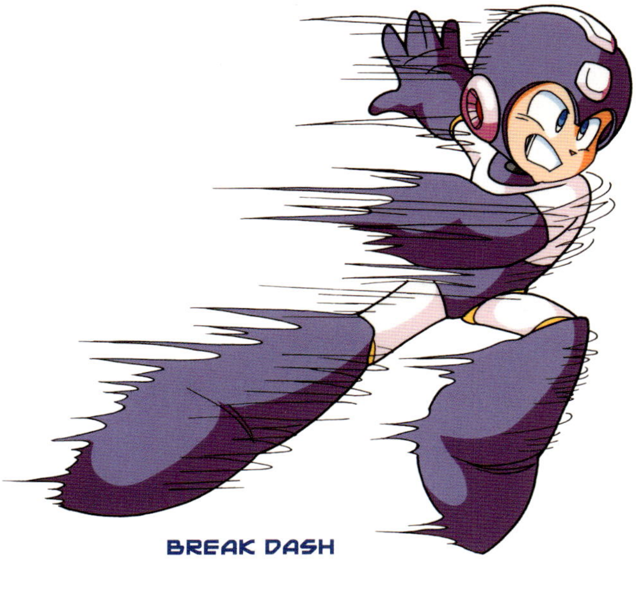

BREAK DASH

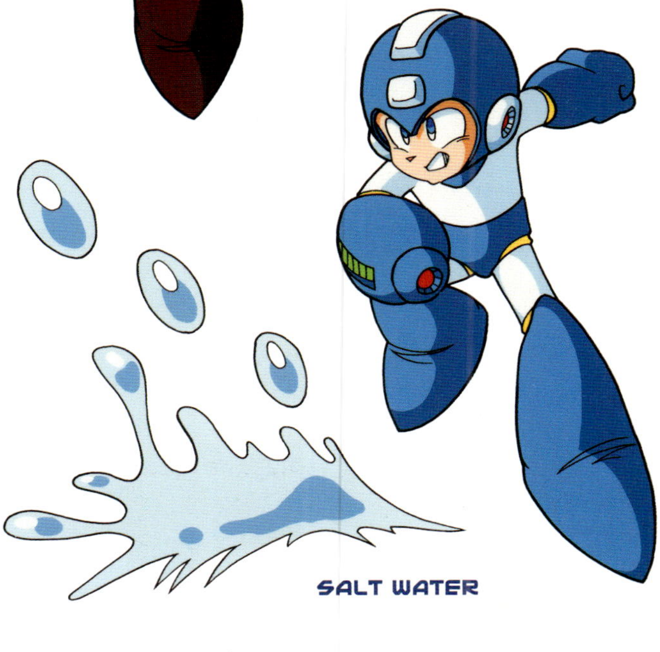

SALT WATER

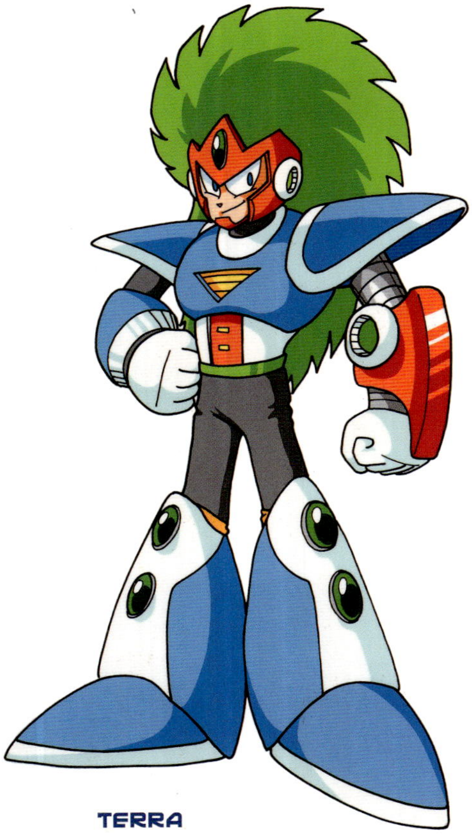

TERRA
SRN.001

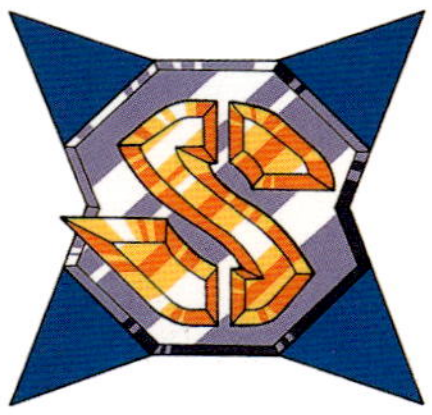

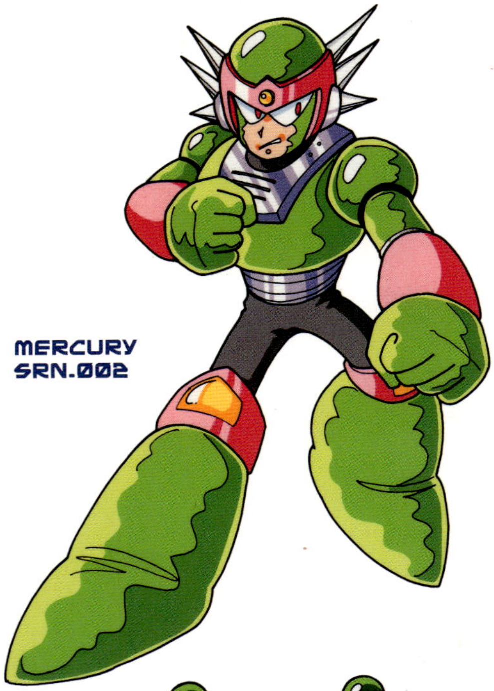

MERCURY
SRN.002

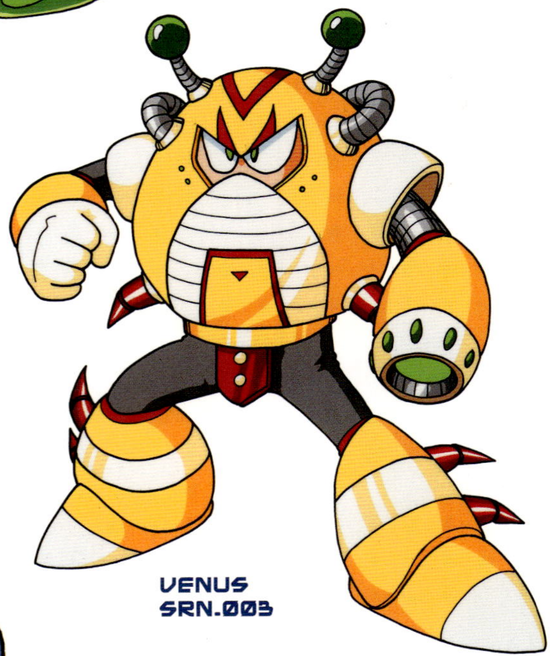

VENUS
SRN.003

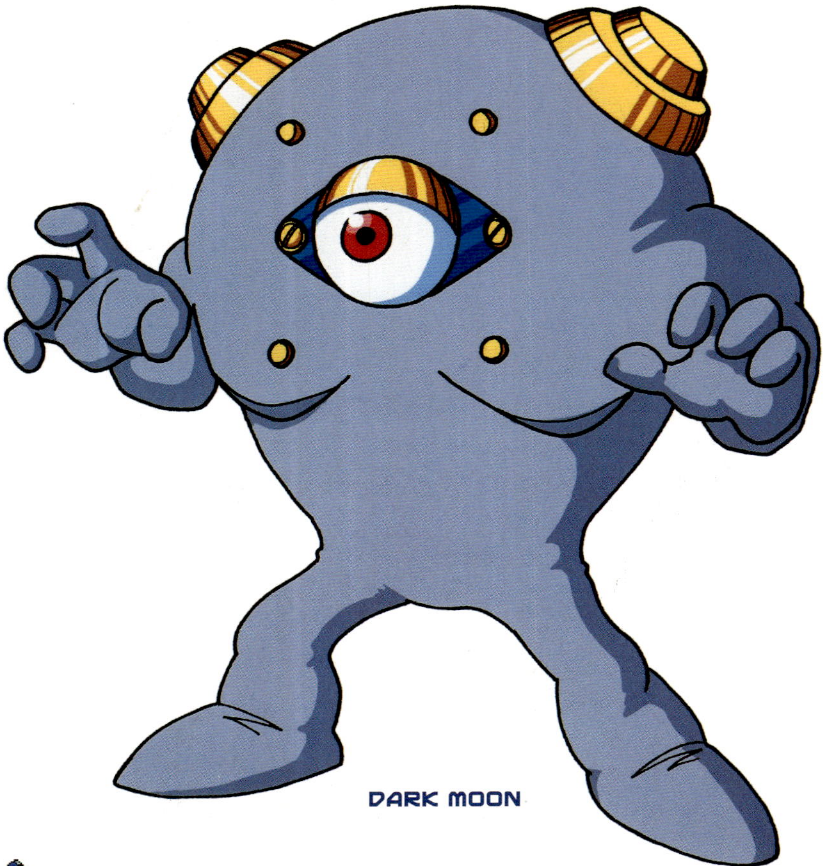

DARK MOON

"Once the concept turned to space, I started coming up with designs based on that concept. When you have a theme to follow, it can make things easier and harder at the same time. Especially with a theme as vague as space, I was like, 'What kind of designs am I supposed to come up with?' (laughs)" (Inafune)

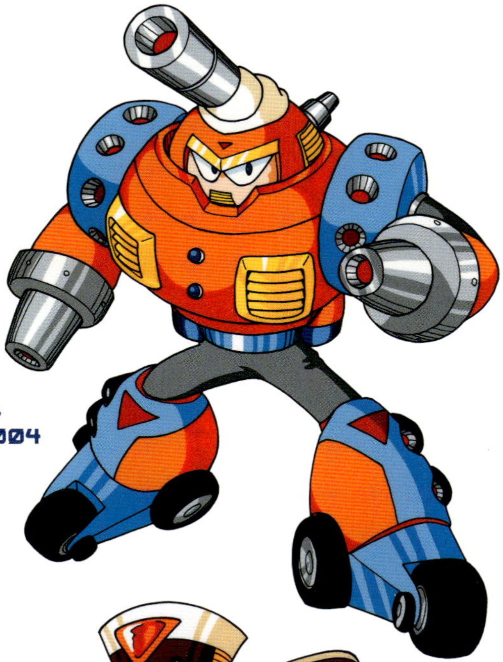

MARS
SRN.004

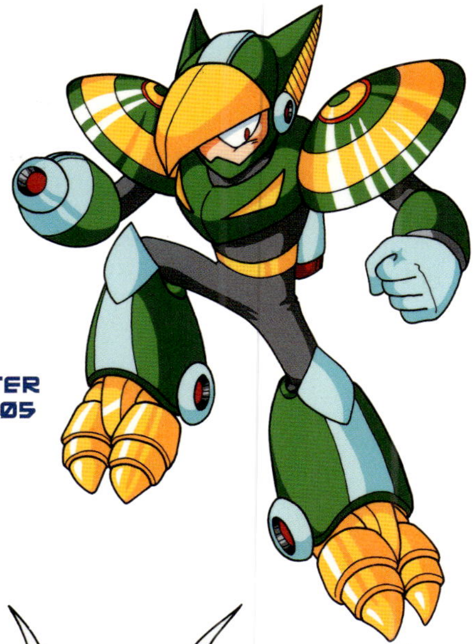

JUPITER
SRN.005

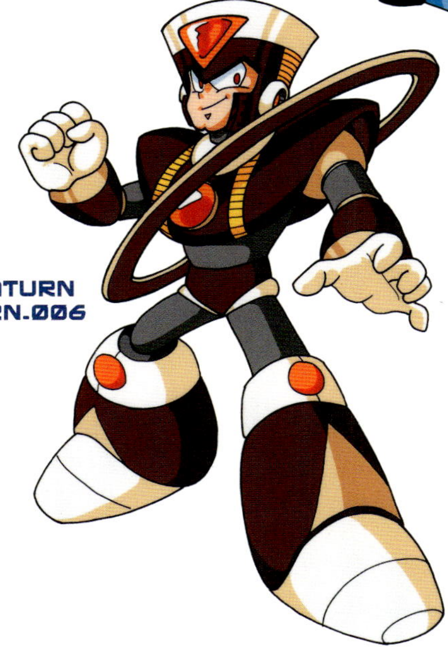

SATURN
SRN.006

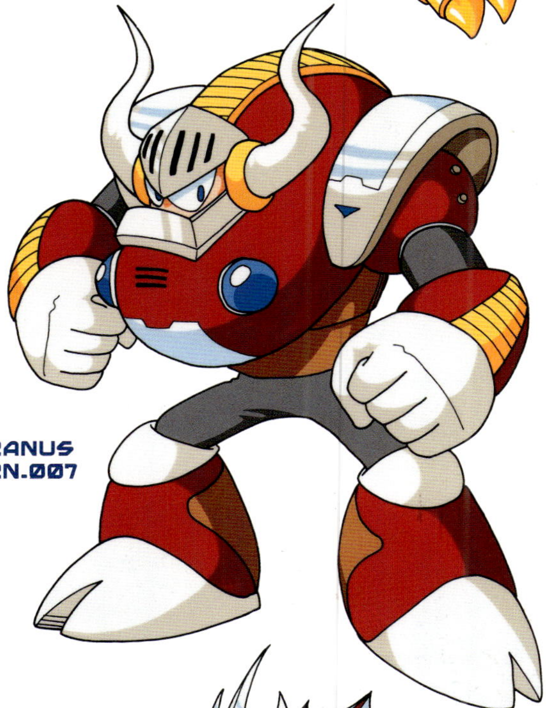

URANUS
SRN.007

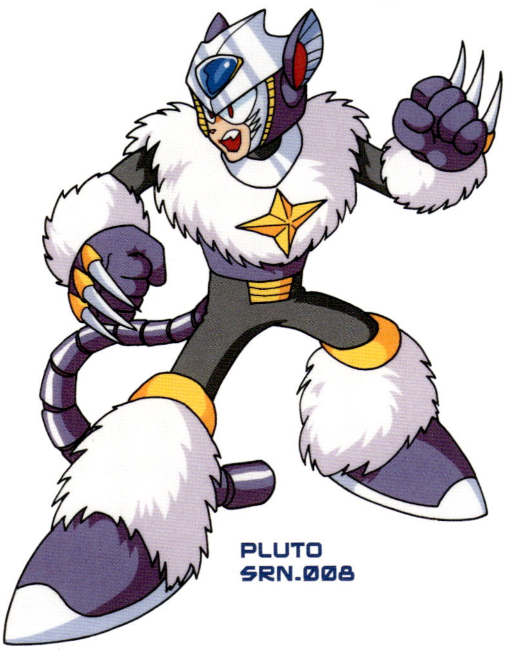

PLUTO
SRN.008

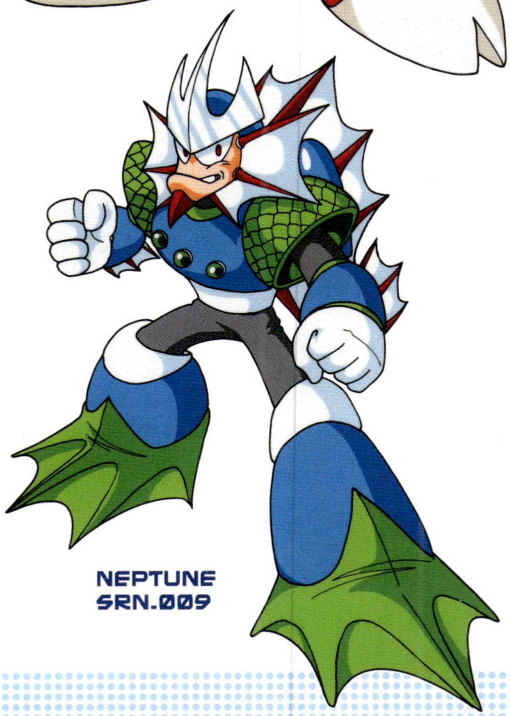

NEPTUNE
SRN.009

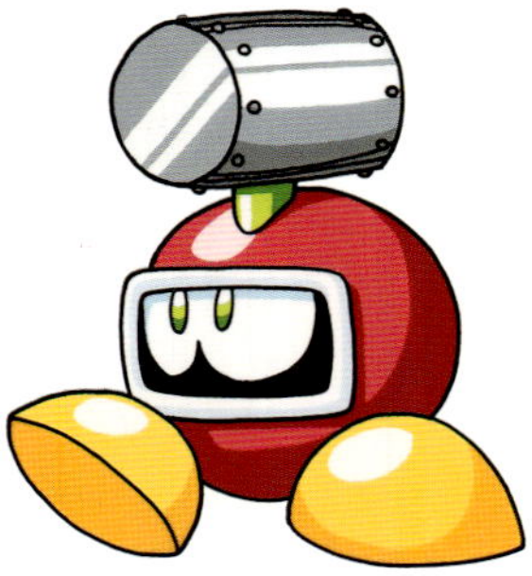

DONCATCH

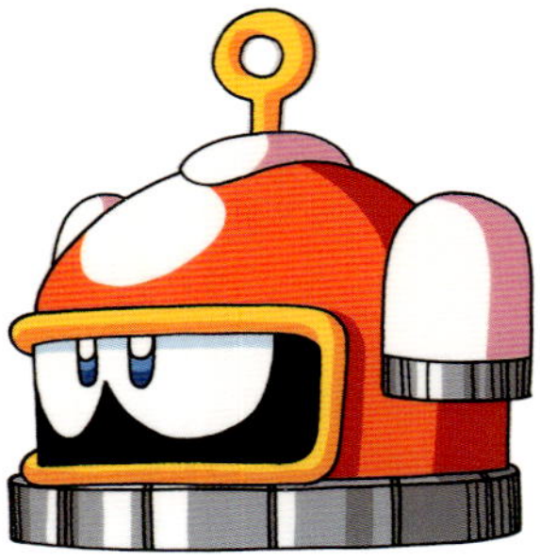

TAMP

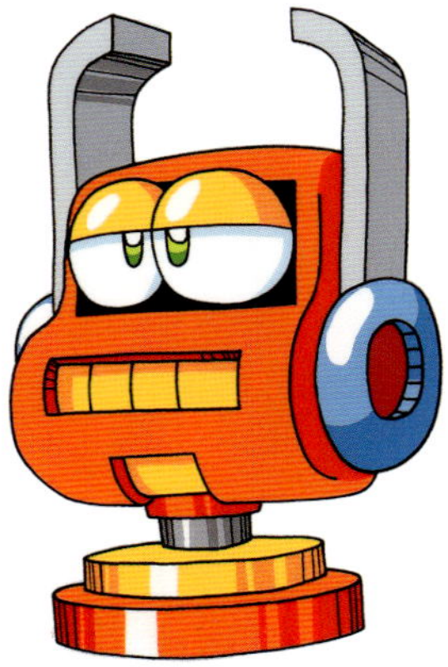

SOSHI BREAKER

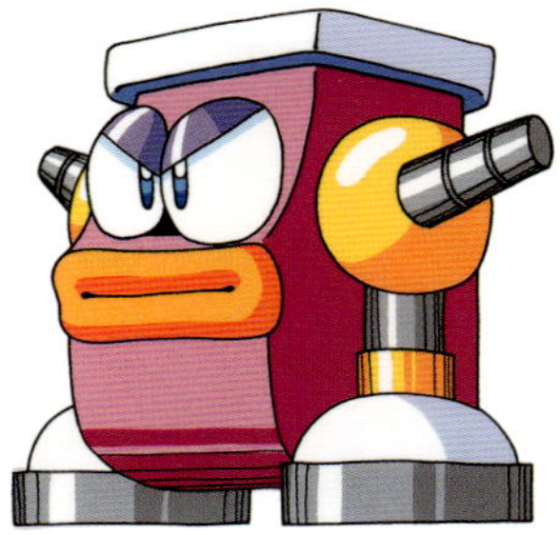

G.S.Q

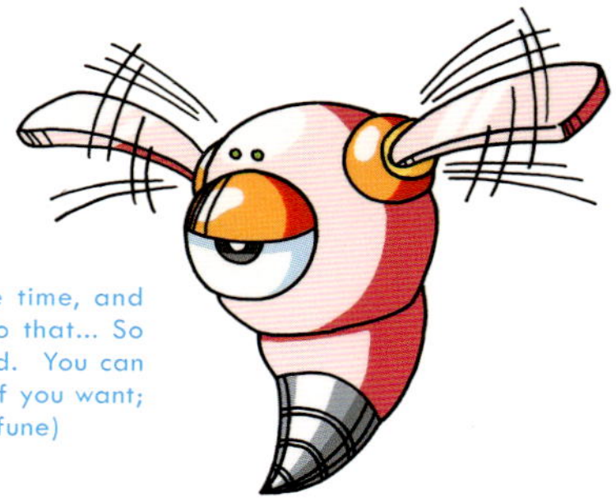

NIBUL

"I had multiple projects going at the same time, and everyone was telling me to draw this or do that... So I've forgotten a lot about the stuff that I did. You can ask me to make a comment about it all now if you want; I'm not really sure what to say. (laughs)" (Inafune)

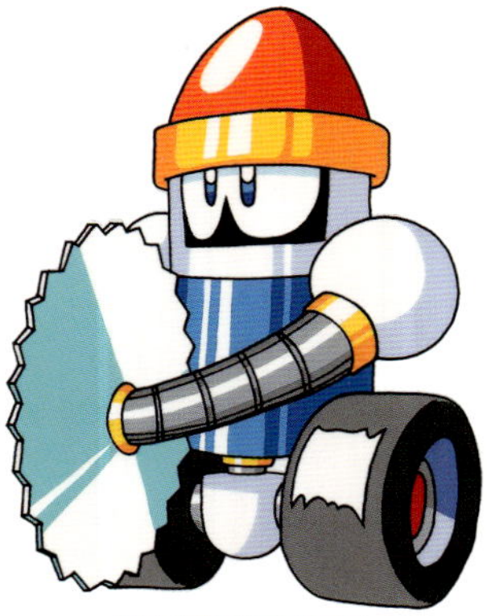

CHAINSOAR

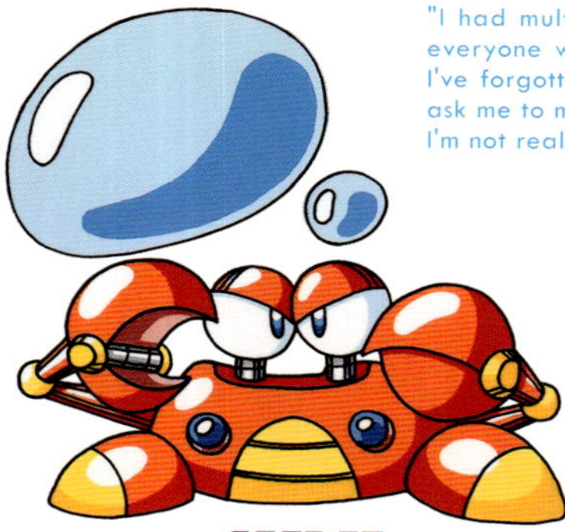

FEEBER

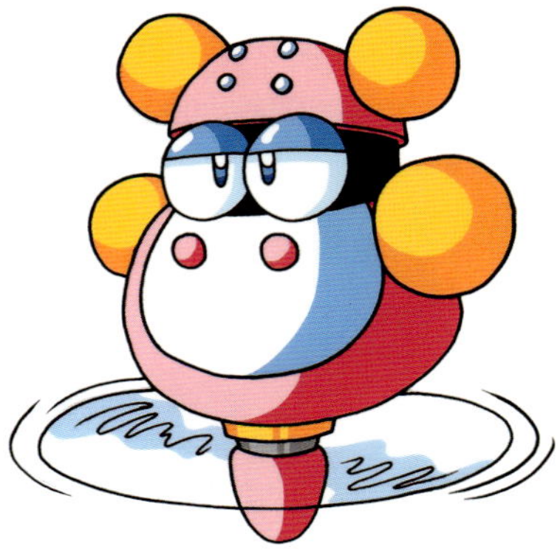

BABY FLIES

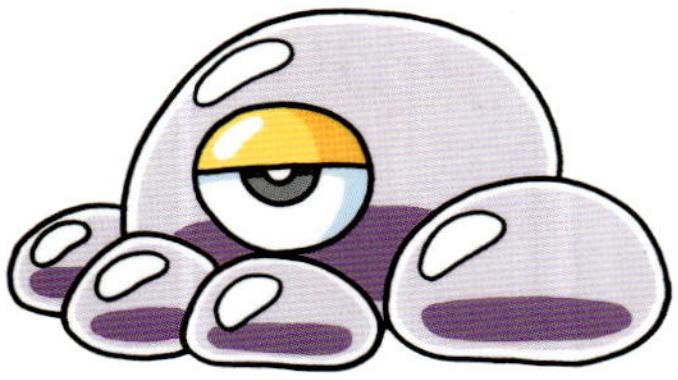

SHABOAN

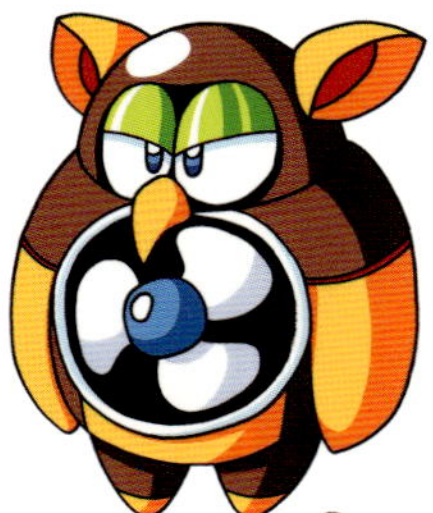

FANKUROW

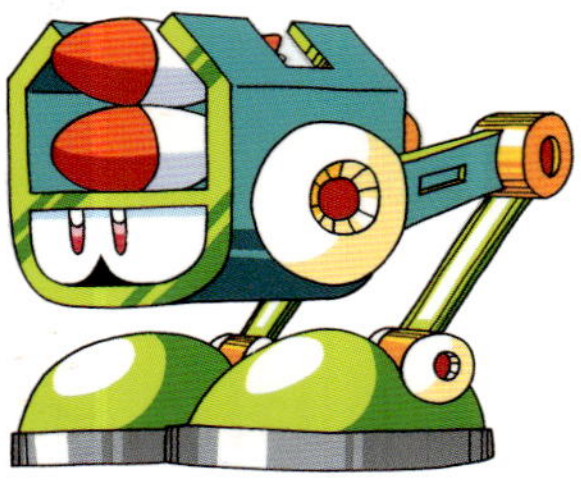

PALMHOPPER

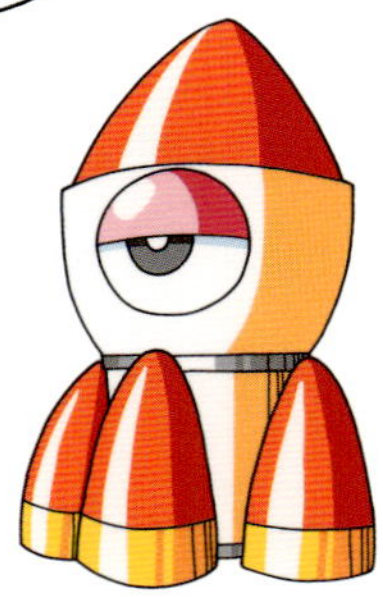

PAROCKET

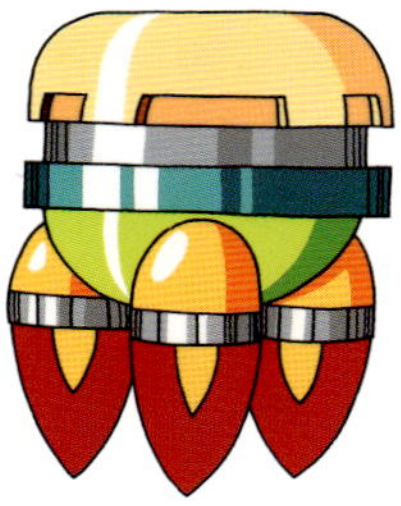

KAMAPOT

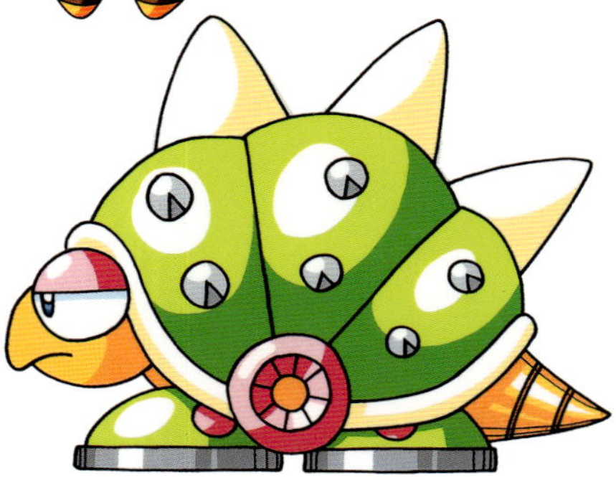

ARMAROID

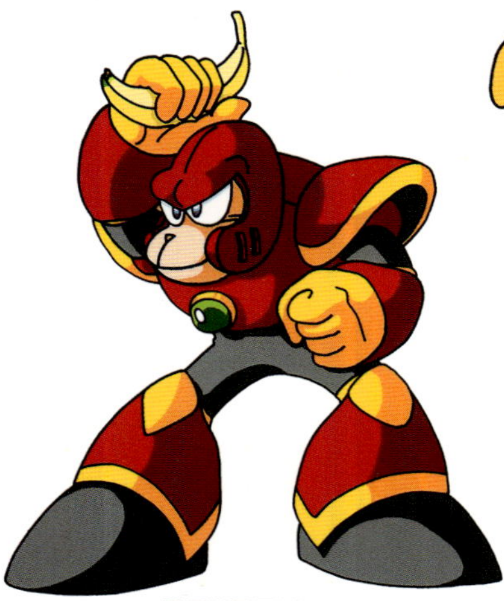

MONKIKKI

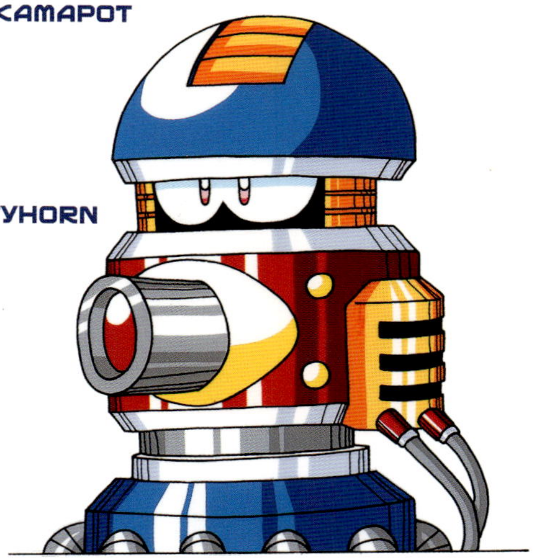

TYHORN

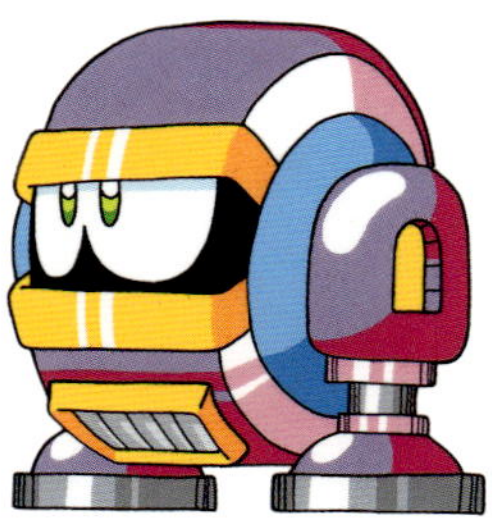

BIKKY BOMB

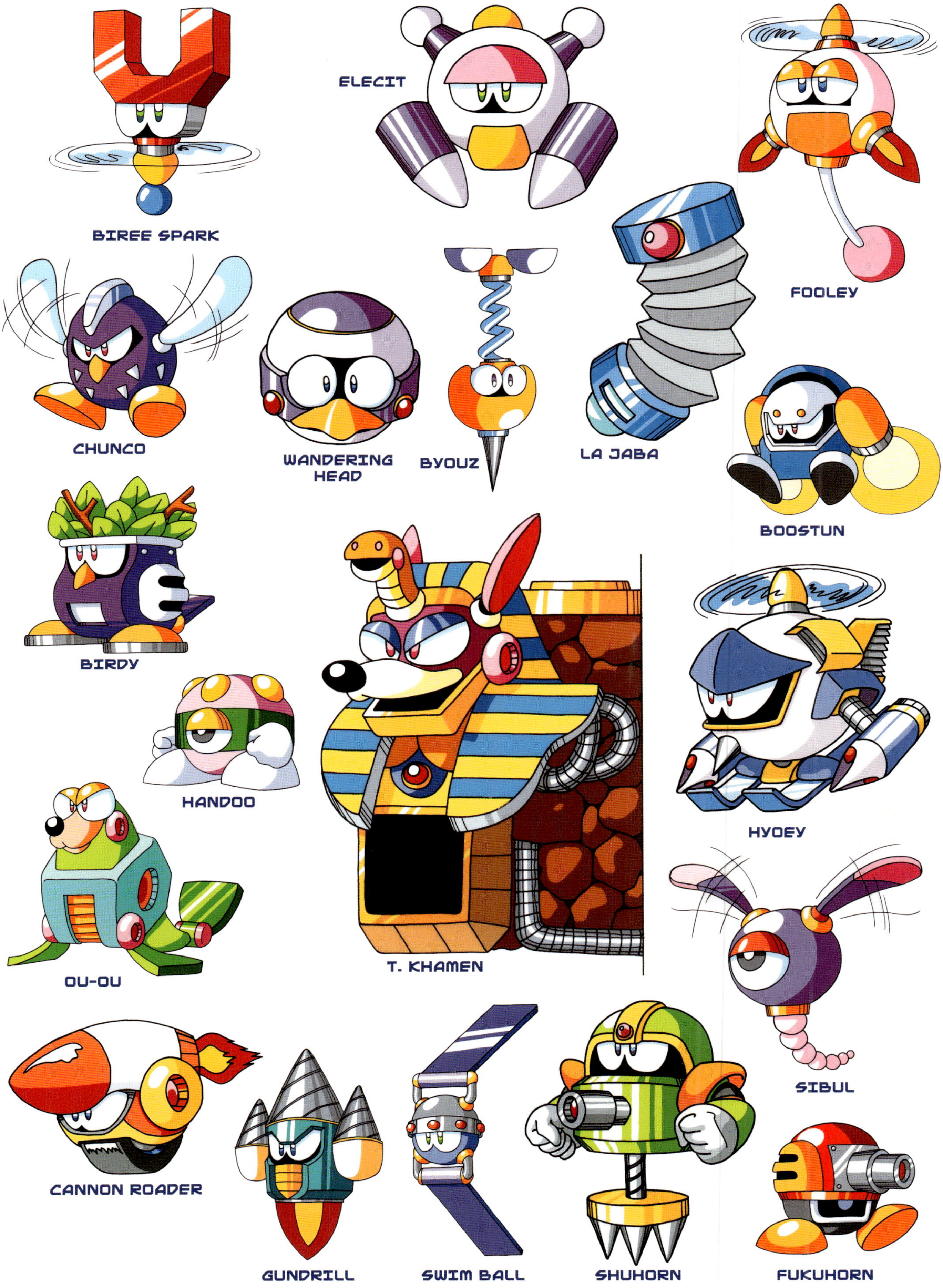
BIREE SPARK
ELECIT
FOOLEY
CHUNCO
WANDERING HEAD
BYOUZ
LA JABA
BOOSTUN
BIRDY
HANDOO
T. KHAMEN
HYOEY
OU-OU
SIBUL
CANNON ROADER
GUNDRILL
SWIM BALL
SHUHORN
FUKUHORN

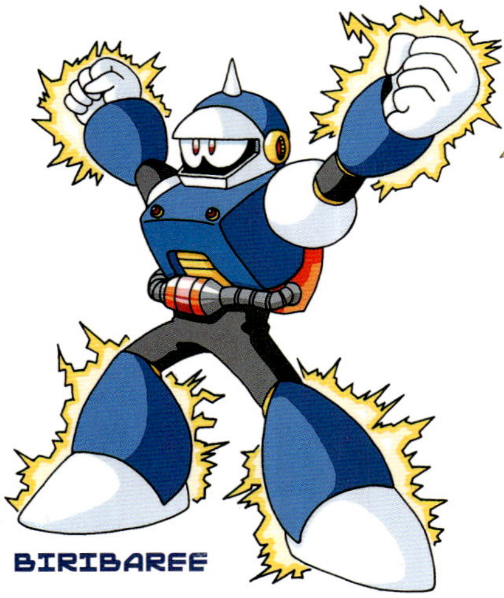

BIRIBAREE

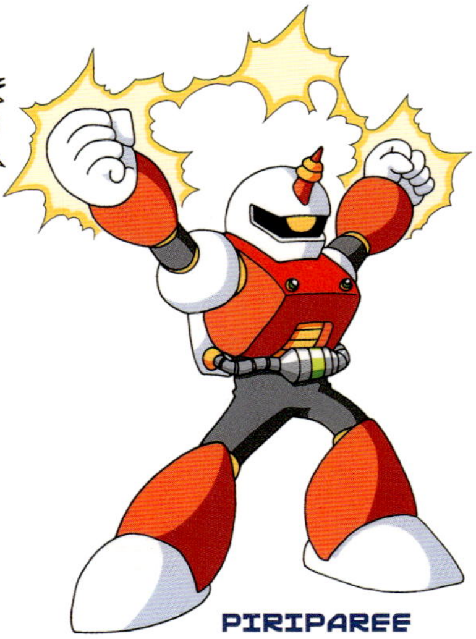

PIRIPAREE

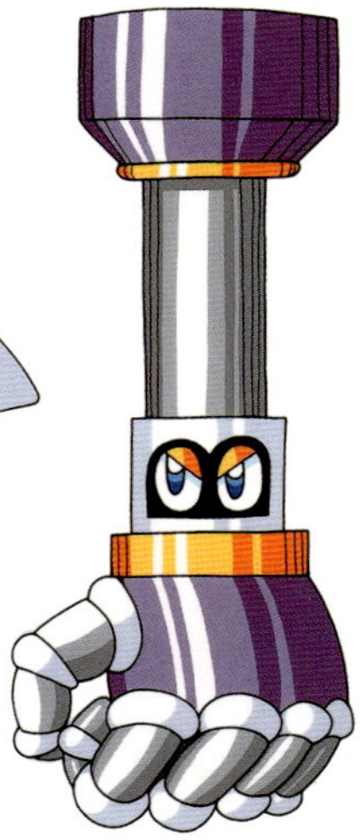

L. KNUCKLE &
R. KNUCKLE

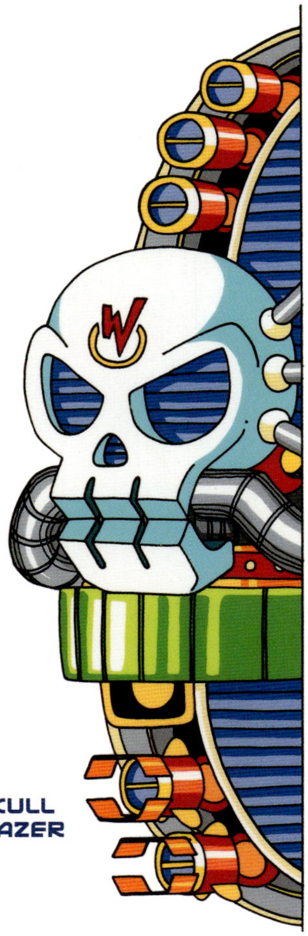

SKULL
BLAZER

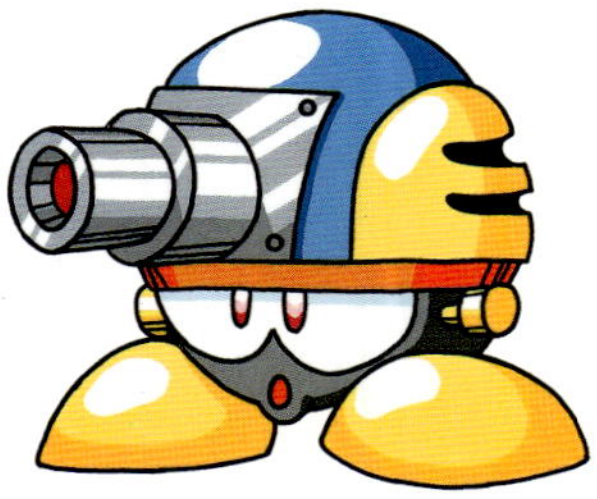

METALL SNIPER

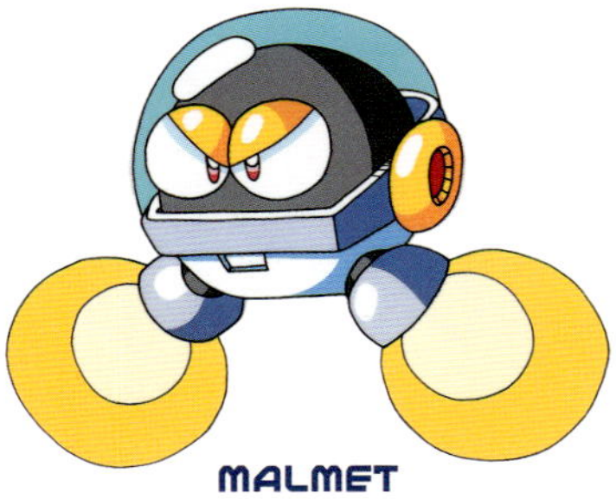

MALMET

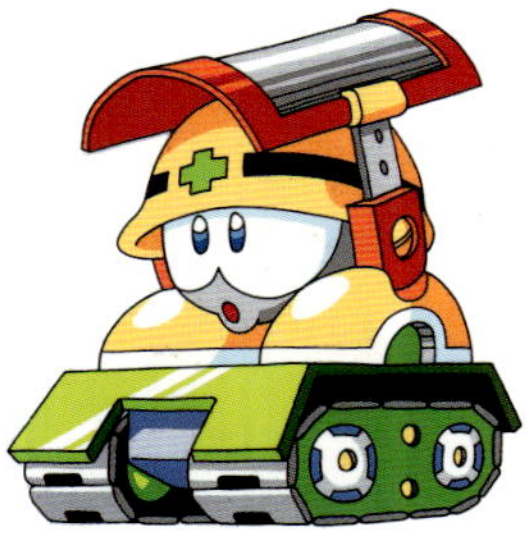

HELL METALL DX

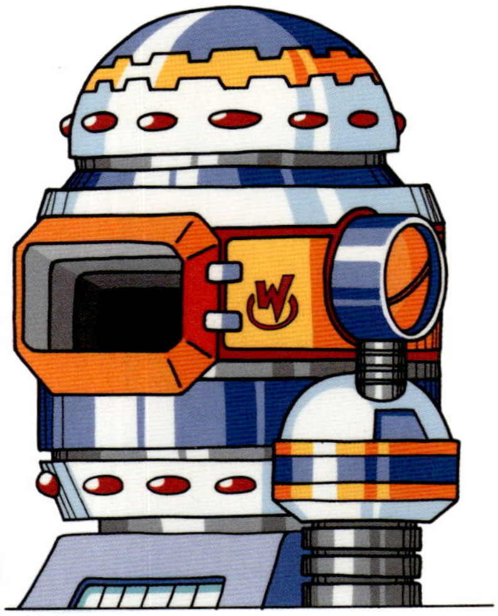

BRAIN CRUSHER

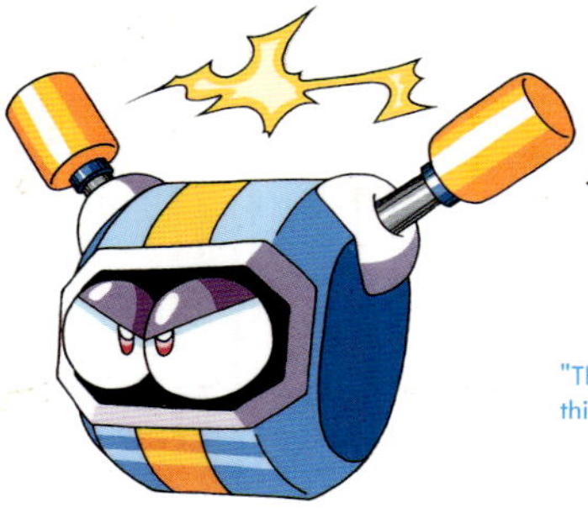

PIKASHU

"This was the last title in the 'World' series. In the end, I think we had a lot of fun working on this series." (Inafune)

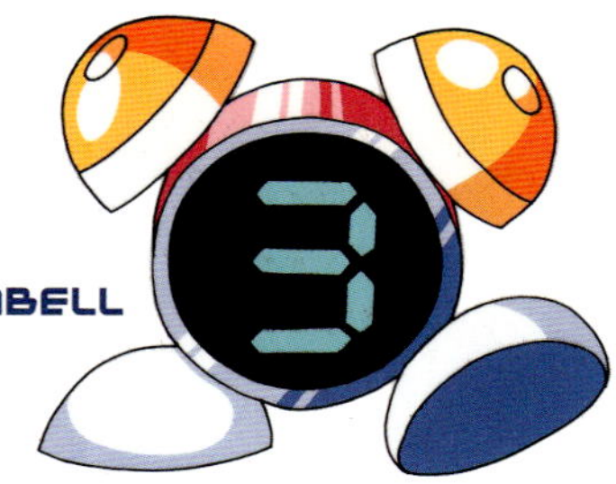

ALABELL

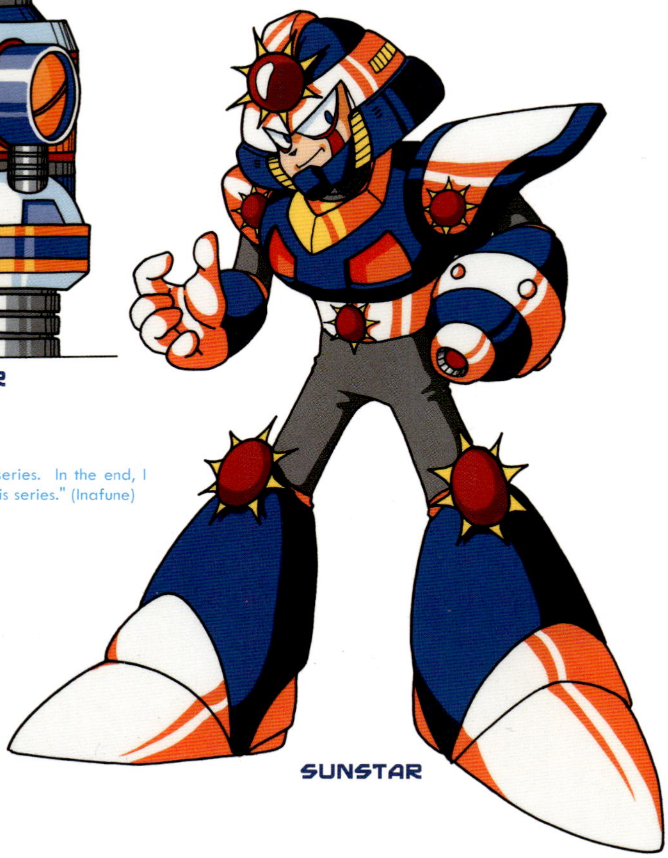

SUNSTAR

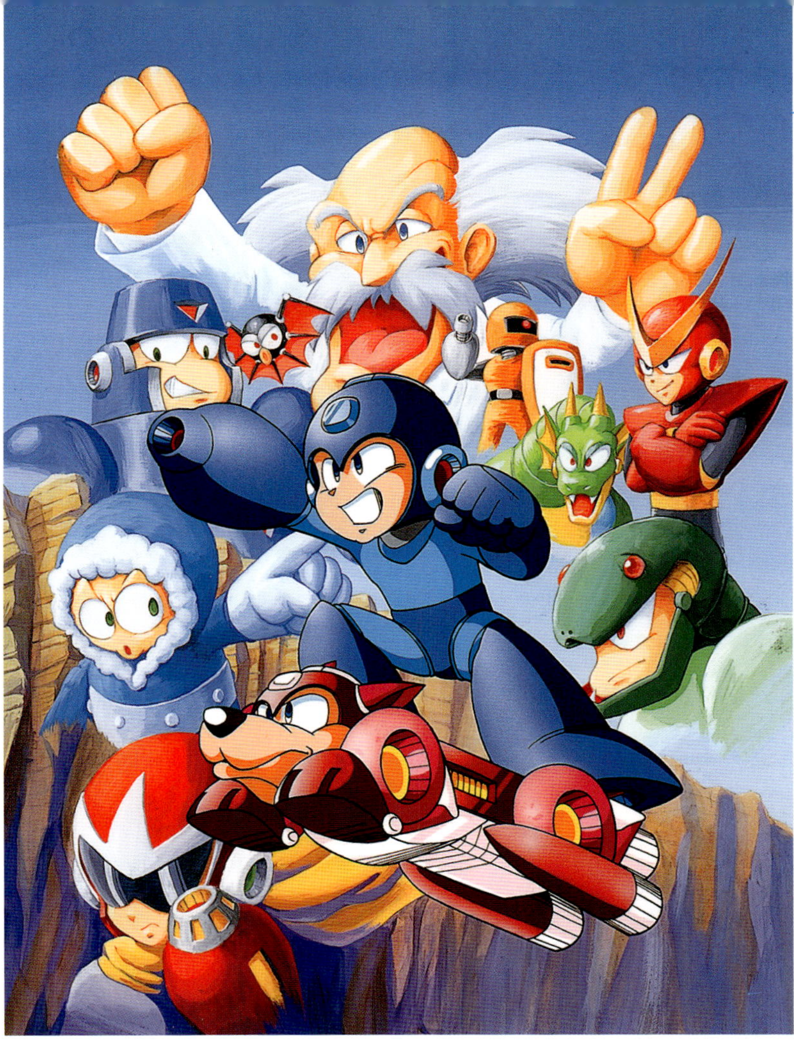

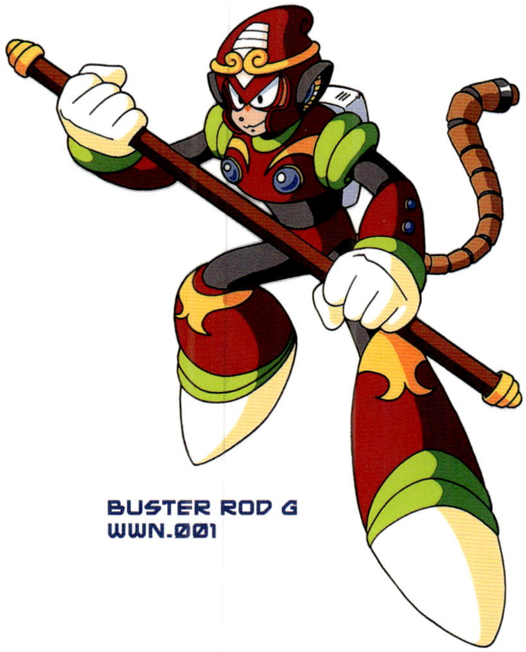

BUSTER ROD G
WWN.001

"We were told that the new theme was going to be the novel 'Journey to the West.' While drawing the boss characters, I tried to take the flavor of the theme and give it that Mega Man twist. I think this kind of blending can be pretty interesting when done right." (Inafune)

ROCKMAN MEGA WORLD

Tired of having his plans foiled every time by Mega Man, Dr. Wily decided to build himself a time machine. Transporting himself into the past, Dr. Wily restored his defeated robots and started causing chaos. At this rate, even the peaceful past was about to be tainted by Dr. Wily's ambitions! In order to stop Dr. Wily, Mega Man was sent into the past in a time machine hastily crafted by Dr. Light.

Mega Man: The Wily Wars
SG 10/21/1994

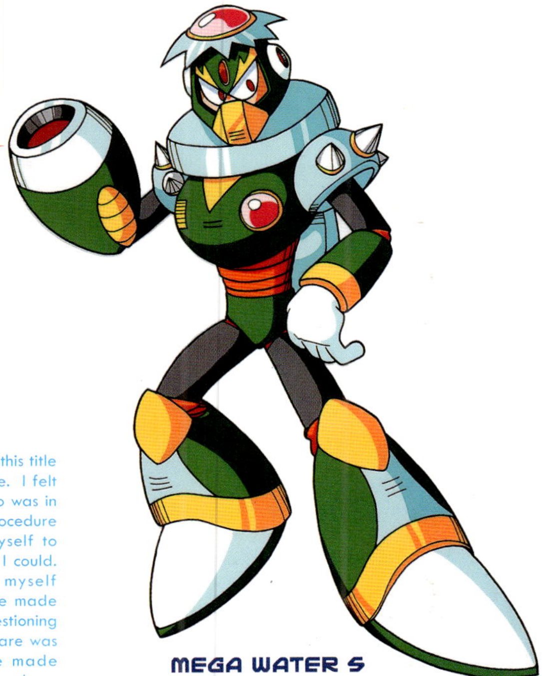

MEGA WATER S
WWN.002

"The bug check phase for this title was an absolute nightmare. I felt so bad for the person who was in charge of the checking procedure that I even jumped in myself to help out in any way that I could. It was so bad, I found myself saying, 'I can't believe we made it out of there alive.' Questioning whether or not this nightmare was 'truly necessary,' we've made some changes in our procedures to hopefully avoid this sort of situation in the future." (Inafune)

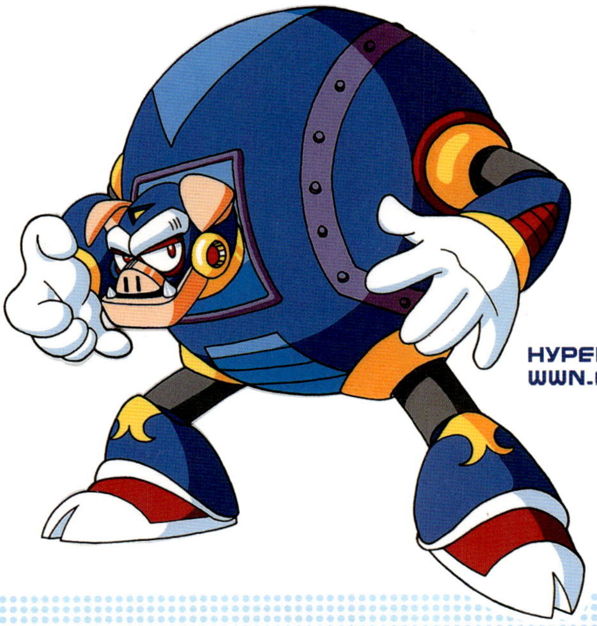

HYPER STORM H
WWN.003

"I barely did anything at all for this title. I did the designs for the 'Journey to the West' bosses, and the Mega Man in the center of the package art, but that's it. Just helping out here and there. We had outsourced this one as well, but they weren't exactly powering through it, so..." (Inafune)

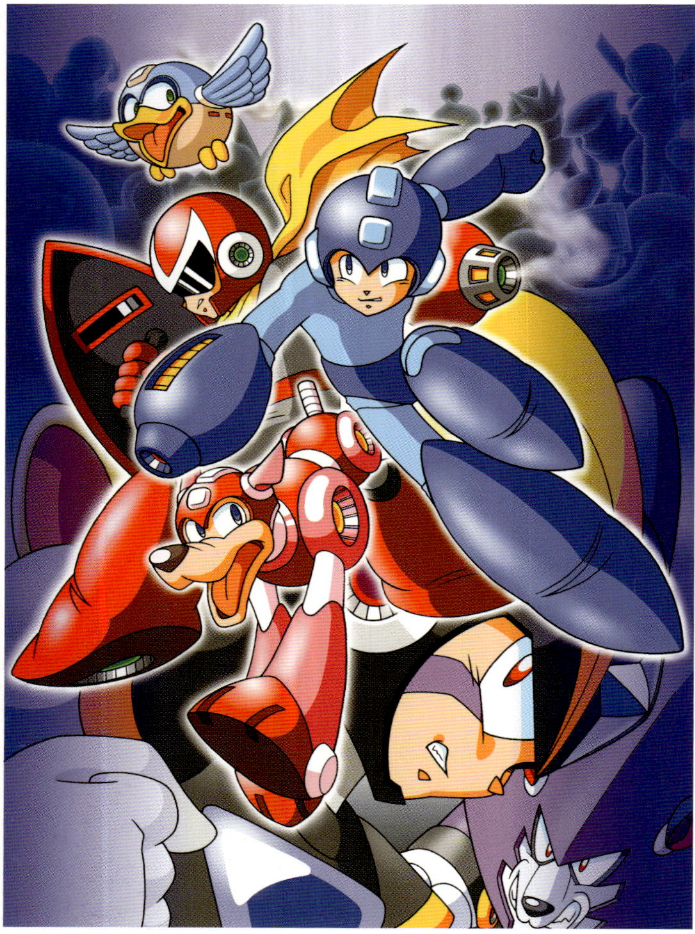

Rockman The Power Battle

Mega Man: The Power Battle
AC 10/1995

Dr. Wily's up to his old tricks again! This time, Dr. Wily has restored the robots defeated by Mega Man in the past and has sent them in for another battle! "How does it feel to be reunited with your old friends, Mega Man? I've powered them up considerably from their original abilities, so I hope you all have a lot of fun." Thus began the greatest battle in history.

"I did the draft of this piece." (Suetsugu)

Rockman 2 The Power Fighters

Mega Man 2: The Power Fighters
AC 08/1996

One day, while Dr. Light was researching an unknown energy source from space, his laboratory was attacked by Wily mechs. The unknown energy source and the new parts that were under development were stolen from the laboratory. To make matters worse, Roll also went missing... With the addition of the mysterious new robot "Duo," a new battle is about to begin!

"I was involved in certain parts of the arcade version. I think this is one of my drawings...? I did drafts, line drawings, and finishing touches, but the work was divided up between so many people... it's hard to remember exactly what I did. Still, it's a real blast from the past to get to see these pieces now." (Hideki)

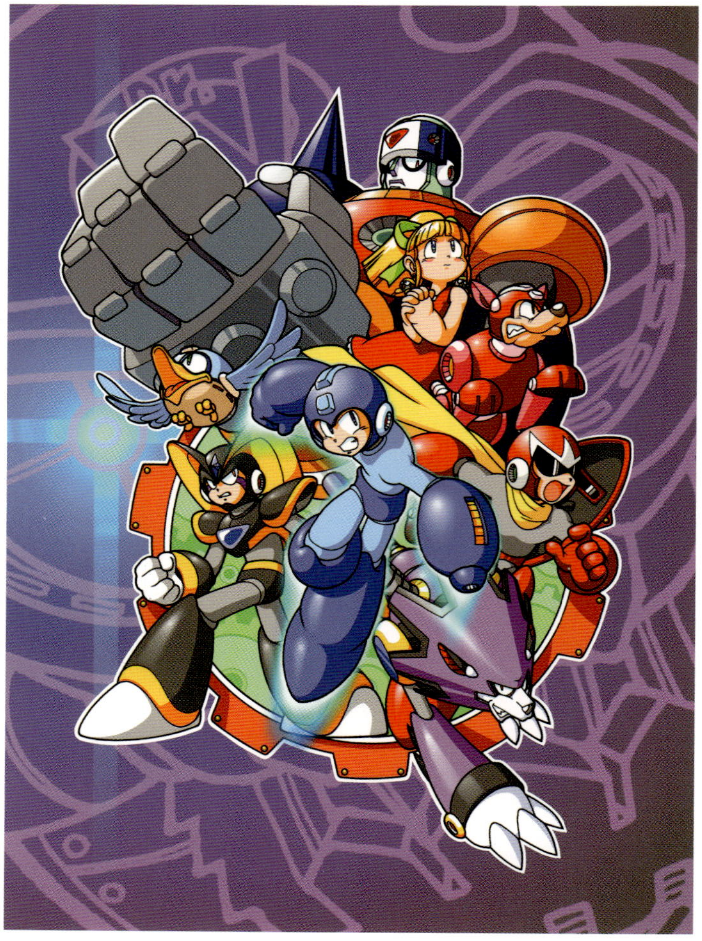

"When we were offered the opportunity to take Mega Man to the arcade, I was like, 'Sure.' With my trusty "Mega Man-fan" team leader in charge of things, I felt confident counting on him. I remember how happy it made me when I saw them redoing the bosses I drew from the NES era into more modern and visually attractive graphics." (Inafune)

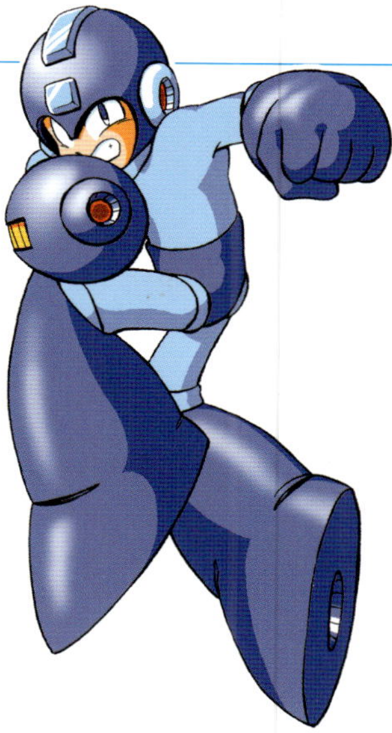

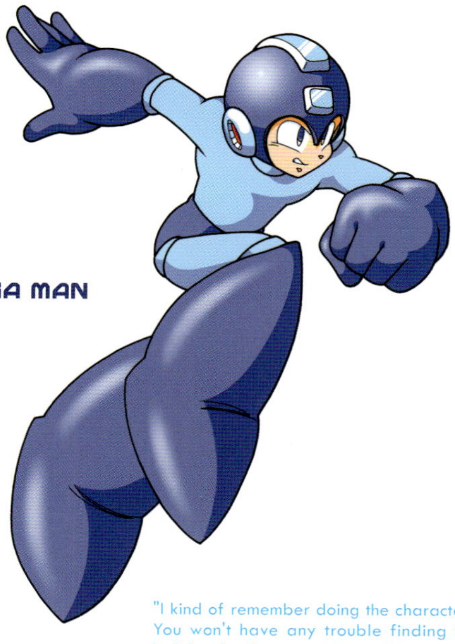

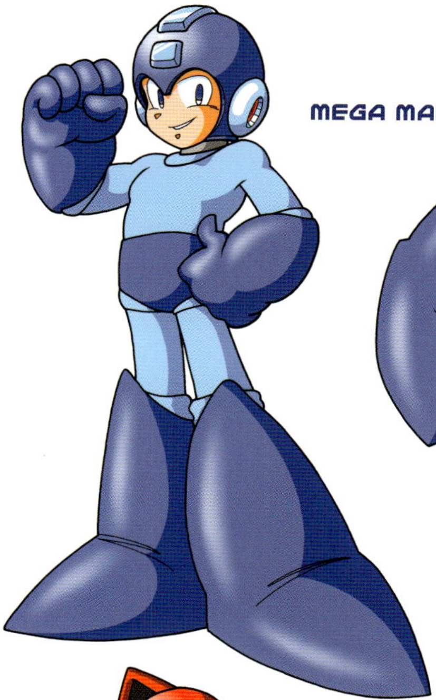

MEGA MAN

"I kind of remember doing the character illustrations. You won't have any trouble finding the ones that I did... the Basses with small heads are all mine. (laughs) I think I also did an illustration of Dr. Wily." (Hideki)

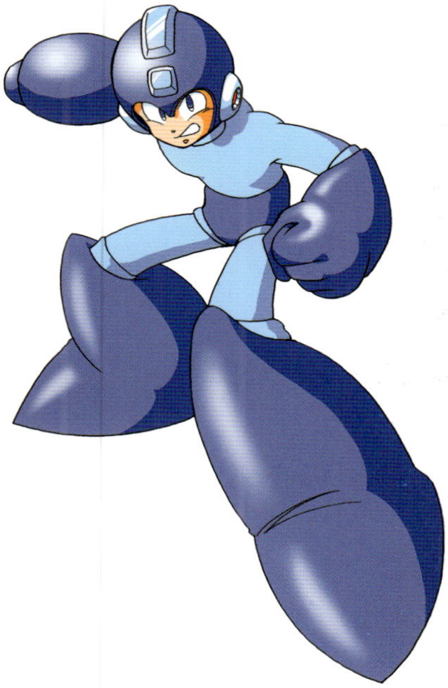

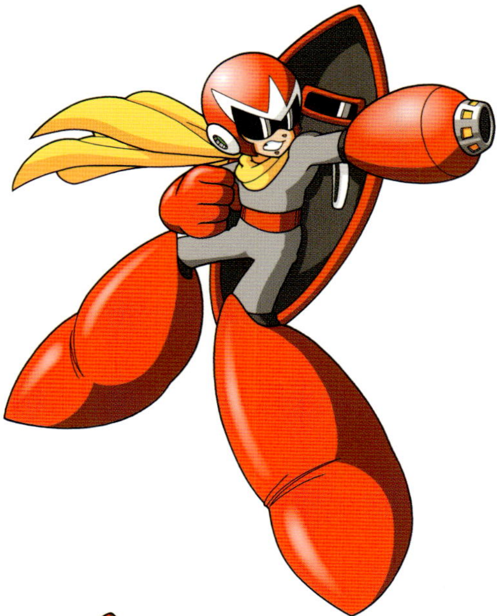

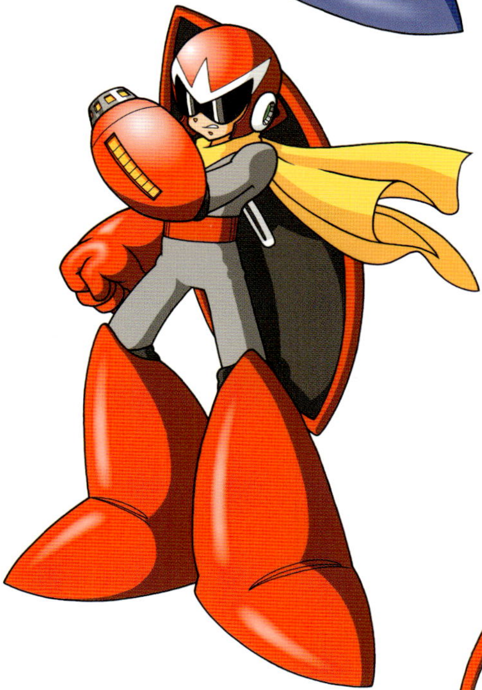

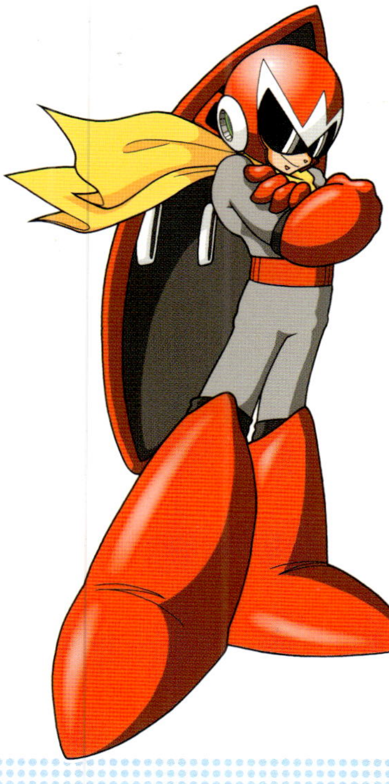

PROTO MAN

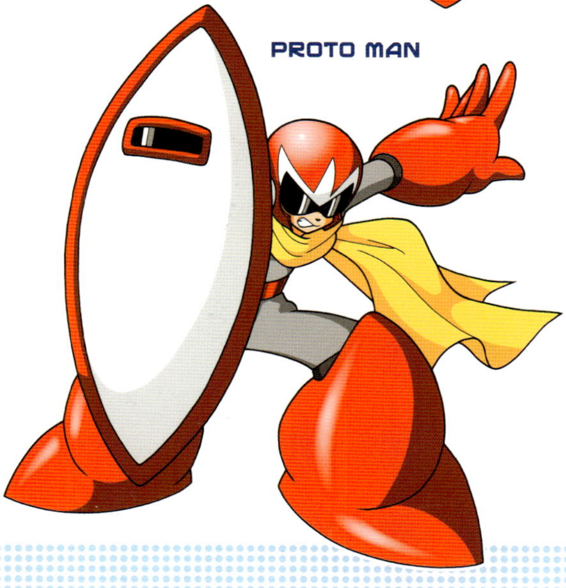

"Oh, yeah! I remember struggling with Proto Man's shield. I wasn't sure how it was attached to his arm, and when I asked Inafune about it, he said something like, 'I don't know... maybe there's a laser beam or whatever that shoots out of the shield all "vyrrm" and wraps around his arm...' Vague would be an understatement. (laughs)" (Hideki)

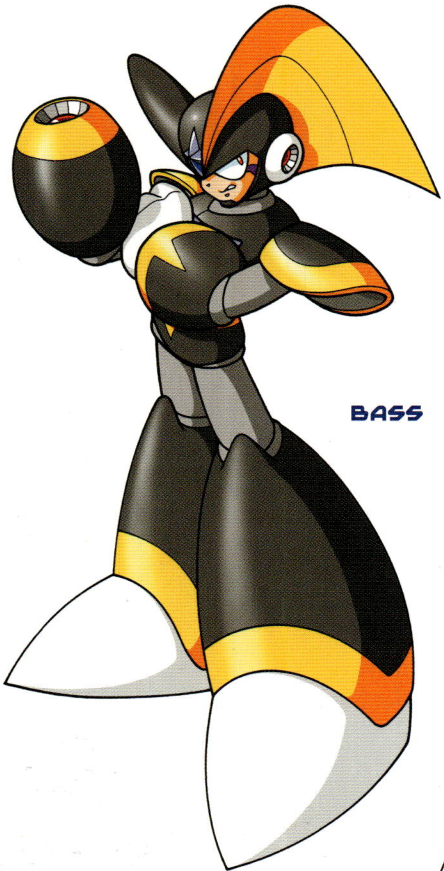

"You can tell from the lines that some of these are clearly Inafune pieces, but then some don't seem to be... We created some, while others were started by Inafune and simply finished up by us. Still others were a conjoined effort. That's how we got through all of these." (Hideki)

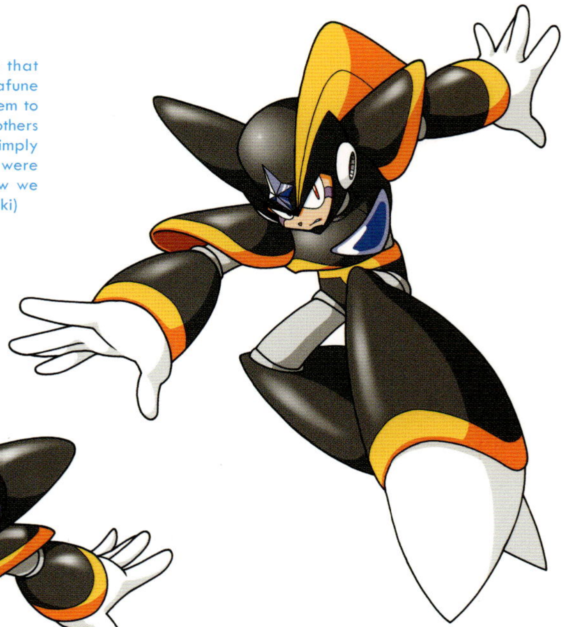

BASS

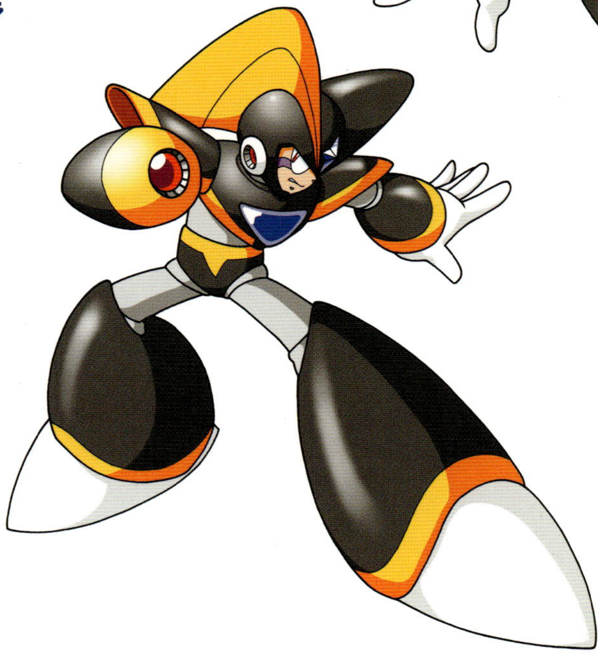

"I think this Duo was done by Kaji, and finished up by someone else...? I could be wrong. I think we were working on the console version of '8' at the same time, so all of my memories are pretty mixed up." (Hideki)

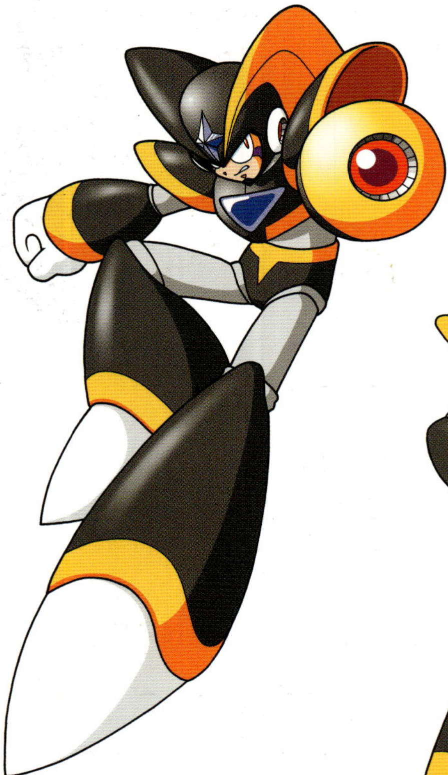

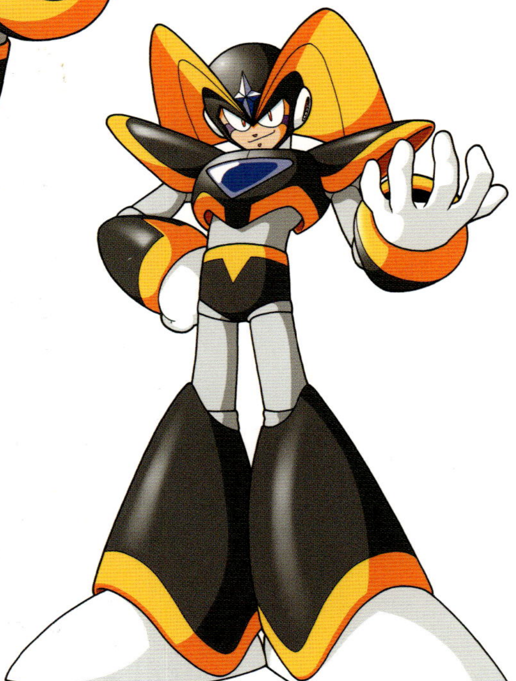

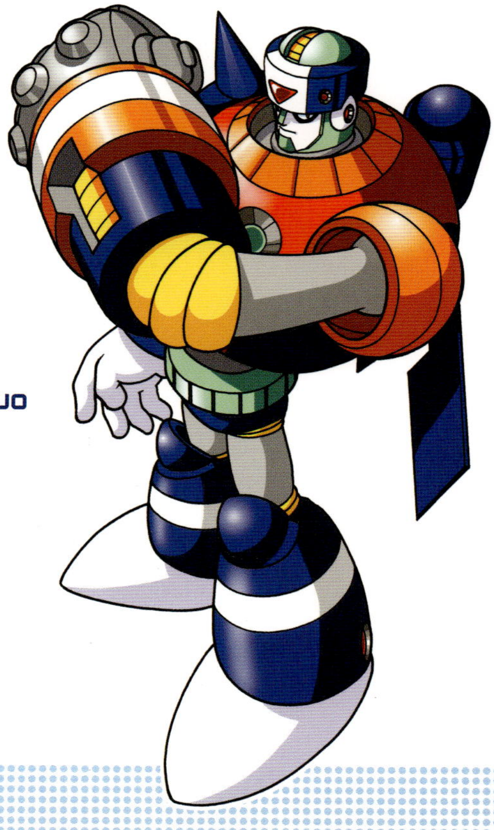

DUO

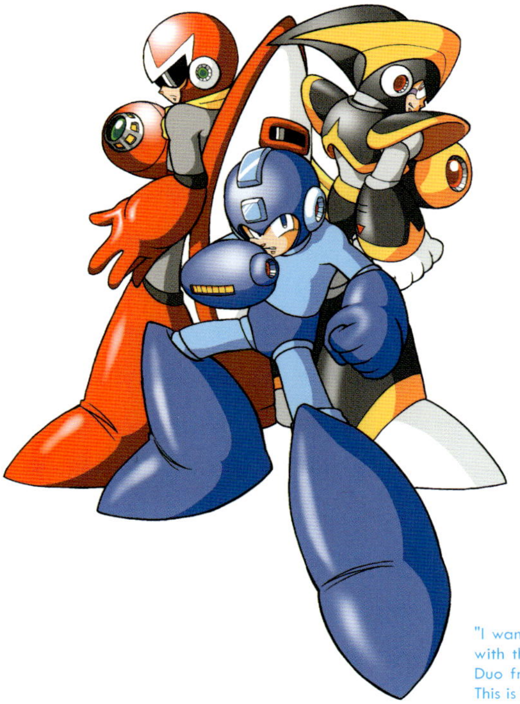

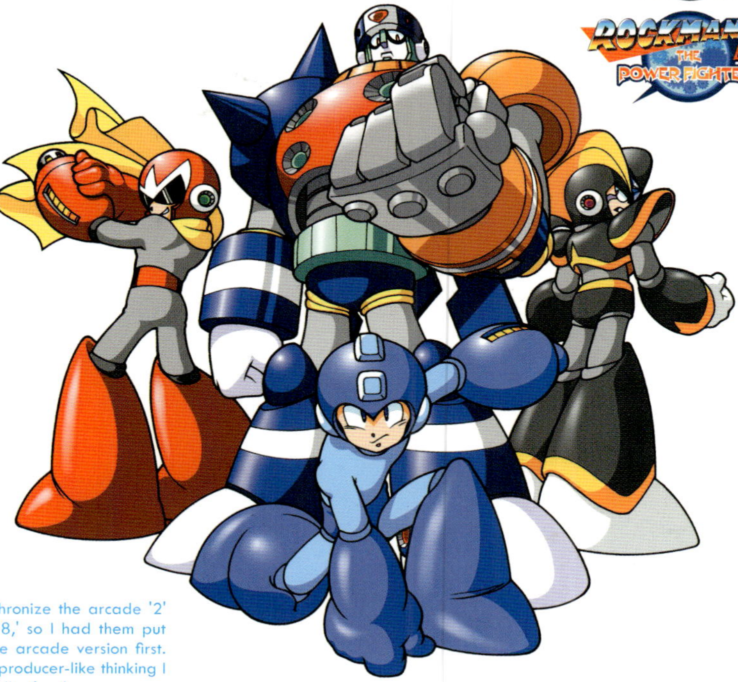

"I wanted to synchronize the arcade '2' with the console '8,' so I had them put Duo from '8' in the arcade version first. This is the kind of producer-like thinking I remember doing." (Inafune)

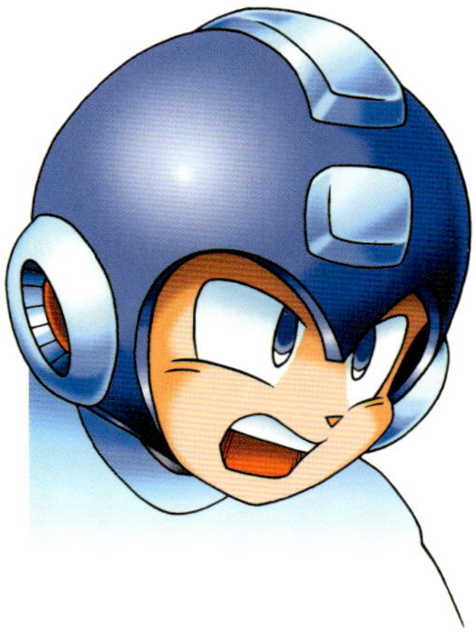

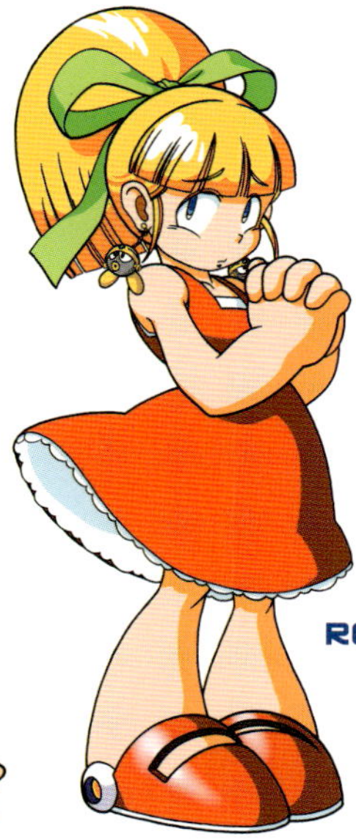

ROLL

DR. LIGHT

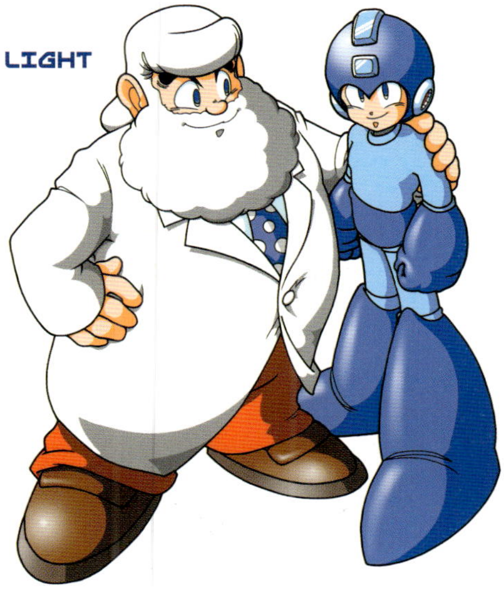

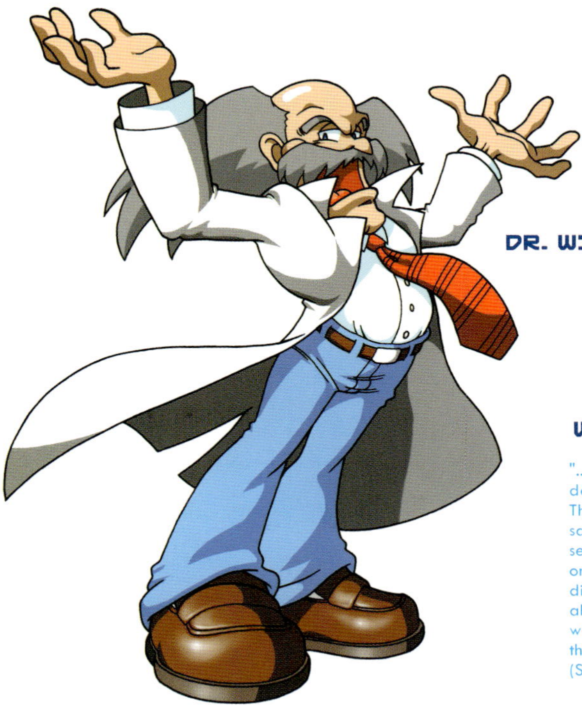

DR. WILY

WILY MACHINE

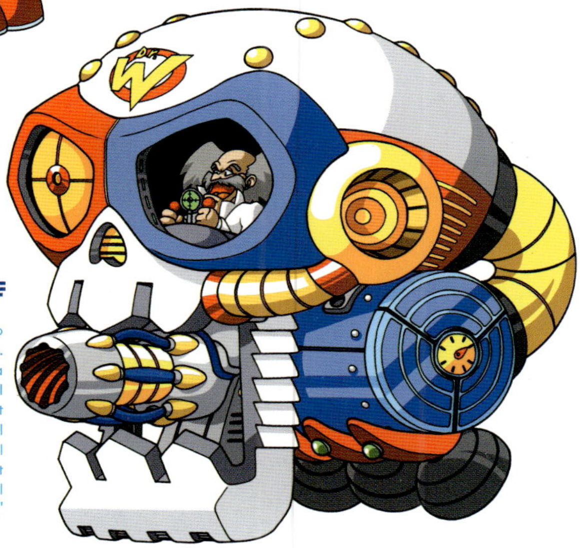

"... Oh! I was the one who designed the Wily mech. The one that looks like a saucer, and chops, and... I see they didn't include that one here. (laughs) Yeah, I didn't work on this one. I also remember helping out with the select screen. I think that's about all I did." (Suetsugu)

"The only things I did for this one were the package illustration and the design for the new character Reggae. I think it's so fun to design mascot characters like Reggae. The package illustration was pretty fun too, since it was the kind of image I don't get to draw very often. As far as the actual game goes, though, I was totally hands-off. (laughs)" (Inafune)

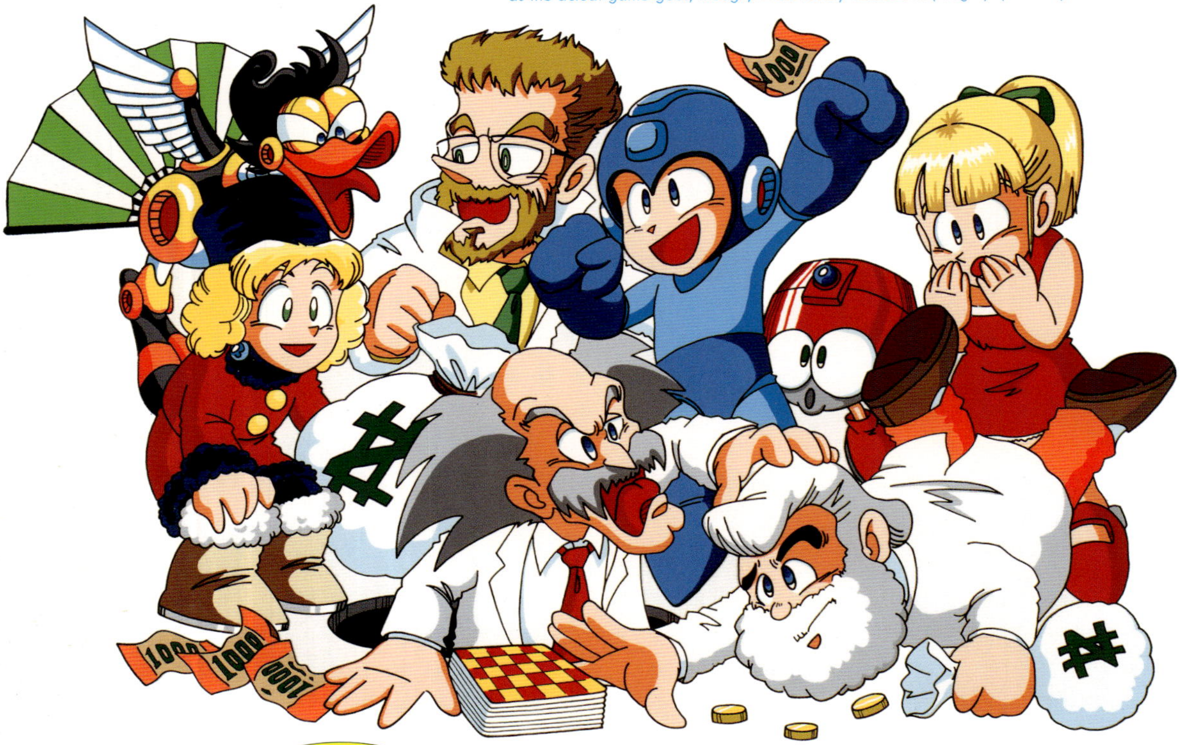

ワイリー&ライトの ROCK BOARD ザッツ☆パラダイス™

Wily & Light's Rock Board ~That's Paradise~
FC 01/15/1993

Who will be the one to run across the expansive field and create their ideal world? The Roulette of Fate will lead them to a fantastical drama that no one can foresee. Everything they are about to go through is just a trial on their path to creating their ideal world. From the use of money, to the buying and selling of land, to the cards that lead to an unimaginable fate... They will make the best of whatever opportunities they can to build their assets and build a wonderful world. THAT'S PARADISE!!

"One day, when I had a day off from work... 'I'm going to play Rock Board today! I'll cover the entire field with hospitals!' So, after a marathon game day, I cleared all of the stages in Battle Royale mode, and the credits started to roll! I wonder if anyone else knows about this? By the way... it took me six hours." (Higurashi)

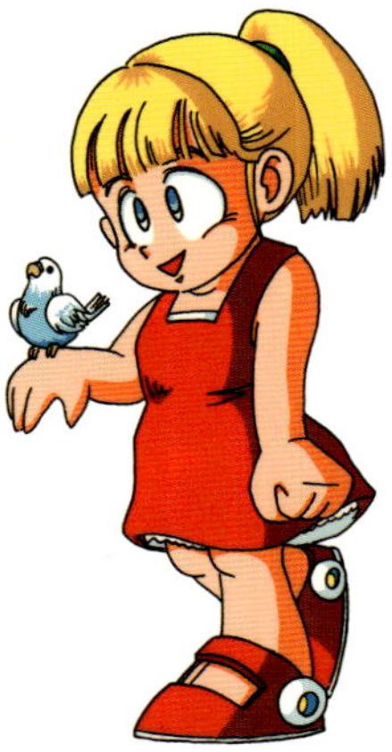

ROLL

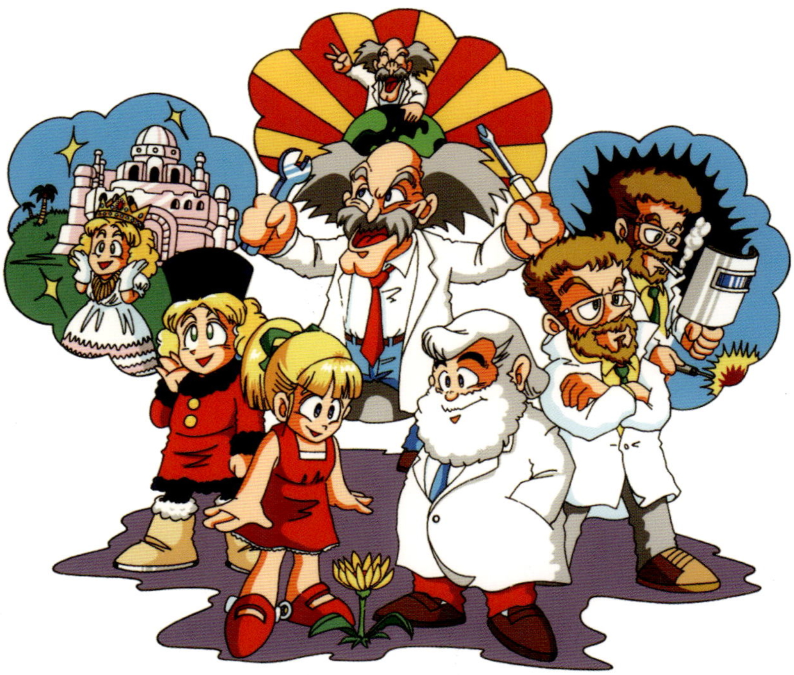

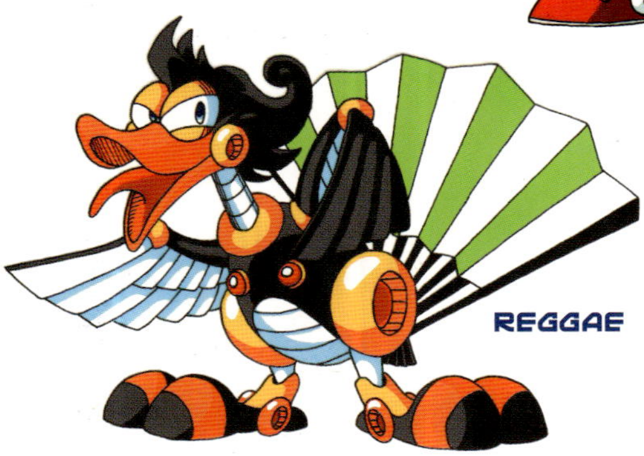

REGGAE

*Though not a developer at the time, we decided to get comments from Higurashi regarding "Rock Board" and "Mega Man's Soccer."

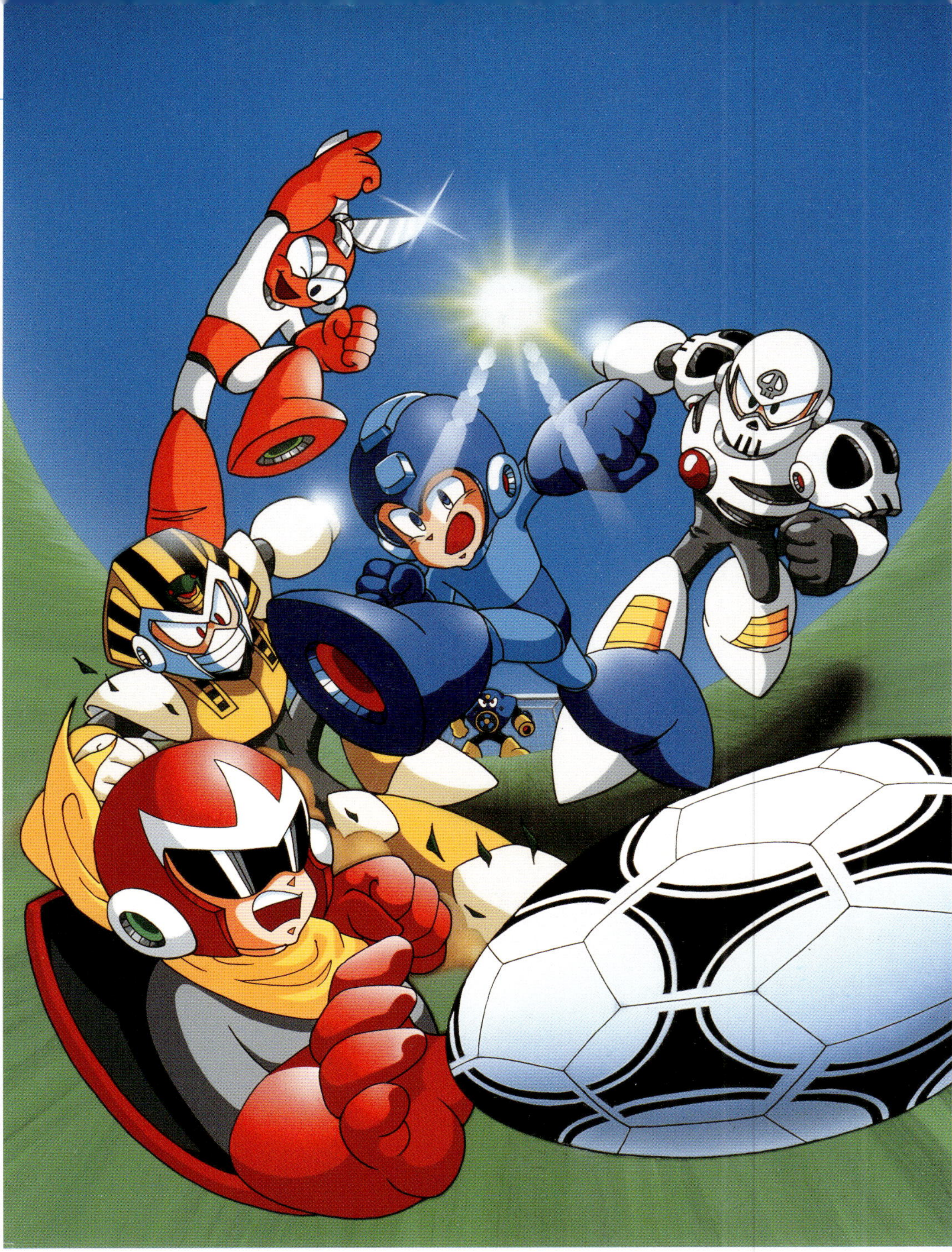

"I'm pretty sure I saw Guts Man and Heat Man in some preview screenshots... I wonder where they went? I asked people about that when I joined the company, and I was told that they planned to include them in the sequel! With the current hardware, it shouldn't be necessary to have only "3 Mega Mans on one team!" We could make teams like the "Light Numbers," or the "Stardroids" (okay, maybe that's not an original name) or something like that! It's like a dream!!" (Higurashi)

ROCKMAN'S SOCCER

Mega Man's Soccer
SNES 03/25/1994

A few months had passed since the battle with Dr. Cossack. One day, soccer fields all over the world were thrown into chaos! Familiar enemy robots restored by Dr. Wily were running out into the field and ruining soccer games. To deal with this emergency situation, Dr. Light modified Mega Man and sent him to make things right. "Go, Mega Man!! You must save soccer, and the dreams of those who love the sport!"

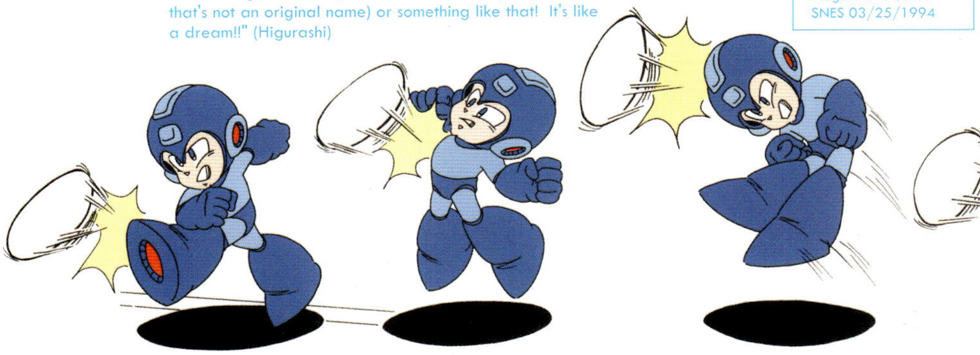

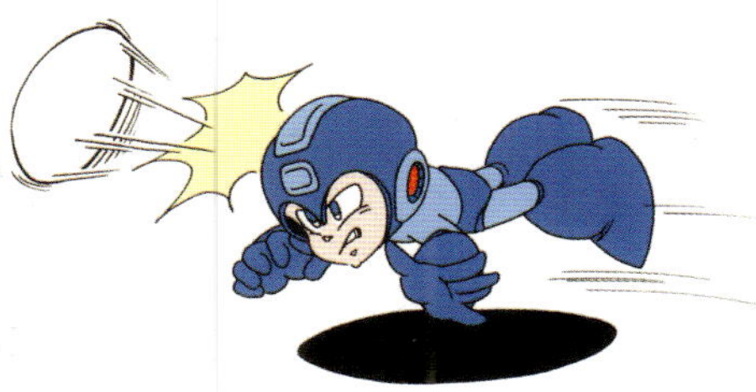

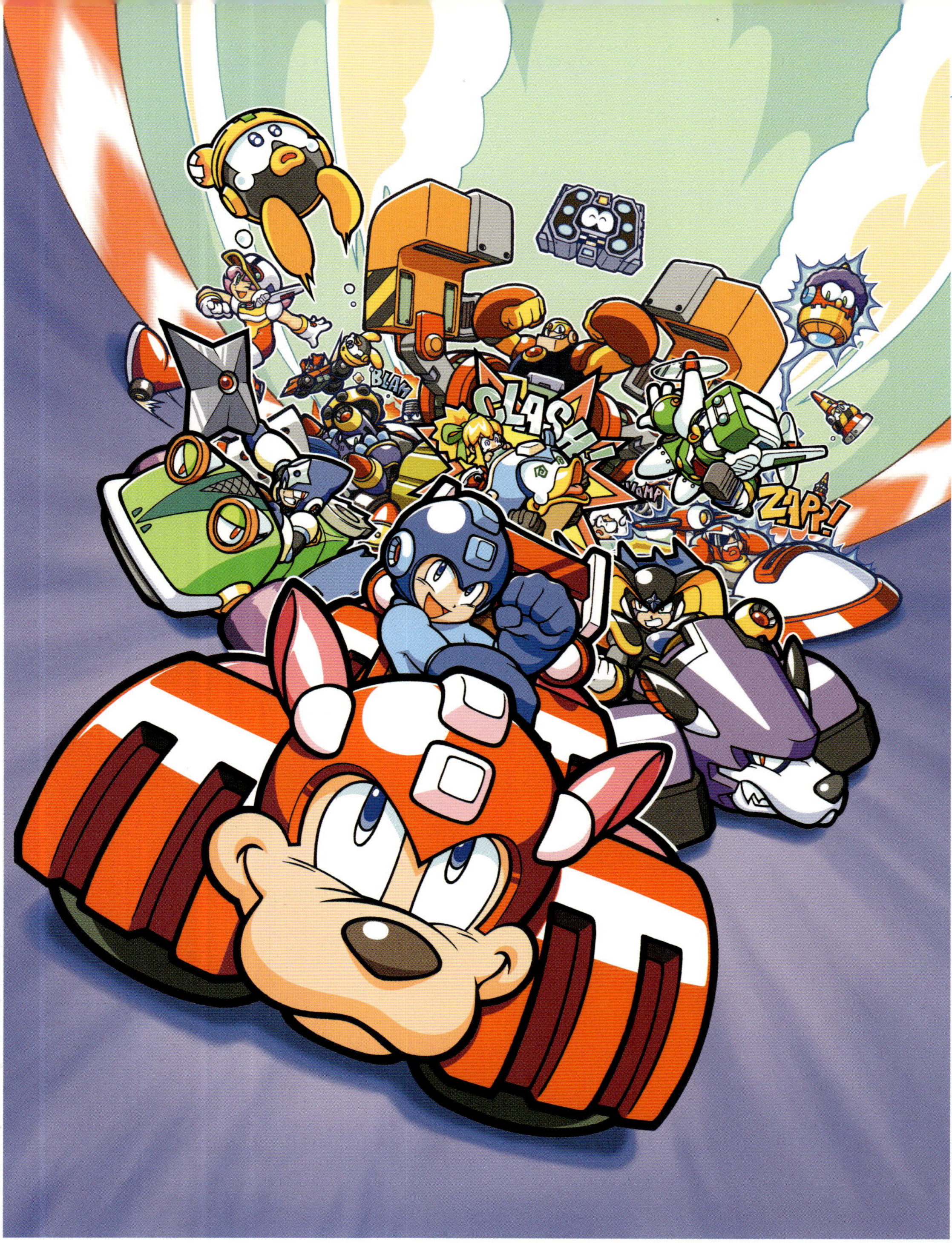

"This was something I've always wanted to do, so I supervised this project with great enthusiasm! Bringing the unique 'beat your enemies and take their stuff' aspect of Mega Man to a racing cart game sounds like it would be a lot of fun, right? When my son started playing video games, this was the one I played with him the most. It's still one of my favorites." (Inafune)

Mega Man Battle & Chase
PS 03/20/1997

Mega Man and the others are entering "Battle & Chase," a car race for robots, where you are allowed to do whatever it takes to win! This battle will involve speed like Mega Man has never experienced before!

ROCKMAN バトル&チェイス

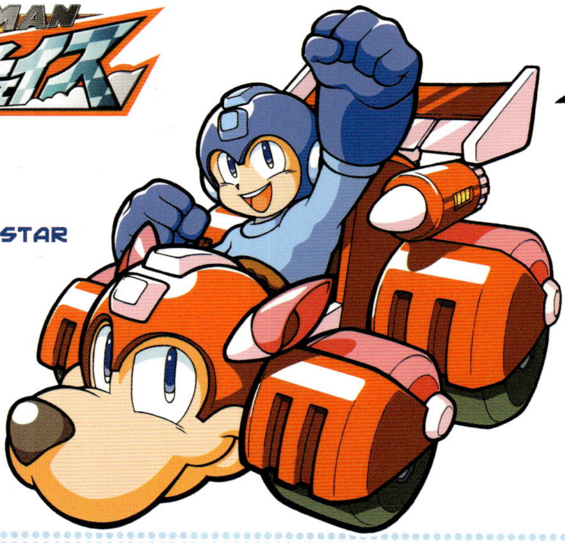

MEGA MAN
RUSH ROADSTAR

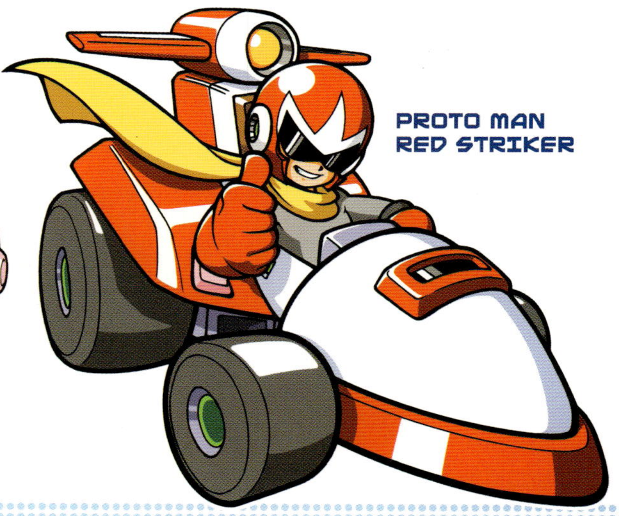

PROTO MAN
RED STRIKER

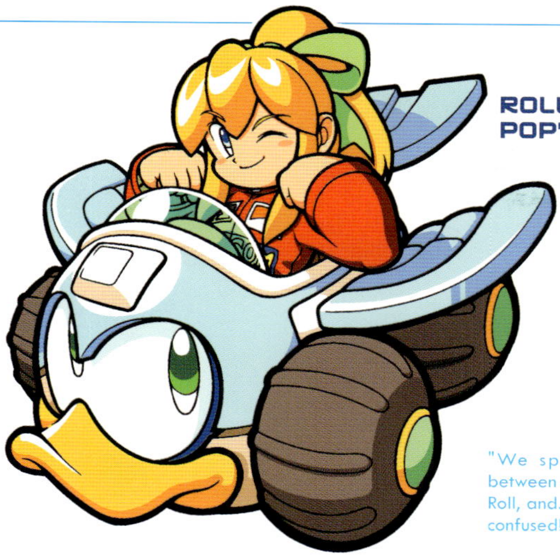

ROLL
POP'N BEAT

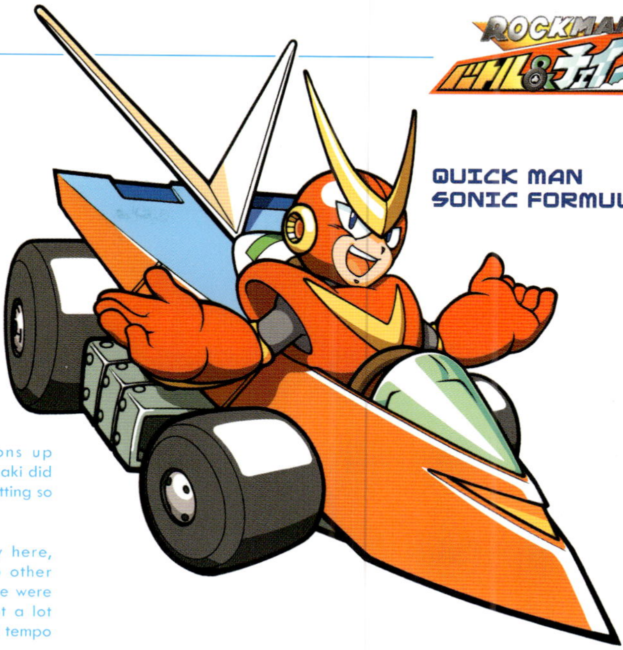

QUICK MAN
SONIC FORMULA

"We split these illustrations up between so many people. Komaki did Roll, and... er... oh, man! I'm getting so confused! (laughs)" (Hideki)

"Ishikawa was the main guy here, assisted by myself and two other people. Compared to when we were working on '8,' I think we got a lot better at matching our overall tempo to each other." (Komaki)

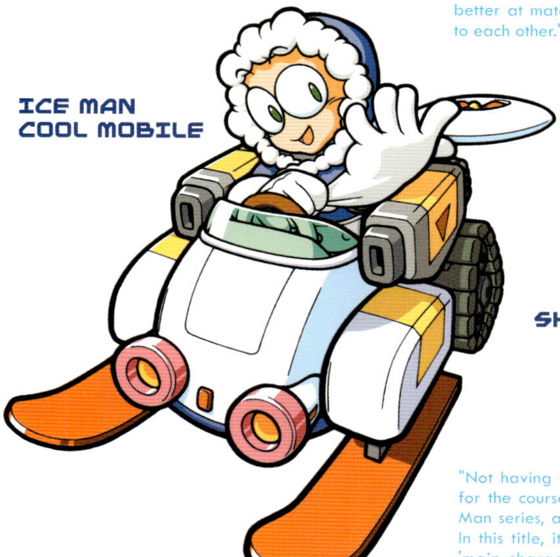

ICE MAN
COOL MOBILE

"I did Roll, Shadow Man, and Guts Man. Ishikawa did Mega Man, Proto Man, Quick Man, Bass, Duo, and Wily. Ice Man, Spring Man, and Napalm Man were handled by someone else. Ishikawa suggested that we try distorting the perspective in our illustrations, so we all focused on that as we worked. I didn't realize how hard it could be to consciously distort perspectives." (Komaki)

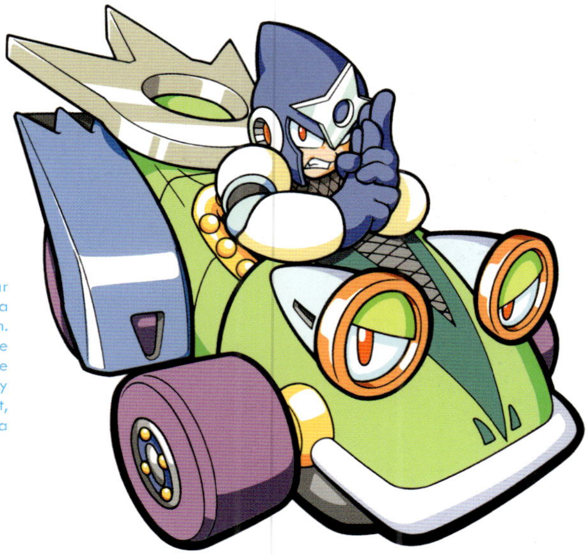

SHADOW MAN
SHINOBI MASTER

"Not having enough time has become par for the course when it comes to the Mega Man series, and this title was no exception. In this title, it's like every character is the 'main character,' and their weapons are pretty interesting. I found it a little scary when the camera swung around really fast, but... the tricks turned out well, and I had a lot of fun." (Hideki)

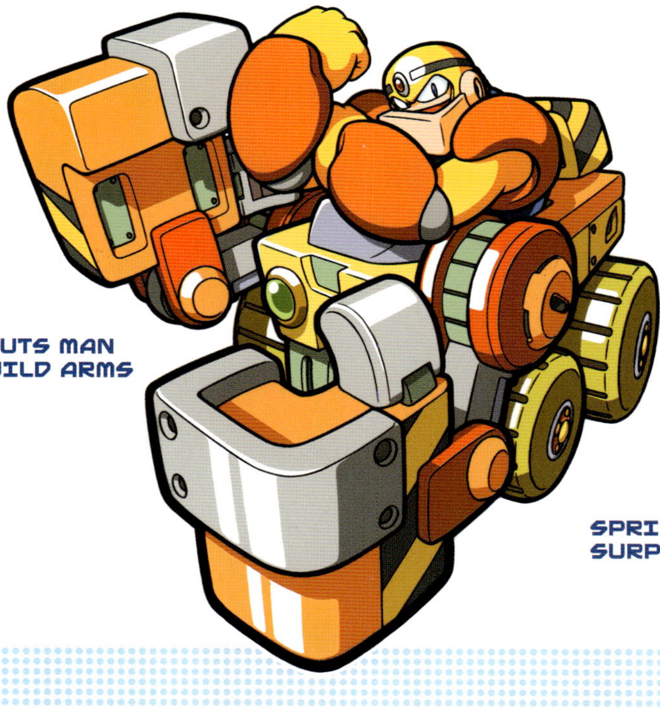

GUTS MAN
WILD ARMS

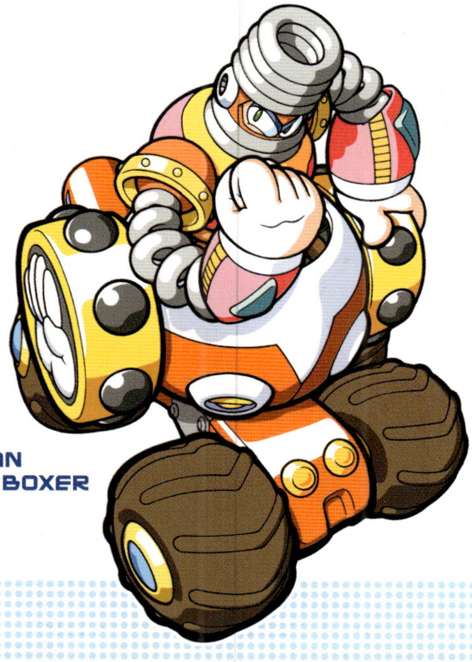

SPRING MAN
SURPRISE BOXER

NAPALM MAN
PATRIOT BOMBER

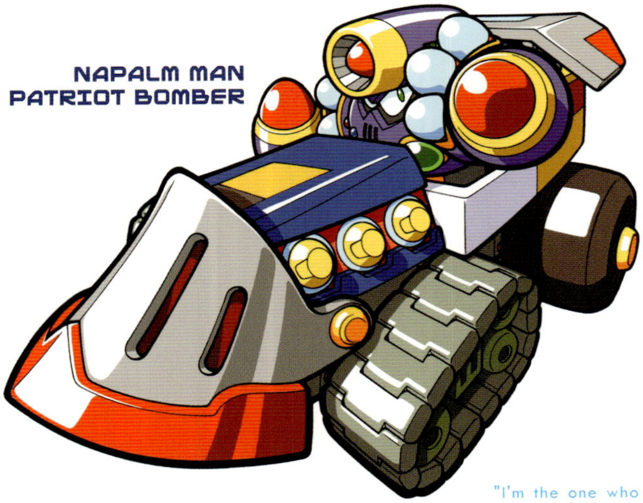

BASS
TREBLE DARKSTAR

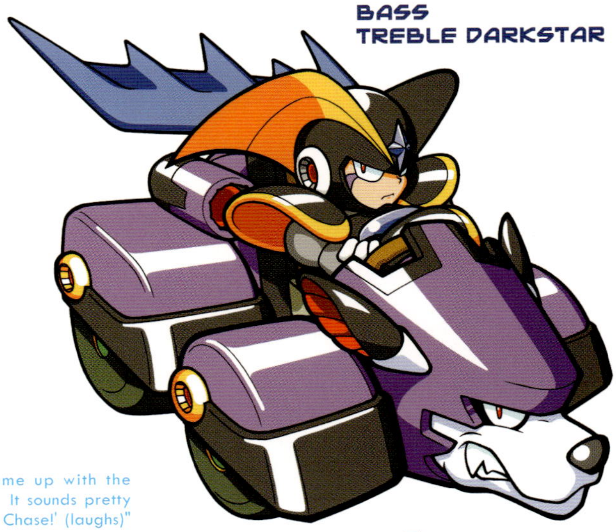

"I'm the one who came up with the title 'Battle & Chase.' It sounds pretty cool, right? 'Battle & Chase!' (laughs)" (Inafune)

DR. WILY
SKULL MACHINE XX

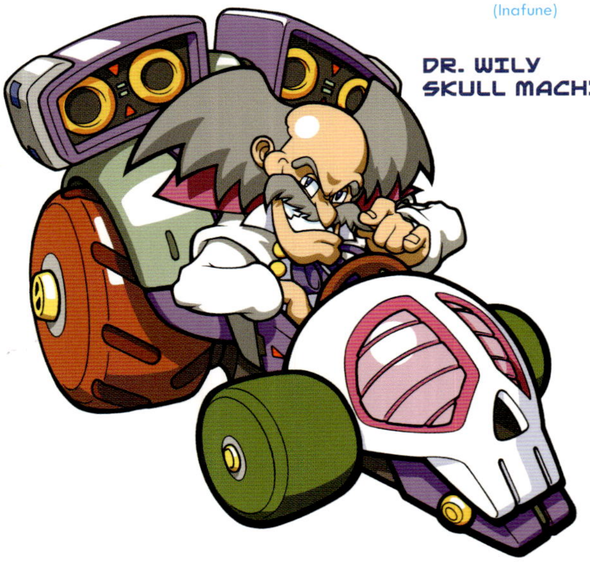

DUO
HARD GRANDEUR

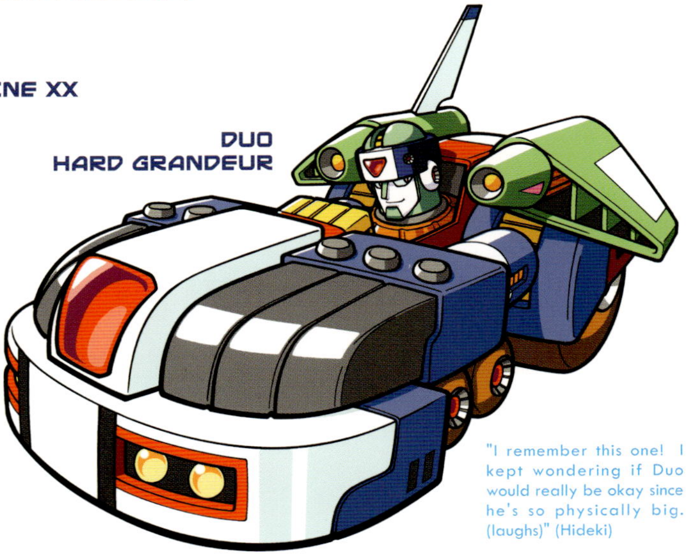

"I remember this one! I kept wondering if Duo would really be okay since he's so physically big. (laughs)" (Hideki)

RIPOT

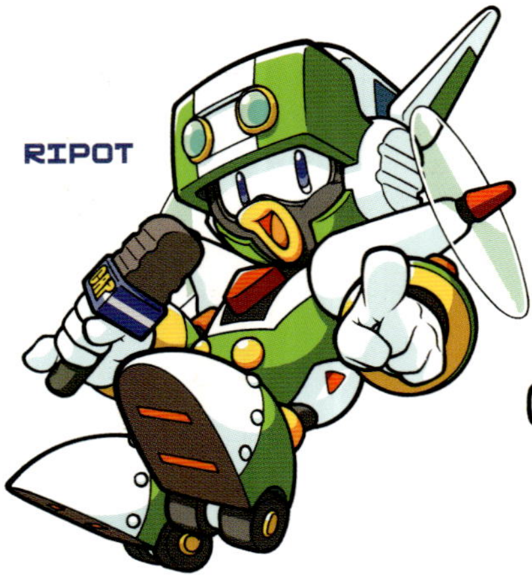

CHEST

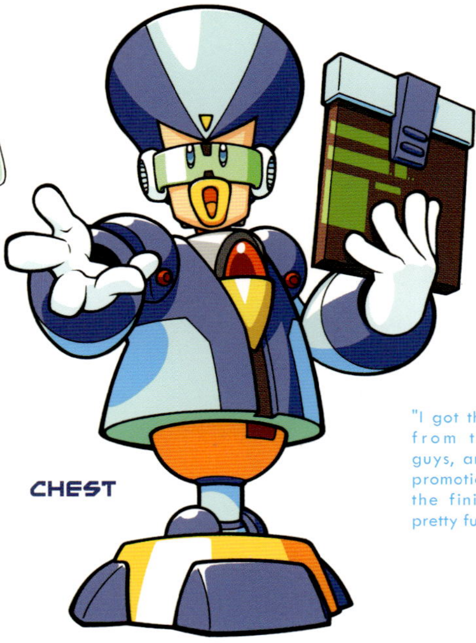

PLUM

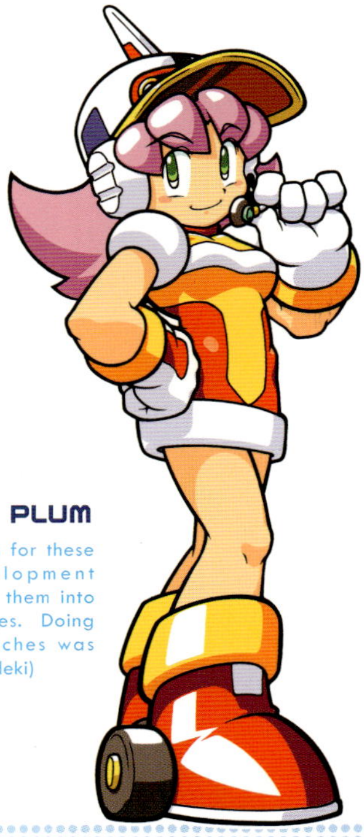

"I got the designs for these from the development guys, and turned them into promotional images. Doing the finishing touches was pretty fun too." (Hideki)

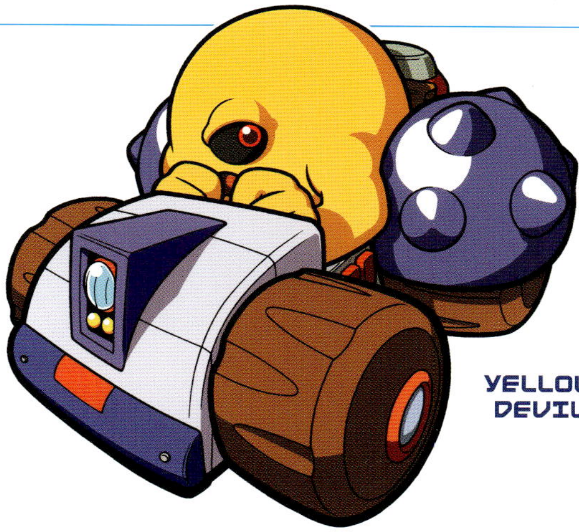

YELLOW DEVIL

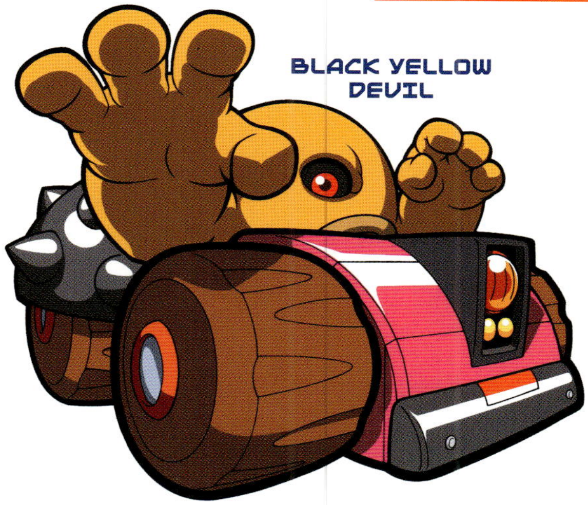

BLACK YELLOW DEVIL

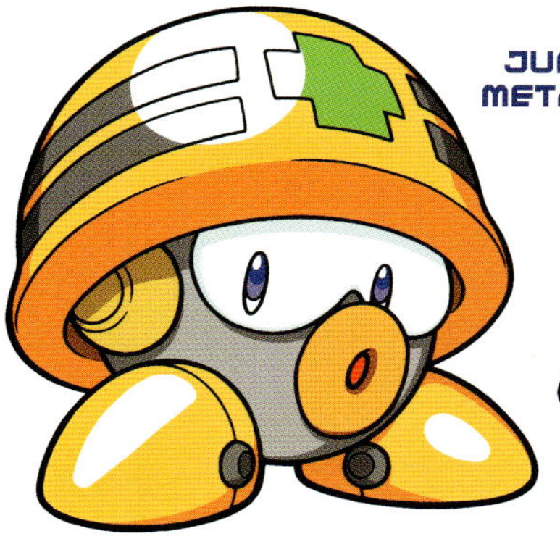

JUMBO METALL F

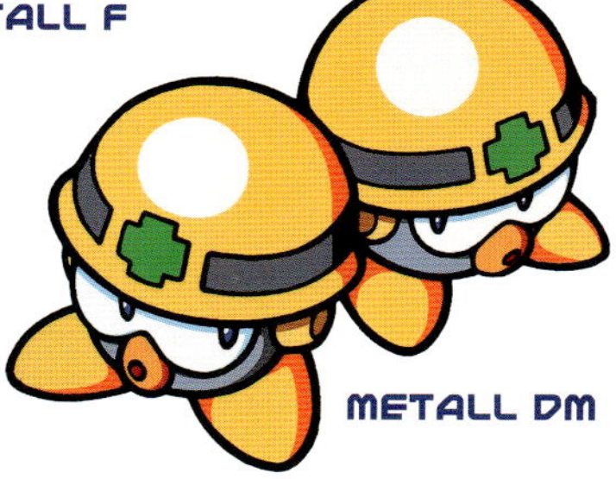

METALL DM

"I drew Black Joe and Black Yellow Devil. I never really understood the whole 'Black Yellow' Devil thing, (laughs) but I guess it just means a Yellow Devil that's a little black?" (Komaki)

"Well, Yellow Devil is Yellow Devil, so we can't make him Black Devil... that's why he's Black Yellow Devil!" (Inafune)

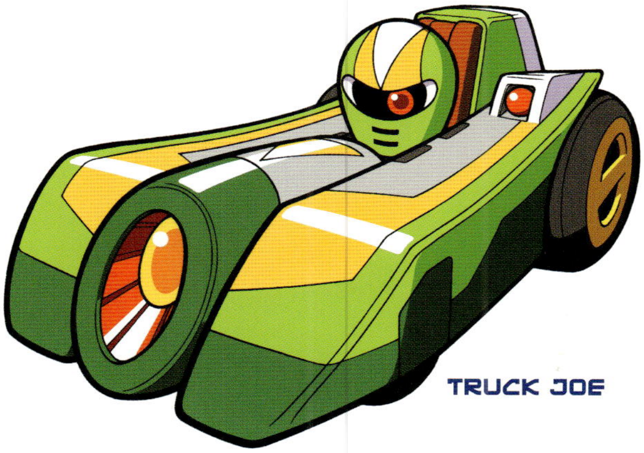

TRUCK JOE

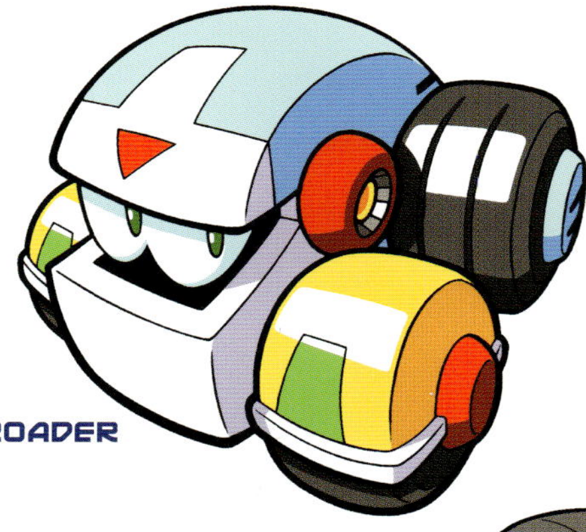

4 ROADER

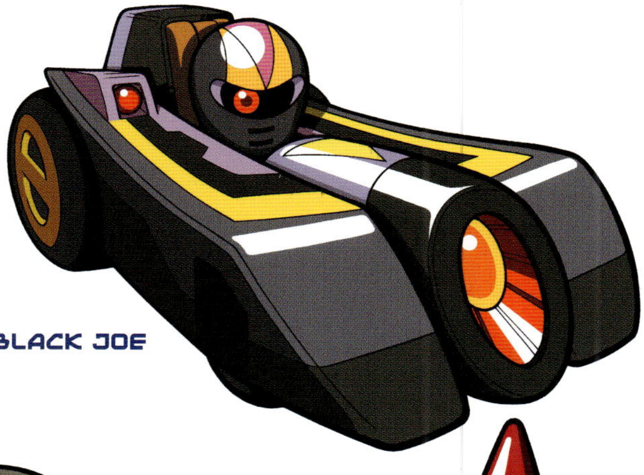

BLACK JOE

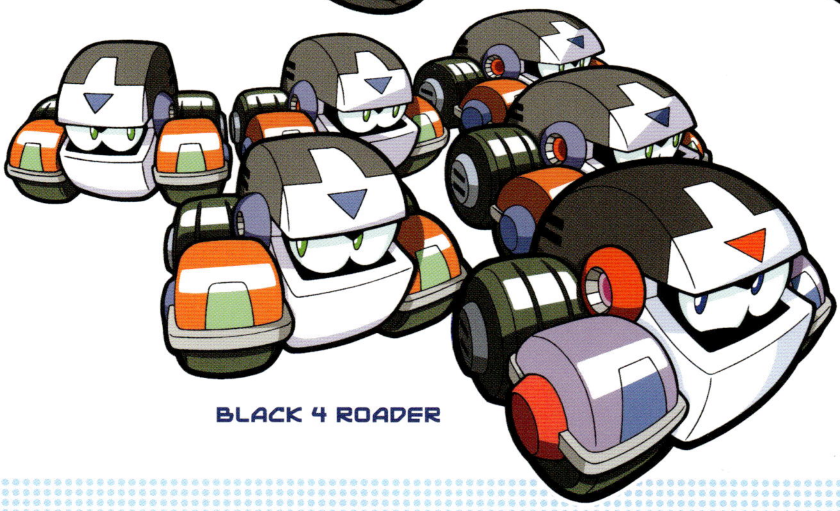

BLACK 4 ROADER

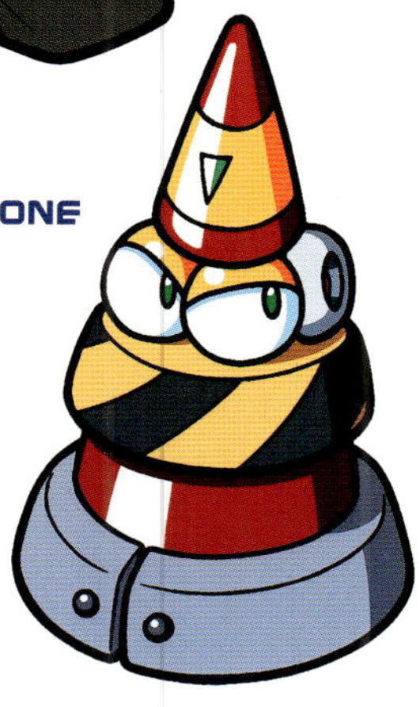

BACCONE

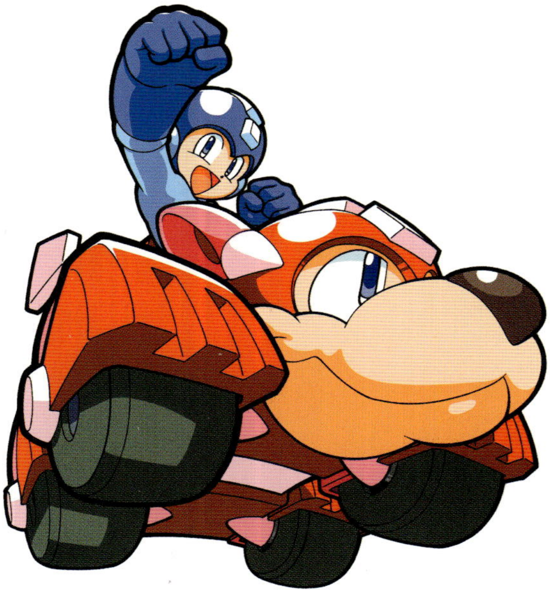

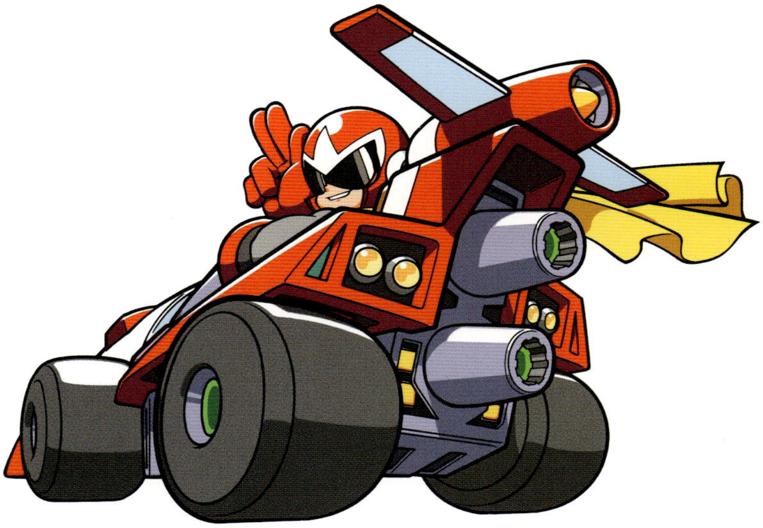

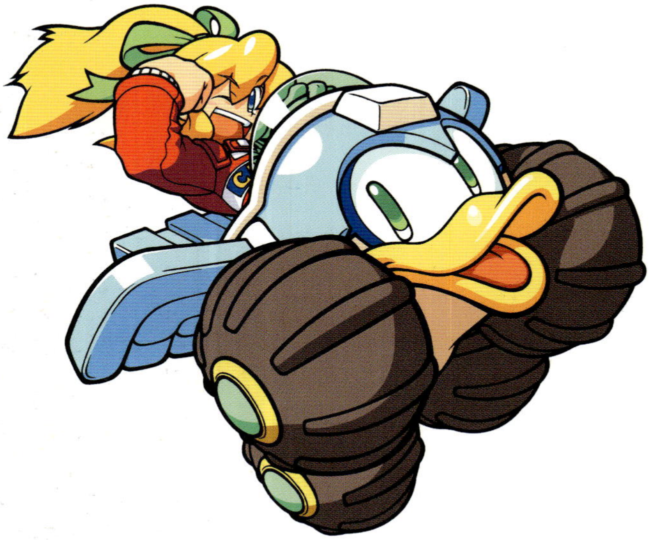

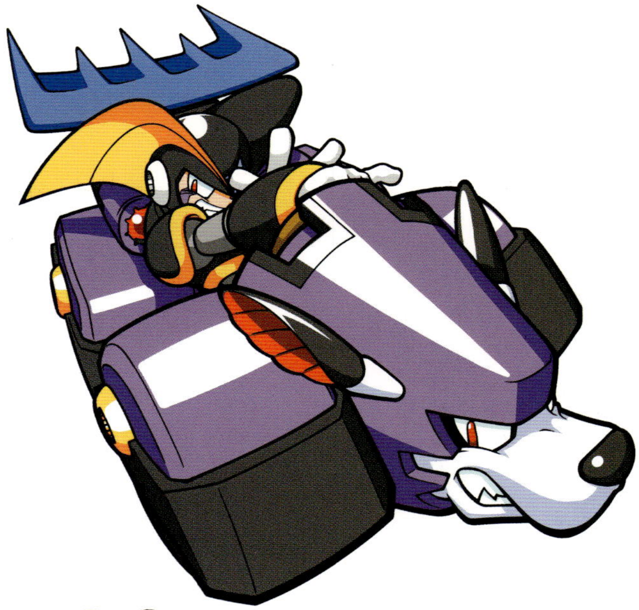

"This Guts Man was done for the overseas versions after we found out his original pose was not acceptable over there. Up to this point, my process involved line drawings, tracing paper, and my Rotring, so having to redraw this was kind of a pain. (laughs)" (Komaki)

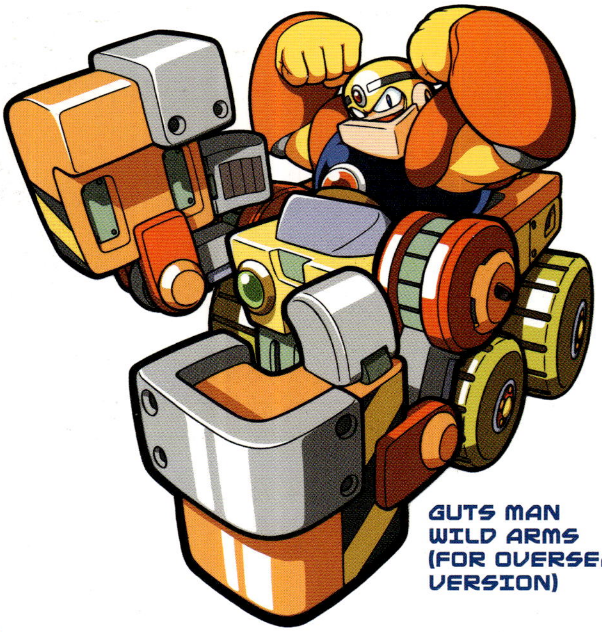

GUTS MAN
WILD ARMS
(FOR OVERSEAS VERSION)

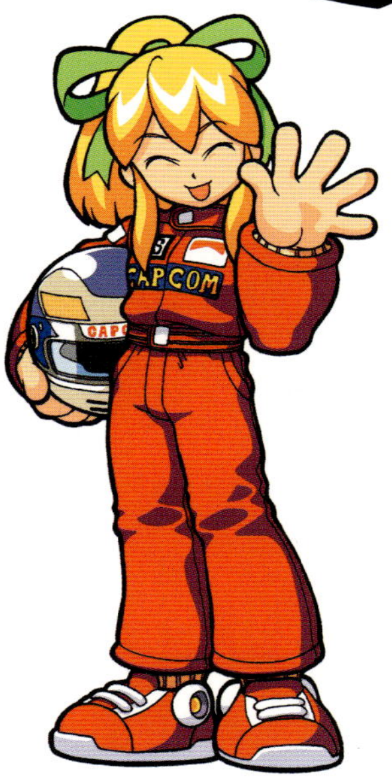

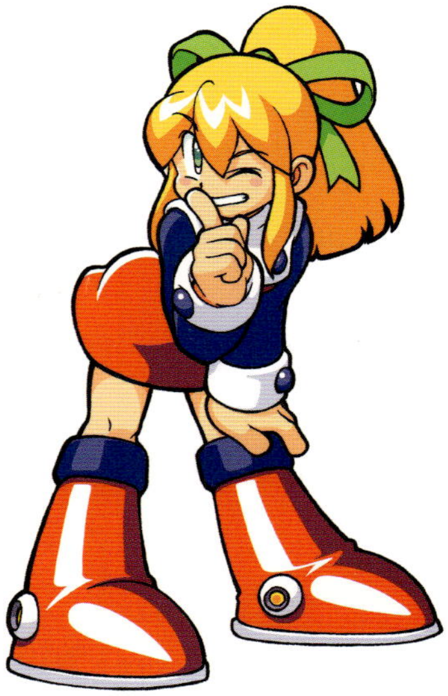

"Ishikawa and I did the images you see here." (Komaki)

"Which ones did Komaki do? Uh... hmm... I can't remember..." (Hideki)

"All of these, except Mega Man and the overseas Guts Man, were done by Ishikawa. (laughs)" (Komaki)

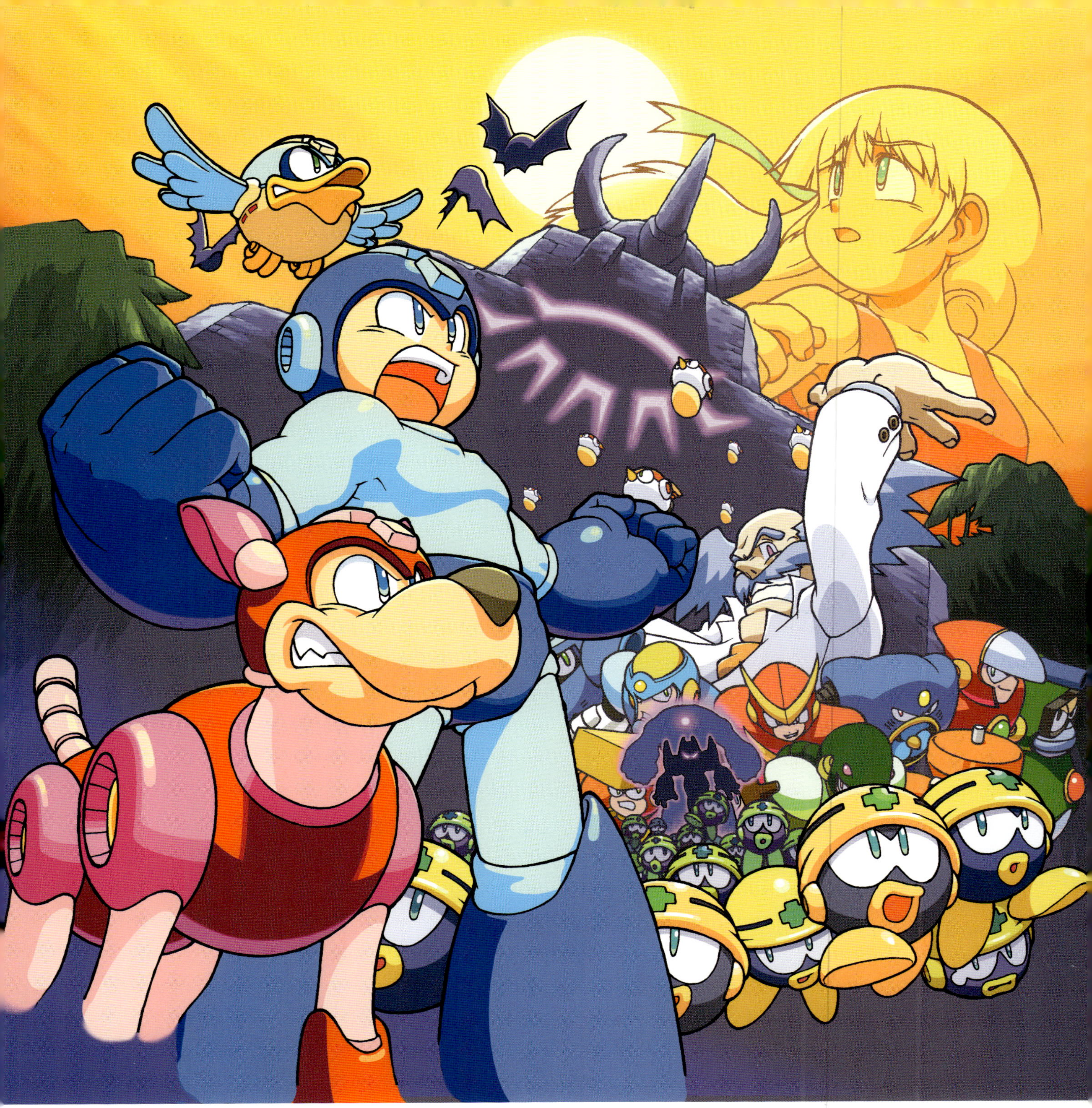

SUPER ADVENTURE ROCKMAN®

スーパーアドベンチャーロックマン

Super Adventure Rockman
PS 06/25/1998 SS 09/23/1998

In the year 20XX, the Lanfront Ruins were discovered in the Amazon rainforest. Dr. Wily headed out to explore the ruins and met the super computer "Ra Moon" there. After finding out about Ra Moon's unique abilities, Dr. Wily pieced together another plan to take over the world using a special electromagnetic pulse. In order to save Earth from this new threat, Mega Man and his friends set their sights on the source of the pulse, the "Temple of Moon" at the center of the ruins.

"To be honest, I feel I owe the players an apology for this one. There was a phase when the company was basically selling Mega Man to the lowest bidder, and I really feel like this title is the worst of the worst. The one who was responsible for the whole project quit rather suddenly, and it was pretty much dropped into my lap. By that time, though, it was at a stage where I couldn't really make any big changes to it. The ultimate unspoken rule about making a game that is geared towards children is that you simply cannot kill anyone, but here you have military helicopters falling out of the sky and people dying in droves. If it had been up to me, I would have at least made it so they all 'got away safely' via parachutes or something. Then, as if that wasn't bad enough, Roll dies... and to top it all off, the whole world is destroyed! I was like, 'Did they really need to go that far!?' I will never let them do something like this ever again. If we, as developers, start getting confused about what 'safe for children' means, we'd not only be betraying our players, but I'd feel like I was betraying every single creator that ever put time into this series." (Inafune)

"All I heard was, 'We don't have a package illustration!' as they dropped this bomb on me. I remember I was wondering what the actual story of the game was as I drew this. I'm really sorry... I didn't have enough time, and I knew they'd crop it anyway, so I didn't draw Rush's legs all the way. (laughs)" (Hideki)

ROCKMAN COMPLETE WORKS (PLAYSTATION)

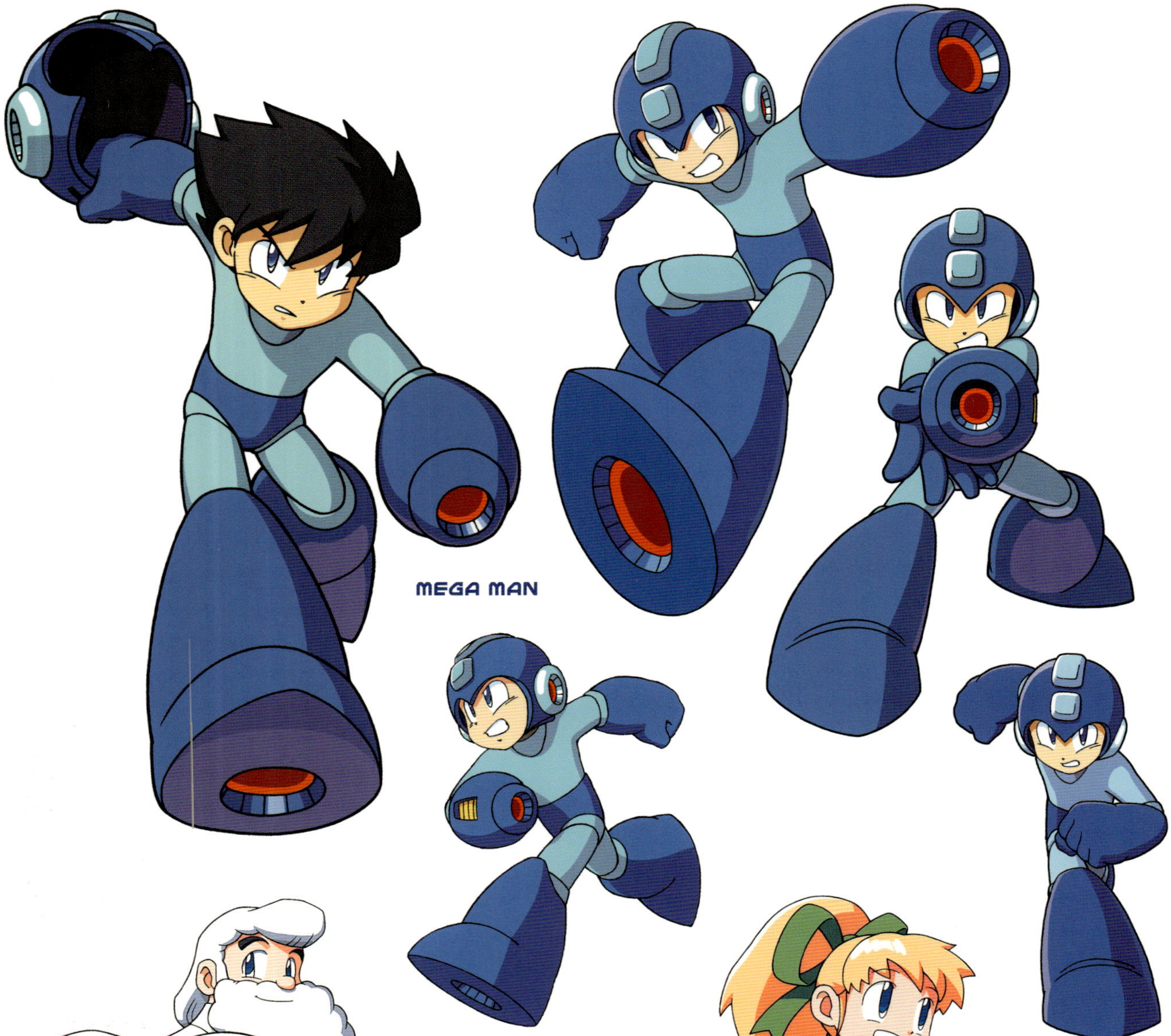

MEGA MAN

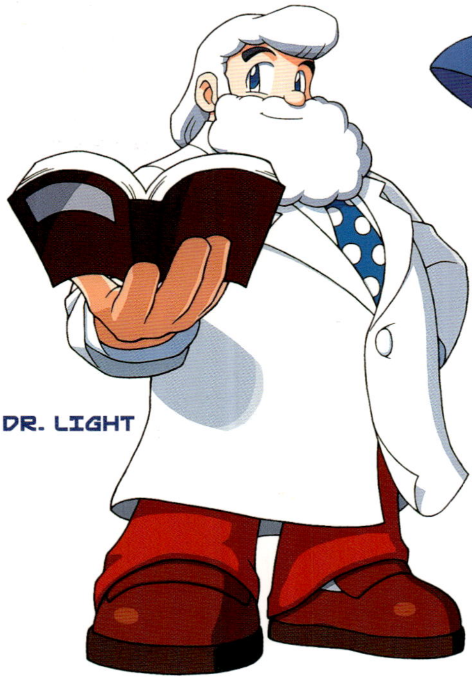

DR. LIGHT

"I drew Rush based on Roll, so I think they pretty much click into place when they're next to each other. I drew Roll's hair this way because I thought, 'I wonder if Roll's hair would get tousled when she runs.' But I may have made the wrong decision. I'm worried that people could think this is just how her hair looks all the time... though I think she looks pretty cute like this, too." (Higurashi)

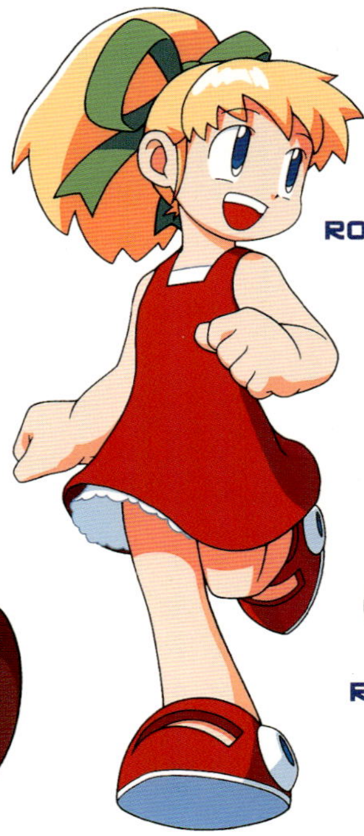

ROLL

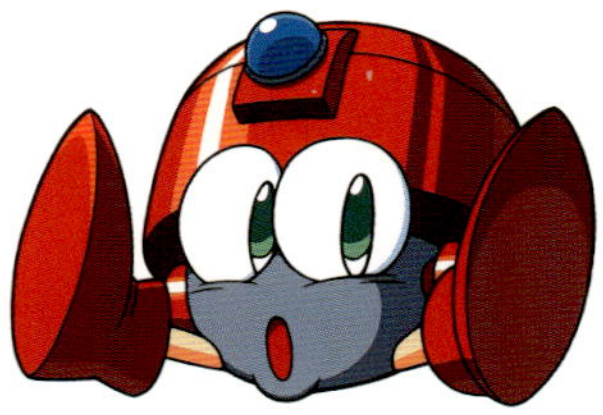

EDDIE

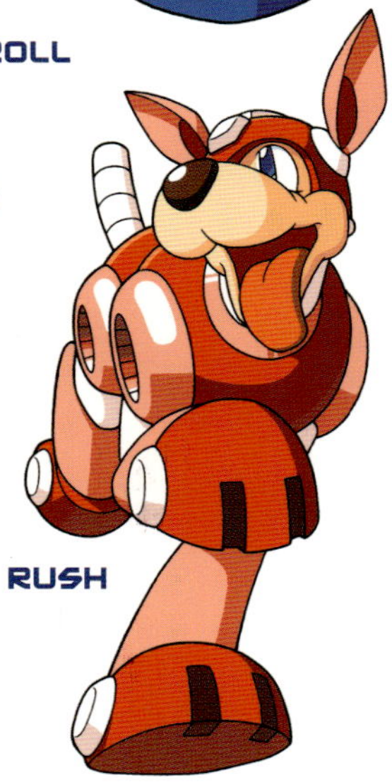

RUSH

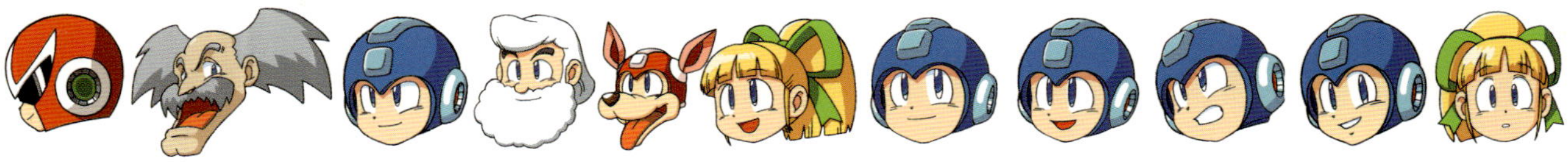

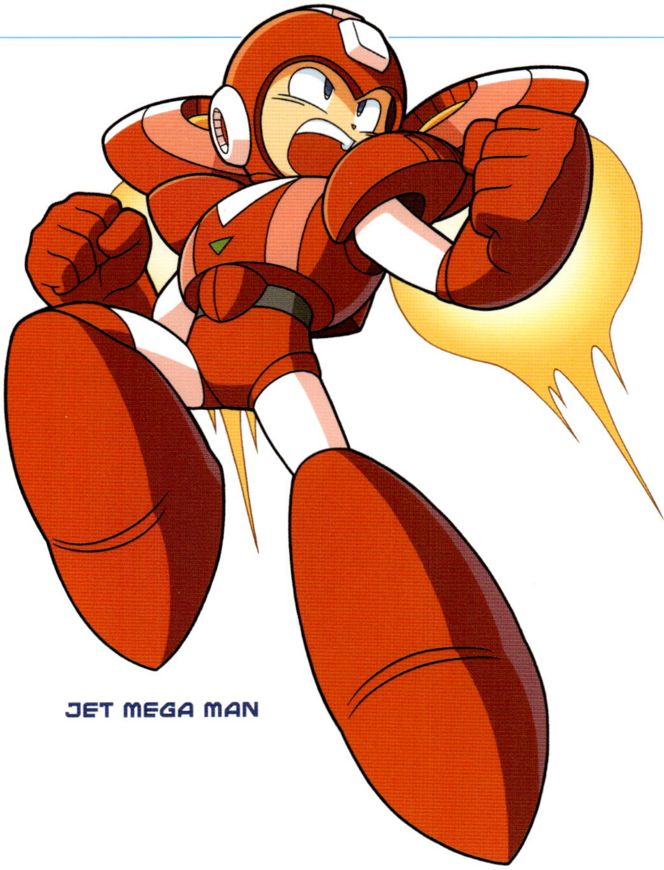

JET MEGA MAN

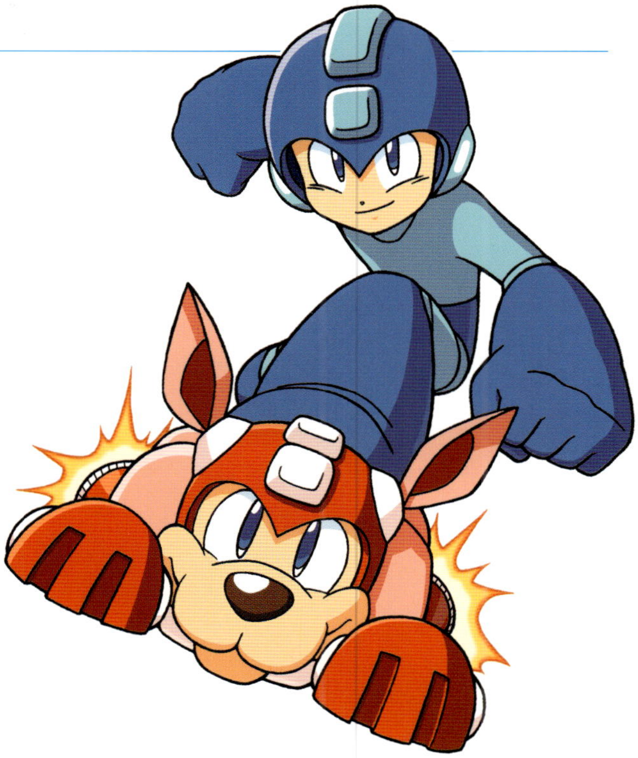

"I find it difficult to look at a lot of my old drawings... but not the ones I actually enjoyed doing! The drawings I did for the PS, for example, always bring a smile to my face even if I think I didn't do a very good job. Even in unused pieces like this Light & Rock & Roll one, I really like the facial expressions. Back then, taking a day off of work was something I never considered, and I remember commuting to the offices on my days off." (Higurashi)

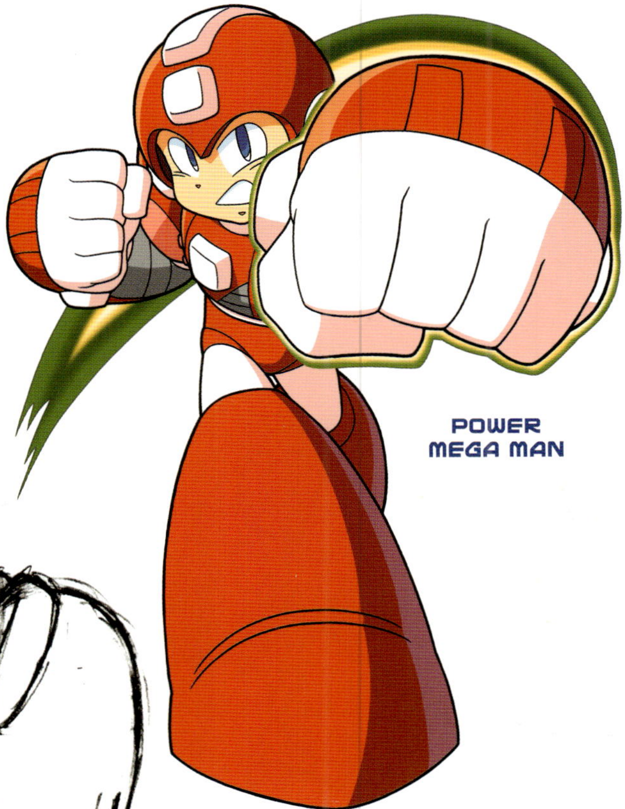

POWER MEGA MAN

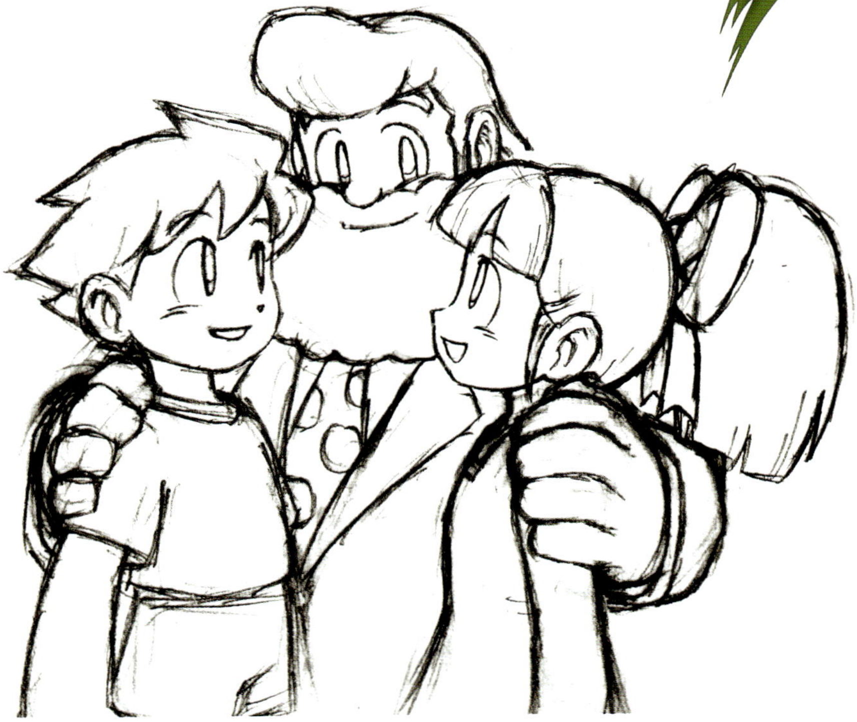

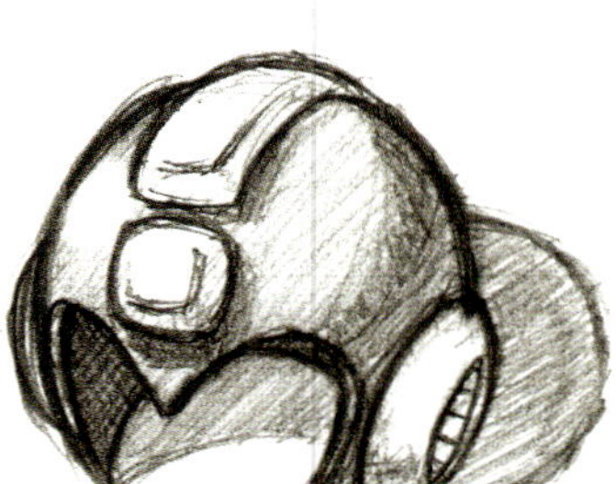

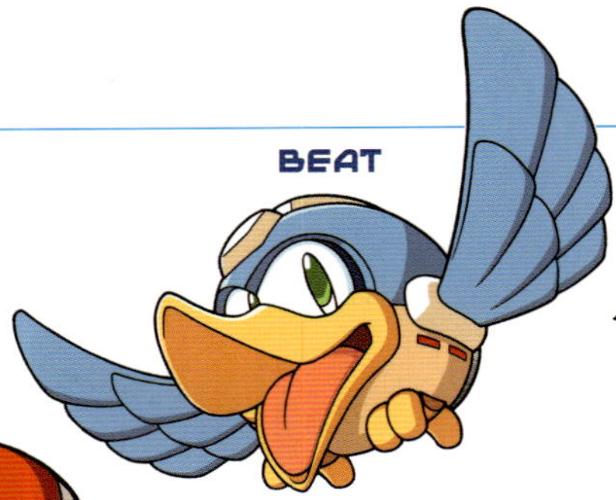

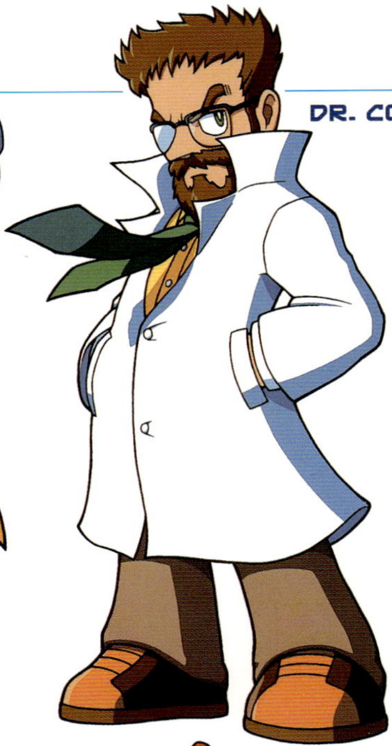

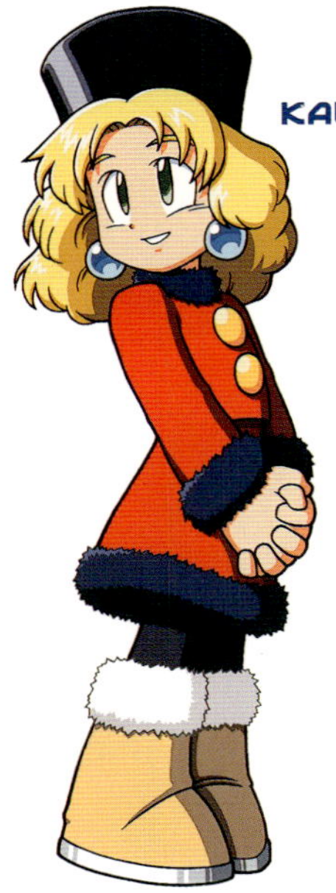

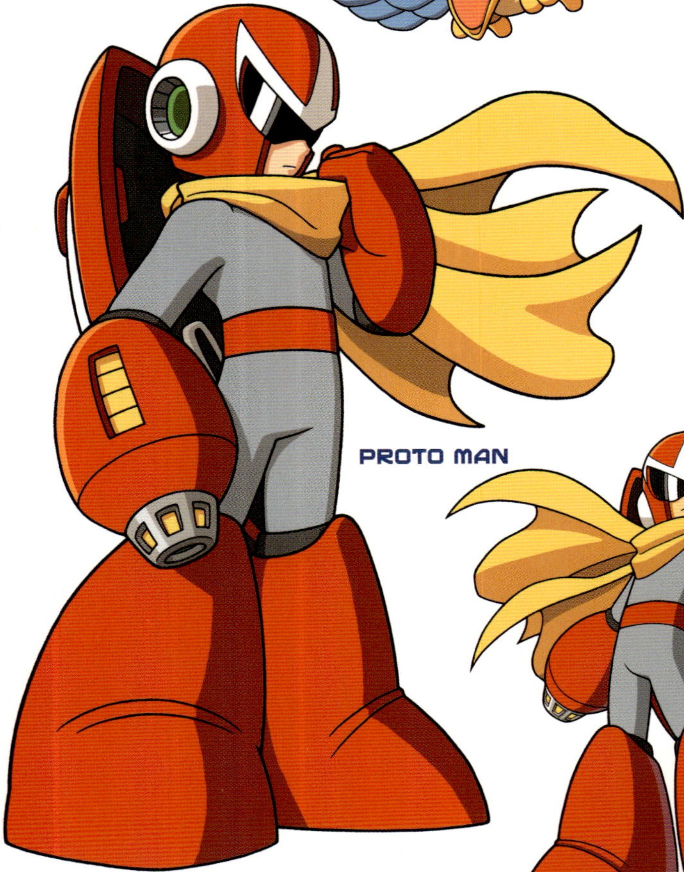

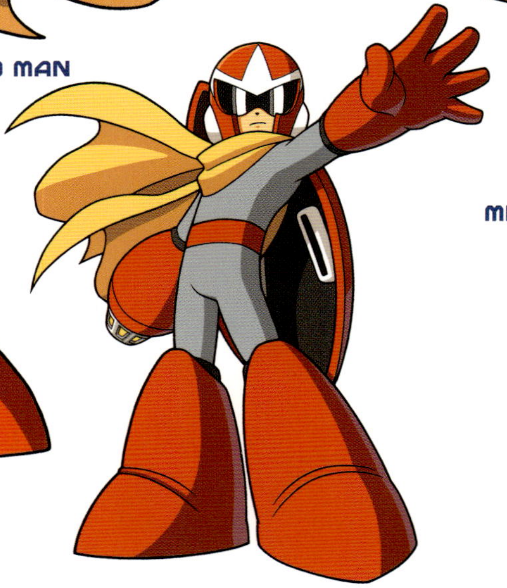

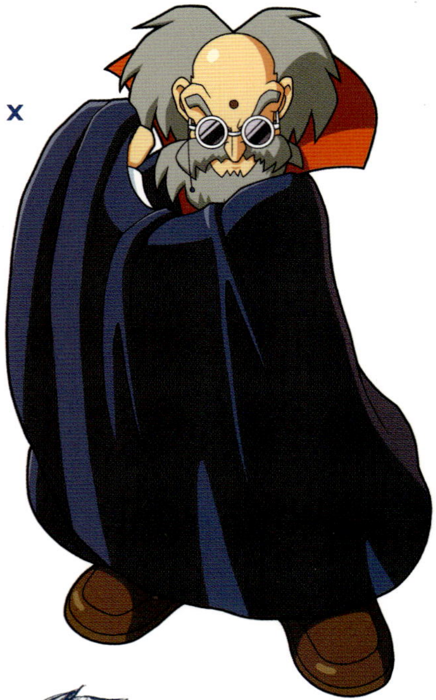

"I like the colorless Cossack the most. Out of the entire series, '4' is my absolute favorite. I loved everything about it, including the game, the music, and the subtitle 'A New Ambition!!' It all made me so excited! Not to mention the new character, Cossack. All of it. Just... all of it! I couldn't tell you how many times I cleared that game." (Higurashi)

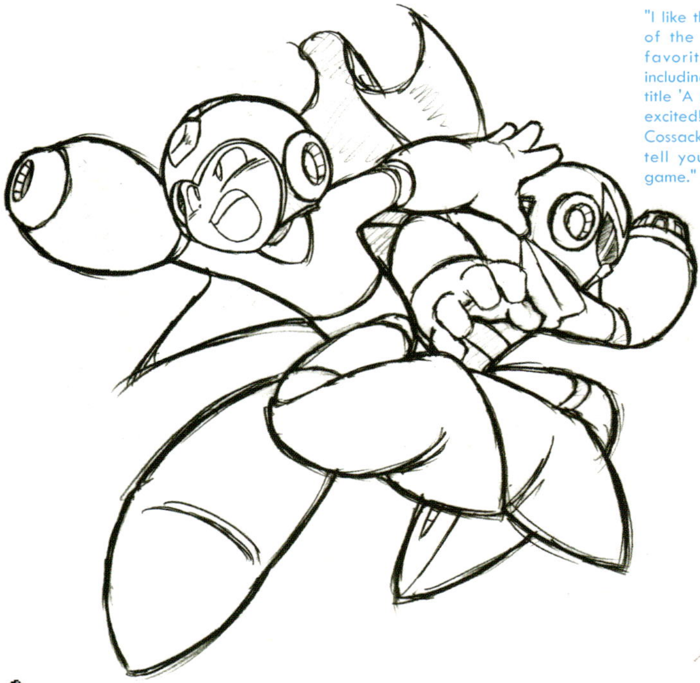

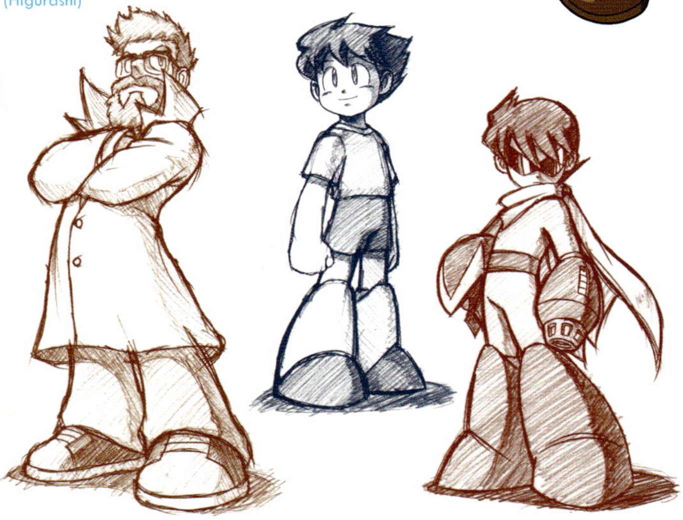

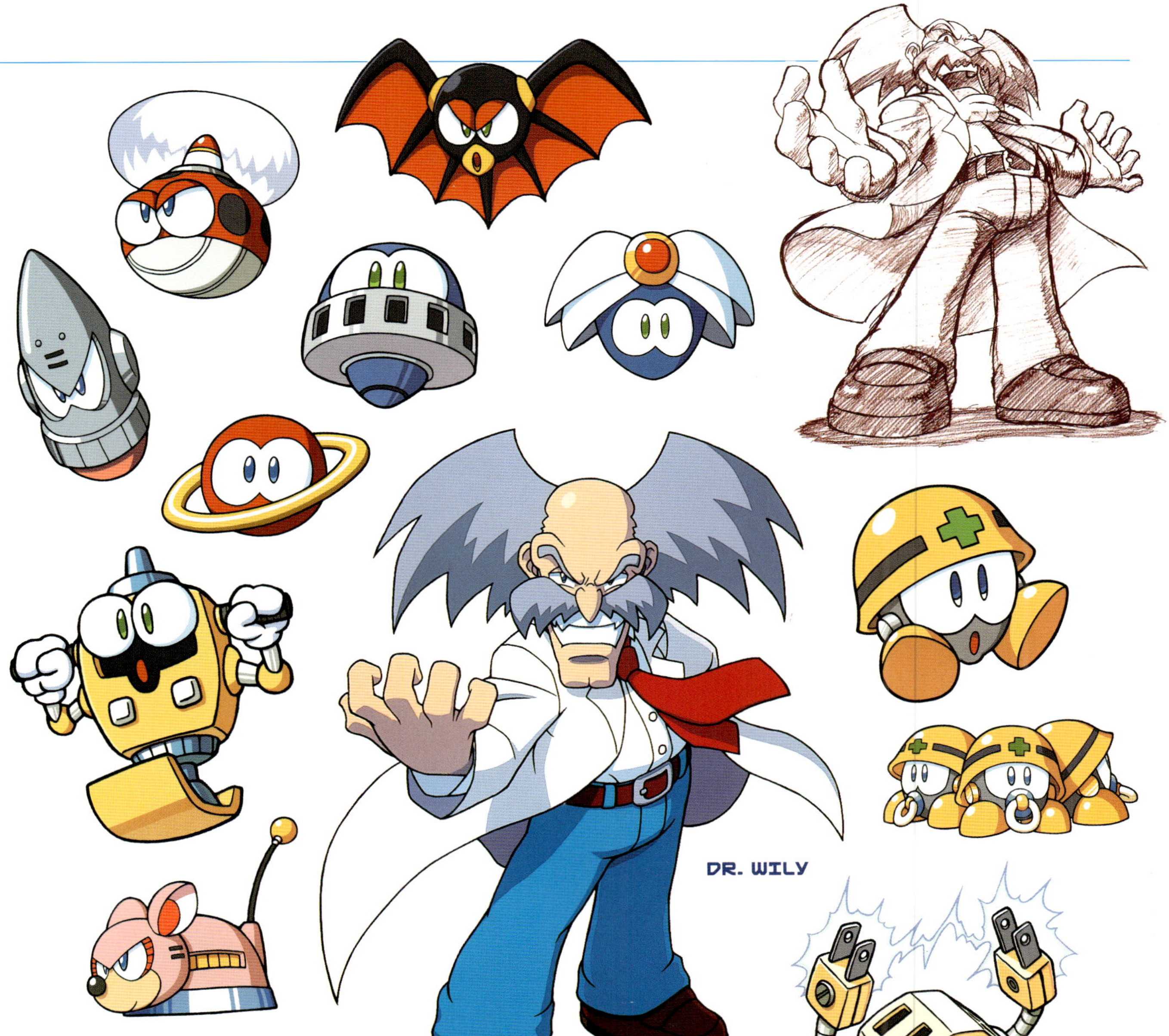

"You can almost see how much fun I had drawing these minor enemy characters! To make it easier to fit them into the manual, I mostly chose to draw characters that would easily fit into squares. Bubukan and Shigaraky were the only ones I chose based solely on personal preference! Shigaraky's so cute! I can't stand it! I wish I had a little Shigaraky doll!" (Higurashi)

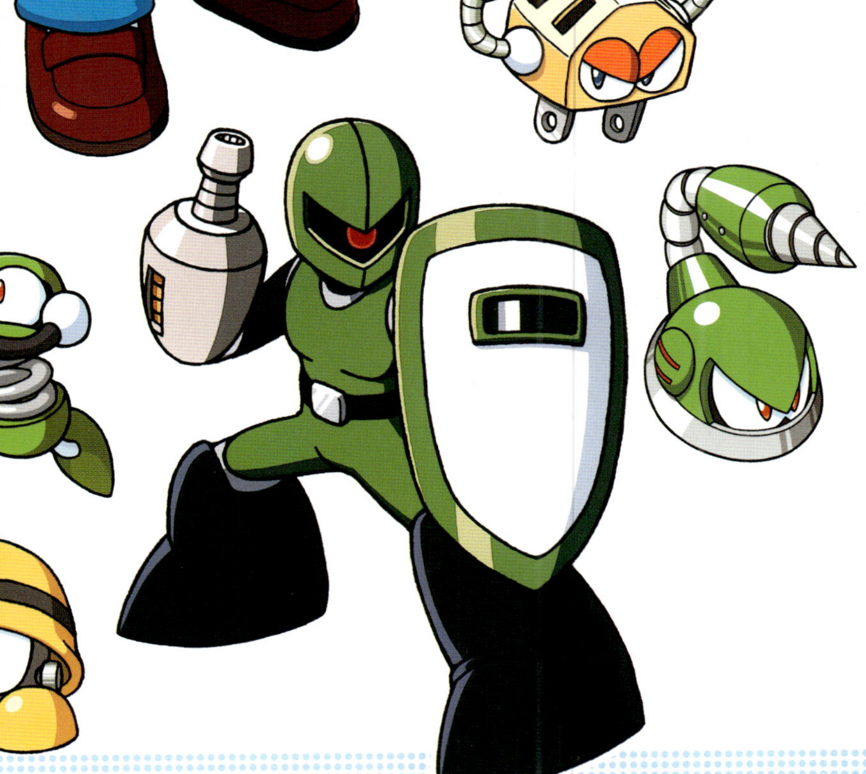

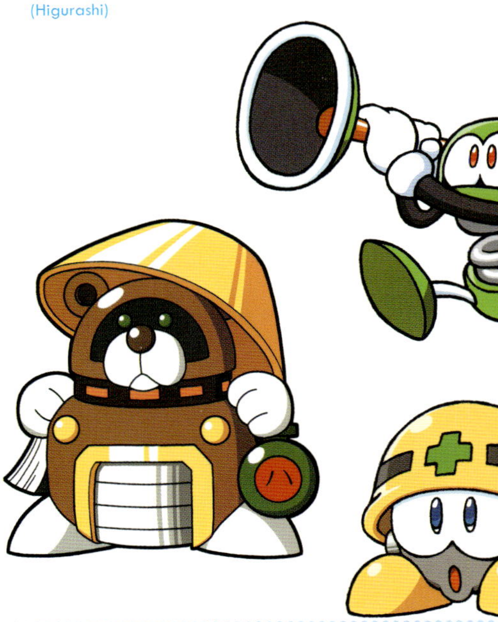

ロックマン

Rockman
PS 08/05/1999

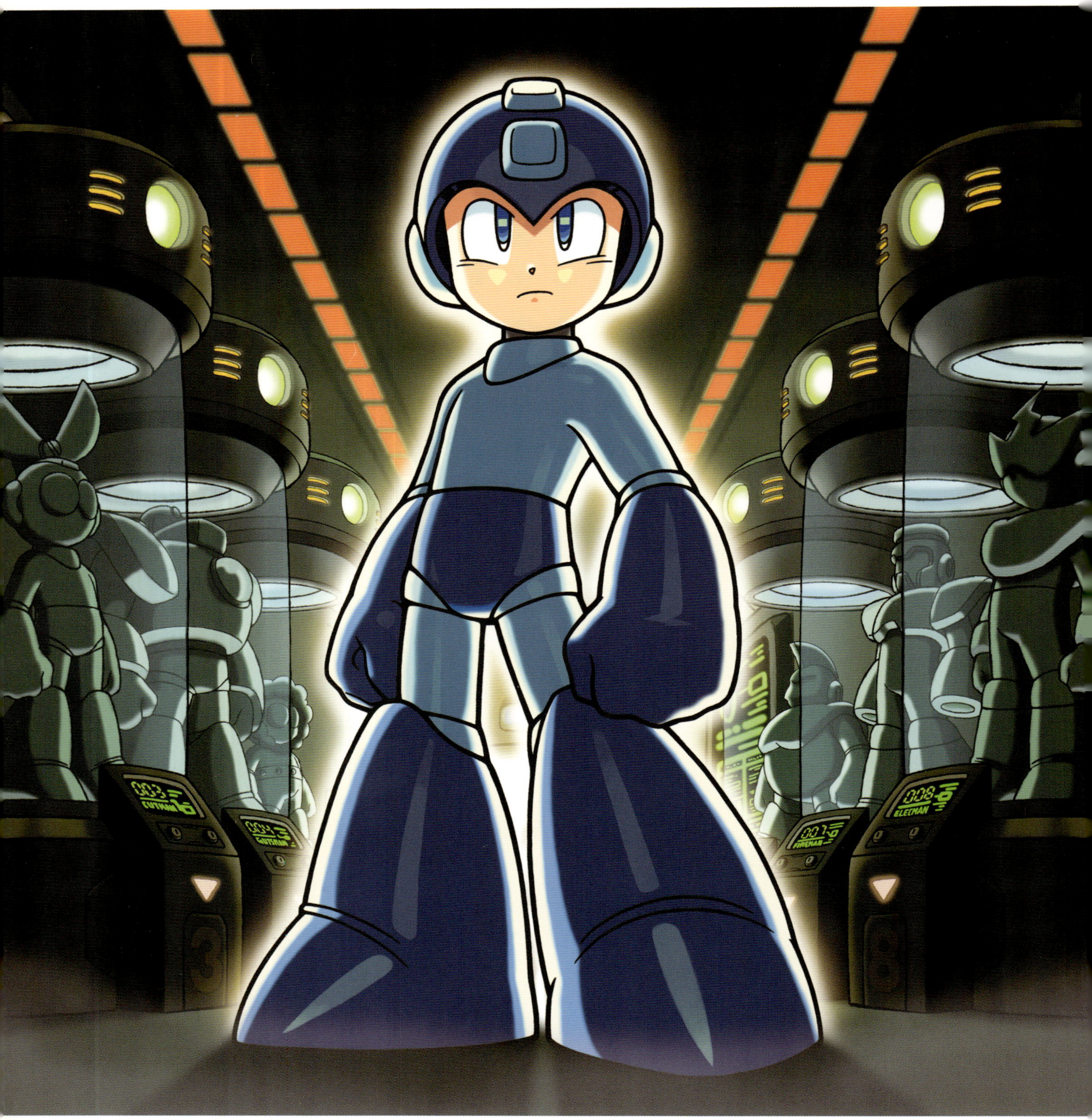

"Initially, we had decided that I would do the main illustrations for all of the odd-numbered titles, and Ishikawa would do the main illustrations for all the even-numbered titles, but due to scheduling issues I ended up doing the illustrations for 1, 3, and 6. The main illustration for '1' was supposed to be Mega Man as he infiltrated Wily's manufacturing plant. Since Guts Man gets mass produced towards the end of the game, I thought maybe they had a room like this in the factory." (Higurashi)

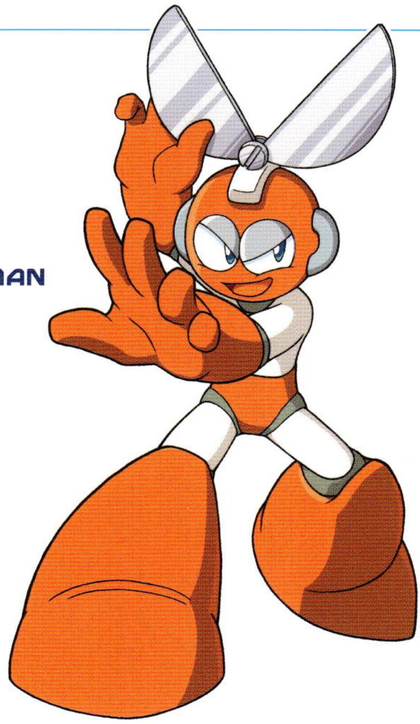

CUT MAN

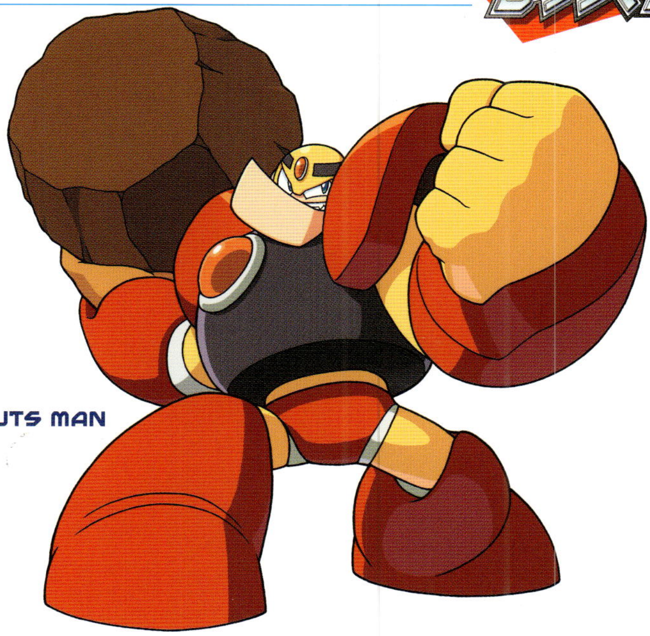

GUTS MAN

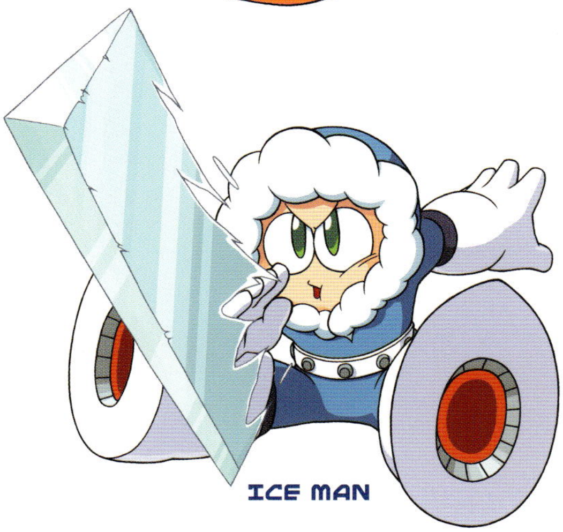

ICE MAN

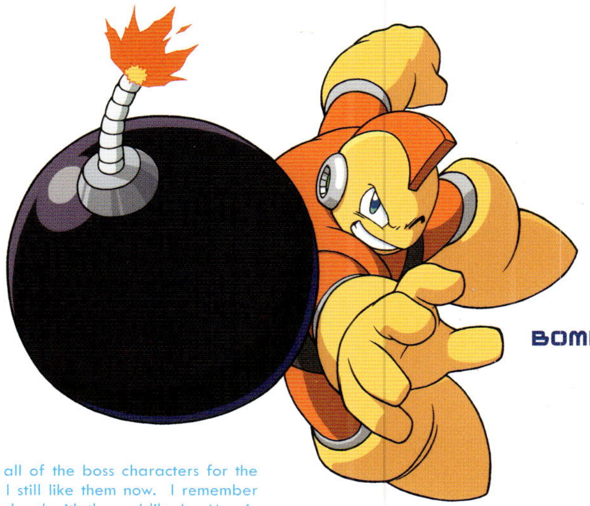

BOMB MAN

"I drew all of the boss characters for the PS, and I still like them now. I remember trying so hard with them. I like Ice Man in particular, since I think he turned out quite cute... though I did struggle quite a bit with the perspective angles on his Ice Slasher. (laughs) I based the look of Fire Man's Fire Storm on the way it looked when Mega Man used it, since there were no illustrations of the special weapons for the PS version." (Higurashi)

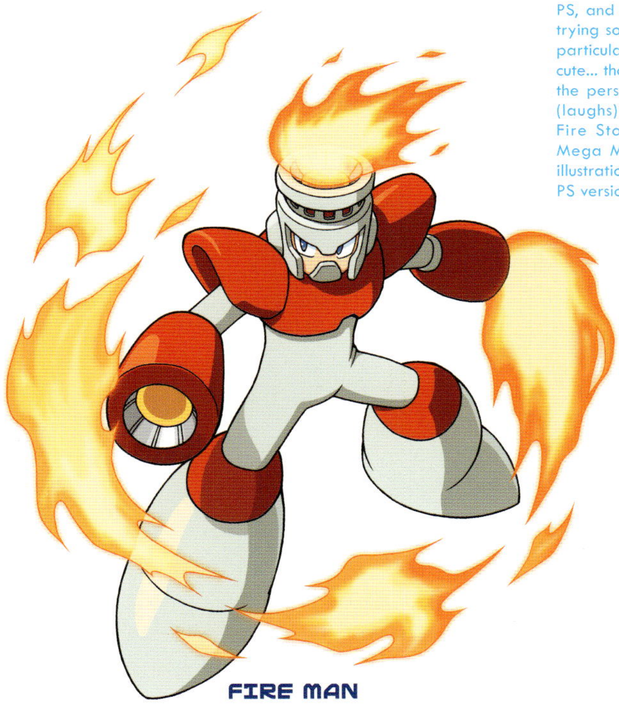

FIRE MAN

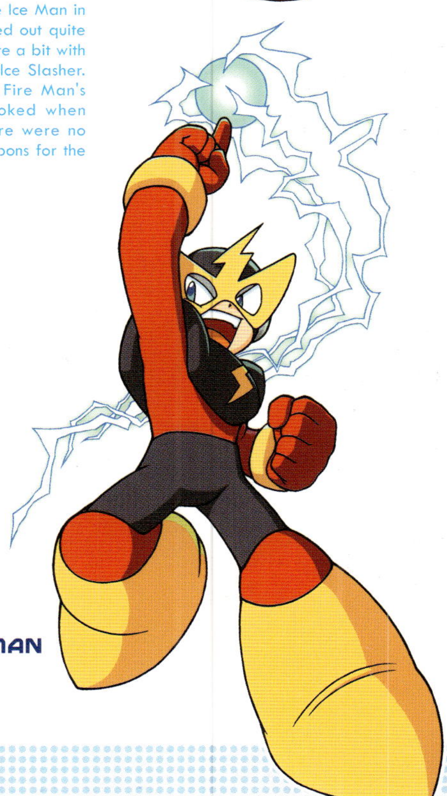

ELEC MAN

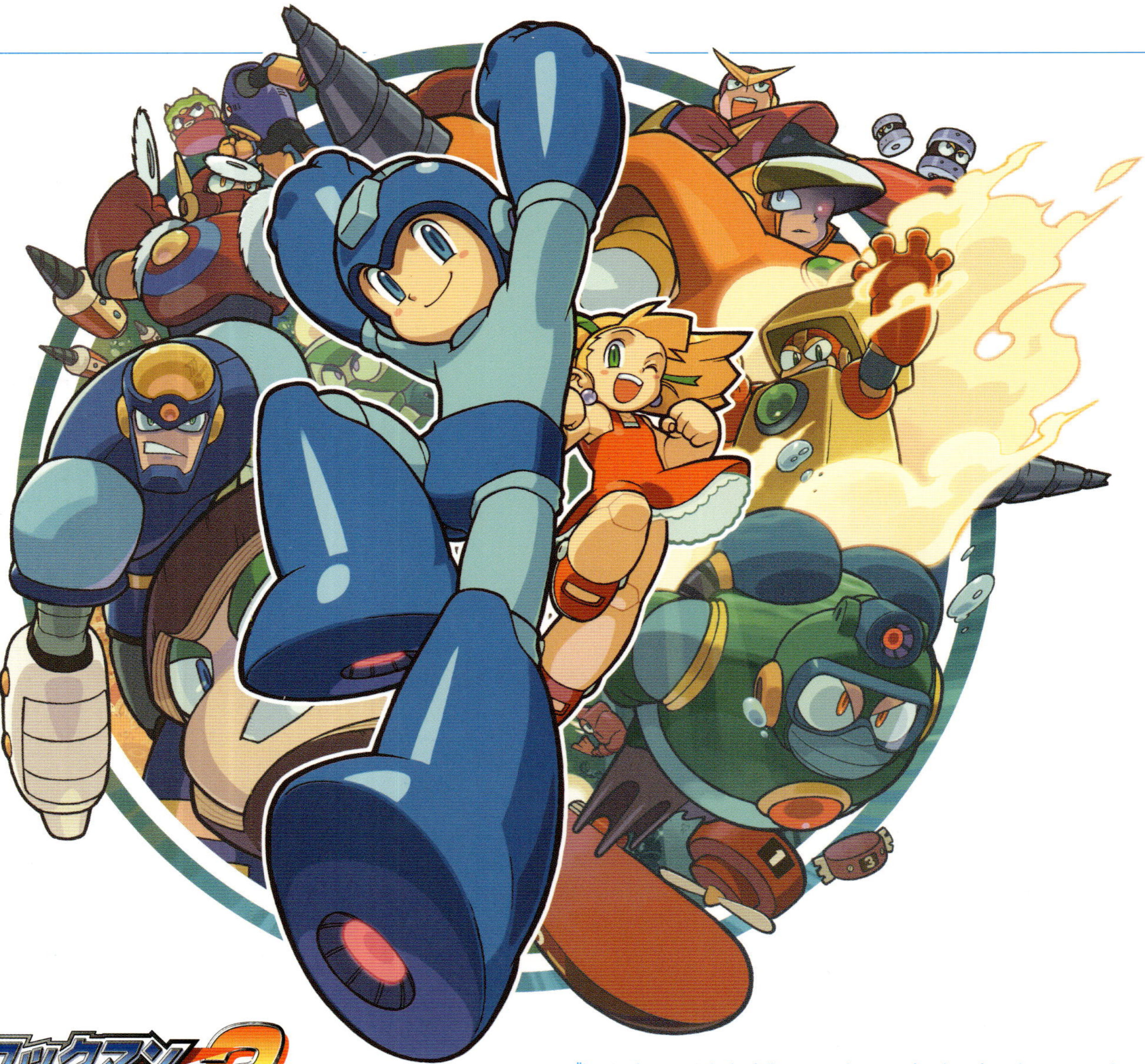

Rockman 2: The Secret of Dr. Wily
PS 09/02/1999

"I noticed a certain lack of illustrations that sort of radiate from the center, and that's why I decided to do this one in this style. Of the entire series, '2' was my favorite. I just loved the Metal Blade. It gave you so much freedom with its blades shooting out in eight directions like, 'gyrrrn gyrrrn!' You could jump, and if there were enemies standing where you were planning on landing, it wouldn't matter because you'd just be like, 'gyrrrn!' (laughs)" (Hideki)

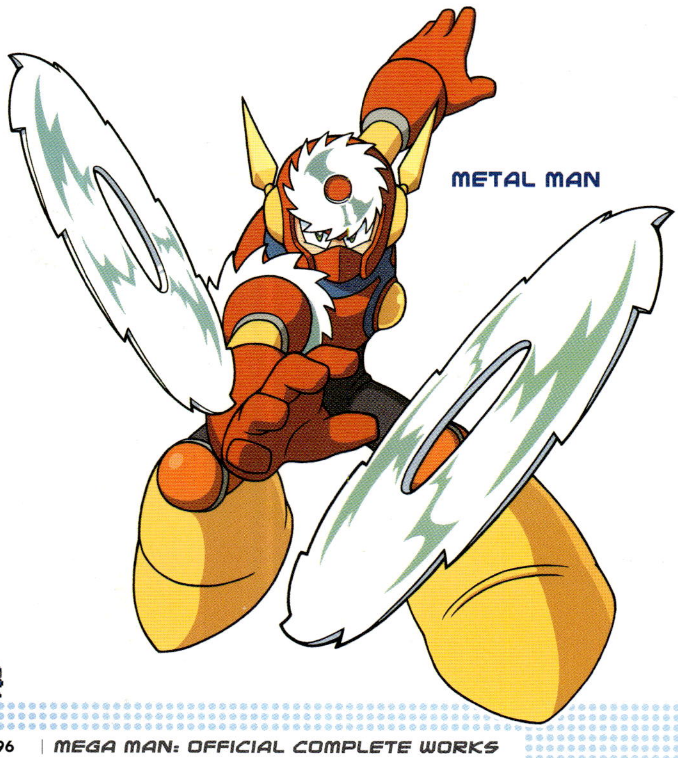

METAL MAN

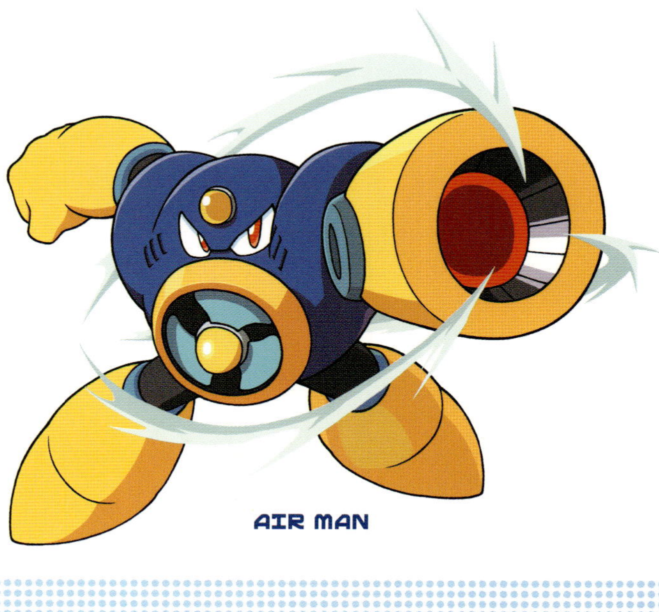

AIR MAN

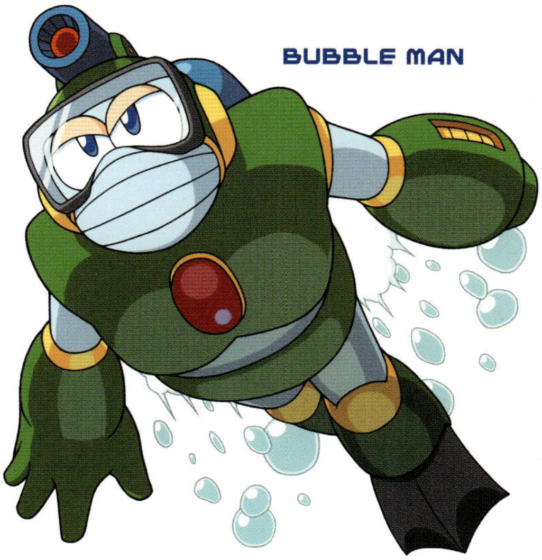

BUBBLE MAN

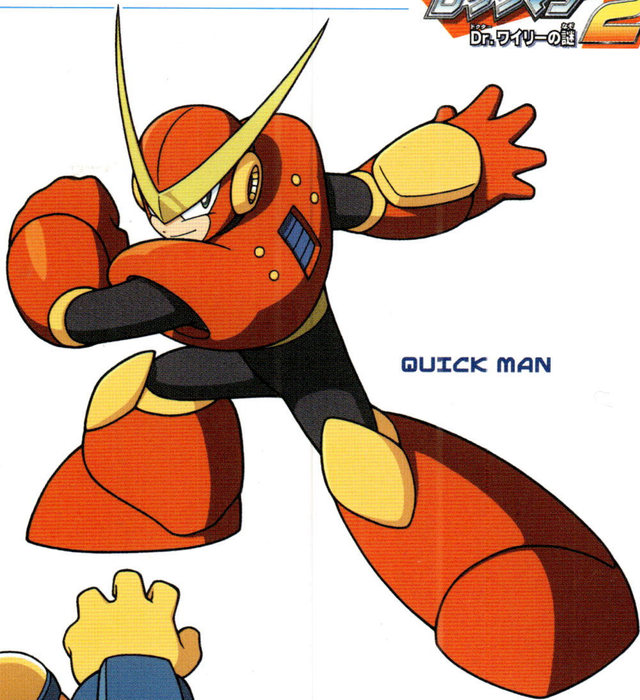

QUICK MAN

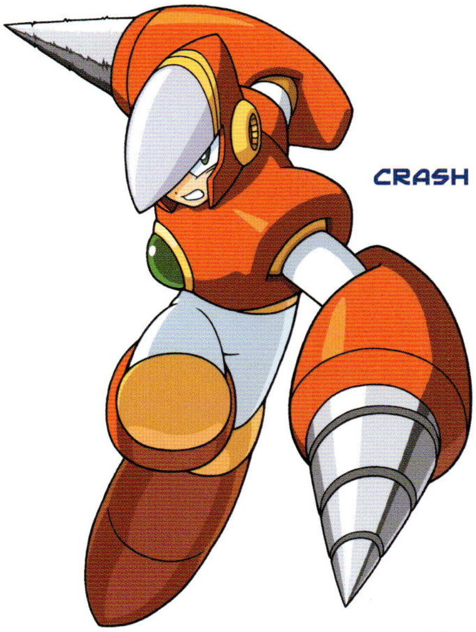

CRASH MAN

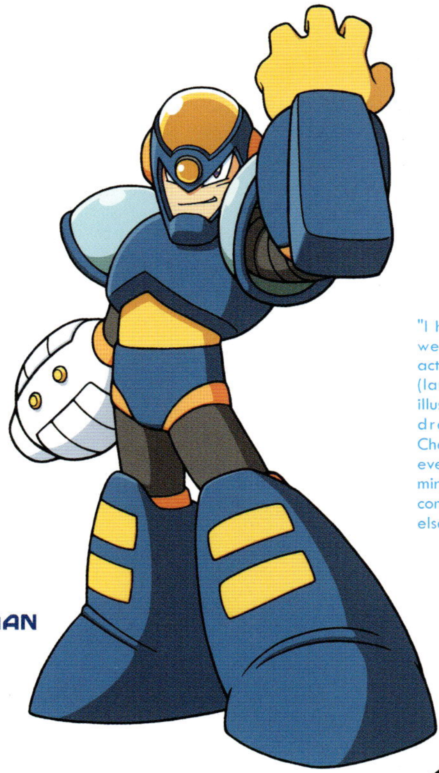

FLASH MAN

"I had to draw all eight boss characters in one week... it was crazy. Metal Man's eyes are actually red, but they somehow turned out green. (laughs) You can see Quick Man's back in my illustration, and the reason why I felt comfortable drawing his back was because I saw the Character Files [later in this book], which showed every side of him. I remember going out of my mind when I saw these files soon after joining the company. I was, after all, just a fan like anyone else. (laughs)" (Higurashi)

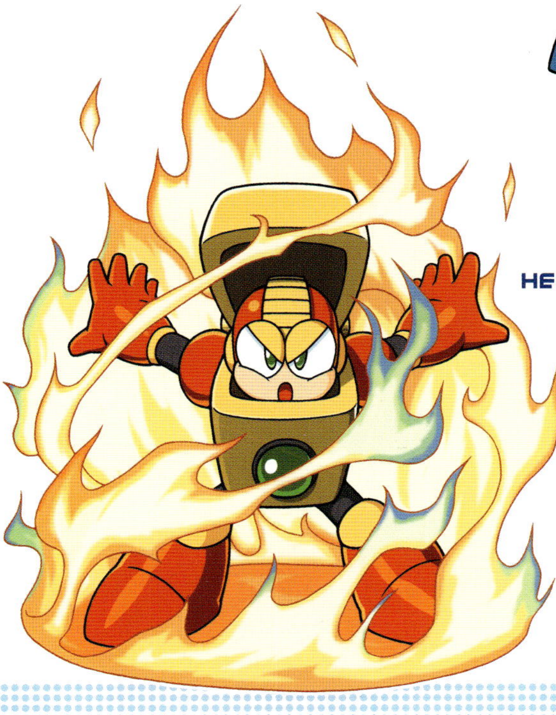

HEAT MAN

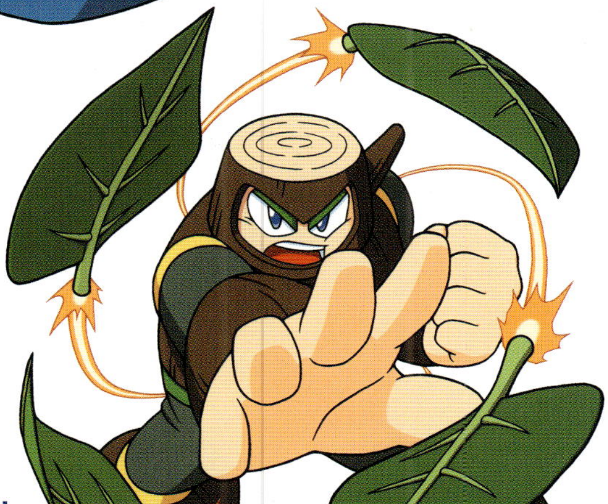

WOOD MAN

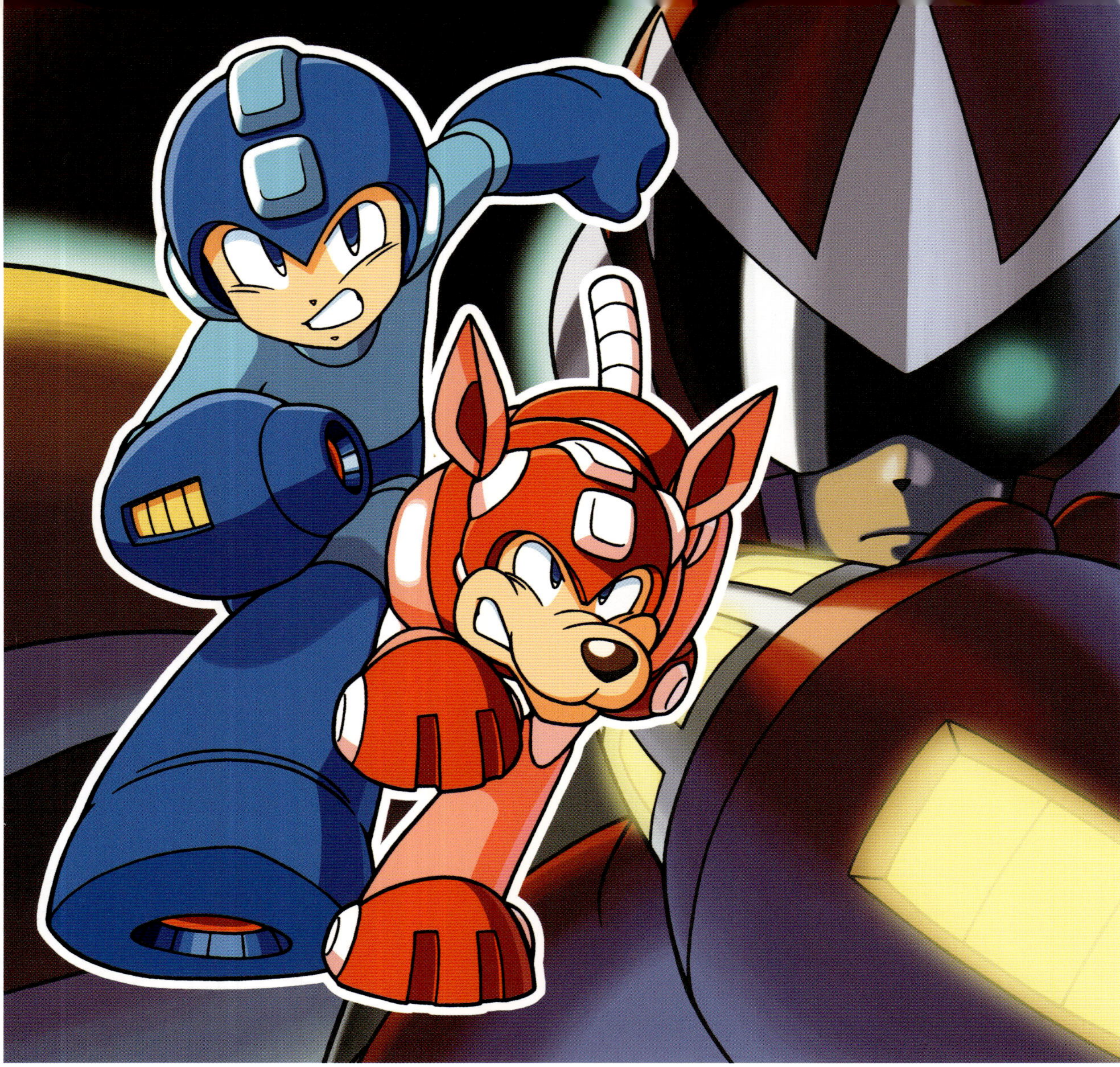

ロックマン3 Dr.ワイリーの最期!?

Rockman 3: The End of Dr. Wily!?
PS 09/14/1999

"I think Proto Man and Rush are the main attractions of '3,' and the green glow you see in Proto Man's eye is something I took from Break Man's image." (Higurashi)

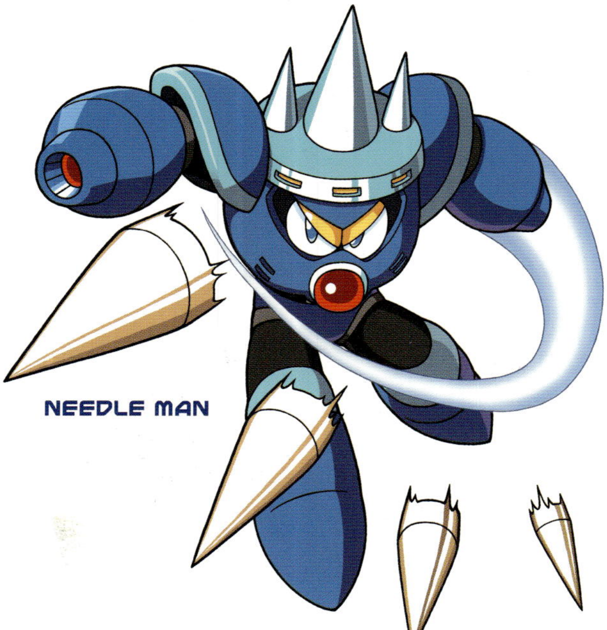

NEEDLE MAN

MAGNET MAN

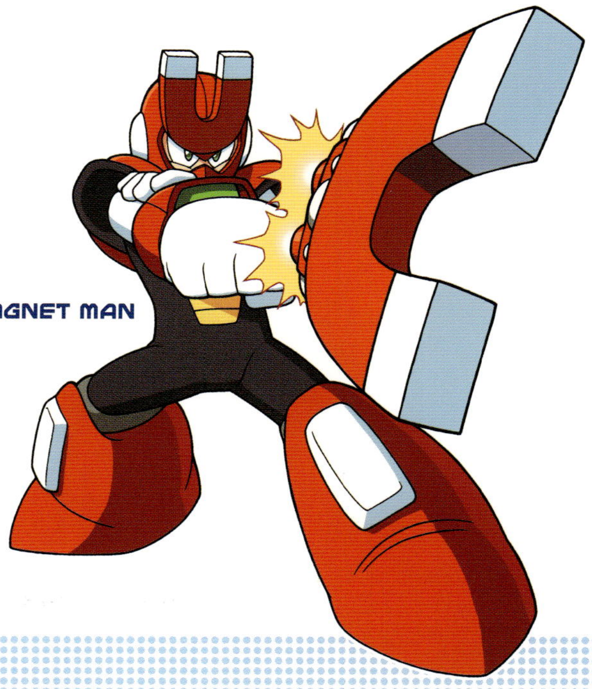

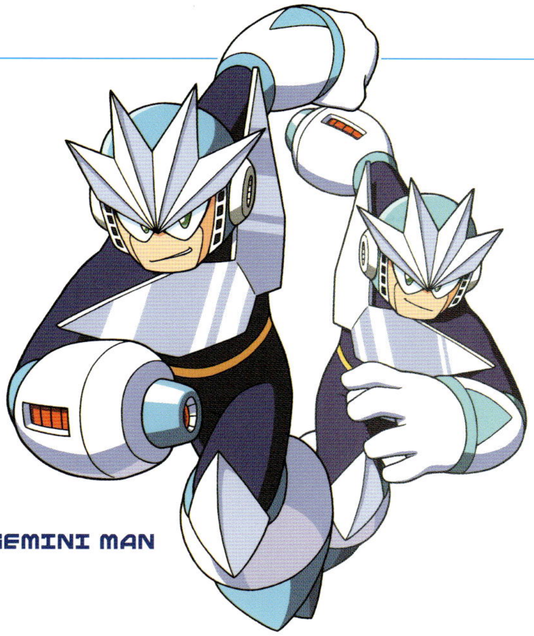

GEMINI MAN

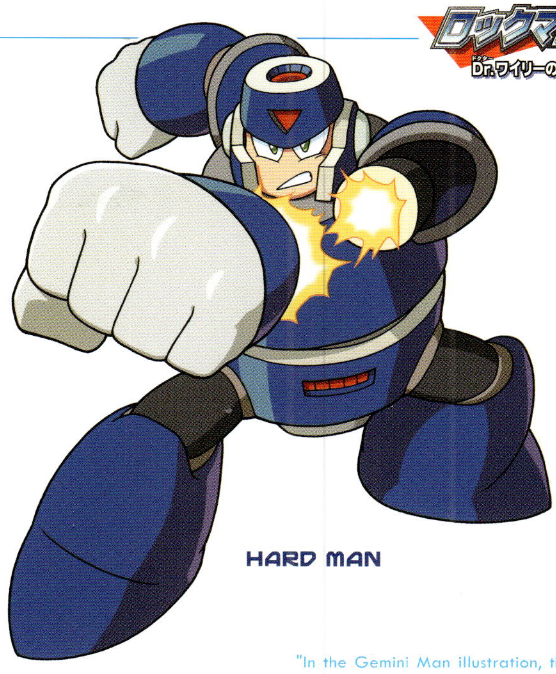

HARD MAN

"In the Gemini Man illustration, the two are slightly different colors. I knew that'd make it totally obvious that one of them is a hologram, but I did it anyway. (laughs) Unlike the illustrations for the NES version, these PS version illustrations mostly show the boss characters actually wielding their weapons or using their attacks. Since I was drawing characters that had already been done before, I figured it'd be pretty pointless if I just drew them in the exact same way. Top Man may be the one exception since I'd have had to draw a bunch of faces if I had drawn him spinning. (laughs)" (Higurashi)

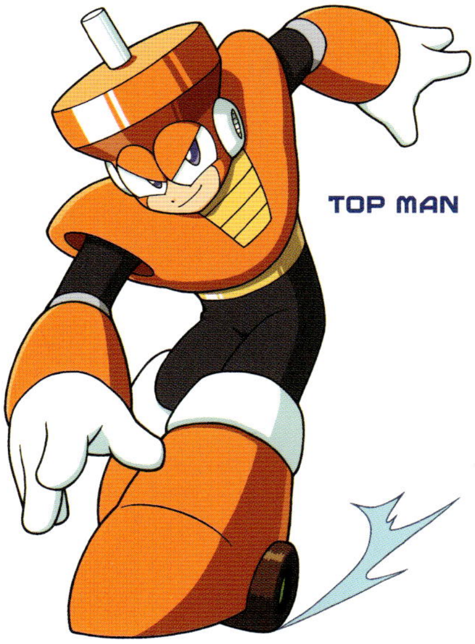

TOP MAN

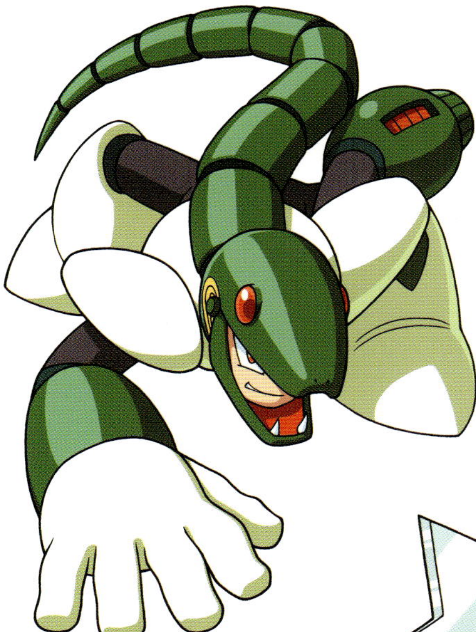

SNAKE MAN

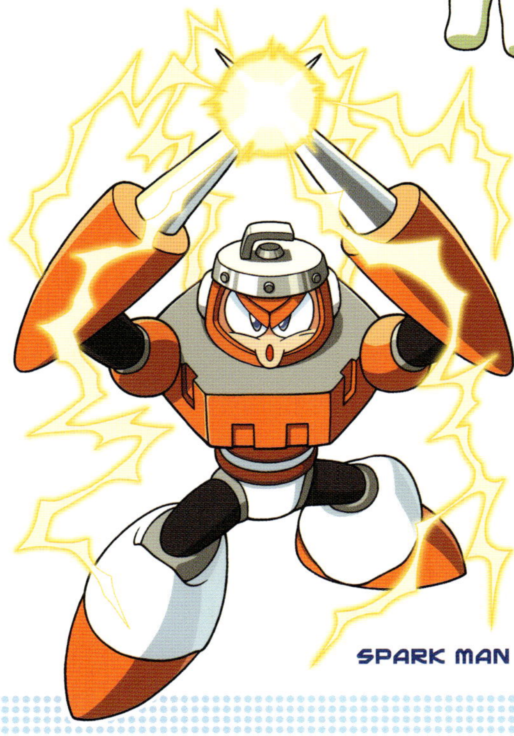

SPARK MAN

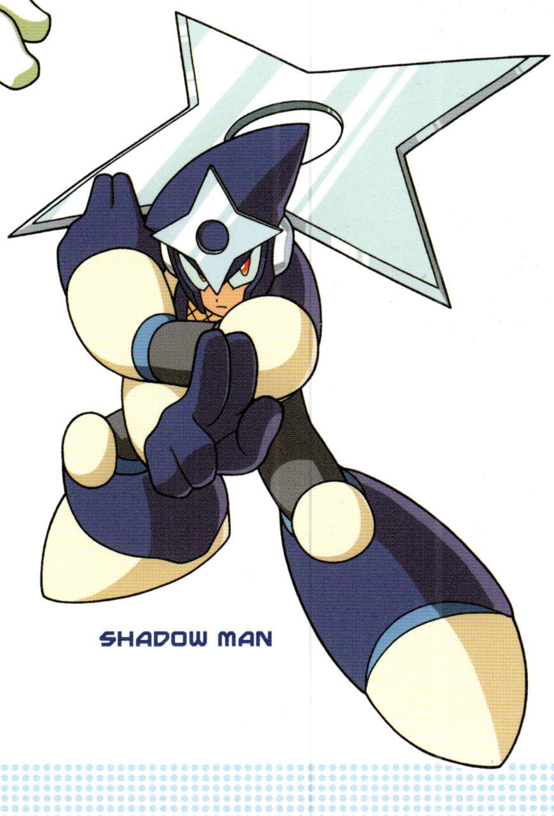

SHADOW MAN

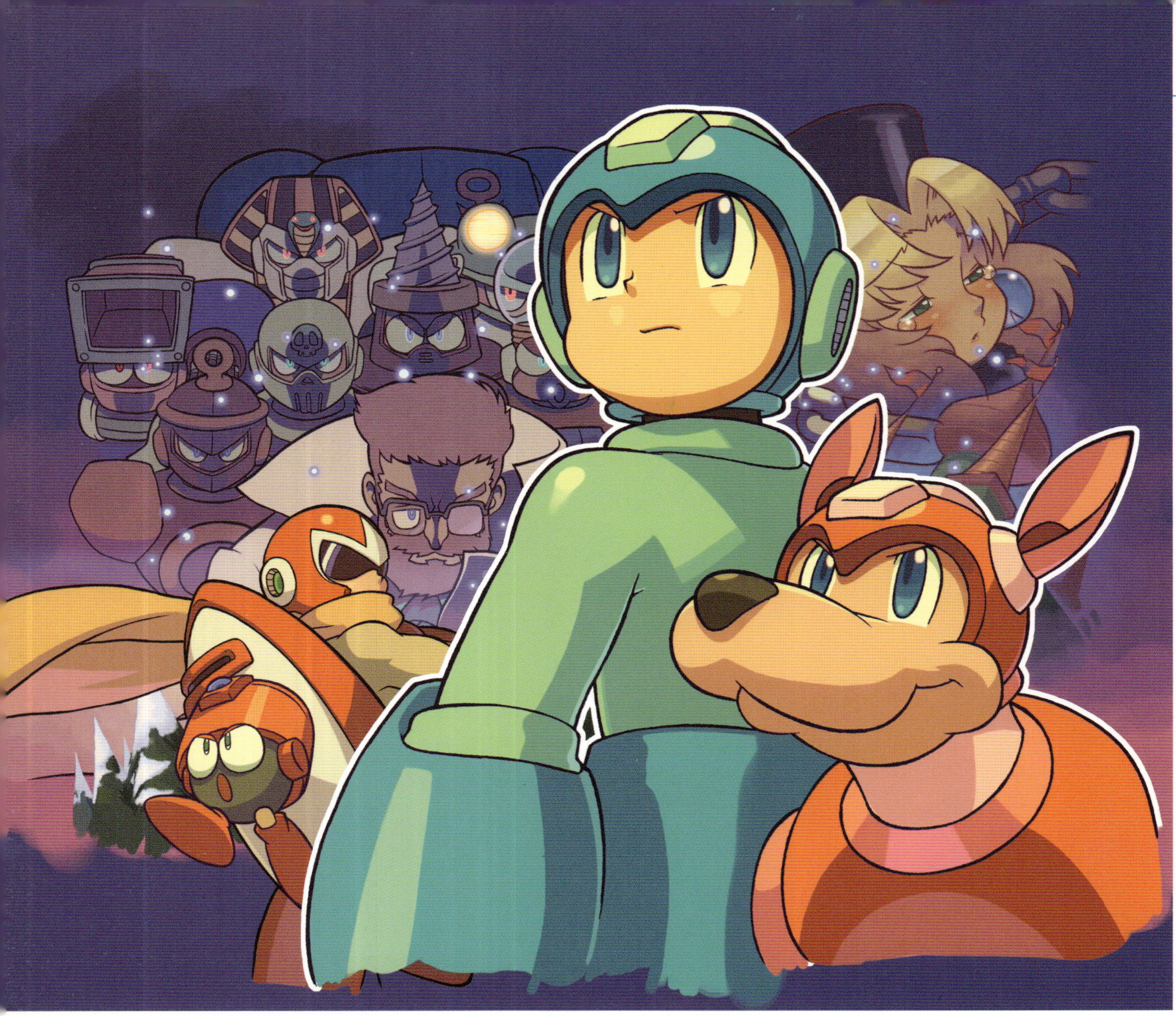

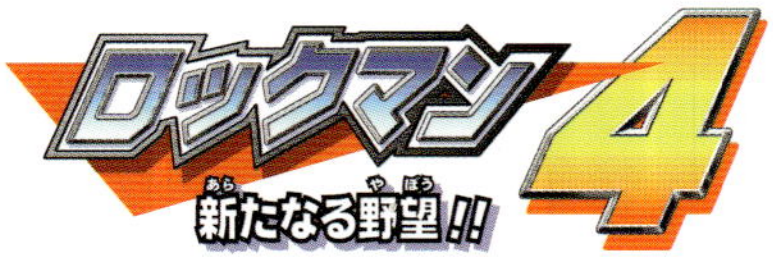

Rockman 4: A New Ambition!!
PS 10/28/1999

"Since this was the title where Cossack made his first appearance, I wanted Cossack to be at the center of this illustration, and added everyone else around him. The reason I didn't finish drawing Dive Man's head and neck is because that part was going to get cropped out anyway. Well... that, and I ran out of time. Higurashi was kind enough to swap places with me for the predetermined illustration allotments. I'd also like to mention just how awesome Higurashi's illustrations are. I remember feeling a wave of nostalgia every time I looked at one of his drawings." (Hideki)

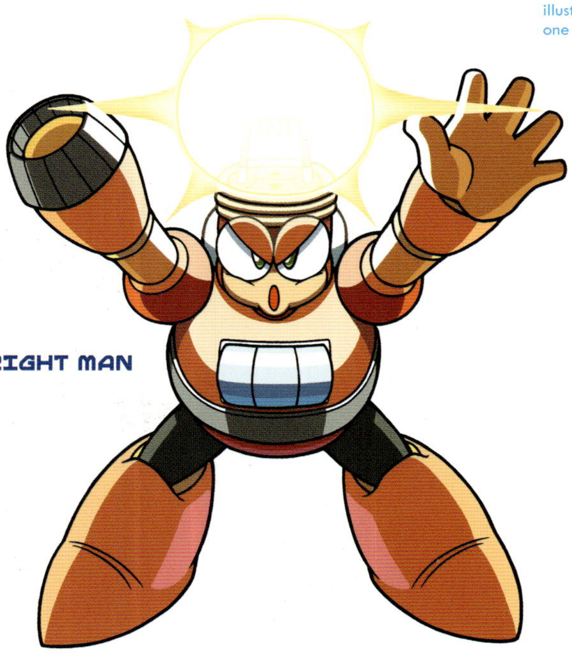

BRIGHT MAN

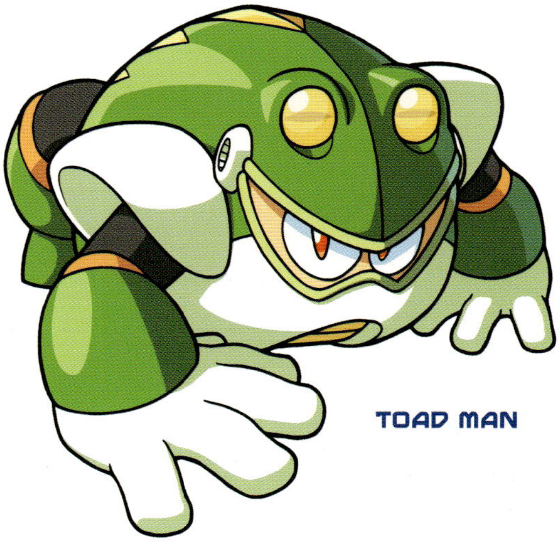

TOAD MAN

"I remember having such a hard time getting Ishikawa to approve my work between '1' and '3,' but from '4' onward, I got better and usually got approved on my first attempts. That coupled with the fact that '4' just happens to be my favorite title meant that I had a lot of fun working on it. As you can see here, I drew Pharaoh Man flying. Do you remember how he would surround himself in an aura and make zombies rain from the sky? That's the image of Pharaoh Man that I have in my mind." (Higurashi)

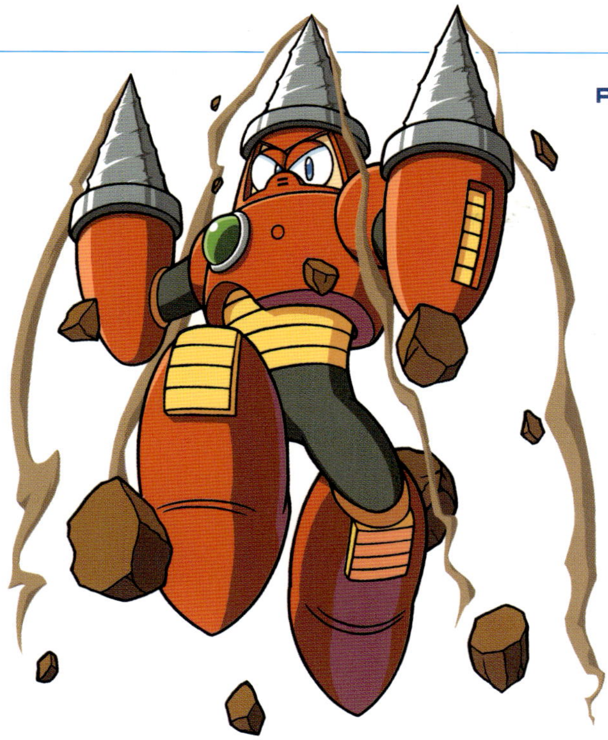

DRILL MAN

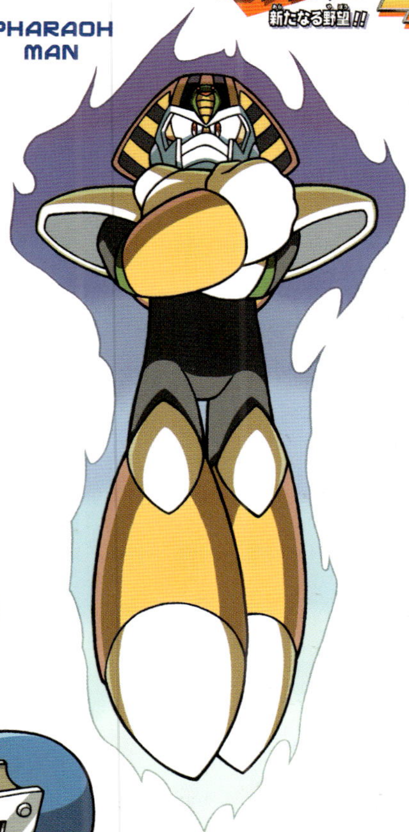

PHARAOH MAN

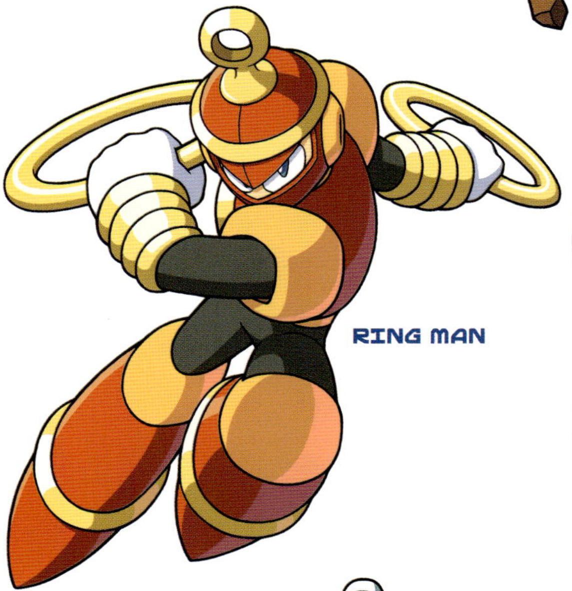

RING MAN

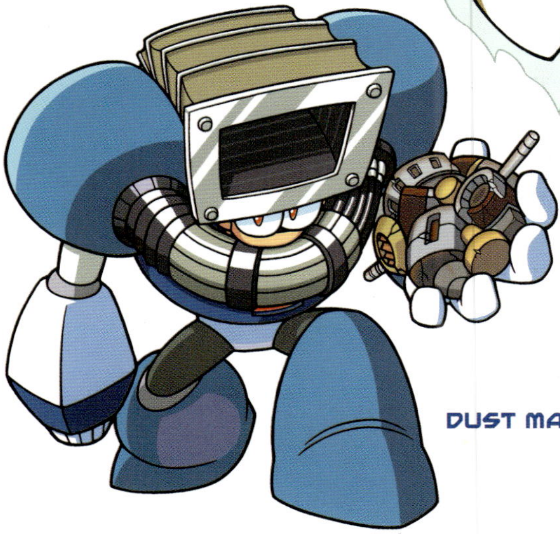

DUST MAN

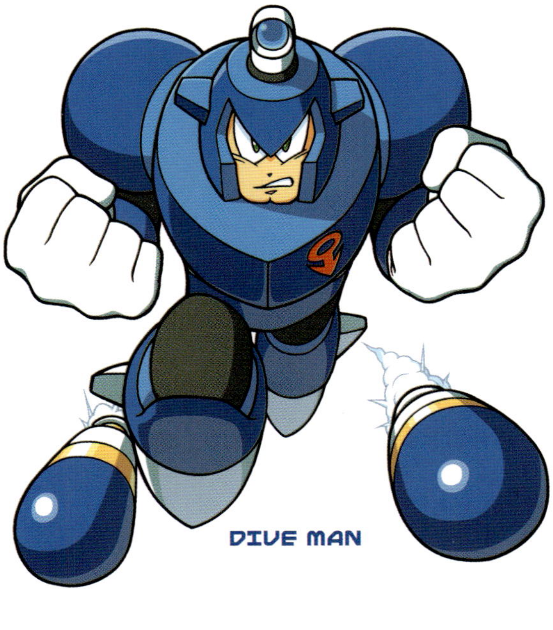

DIVE MAN

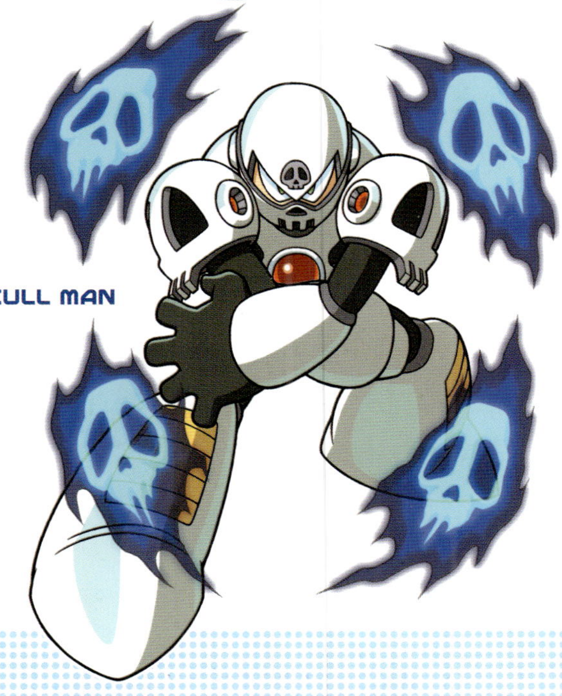

SKULL MAN

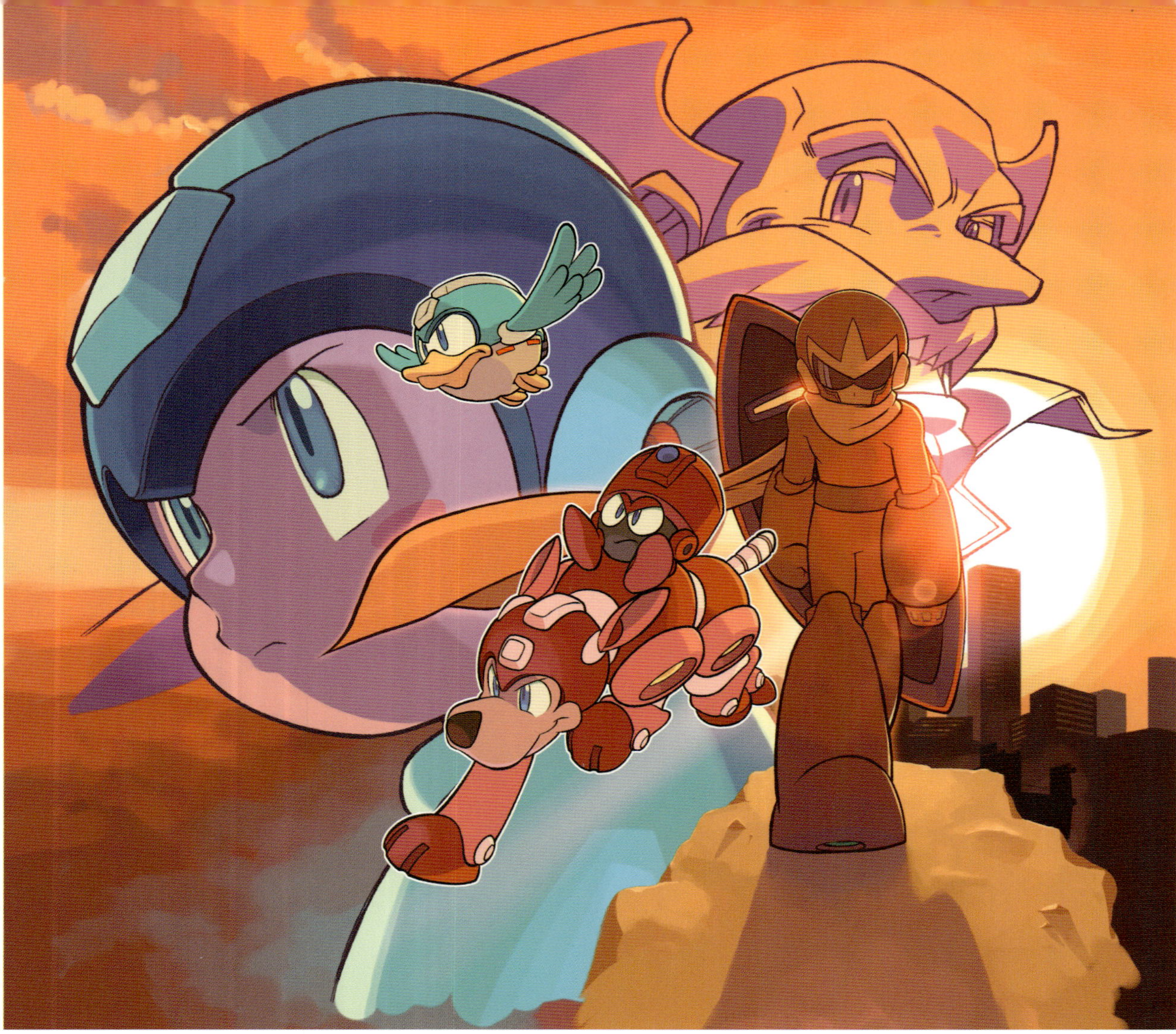

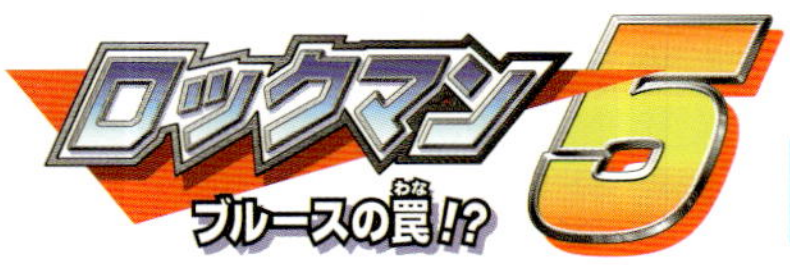

Rockman 5: Blues' Trap!?
PS 11/25/1999

"I'm happy to say, I didn't have to draw all of the boss characters for '5.' (laughs) Scheduling had a lot to do with it, but I wanted to try a change of pace for the package illustration. There were fewer characters, and a lower resolution, so I thought it would be worthwhile to focus on visibility. With '5' being 'Blues' Trap!?,' I planned it out so that people's eyes would naturally be drawn to Proto Man." (Hideki)
[Editor's note: Proto Man is known as Blues in Japan]

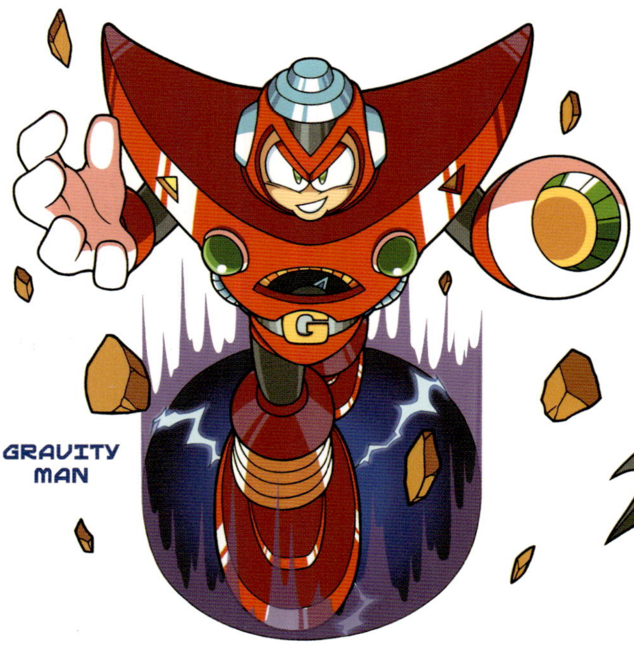

GRAVITY MAN

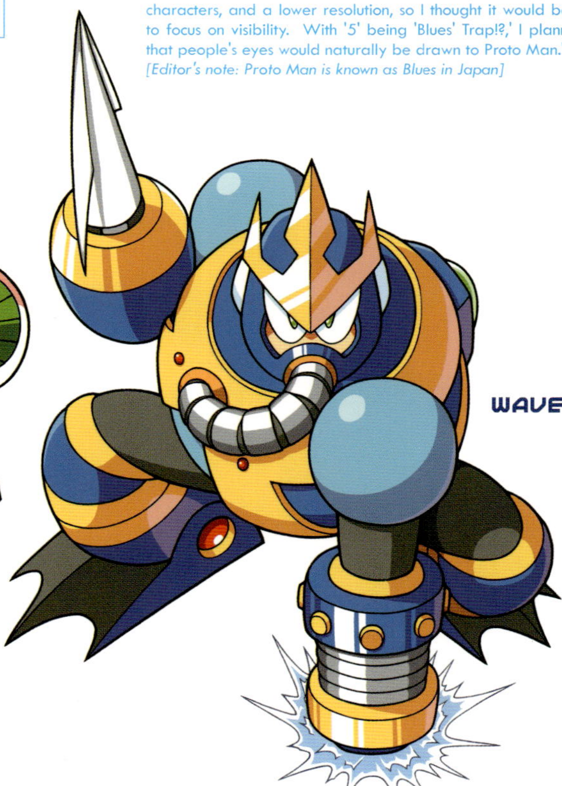

WAVE MAN

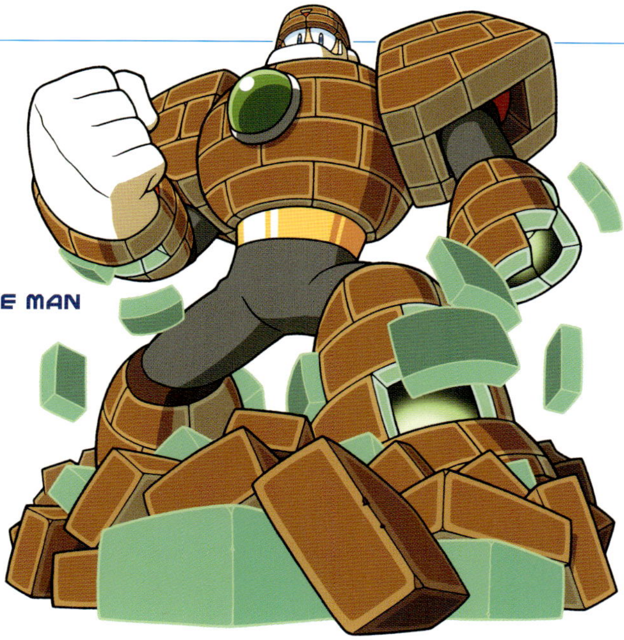

STONE MAN

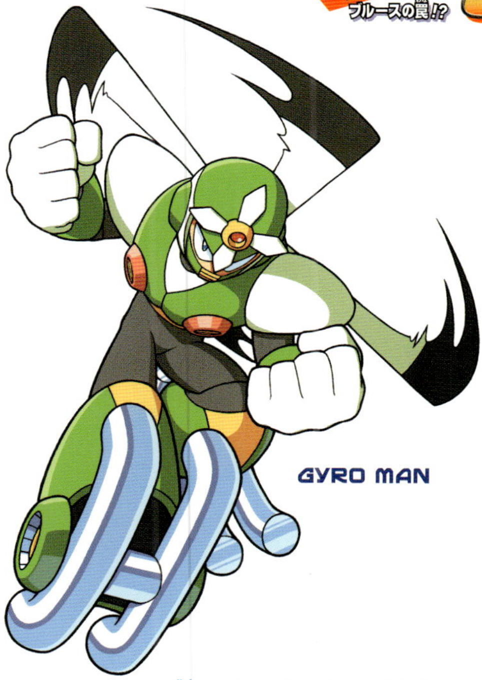

GYRO MAN

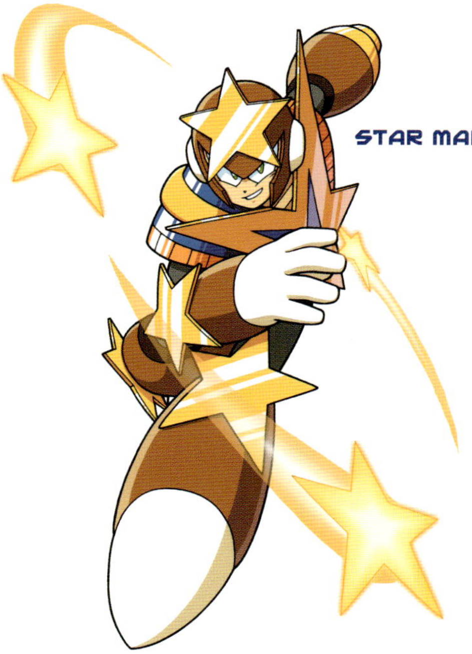

STAR MAN

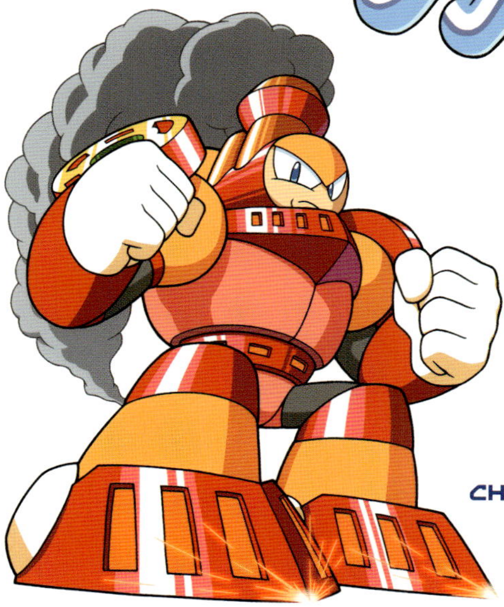

CHARGE MAN

"I'm not sure how to explain it, but they wanted me to do the drawings based on the theme of each character. For Gravity Man, I remember being like, 'How am I supposed to visually express gravity!?' (laughs) Stone Man was a little easier, as I just drew stones lifting up off the ground and coming together. I also tried adding little details, like the sparks at the tips of Charge Man's feet. I struggled a bit with ideas for Crystal Man, but ended up going with a 'forming a Crystal Eye' image." (Higurashi)

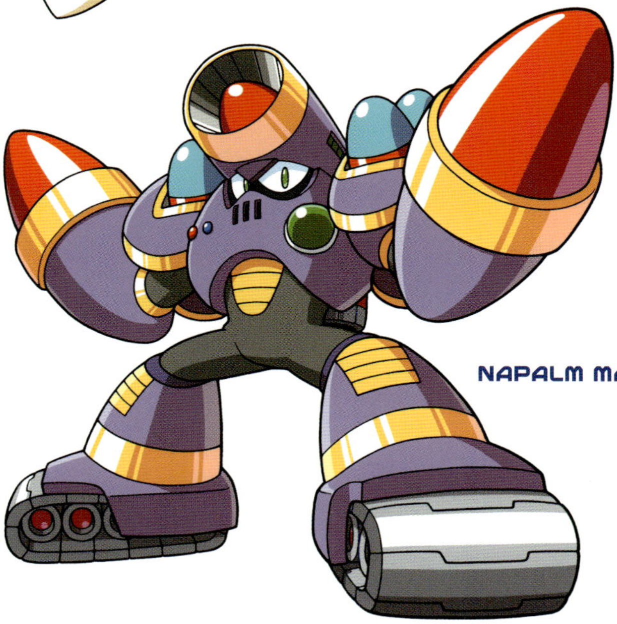

NAPALM MAN

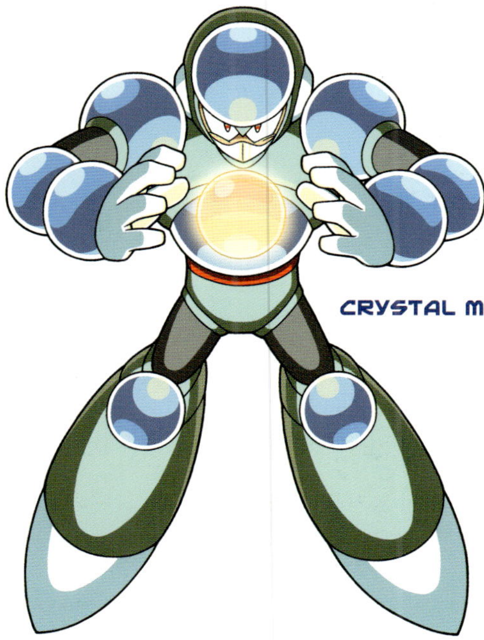

CRYSTAL MAN

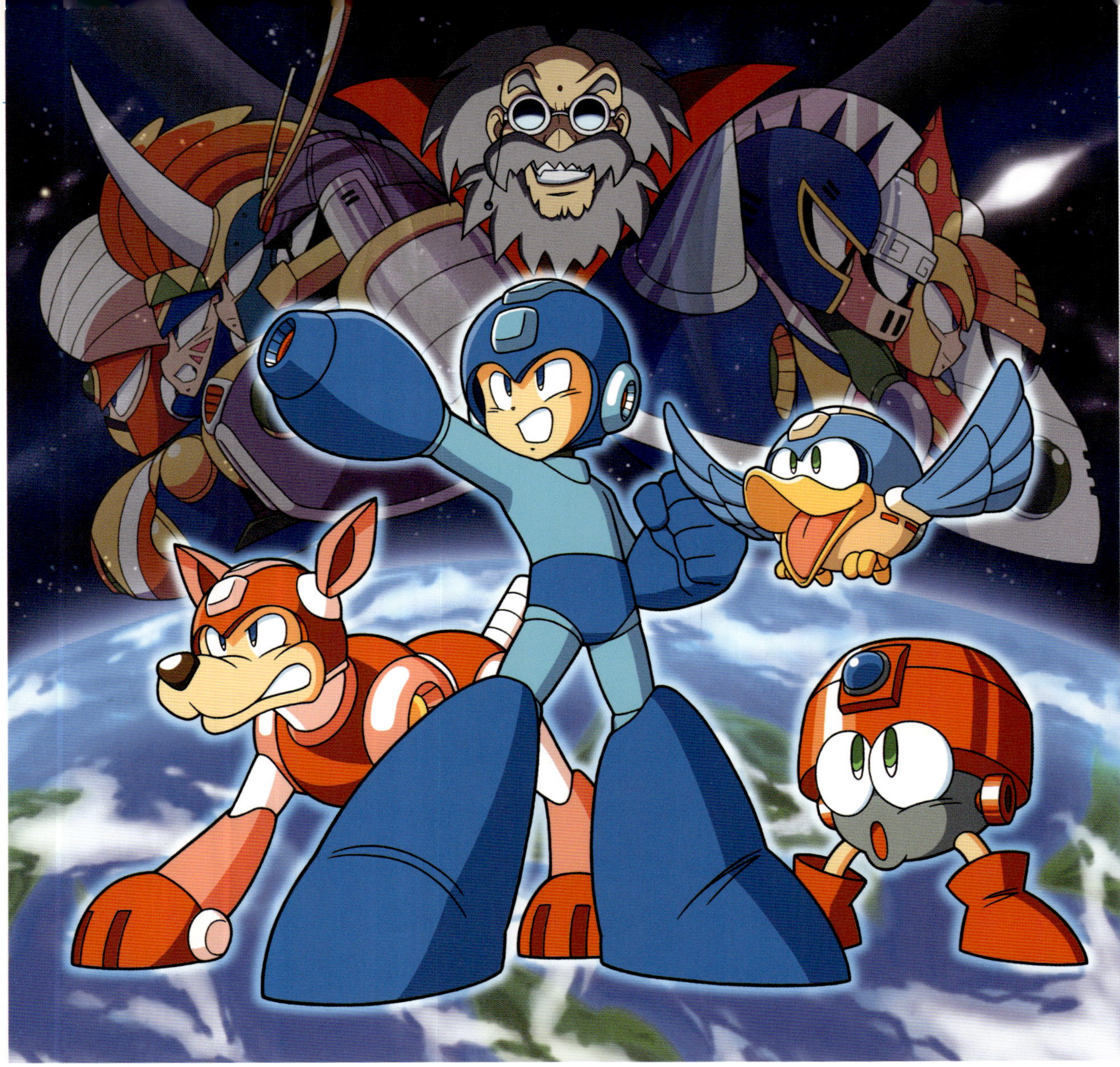

ロックマン6 史上最大の戦い!!

Rockman 6: The Greatest Battle of All Time!!
PS 12/09/1999

"They were granting me more and more responsibility and autonomy, so I felt like I was doing whatever I wanted. As you can see, I basically ripped off the NES package illustration for this one. (laughs) I really wanted to include Metall too, but didn't have enough space. The Earth itself is looking a little rough, and I probably would redo it if I had the chance. Considering my skills at the time, though, I'd say I did pretty well with this one." (Higurashi)

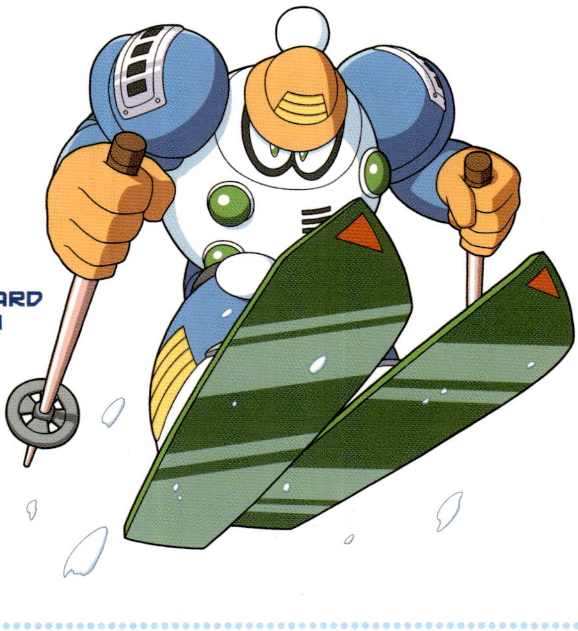

BLIZZARD MAN

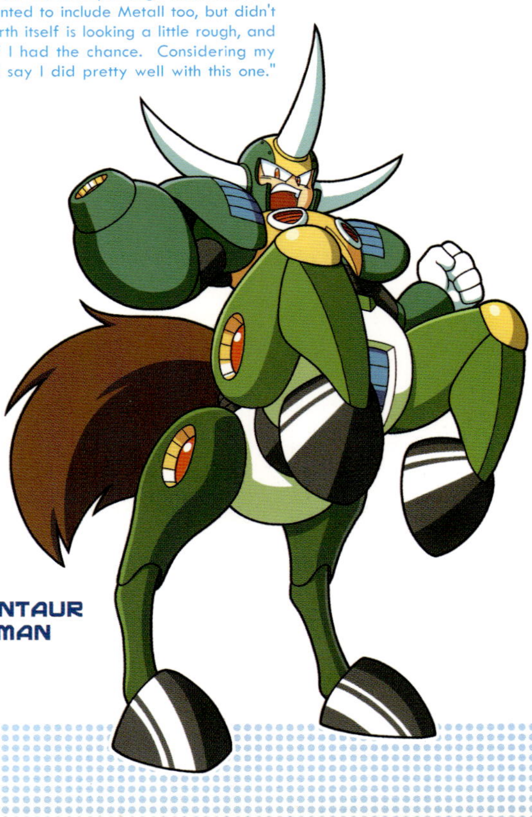

CENTAUR MAN

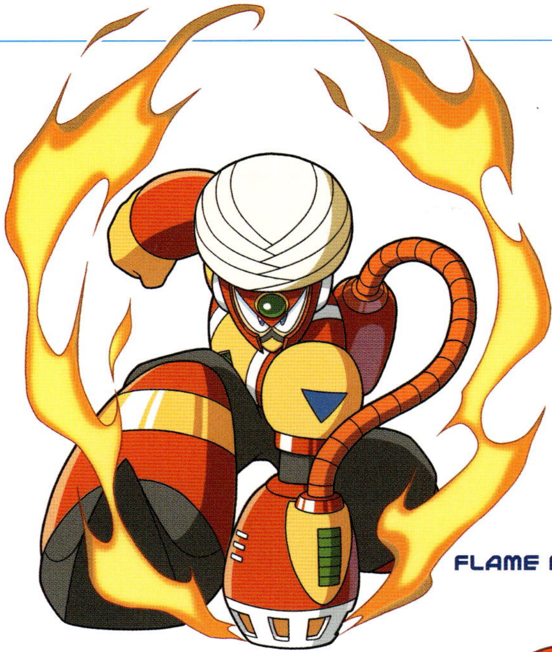

FLAME MAN

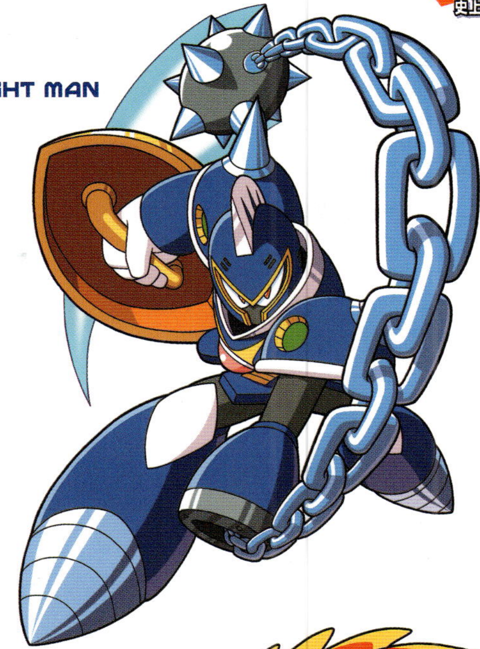

KNIGHT MAN

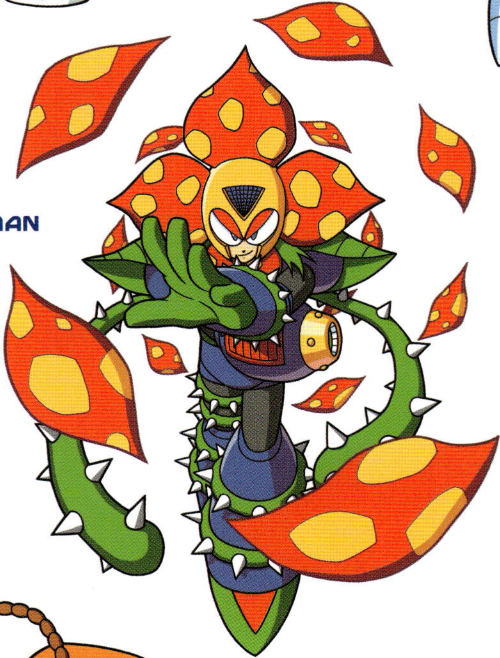

PLANT MAN

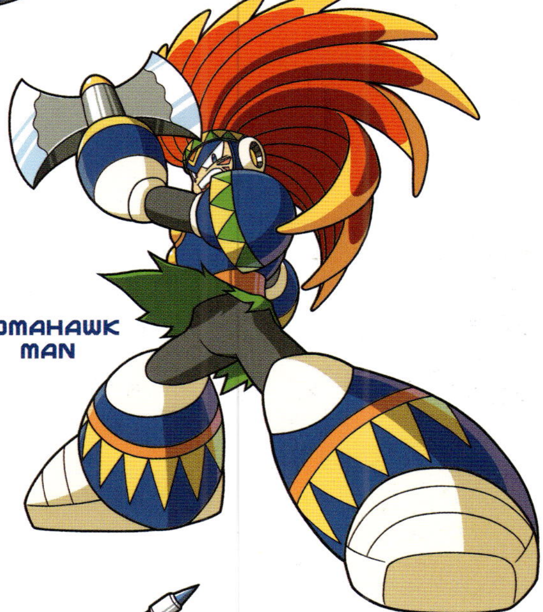

TOMAHAWK MAN

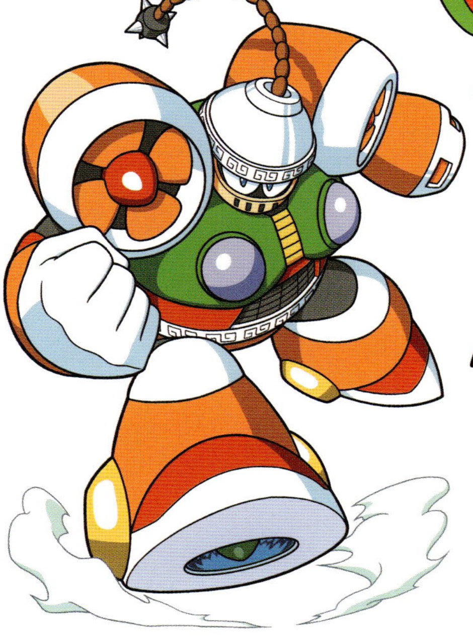

WIND MAN

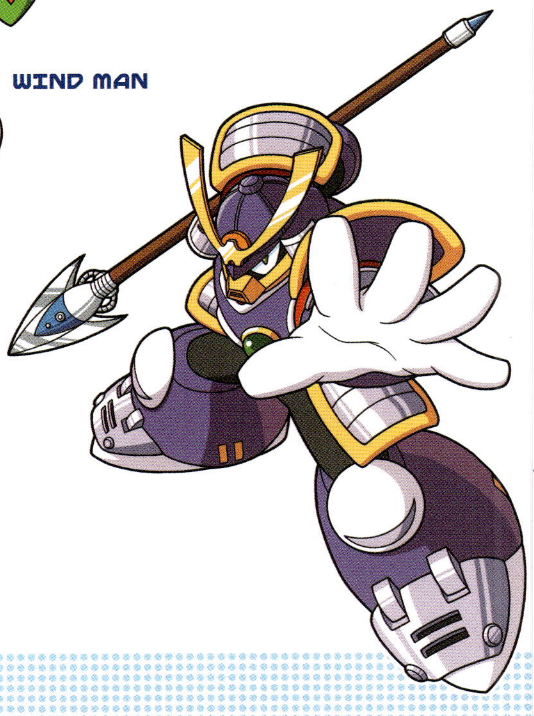

YAMATO MAN

"Blizzard Man is my favorite boss in '6.' I drew him while looking at some pictures of people skiing. Since I couldn't really show Wind Man's weapon, I drew him floating off the ground a bit to express his 'wind' theme. I really like Musha Gundam and Knight Gundam, so drawing Yamato Man and Knight Man was a total joy. I used to be a loyal 'BonBon' reader. (laughs)" (Higurashi)

ロックマン® バトル&ファイターズ™

Rockman Battle & Fighters
NGP 07/06/2000

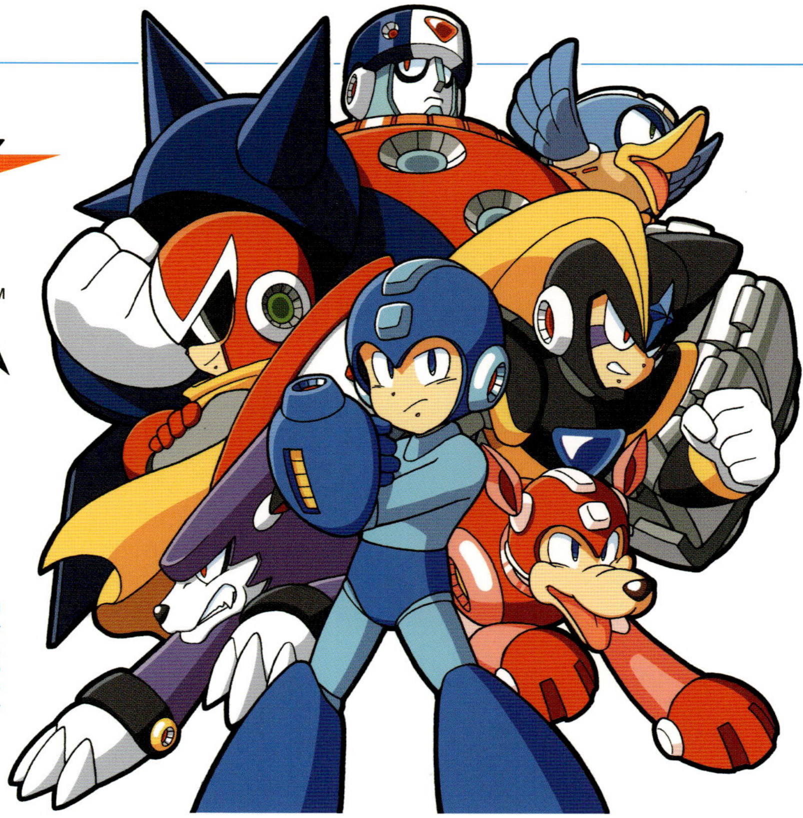

"When the arcade version came out, I couldn't afford the PCB [Printed Circuit Board]. I was pretty upset about it, and decided that if I couldn't collect them all, I didn't want any of my other collectables either! So I took all of my Mega Man stuff, except for my game cartridges (still a lot of stuff), and got rid of it. What a waste!!" (Higurashi)

ロックマン&フォルテ

Mega Man & Bass
GBA 08/10/2002

"Somehow Mega Man & Bass, which was difficult enough to begin with, seems all the more tricky in widescreen format. As far as the illustration goes, I think Mega Man's facial expression looks pretty good. Overall, I find the illustration a little dull, and I wouldn't mind redrawing it... but I just can't get over how much difficulty I had with the widescreen format." (Higurashi)

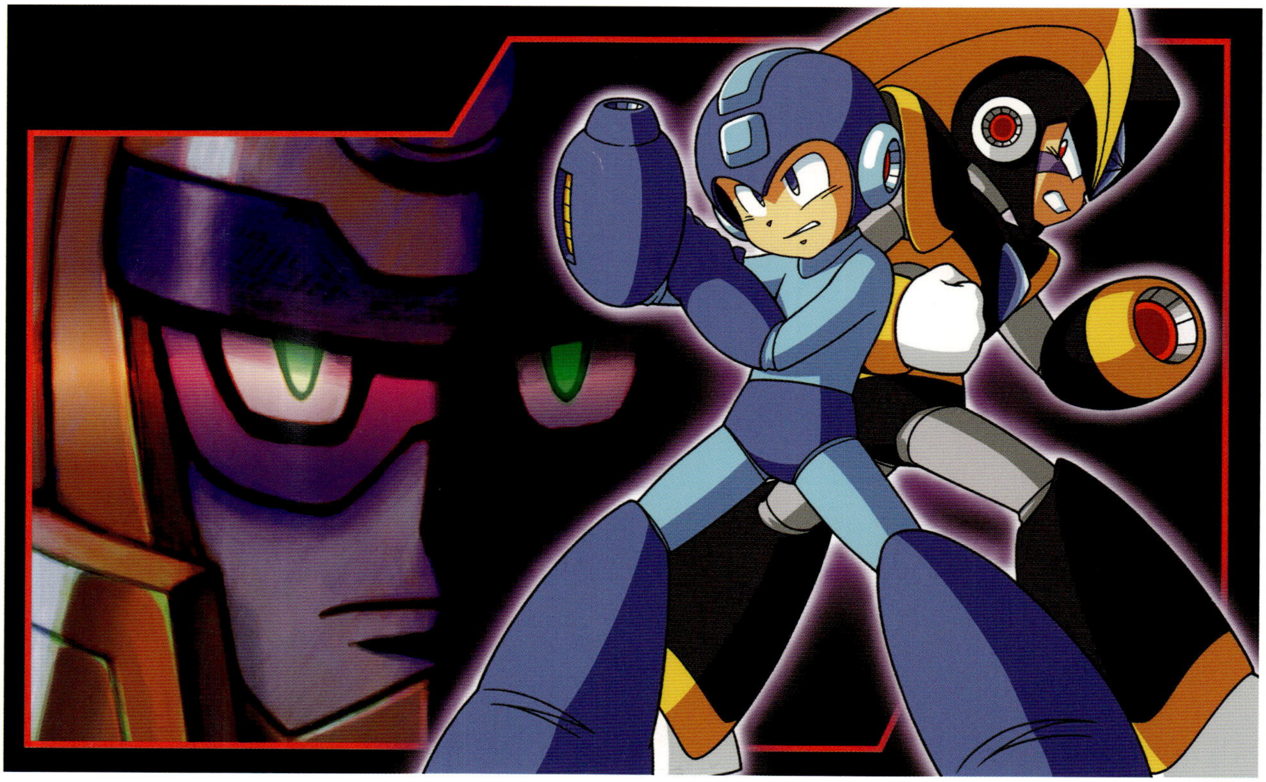

ロックマン パワーバトルファイターズ

Rockman Power Battle Fighters
PS2 08/05/2004

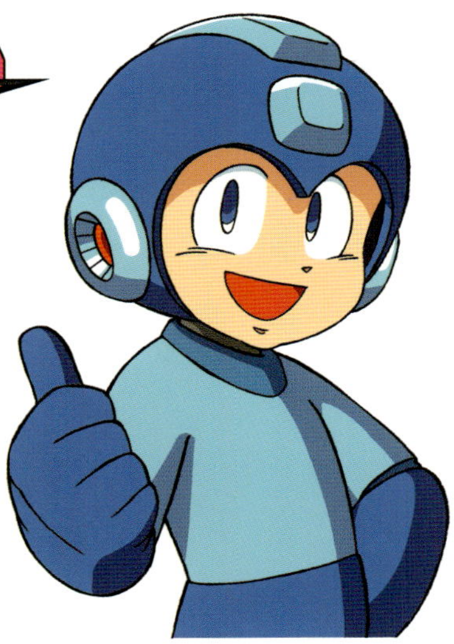

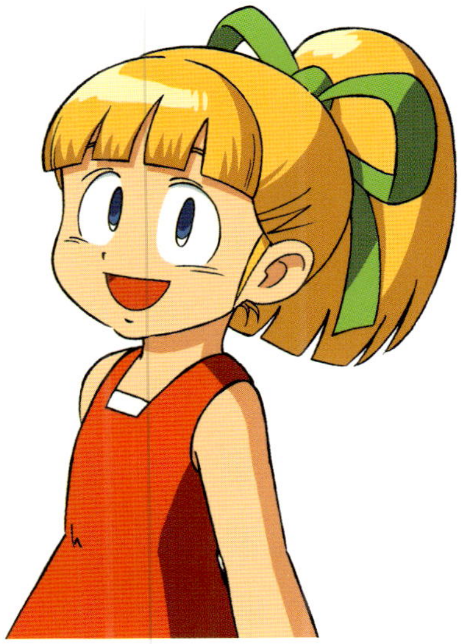

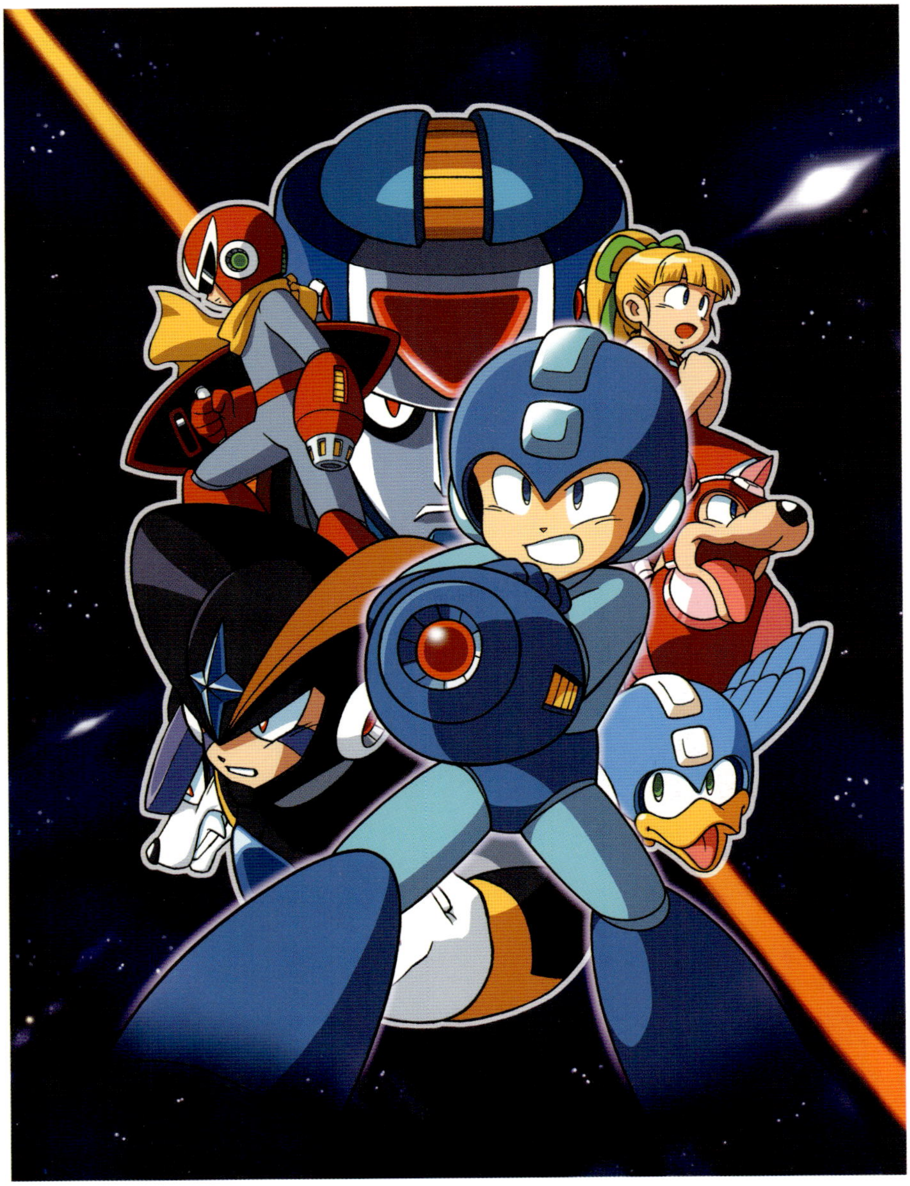

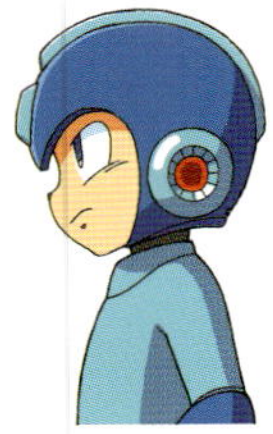

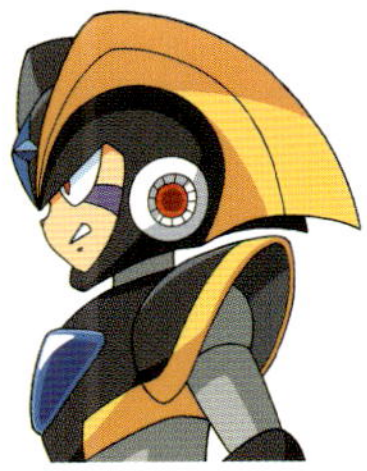

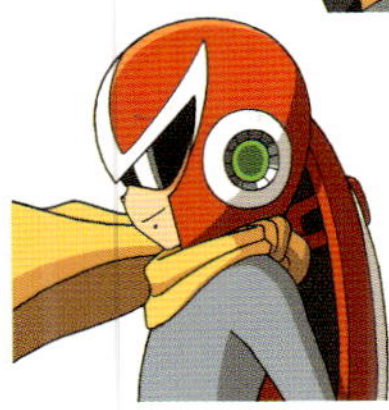

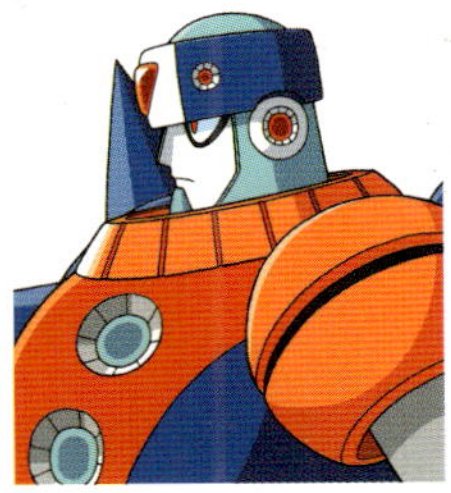

"I had been wishing and waiting for this arcade game to be brought to console! I was so psyched about this, and as a result, I ended up with an illustration that I am really happy with. I drew the rough draft in about 15 minutes, and got immediate approval from Inafune. I spent four days finishing it up. I was actually planning on spending another day on it to make the space background a little cooler, but I had some more work come in and I didn't have the time. Too bad...!" (Higurashi)

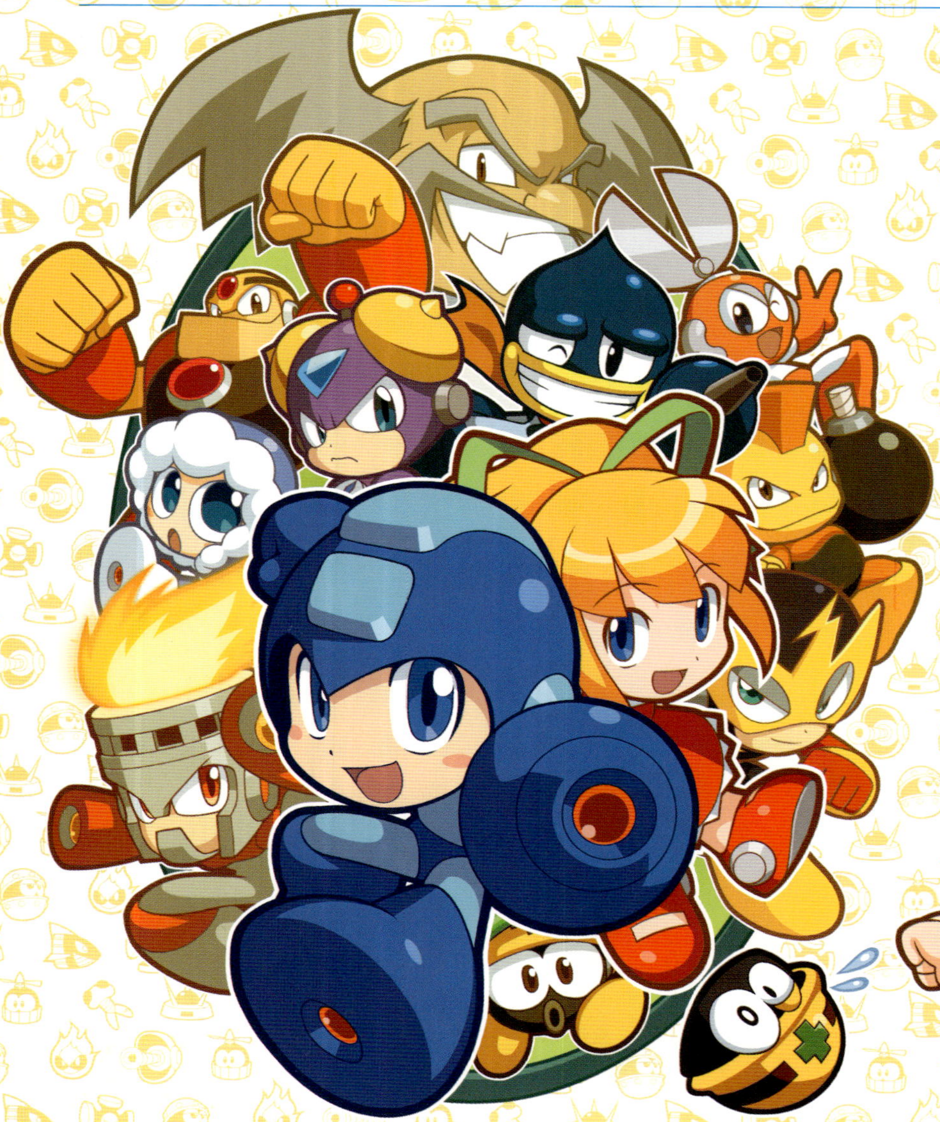

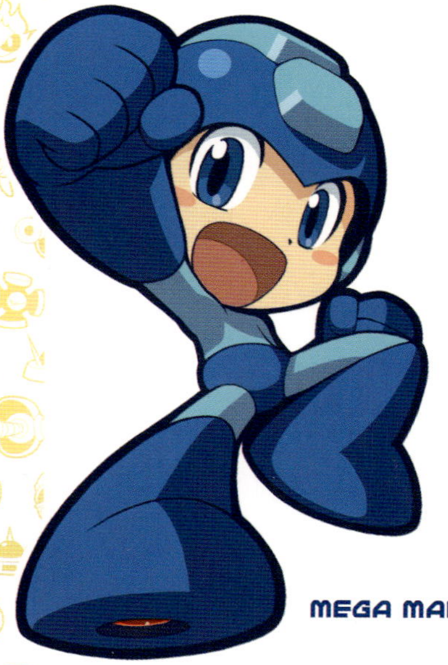

MEGA MAN

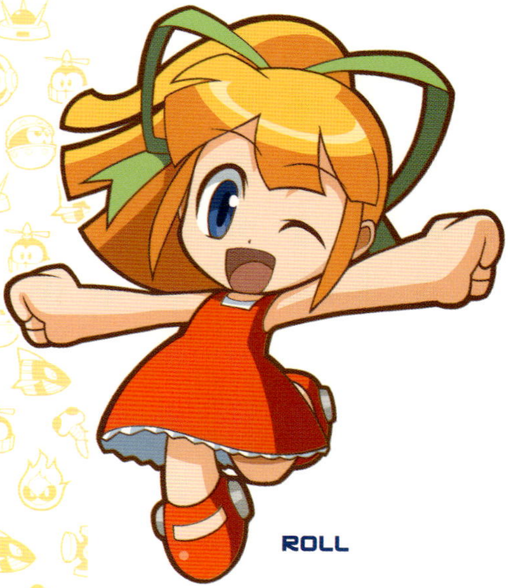

ROLL

ロックマンロックマン®

Mega Man: Powered Up
PSP 03/02/2006

In the not-too-distant future, humans and robots live in harmony. One day, Dr. Light created a peace-loving robot and named him "Rock." The good professor's laboratory was suddenly attacked by the evil genius Dr. Wily, and all of Dr. Light's robots were abducted. After much hesitation and thought, Dr. Light reconfigured Rock into a combat robot. "Go, Rock... No, wait... Starting today, you shall be known as Mega Man!"

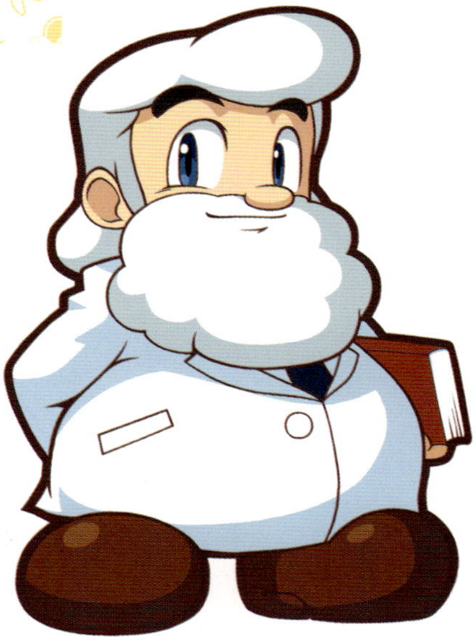

DR. LIGHT

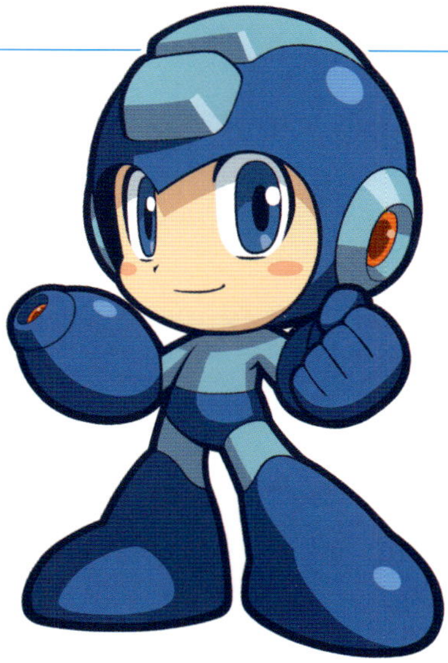

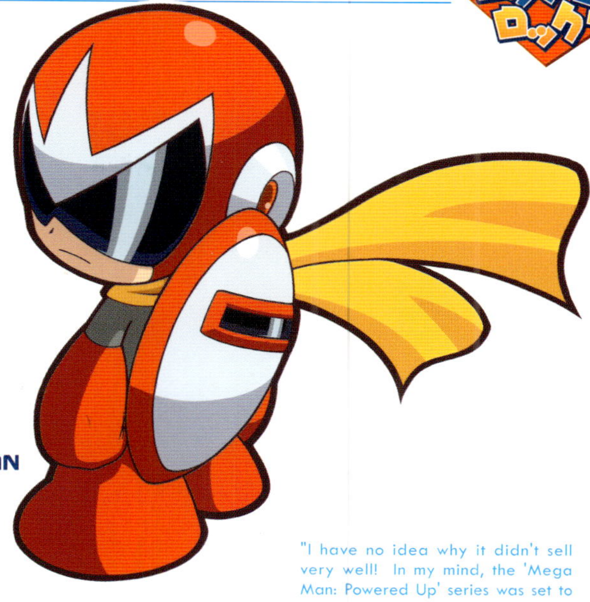

PROTO MAN

"I have to say, 'Mega Man: Powered Up' is the greatest! With its massive volume and fun construction, its replay value is immeasurable. The staff that worked on it had so much invested in Mega Man, too. I promise I didn't tell them to make such an intense game; they did that all by themselves. (laughs)" (Inafune)

"My participation in the 'Mega Man: Powered Up' project was at the concept level. I guess you could say I was the general supervisor." (Yoshikawa)

"I have no idea why it didn't sell very well! In my mind, the 'Mega Man: Powered Up' series was set to have multiple sequels! (laughs) I truly believe that this is definitely one game that any self-respecting Mega Man fan must have! You there... it's not too late to get your copy, you know! (laughs)" (Inafune)

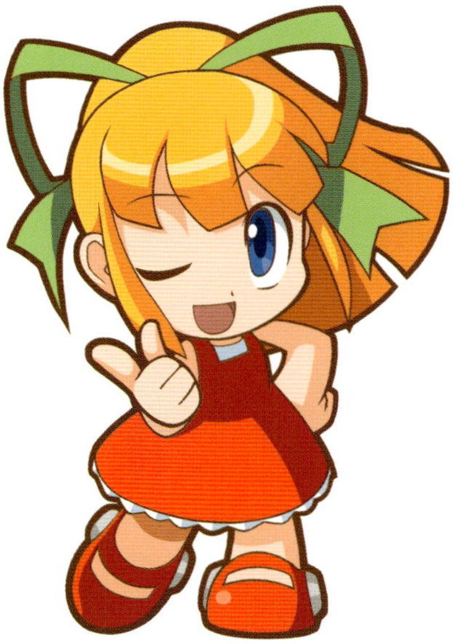

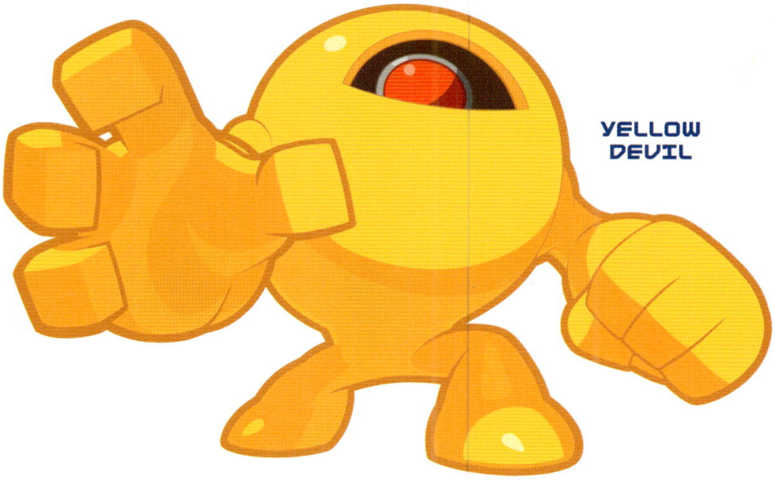

YELLOW DEVIL

"The concept for these designs was 'toys.' We wanted cute designs geared towards little kids... the kinds of characters that you'd see hanging off of keychains and such. Not only that, I made sure to tell the designers not to skimp on any of the original Mega Man details. We wanted their proportions and movements to be accurately reflected in these designs as well." (Yoshikawa)

"They let us do some of the finishing touches on the early Mega Mans." (Higurashi)

"That they did." (Komaki)

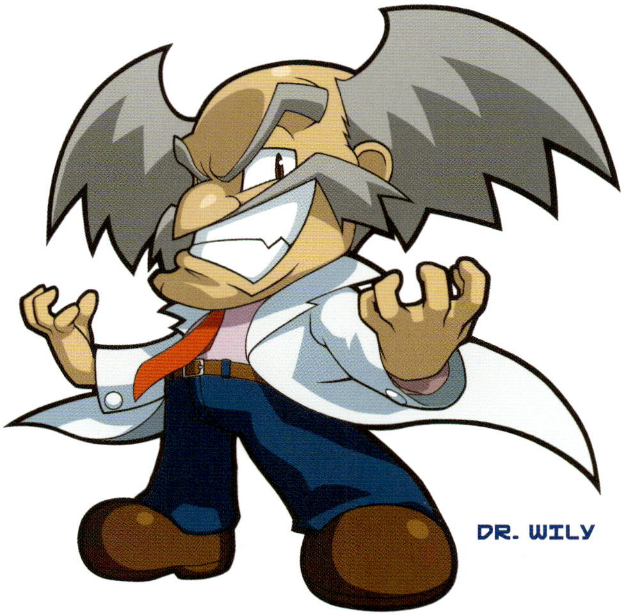

DR. WILY

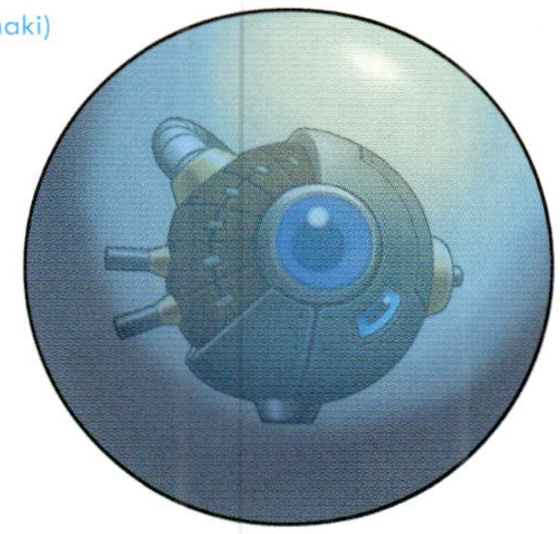

CWU-01P

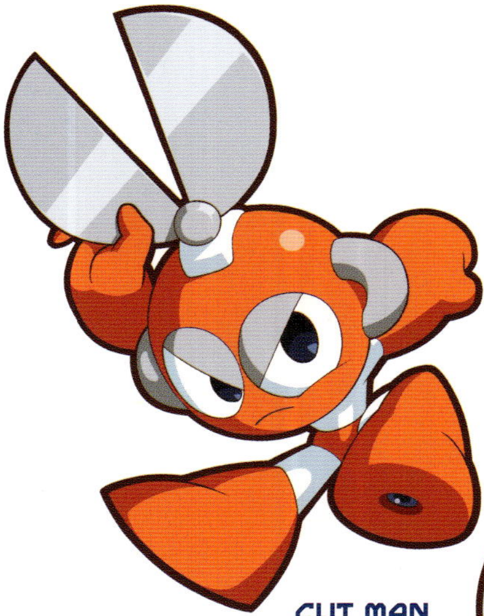

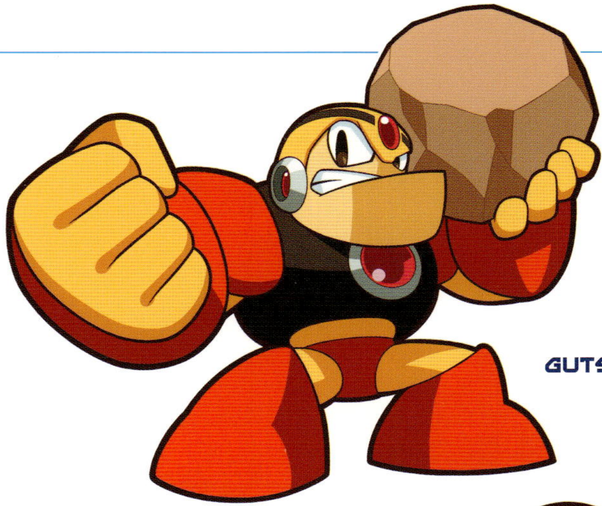

GUTS MAN

CUT MAN

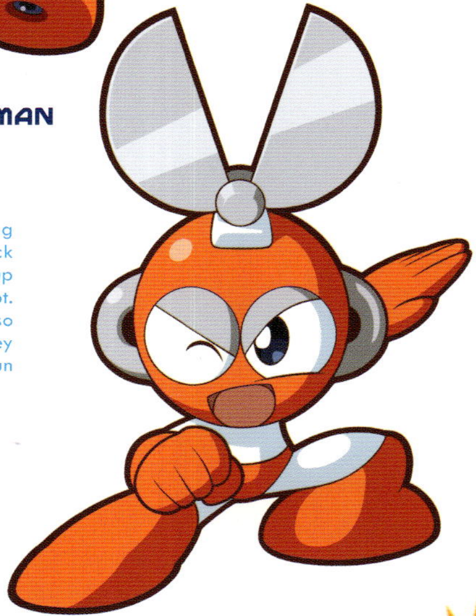

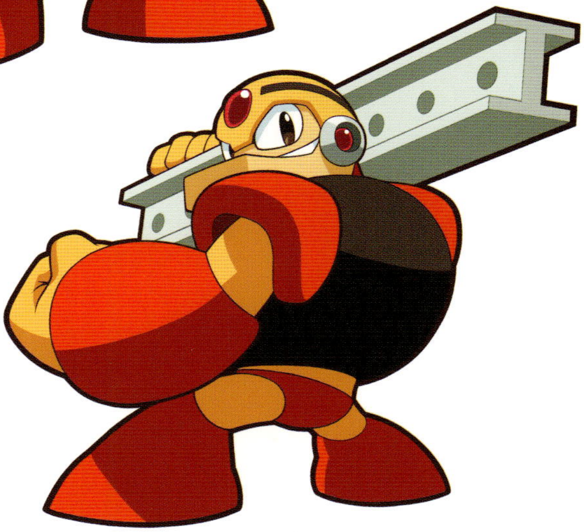

"Development was progressing parallel to 'Mega Man: Maverick Hunter X,' so I basically left it all up to the staff beyond the initial concept. They were all Mega Man lovers, so everything went pretty smoothly. They seemed to be having a lot of fun working on this one." (Yoshikawa)

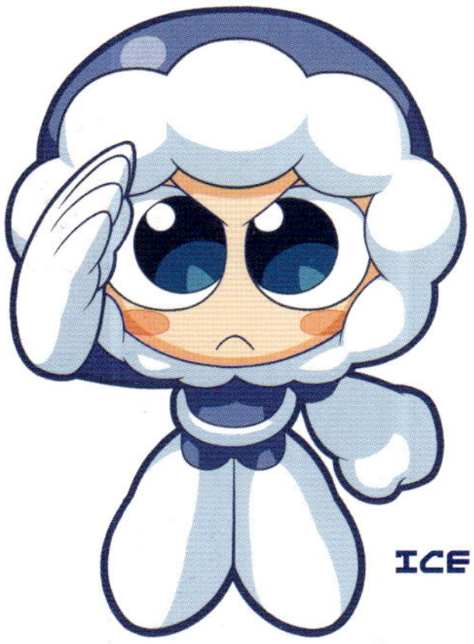

"I did the line drawings for the Ice Man and Elec Man pieces." (Higurashi)

"I think I remember those... (laughs) I colored Ice Man." (Komaki)

"Come to think of it, I may have colored Fire Man too. (laughs)" (Higurashi)

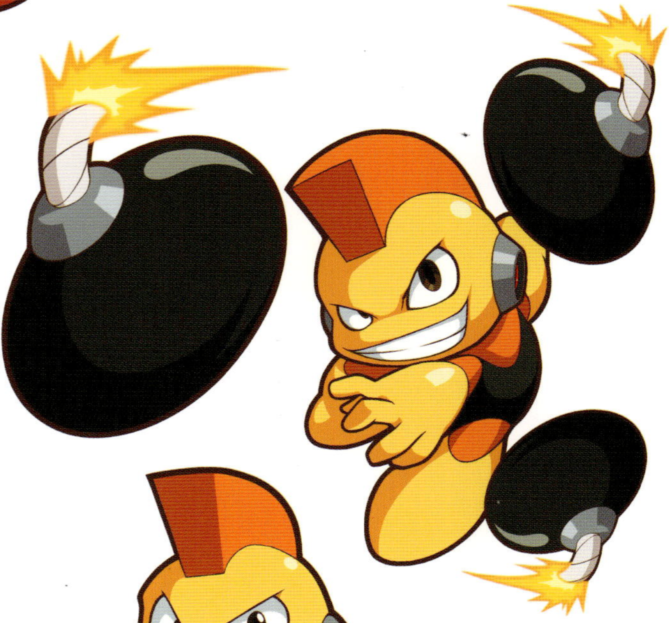

ICE MAN

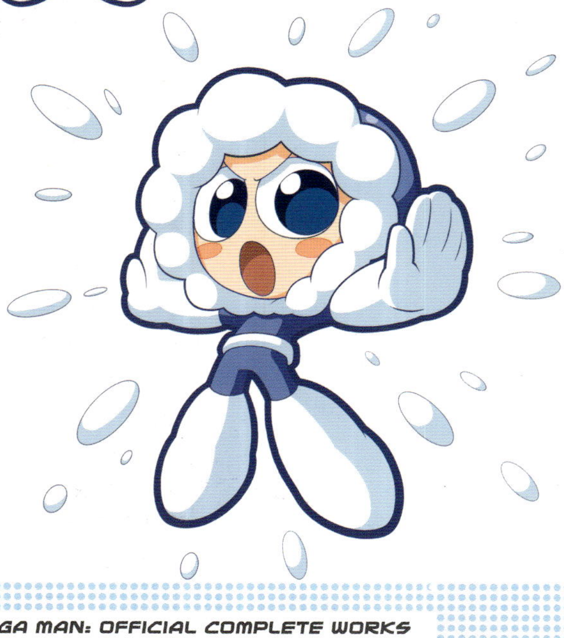

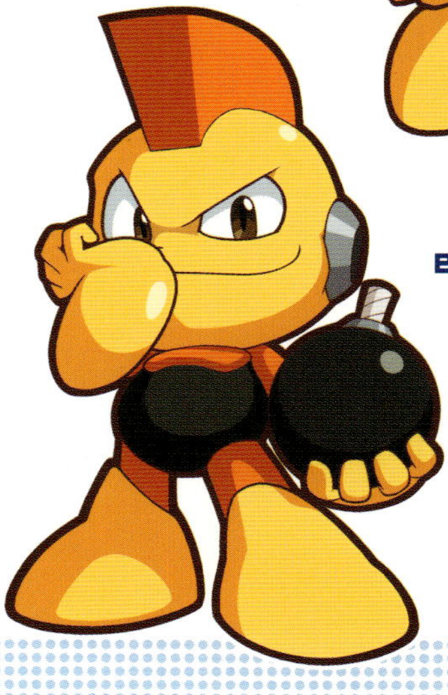

BOMB MAN

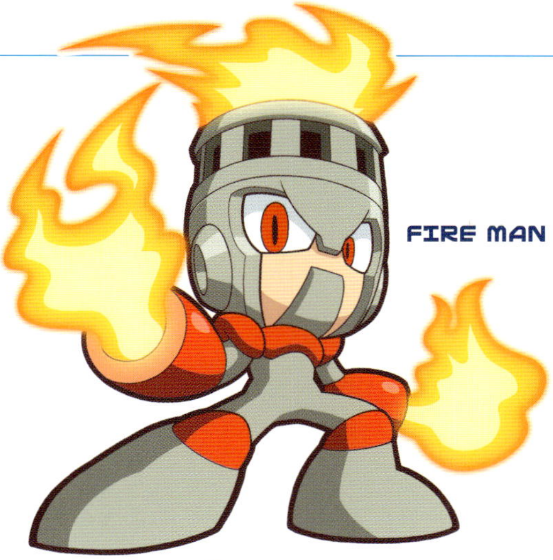

FIRE MAN

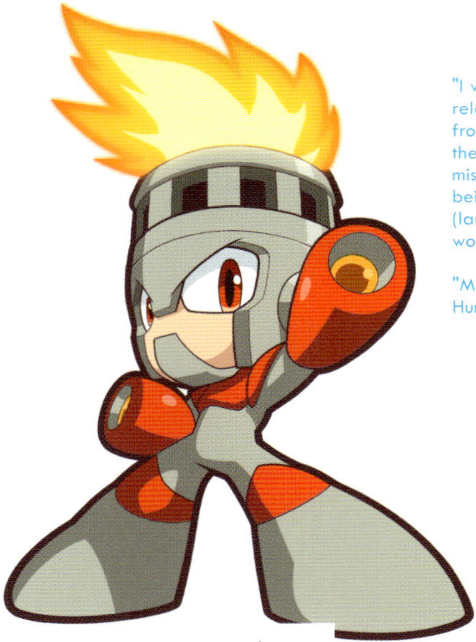

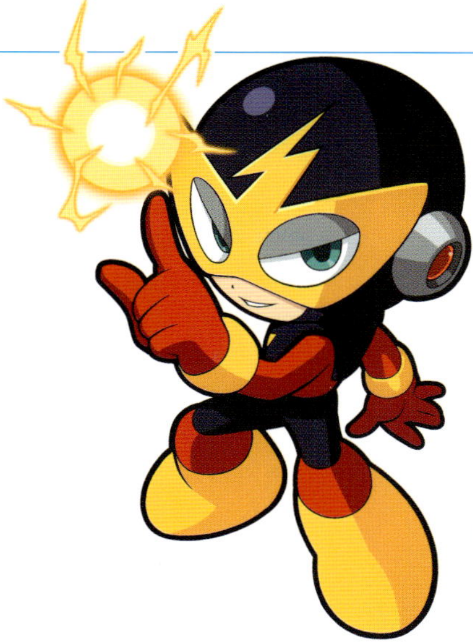

ELEC MAN

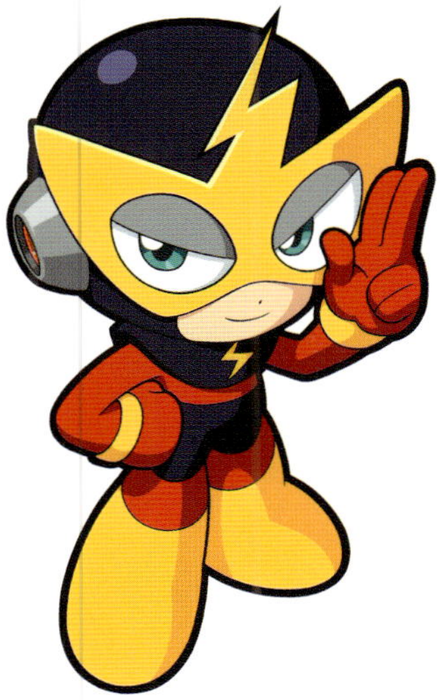

"I was the one they put in charge of all the illustration-related work. Being a newbie, I got a lot of advice from my predecessors while drawing these. I added the rosy cheeks on Mega Man as a little streak of mischief when doing the finishing touches. I remember being a little surprised when they went ahead with it. (laughs) I was trying so hard to convey how fun this world is." (Mizuno)

"Mizuno and I both worked on 'Mega Man: Maverick Hunter X' too. We're like a set." (Komaki)

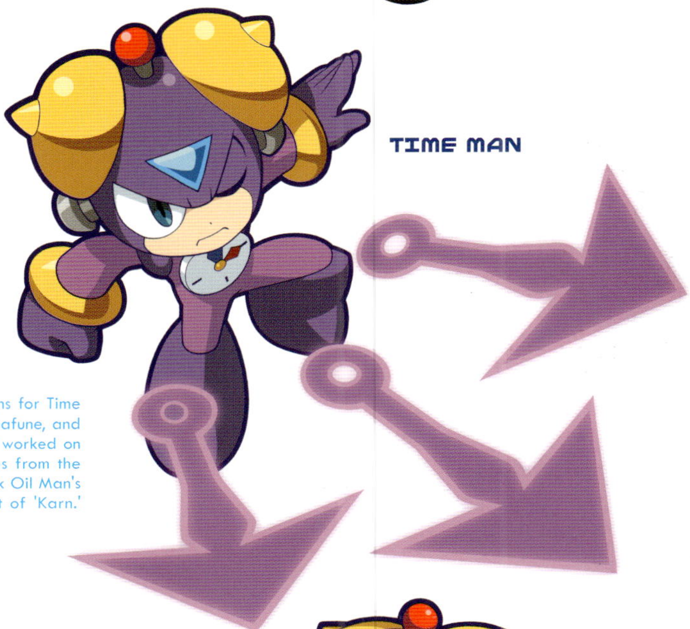

TIME MAN

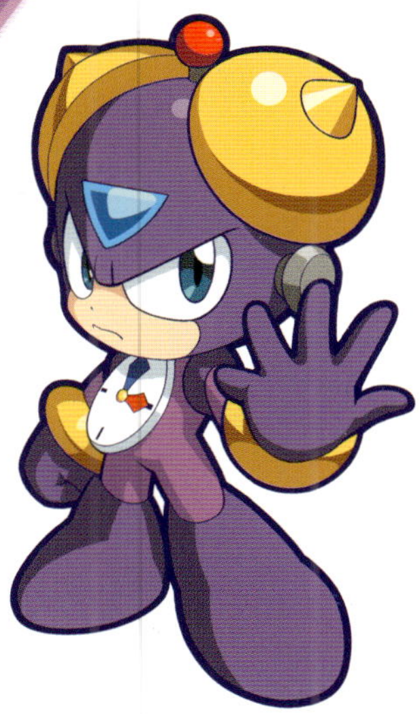

"We got the initial designs for Time Man and Oil Man from Inafune, and refined them ourselves. I worked on the 'Breath of Fire' series from the very beginning, and I think Oil Man's face is pretty reminiscent of 'Karn.' (laughs)" (Yoshikawa)

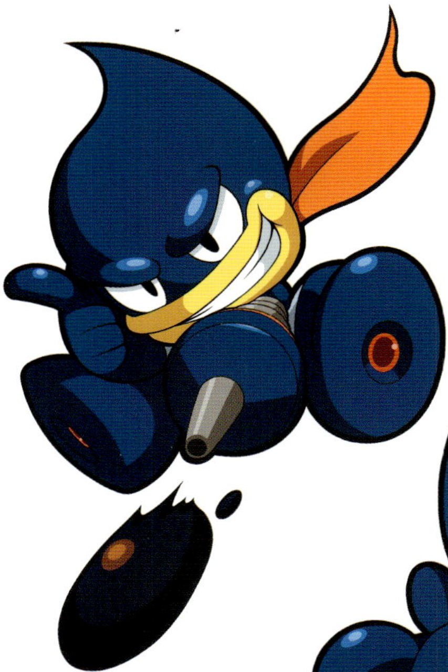

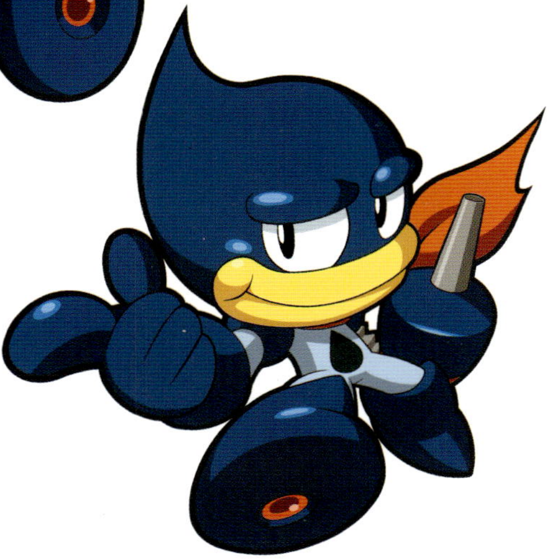

OIL MAN

MEGA MAN SERIES DATA

MEGA MAN *("Rockman" in Japan)*
Mega Man was first created by Dr. Light to be a helper robot, and was named Rock. He lived peacefully with Dr. Light until Dr. Wily's ambitions forced Dr. Light to reconfigure Rock into a combat robot. Mega Man is a kind boy with a strong sense of justice.

PROTO MAN *("Blues" in Japan)*
Proto Man was Dr. Light's first attempt at a humanoid robot, and is considered to be Mega Man's older brother. After he was created, it was discovered that Proto Man's energy processing device had a fatal defect. Realizing that his death was now inevitable, Proto Man disappeared without a trace. Moments before he shut down, however, he was taken by Dr. Wily. Because of the alterations Dr. Wily performed, Proto Man was able to narrowly avoid death.

BASS *("Forte" in Japan)*
Bass is one of the combat robots in the Special Wily Numbers, developed by Dr. Wily. Bass' greatest desire is to defeat Mega Man, and he will often take action without regard for Dr. Wily's orders.

DR. LIGHT *("Dr. Right" in Japan)*
Dr. Light's full name is Thomas Light. He is the one who created Mega Man, and is the leading mind in the world of robotics. After graduating at the top of his class in electronic engineering from the Robot Institute of Technology, Dr. Light devoted his life to the research and development of robots that aid in world peace.

ROLL
Roll is a domestic helper robot created by Dr. Light, and is considered to be Mega Man's little sister. She is a kind-hearted girl who is proficient at cooking and cleaning. Roll is constantly praying for Mega Man's safety.

RUSH
Rush is a support robot that Dr. Light created to aid Mega Man. Among other forms, Rush can transform into the Rush Coil, Rush Jet, and Rush Marine, according to Mega Man's transportation needs. Later on, Rush was also modified to be able to physically merge with Mega Man.

EDDIE
Eddie is an item storage robot created by Dr. Light. Due to a sudden attack by Dr. Wily, Eddie was forced to mobilize before he was perfected.

TANGO
Tango was created by Dr. Light to be a pet cat robot. Modified with attack capabilities, Tango will physically ram enemies to aid Mega Man.

AUTO *("Rightot" in Japan)*
Auto is an assistant robot that works at Dr. Light's laboratory. Being a bit absent-minded, Auto misplaced one of the bolts from his head while he was out running an errand. He rides his truck to get around.

DR. WILY
Dr. Wily's full name is Albert W. Wily. A former schoolmate of Dr. Light's, Dr. Wily was never quite able to match Dr. Light in skill, and eventually developed a desire to take over the world. Dr. Wily's hobbies include ping pong.

REGGAE
Reggae was created by Dr. Wily to relieve some of the constant loneliness he felt. Reggae is a bird robot, and does not have any combat abilities.

TREBLE *("Gospel" in Japan)*
Treble is a wolf robot that travels with Bass and offers support as needed. It is rumored that Treble's combat abilities are superior to those of the Wily Numbers'. Treble is able to turn into a flight booster and merge with Bass.

DR. COSSACK
Dr. Cossack's full name is Mikhail Sergeyevich Cossack. When his daughter Kalinka was taken hostage by Dr. Wily, Dr. Cossack had no choice but to send his robots into battle against Mega Man. After the battle was over, Dr. Cossack devoted himself to helping Dr. Light in the pursuit of peace. Dr. Cossack's hobbies include watching ballet performances.

KALINKA
Kalinka is Dr. Cossack's daughter. Dr. Wily took her hostage and used her to manipulate Dr. Cossack. Kalinka enjoys listening to classical music.

BEAT
Beat is a bird robot created by Dr. Cossack to aid Mega Man in the battle for world peace. Beat follows the signal sent by the Beat Plates to find Mega Man and swoop in to attack enemies.

MR. X
Everything about Mr. X is a mystery, except for the fact that he is the owner of the X Foundation. He provided financial support to the Global Robot Alliance, and was the one who suggested a contest to determine the most powerful peace-supporting robot. He was later discovered to be Dr. Wily in disguise when he stole the strongest robots from the tournament in an attempt to take over the world.

CHEST
Chest acts as a robot host in "Battle & Chase," providing explanations of each course.

RIPOT
In "Battle & Chase," Ripot provides live coverage of the races and helps drive the excitement level through the roof.

PLUM
Plum is a girl who serves as an announcer for "Battle & Chase."

DUO
Duo is a mysterious robot who fell to Earth while battling evil robots in space. After being discovered on a deserted island by Mega Man, Duo is repaired by Dr. Light. Sensing evil energy readings somewhere on Earth, Duo leaves to pursue their source.

KING
King is a robot who attempts to take over the world in the hopes of creating a new world where humans are dominated by robots. Stealing the data of the robots created by Dr. Light and Dr. Wily, King forms his own legion. King's hobbies include chess.

MEGA MAN SERIES RELEASE CHART

1987	12/17	Mega Man (NES)
1988	12/24	Mega Man 2 (NES)
1990	09/28	Mega Man 3 (NES)
1991	07/26	Mega Man: Dr. Wily's Revenge (GB)
	12/06	Mega Man 4 (NES)
	12/20	Mega Man II (GB)
1992	12/04	Meg Man 5 (NES)
	12/11	Mega Man III (GB)
1993	01/15	Wily & Light's Rock Board ~That's Paradise~ (NES)
	10/29	Mega Man IV (GB)
	11/05	Mega Man 6 (NES)
1994	03/25	Mega Man's Soccer (SNES)
	07/22	Mega Man V (GB)
	10/21	Mega Man: The Wily Wars (SG)
1995	03/24	Mega Man 7 (SNES)
	October	Mega Man: The Power Battle (AC)
1996	August	Mega Man 2: The Power Fighters (AC)
	12/17	Mega Man 8 (PS)
1997	01/17	Mega Man 8 (SS)
	03/20	Mega Man Battle & Chase (PS)
1998	04/24	Rockman & Forte (SNES)
	06/25	Super Adventure Rockman (PS)
	09/23	Super Adventure Rockman (SS)
1999	08/05	Rockman (PS)
	09/02	Rockman 2: The Secret of Dr. Wily (PS)
	09/14	Rockman 3: The End of Dr. Wily!? (PS)
	10/28	Rockman 4: A New Ambition!! (PS)
	11/25	Rockman 5: Blues' Trap!? (PS)
	12/09	Rockman 6: The Greatest Battle of All Time!! (PS)
2000	07/06	Rockman Battle & Fighters (NGP)
2002	08/10	Mega Man & Bass (GBA)
2004	08/05	Rockman Power Battle Fighters (PS2)
2006	03/02	Mega Man: Powered Up (PSP)

ROUGH SKETCH

ラフスケッチ

With permission from the Capcom Design Department, we have gathered some of the art from Keiji Inafune's sketch book in this section. By going through these pages, we get to have an exclusive look at the process behind the illustrations, as well as the trials and tribulations Inafune faced. We are also fortunate enough to have some comments from Inafune himself to accompany these sketches.

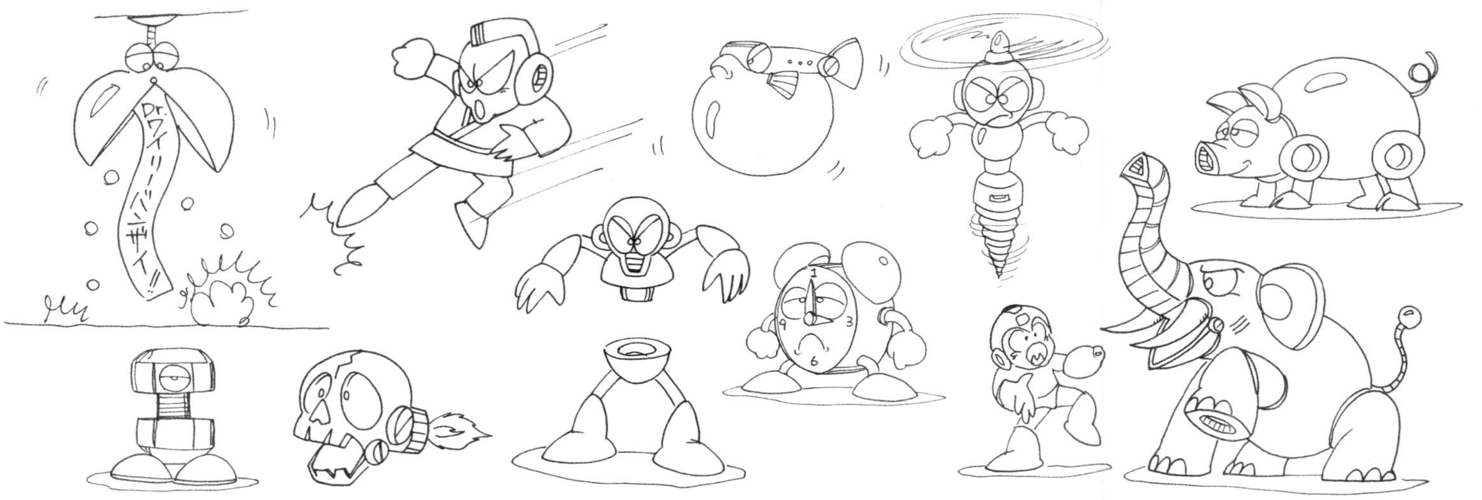

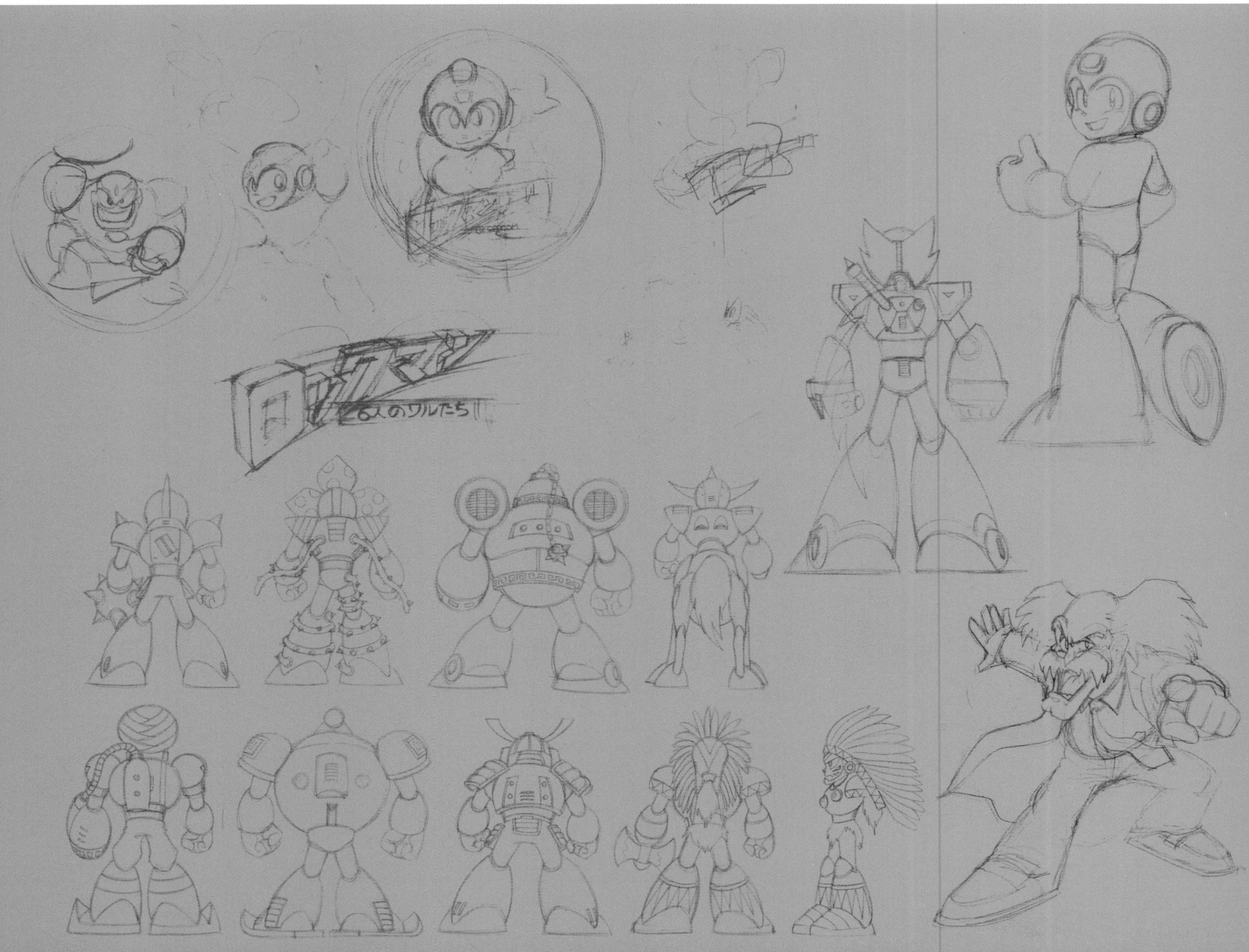

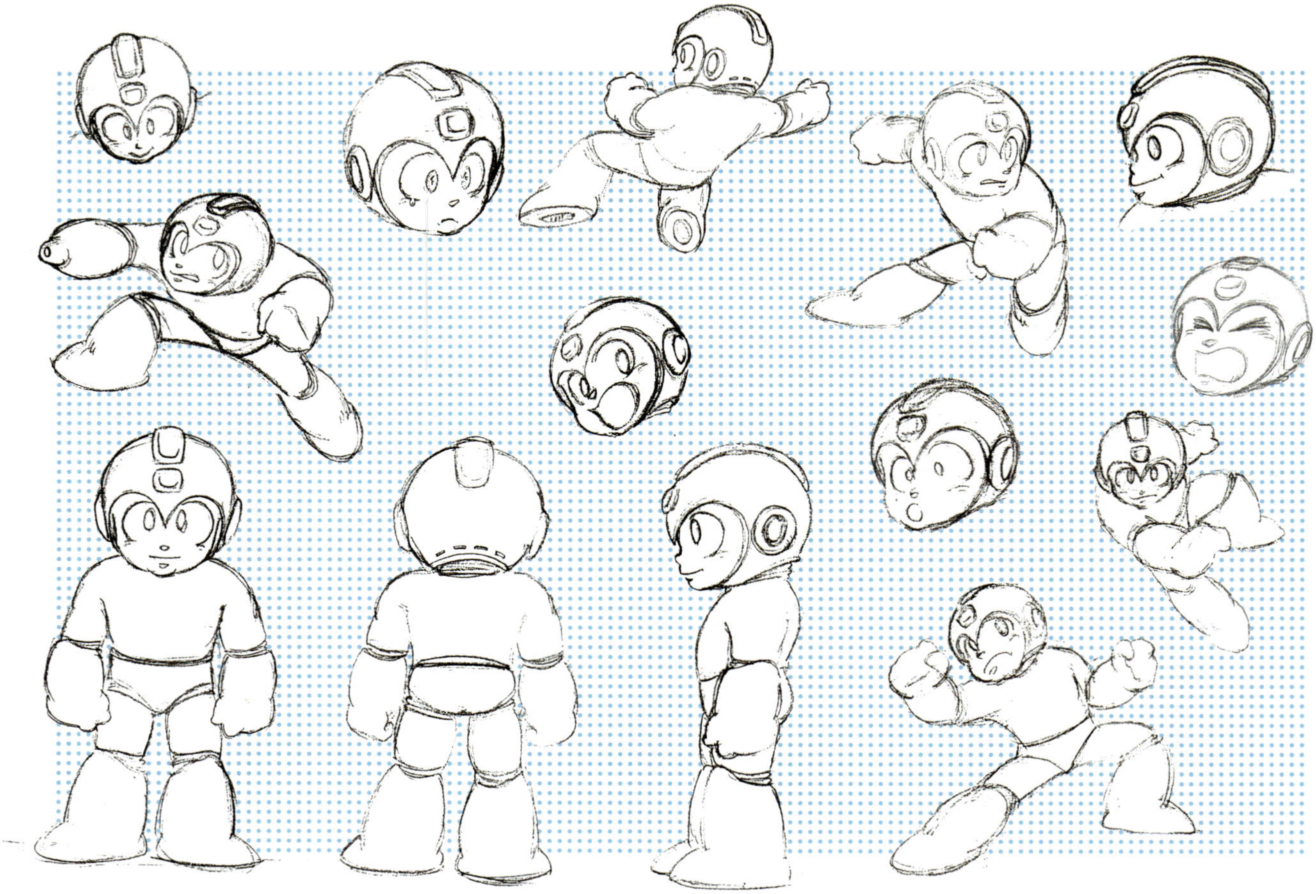

"By the time I joined the development team, the planner (my mentor) had already hammered out some basic dot images for Mega Man." (Inafune)

Inafune added any missing patterns, and moved on to create the main visuals for the character. We believe these sketches were part of his process to solidify the image of Mega Man.

While doing the dot work, his sketch book was always sitting next to his computer.

"These are sketches I did while trying to figure out what Elec Man would look like. You can see the transition from an early model to something that looks more like the final character design." (Inafune)

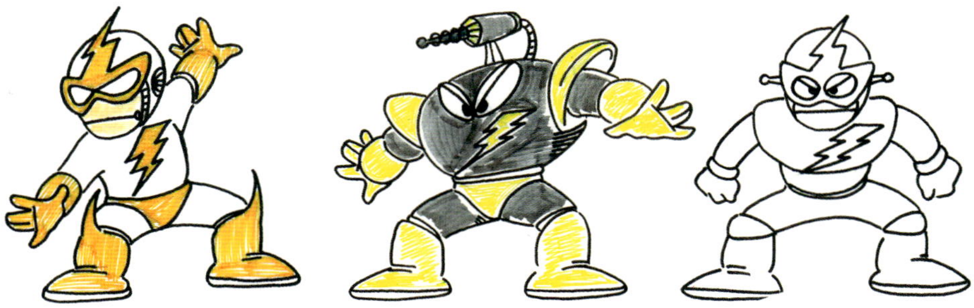

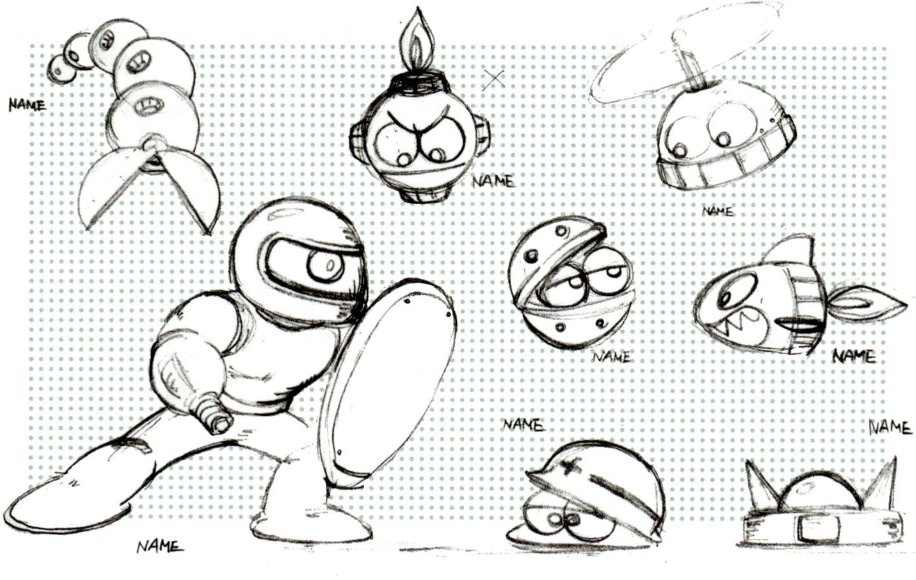

It was always necessary to keep the limits of the NES's capabilities in mind while designing characters. Inafune had to supress a lot of his desire for more detail while he pushed out the dots and added sketches to his book.

"I guess I could have enjoyed more freedom with my designs if I had simply ignored the limitations I was presented with... but in some ways, working within certain limitations can actually lead to really interesting designs." (Inafune)

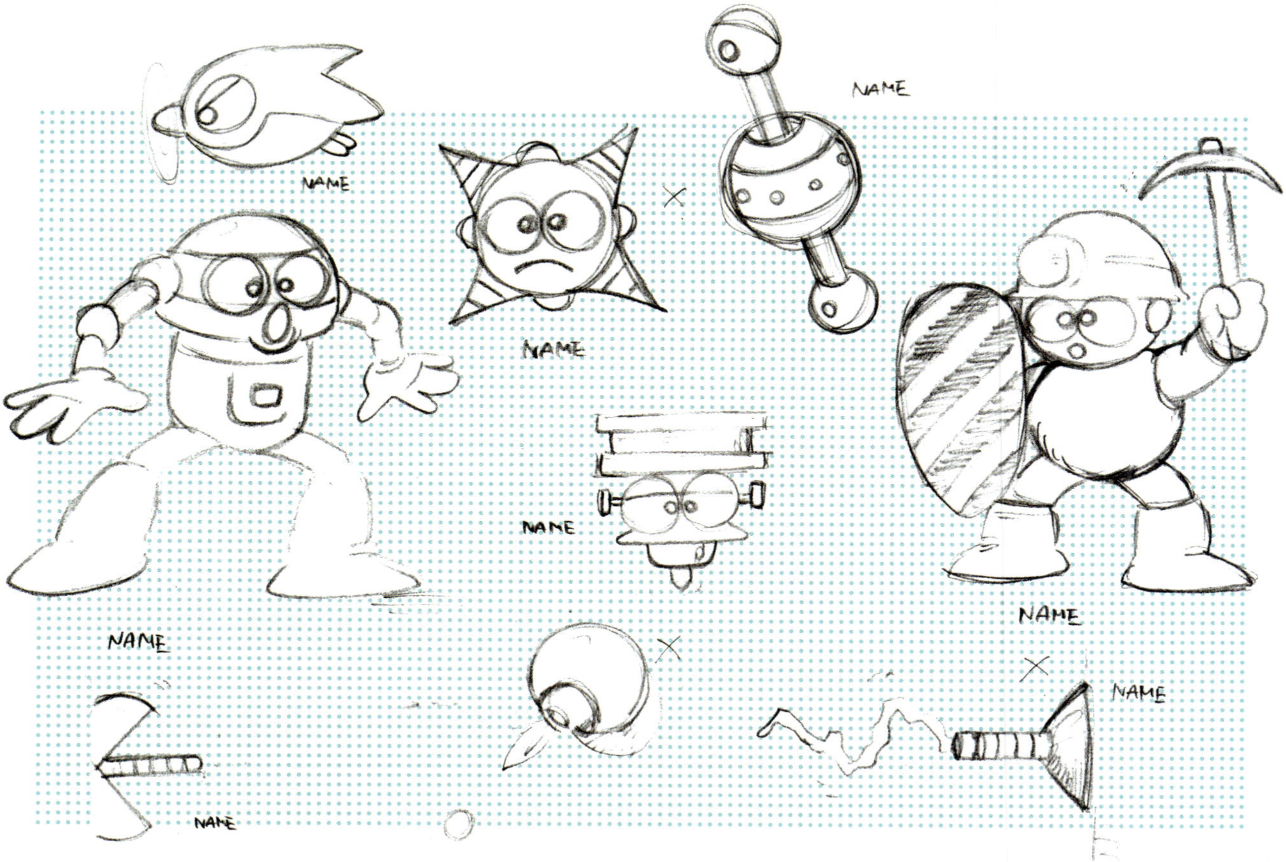

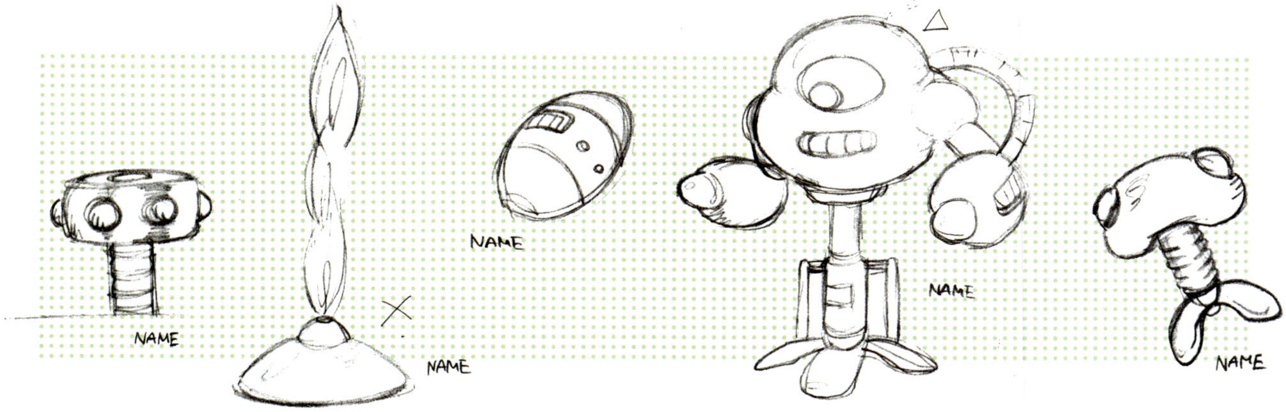

According to Inafune, the on-screen graphics were "quite limited," and keeping these limitations in mind while designing characters for the NES proved quite challenging.

Here we can see the early form of Springer from Mega Man 2. A lot of the characters who were sketched out but not used in the first game were reused later on as base concepts for characters in future titles.

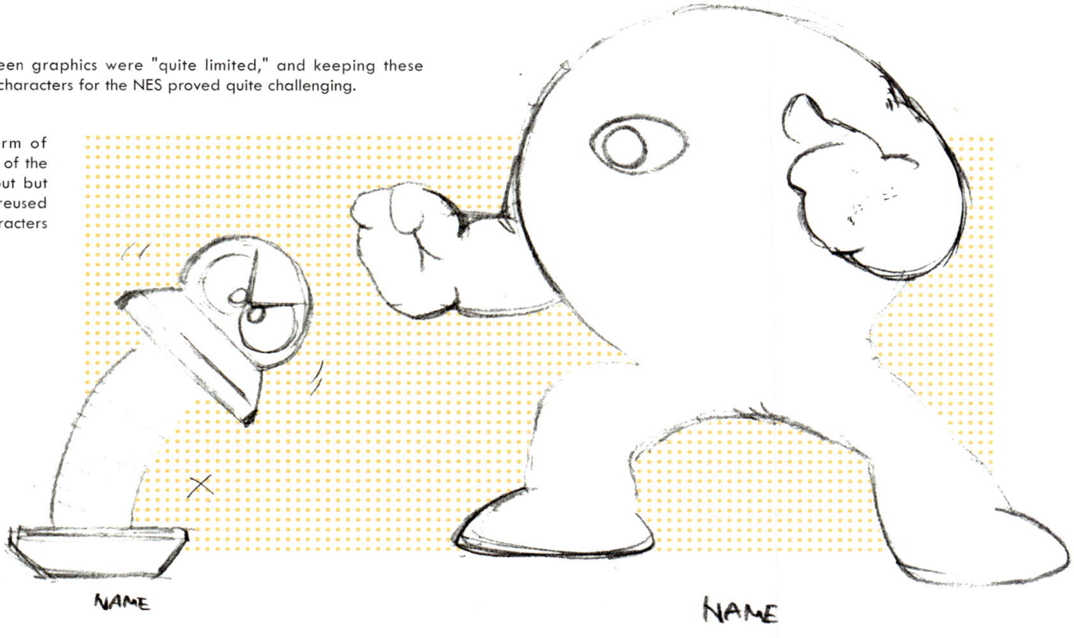

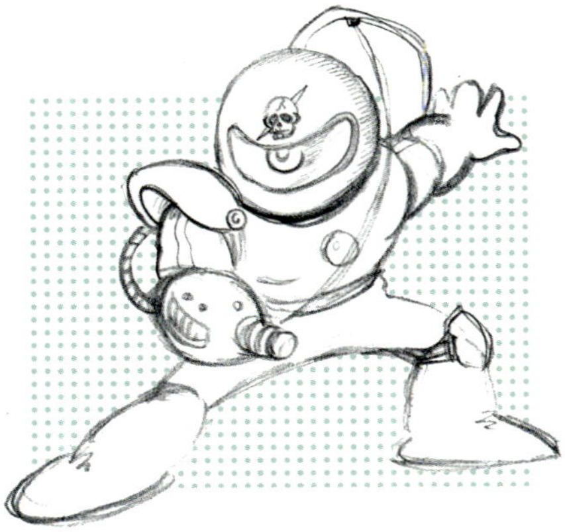

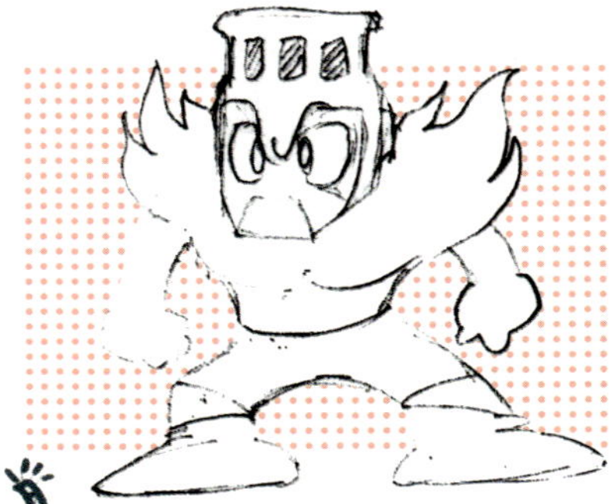

A Fire Man with flaming shoulders, and a Sniper Joe with more details in his design.

"I'd draw sketches in my book, try to create a dot image, then go back and forth between the two to figure out exactly what I could and could not make happen. I'd be like, 'Hmm... I don't think this is possible,' or 'Oh! I can totally make that work!' That's how my process worked." (Inafune)

"I had so much trouble getting Bomb Man approved." (Inafune)

By struggling through the constant rejection of his submissions, Inafune eventually settled on the Bomb Man below.

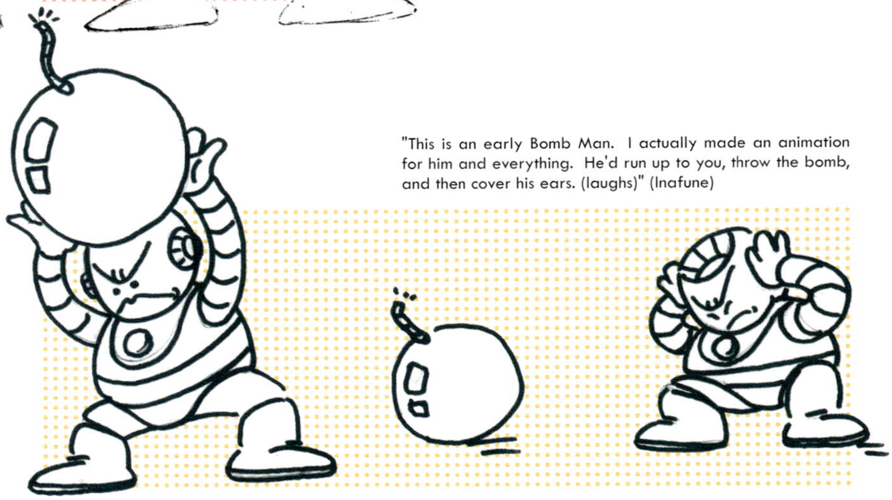

"This is an early Bomb Man. I actually made an animation for him and everything. He'd run up to you, throw the bomb, and then cover his ears. (laughs)" (Inafune)

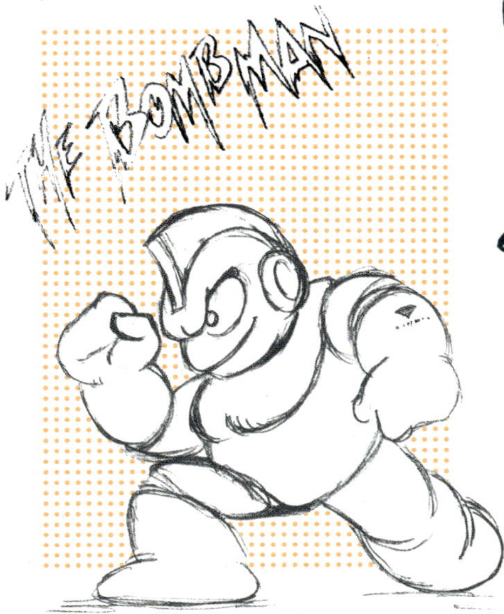

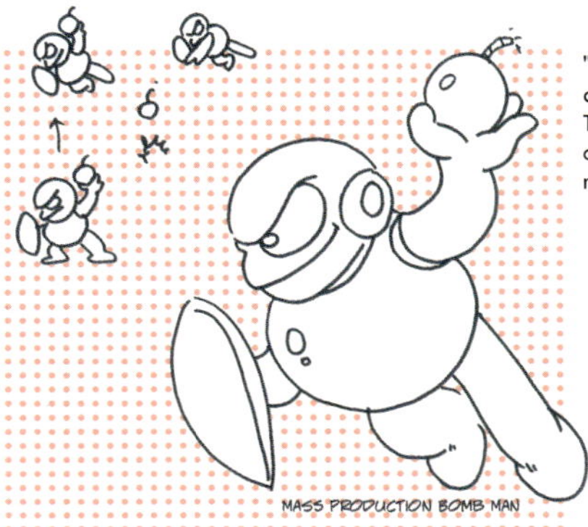

"Mass Production Bomb Man? What the... I don't remember drawing this at all. (laughs) This was probably a design for some minor character to go along with Sniper Joe... maybe. (laughs)" (Inafune)

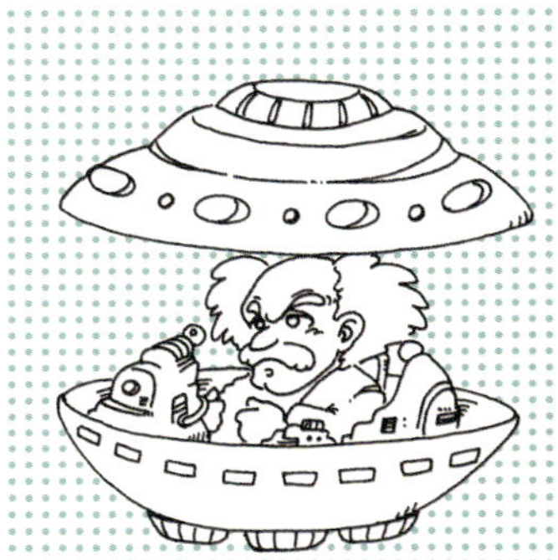

"The initial plan was to have eight boss characters, but that number was reduced to six due to resource issues." (Inafune)

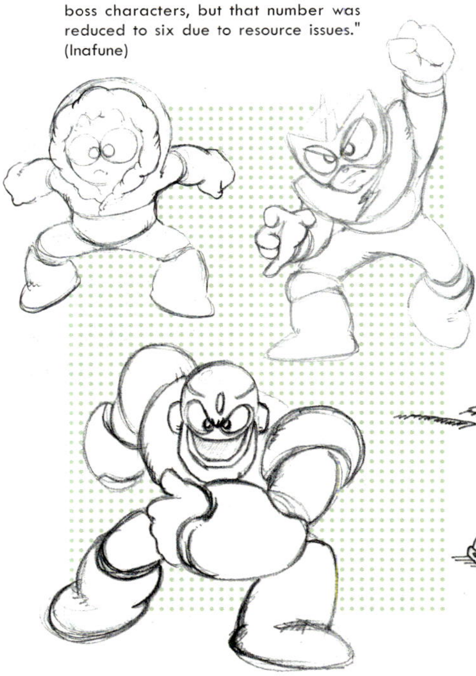

While Inafune was working on character designs, he also had to come up with designs for the backgrounds. The sketch below is of Wily's base. Note what appears to be a Wily UFO parked on the very top of the building.

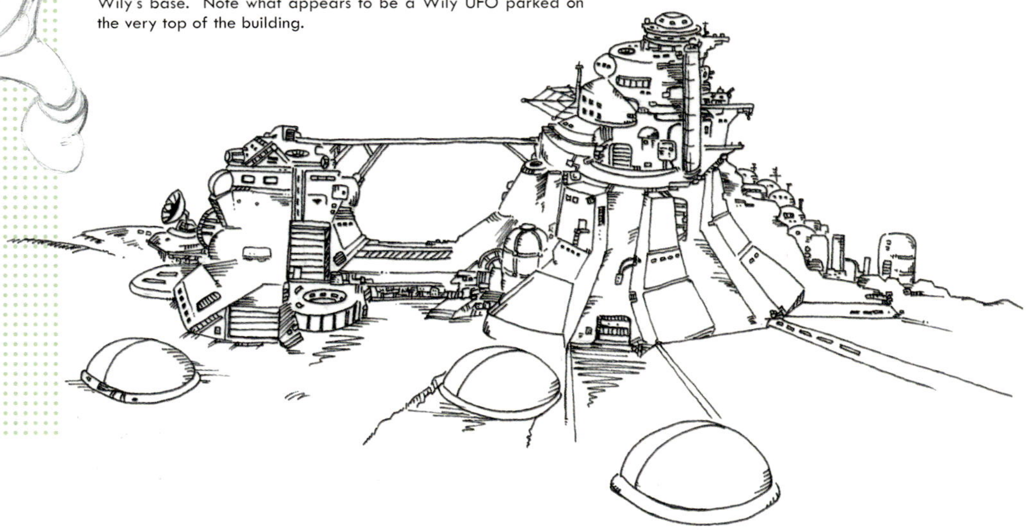

Early designs of Dr. Light and Dr. Wily. Their designs were further refined from these sketches, with Light being based off of Santa Claus and Wily being based off of Einstein.

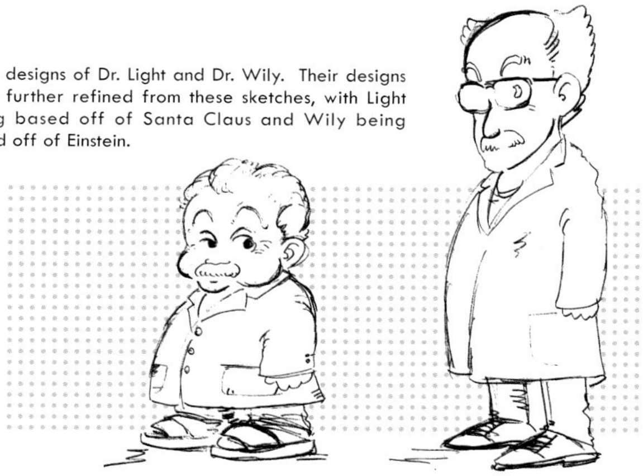

A rough sketch of the Wily Machine. The UFO had always been a part of the concept.

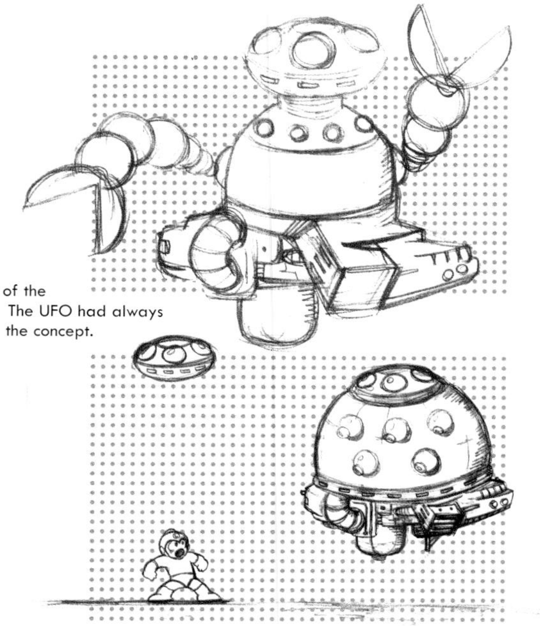

The title design was also done by Inafune. We can see from these sketches that there were a number of ideas being tossed around before they settled on "Rockman."

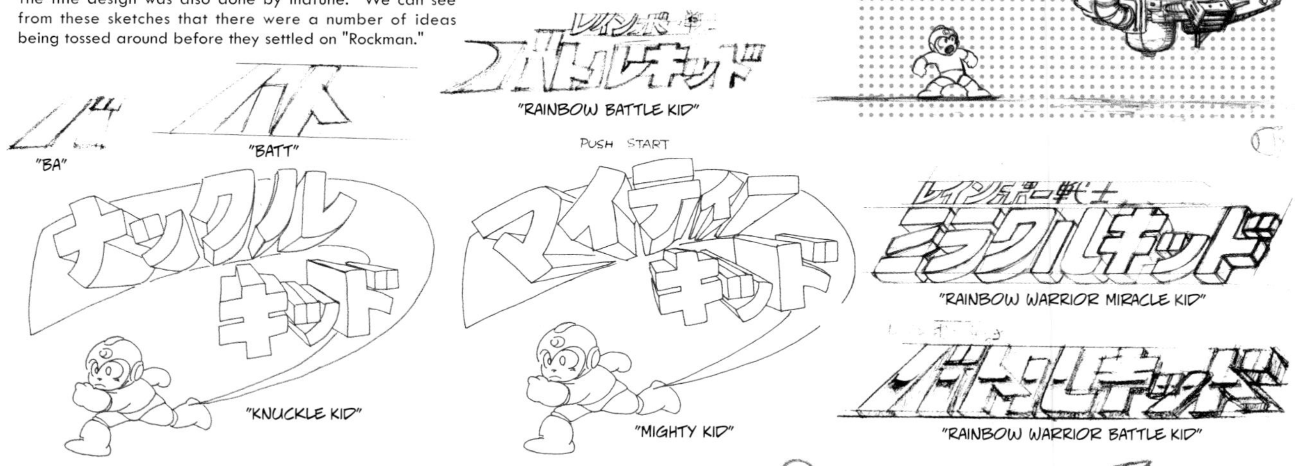

Even after they had settled on "Rockman," there were still quite a few ideas for the title design.

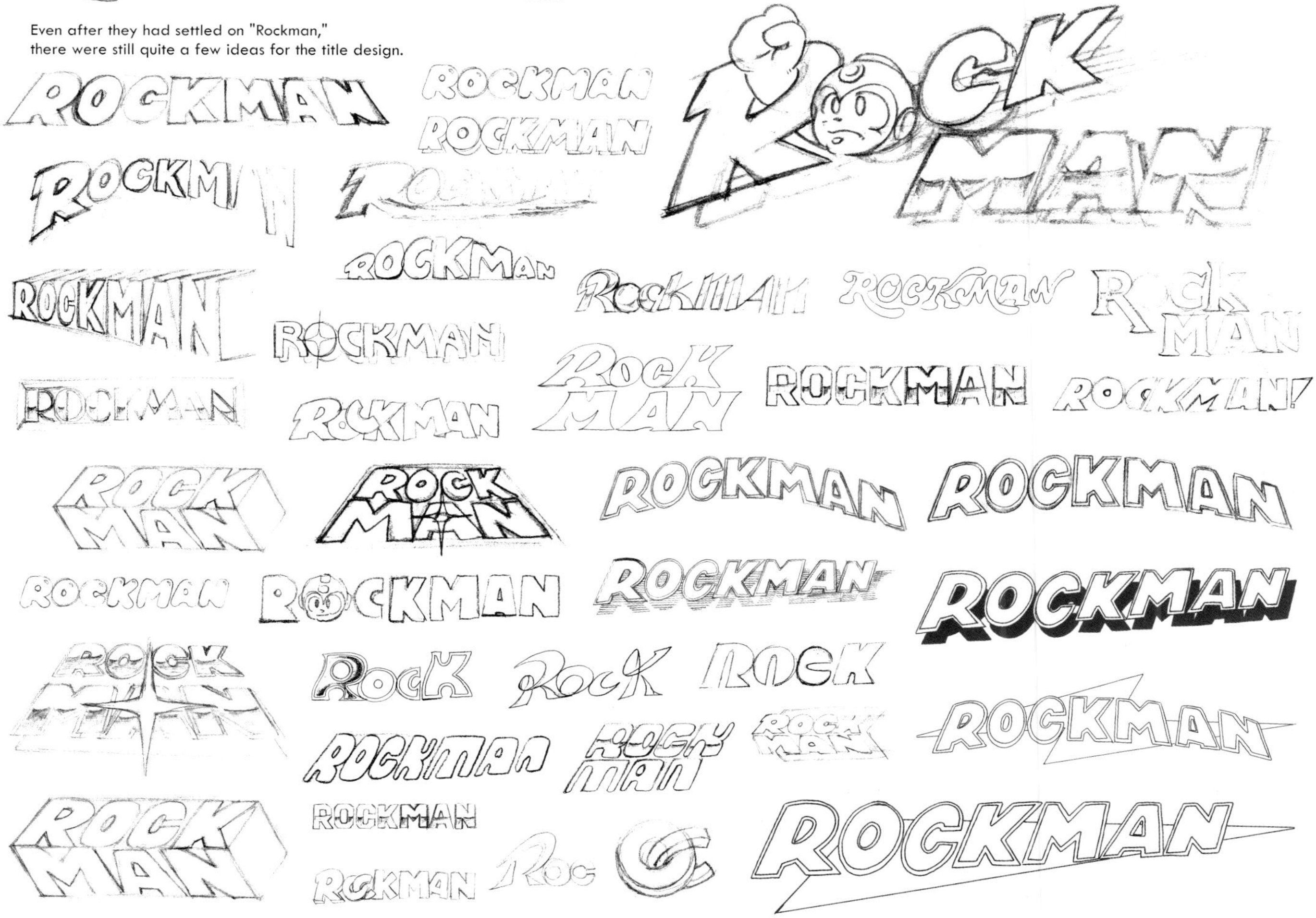

THE ROAD TO THE BOSS CHARACTERS OF MEGA MAN 2

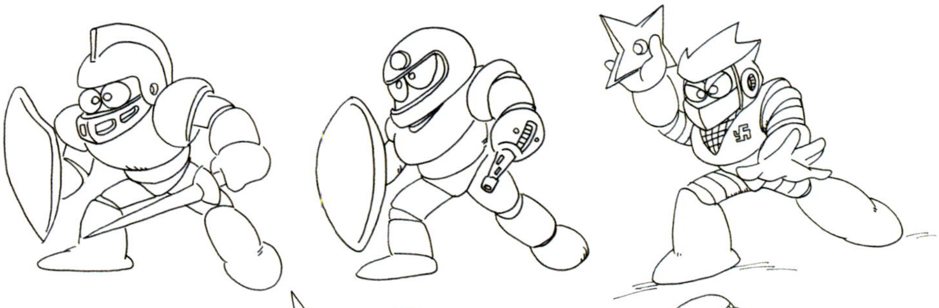

"Although the boss characters were open to public submissions, we couldn't wait until after the submissions had arrived and we had selected the winners to start development. If we went that route, we never would have made our deadlines. Instead, we had to plan out the various stages and have a loose idea of what kind of boss we would want for each stage." (Inafune)

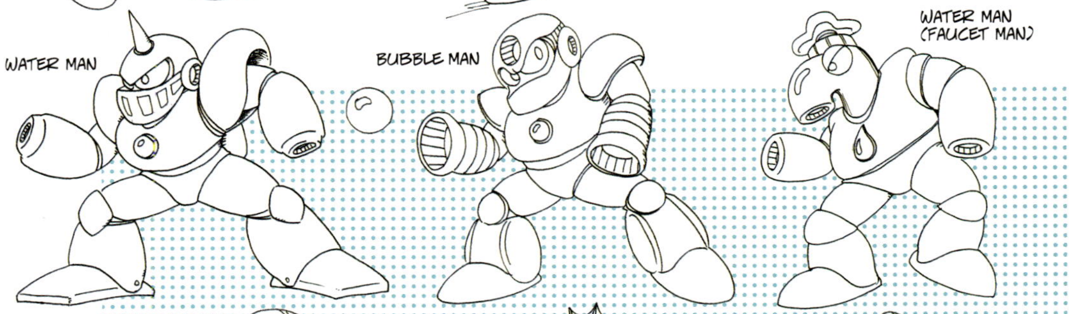

"We selected the motifs we were most interested in from out of the many submissions. I really enjoyed working off of our players' ideas, cleaning them up and redesigning them as necessary." (Inafune)

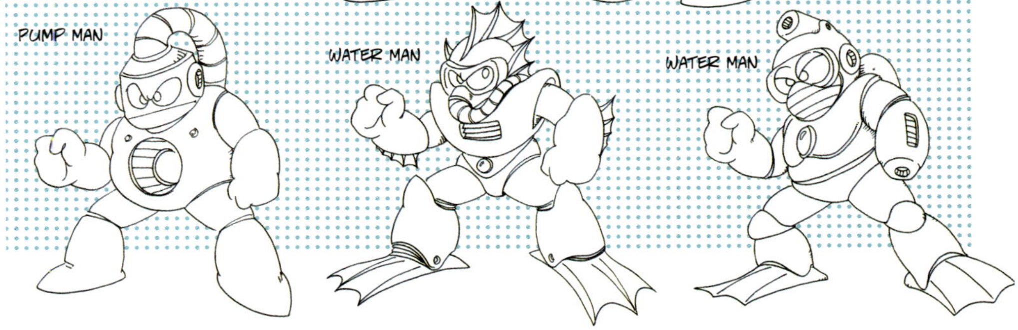

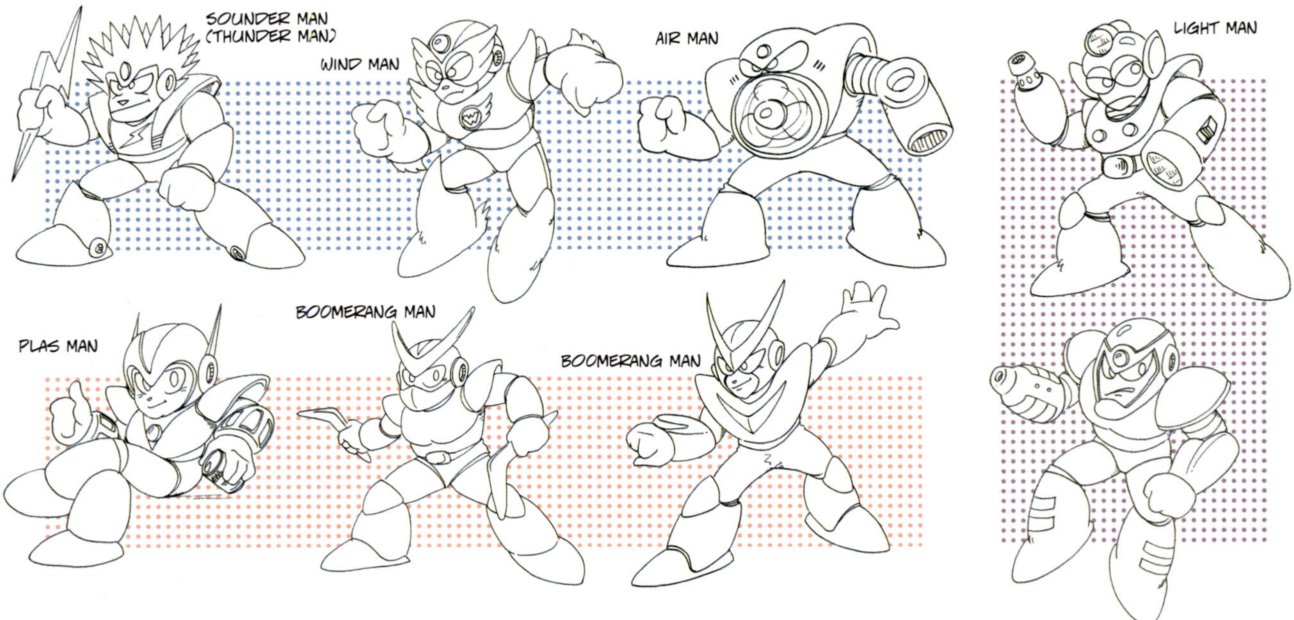

Inafune took designs from the selected entries and cleaned them up a bit before he and his team made their final selections.

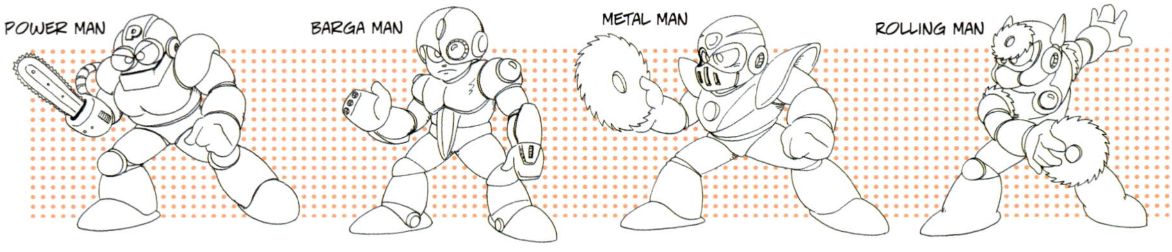

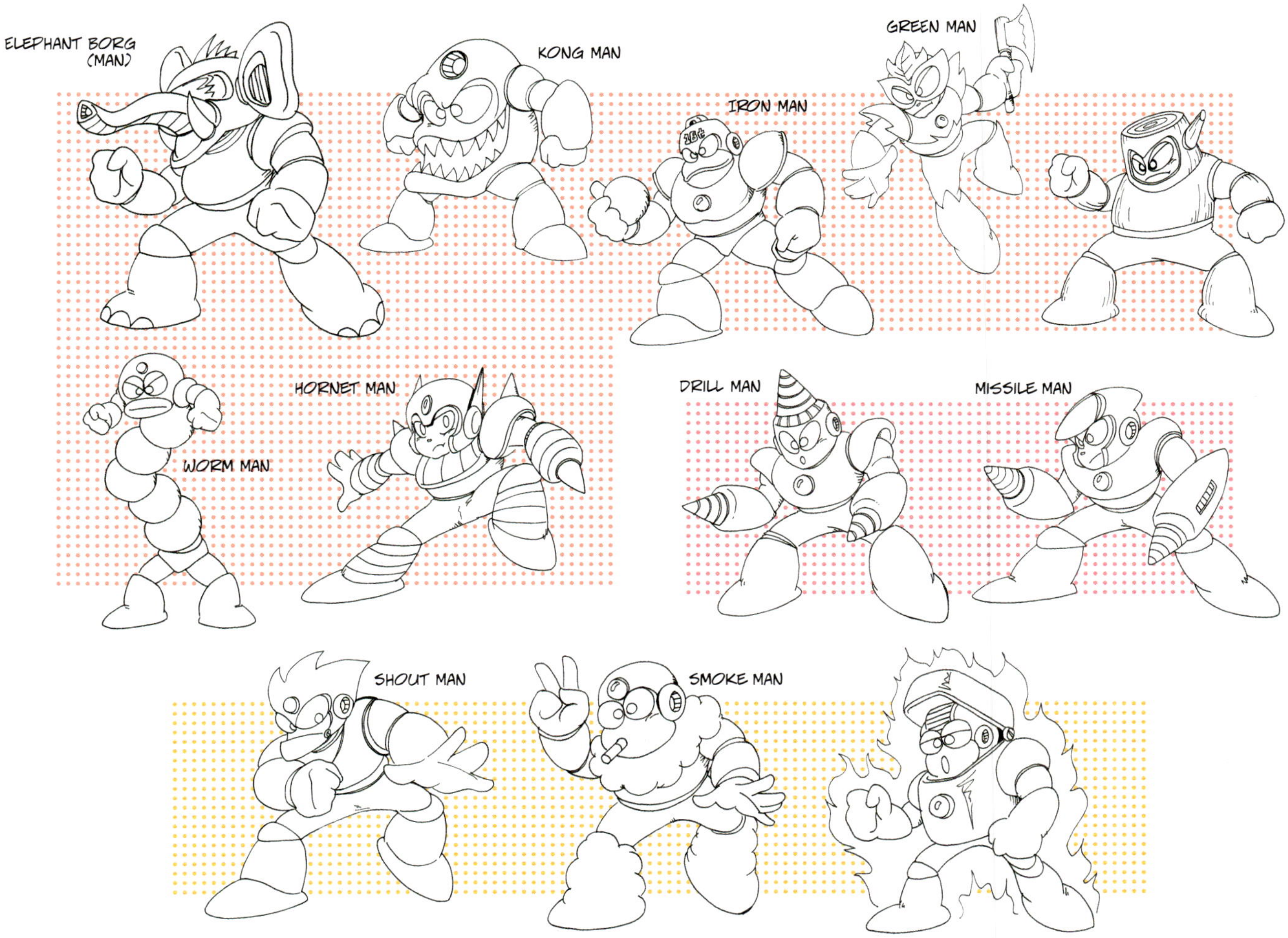

WORK ON THE STAGE ENEMIES WAS PROGRESSING EVEN BEFORE THE BOSS CHARACTER SUBMISSIONS WERE IN.

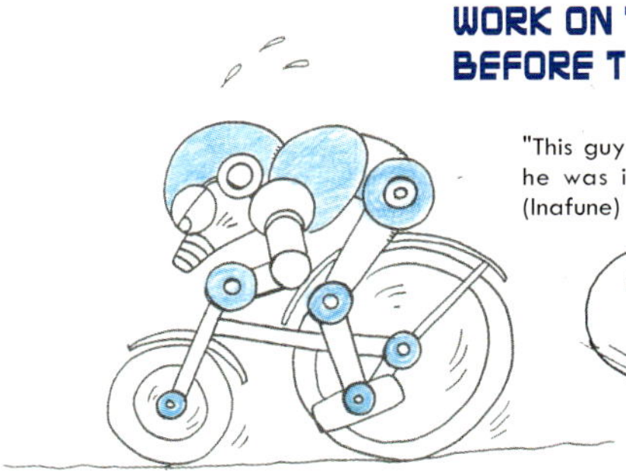

"This guy who's kicking something... I think he was intended for Air Man's stage." (Inafune)

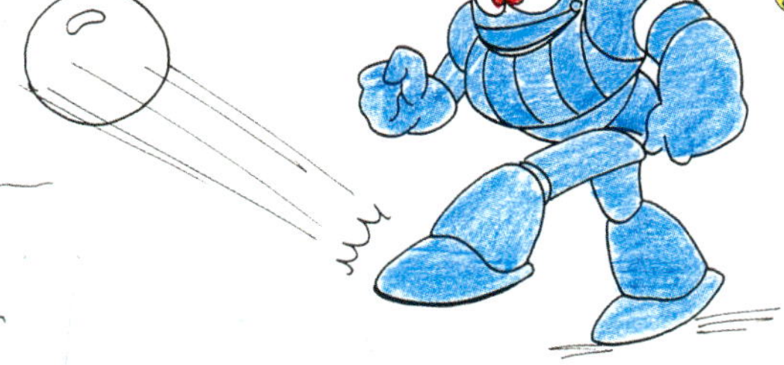

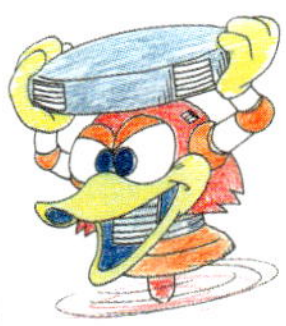

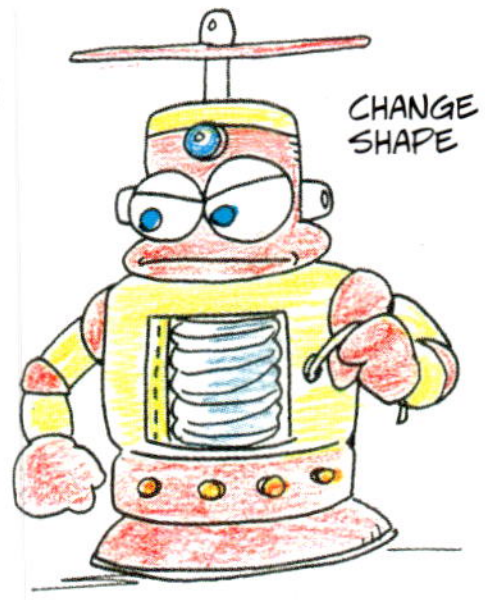

We believe this sketch is the original design for Fly Boy. The words "change shape" can be seen next to the sketch.

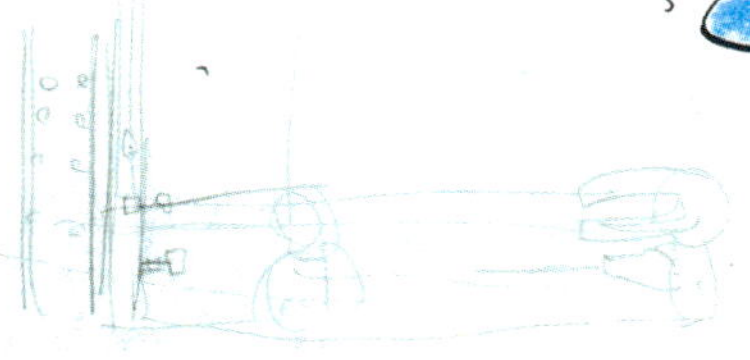

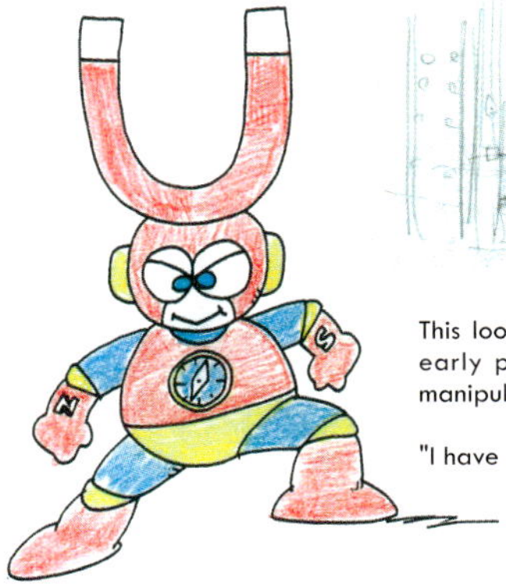

This looks like it was an idea for a boss character based on the early plans for a stage. It looks like he is using his magnet to manipulate screws as a way to attack the player... is this correct?

"I have no idea. (laughs) It was such a long time ago." (Inafune)

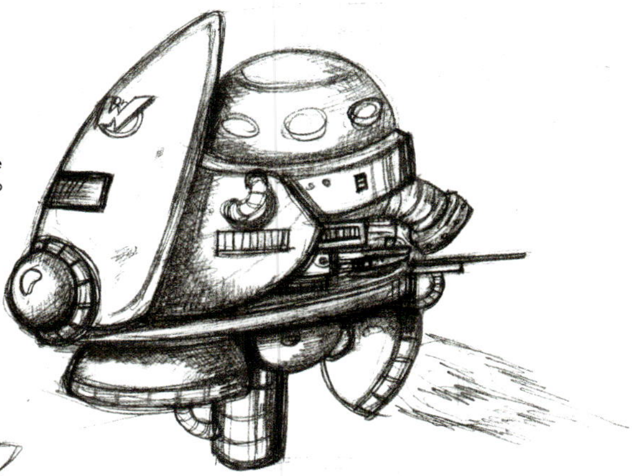

A sketch of Wily Machine 2.

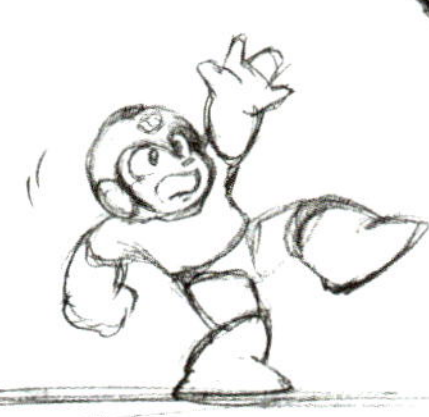

"The guy behind '1' and '2,' my mentor, was so hardcore. I learned so many valuable lessons from him... things like how to make a character seem bigger than the NES's limitations technically allow, the unwritten laws of making a game, and what is absolutely not acceptable according to those laws. By working with him, I really learned how deep you need to get in order to make a great game. I learned even more while working on '2.'" (Inafune)

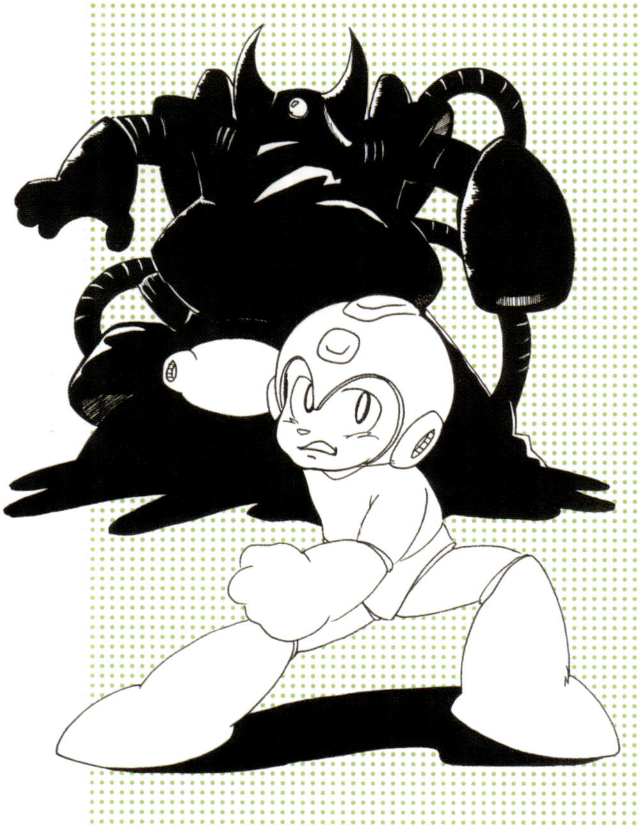

"This is something I did while working on Gamma." (Inafune)

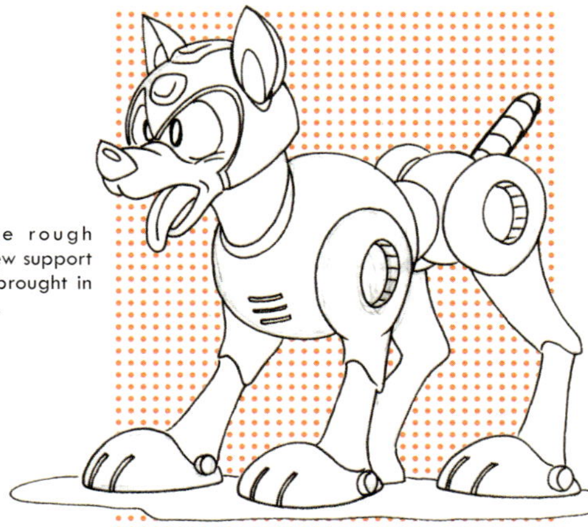

These were the rough sketches for the new support character being brought in with Mega Man 3.

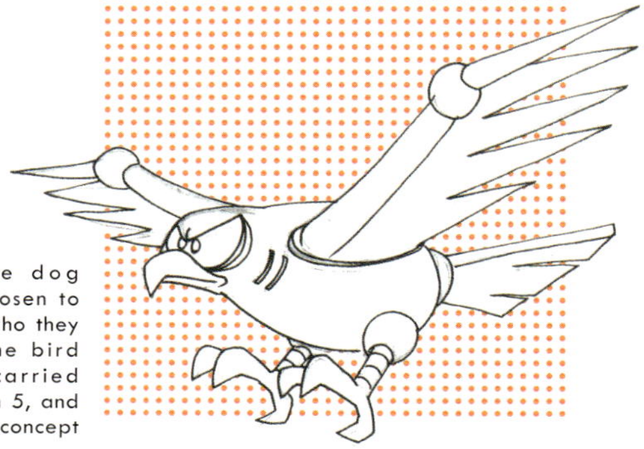

In the end, the dog character was chosen to be in the game, who they named Rush. The bird character was carried over to Mega Man 5, and became the base concept for Beat.

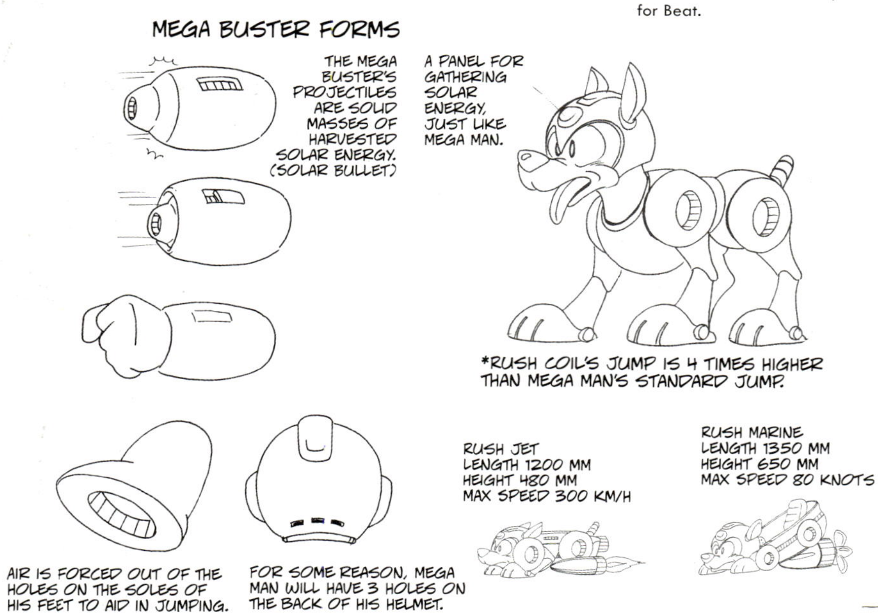

For Mega Man 3, the designs were further refined. These are a few of the sketches for Mega Man and Rush.

Starting with Mega Man 3, Infaune was not only doing the character designs and the backgrounds, he was also heavily involved in the planning aspects of the game.

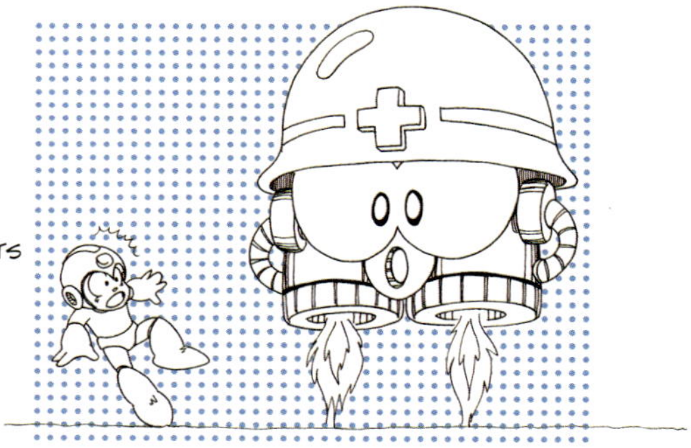

"With '2,' we were pretty tight on time, so I pitched in with the planning as well. Guts Tank, for instance, was all me. For '3,' I was involved in the planning from the very beginning. I had to consider things like how to make the giant snake in Snake Man's stage wriggle properly, and I also had to redo certain characters and stages. I learned so much from my experience with '2,' and I put that knowledge to good use." (Inafune)

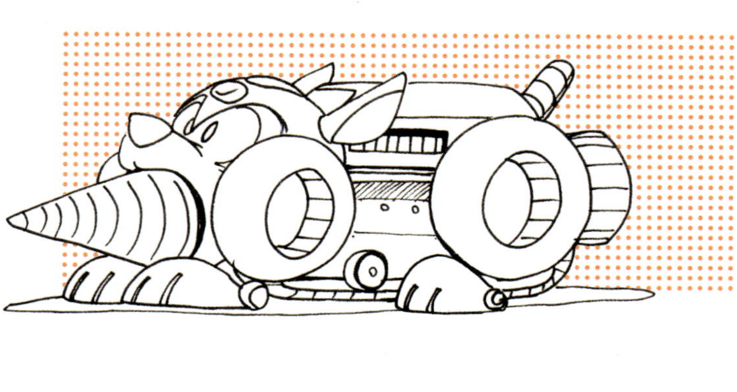

One of Rush's forms that didn't end up making the final cut. It seems like they were thinking about having this drill burrow through the stage map to make a path for the player. The giant drill coming out of Rush's mouth has a pretty strong impact.

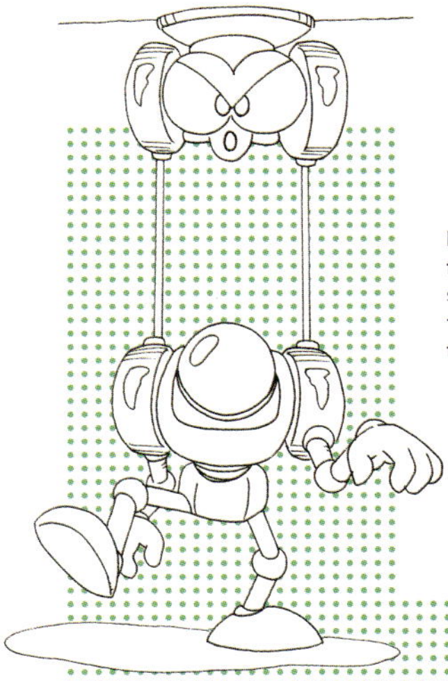

Enemy designs, and one of the designs for an event scene. We spotted Yudon from Mega Man 5 among these sketches.

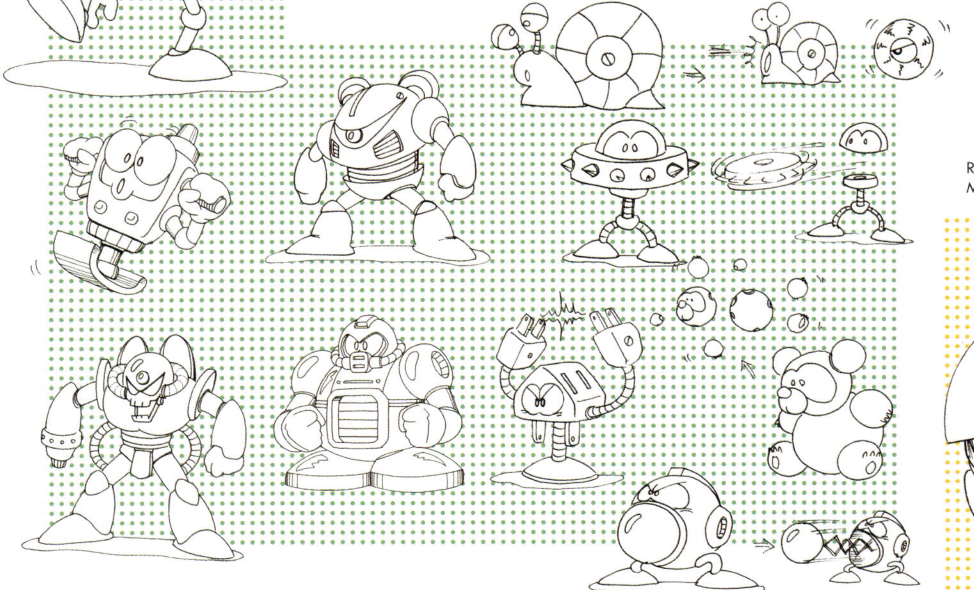

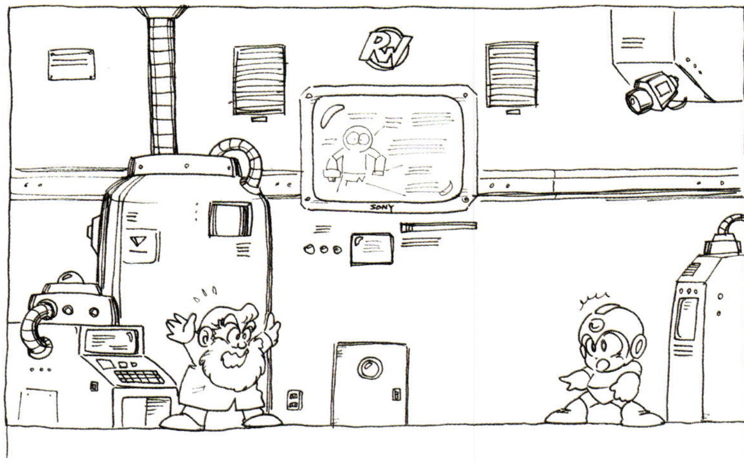

Roll's first close-up, from the Mega Man 3 ending.

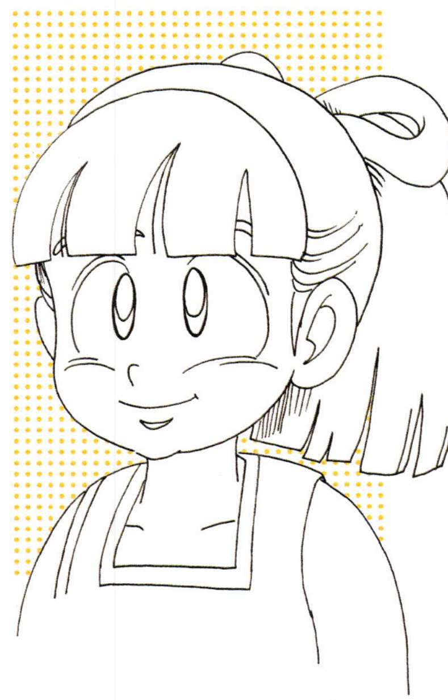

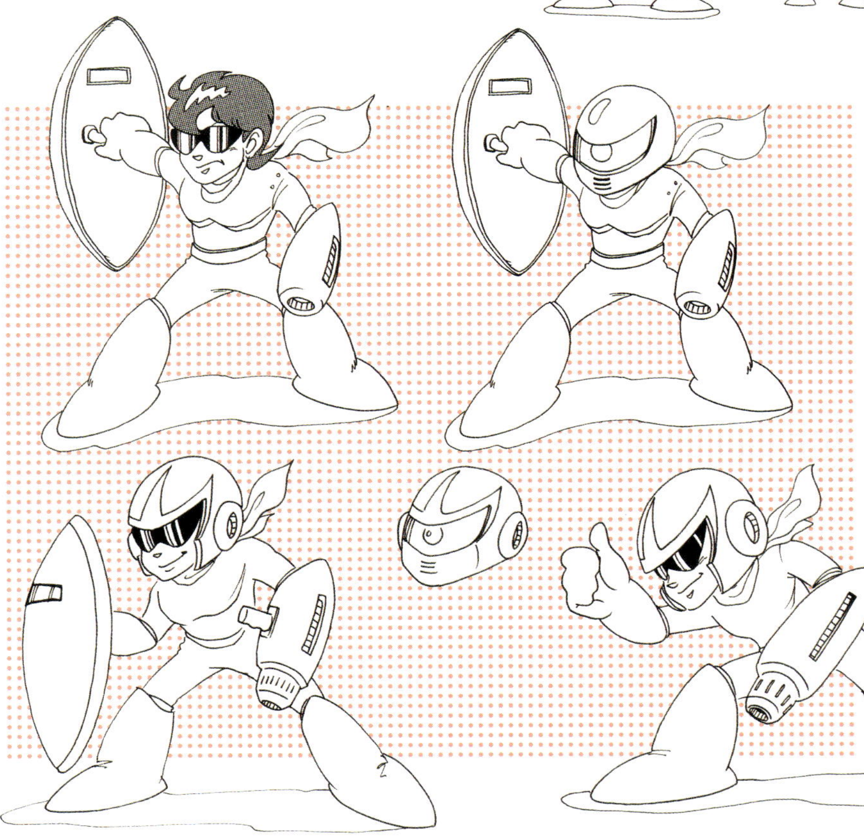

Through multiple stages of trial and error, Proto Man comes to life.

"We initially were going to have him with hair, but that just made it look like Mega Man was being mean to a human being, so... (laughs)" (Inafune)

The result of these designs was a Proto Man with an open-face helmet, who was used for both television commercials and the manual.

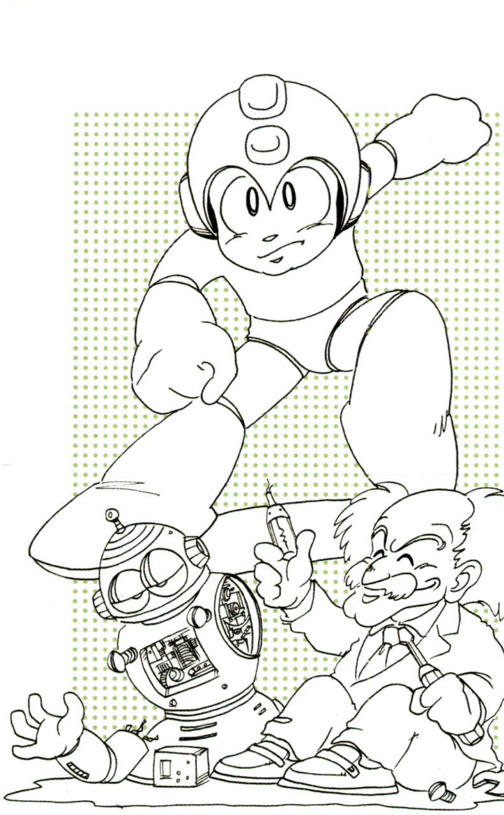

These sketches of Mega Man and Dr. Wily were for the boss character submission ads.

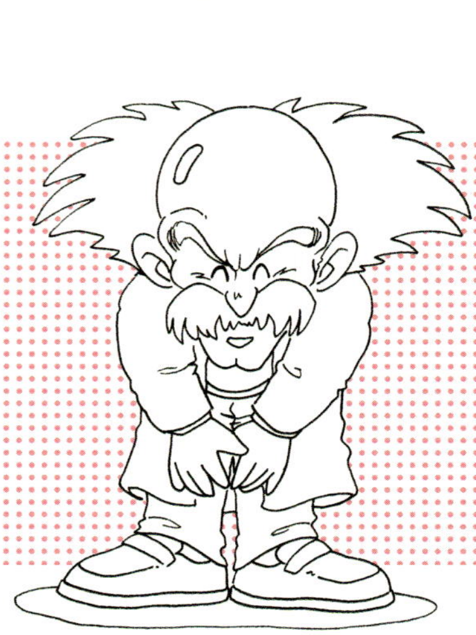

"This is the 'Thank you for all the submissions!' Wily." (Inafune)

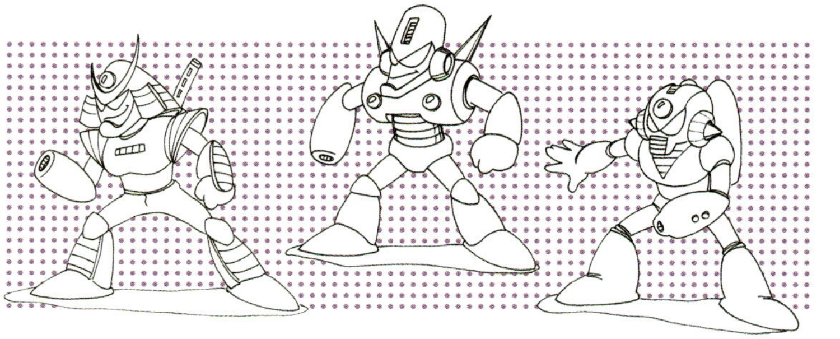

Then came the process of sifting through the submissions that came in from all over the country.

"There's so many... I can't remember which ones were from submissions, and which ones were the ones I did while planning out the stages." (Inafune)

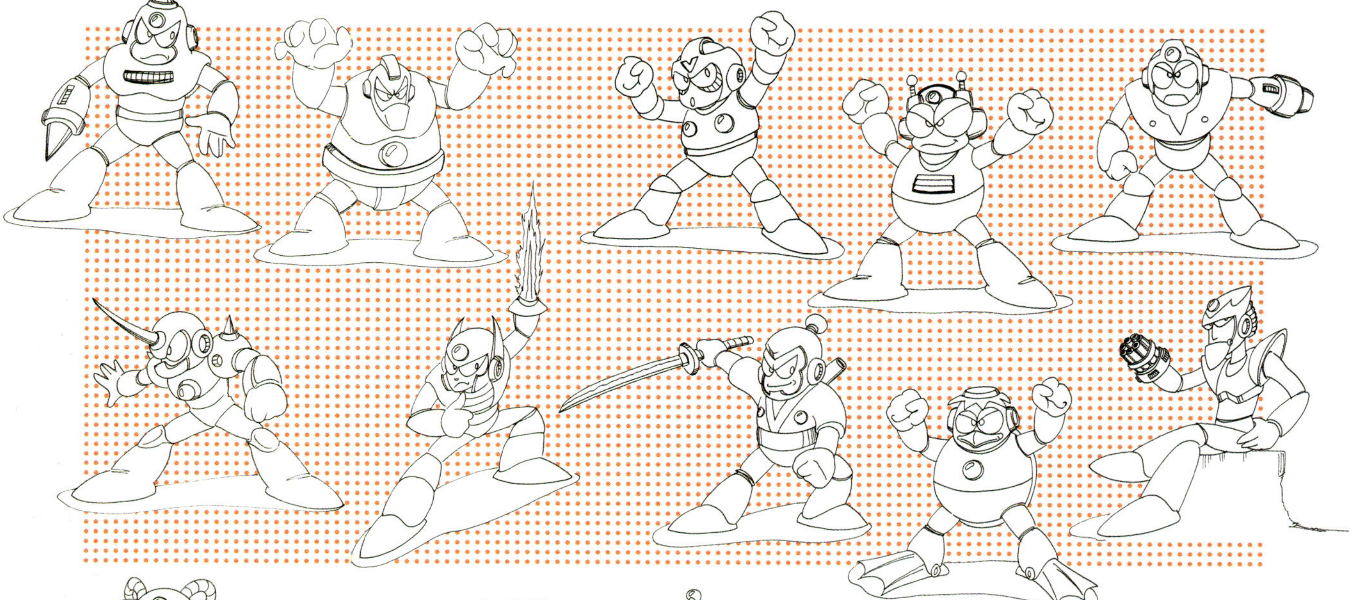

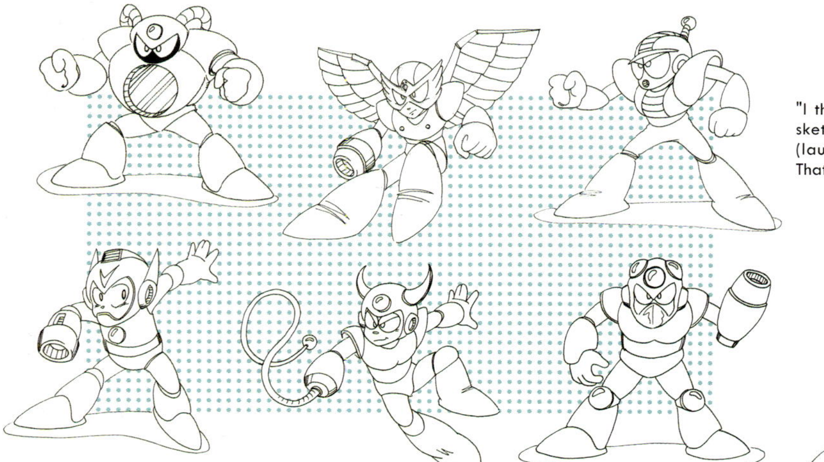

"I think it's so fun when we find sketches that I don't recognize. (laughs) But... they're all mine. That's for sure. (laughs)" (Inafune)

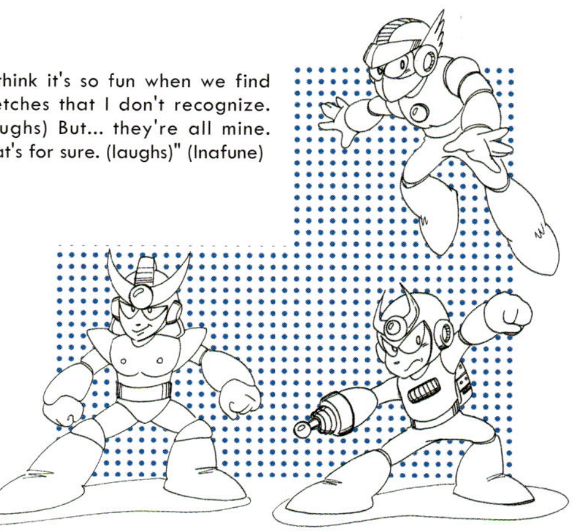

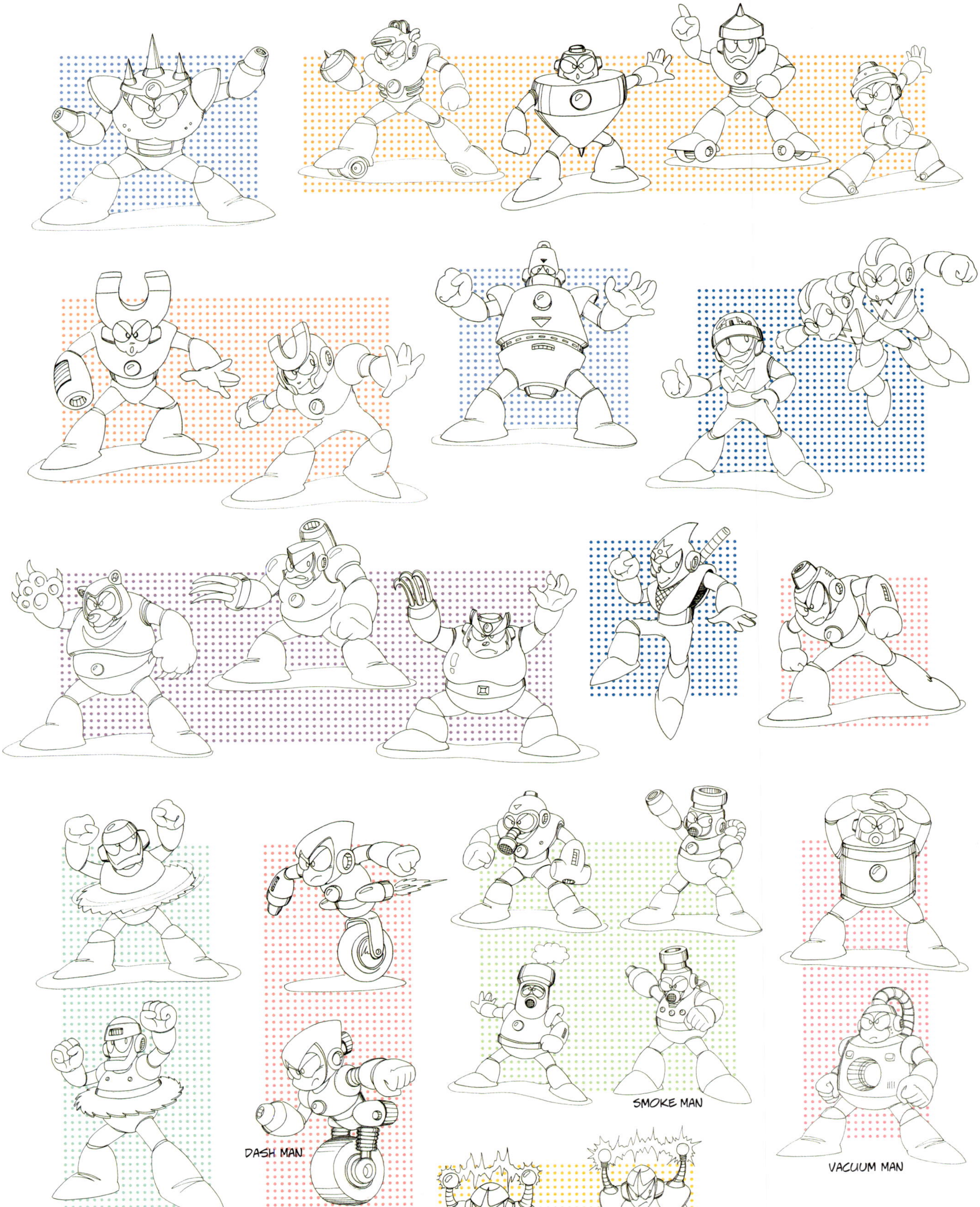

There were even more boss character submissions for Mega Man 3 than there were for Mega Man 2. From the sheer volume of sketches that Inafune made based on the submissions, it is clear that the competition between the Mega Man 3 submissions was also more intense.

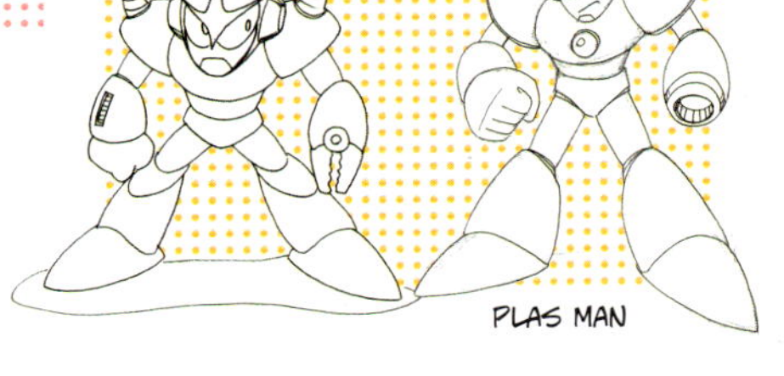

We can see that some of these sketches look very close to the final designs. The designs that were not used in the games are still just as fun as those that were. I wonder how far along in production they swapped out the chosen bosses with the placeholders?

Designs for Wily Machine 3

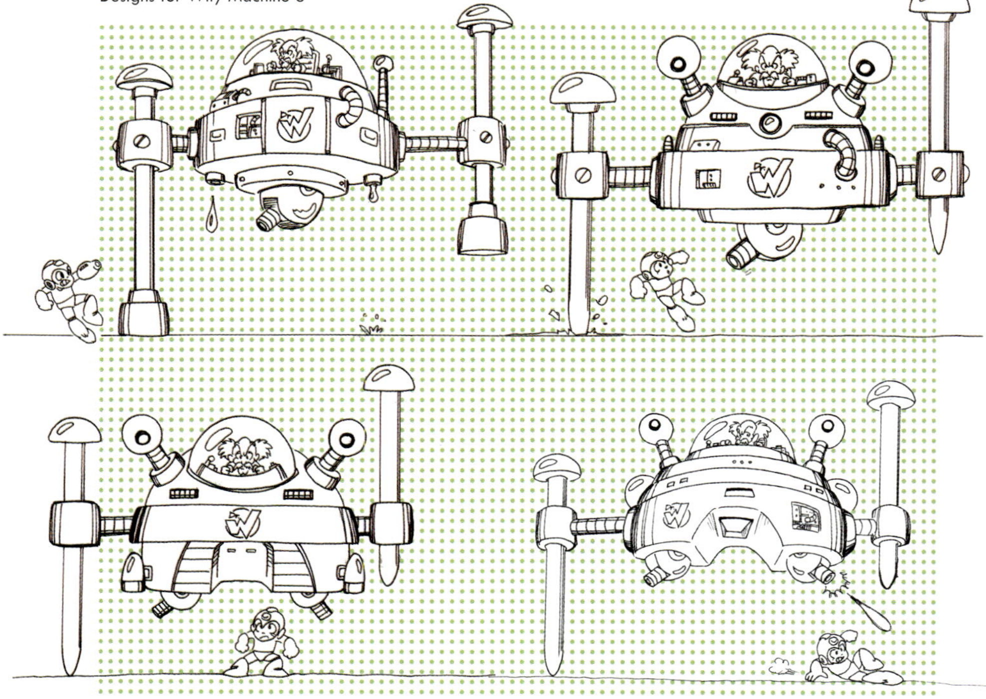

They traded in the acid drops for the stakes to perform vertical attacks, and gradually went from just one cannon to two cannons. These changes were made to give the player more opportunities to use the new "sliding" feature that was introduced in Mega Man 3.

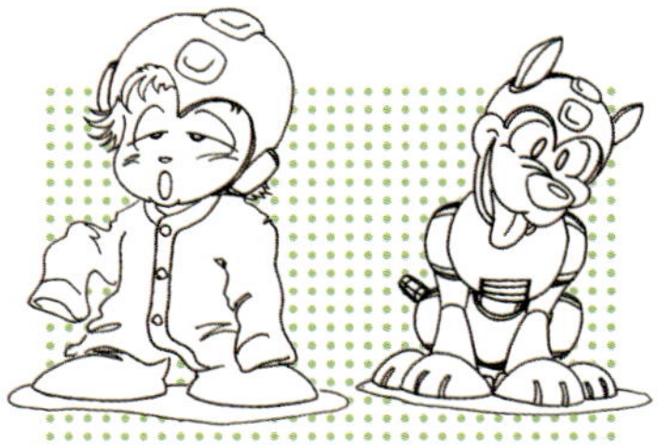

Mega Man and Rush sketch for the Rockman 3 box thumbnail.
"We didn't end up using either of these." (Inafune)

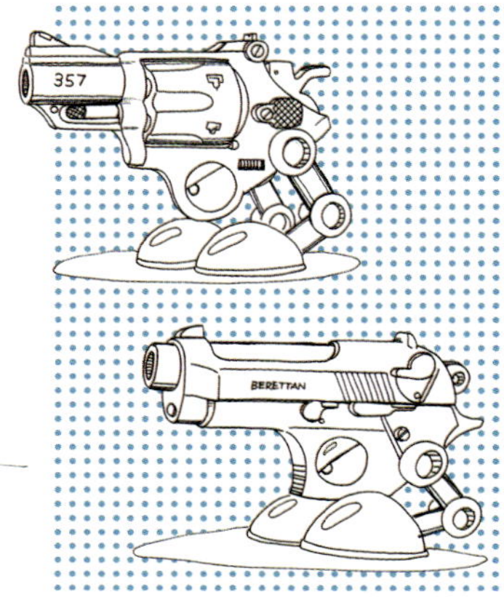

"What the heck is this!? Berettan... (laughs) There's no way we could get away with something like this now." (Inafune)

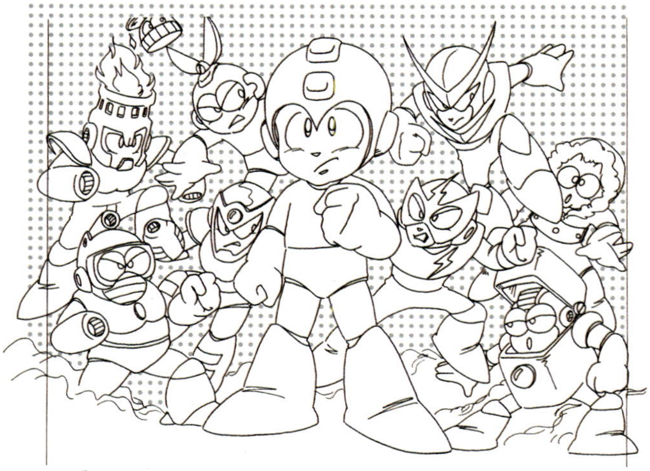

Some ideas for the package art for Rockman World ["Mega Man: Dr. Wily's Revenge" in North America] on the Game Boy. At this stage, the general set up closely resembles that of the NES versions, but is quite different from the final product.

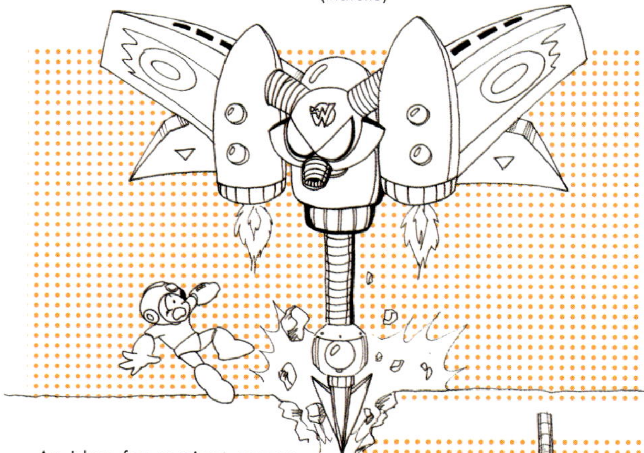

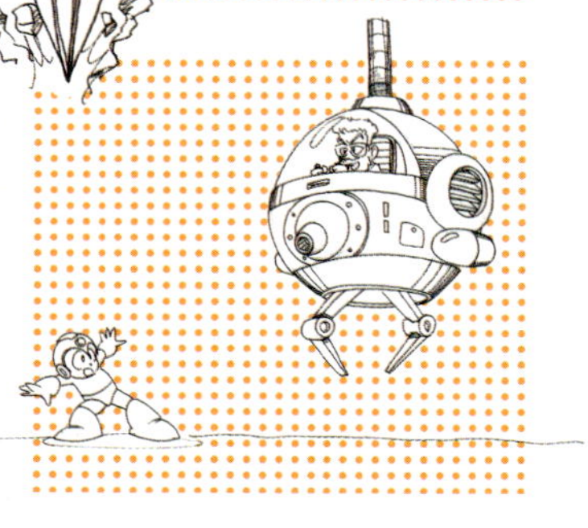

An idea for a giant enemy character in Mega Man 4. The details of a design are usually refined on the fly while doing the dots for any given character.

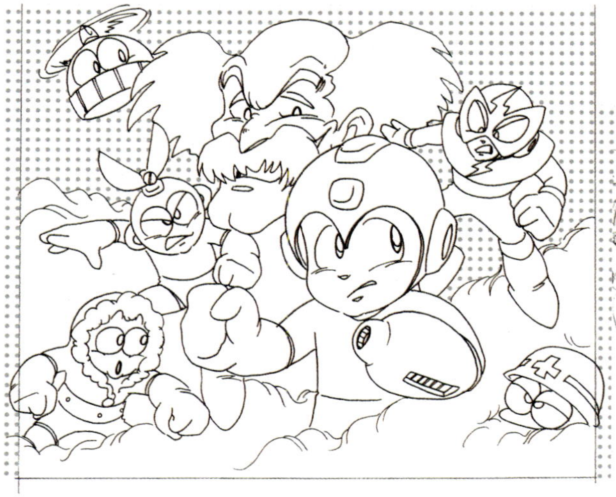

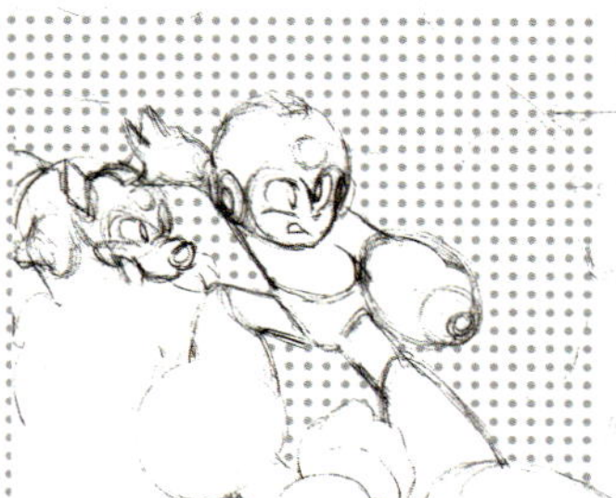

"Since this title was sort of a spin-off, I wanted to make the package look really different from what you saw with the main titles. I basically went with something that looked like we were seeing him in the middle of a heated battle, which included the backs of certain characters and visible wounds all around." (Inafune)

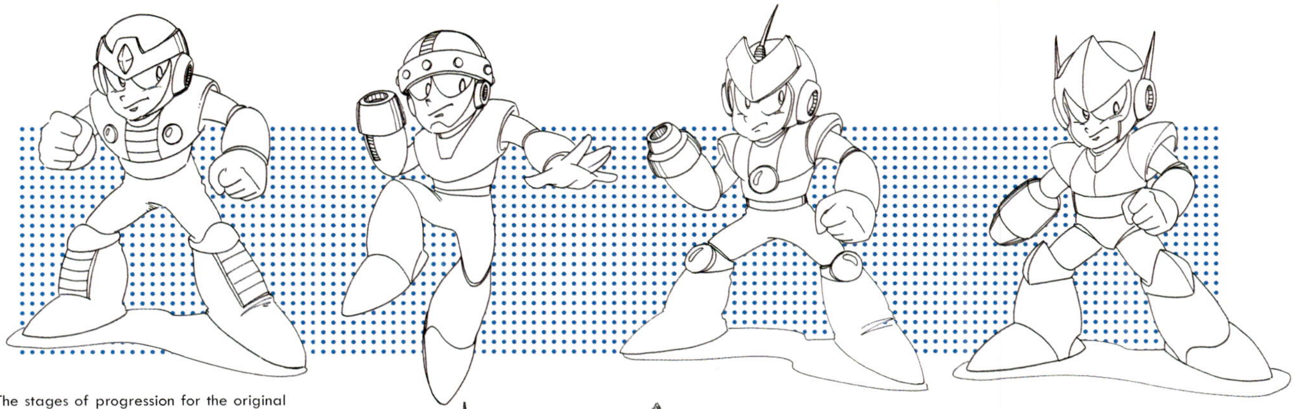

The stages of progression for the original boss that they came up with for the Game Boy version: the Mega Man Killer, Enker.

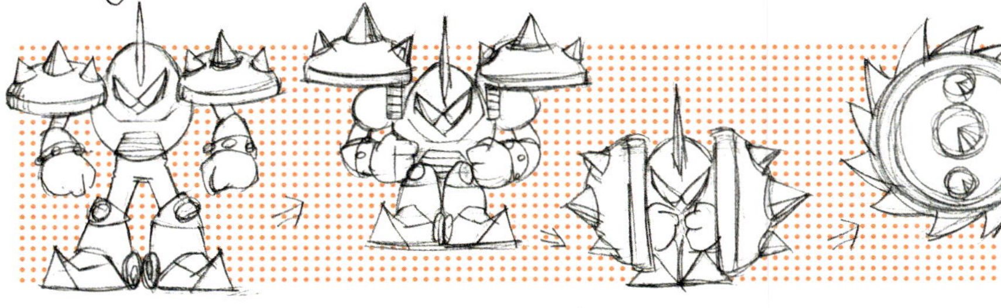

The different transformation stages of the Mega Man Killer, Punk.

"I really got into these designs, except for 'World 2' ['Mega Man II' in America]. (laughs) I especially liked Punk, and when it was decided that he'd make an appearance in 'Battle Network,' I insisted on redesigning him myself. (laughs)" (Inafune)

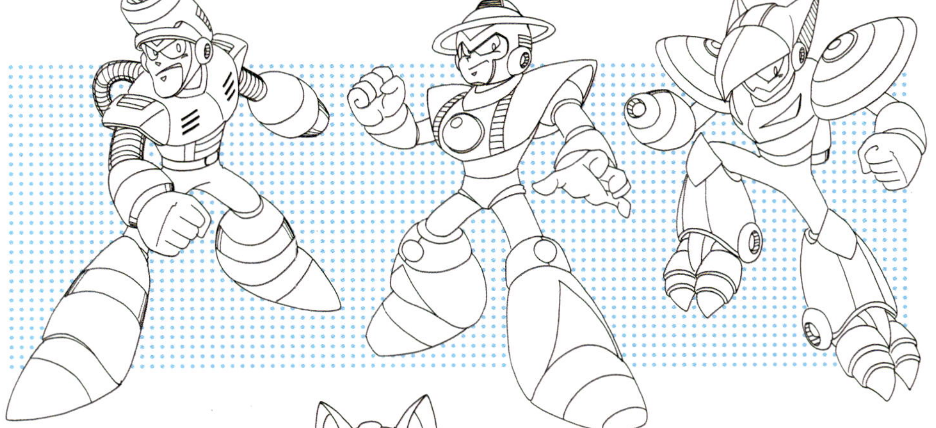

These sketches were for the Stardroids in Mega Man V.

"With all of the 'World 5' ['Mega Man V' in America] boss characters being new originals, I remember I had a lot of reservations while designing them. I did wonder what it would be like if we took the whole game out into space, but I guess that's an idea for another spin-off." (Inafune)

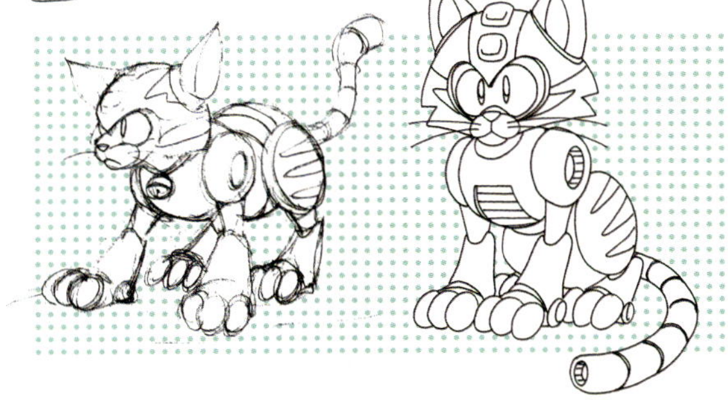

"Oh, are we already into Tango? (laughs) When we discussed bringing in a new support character, I got the request to make it a cat. I had no problem with that, as I'm quite the cat lover myself. I had a lot of fun designing sub characters based on animals." (Inafune)

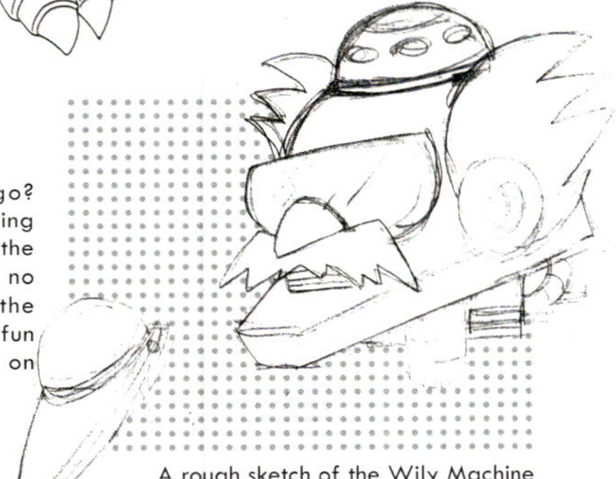

A rough sketch of the Wily Machine for the first Game Boy version.

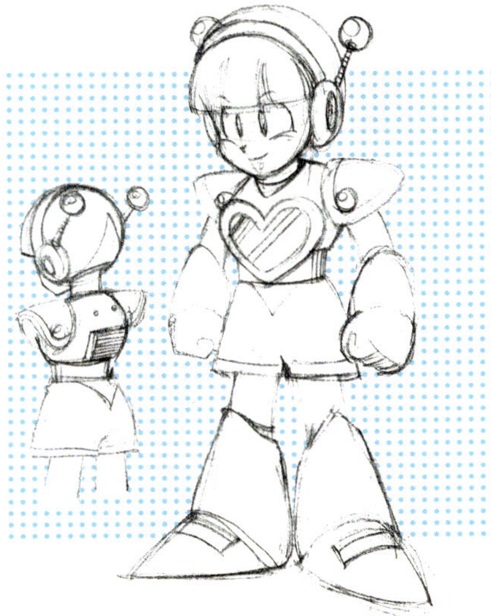

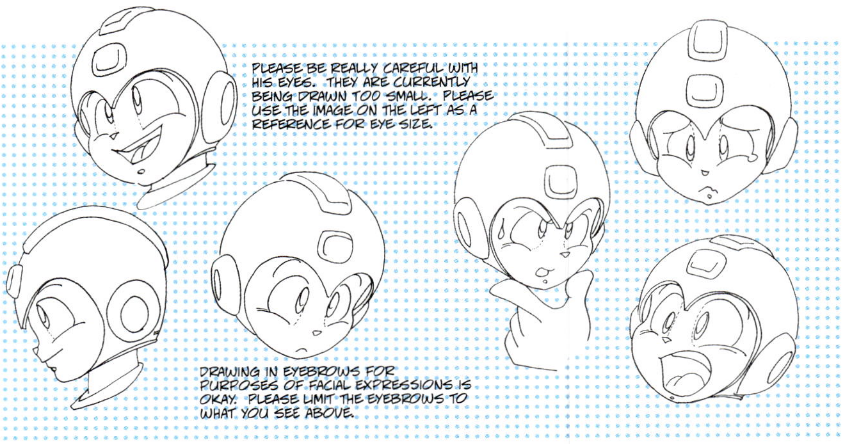

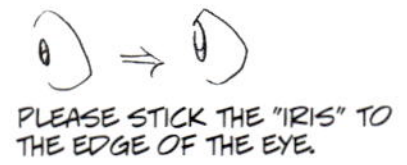

Mega Man was chosen to become an anime, not as a traditional television series or an OVA, but rather as an anime that would be used to introduce Japanese culture to other countries. These are the sketches I did for that project.

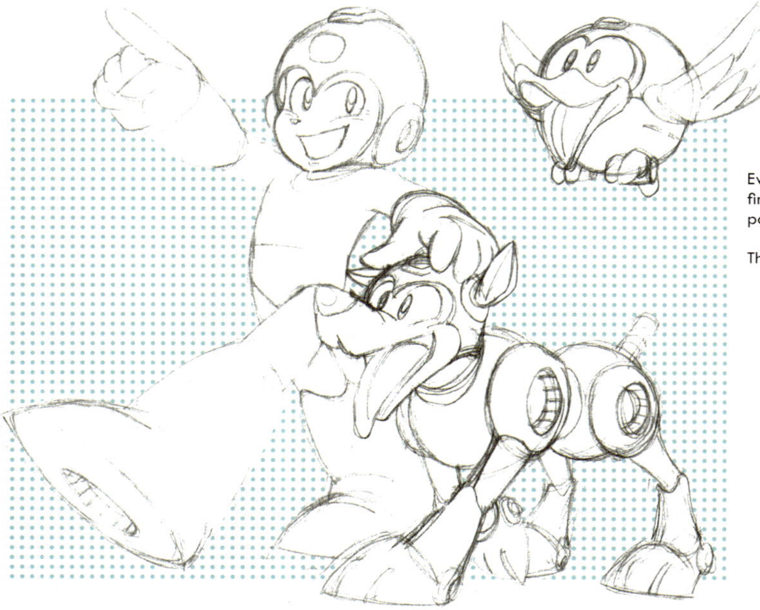

Even after the X series found its groove, the first-generation Mega Man series was still very popular and enjoyed many more sequels.

This is a sketch that was done for Mega Man 7.

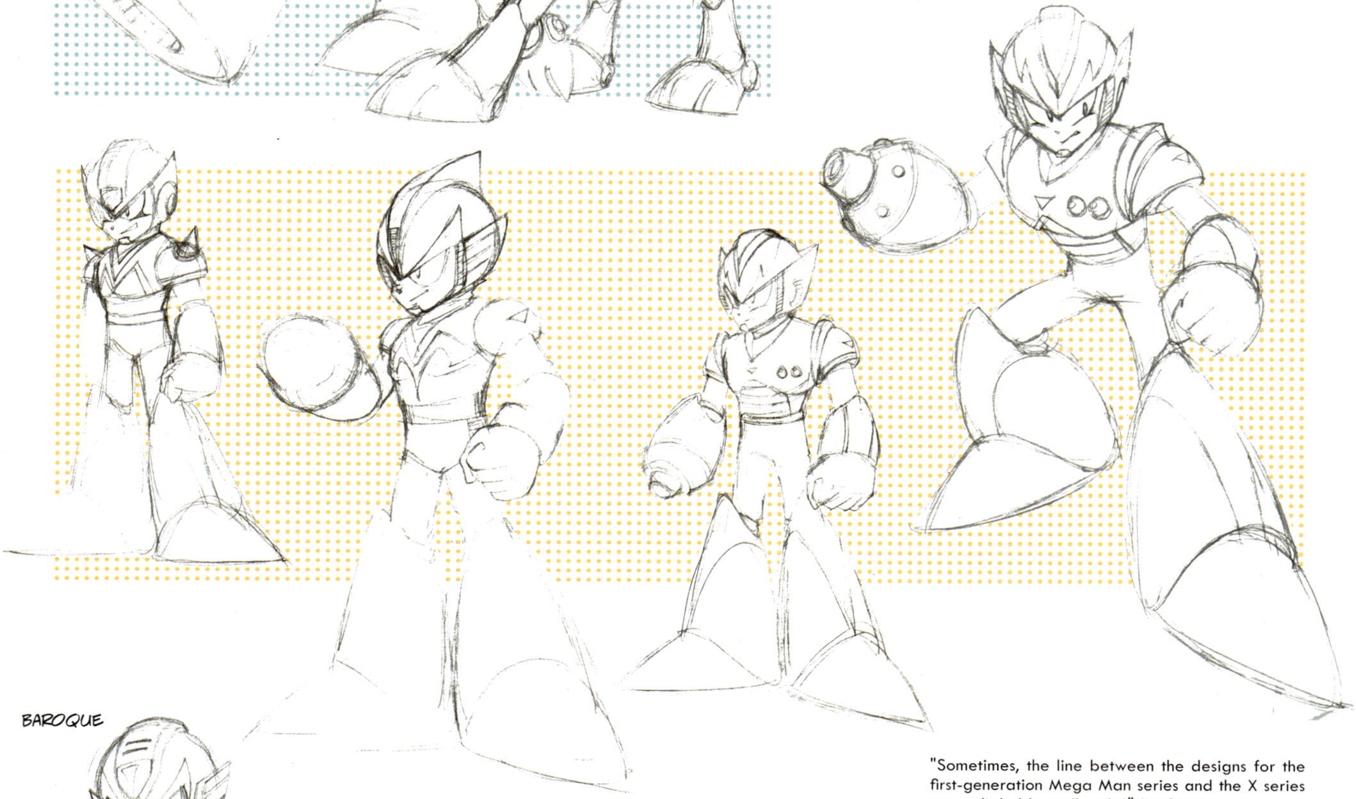

"Sometimes, the line between the designs for the first-generation Mega Man series and the X series gets a little blurry. (laughs)" (Inafune)

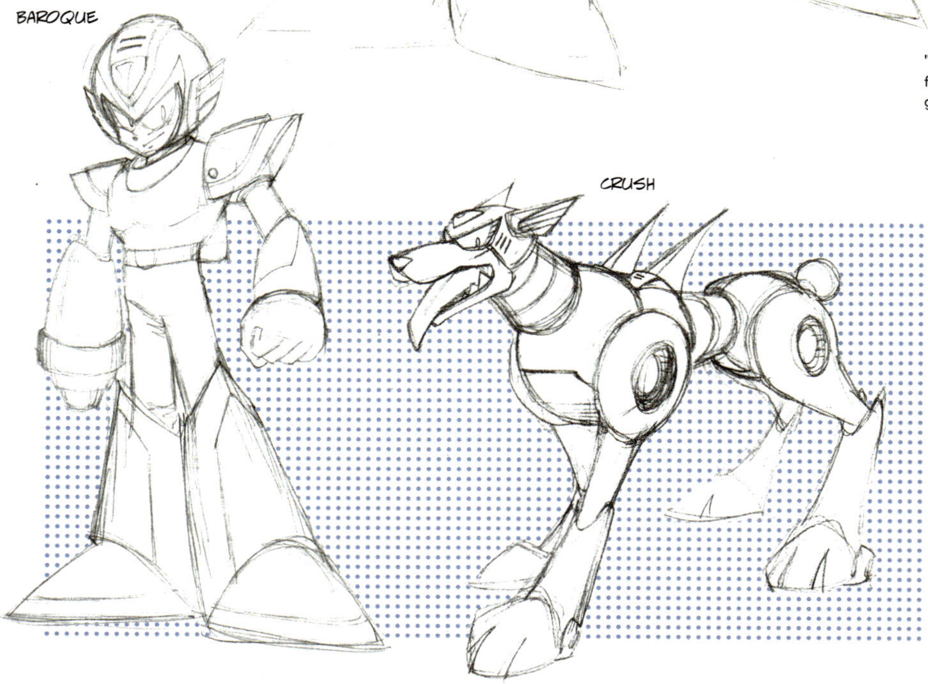

"Baroque" and "Crush" are the designs that Bass and Treble were based off of.

"Since Proto Man was kind of straddling the fence, I wanted to bring in a full-time rival for Mega Man. I wanted a guy who was extremely competitive, and absolutely hated to lose." (Inafune)

As Inafune mentioned, it was sometimes difficult to keep the designs for the Mega Man series and the X series distinct. This is a sketch of Auto that was done for the Mega Man series, and we can see how Inafune was trying different things to keep the two series separate as far as designing was concerned.

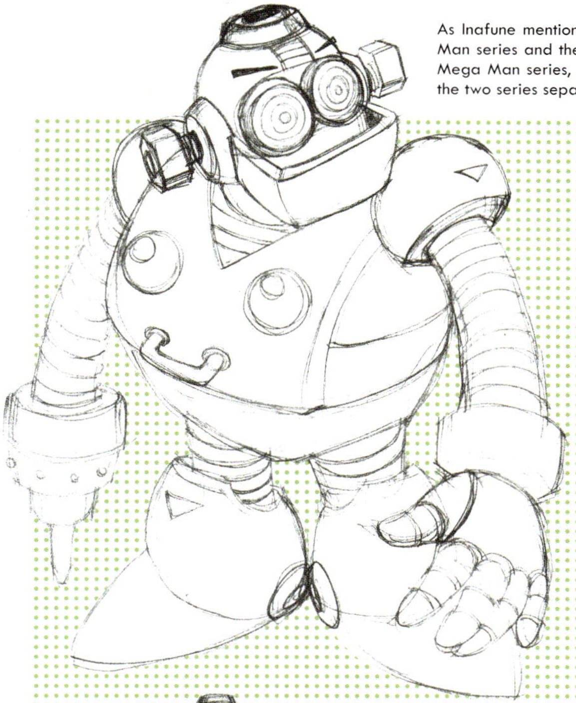

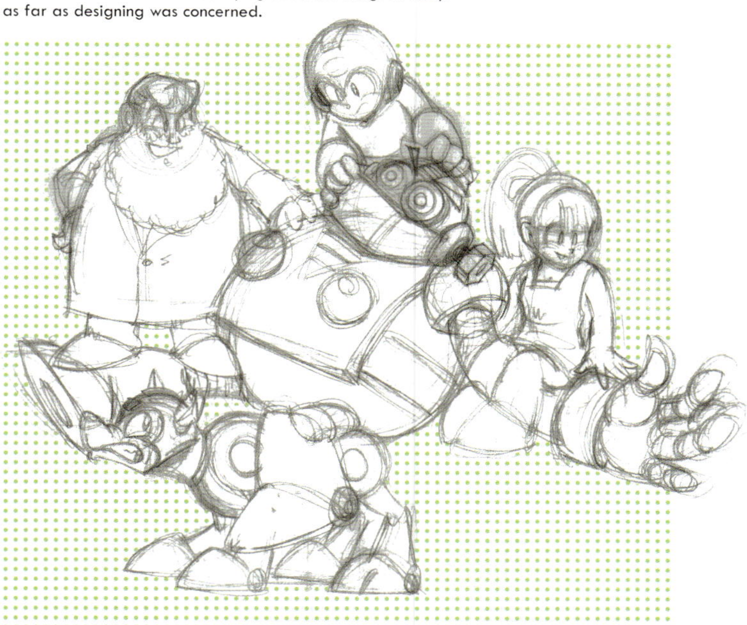

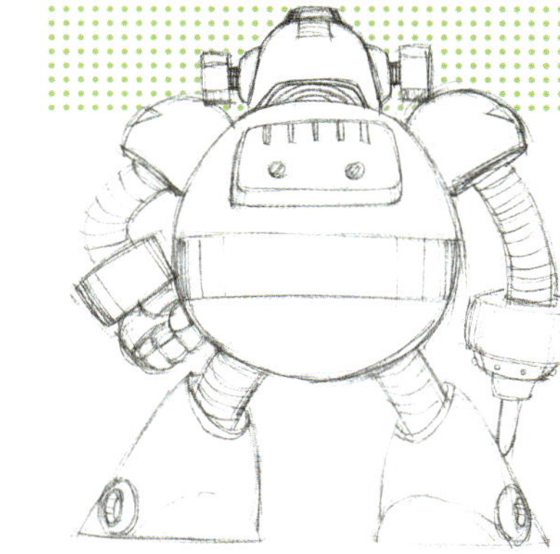

"Auto's pretty... complex, isn't he? It got to the point where I wasn't even sure what made him so amazing. (laughs) Sometimes, I can't believe that I actually drew him." (Inafune)

The rough draft of the package art for Rockman's Soccer. Guts Man was initially slated to join the cast for this title, but when he was pulled out of the final game, he was replaced with Proto Man in the illustration.

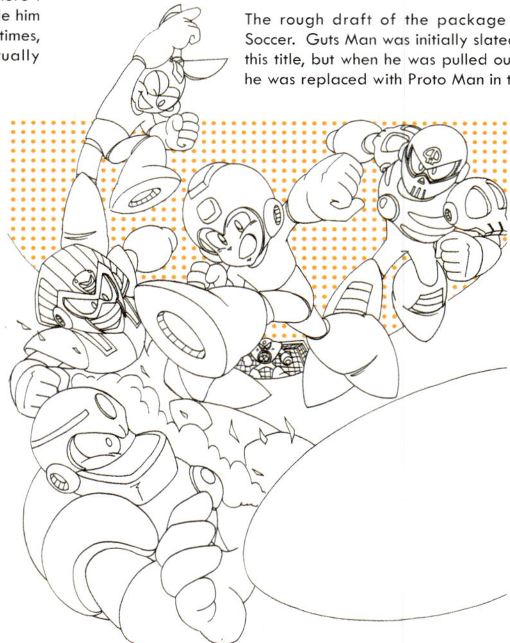

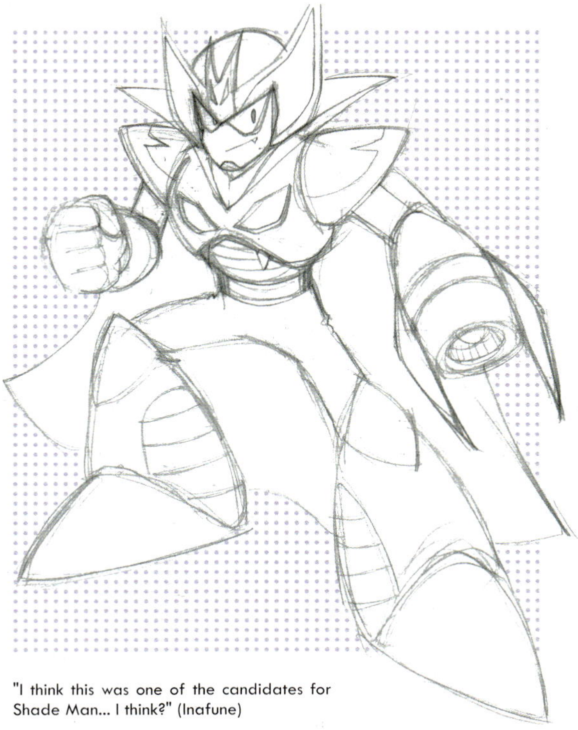

"I think this was one of the candidates for Shade Man... I think?" (Inafune)

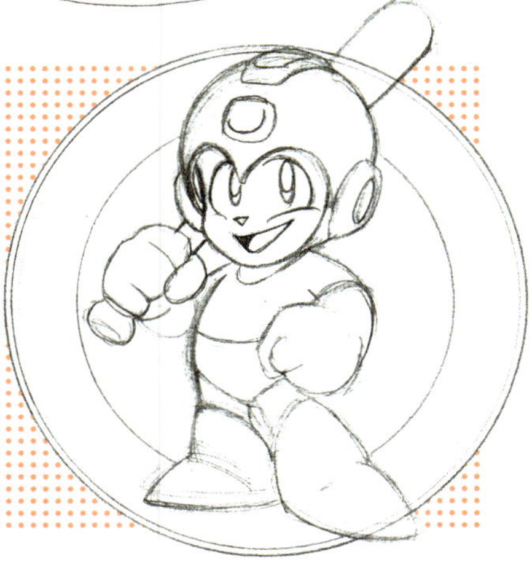

Could this be an illustration that was done sometime before or after Mega Man's Soccer? Perhaps there were plans for a Mega Man baseball game?

"I have no idea when I drew this, not to mention what I drew it for. (laughs)" (Inafune)

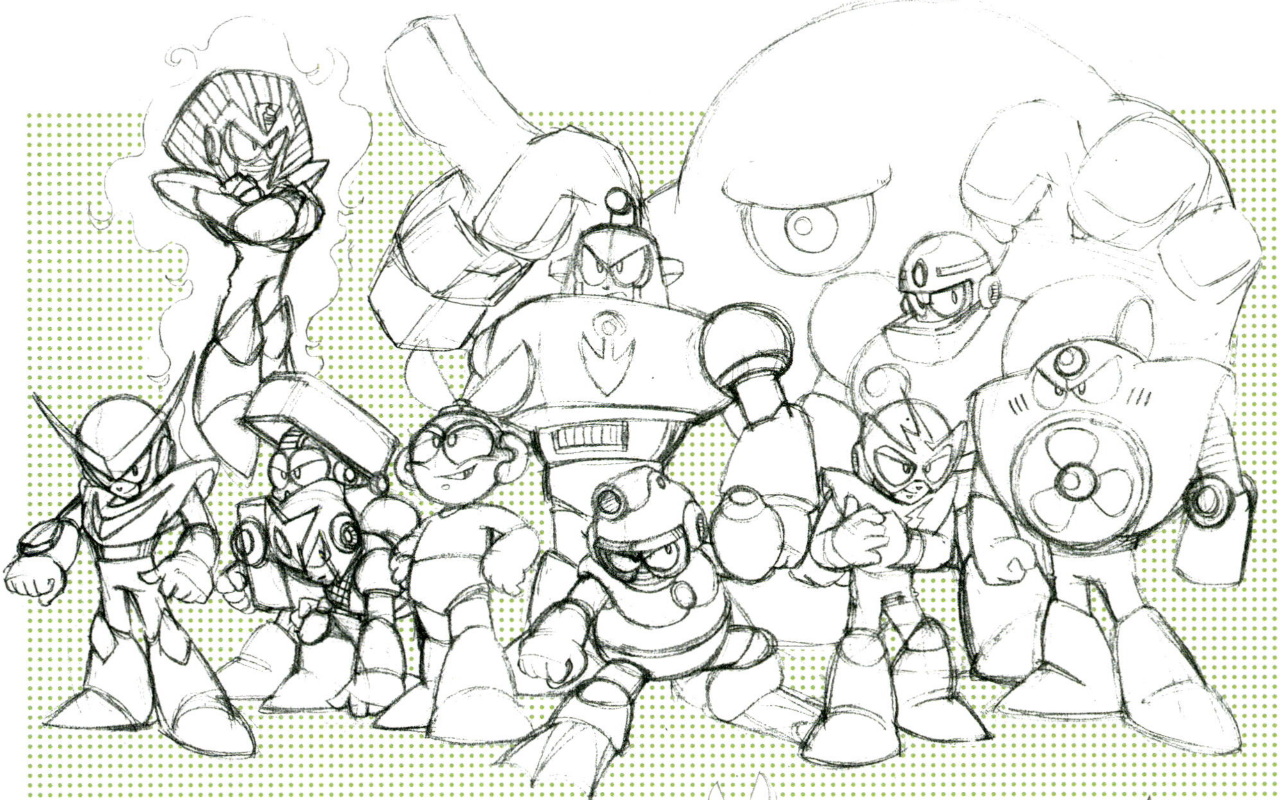

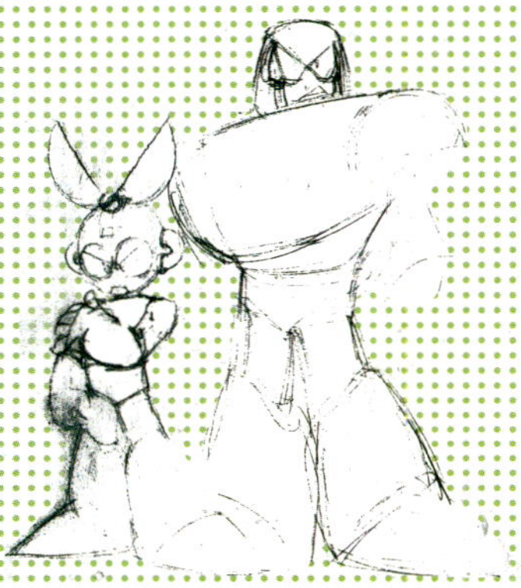

These sketches were done around the release of the arcade game. Inafune seemed to make minor touch-ups to the familiar characters as he drew them, almost as if he was exploring what they would be like if he drew them now for the first time.

"They were able to do so much more with the details in the graphics. It made me really happy with regard to the designing aspect of it all." (Inafune)

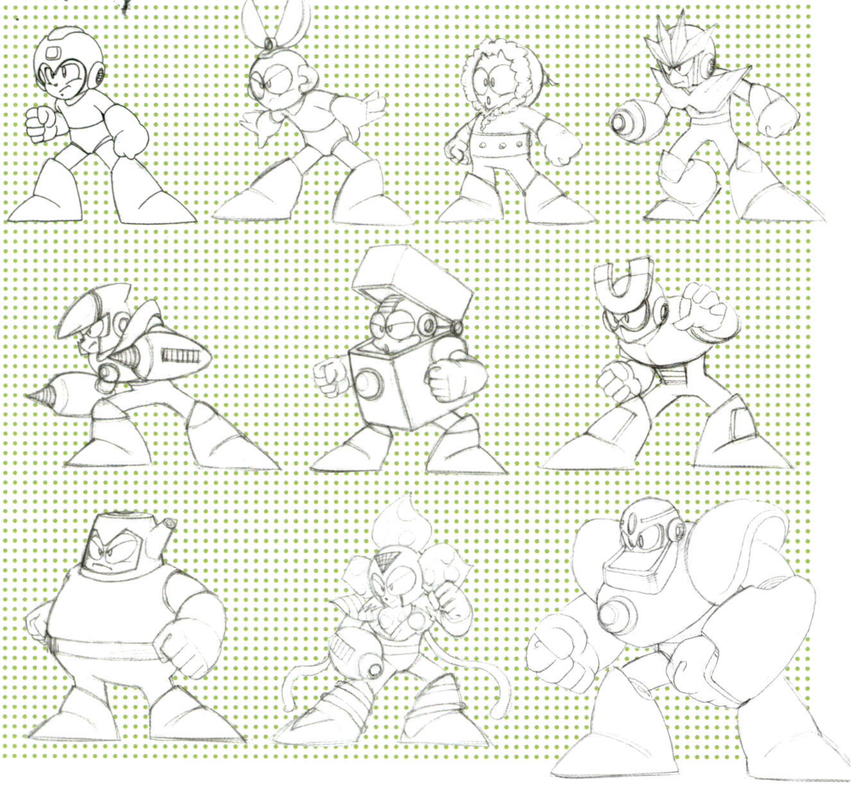

"Wood Man was so easy to make because once we had the main body, all we had to do was make his leaves spin. That's the main reason why we decided to reuse him in the Sega Saturn version of '8.' (laughs)" (Inafune)

Wood Man was used in the overseas versions of the game as well.

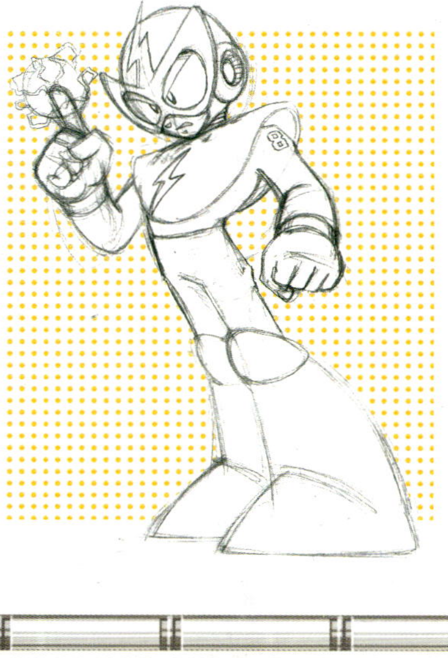

This is the Elec Man that was included in the Grand Rockman Exposition in the Capcom Secret File celebrating the 10th anniversary of Mega Man.

Sketches of Proto Man that were done during the development stages of Mega Man 8.

"I thought it'd be really funny if Proto Man had this crazy head of hair when he took his helmet off. (laughs)" (Inafune)

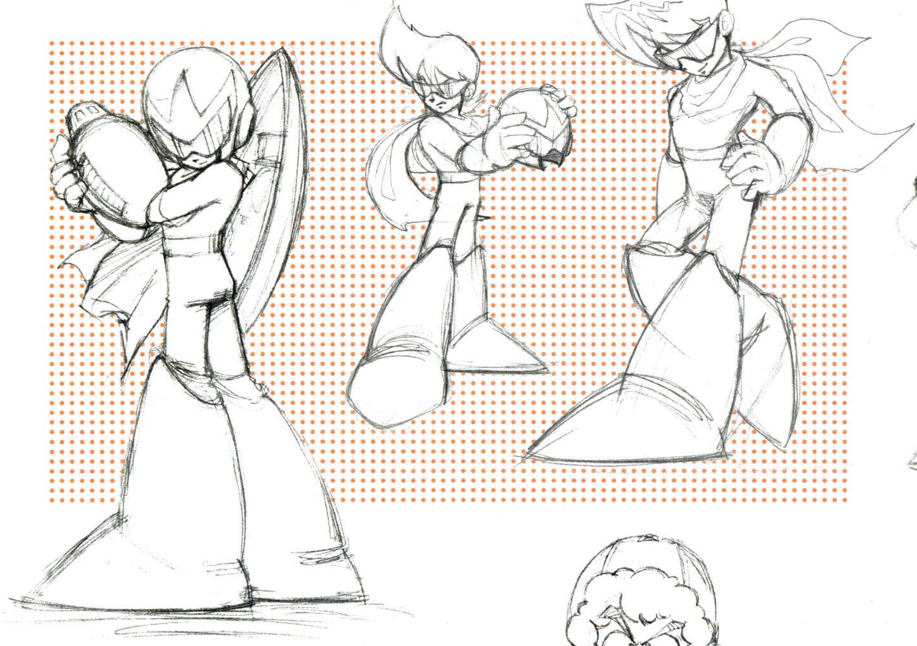

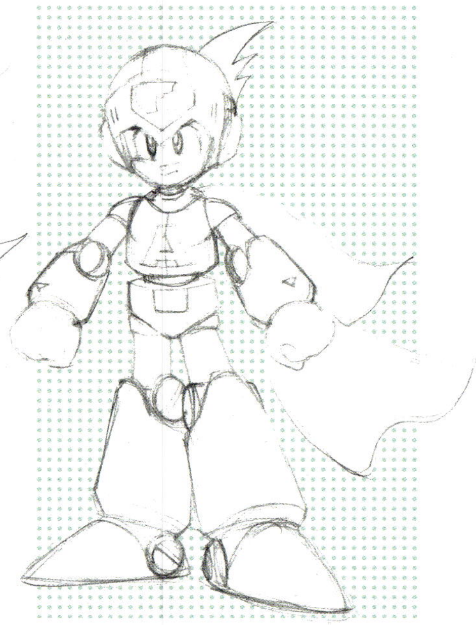

"I don't remember this one..." (Inafune)

The shape of the legs is more reminiscent of Mega Man Legends than the first-generation Mega Man or X.

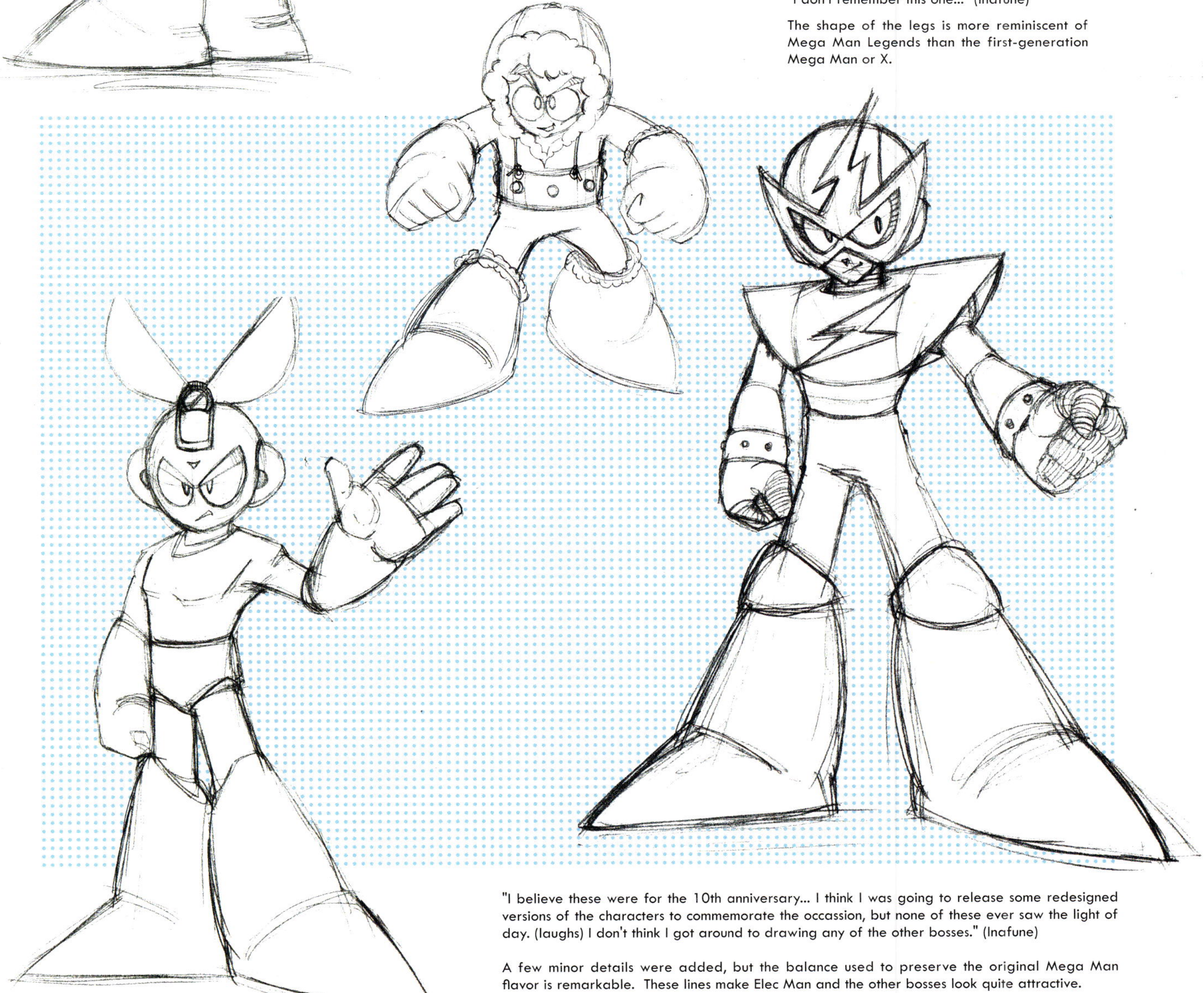

"I believe these were for the 10th anniversary... I think I was going to release some redesigned versions of the characters to commemorate the occassion, but none of these ever saw the light of day. (laughs) I don't think I got around to drawing any of the other bosses." (Inafune)

A few minor details were added, but the balance used to preserve the original Mega Man flavor is remarkable. These lines make Elec Man and the other bosses look quite attractive.

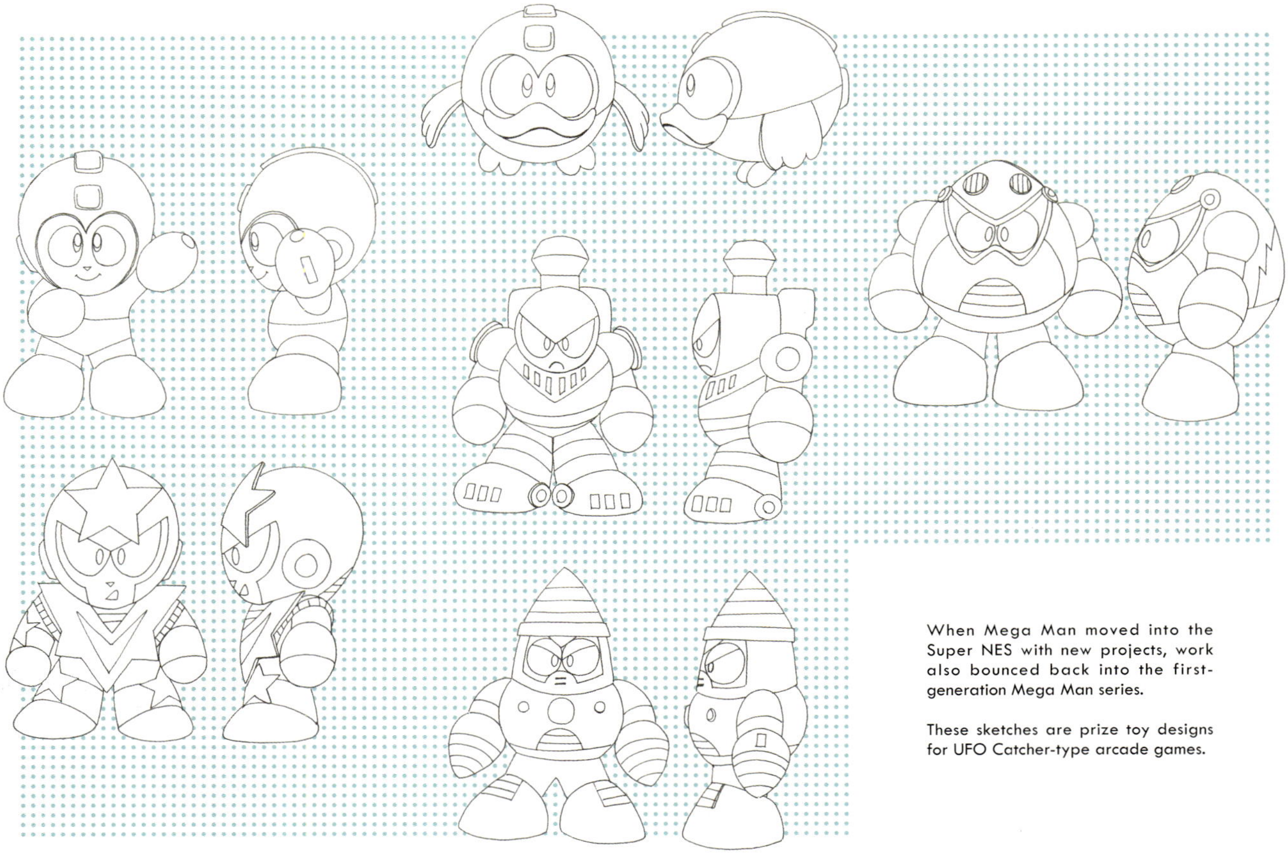

When Mega Man moved into the Super NES with new projects, work also bounced back into the first-generation Mega Man series.

These sketches are prize toy designs for UFO Catcher-type arcade games.

The cover illustration for one of the Capcom Fan Club bulletins. Mega Man appears together with some Street Fighter II characters and a Red Arremer. *[Editor's note: "Red Arremer" is an enemy from another Capcom game series, "Ghosts 'n Goblins."]*

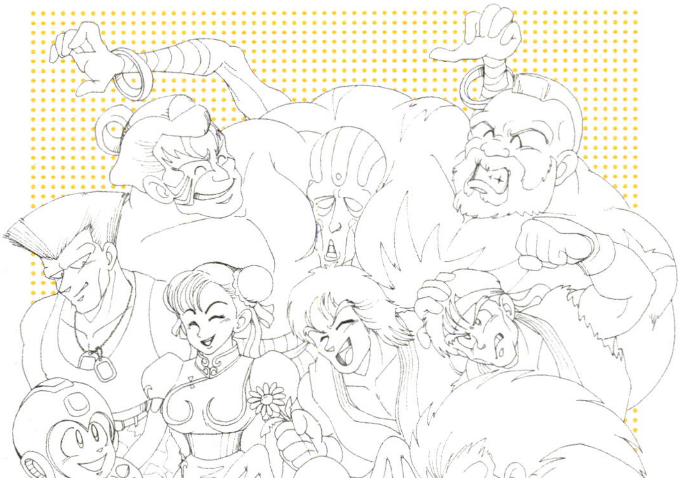

These sketches of cute and miniature versions of Mega Man and Proto Man serve no particular purpose.

"Every now and then, I'd have some spare time between tasks at work. These bouts of free time often led to my experimenting with different styles and ideas." (Inafune)

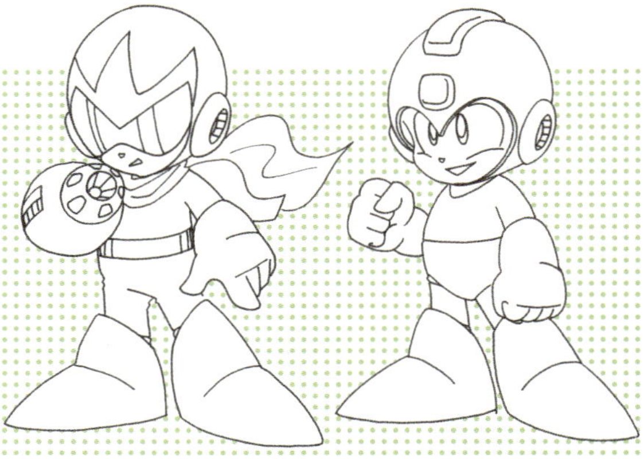

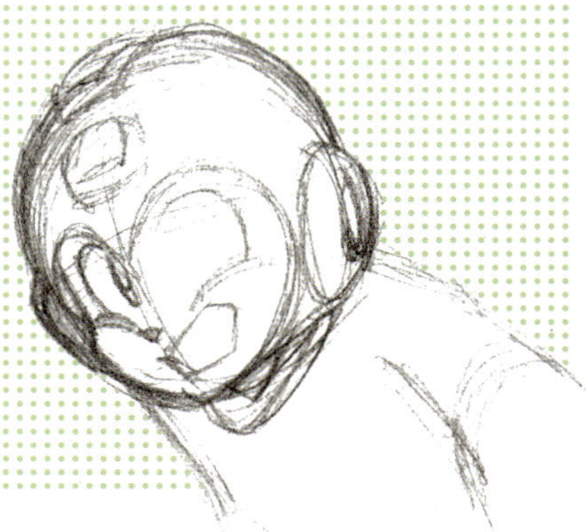

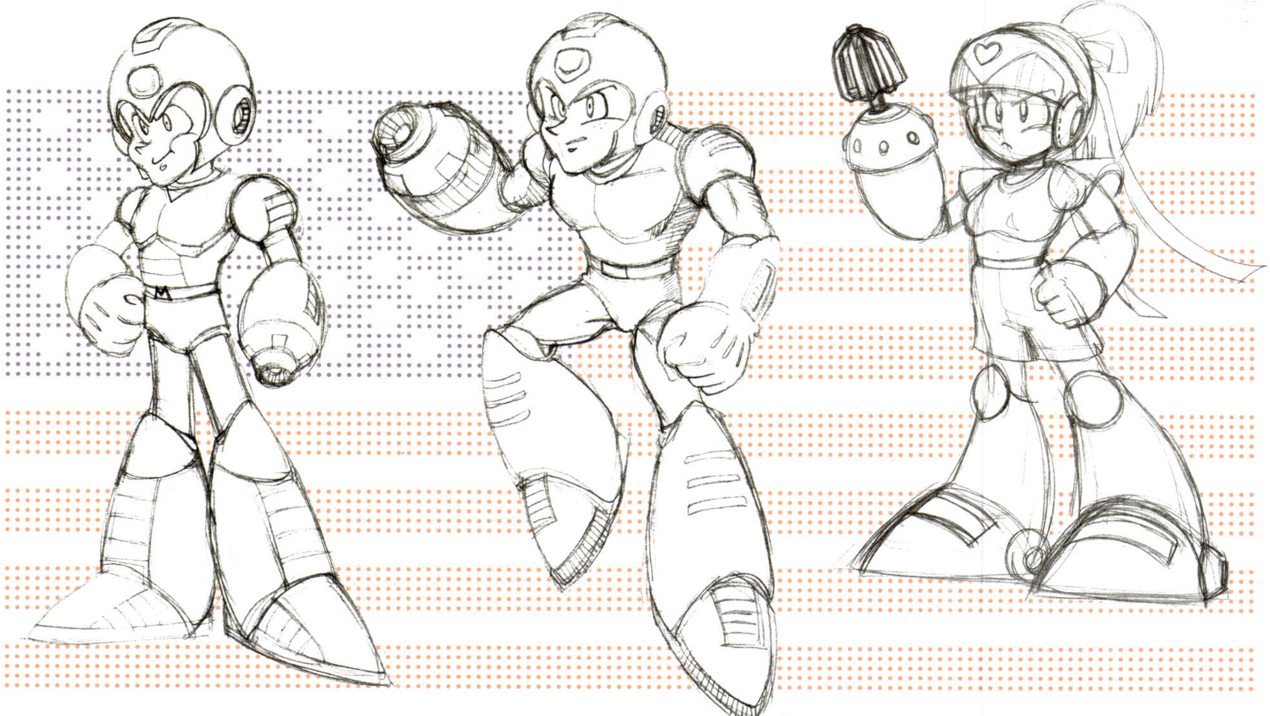

"These are some sketches I did in my spare time. I was wondering how I would depict an American 'Mega Man.' (laughs) I tried to make Roll more obvious in her role as a domestic helper, and I also tried to consider what would make these characters appealing to our English-speaking players. (laughs)" (Inafune)

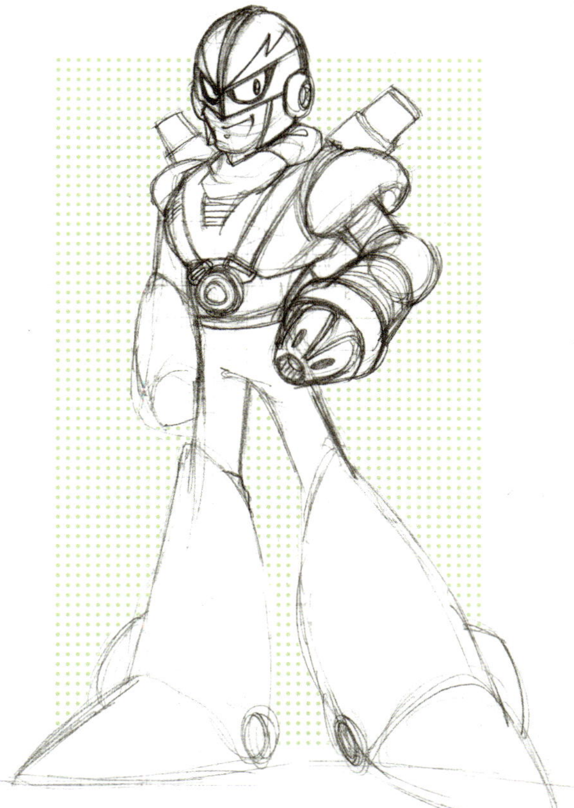

"Who's this supposed to be? I don't remember drawing him. From the look of his face, I'd guess he was meant to be an ally, not an enemy. He has a harness on his torso. This must have been some random sketch I did while trying to come up with ideas for new allies... maybe. (laughs)" (Inafune)

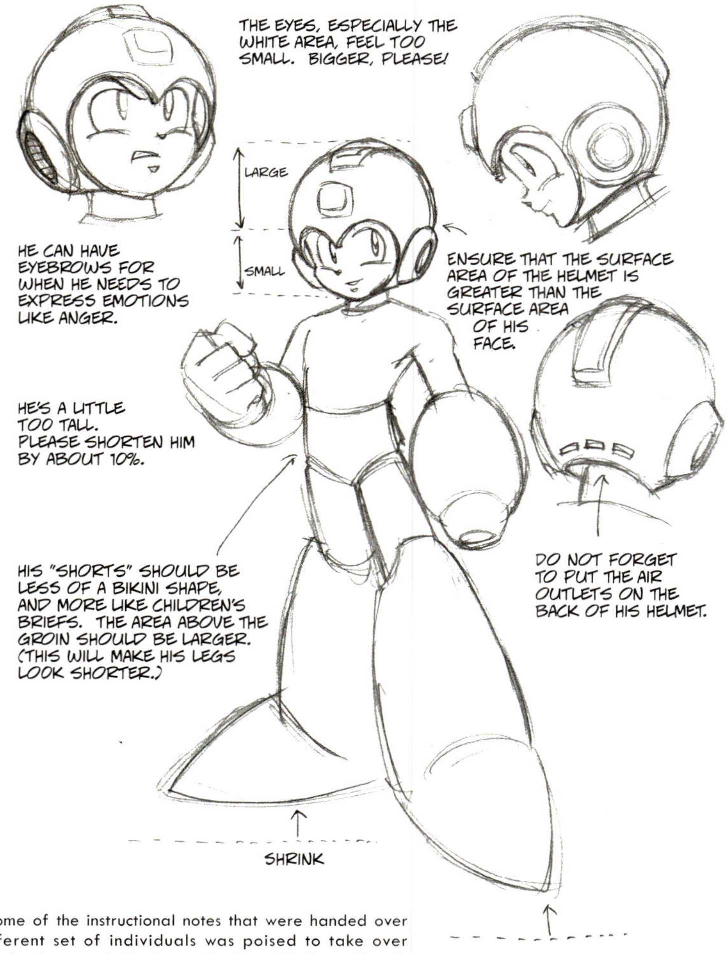

These are some of the instructional notes that were handed over when a different set of individuals was poised to take over responsibility for the copyrighted art. Starting with Mega Man 8, Inafune began focusing more on his duties as a producer.

GALLERY

ギャラリー

This section includes many rare illustrations, including promotional pieces on various mediums as well as unique designs for foreign versions of Mega Man games. Anniversary illustrations and other works with a lot of details have been blown up to better show off their features.

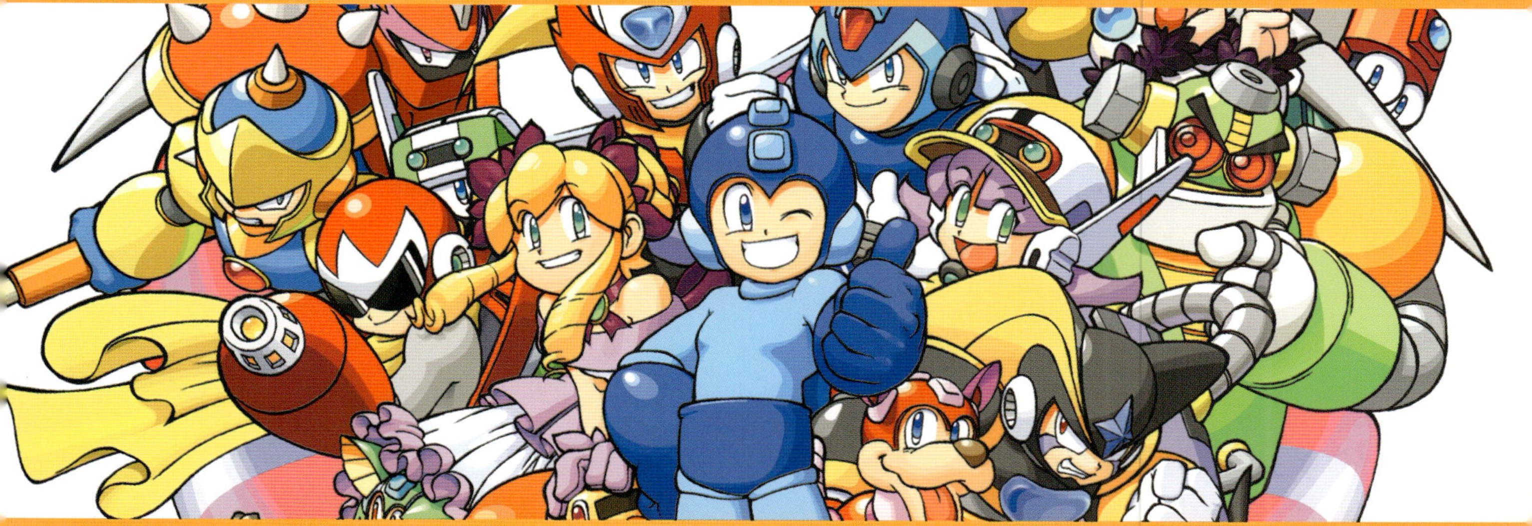

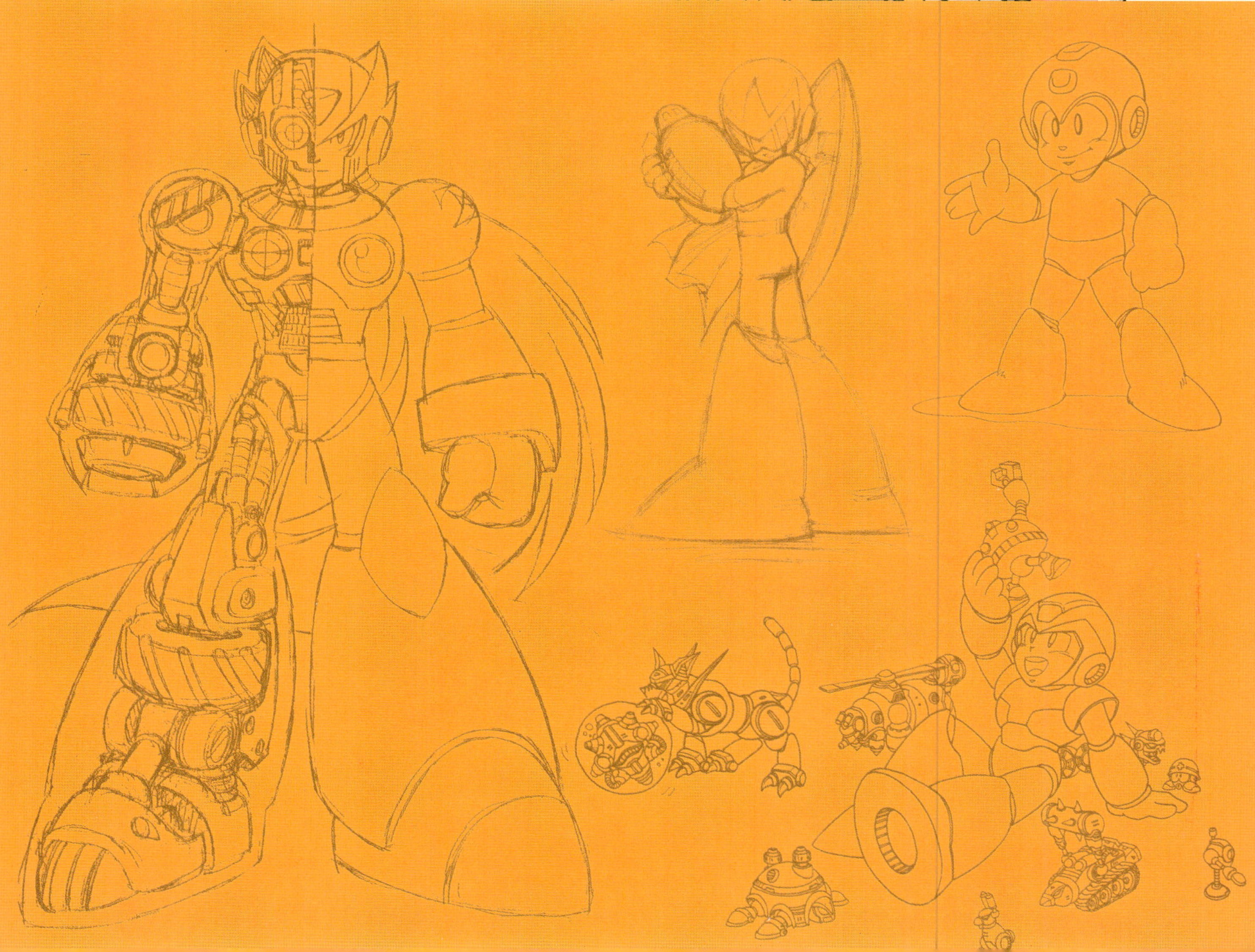

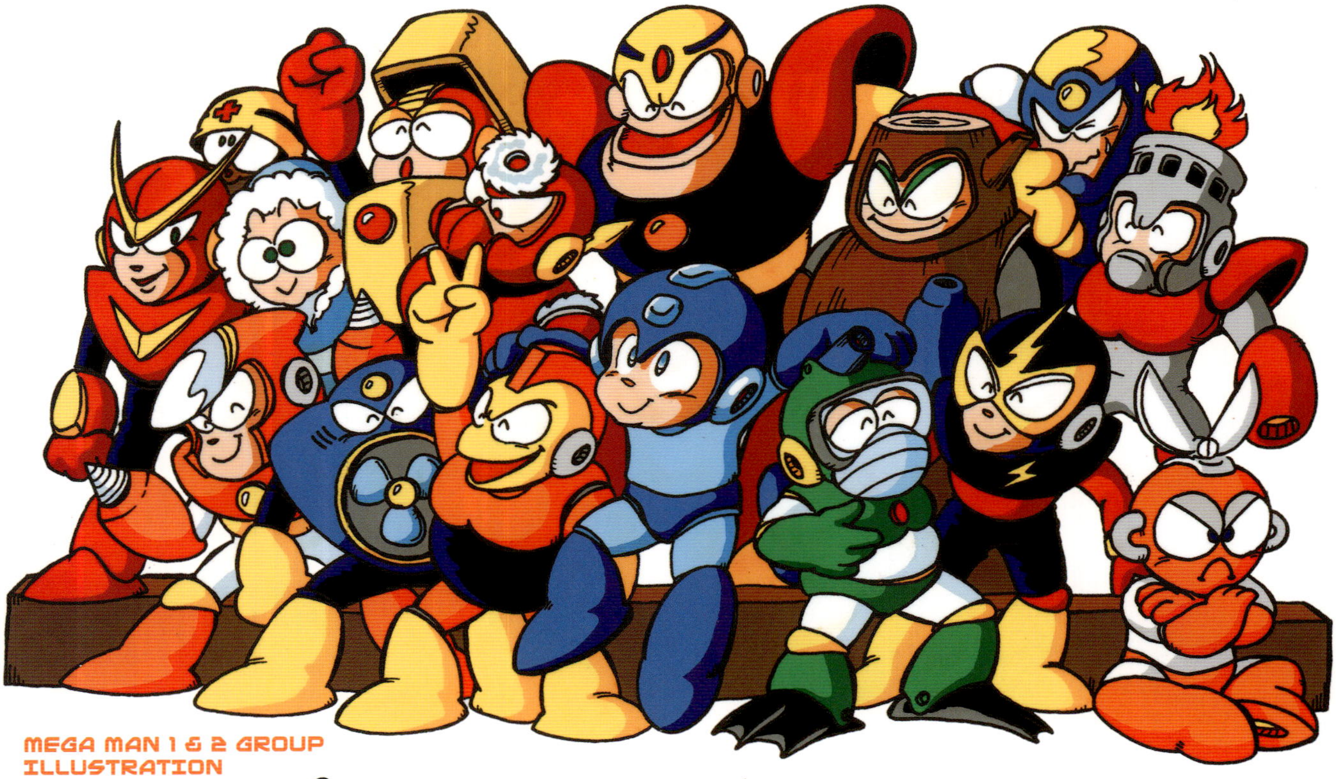

MEGA MAN 1 & 2 GROUP ILLUSTRATION

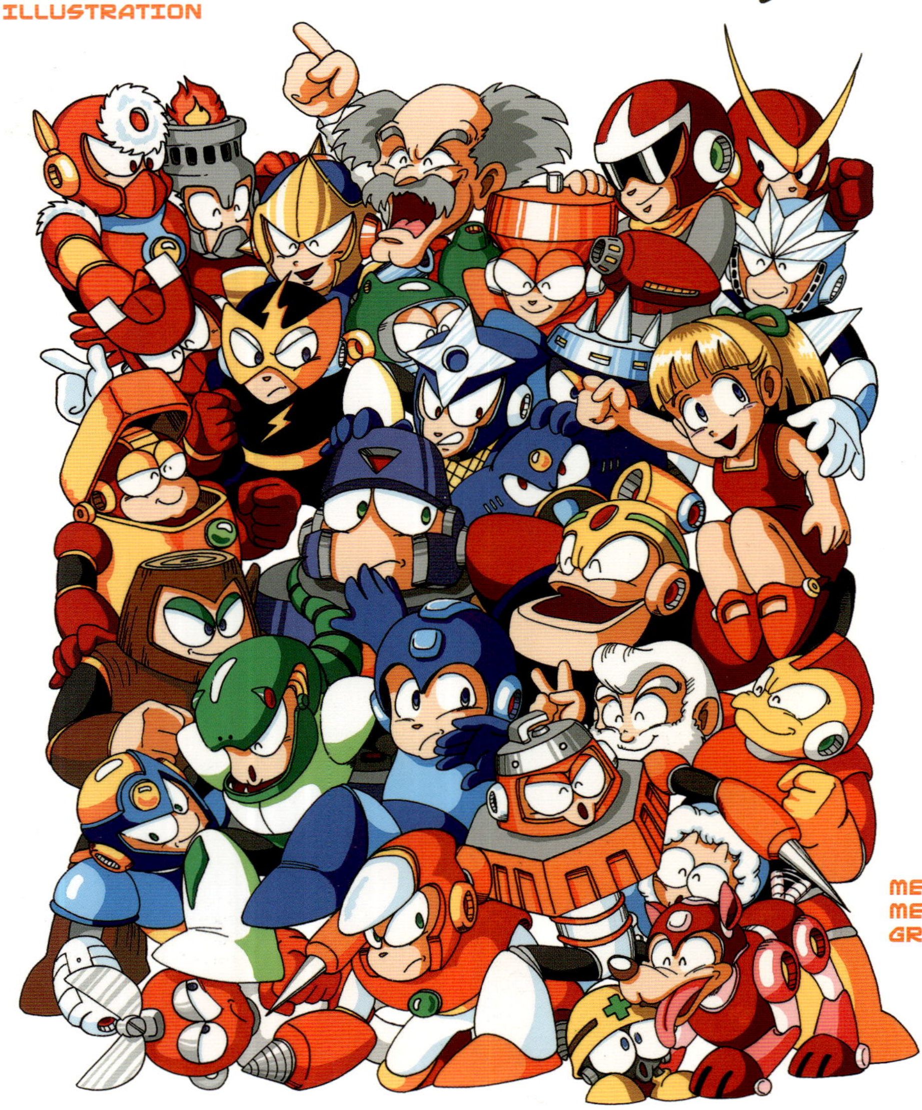

MEGA MAN 1 ~ 3 + MEGA MAN: DR. WILY'S REVENGE GROUP ILLUSTRATION

10TH ANNIVERSARY ILLUSTRATION

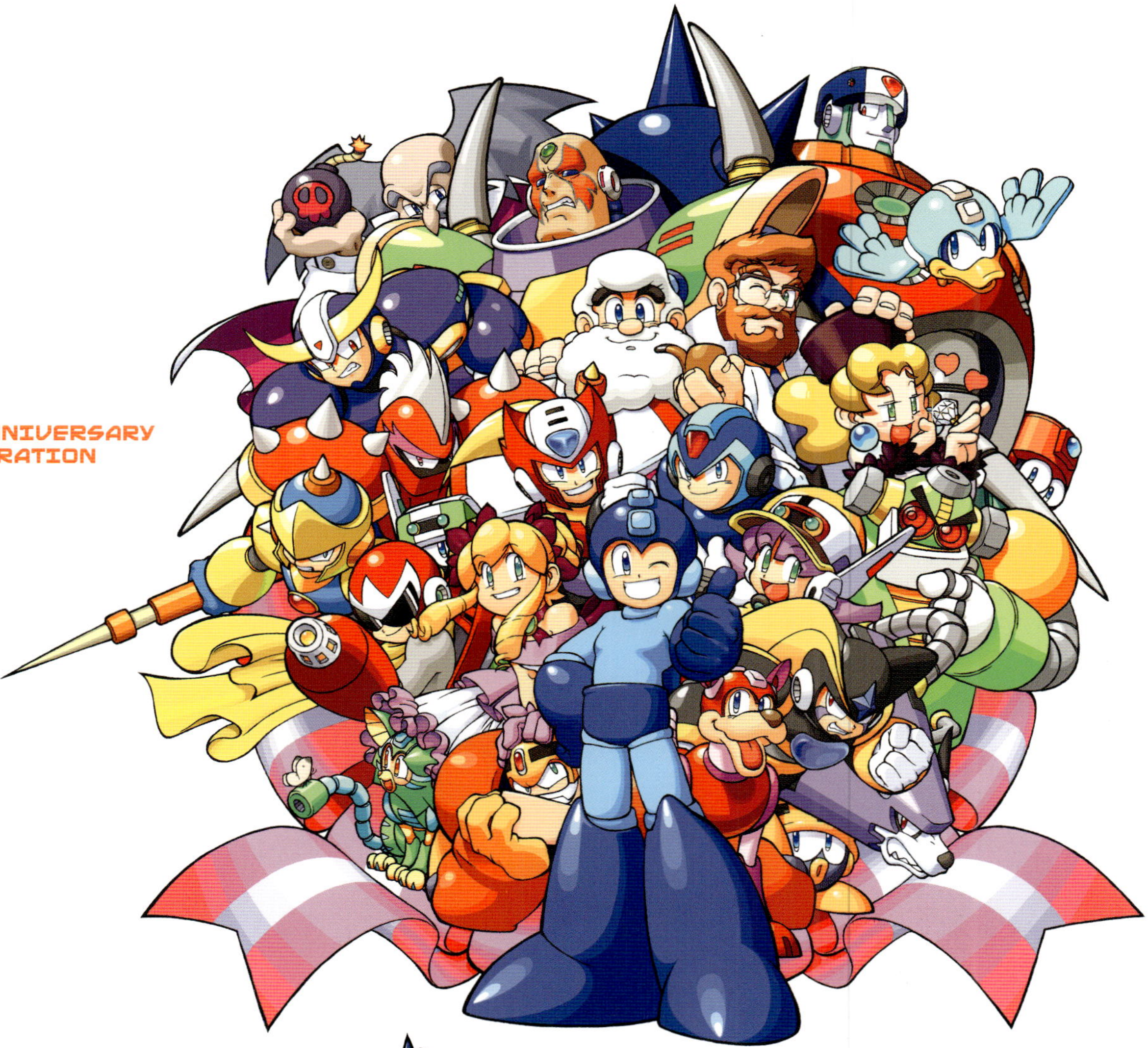

10TH ANNIVERSARY ILLUSTRATION (LEGENDS)

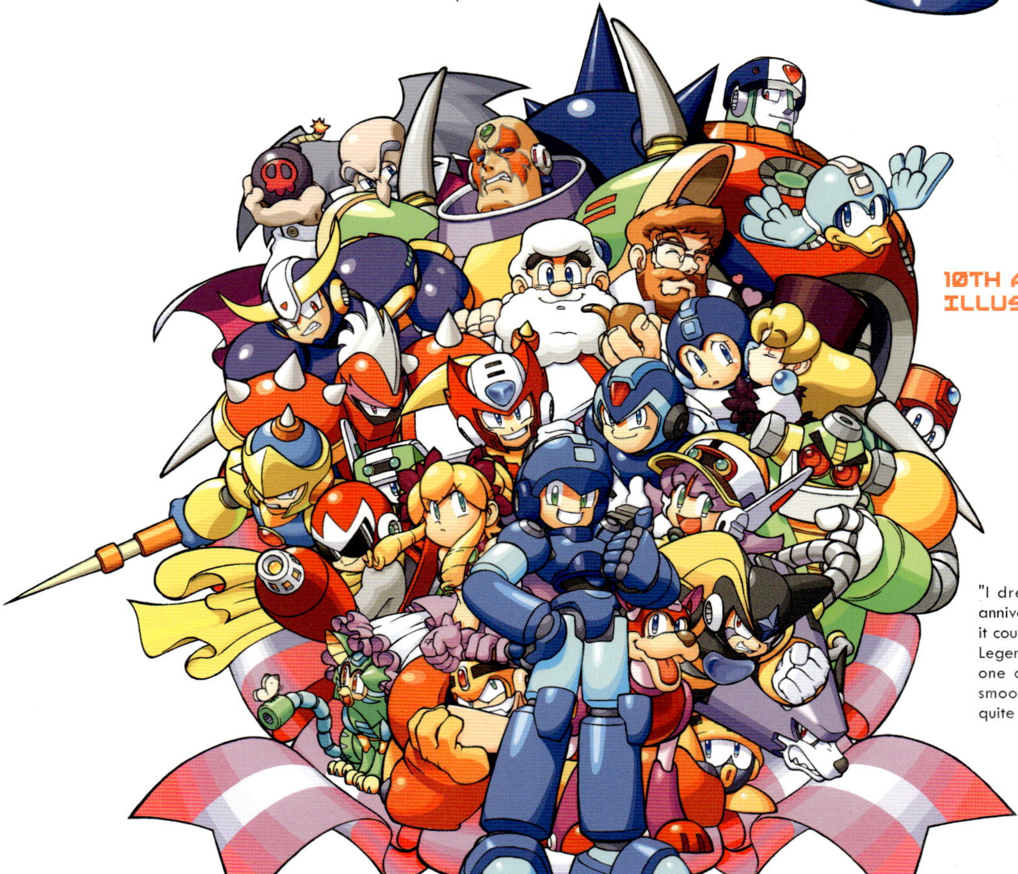

"I drew two different versions of the 10th anniversary piece. I made the second so that it could be used for promotional purposes for Legends. In the Legends version, we can see one of the additional Mega Mans getting smooched by Kalinka, and Roll is looking quite unhappy about it." (Hideki)

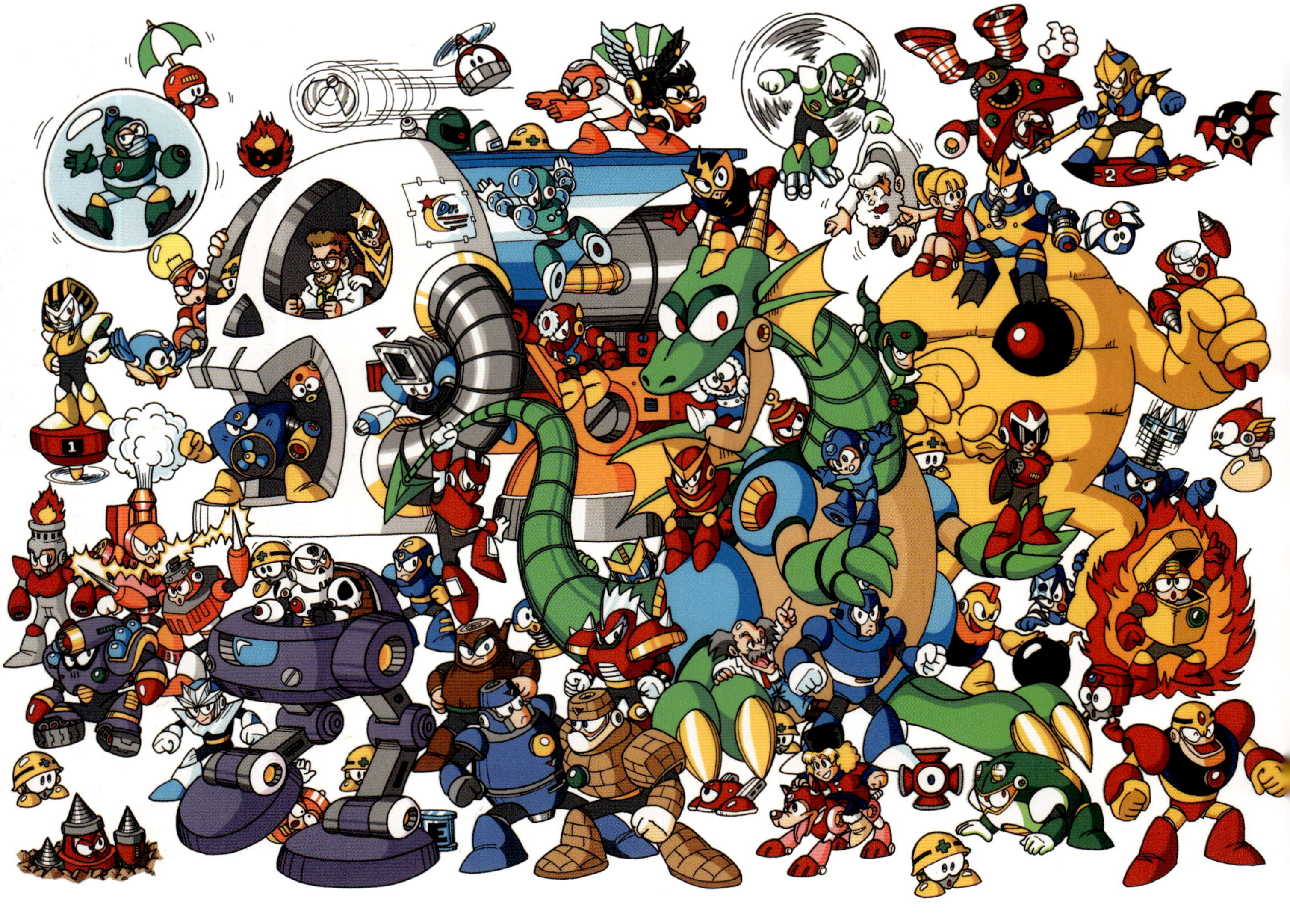

"CLUB ☆ CAPCOM" POSTER

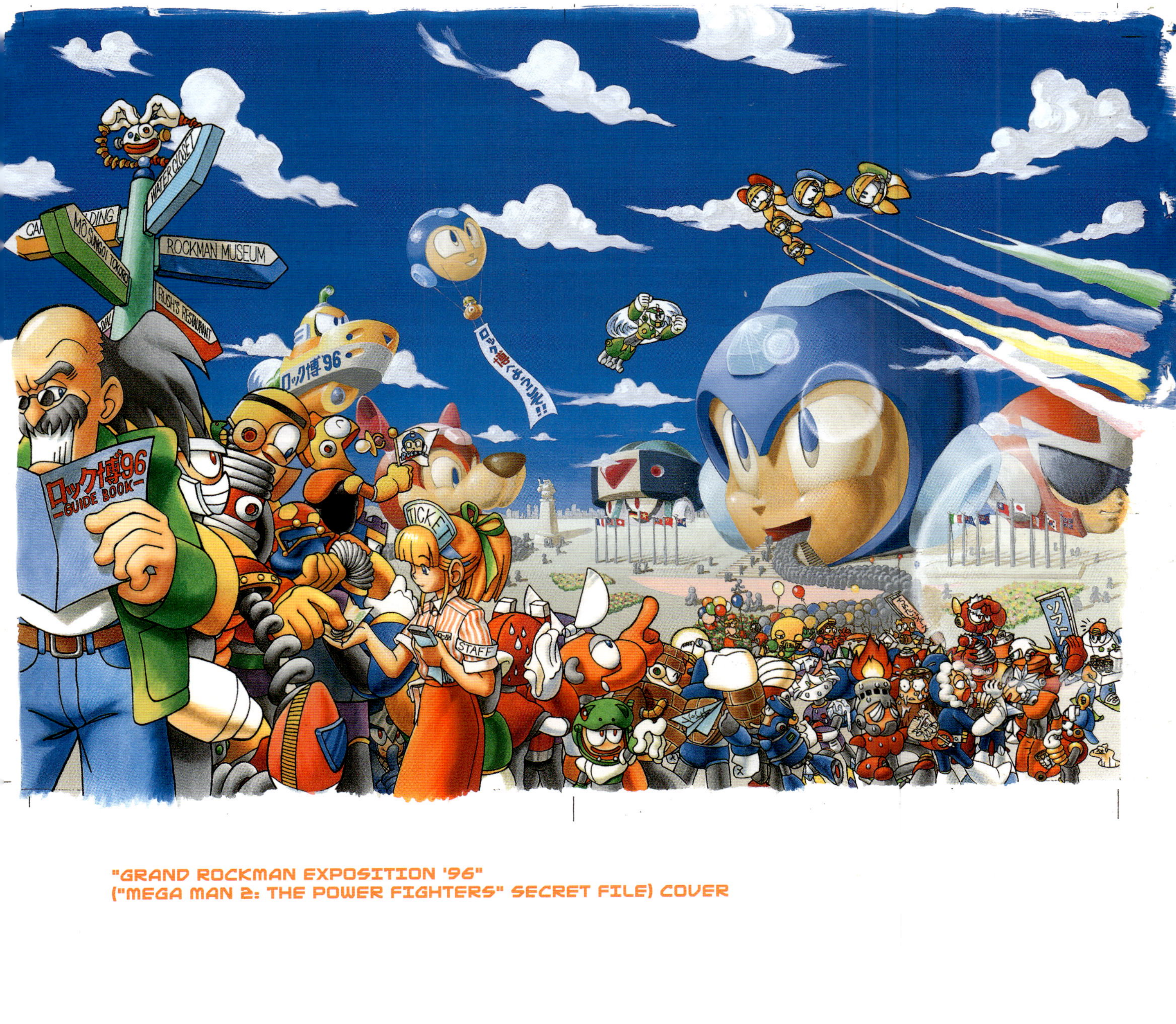

"GRAND ROCKMAN EXPOSITION '96"
("MEGA MAN 2: THE POWER FIGHTERS" SECRET FILE) COVER

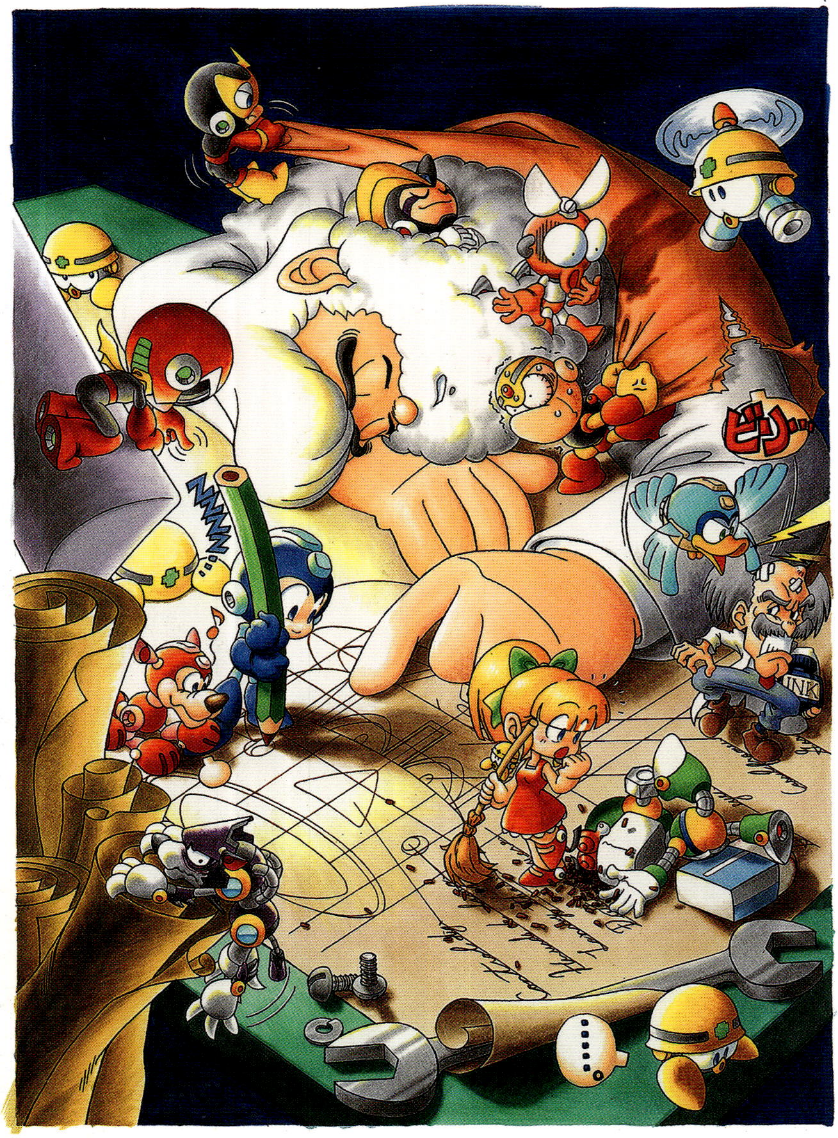

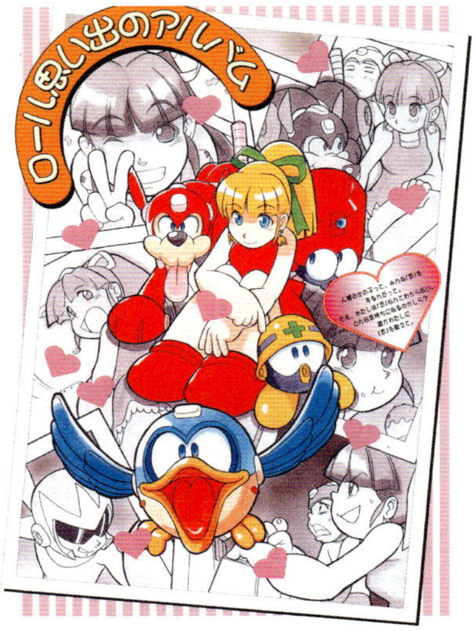

"GRAND ROCKMAN EXPOSITION '96"

"GRAND ROCKMAN EXPOSITION '96"

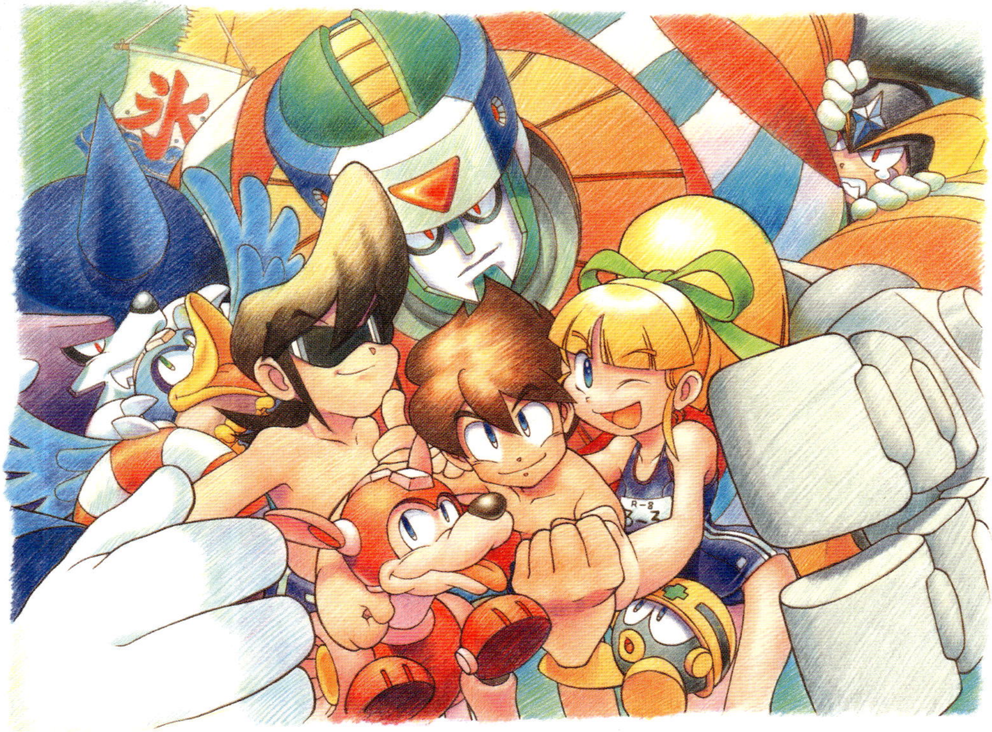

"This is supposed to be a drawing from Roll's diary, so I did it all with colored pencils. The theme was 'Summer Holidays,' so I wanted to draw something that people would relate to easily." (Hideki)

"GRAND ROCKMAN EXPOSITION '96"

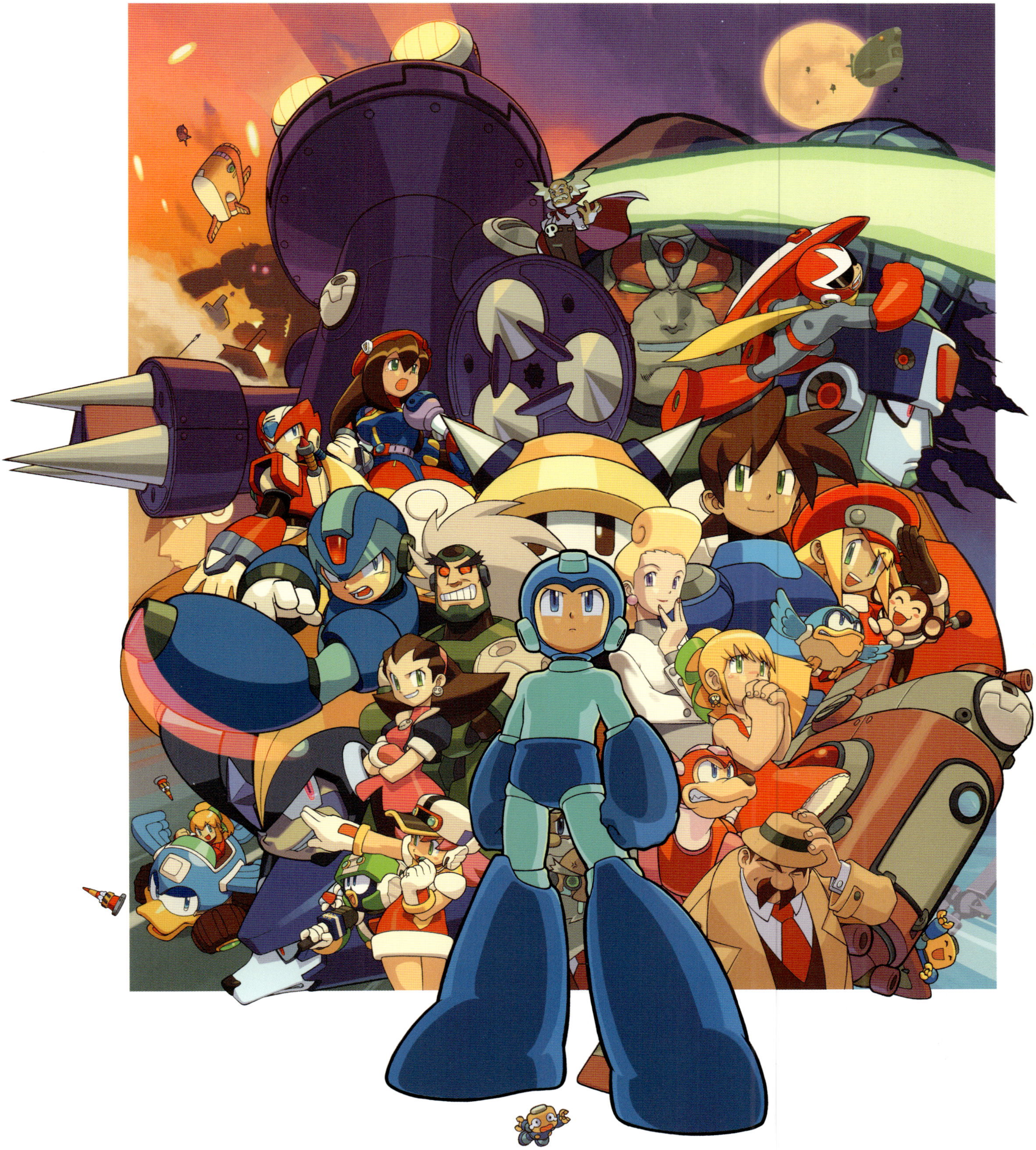

SALES CAMPAIGN

"Once I started doing art using the PC, I learned that I could use these things called layers. I got overzealous and made about 50 layers, which was great until it took 20 minutes to save my work. (laughs) I made so many layers because I kept thinking I may want to go back and alter parts of the layout. Now, though, I often just rip through it all in one layer. (laughs)" (Hideki)

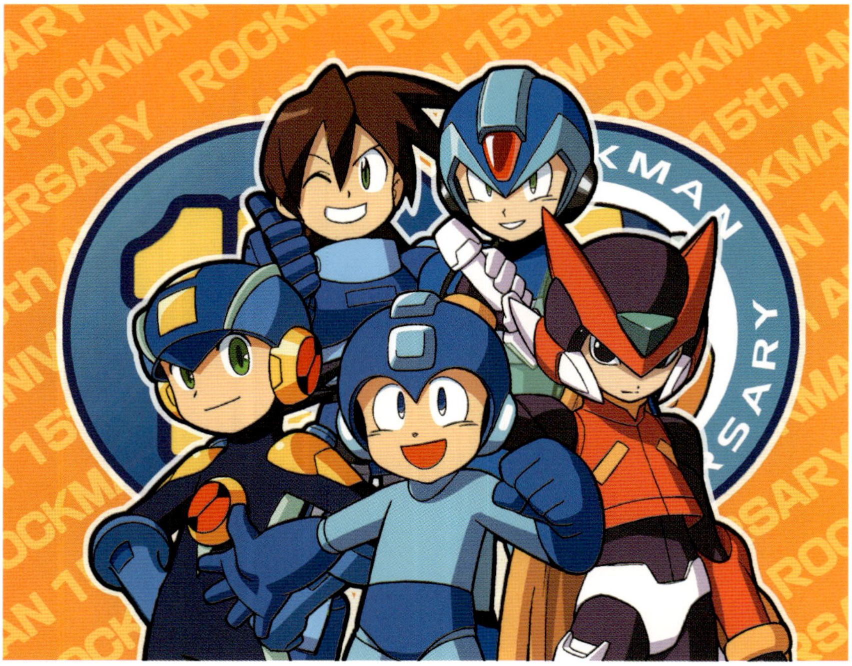

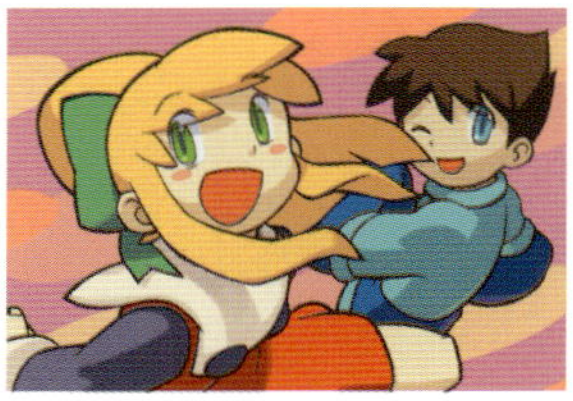

FAN CLUB BULLETIN

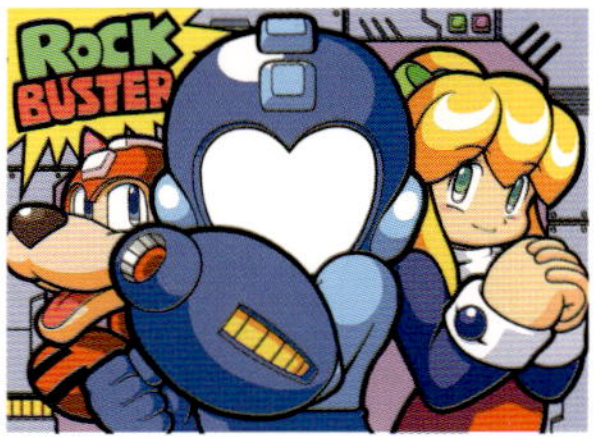

PHOTO STICKER

15TH ANNIVERSARY ILLUSTRATION

"I did this piece for the Capcom Fan Club. It was the first time I got to draw Zero, so that was very exciting for me. I worked on the PSP version of 'Legends,' and did a wallpaper for 'ZX,' so I guess you could say I had a hand in every series! (laughs)" (Higurashi)

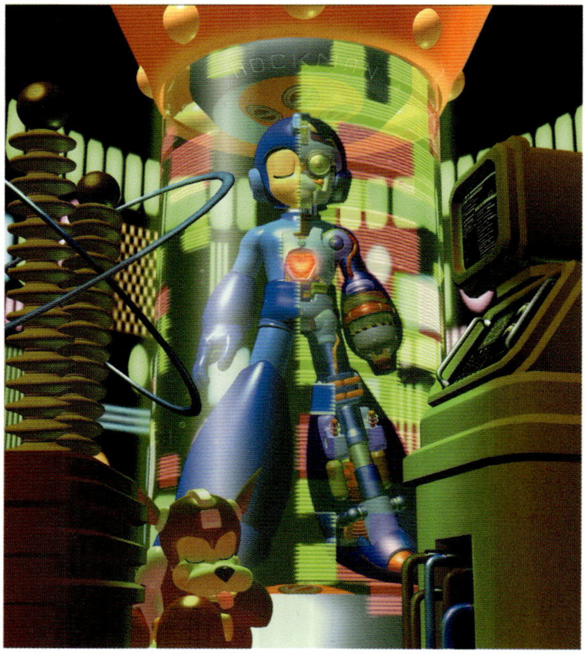

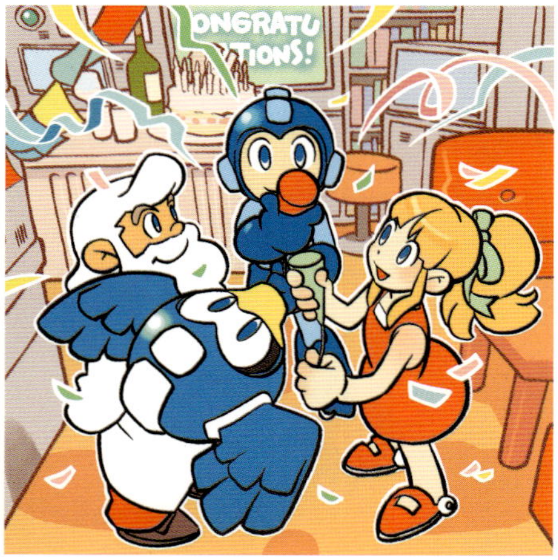

15TH ANNIVERSARY ILLUSTRATION

10TH ANNIVERSARY BOOK COVER

"I'm not the one who actually did this one, but at the time my priority was collecting as much knowledge as I could about working with CG and polygons. This piece was just a part of that learning curve." (Hideki)

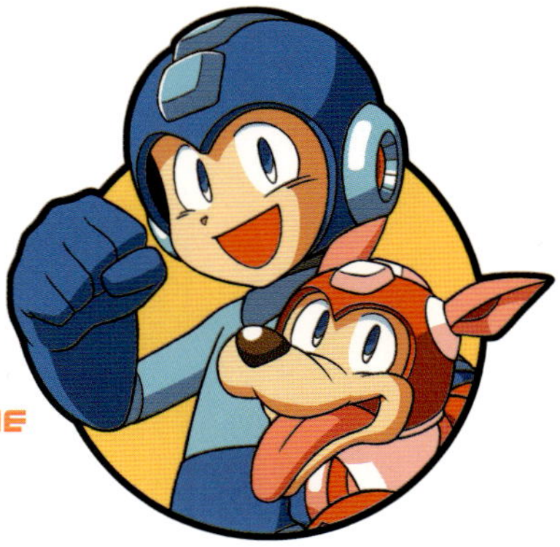

MAGAZINE COVER

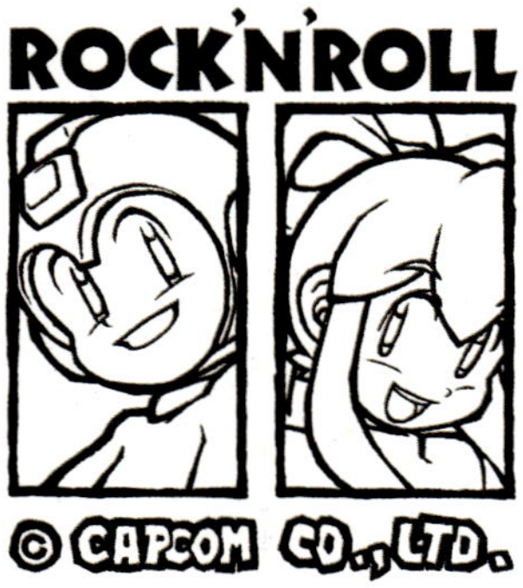

10TH ANNIVERSARY T-SHIRT

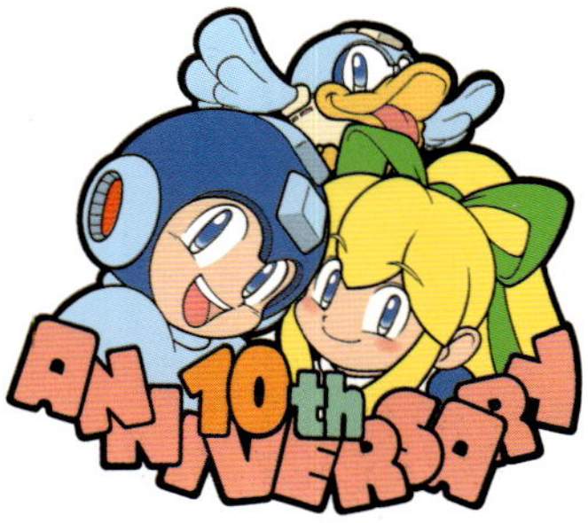

10TH ANNIVERSARY ILLUSTRATION

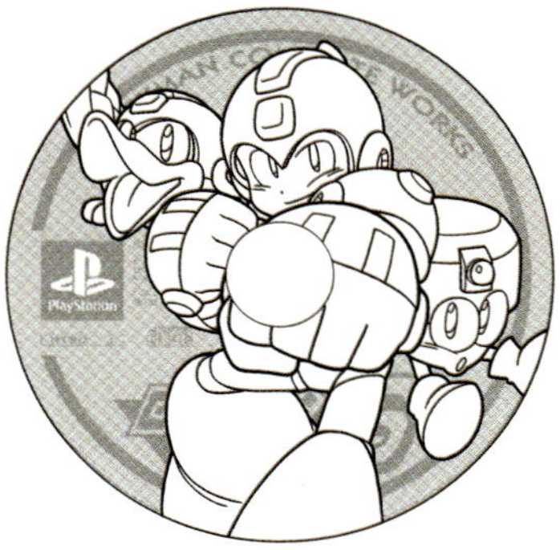

ROCKMAN 6 (PS VERSION) CD LABEL

"Since this basically marked the end of the PS versions, I put a lot of energy into making this label. Since he is in Power Mega Man form, Rush does not appear alongside him." (Higurashi)

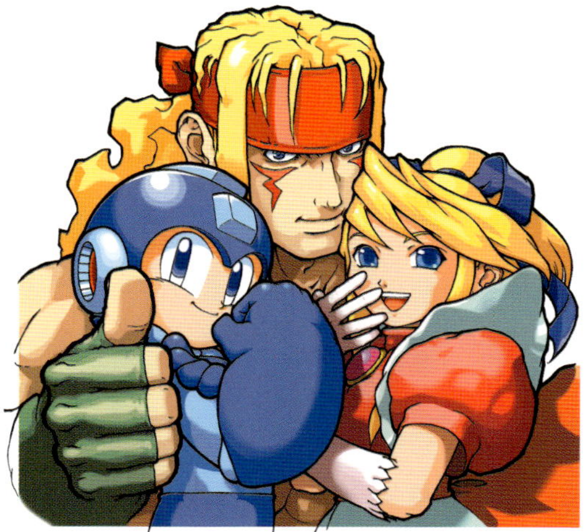

FAN CLUB BULLETIN

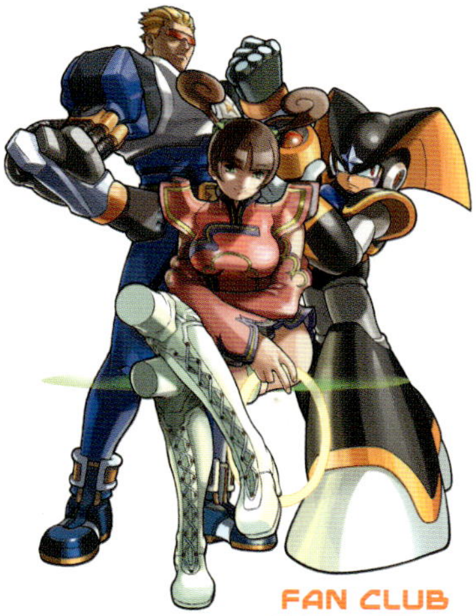

FAN CLUB BULLETIN

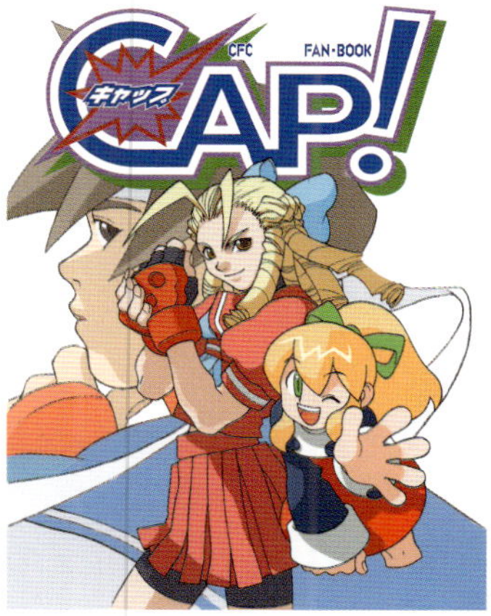

FAN CLUB BULLETIN

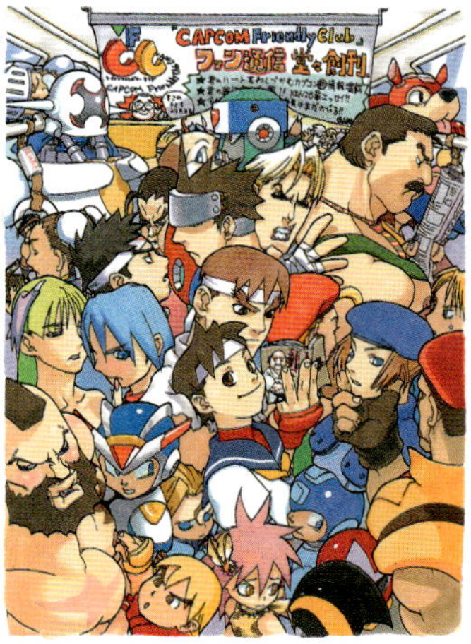

FAN CLUB BULLETIN

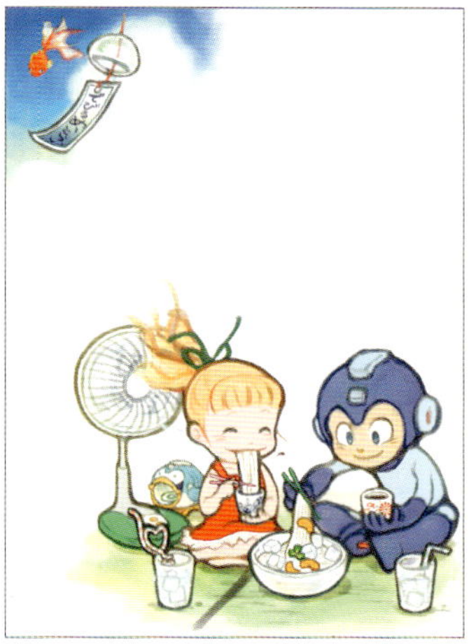

SUMMER POSTCARD

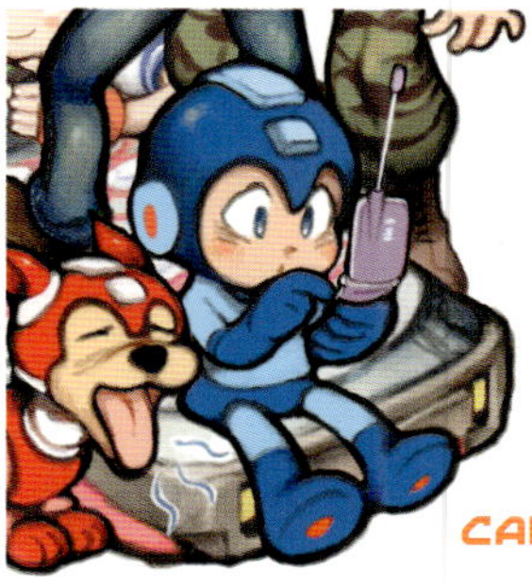

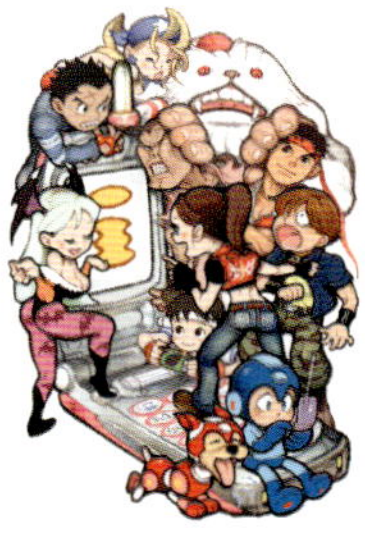

CAPCOM MOBILE

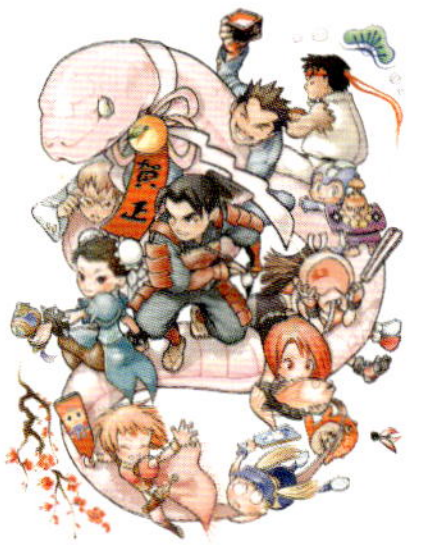

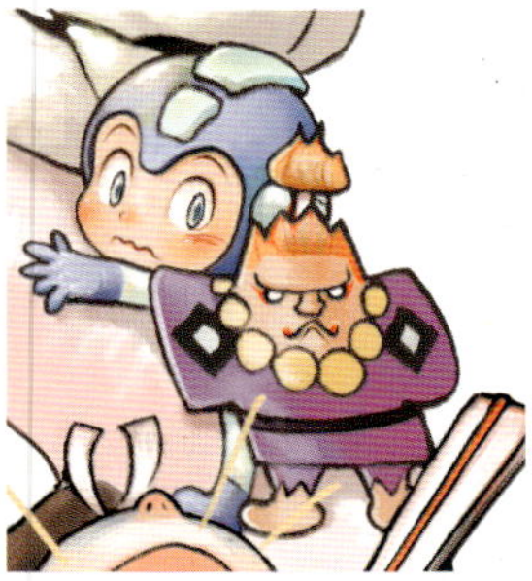

YEAR-END CAMPAIGN

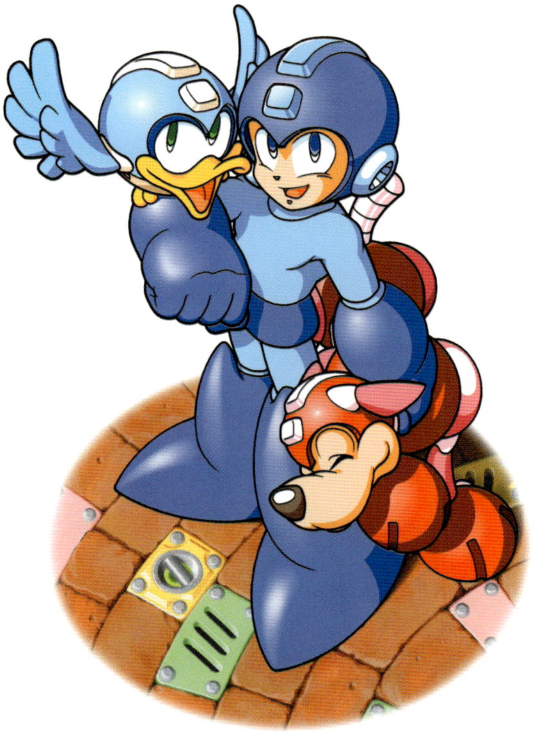

TELEPHONE CARD ILLUSTRATION (FAN CLUB GIFT)

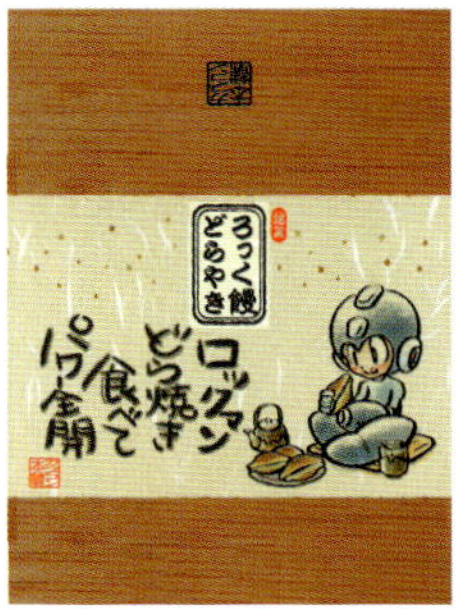

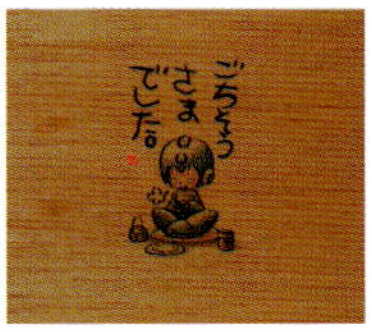

ROCKMAN DORAYAKI PACKAGE

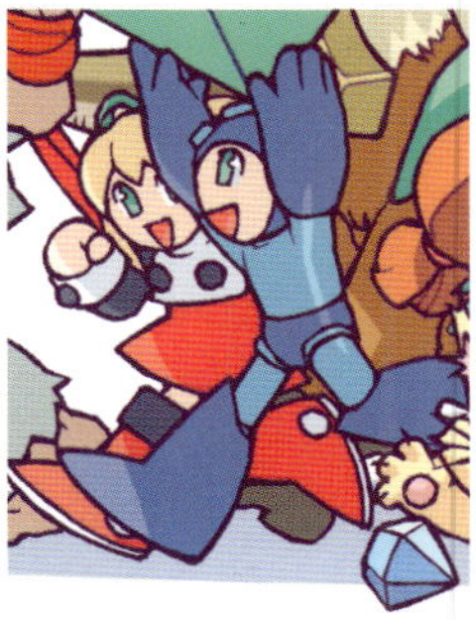

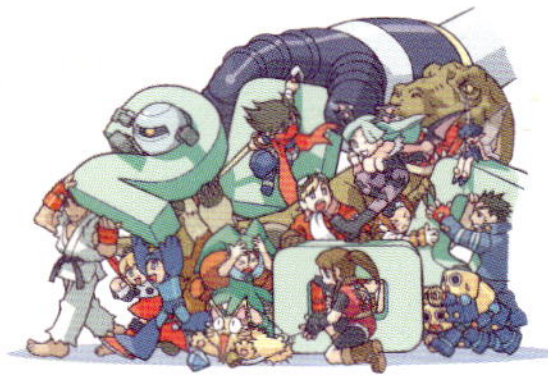

OFFICIAL NEW YEAR'S POSTCARD

DESIGN STUDIO ART BOOK COVER

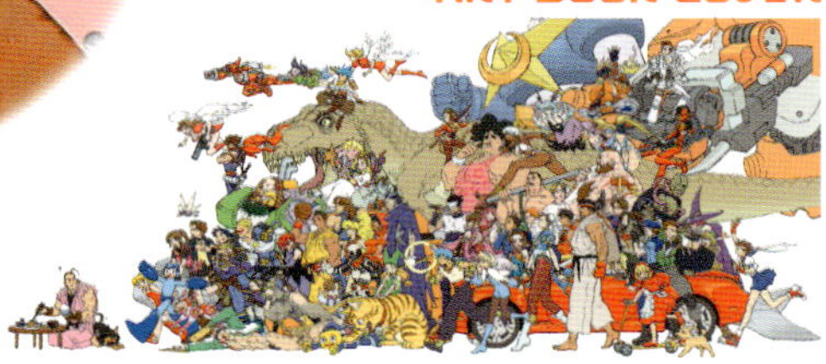

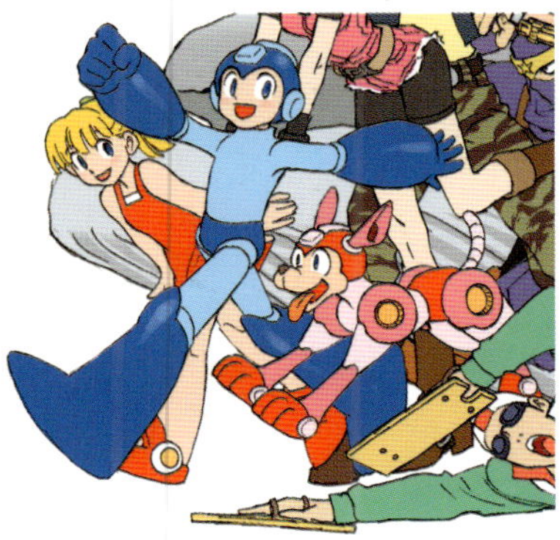

FAN CLUB BULLETIN

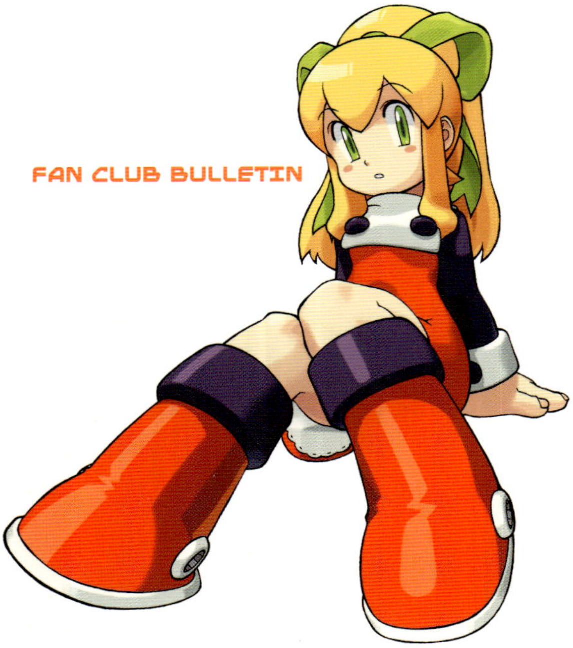

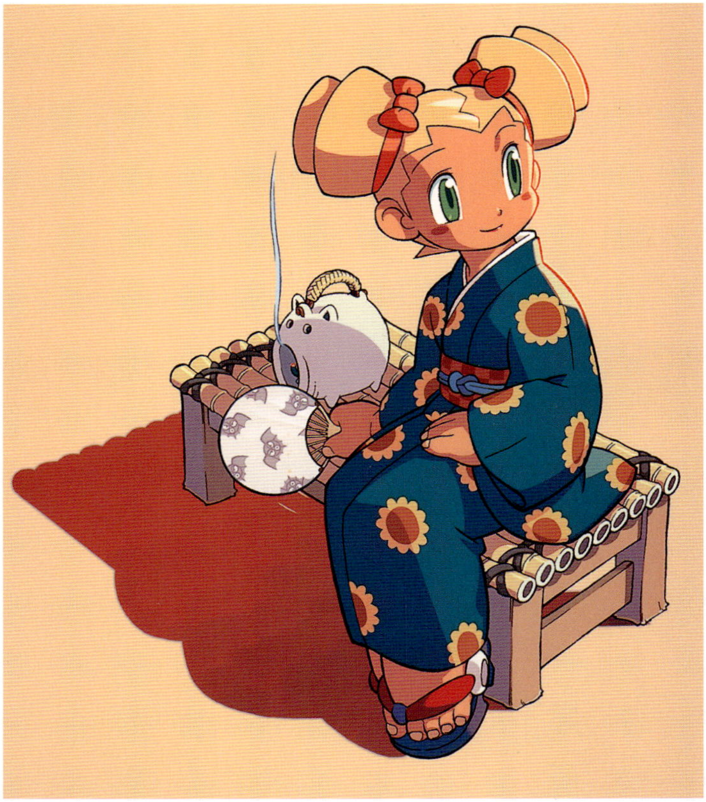

PS VERSION INSTRUCTION MANUAL ILLUSTRATION

"I started wondering what Rock and Roll would wear casually. I tried dressing them in modern clothes as well as futuristic clothes, but it just didn't seem to fit within their world. I just happened to be really into '50s fashion at the time, and that's how they ended up dressed like this in the drawings on the next page. (laughs)" (Hideki)

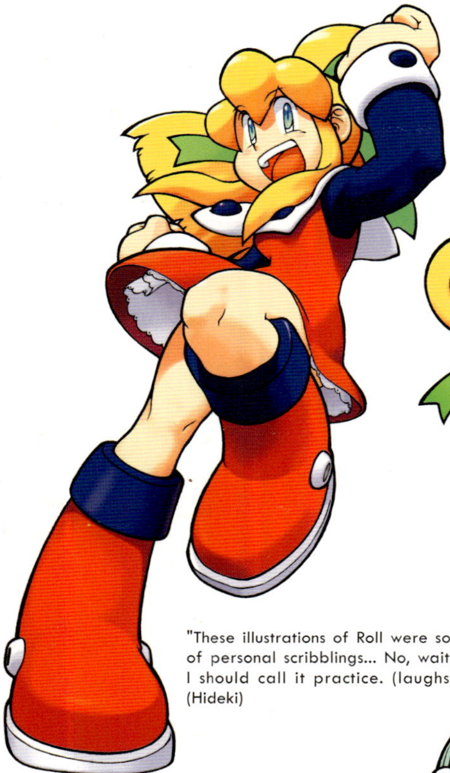

"These illustrations of Roll were sort of personal scribblings... No, wait... I should call it practice. (laughs)" (Hideki)

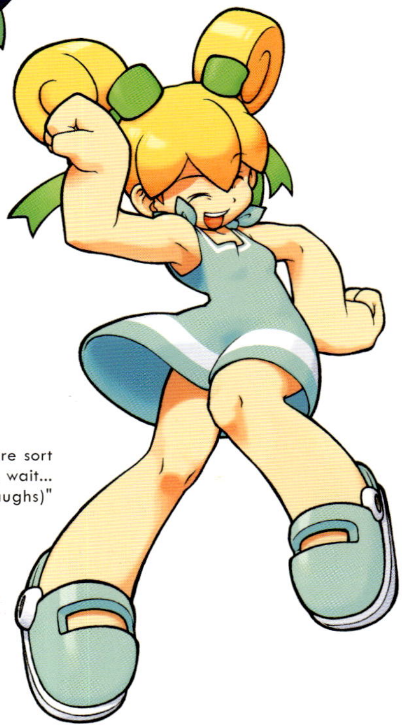

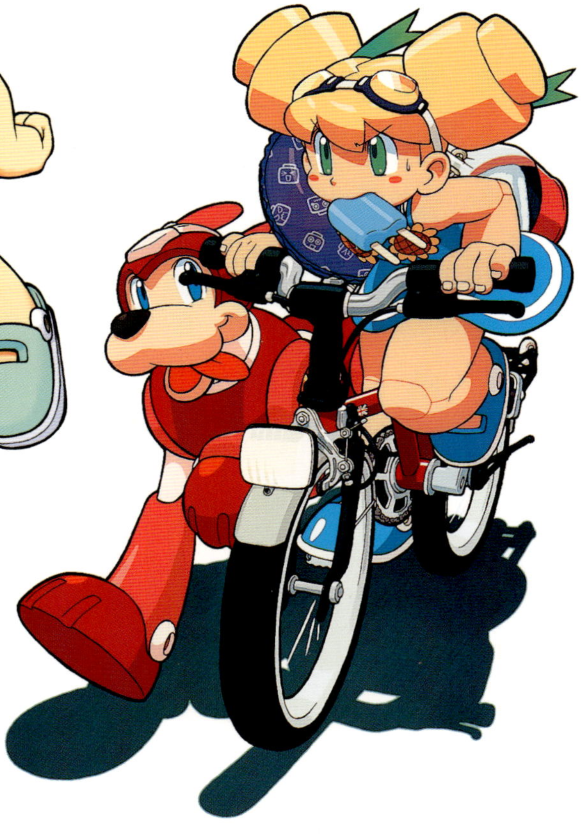

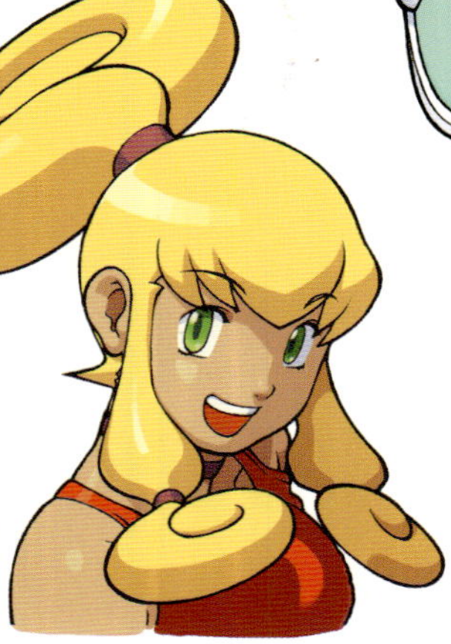

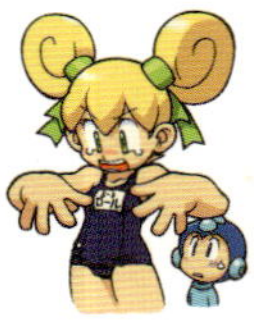

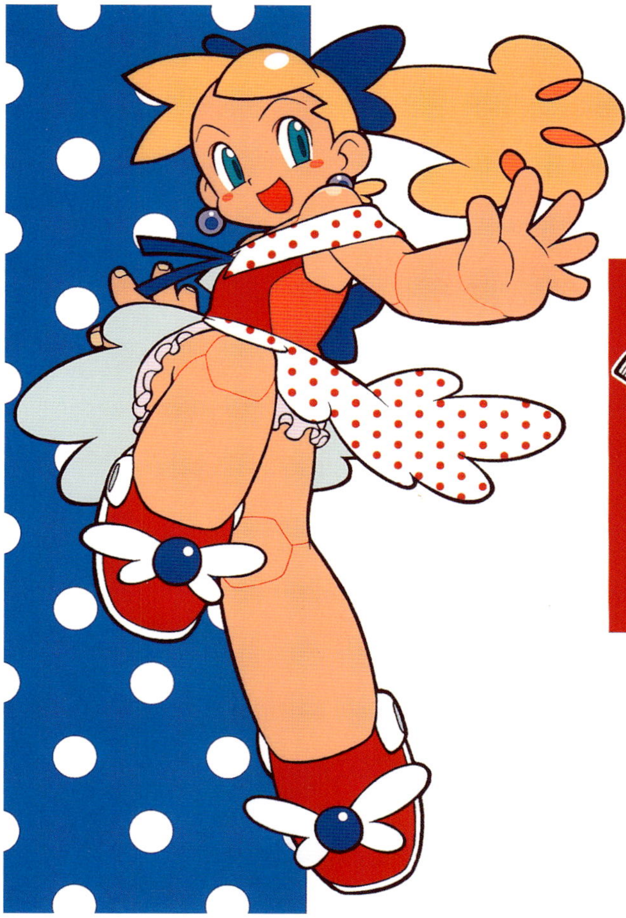
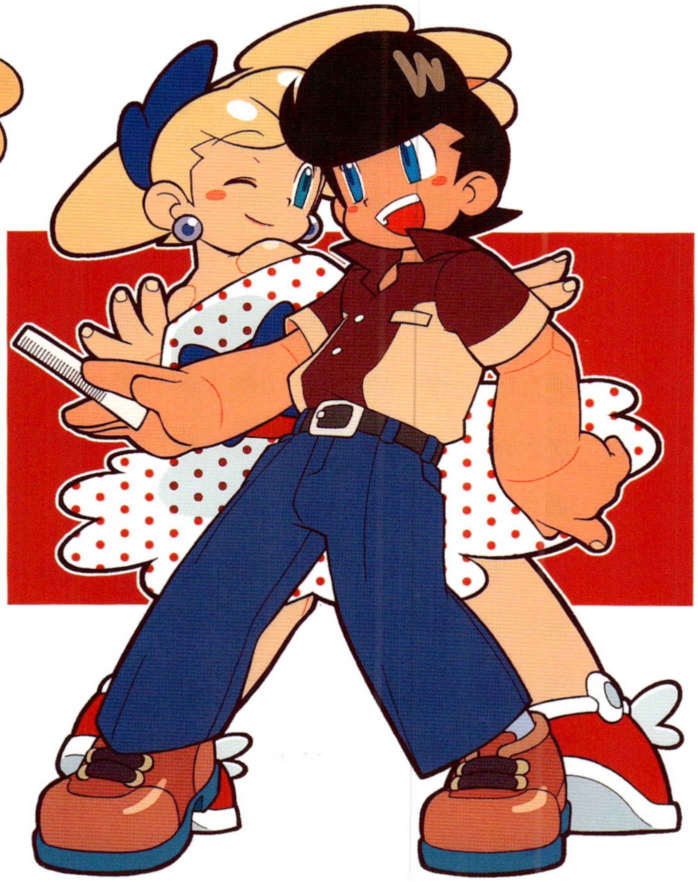
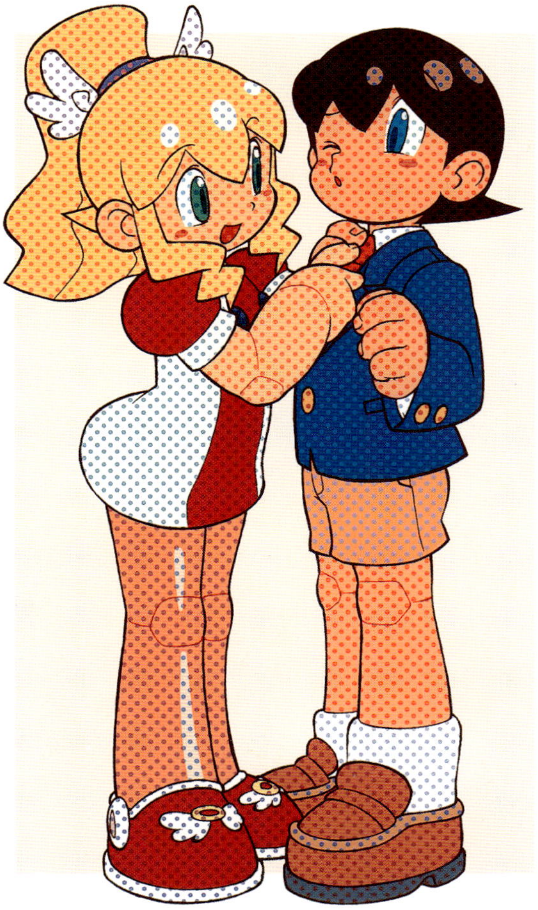
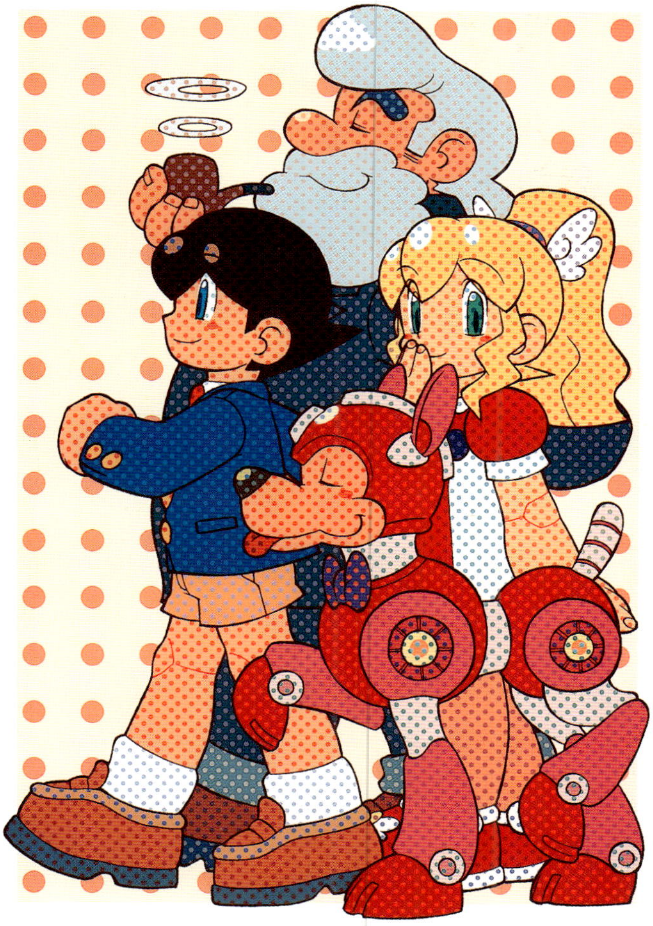

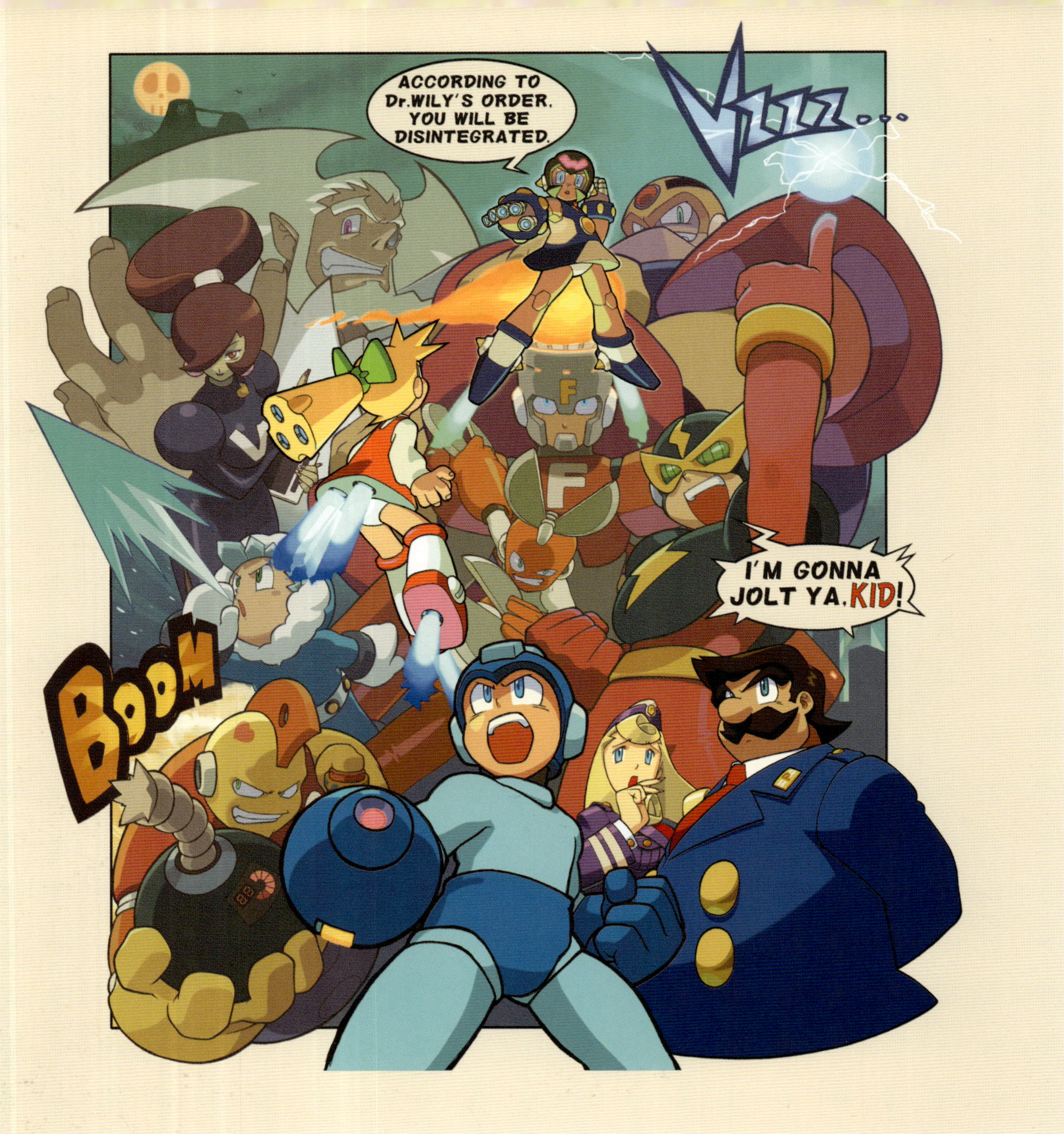

FAN CLUB BULLETIN "I was told I could do whatever I wanted with this piece, so I went with a sort of 'parallel universe' idea. If Mega Man has girls on his side, why couldn't Dr. Wily have girls on his side too, right? I also altered Dr. Wily slightly, as you can see in the upper left. I actually think he looks like someone who could get in bigger trouble than the Dr. Wily from the actual games. (laughs)" (Hideki)

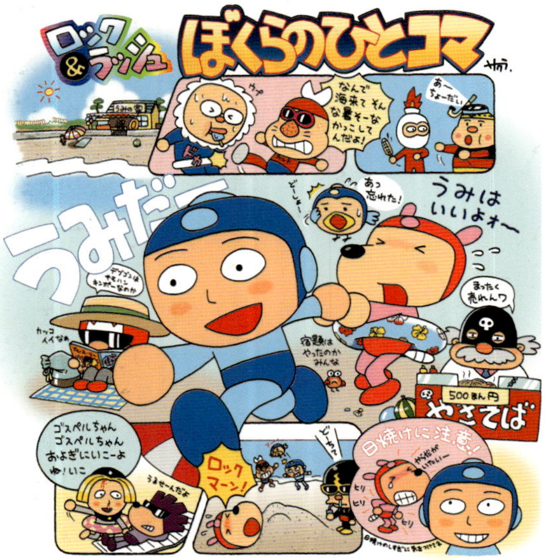

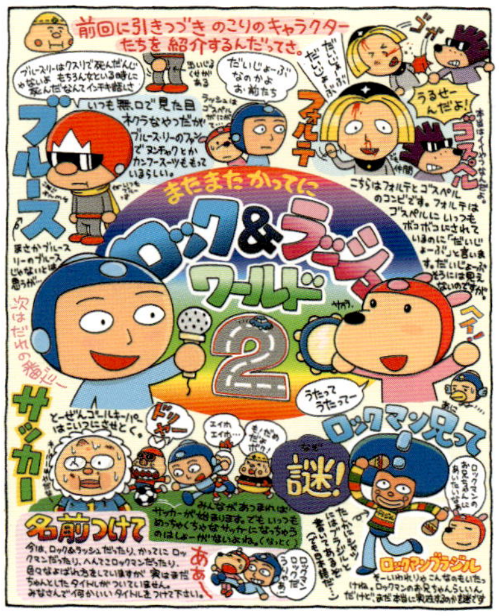

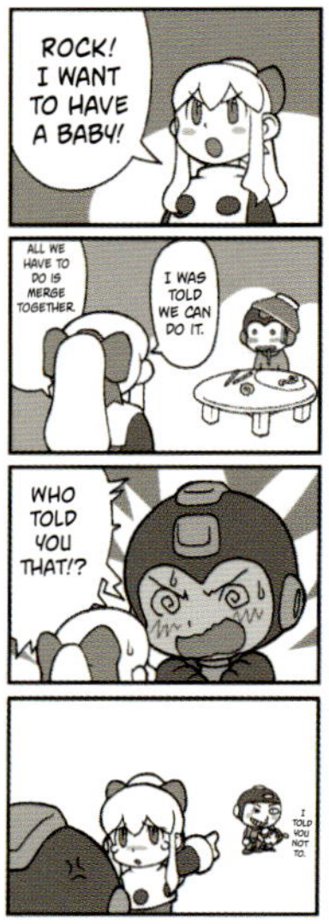

Rockman comics by Sakura, presented in Secret Files, etc.

"CLUB ☆ CAPCOM" COVER

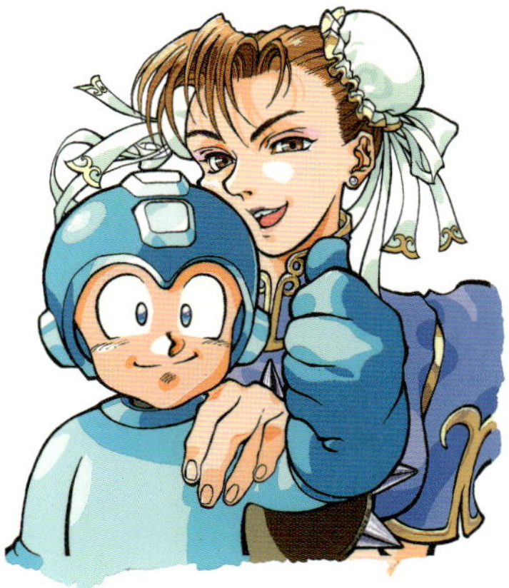

"EVERYTHING CAPCOM CAMPAIGN" (PSP) ILLUSTRATION

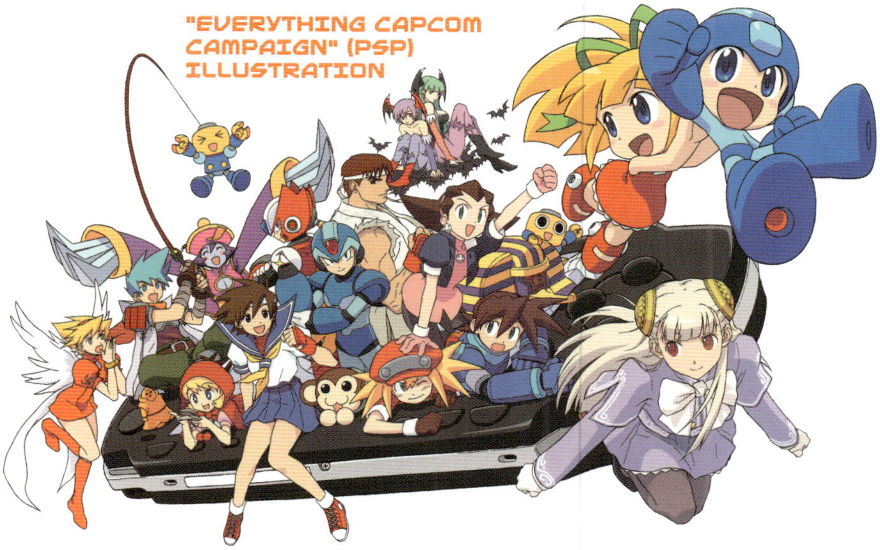

"Since I had been drawing Mega Man characters for so long, I felt a ton of pressure when I was trying to draw Street Fighter characters. (laughs) But I was really happy that I got another chance to draw the 'Legends' characters, who I had drawn for the PSP package art." (Higurashi)

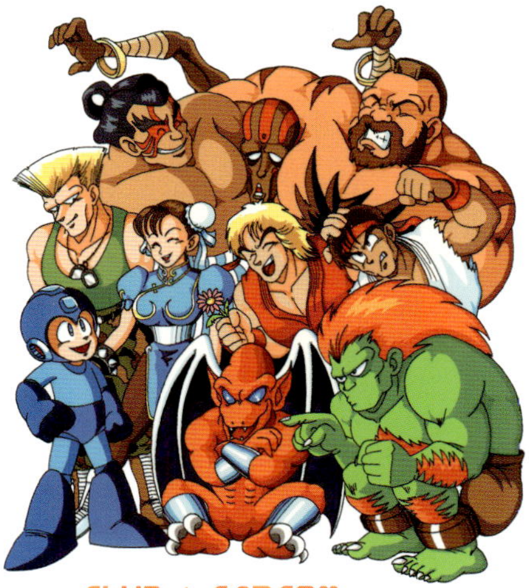

CLUB ☆ CAPCOM

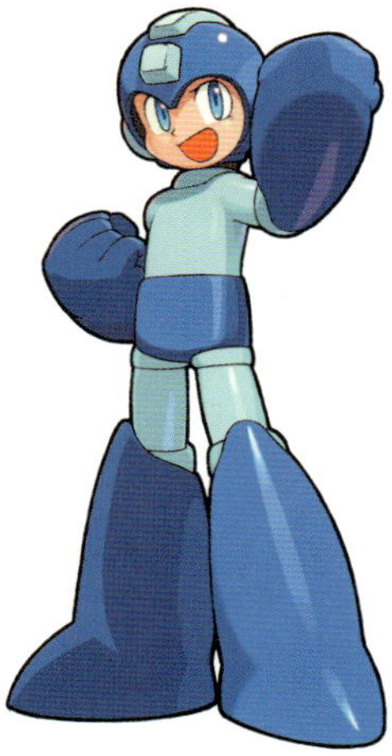

"CANNON SPIKE" MEGA MAN

"I colored Mega Man a bit differently so that there didn't seem to be as much of a gap between the weights of the textures for the character I drew and the characters Kinu Nishimura drew." (Hideki)

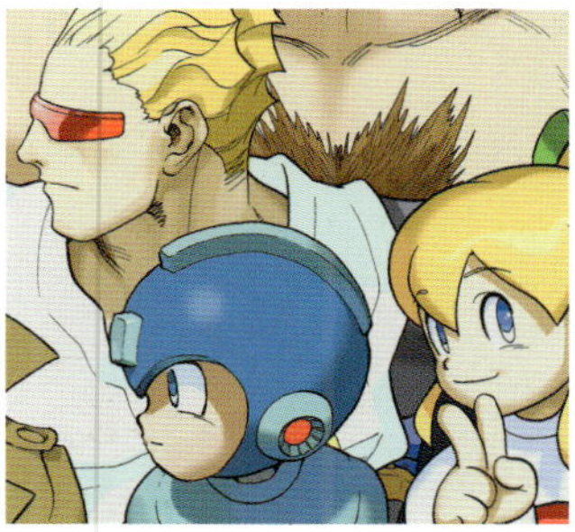

"MARVEL VS. CAPCOM" MAIN ILLUSTRATION

"MARVEL VS. CAPCOM" SECRET FILE

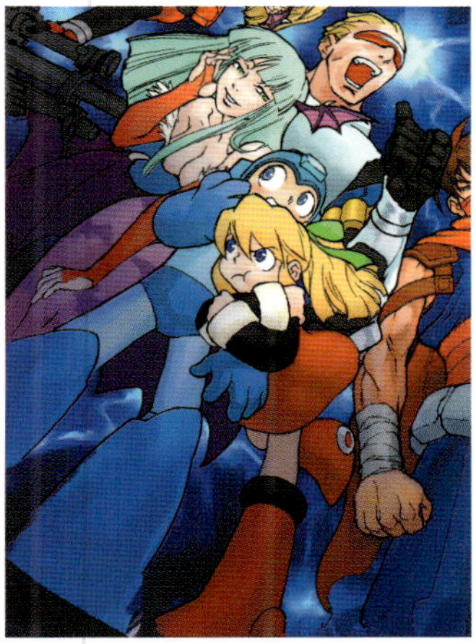

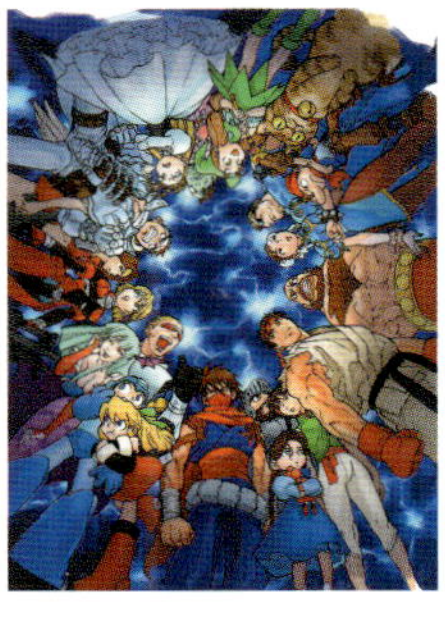

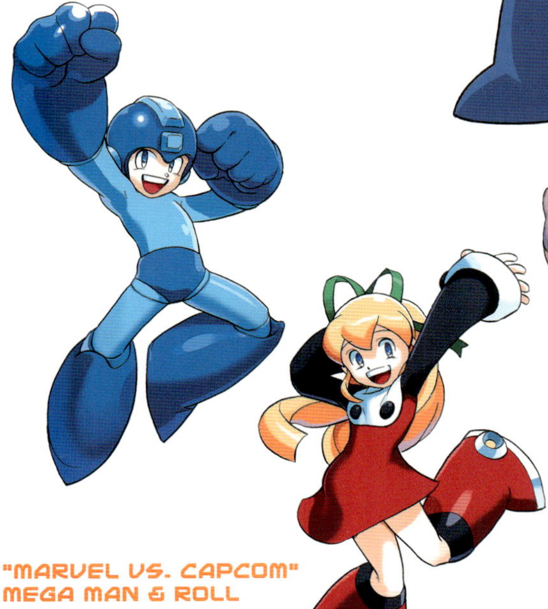

"MARVEL VS. CAPCOM" MEGA MAN & ROLL

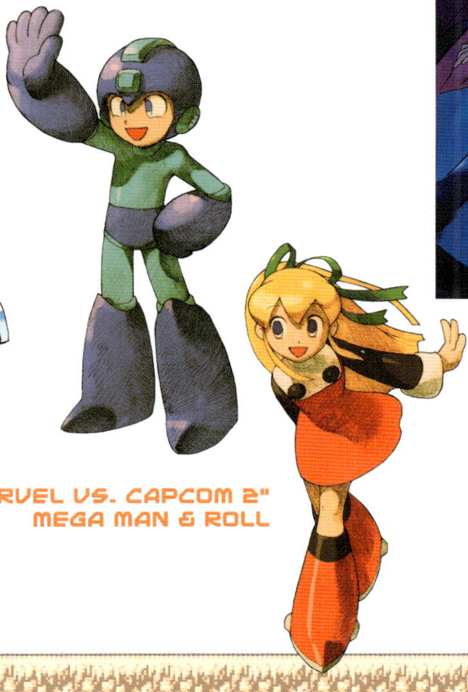

"MARVEL VS. CAPCOM 2" MEGA MAN & ROLL

ROCKMAN MANGAS

A few of the Mega Man mangas that ran in Kodansha's "Comic Bon Bon," complete with authors' comments.

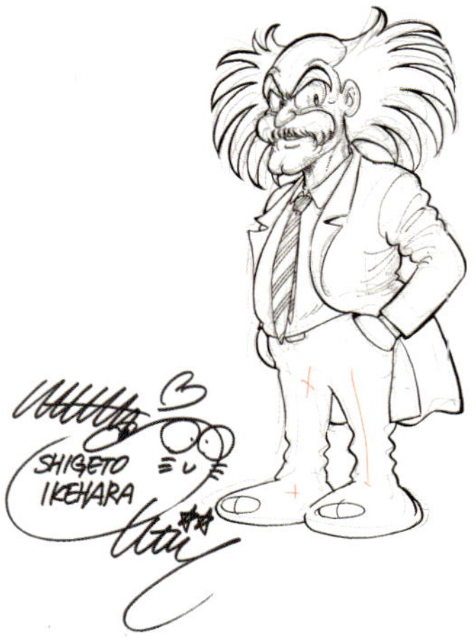

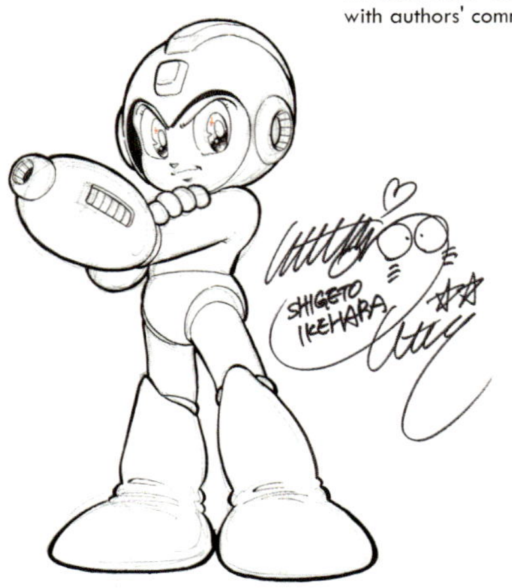

"Ikehara gave me these two autographed illustrations when I went to visit him at his workplace. He drew them up right in front of my eyes." (Ariga)

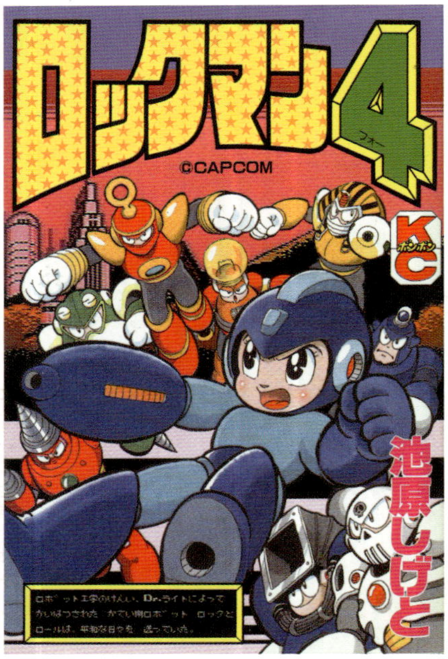

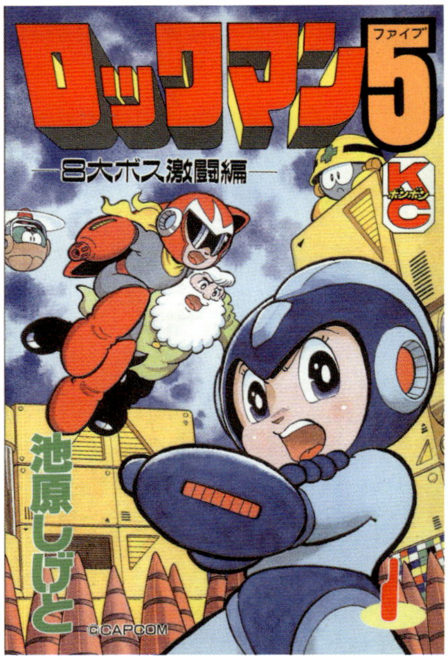

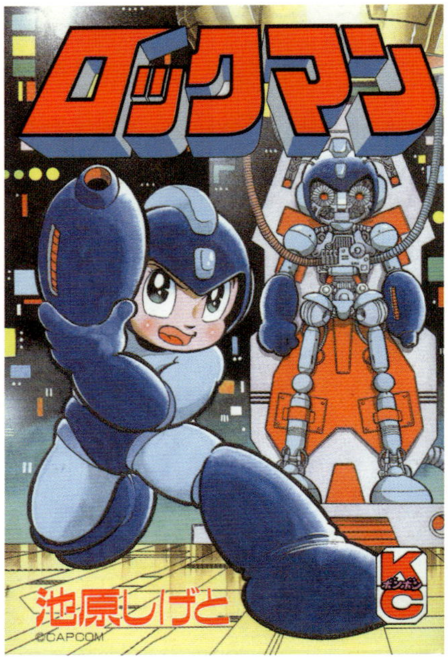

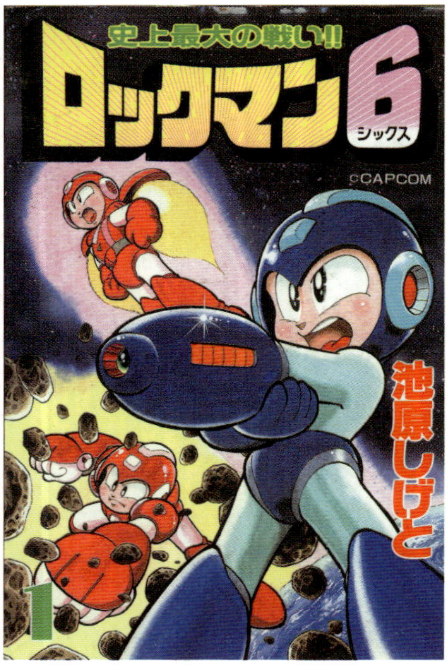

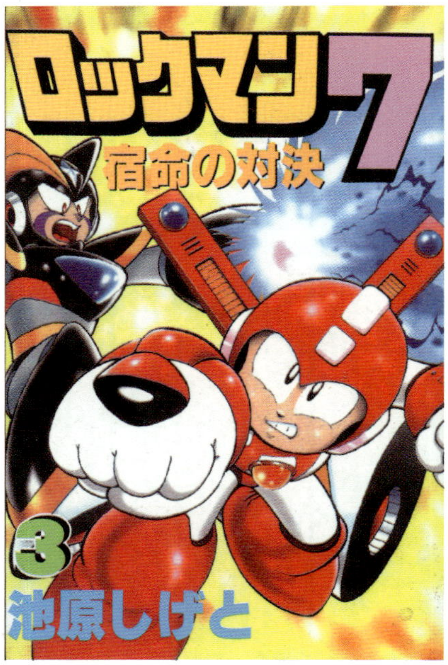

Shigeto Ikehara

"I drew Mega Man so much. I initially got started drawing game guide mangas, but they gradually gave me more and more freedom with the content until I ended up doing a whole original story. Hmm... Ariga, I don't see the cover that I like here...? (laughs)" (Ikehara)
"You mean 'Blues Reborn,' right? Yeah, I wanted to include that one too since I had a small hand in it, but... (sweats)" (Ariga)
"Oh well. Thanks for calling me in on this project anyway. (laughs)" (Ikehara)

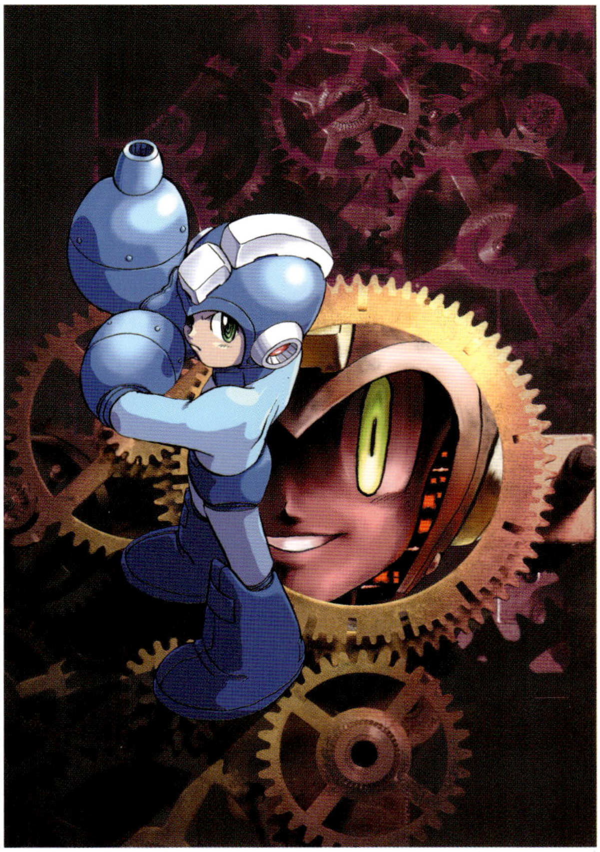

Hitoshi Ariga

"Since Ikehara's work was the generally accepted mainstream Mega Man manga, I always considered my work to be more of a spin-off, or maybe an OVA eventually. I was such a huge Mega Man fan... I put my heart and soul into every manga that I drew. The whole theme of robotics is such a deep interest of mine, these works will always have a special place in my memories. I am currently working on more volumes." (Ariga)

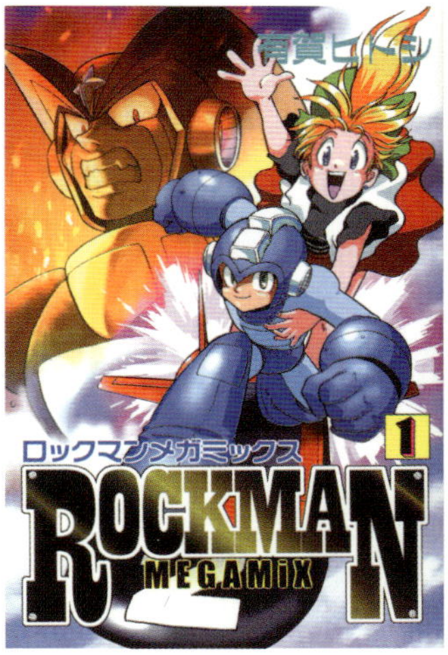

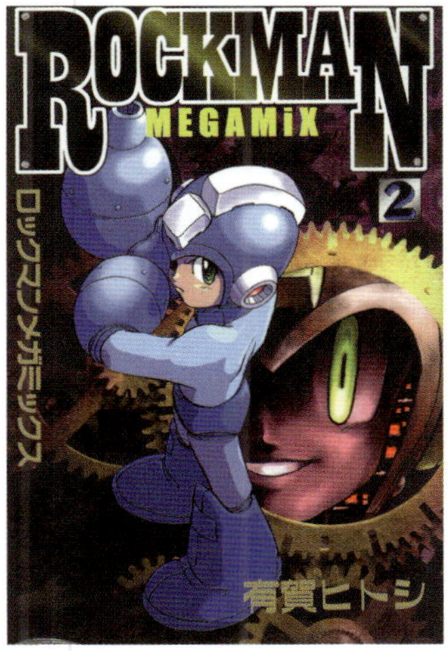

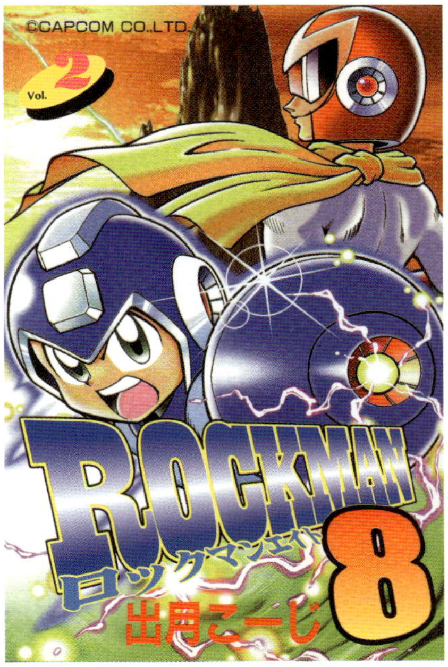

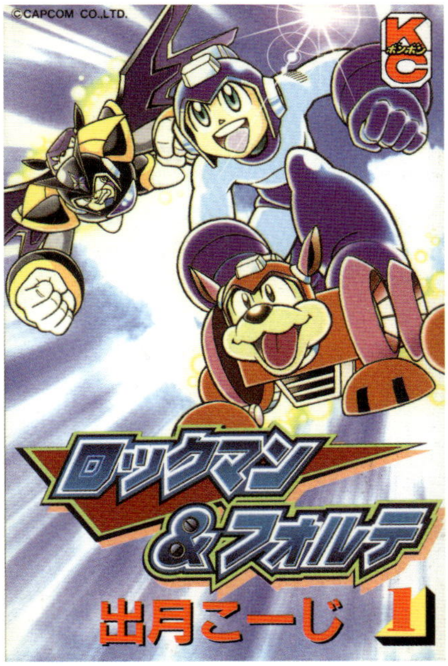

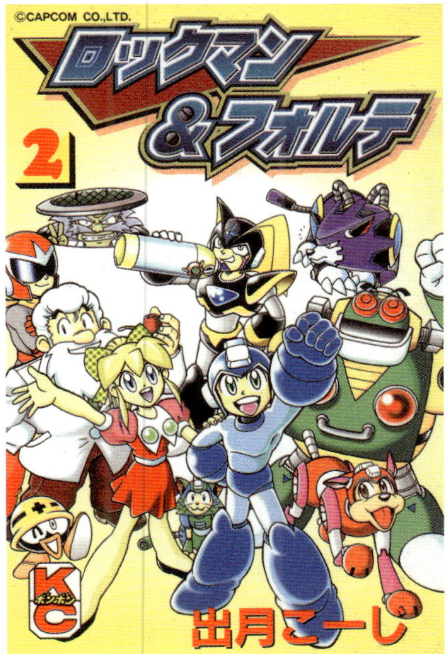

Koji Izuki

"The contrail you see on the cover of Rockman 8 Volume 2 is my tribute to Duo. I didn't get to send him back home to space in the actual book, so I wanted to at least do that for him on the cover." (Izuki)

OVERSEAS MEGA MAN

All the different Mega Mans have had such a strong impact. The overall setting of the game hasn't been changed, so the good guys still report back to Dr. Light after battle... or at least they should.

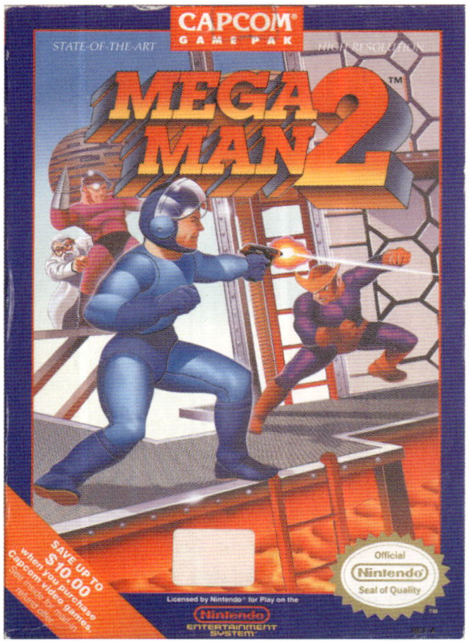

"MEGA MAN 2"

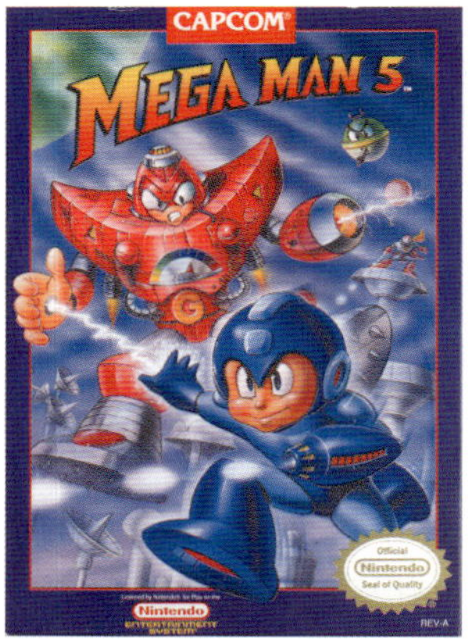

"MEGA MAN 5"

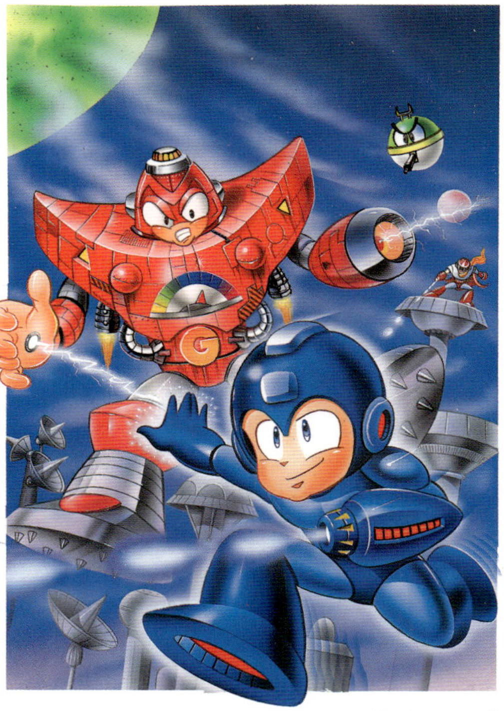

"MEGA MAN 5"
Original package art

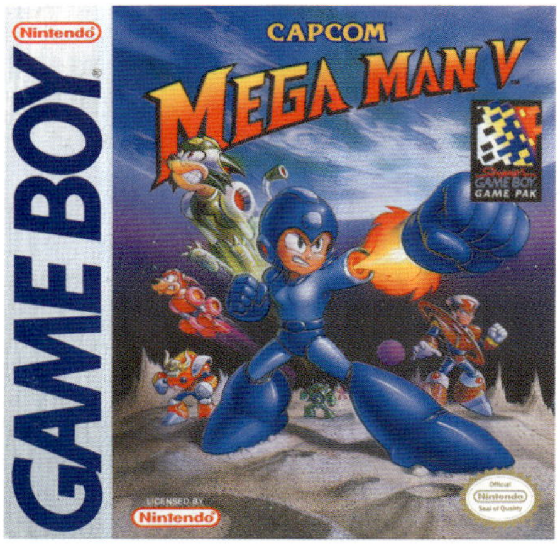

"MEGA MAN V"

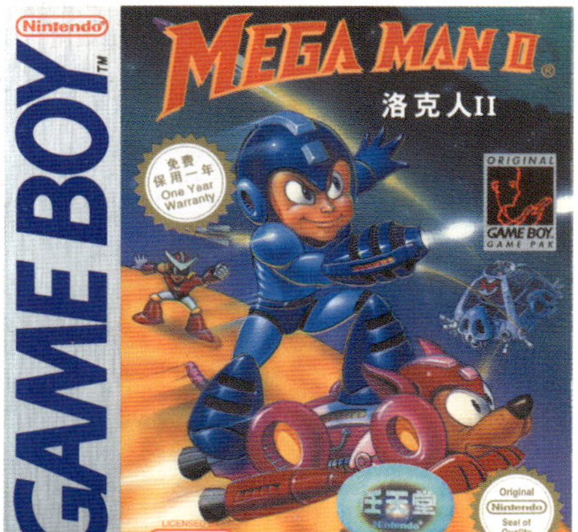

"MEGA MAN II" (ASIAN VERSION)

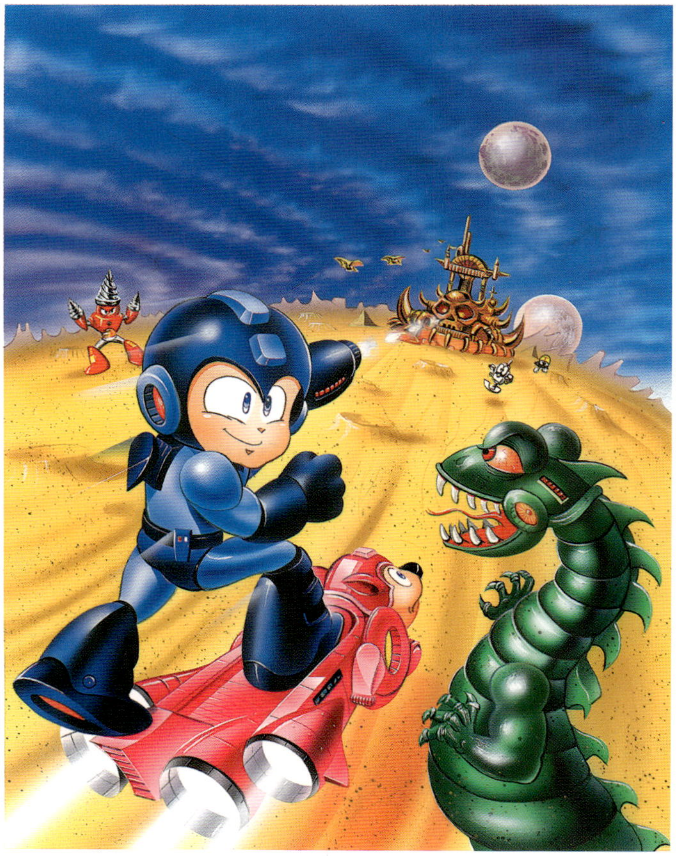

"MEGA MAN III"
Original package art

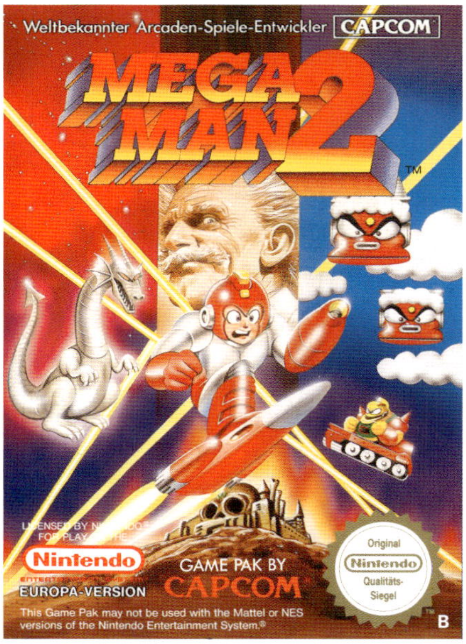

"MEGA MAN 2"
(European Version)

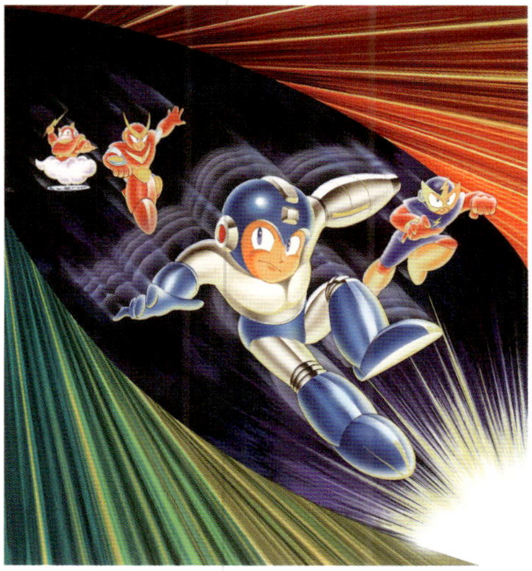

"MEGA MAN"
(European Version)

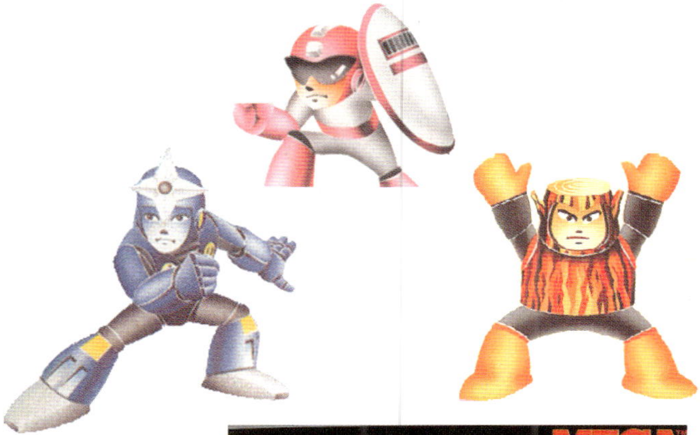

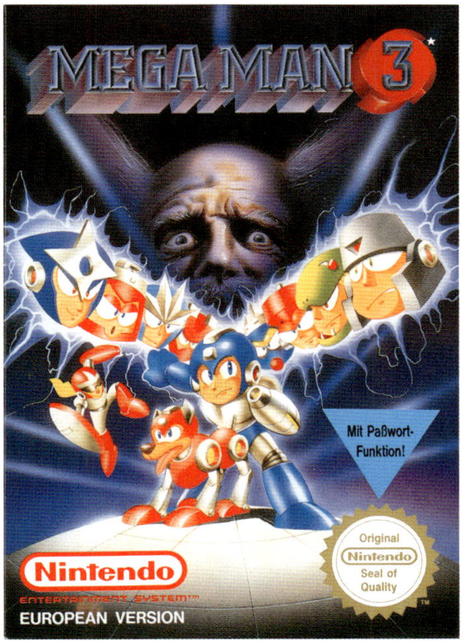

"MEGA MAN 3"
(European Version)

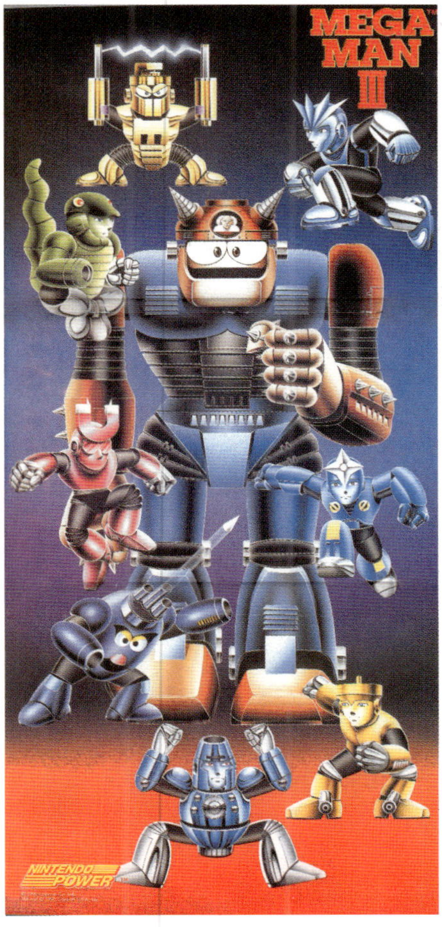

"MEGA MAN 3" POSTER

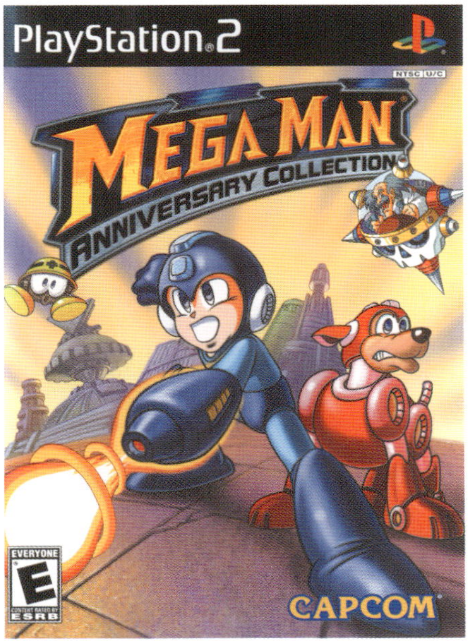

"MEGA MAN ANNIVERSARY
COLLECTION"

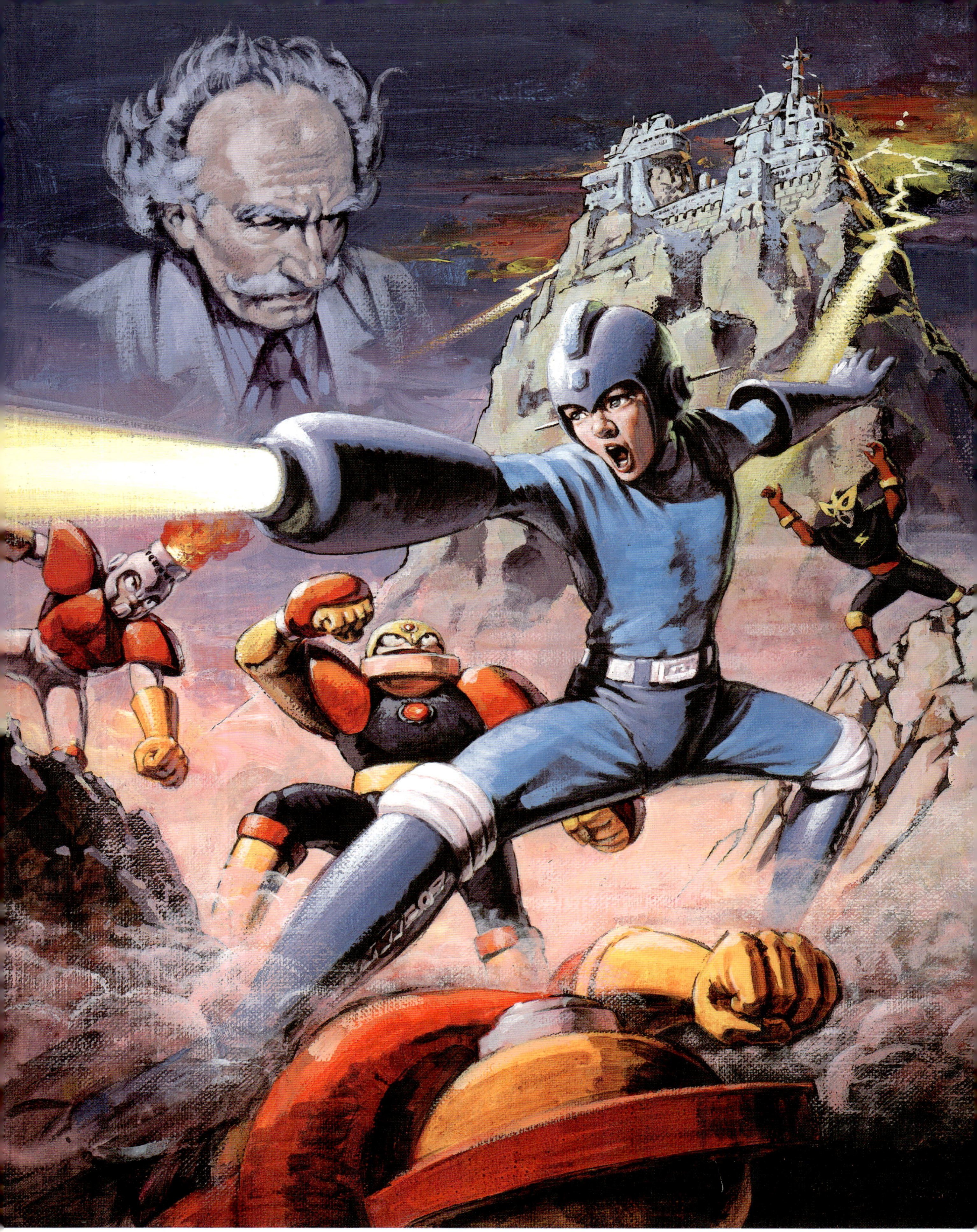

"MEGA MAN" (European version) Original package art

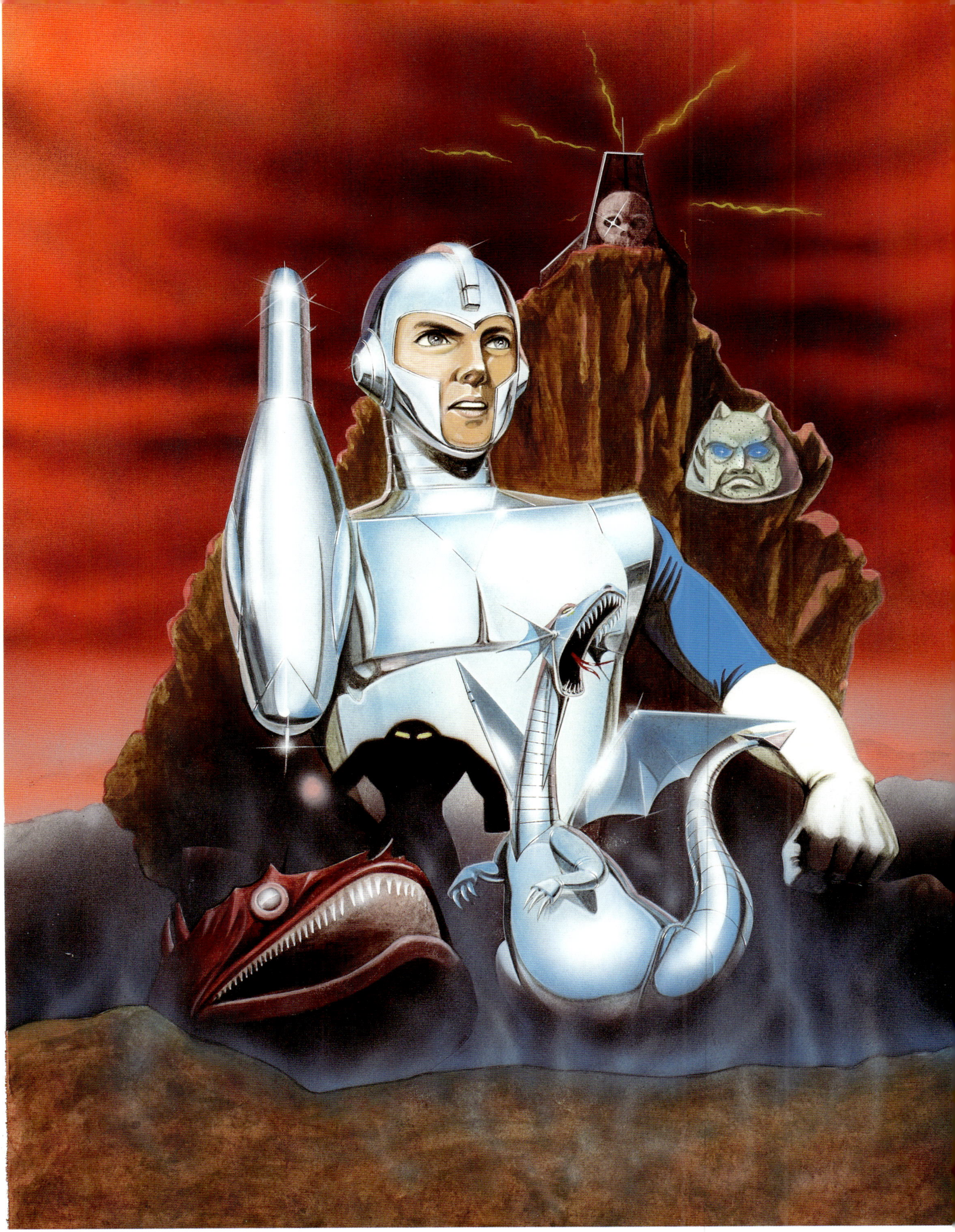

"MEGA MAN 2" (European version) Original package art

COMIC ADAPTATIONS

All four issues of the comic series "Mega Man" published by the Canadian company Dreamwave Productions in 2003.

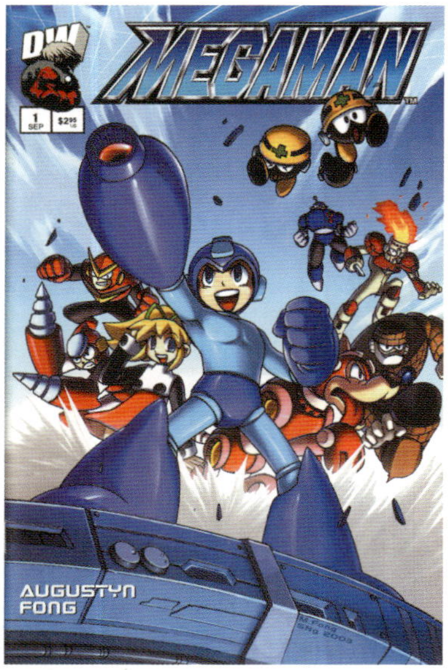

Issue 1

Mega Man attends school as a normal boy, his identity hidden from his schoolmates. Meanwhile, crimes involving robots are on the rise in the city.

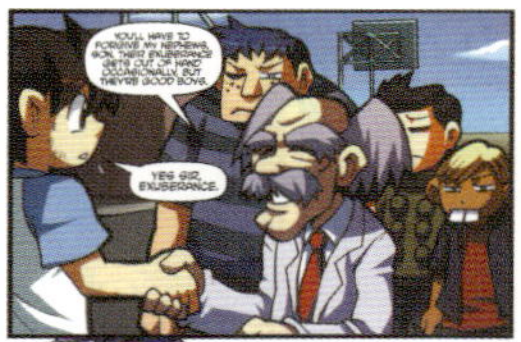

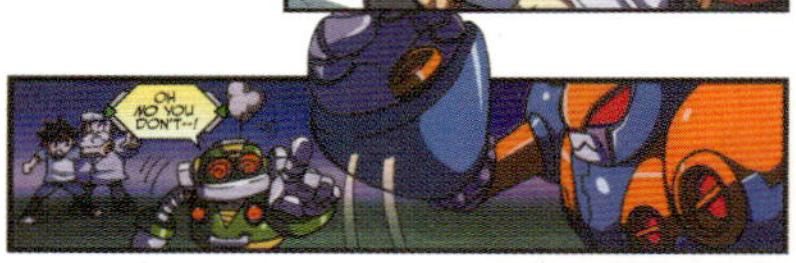

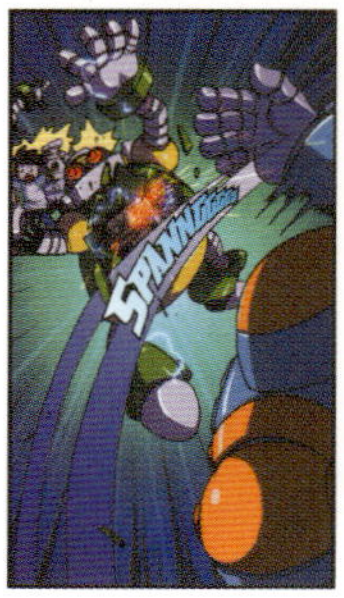

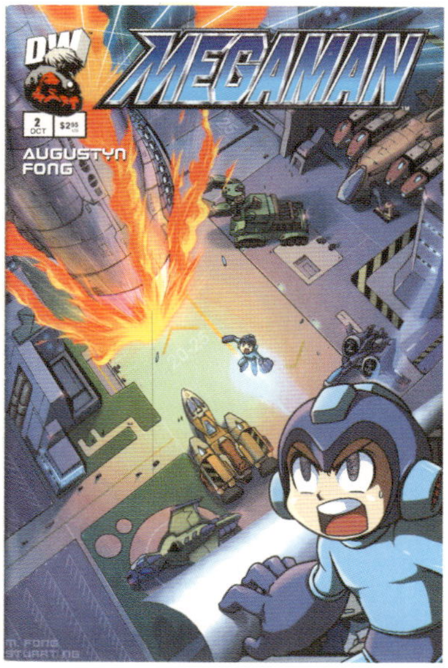

Issue 2

Bullies can make school life so hard. To make matters more confusing, the school bully's uncle looks strangely familiar.

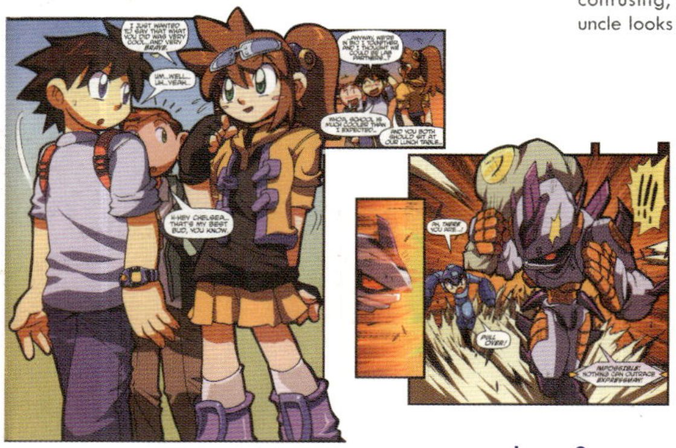

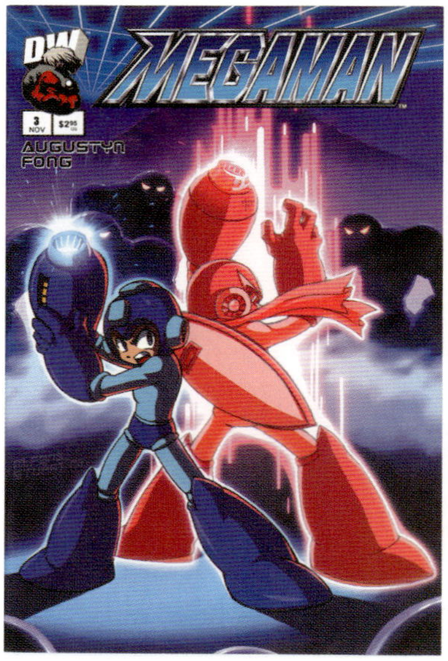

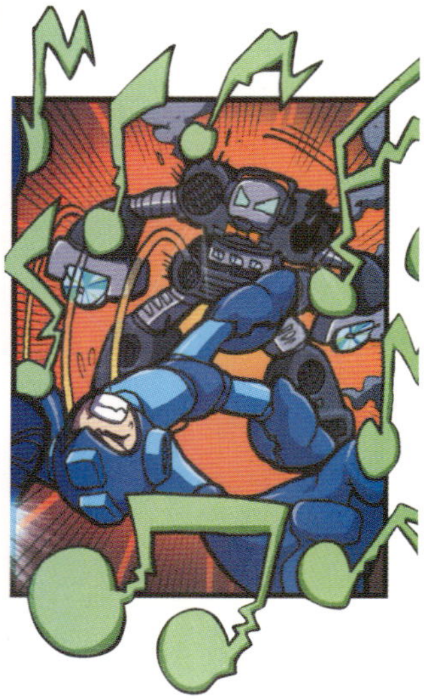

Issue 3

Mega Man was on top of the world after attending a dance party with his classmate Chelsea, but things take a turn for the worse when Dr. Light gets kidnapped.

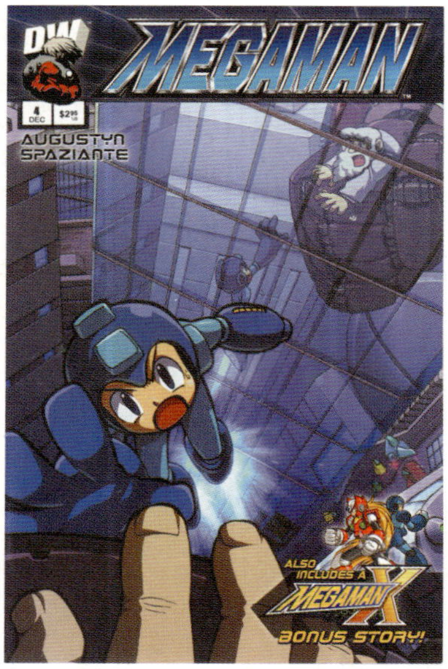

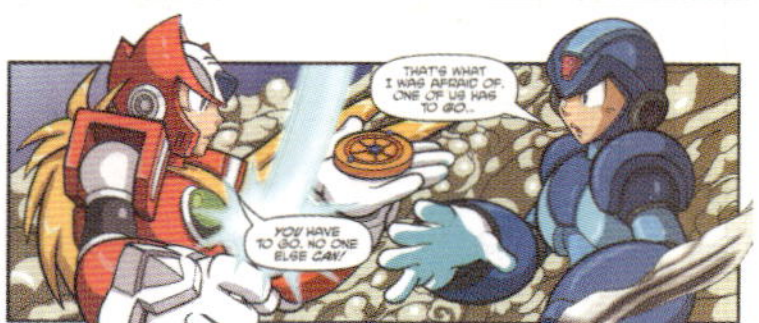

Issue 4

Mega Man and Proto Man head out together to find and rescue Dr. Light. The situation only gets more complicated when Wily's giant robot shows up!

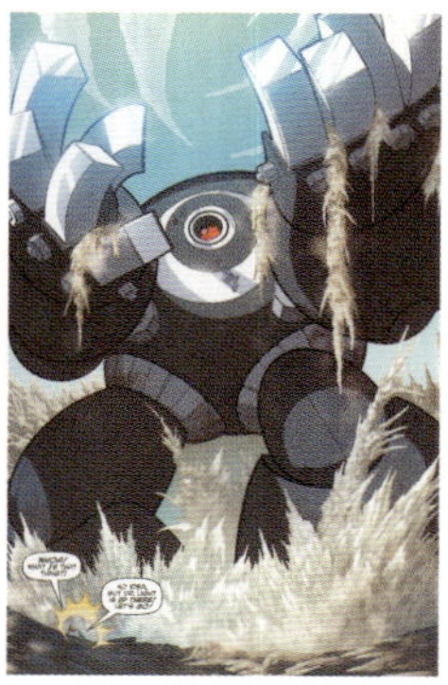

Mega Man issue 4 included an ad for issue 1 of the "Mega Man X" comic series. (Sadly, the Mega Man X series was never published).

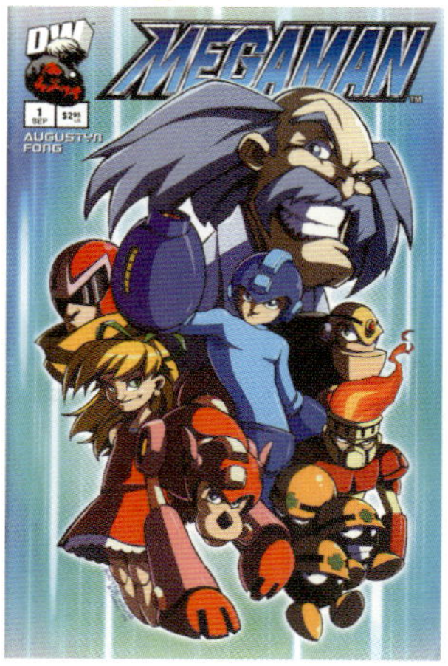

Issue 1 alternate cover

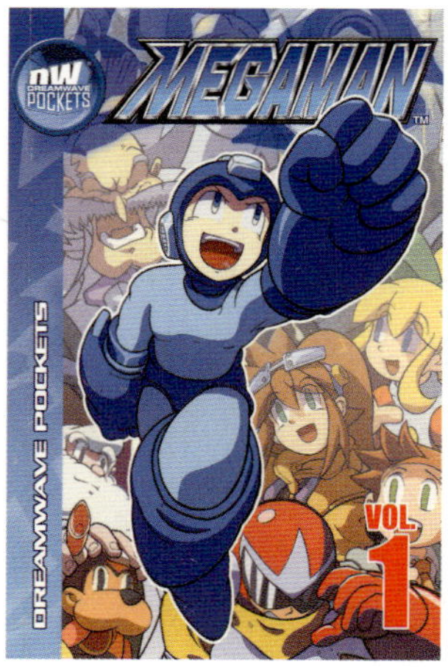

Issues 1-4 collected into a single book.

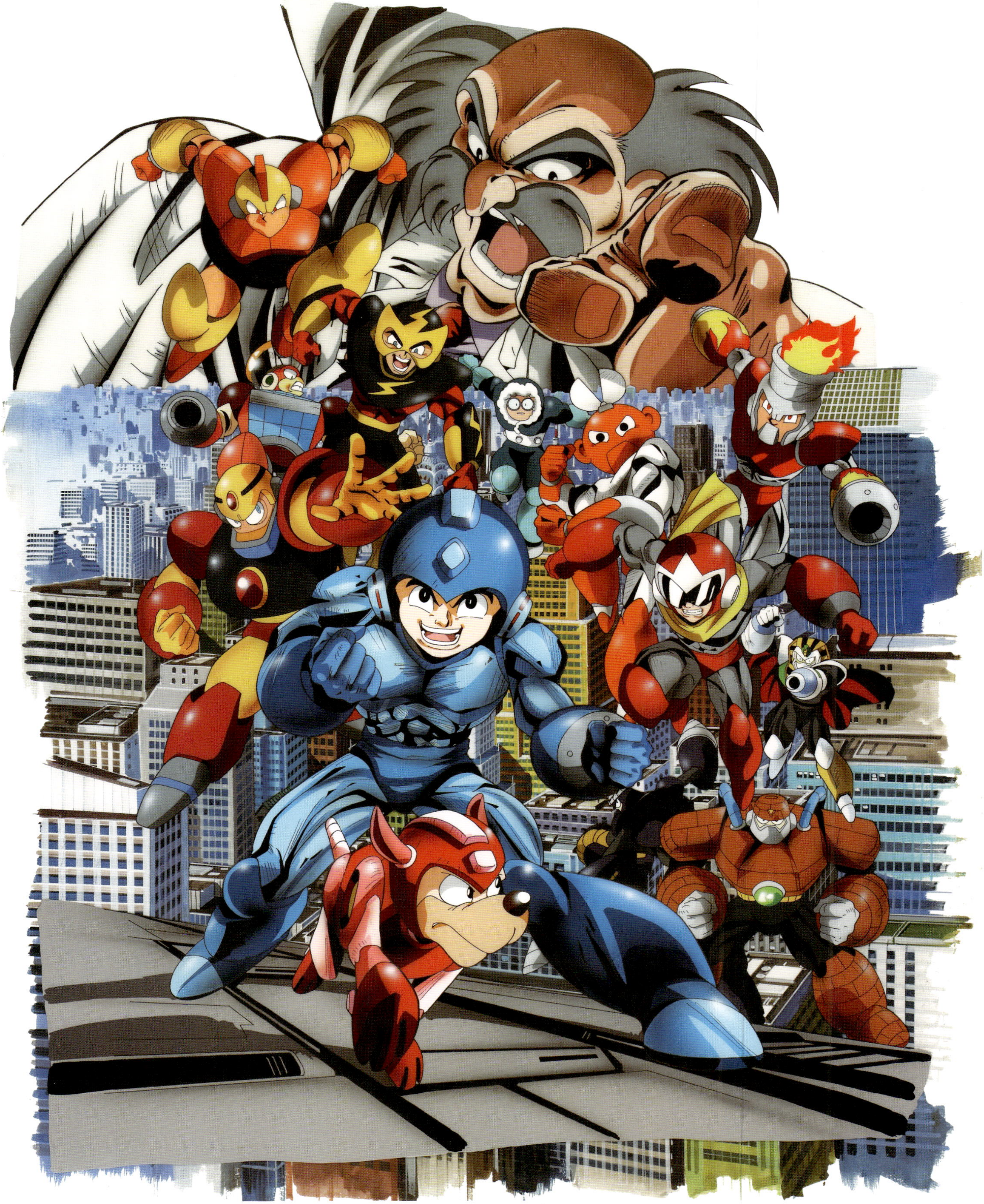

Illustration for the "Mega Man" cartoon

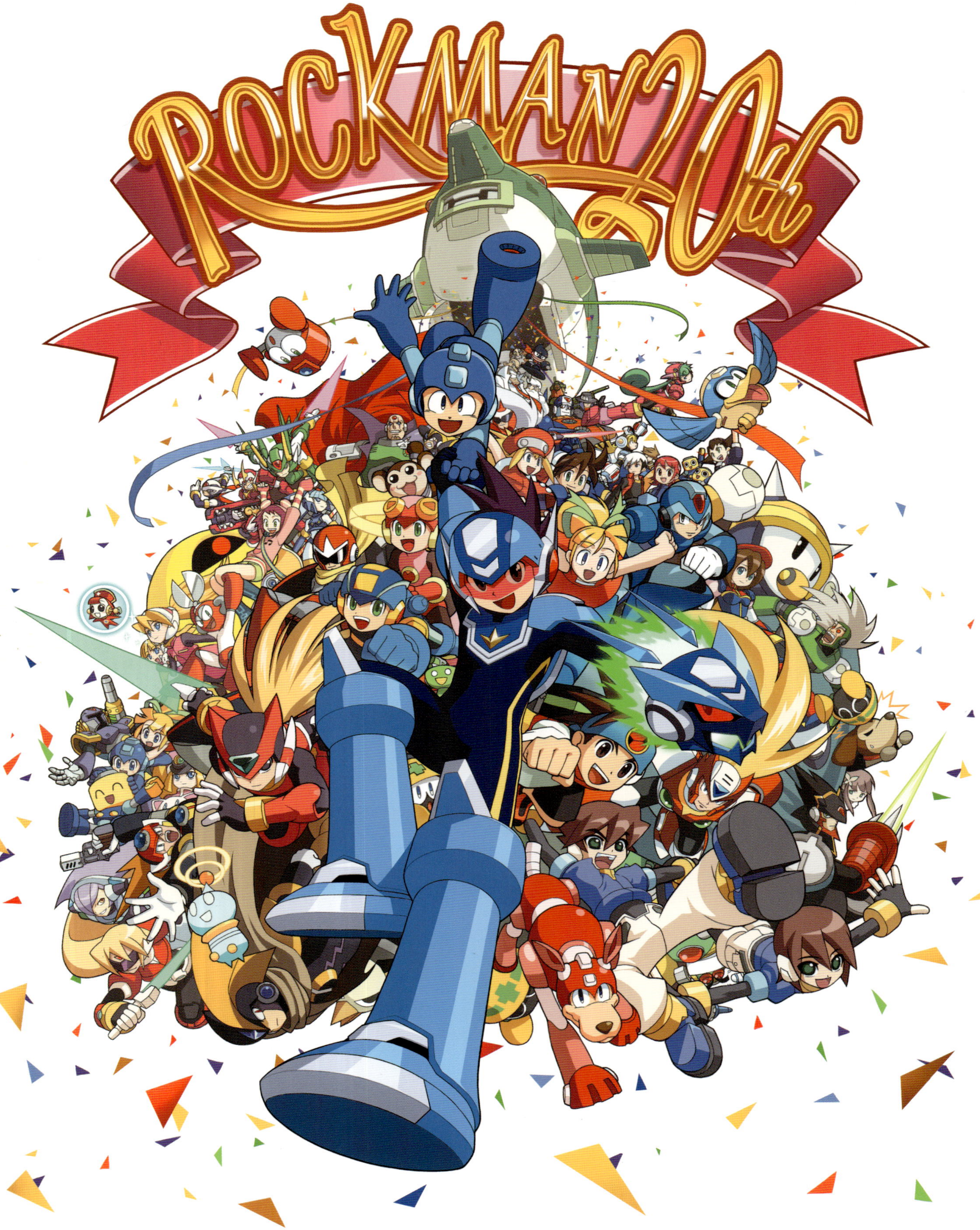

20TH ANNIVERSARY ILLUSTRATION #1

"This was my first high volume illustration, and I remember having a lot of trouble with it. I thought back on all 20 years of Mega Man and basked in the nostalgia while drawing this. I personally selected each and every character included in this illustration. I hope everyone likes it." (Mizuno)

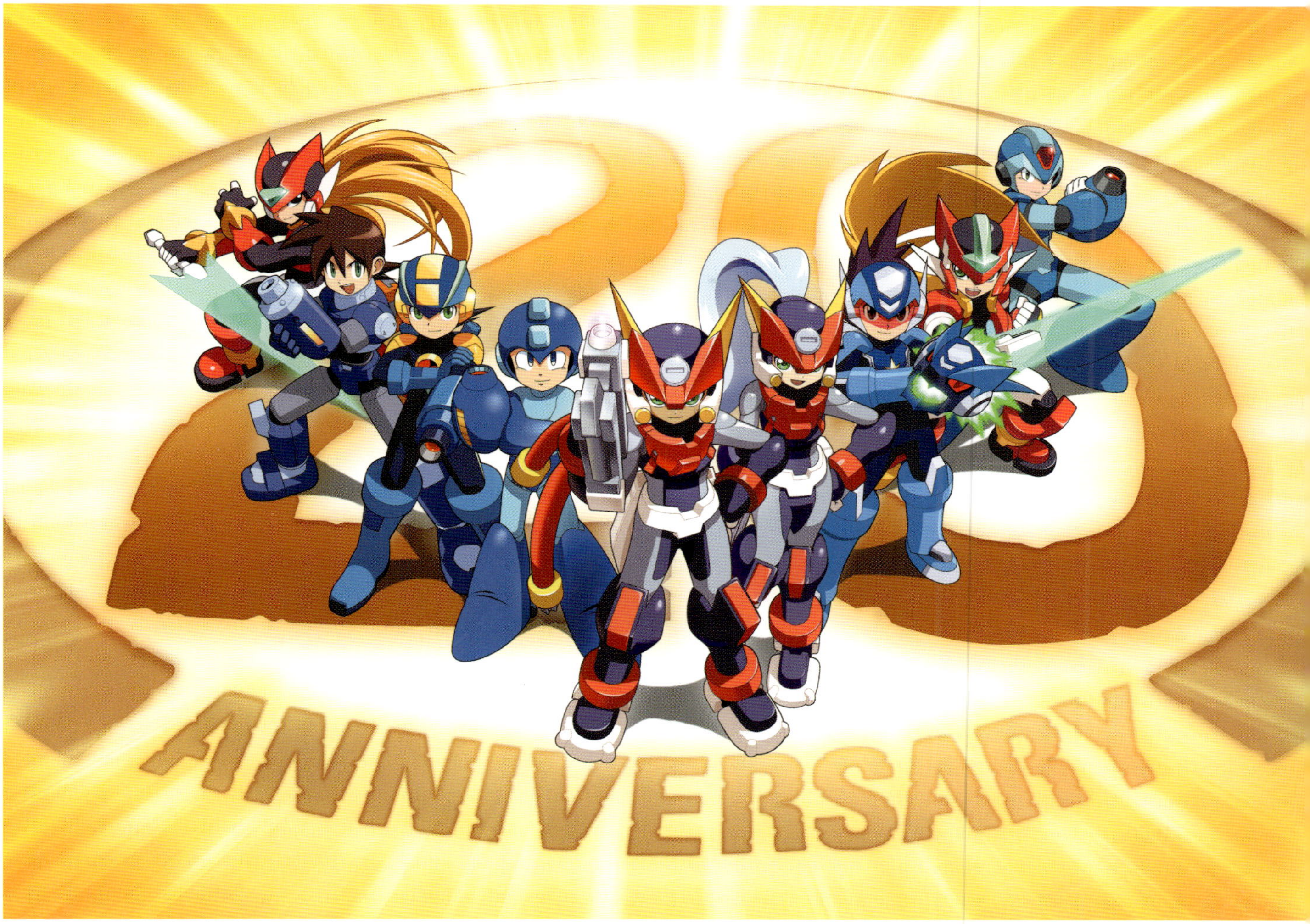

20TH ANNIVERSARY ILLUSTRATION #2

"Unlike the first 20th anniversary illustration, I went with more of a 'hero' concept for this one. I tried to focus on the 'cool factor' of Mega Man. Initially, this image was distributed online as a desktop wallpaper, and I started to think that would be the end of it. That's why I was so touched when I saw that they made it a huge feature in the event hall during the 20th anniversary event." (Mizuno)

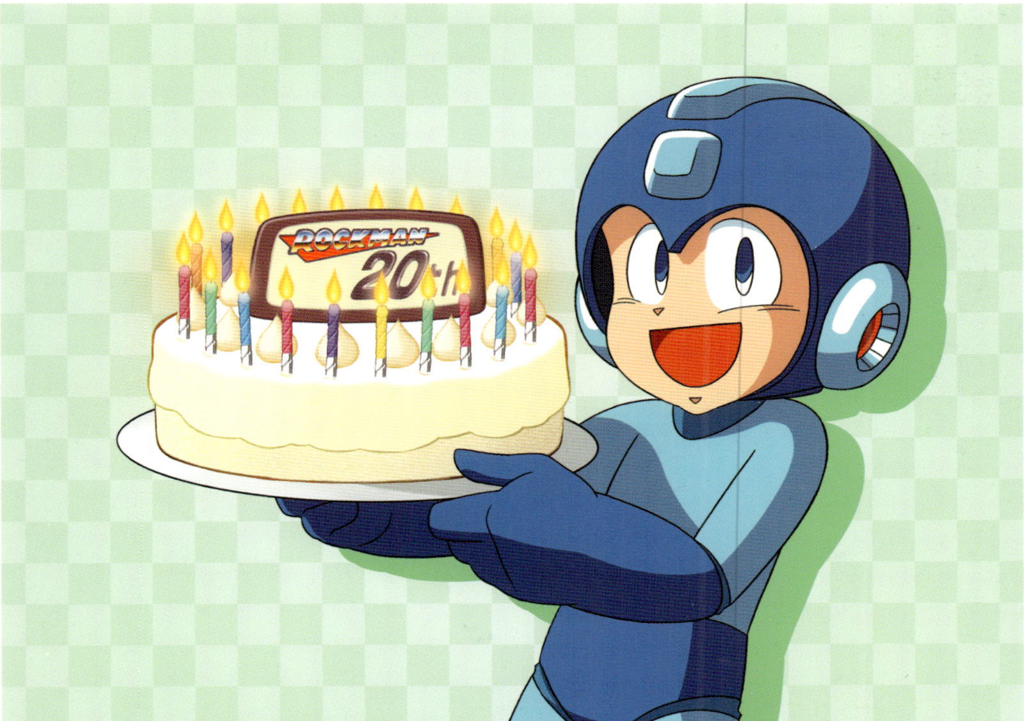

OFFICIAL WEBSITE IMAGE FOR 20TH ANNIVERSARY

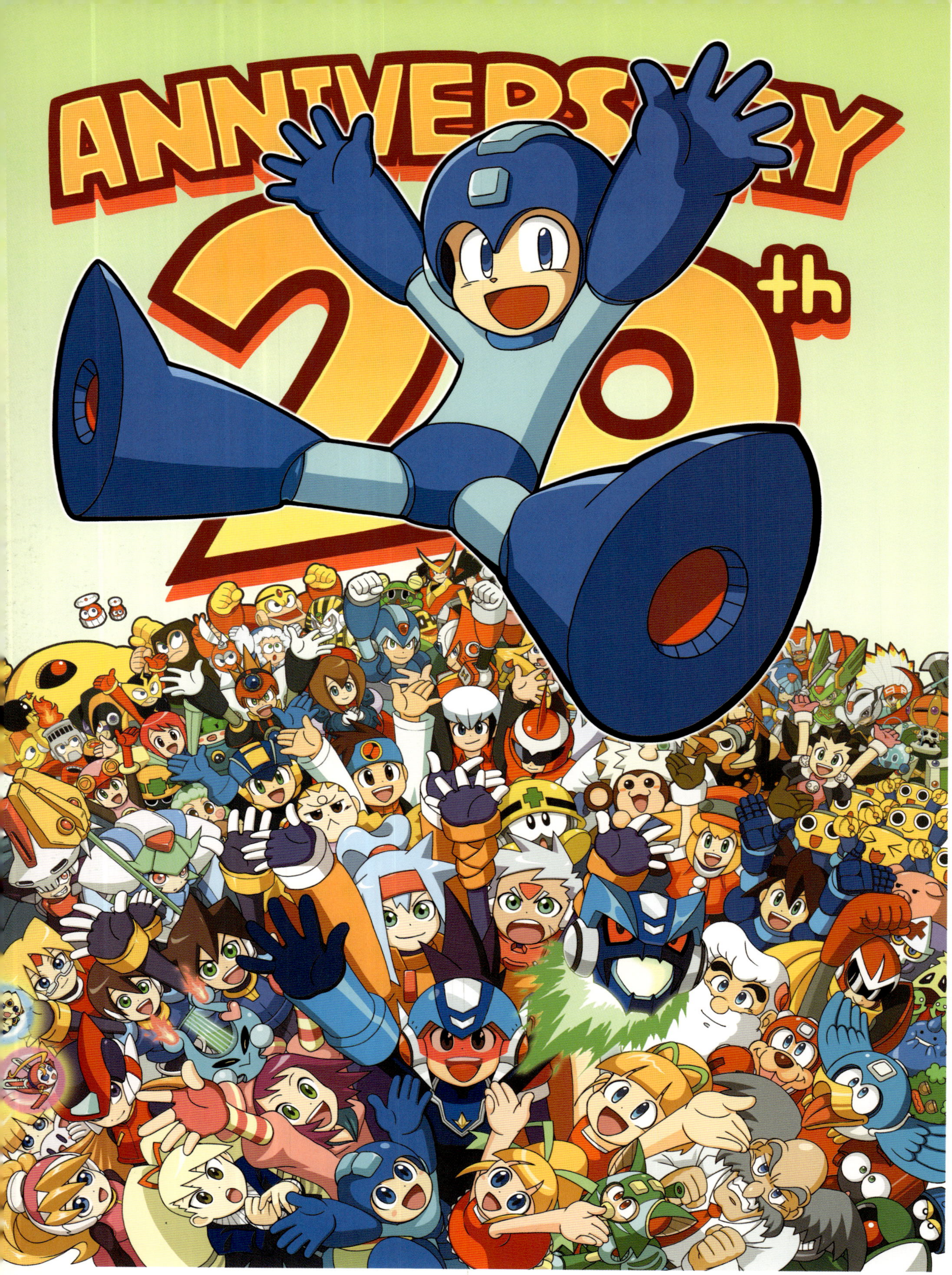

20TH ANNIVERSARY ILLUSTRATION #3

"I was so nervous when they asked me to draw such a big illustration soon after I joined the company. I struggled with bringing out the Mega Man flavor, but it was an amazing opportunity to draw all the characters I had been wanting to draw, so I had a lot of fun." (Yuri Kataiwa)

ARCHIVES

アーカイブ

Here you will find a veritable treasure trove of development resources, including things that have never before been released to the public. Detailed character files, rough drafts, and illustrations brimming with ideas... all the things that any true fan would want to see with their own eyes.

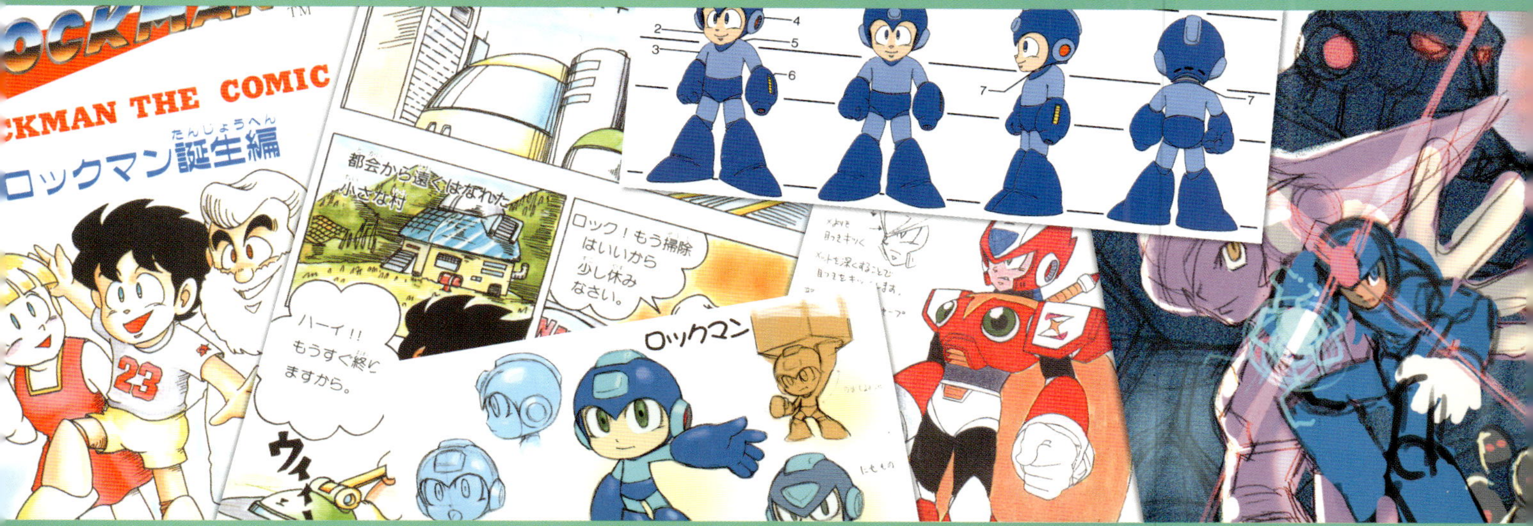

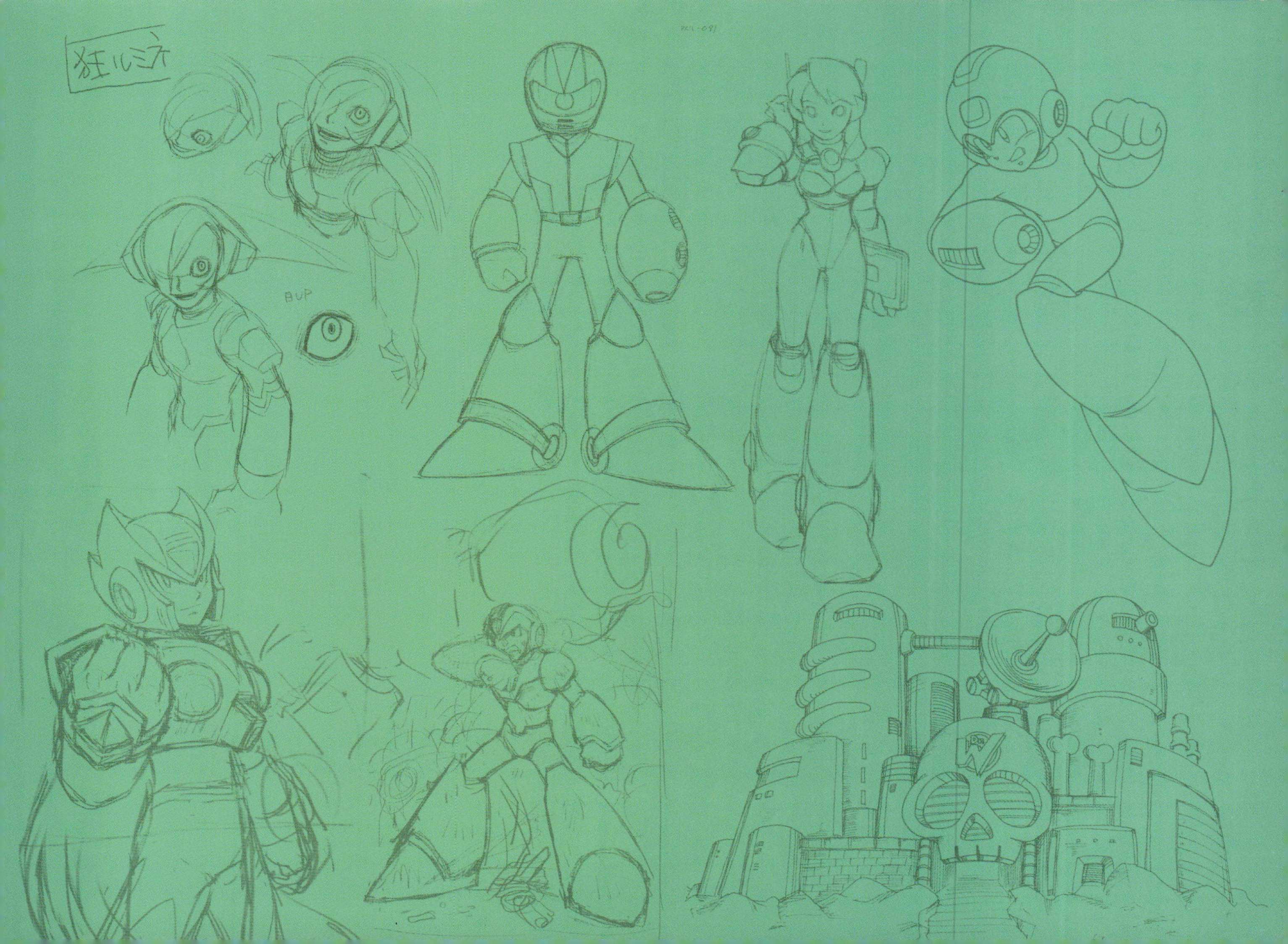

DLN.001 MEGA MAN

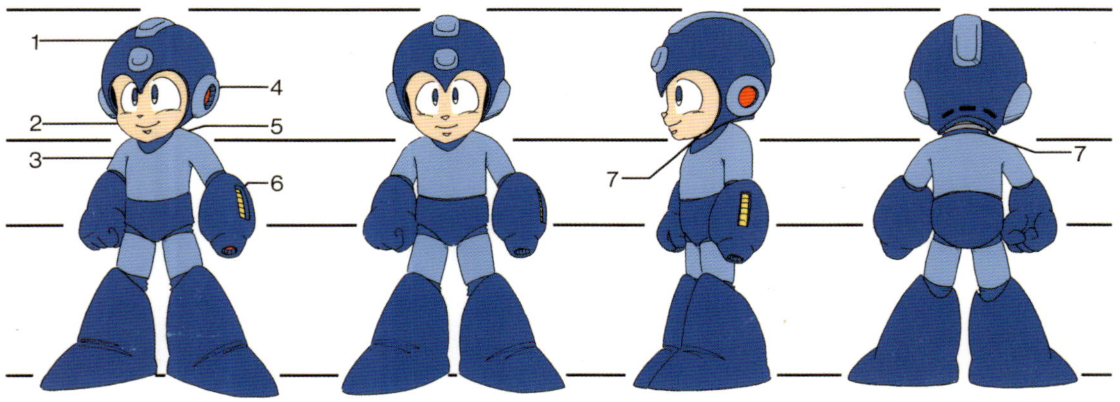

DLN.002 ROLL

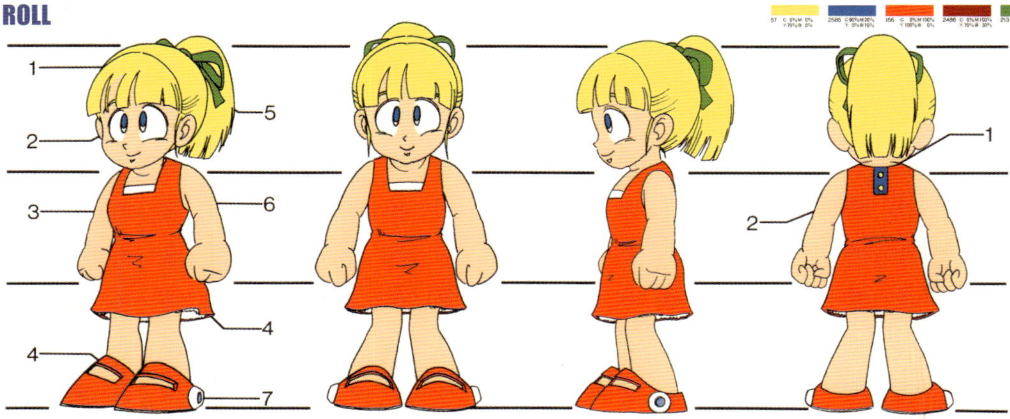

DLN.003 CUT MAN

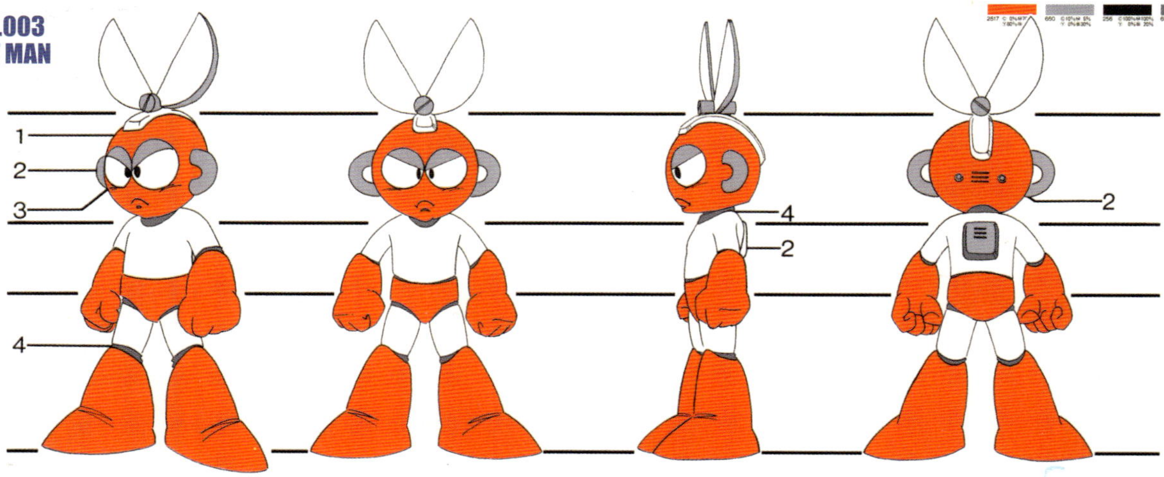

DLN.004 GUTS MAN

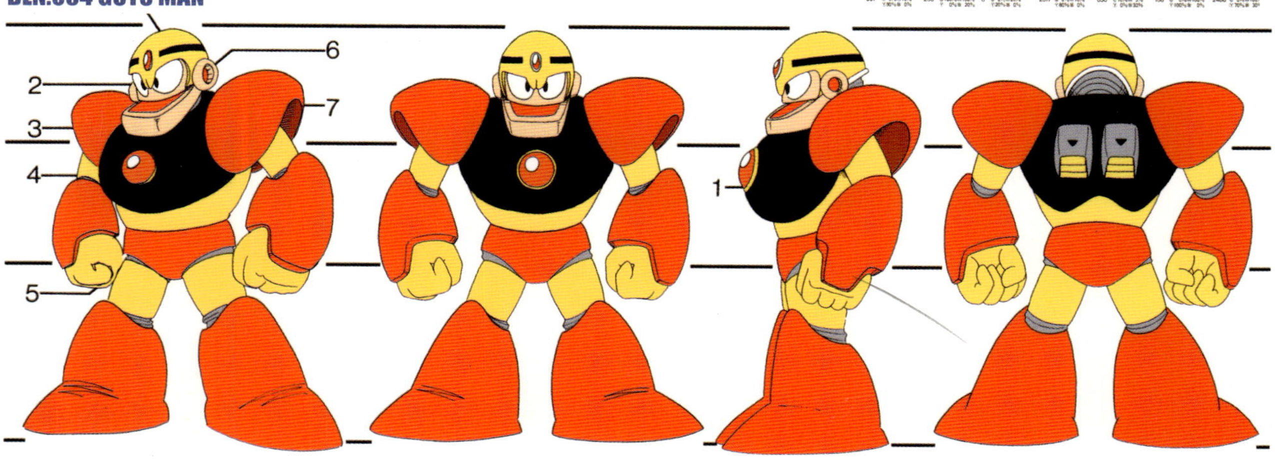

DLN.005 ICE MAN

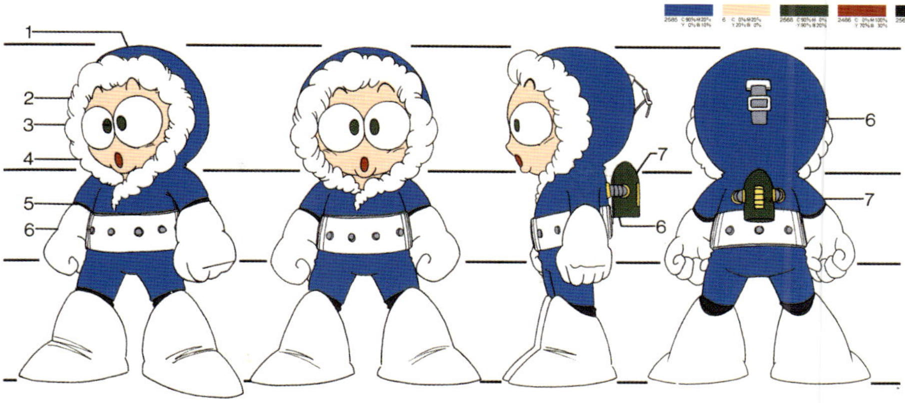

DLN.006 BOMB MAN

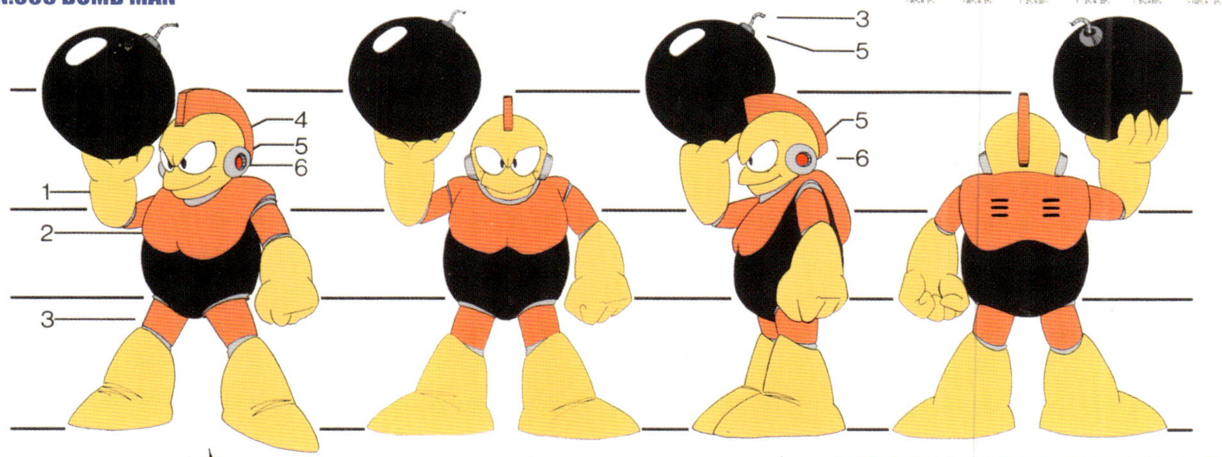

DLN.007 FIRE MAN

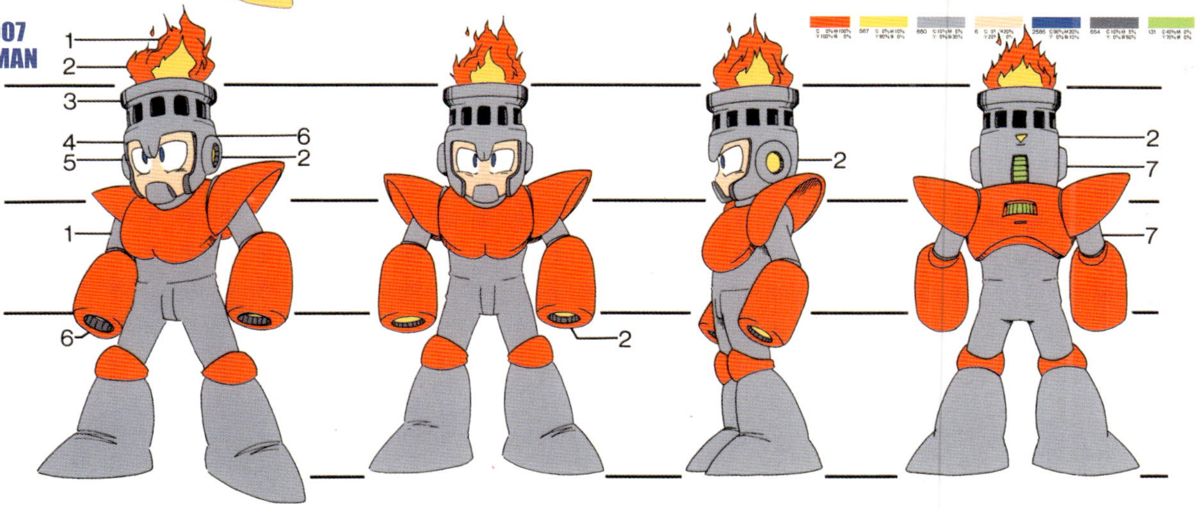

DLN.008 ELEC MAN

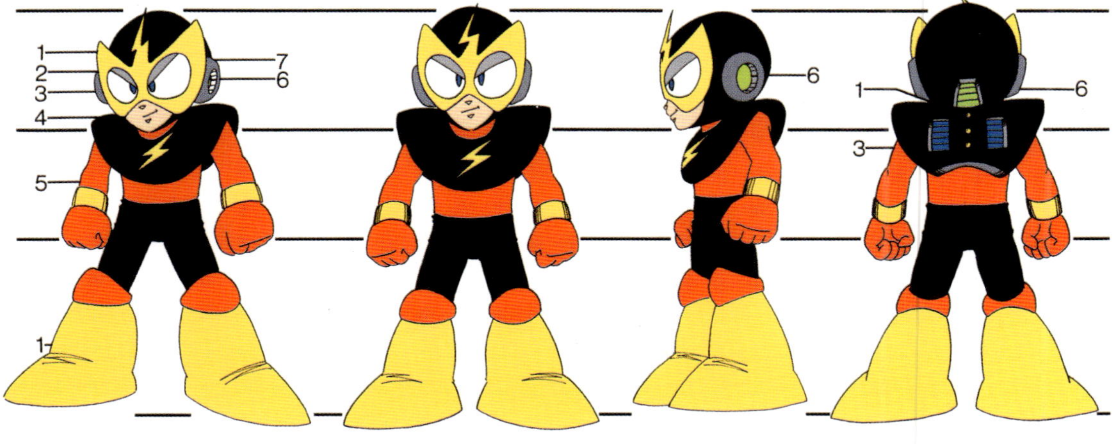

THOMAS X. LIGHT

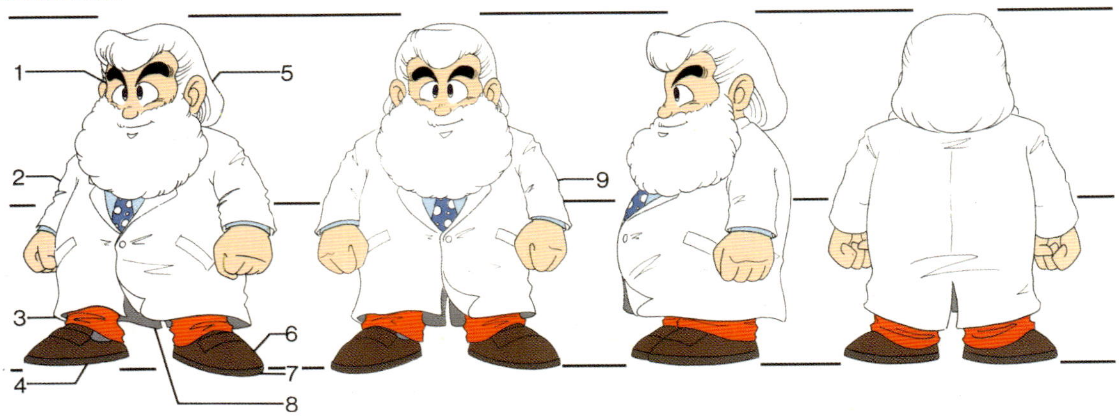

EDDIE

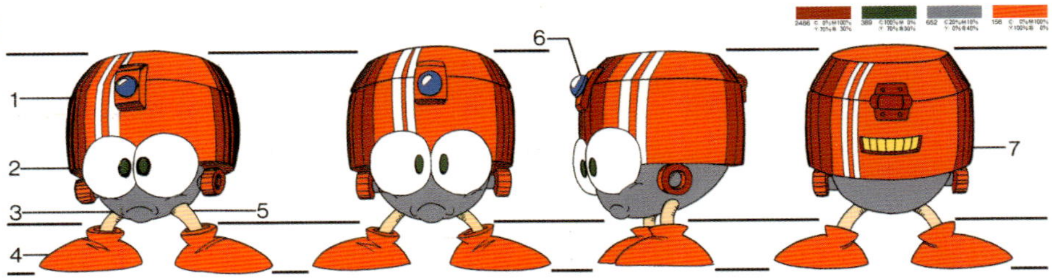

BEAT

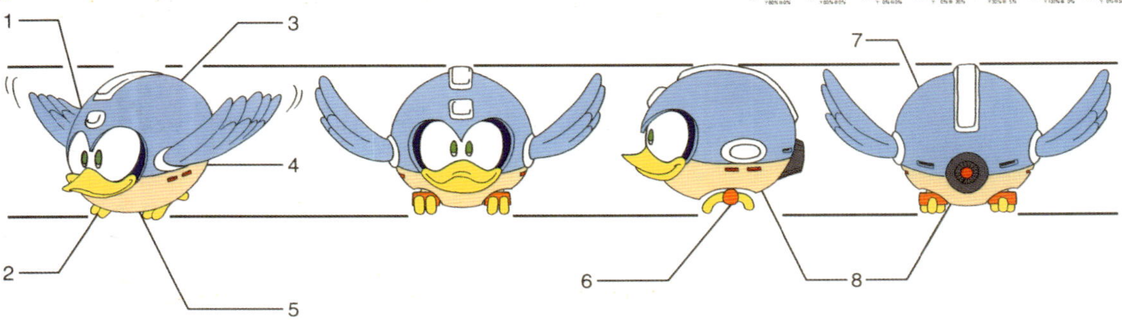

RUSH

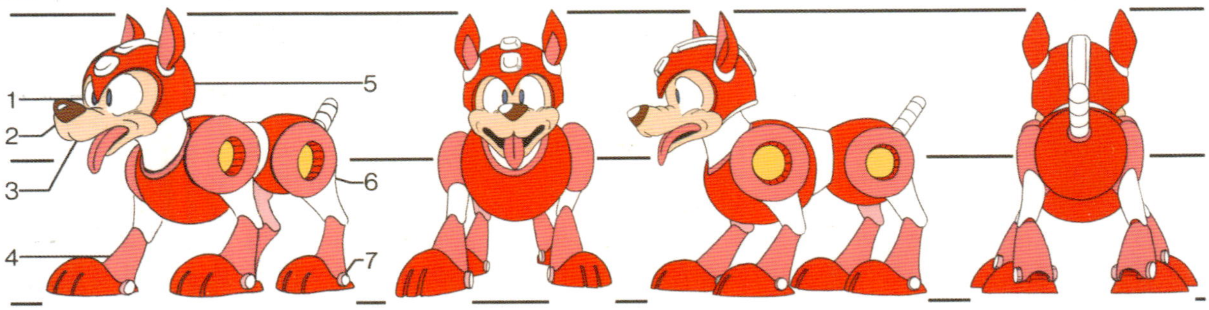

RUSH COIL

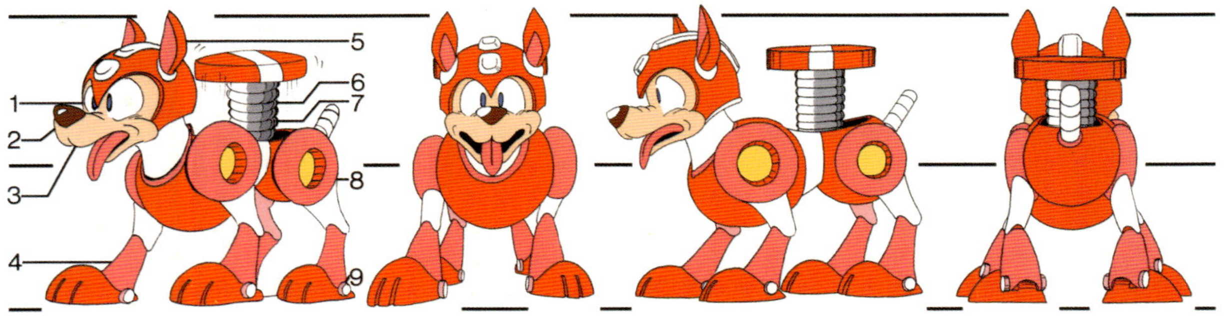

RUSH JET

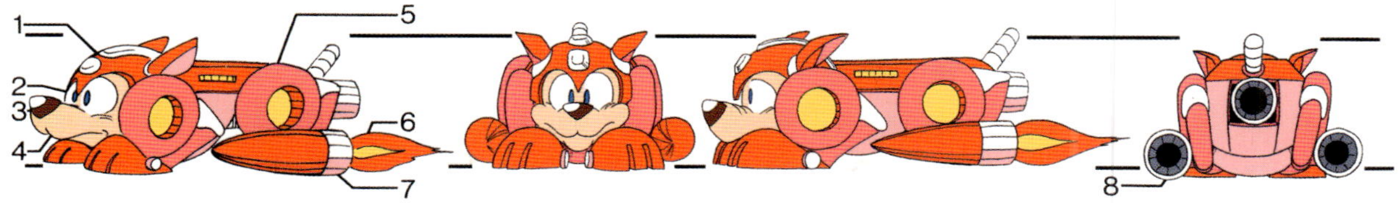

RUSH MARINE

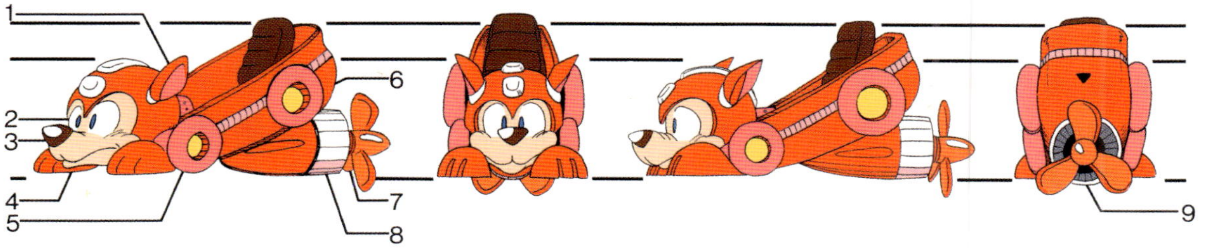

NEW RUSH COIL

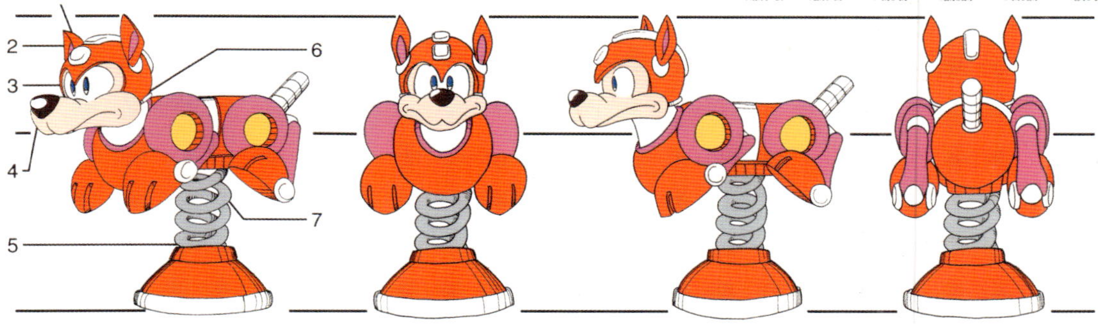

POWER MEGA MAN

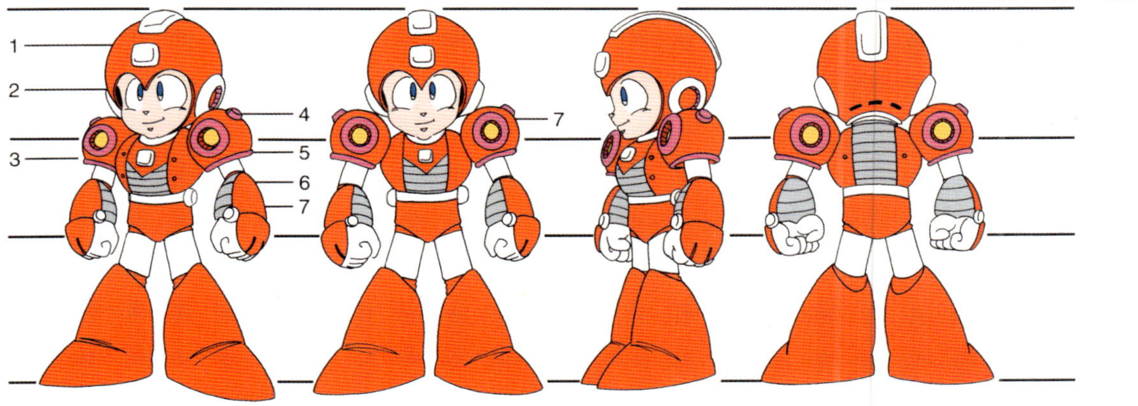

JET MEGA MAN

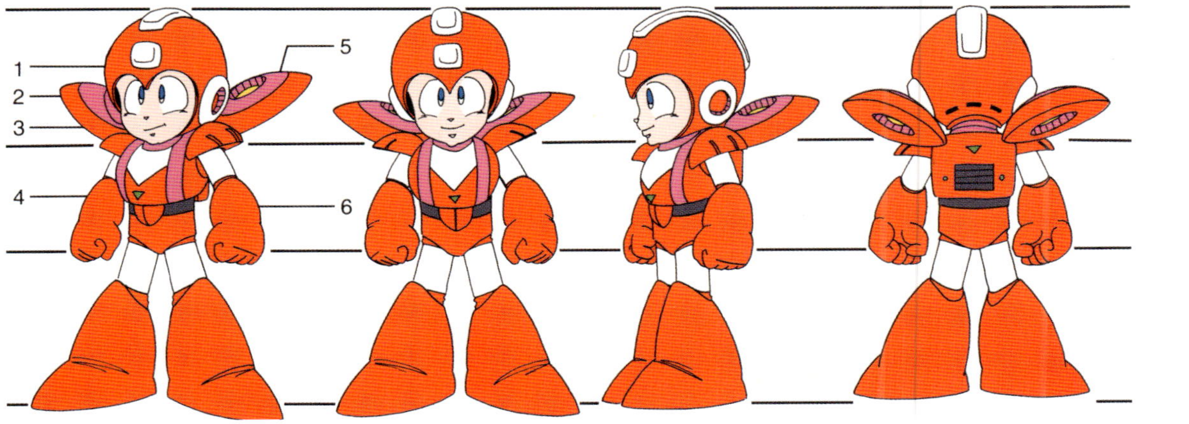

ALBERT W. WILY

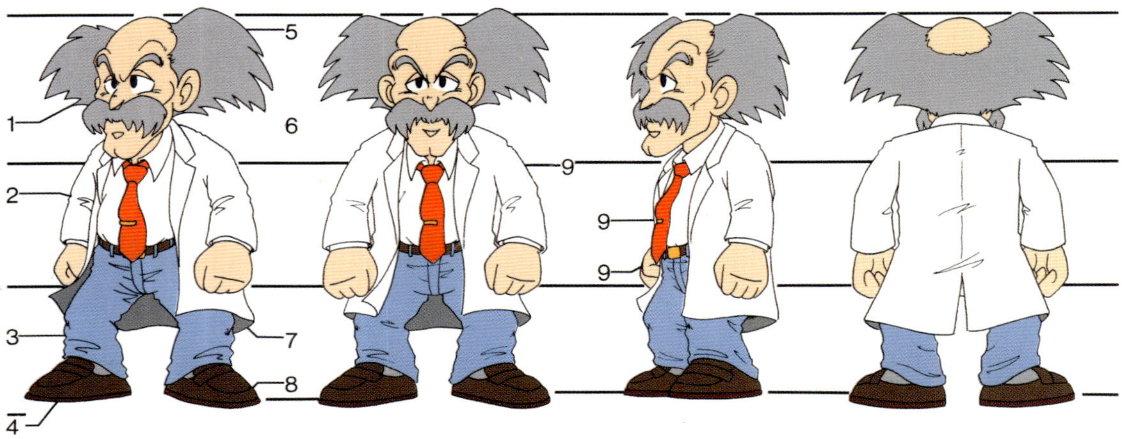

DLN.000 PROTO MAN

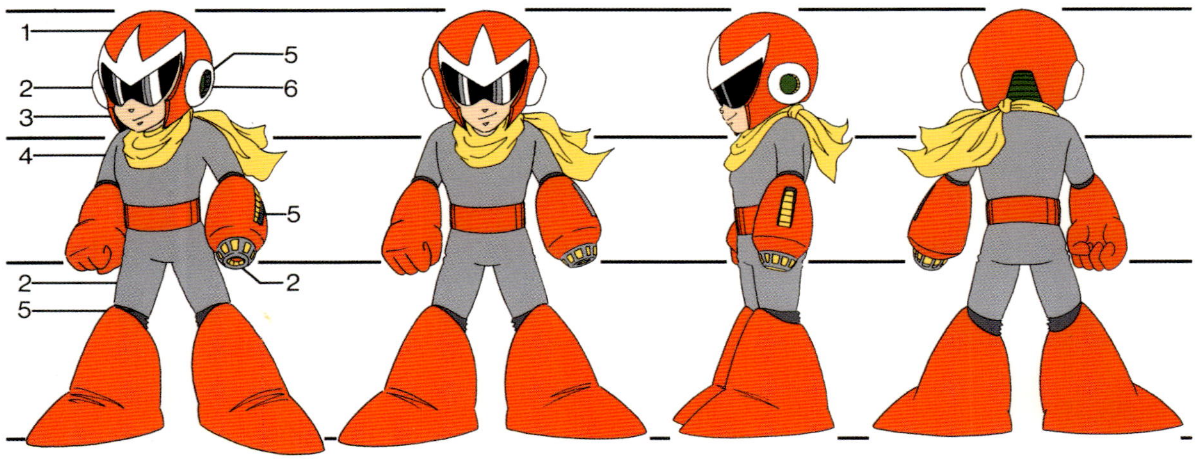

SNIPER JOE

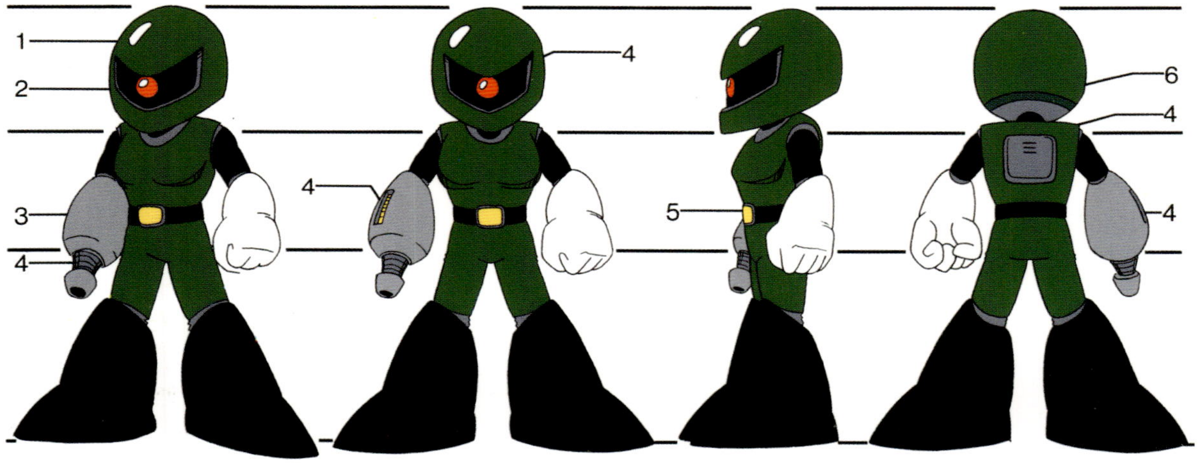

METALL

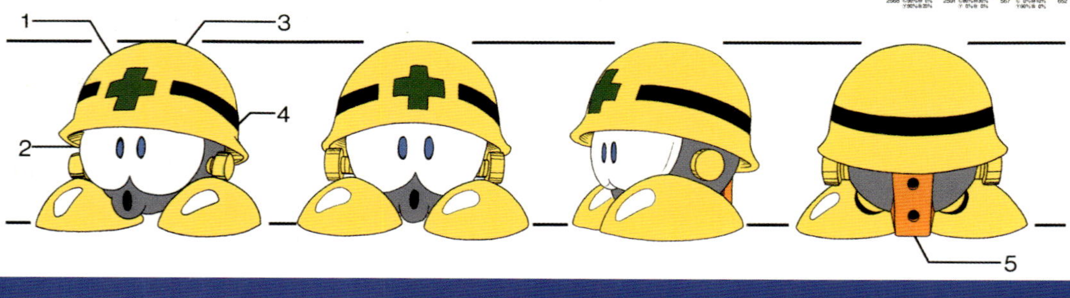

BATTON

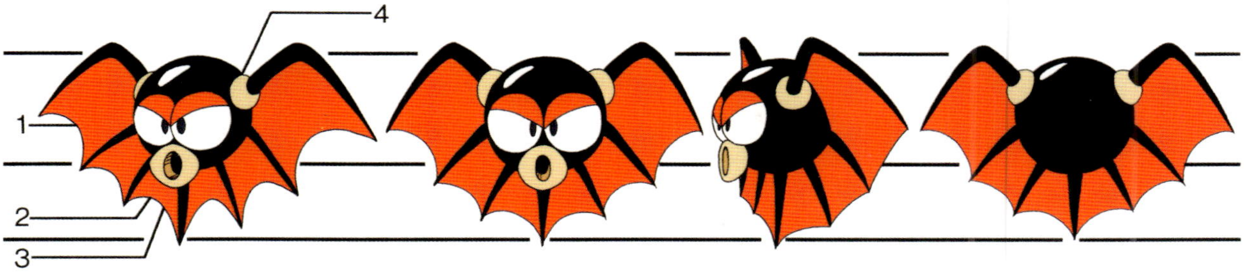

PIPI

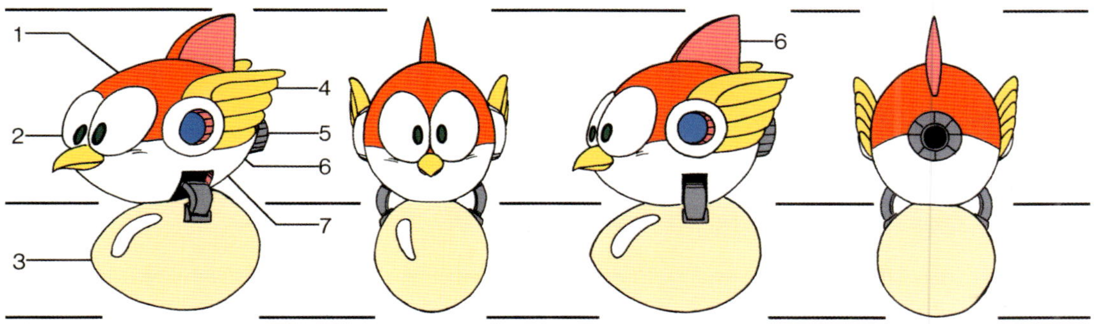

MONKING

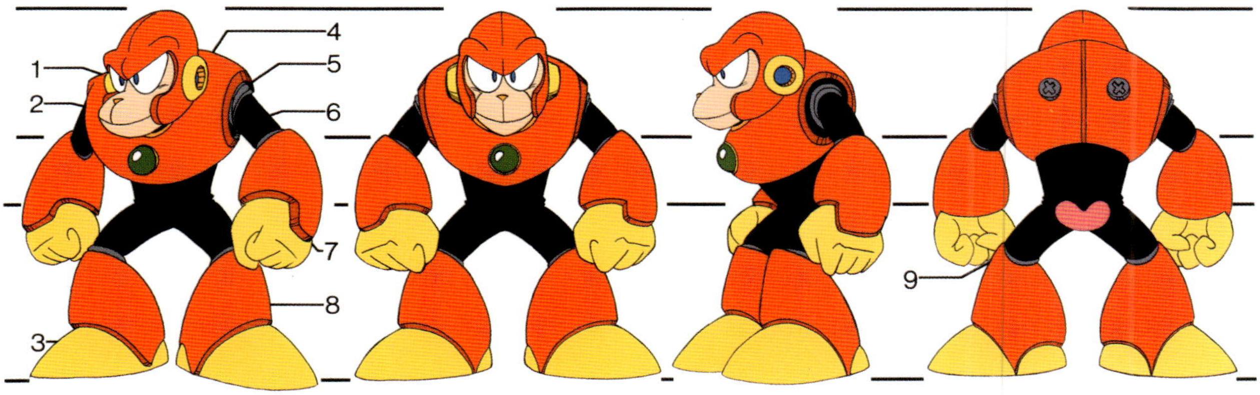

REGGAE

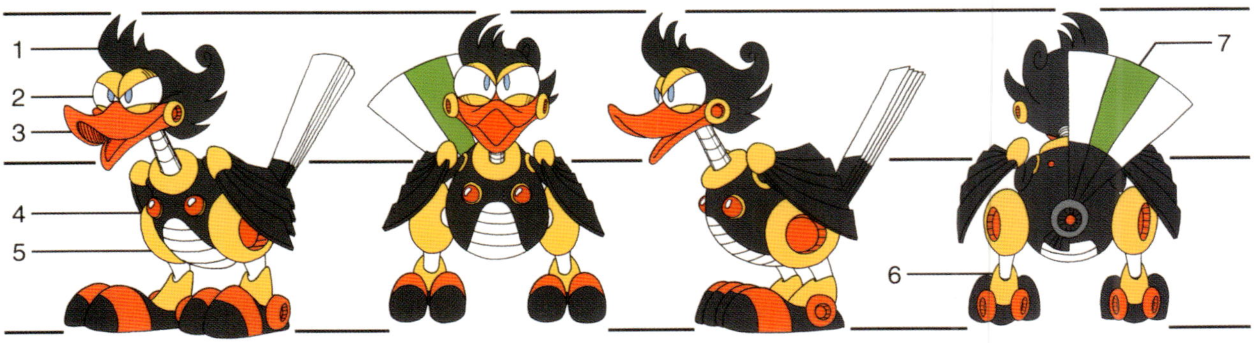

DWN.009 METAL MAN

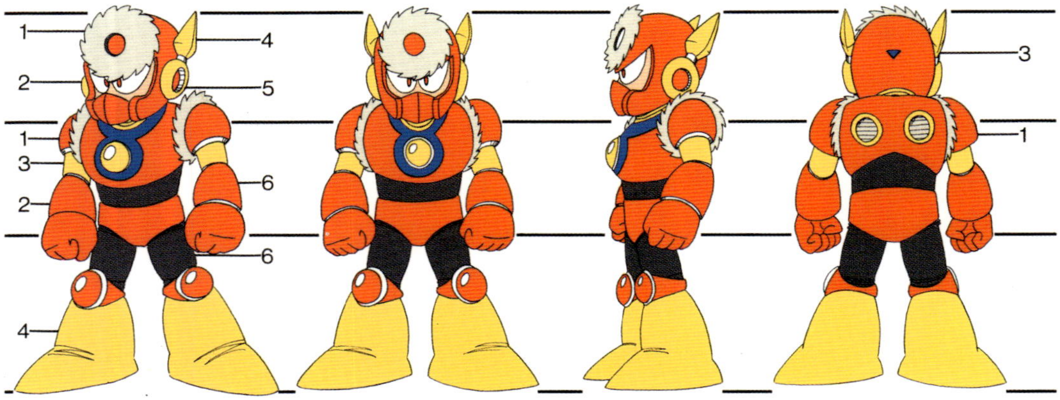

DWN.010 AIR MAN

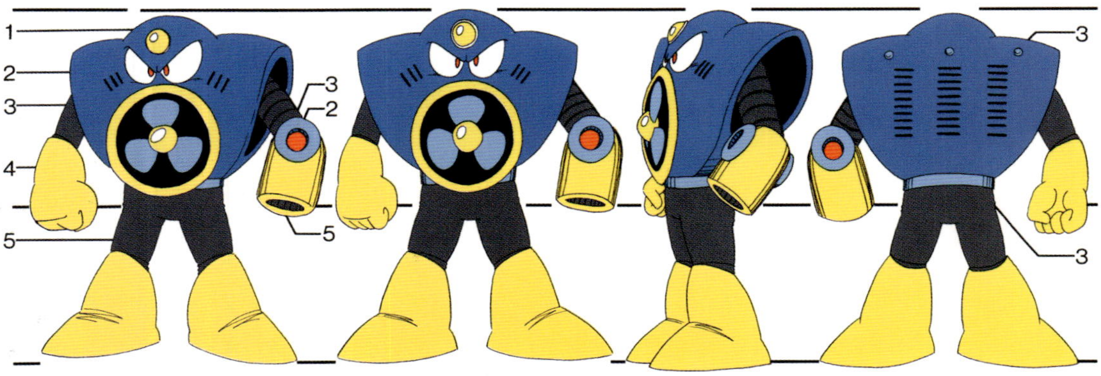

DWN.011 BUBBLE MAN

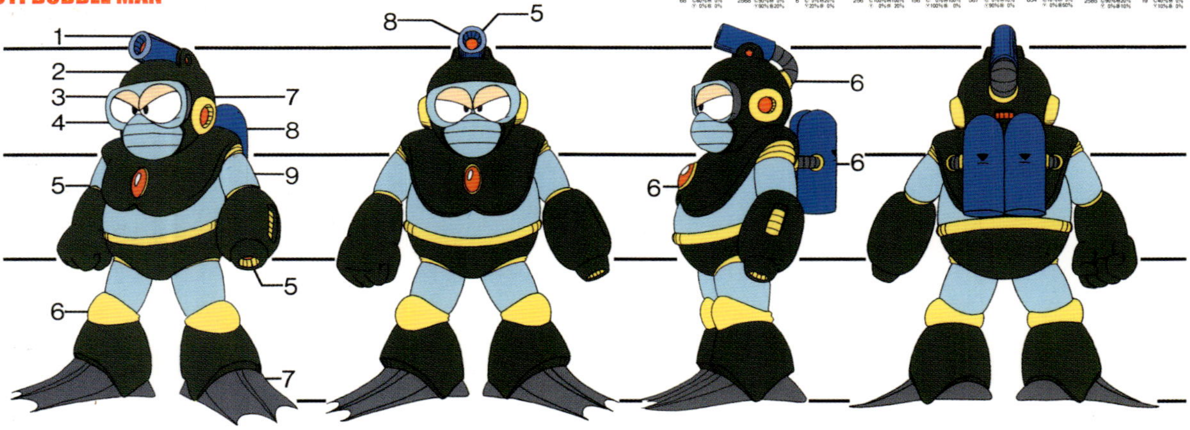

DWN.012 QUICK MAN

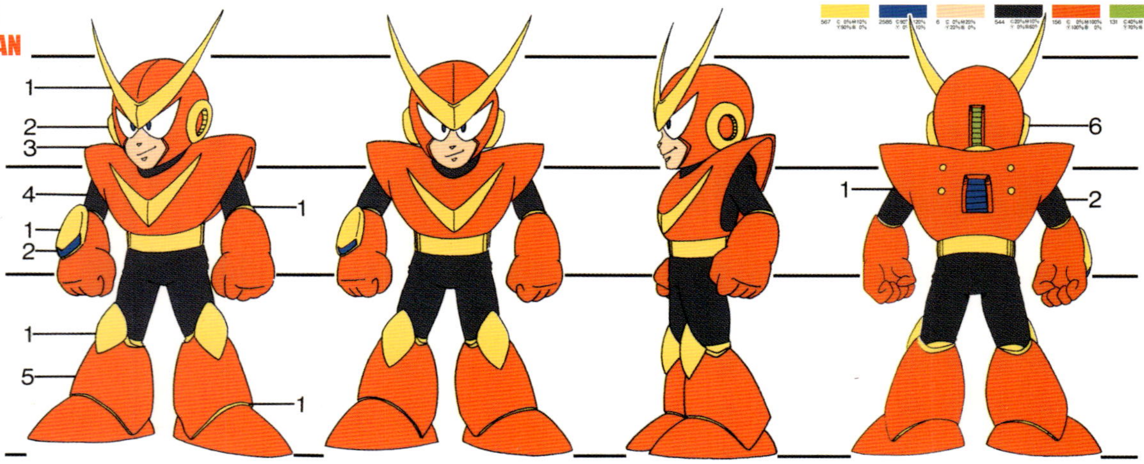

DWN.013 CRASH MAN

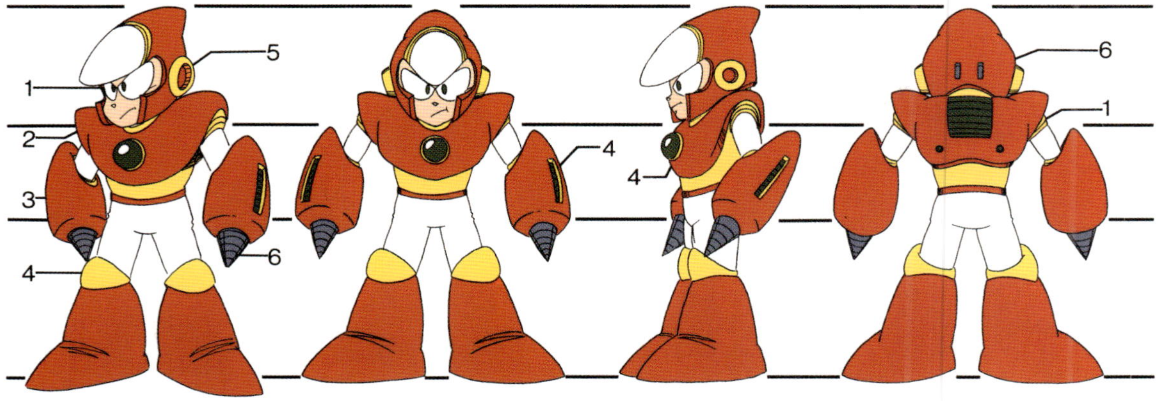

DWN.014 FLASH MAN

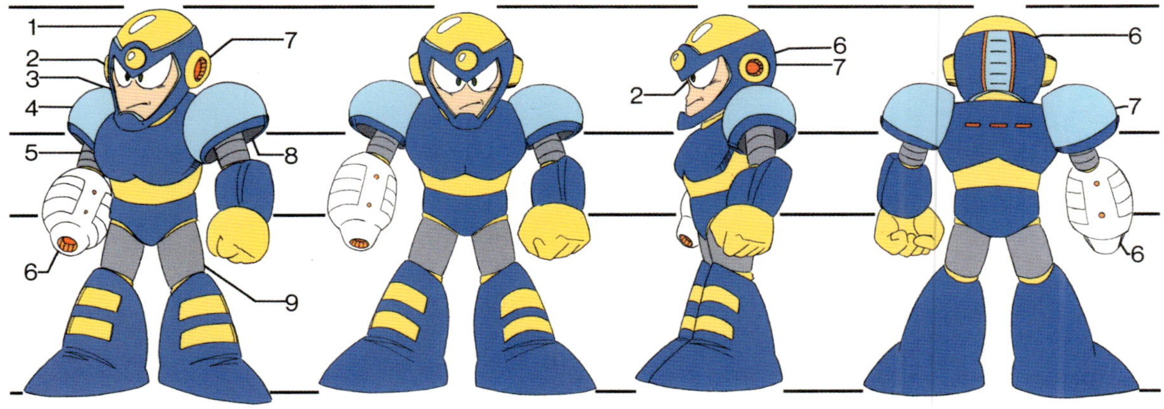

DWN.015 HEAT MAN

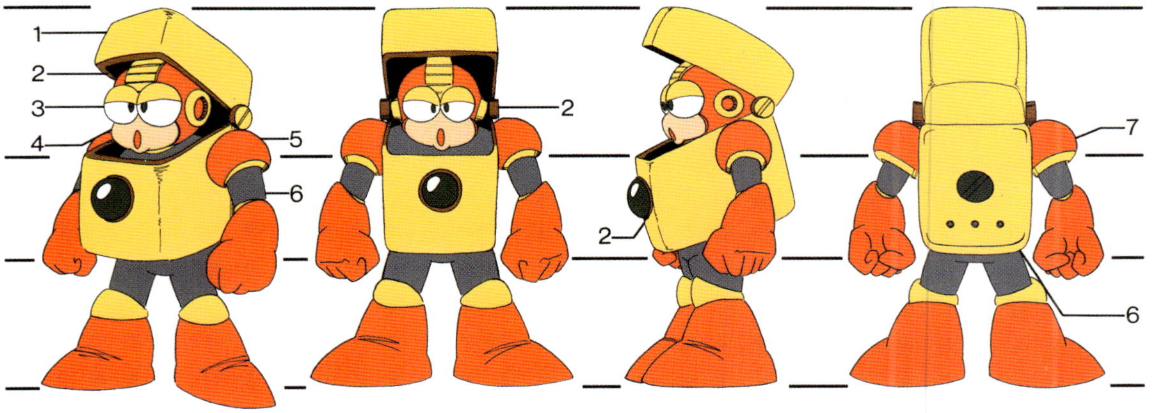

DWN.016 WOOD MAN

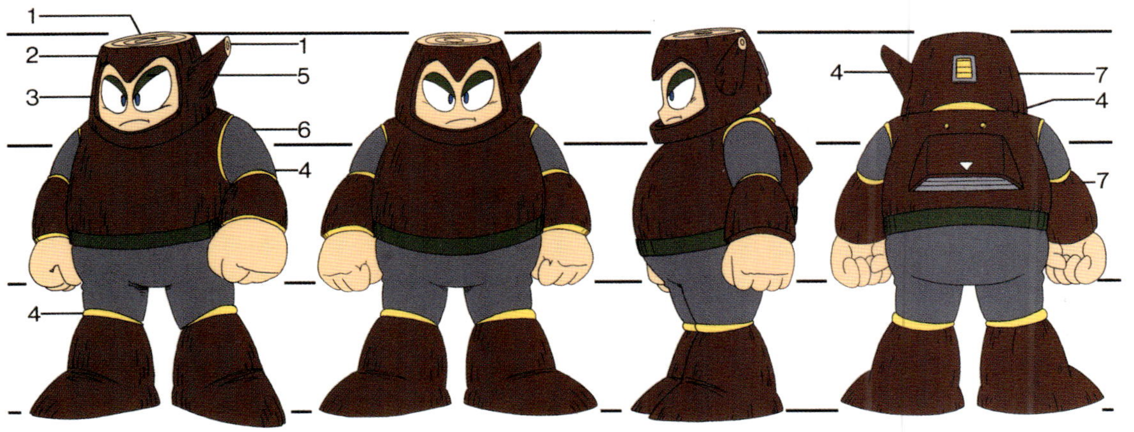

DWN.017 NEEDLE MAN

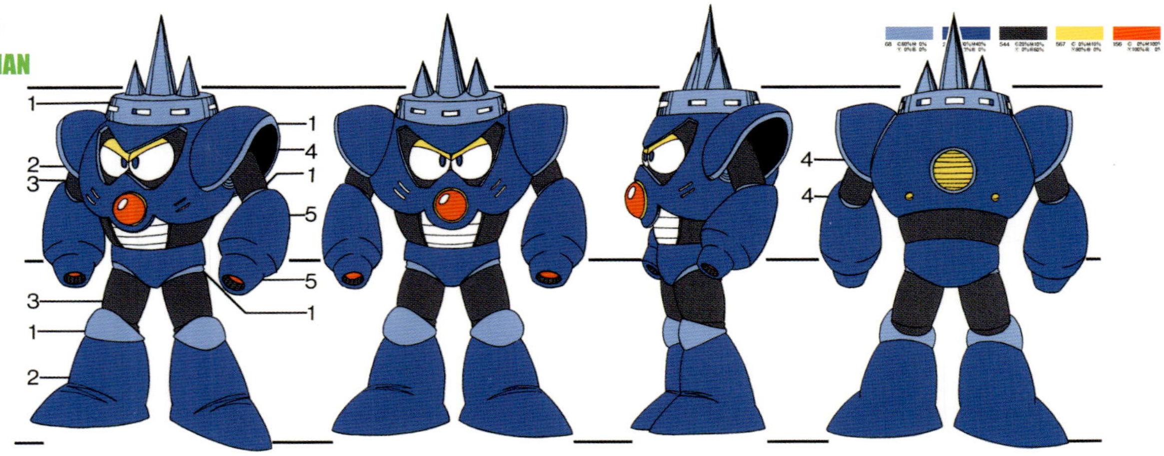

DWN.018 MAGNET MAN

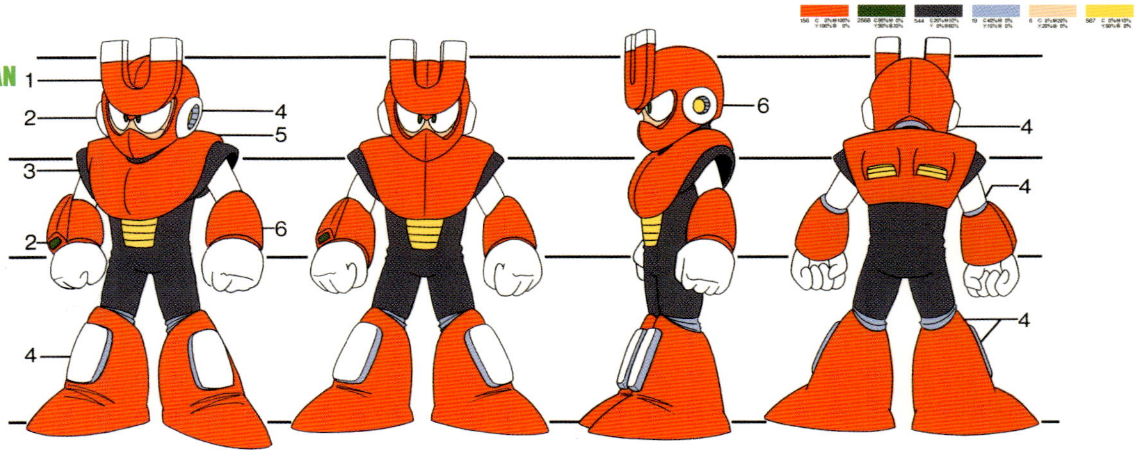

DWN.019 GEMINI MAN

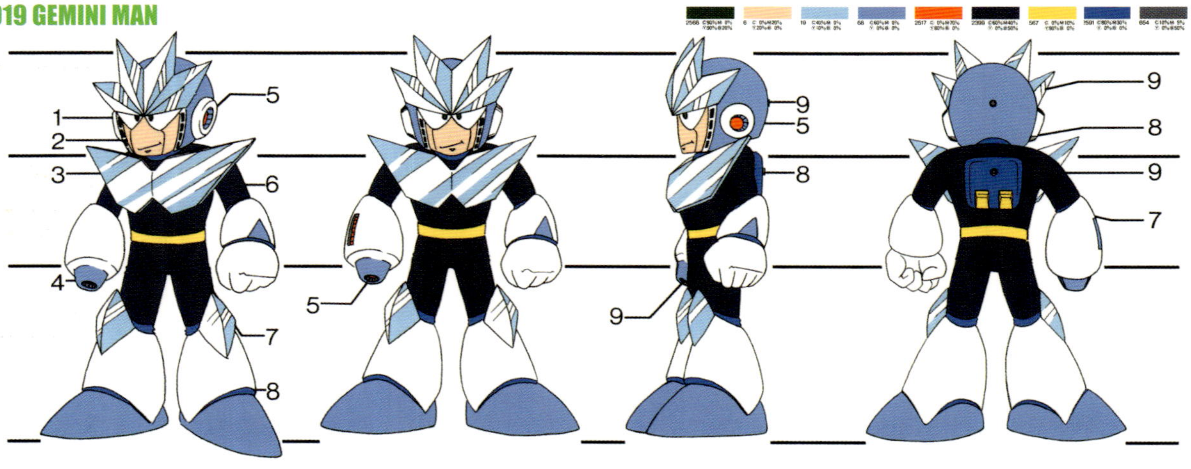

DWN.020 HARD MAN

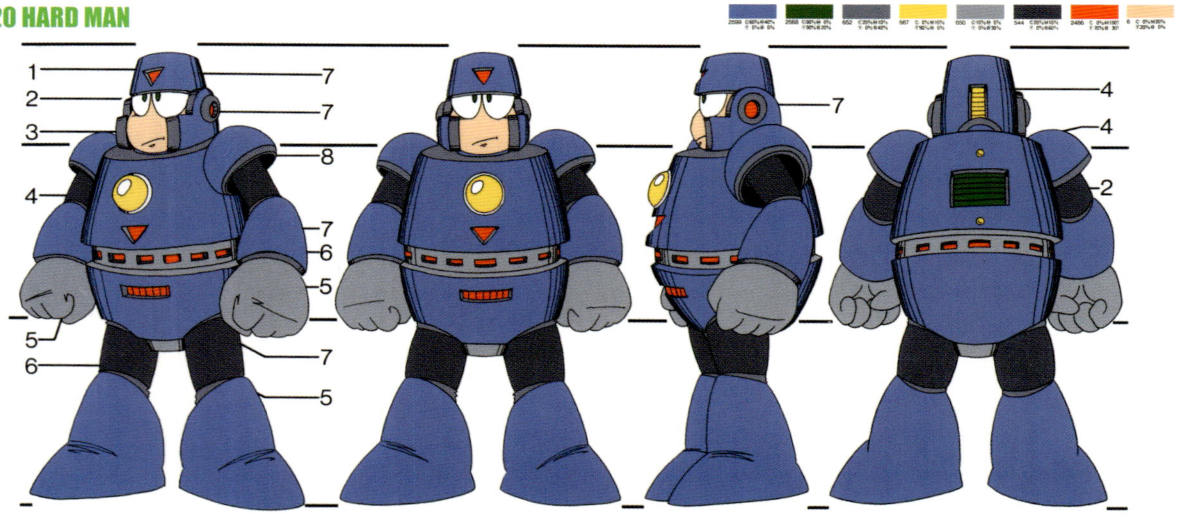

DWN.021 TOP MAN

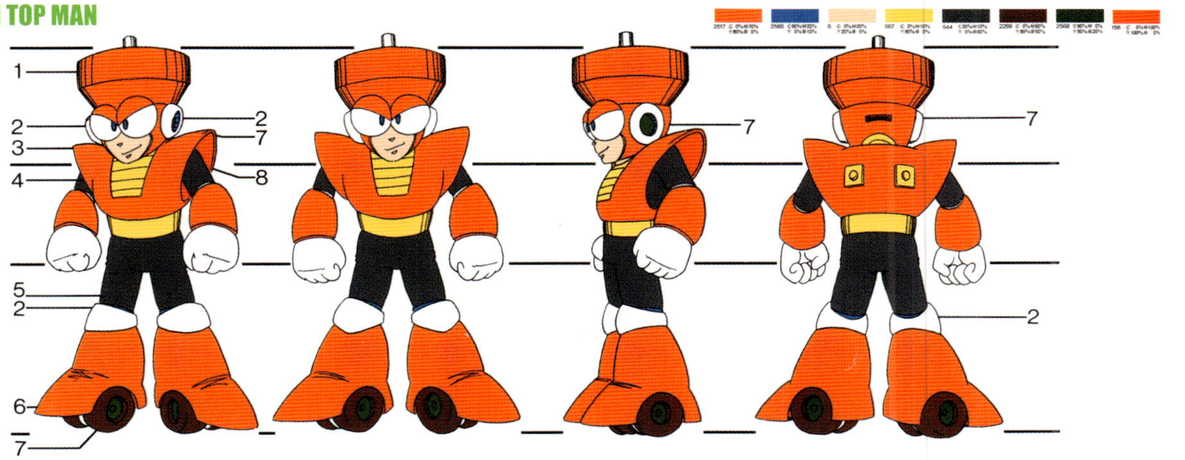

DWN.022 SNAKE MAN

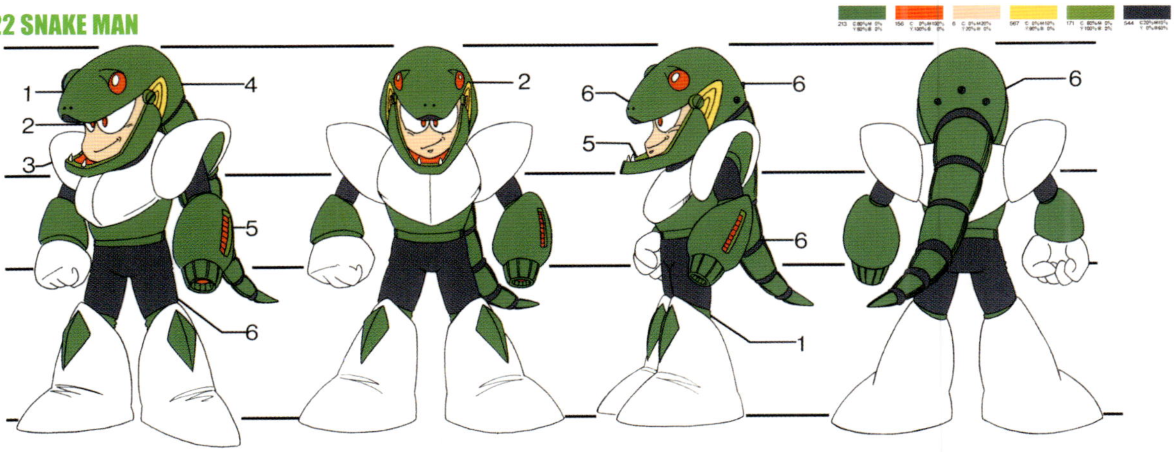

DWN.023 SPARK MAN

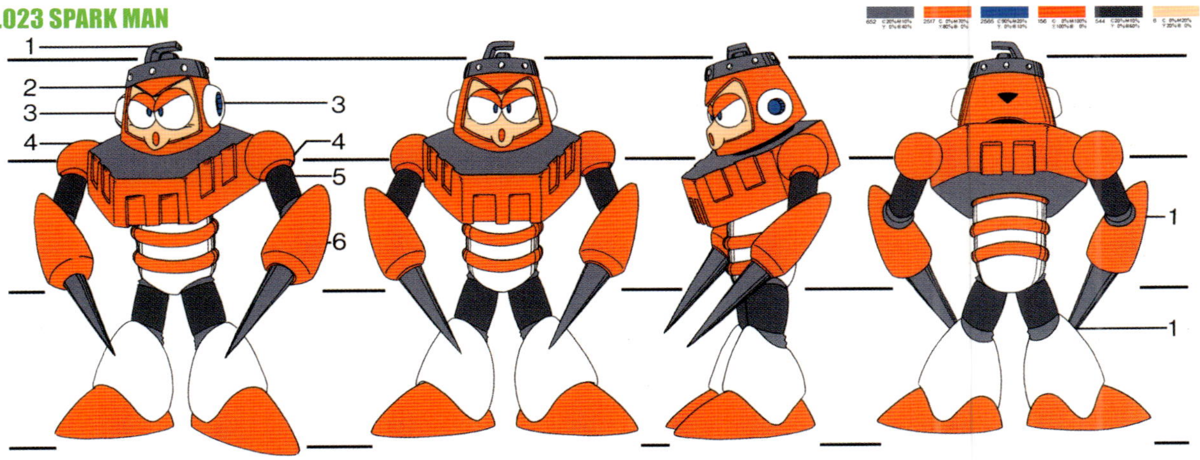

DWN.024 SHADOW MAN

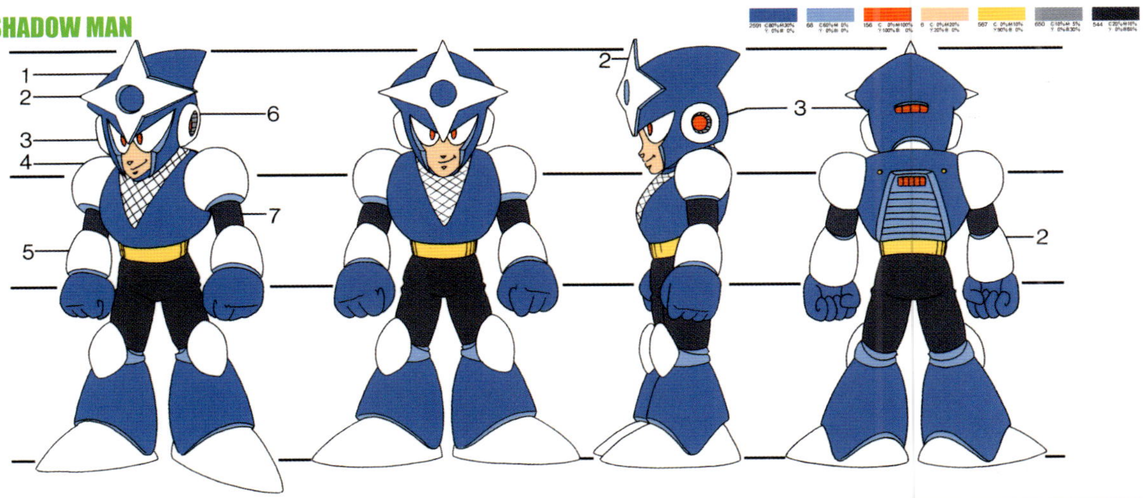

DWN.025 BRIGHT MAN

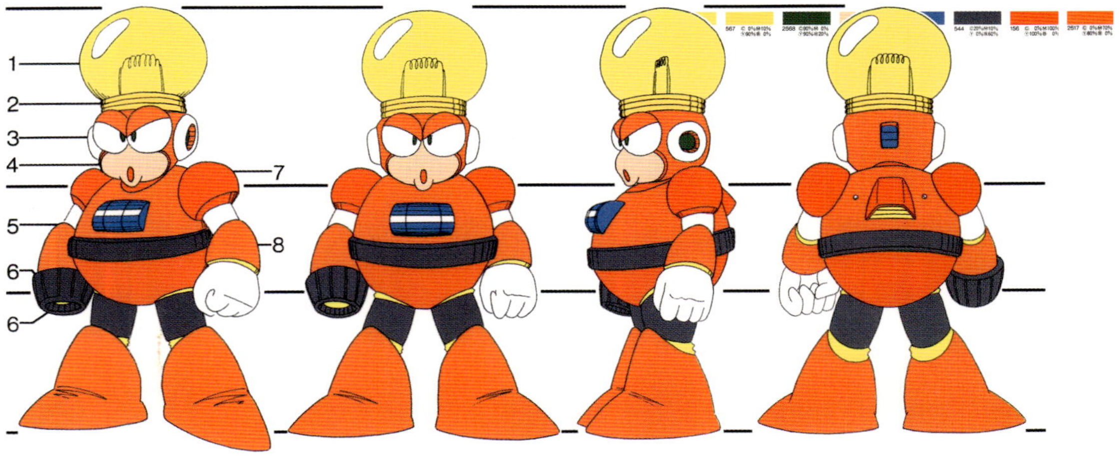

DWN.026 TOAD MAN

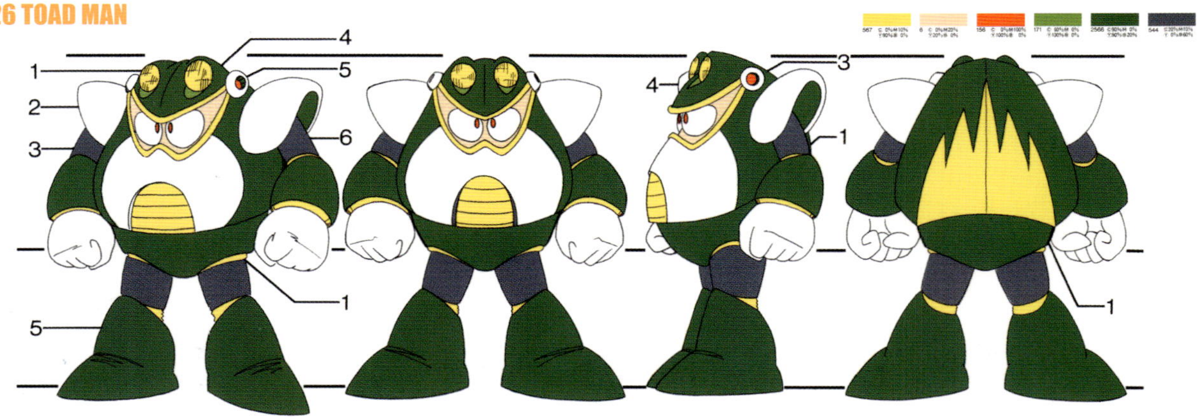

DWN.027 DRILL MAN

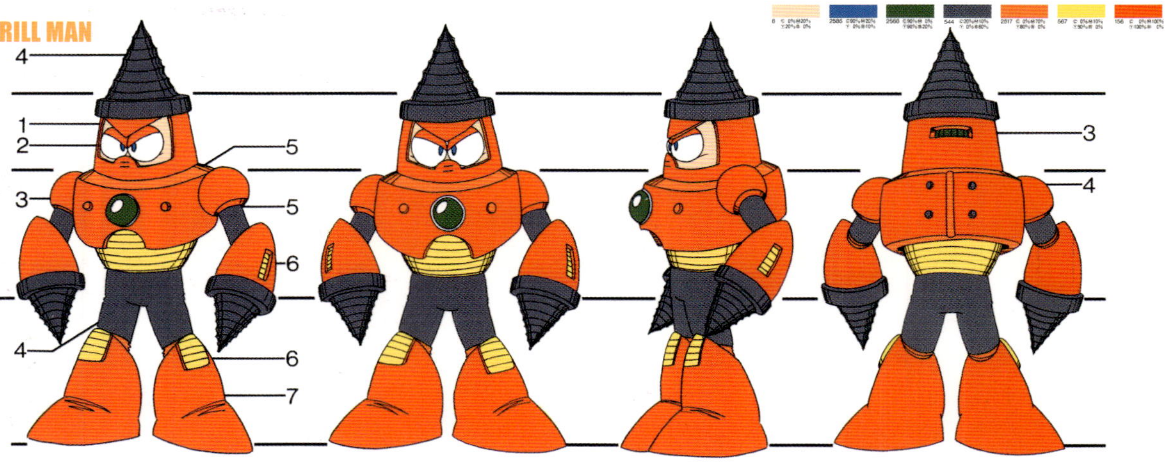

DWN.028 PHARAOH MAN

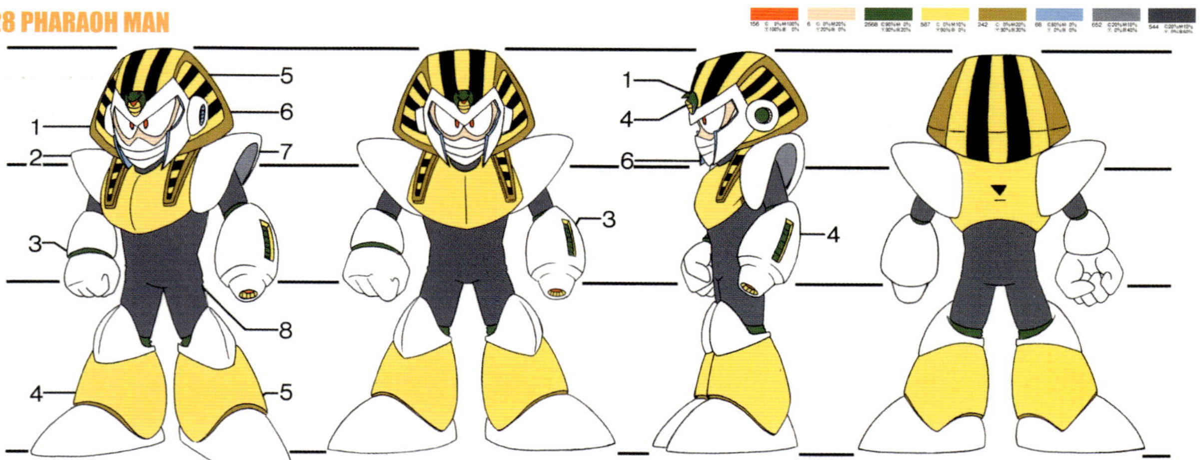

DWN.029 RING MAN

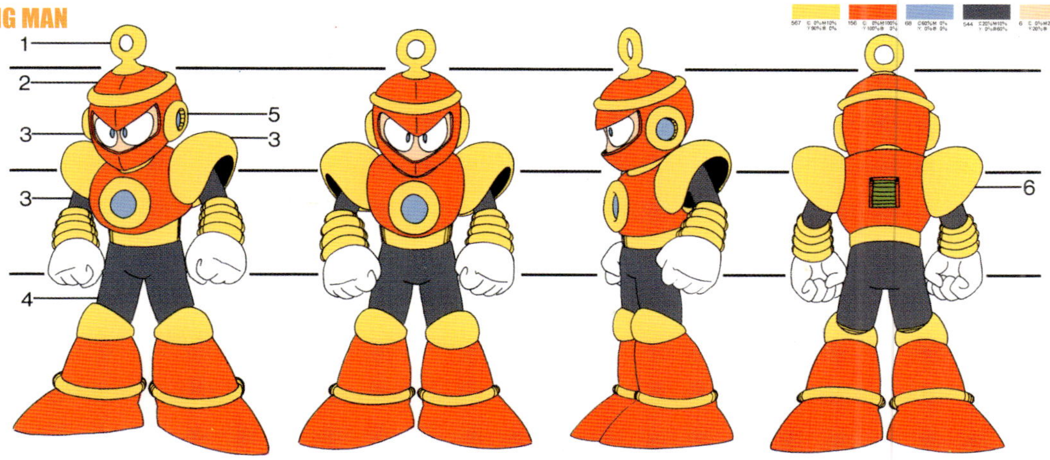

DWN.030 DUST MAN

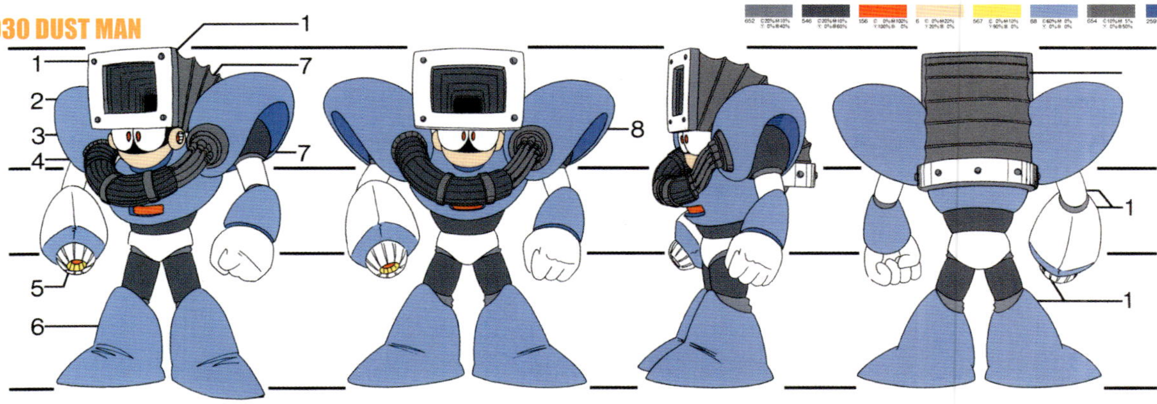

DWN.031 DIVE MAN

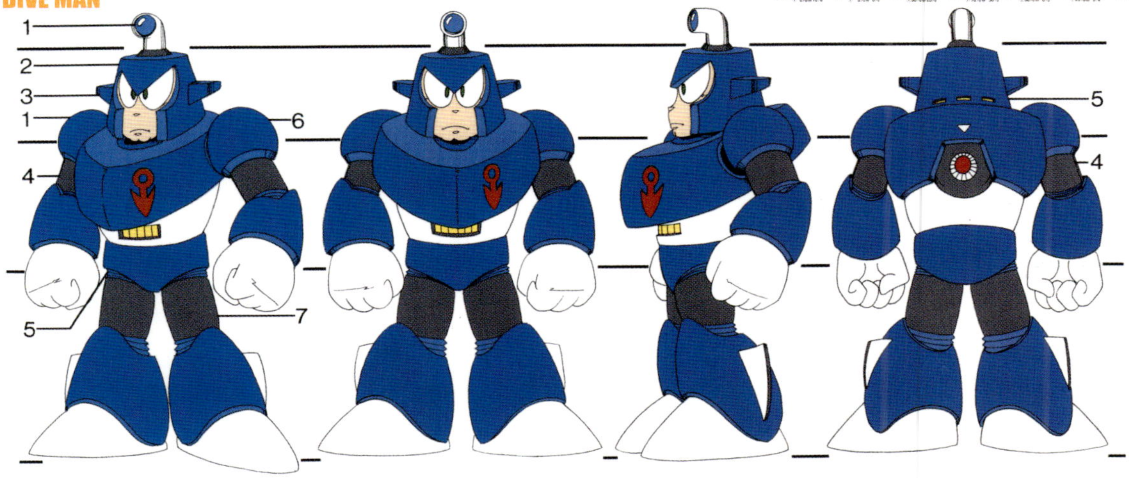

DWN.032 SKULL MAN

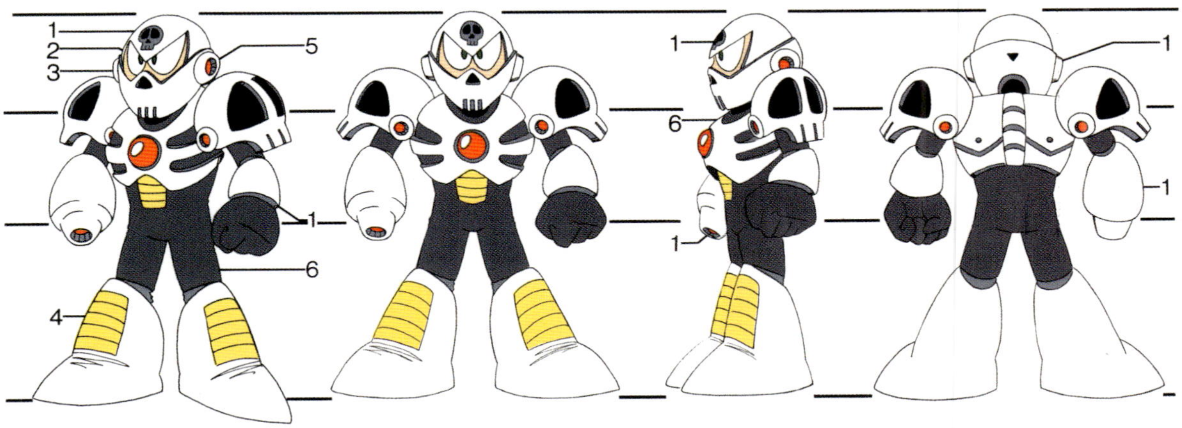

DWN.033 GRAVITY MAN

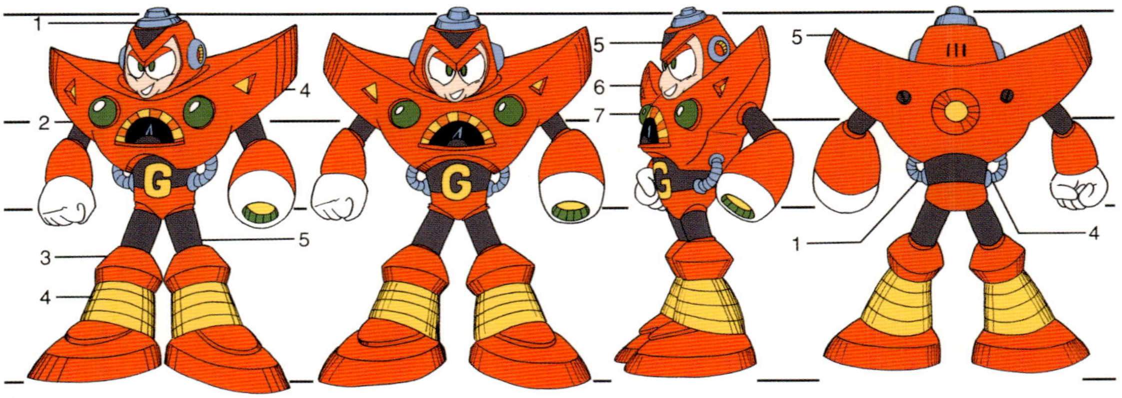

DWN.034 WAVE MAN

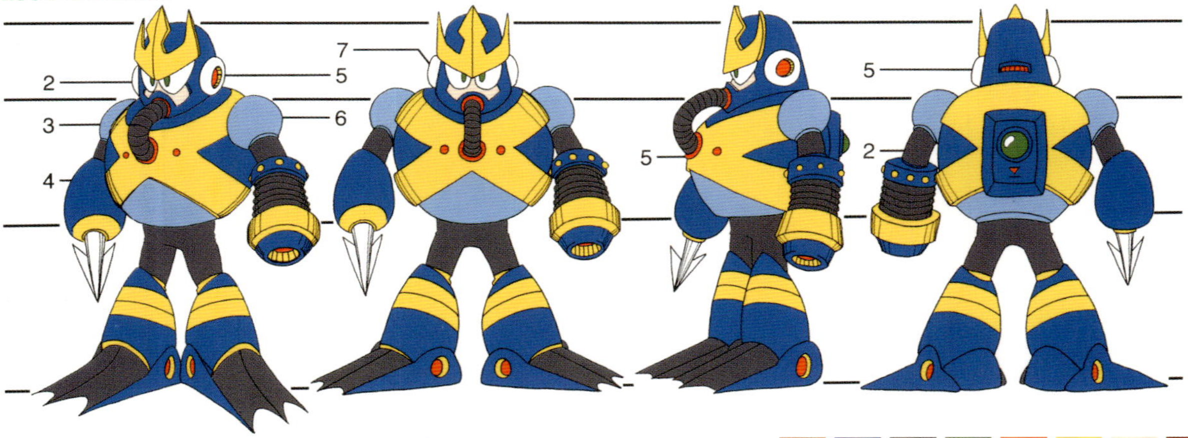

DWN.035 STONE MAN

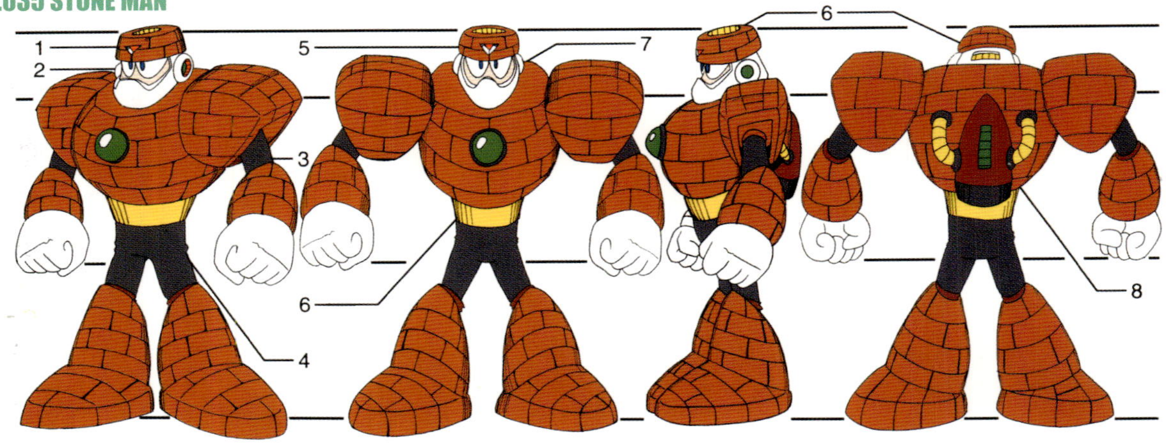

DWN.036 GYRO MAN

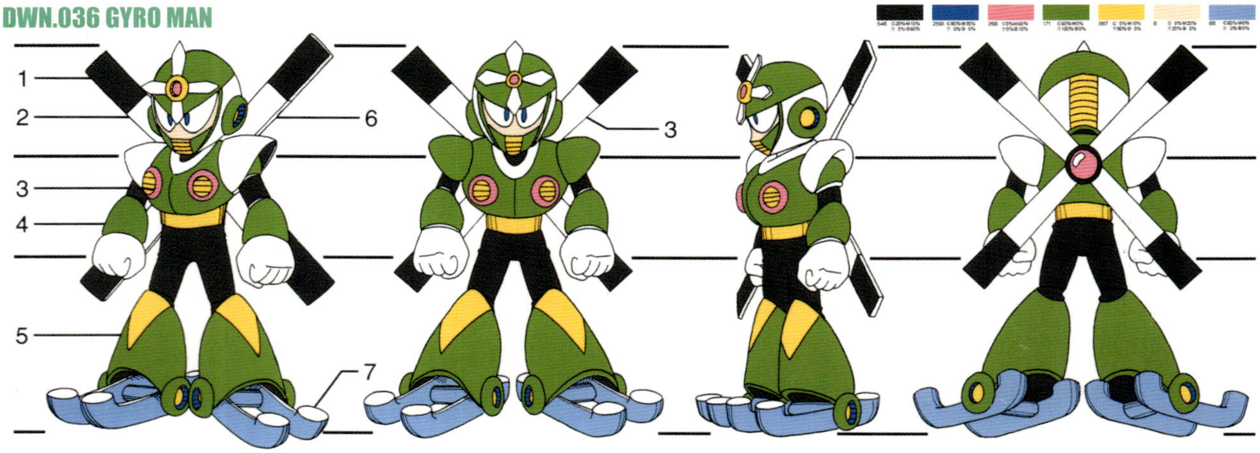

DWN.037 STAR MAN

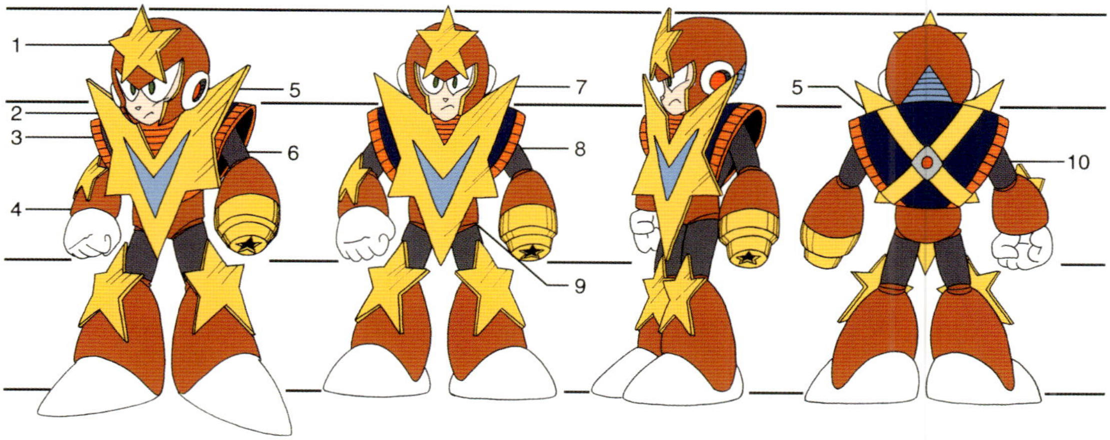

DWN.038 CHARGE MAN

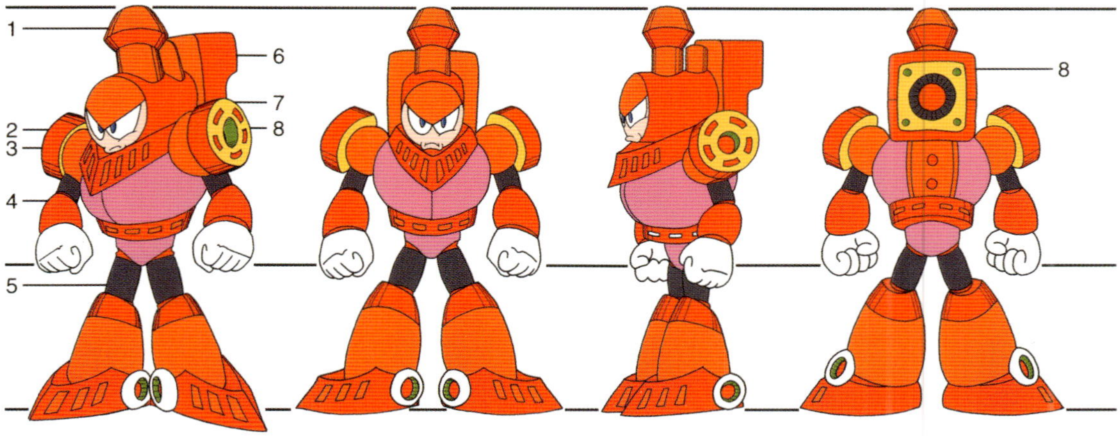

DWN.039 NAPALM MAN

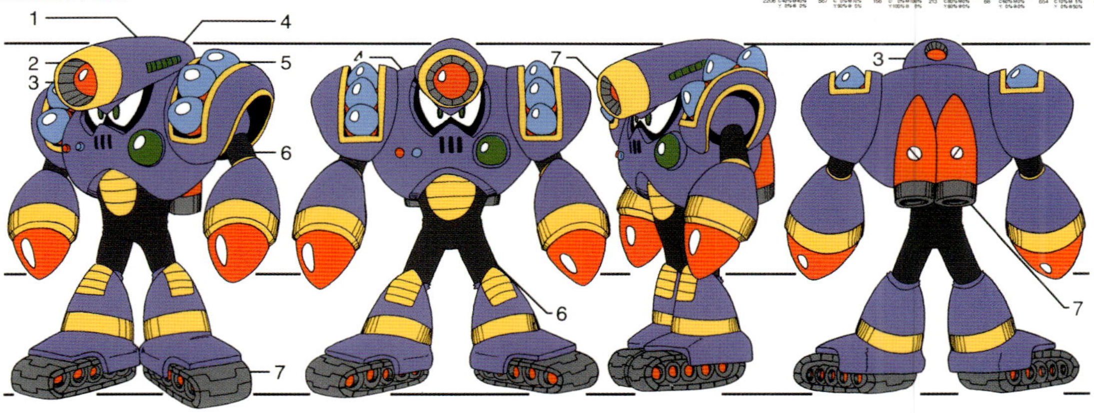

DWN.040 CRYSTAL MAN

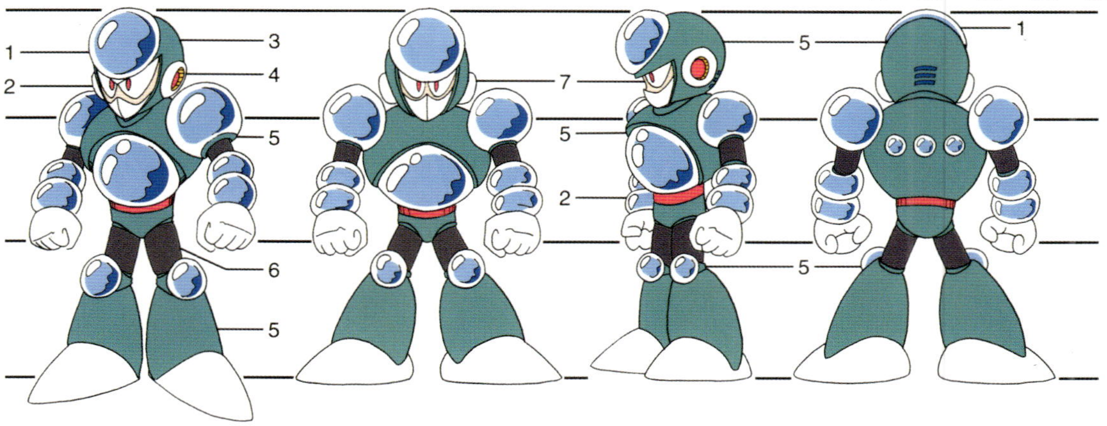

DARK MAN 1

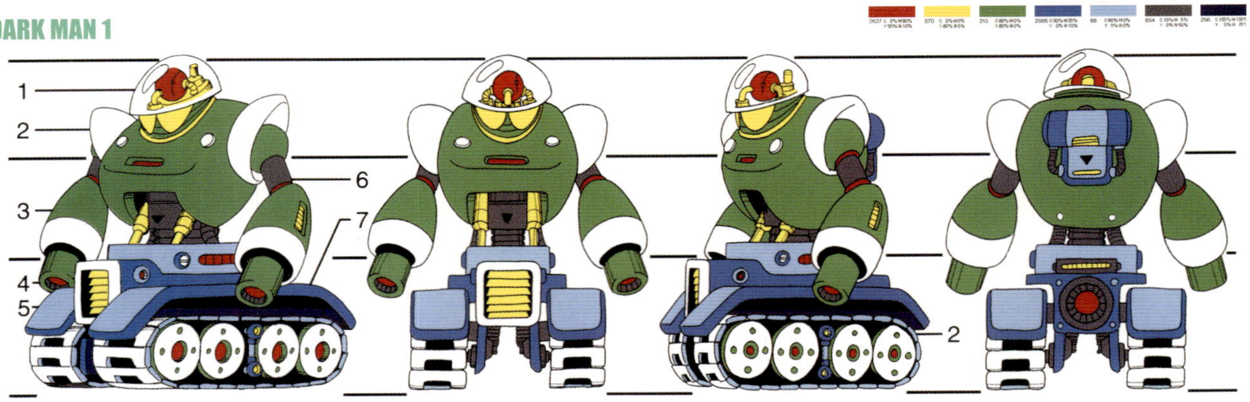

DARK MAN 2

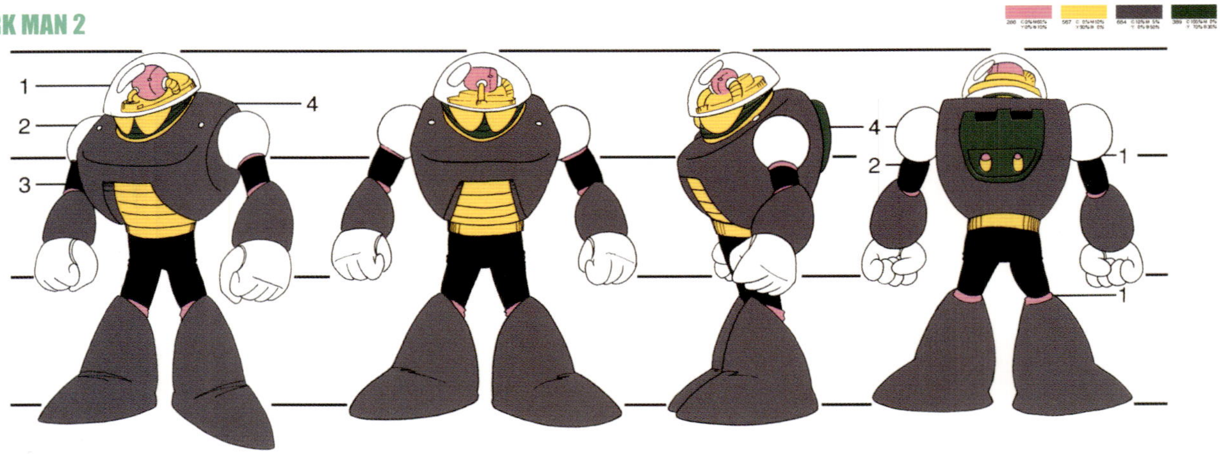

DARK MAN 3

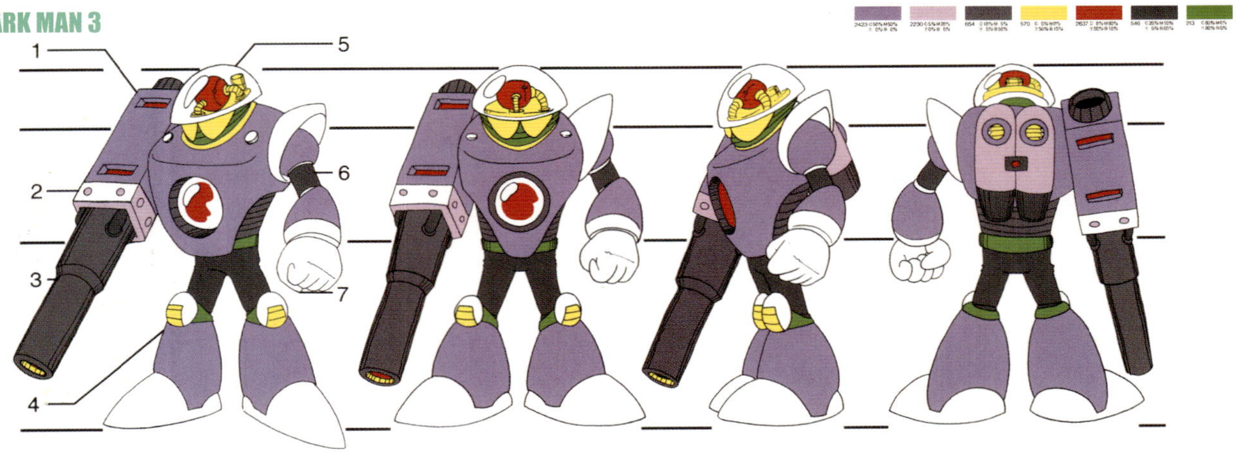

DARK MAN 4

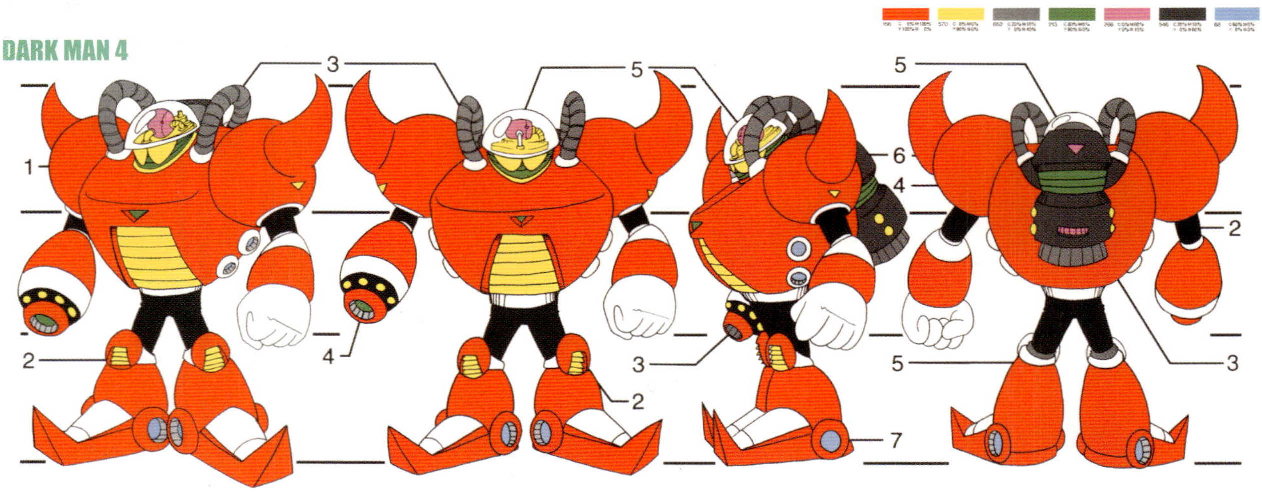

MKN.001 ENKER

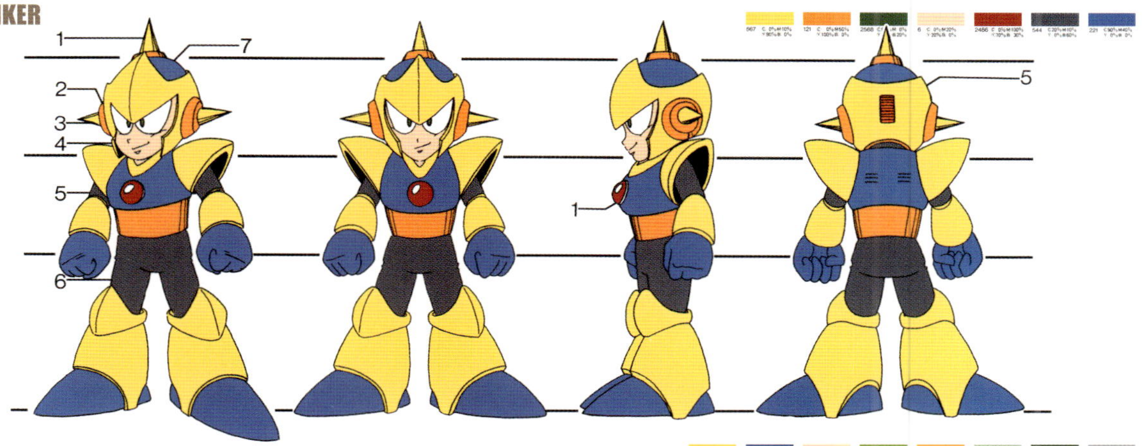

QUINT

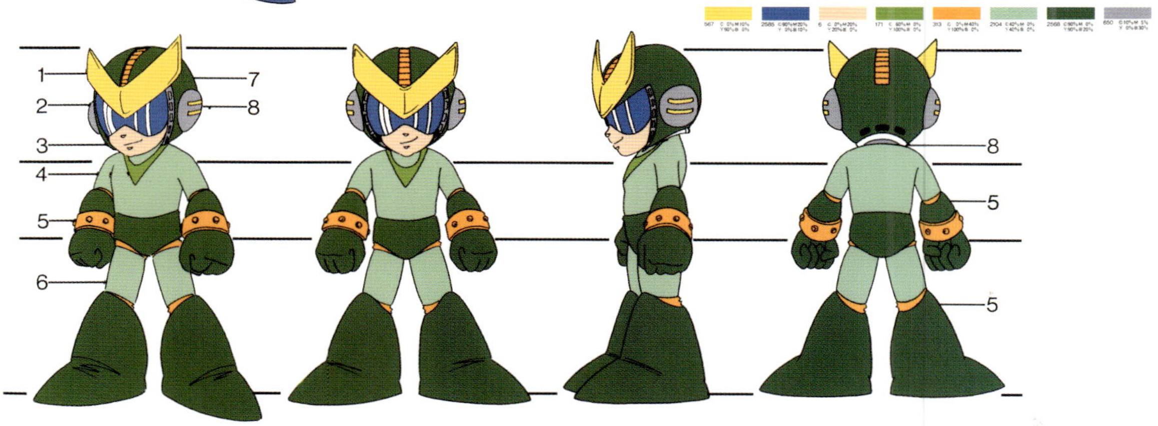

MKN.002 PUNK

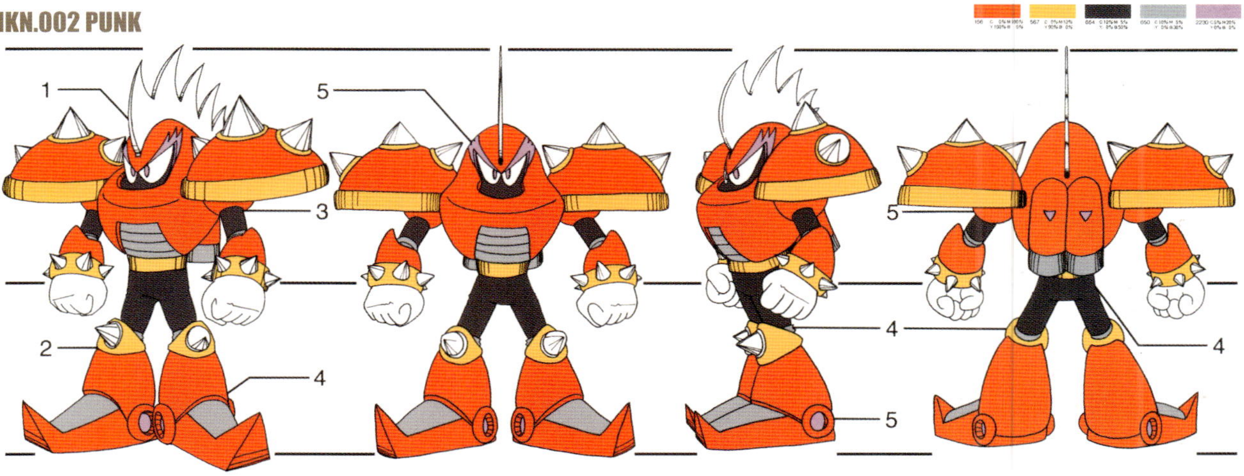

MKN.003 BALLADE

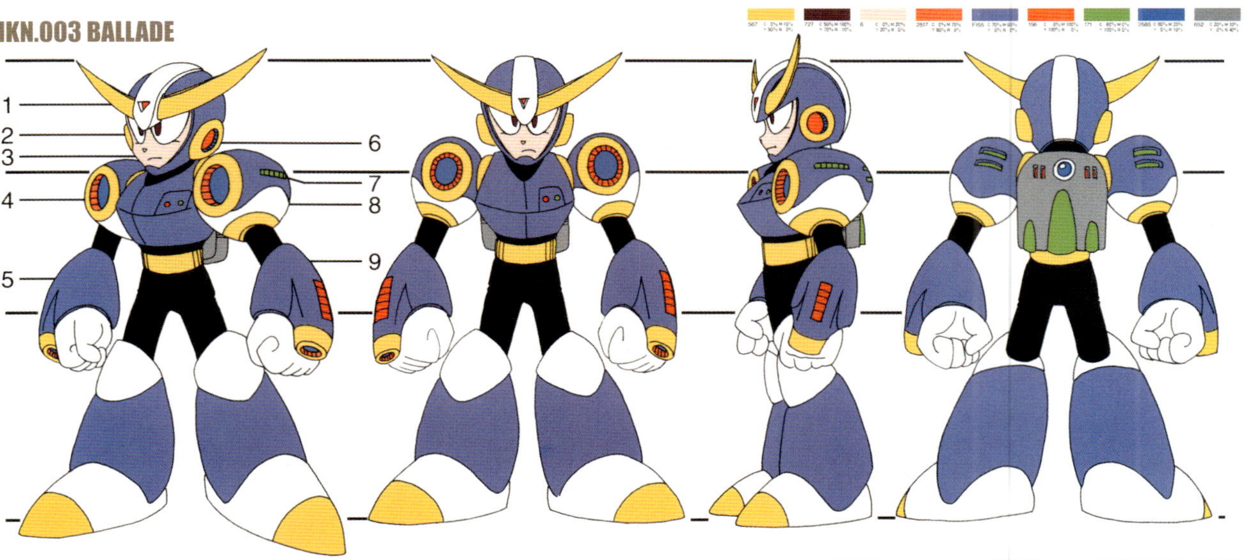

DWN.041 BLIZZARD MAN

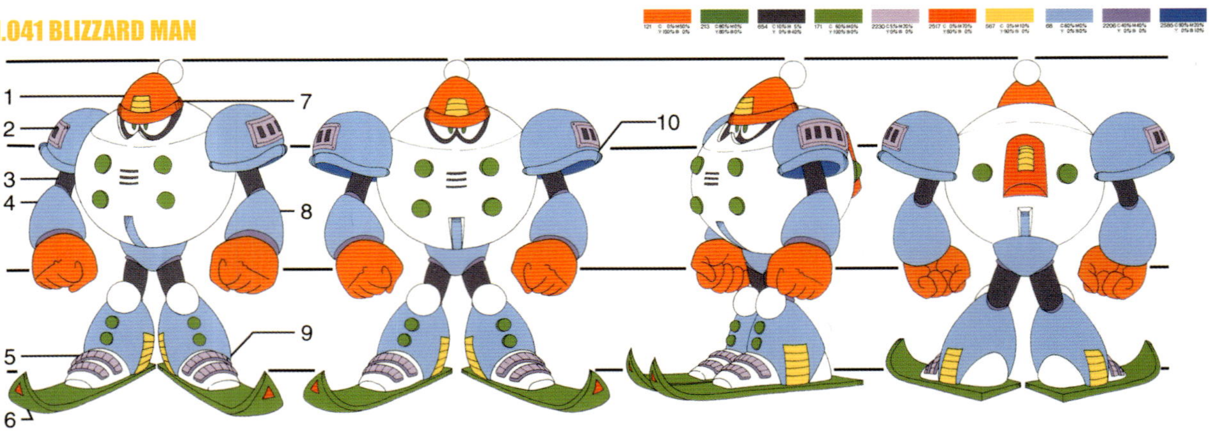

DWN.042 CENTAUR MAN

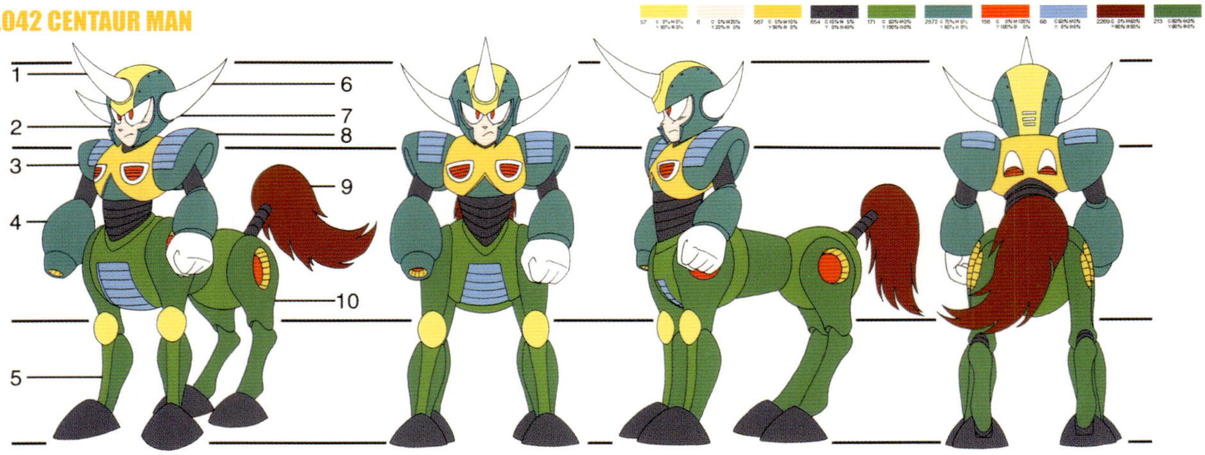

DWN.043 FLAME MAN

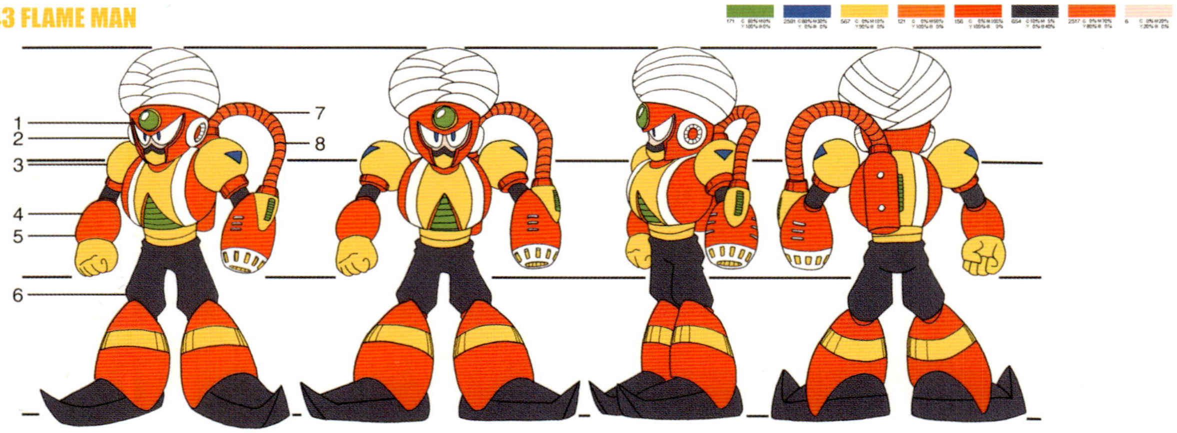

DWN.044 KNIGHT MAN

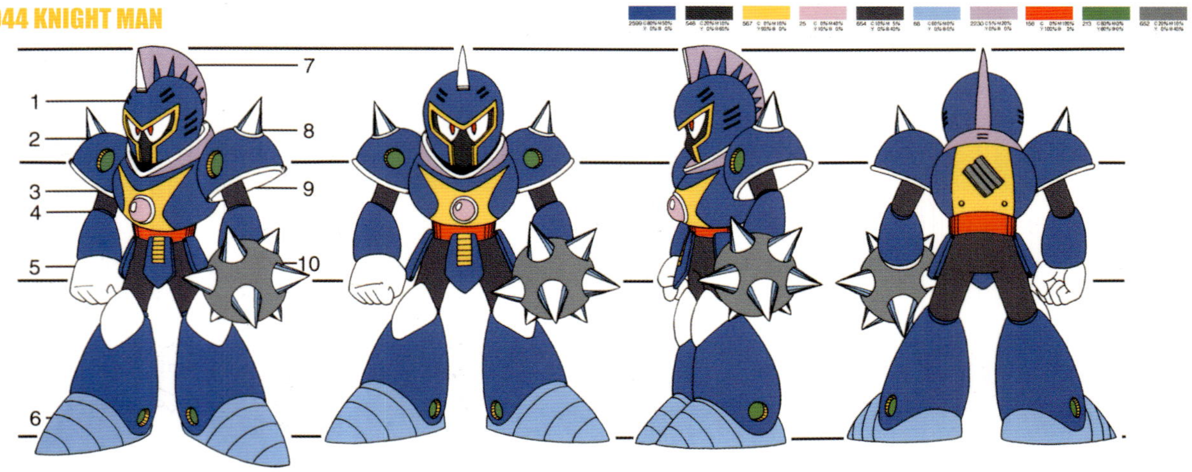

DWN.045 PLANT MAN

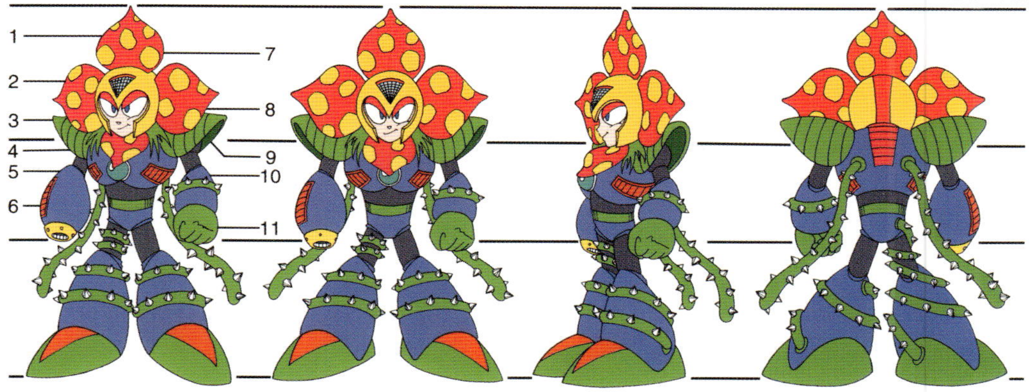

DWN.046 TOMAHAWK MAN

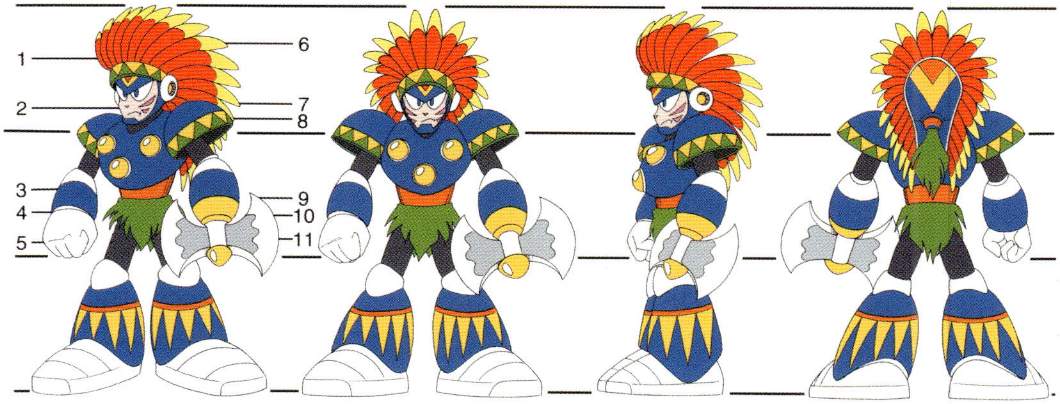

DWN.047 WIND MAN

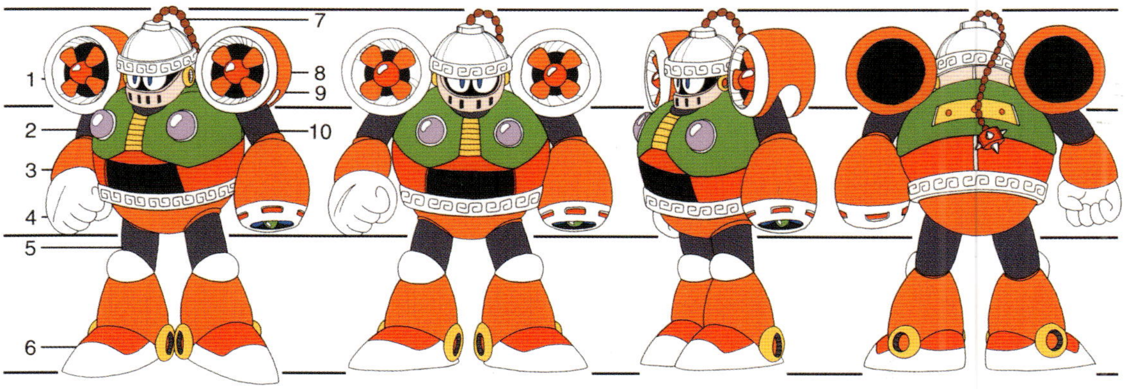

DWN.048 YAMATO MAN

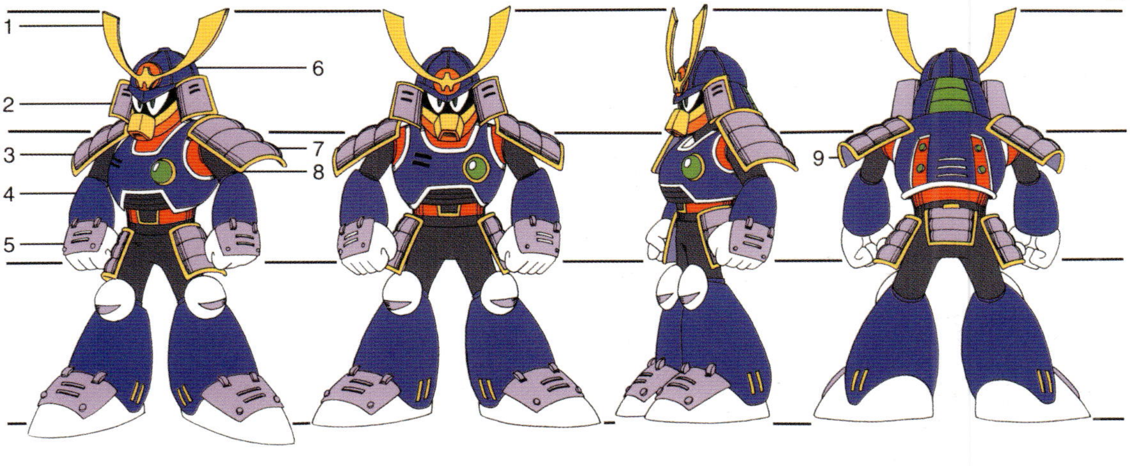

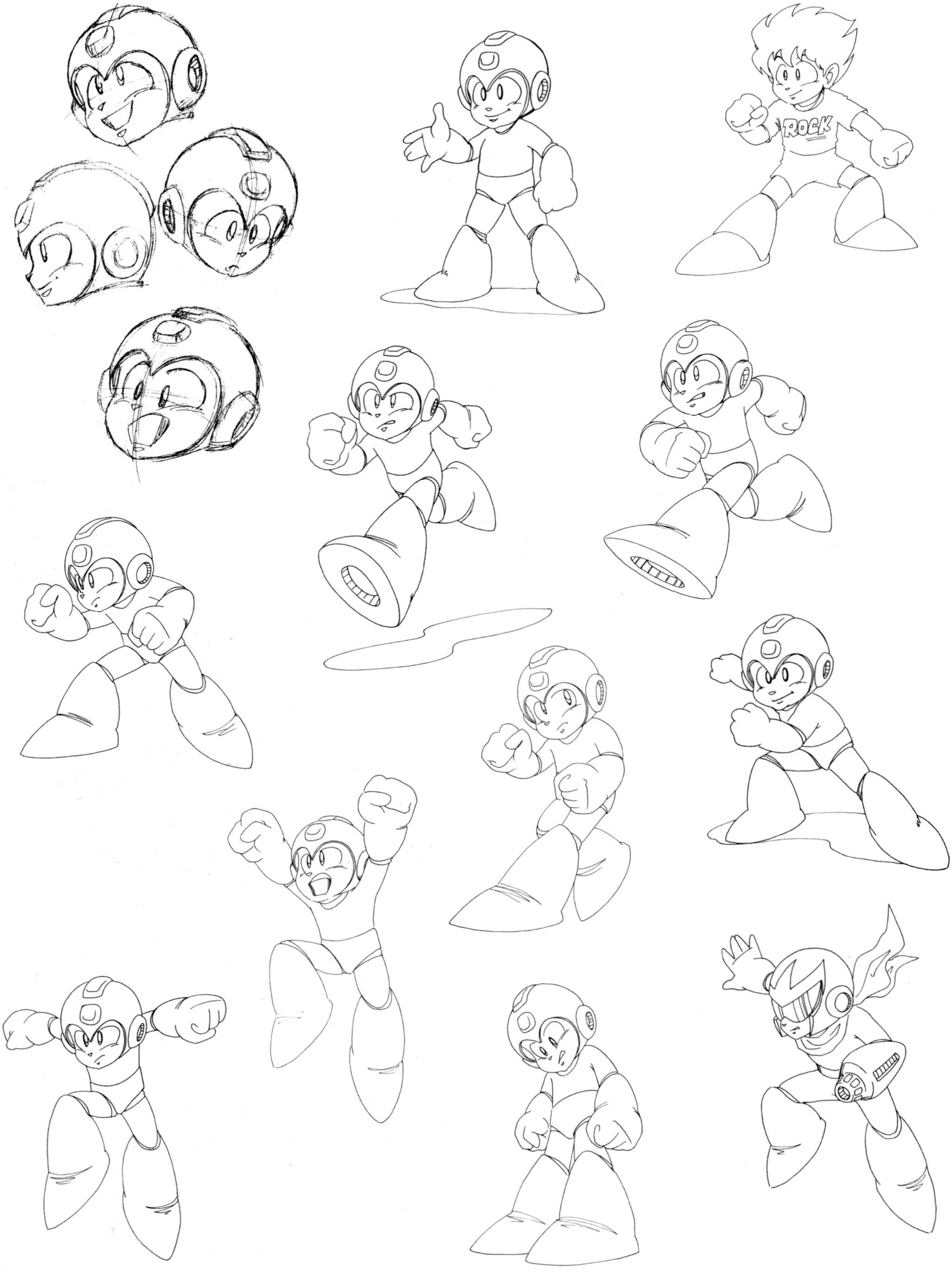
ROCK

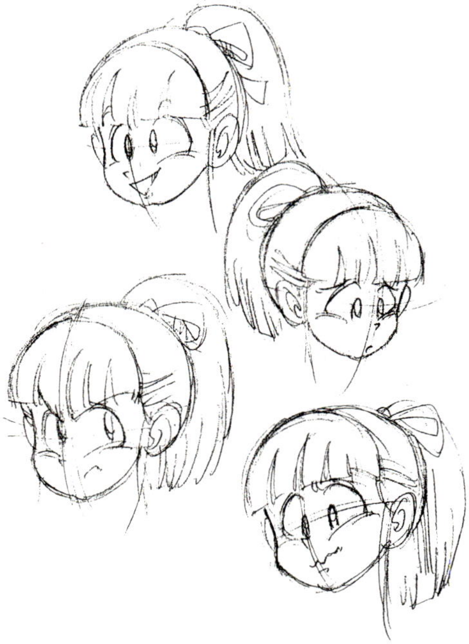

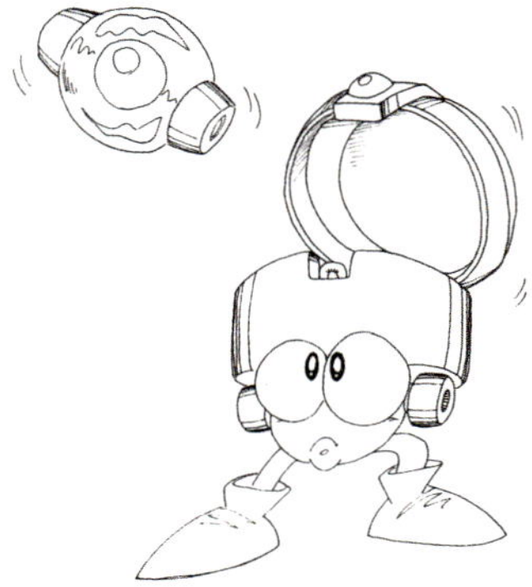

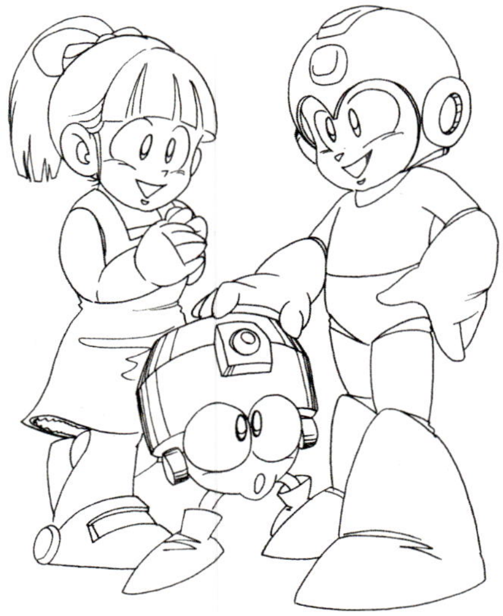

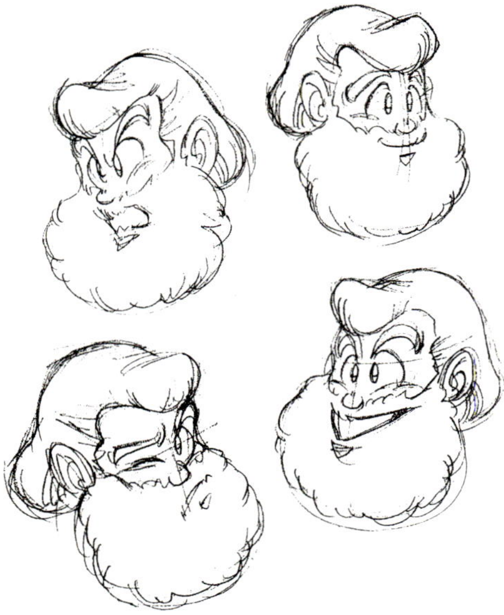

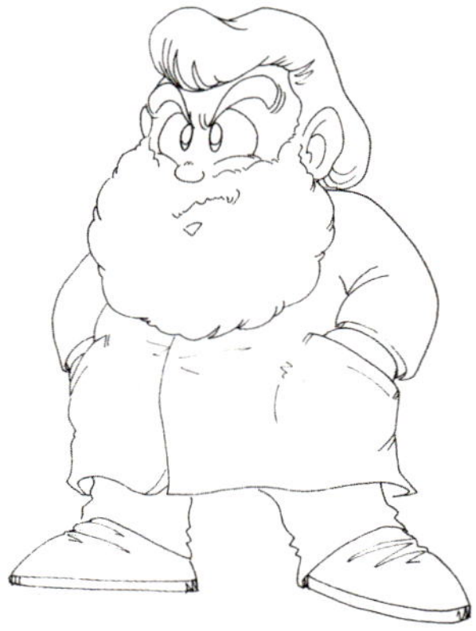

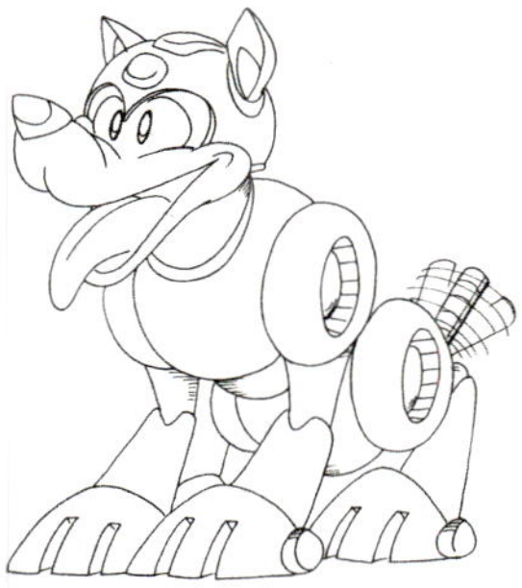

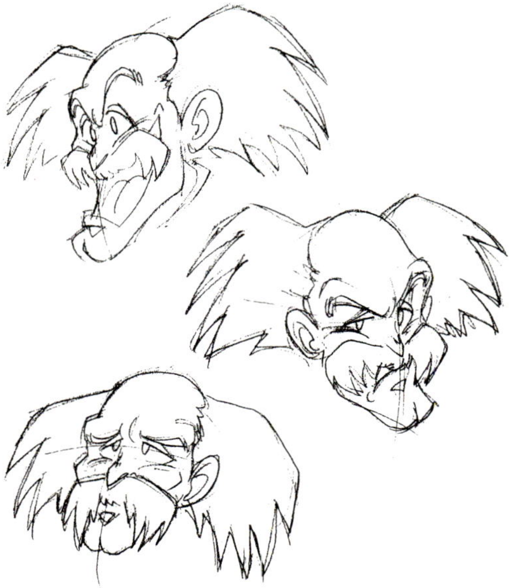

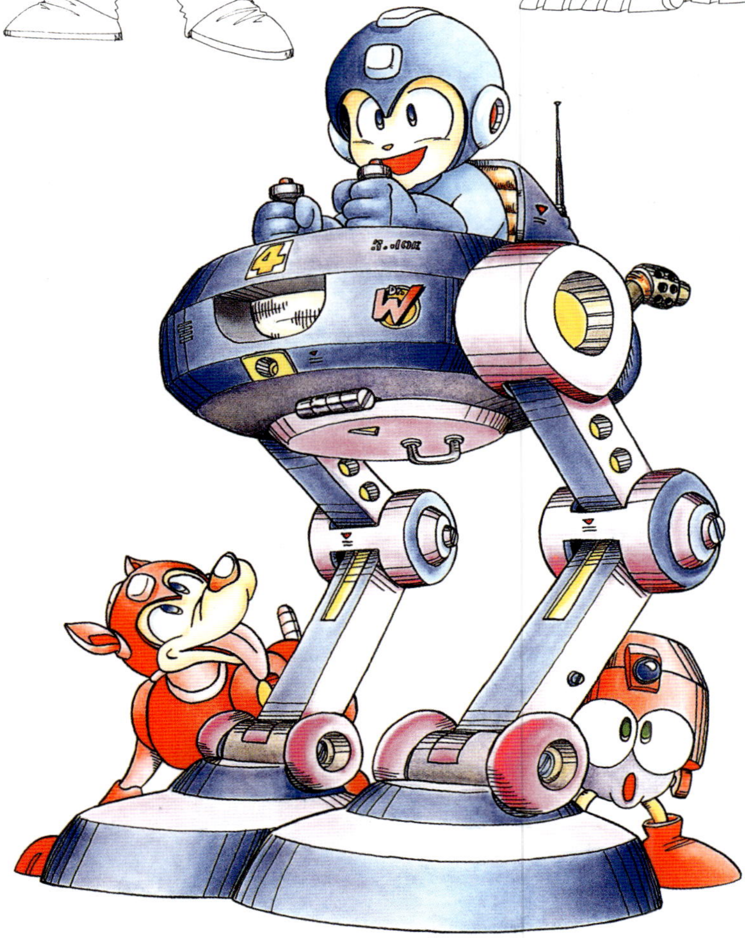

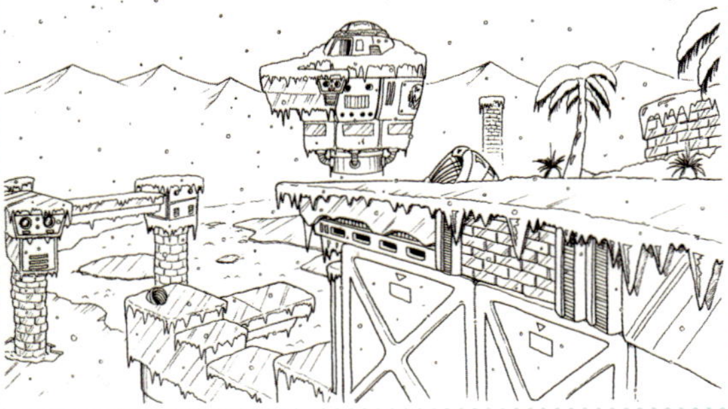

MEGA MAN
ICE MAN STAGE

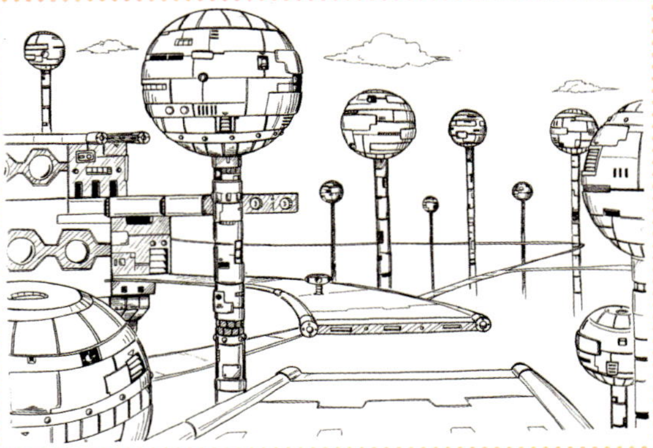

MEGA MAN
BOMB MAN STAGE

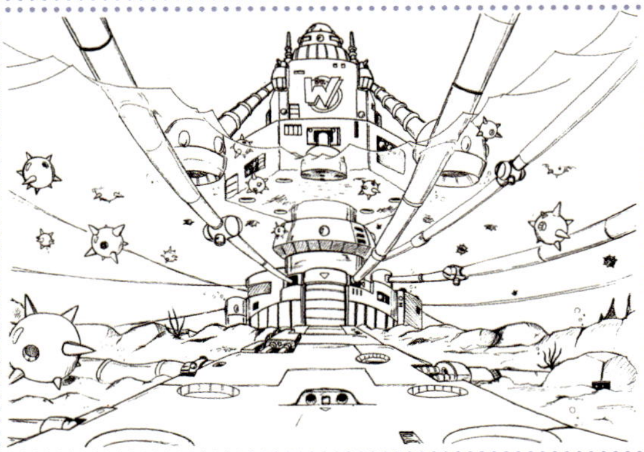

MEGA MAN 2
BUBBLE MAN STAGE

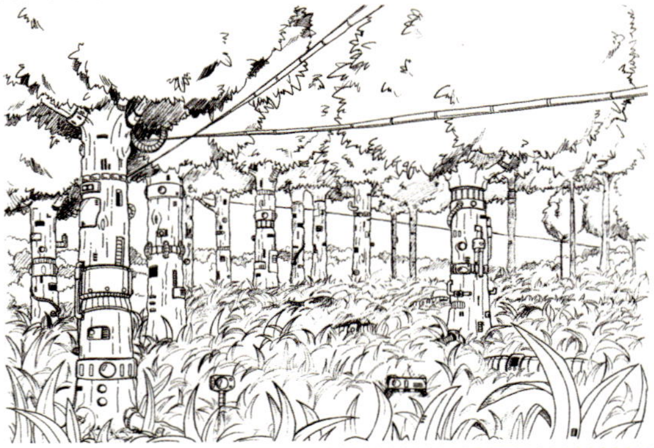

MEGA MAN 2
WOOD MAN STAGE

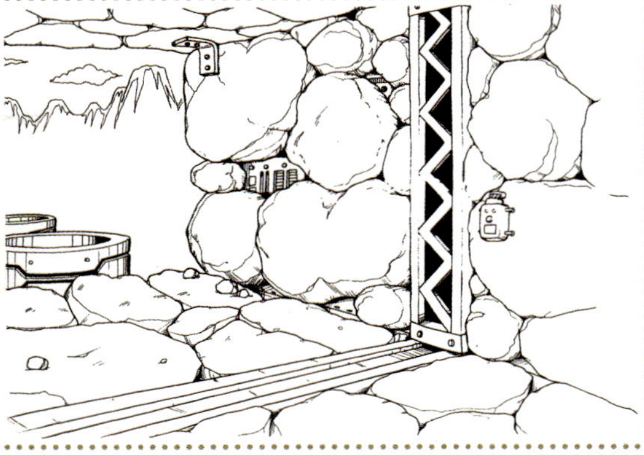

MEGA MAN 3
HARD MAN STAGE

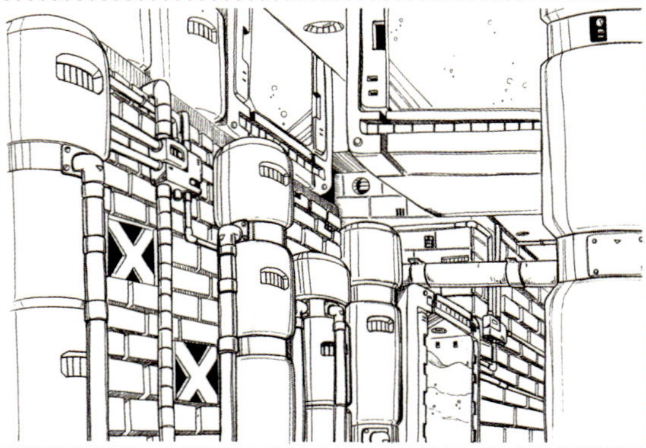

MEGA MAN 3
SHADOW MAN STAGE

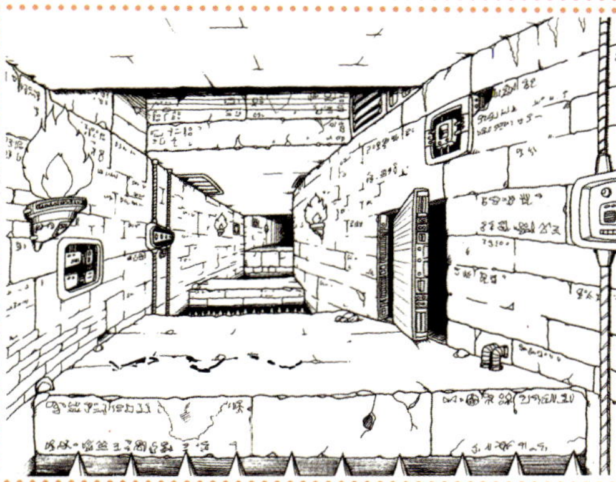

MEGA MAN 4
PHARAOH MAN STAGE

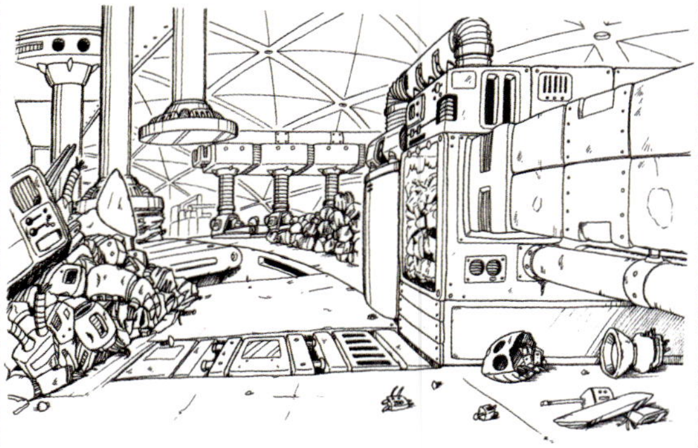

MEGA MAN 4
DUST MAN STAGE

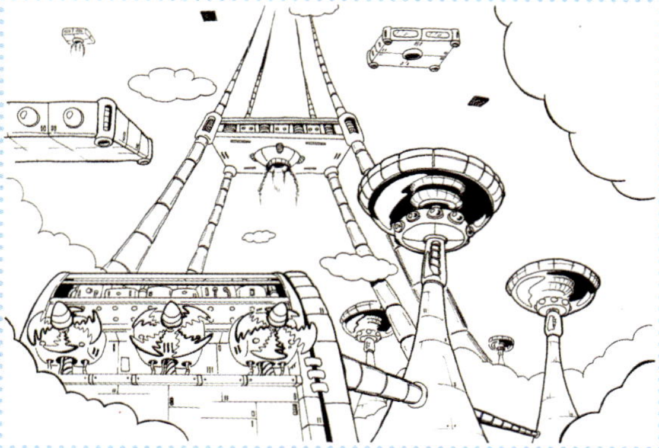

MEGA MAN 5
GYRO MAN STAGE

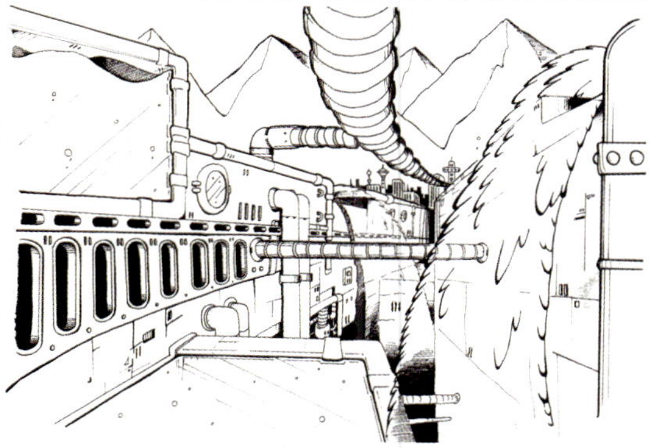

MEGA MAN 5
WAVE MAN STAGE

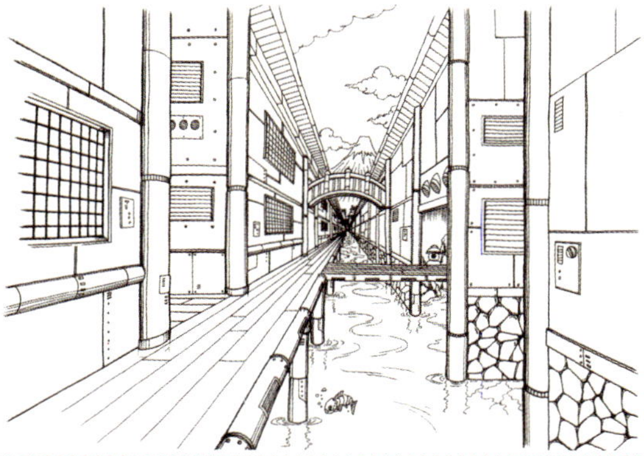

MEGA MAN 6
YAMATO MAN STAGE

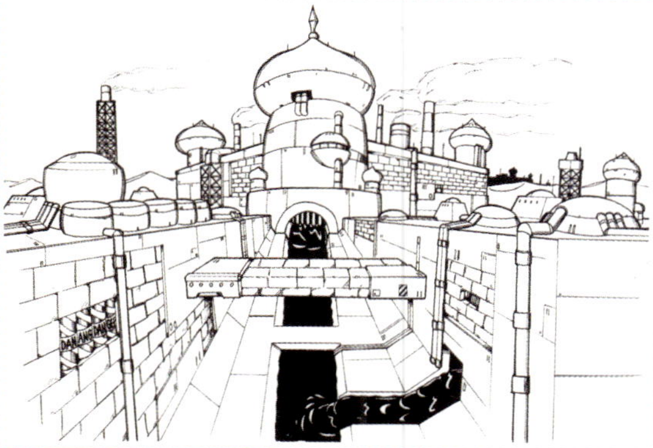

MEGA MAN 6
FLAME MAN STAGE

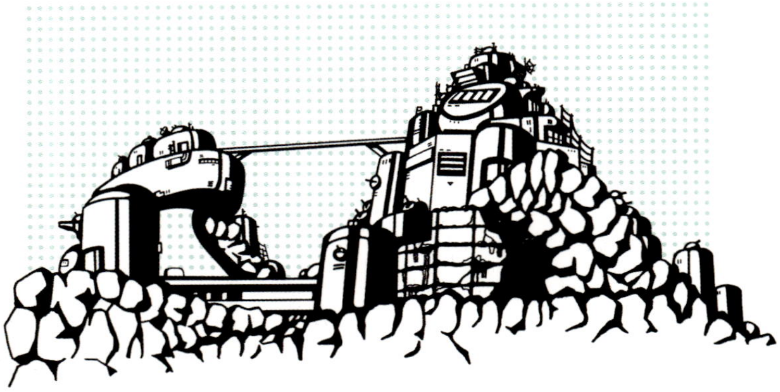

MEGA MAN
DR. WILY'S ROBOT MANUFACTURING PLANT

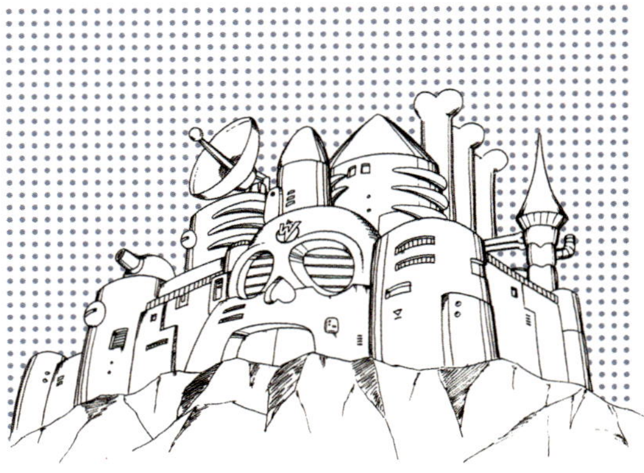

MEGA MAN 2 WILY CASTLE

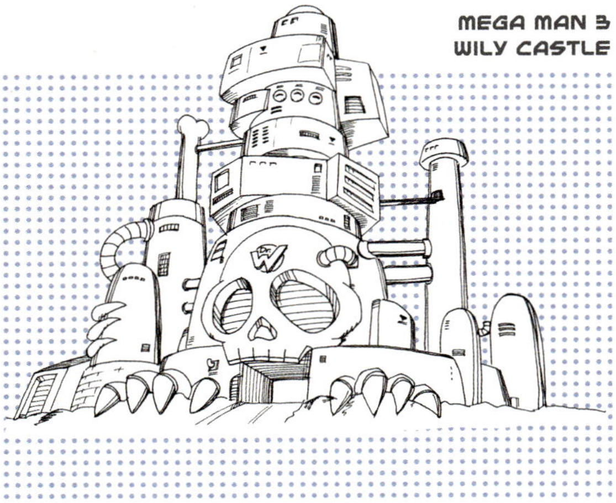

MEGA MAN 3
WILY CASTLE

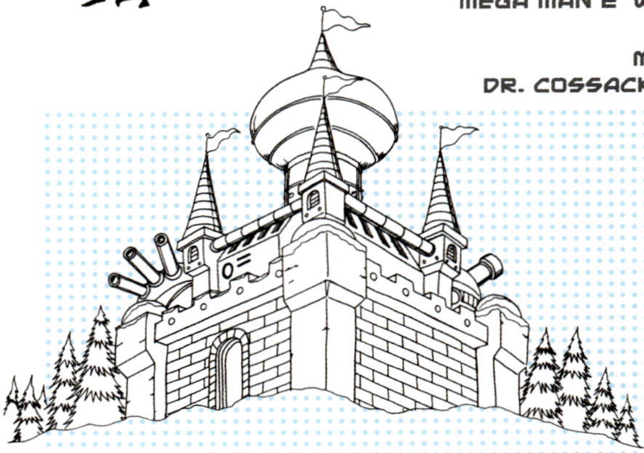

MEGA MAN 4
DR. COSSACK'S CITADEL

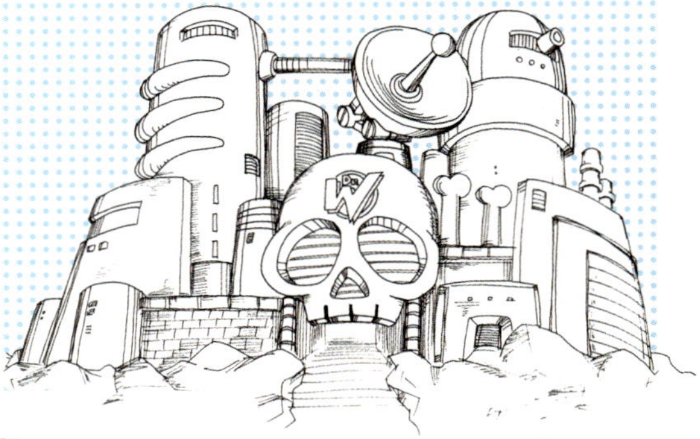

MEGA MAN 4 WILY CASTLE

MEGA MAN 5 PROTO MAN'S CASTLE

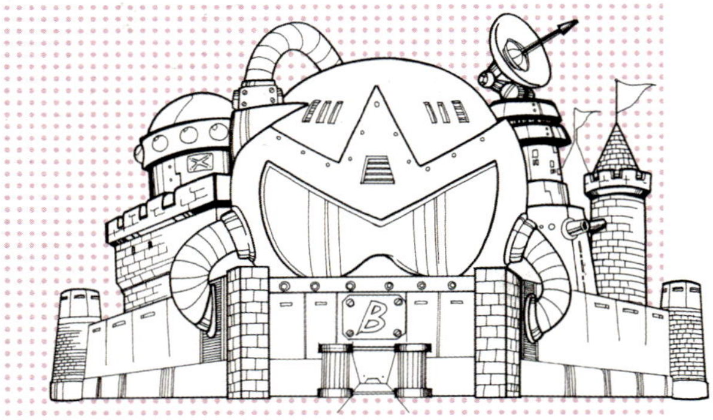

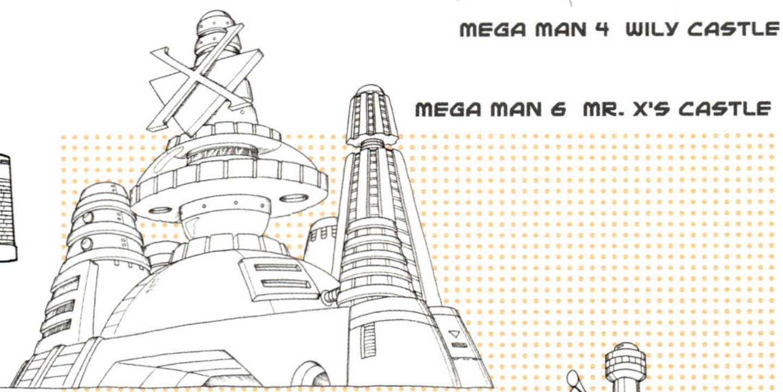

MEGA MAN 6 MR. X'S CASTLE

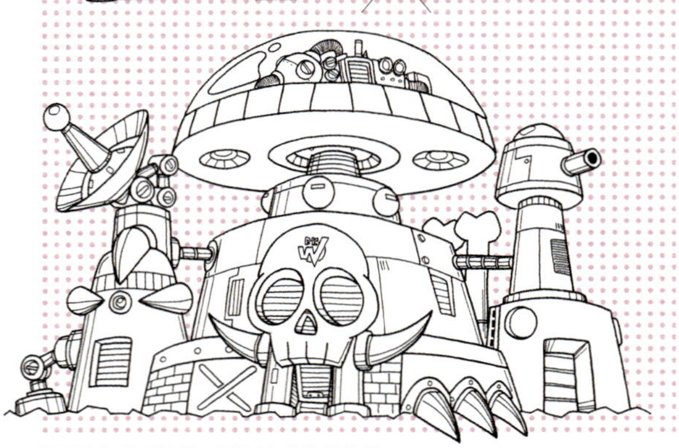

MEGA MAN 5 WILY CASTLE

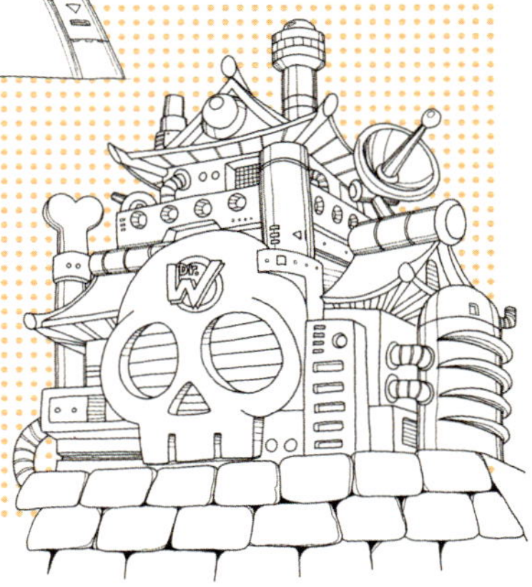

MEGA MAN 6 WILY CASTLE

MEGA MAN: DR. WILY'S REVENGE WILY CASTLE

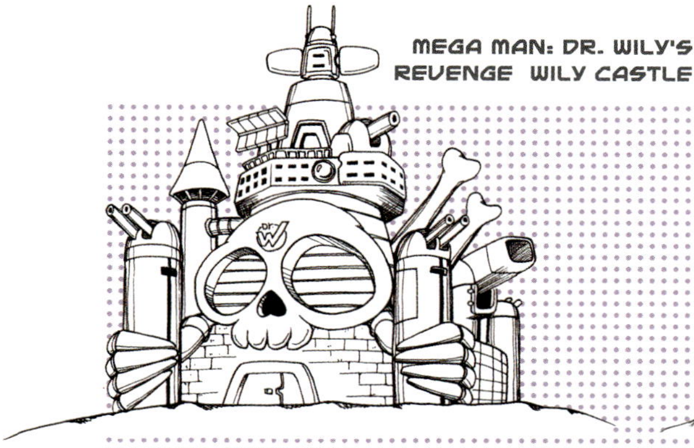

MEGA MAN II WILY CASTLE

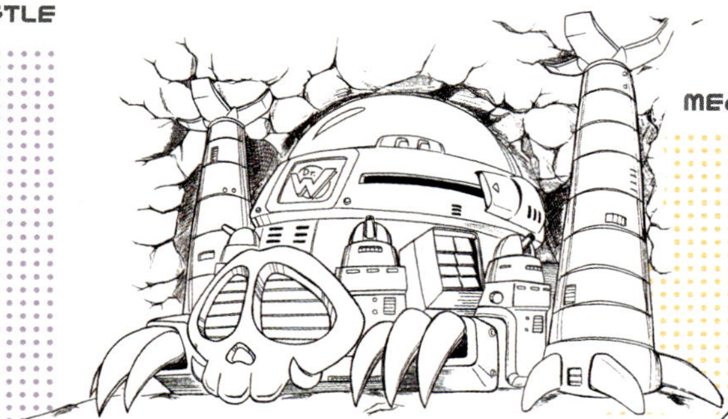

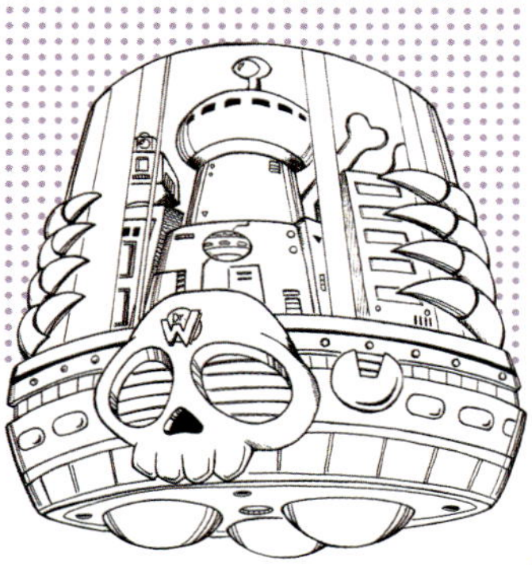

MEGA MAN: DR. WILY'S REVENGE WILY STATION

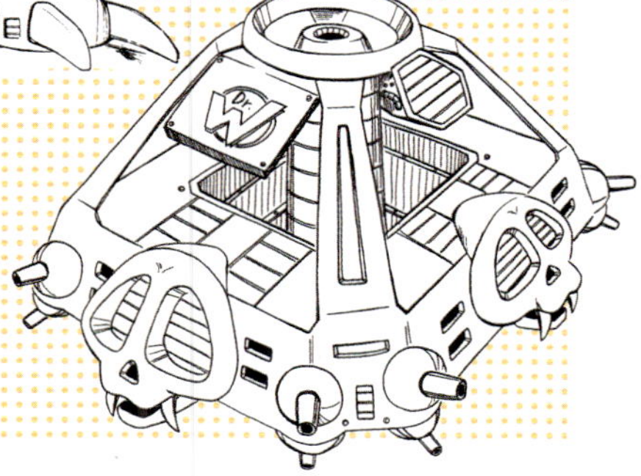

MEGA MAN II WILY STATION

MEGA MAN IV WILY STATION

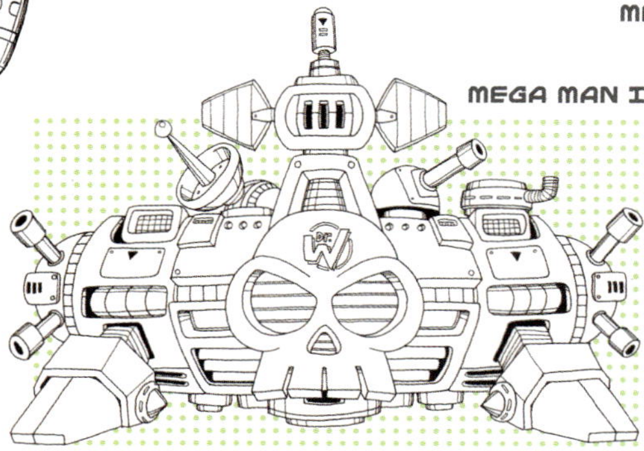

MEGA MAN III WILY CASTLE

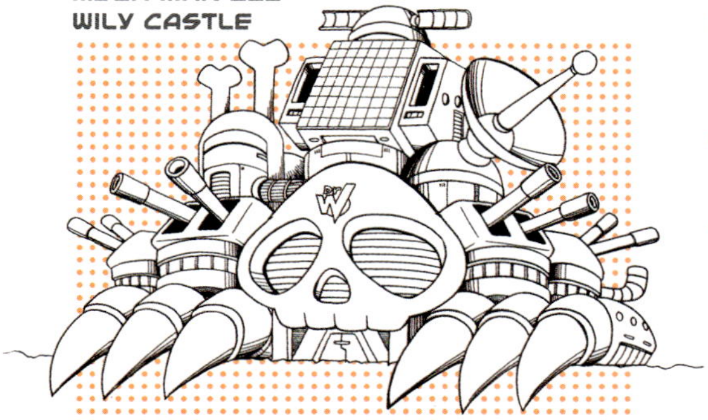

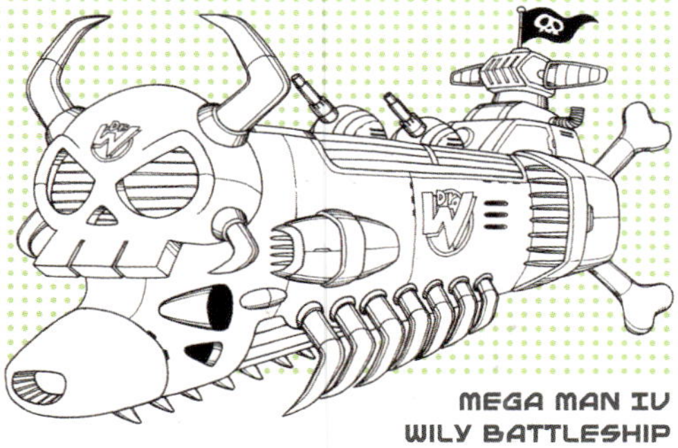

MEGA MAN IV WILY BATTLESHIP

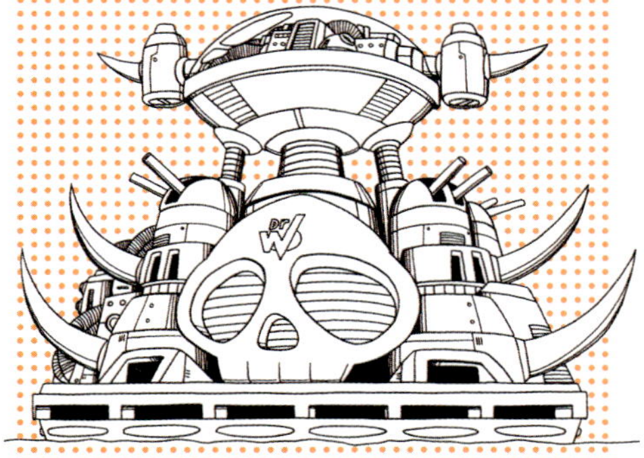

MEGA MAN III WILY STATION

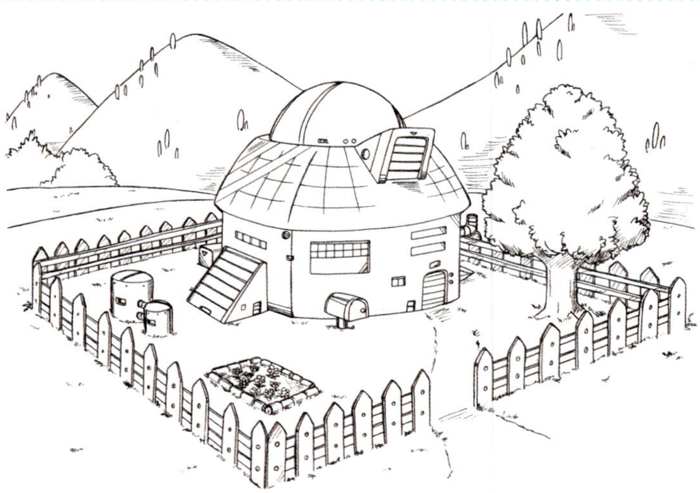

DR. LIGHT'S RESEARCH LABORATORY

"MEGA MAN" SPECIAL WEAPONS (1)

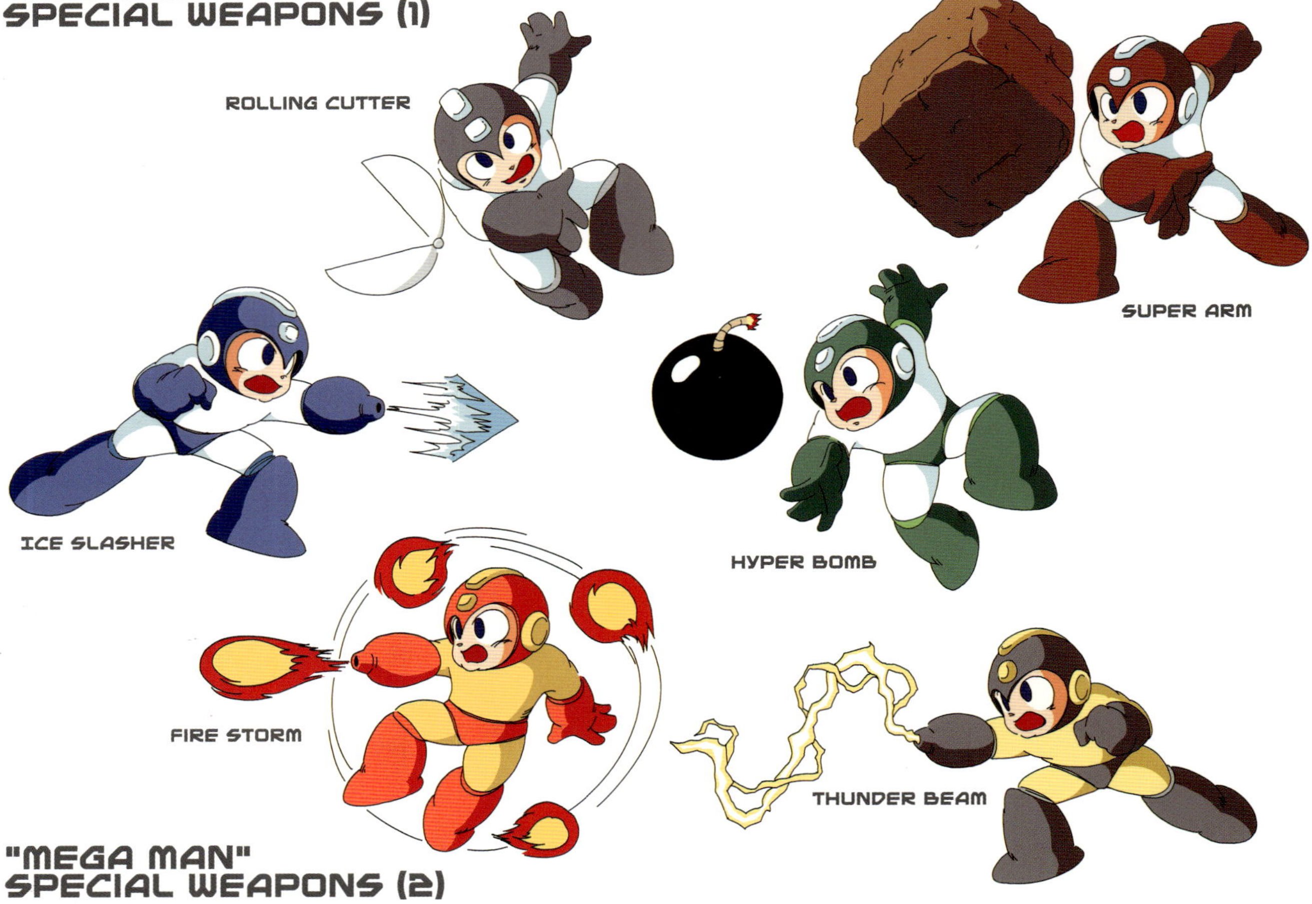

"MEGA MAN" SPECIAL WEAPONS (2)

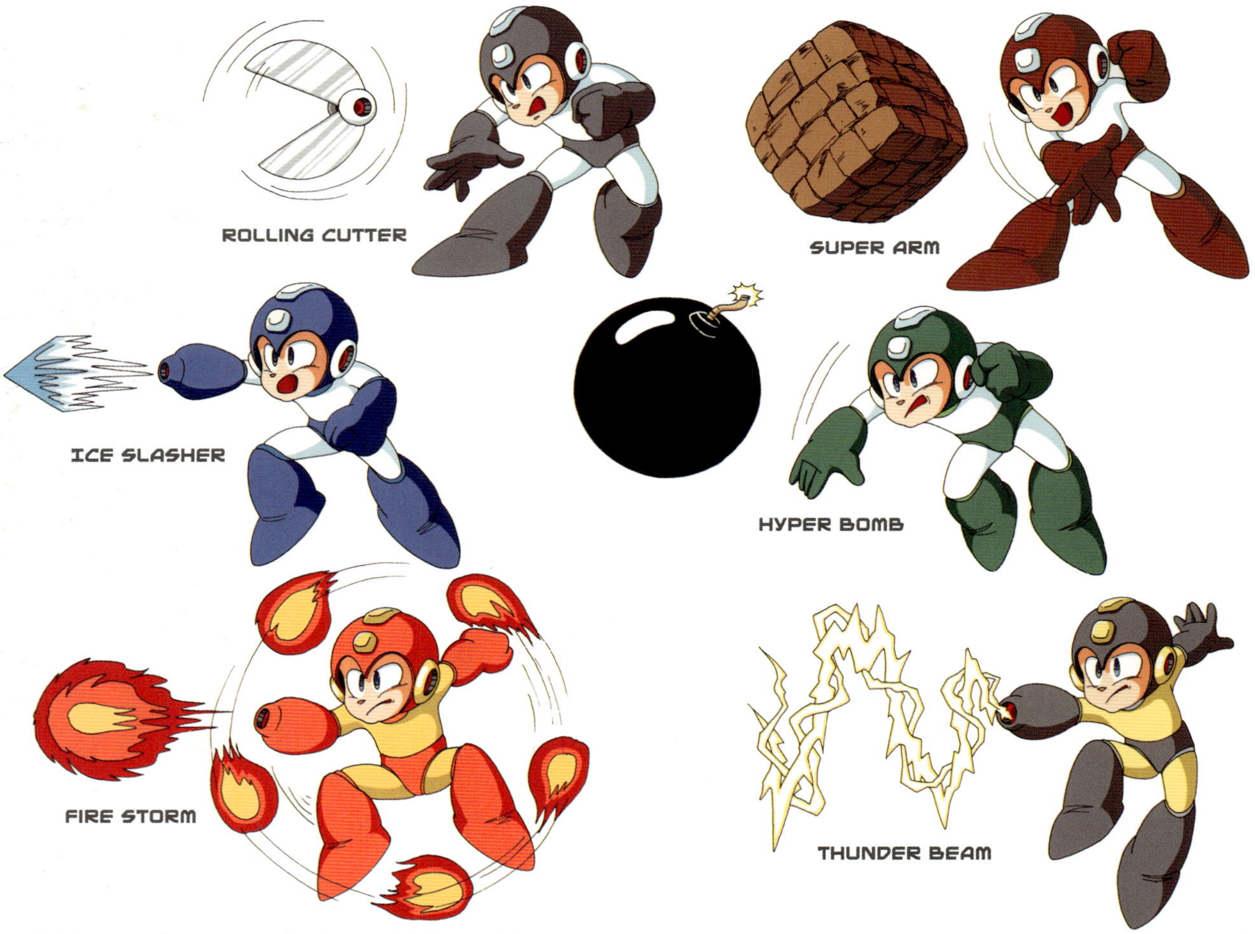

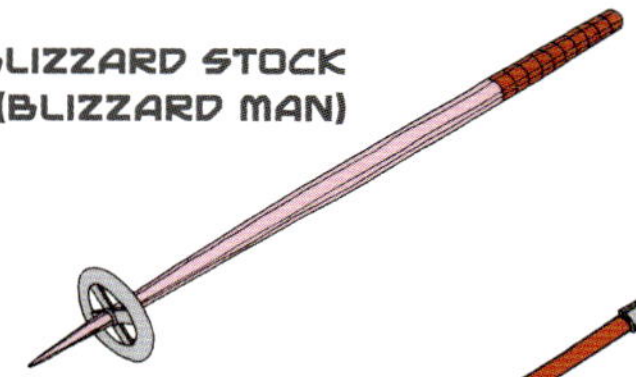

BLIZZARD STOCK
(BLIZZARD MAN)

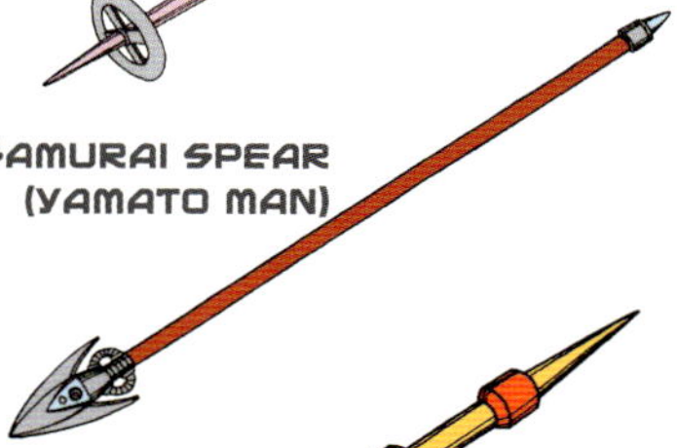

SAMURAI SPEAR
(YAMATO MAN)

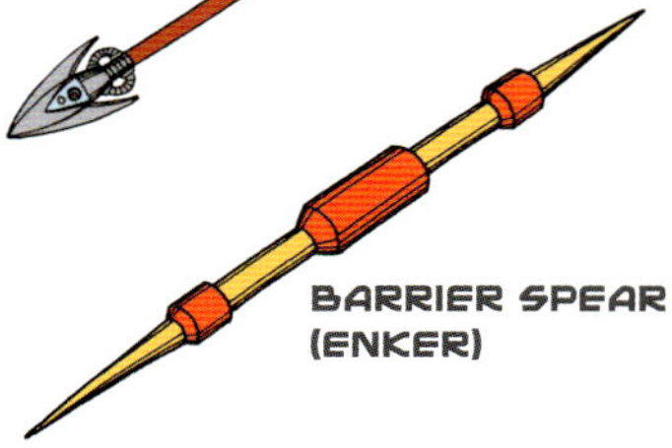

BARRIER SPEAR
(ENKER)

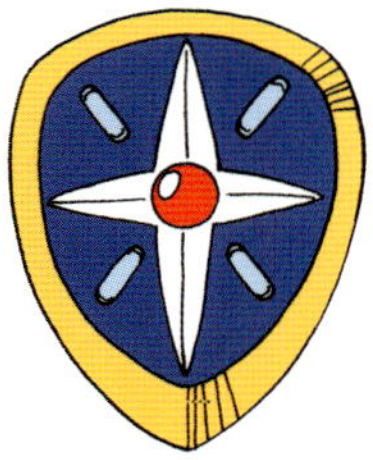

KNIGHT SHIELD
(KNIGHT MAN)

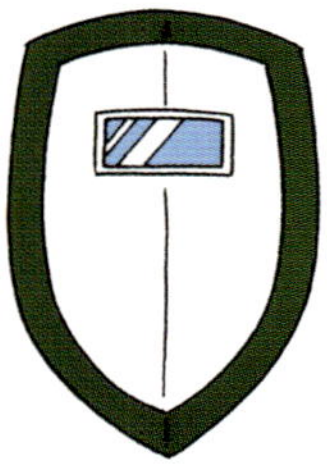

SNIPER SHIELD
(SNIPER JOE)

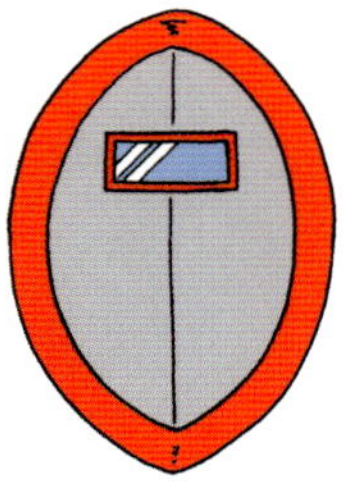

PROTO SHIELD
(PROTO MAN)

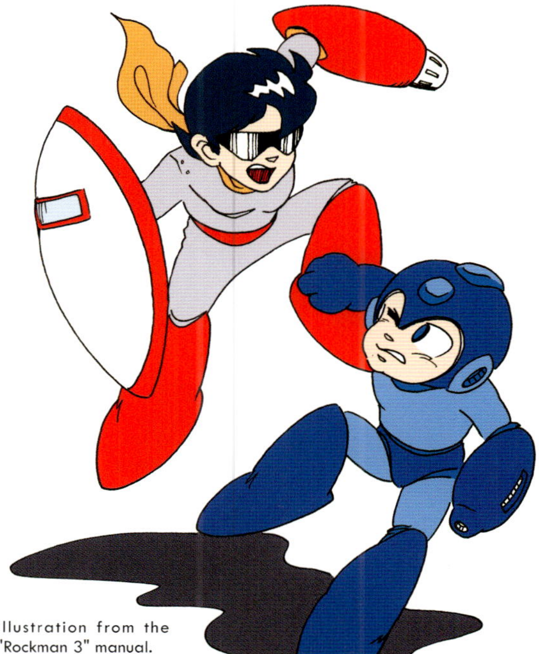

Illustration from the "Rockman 3" manual.

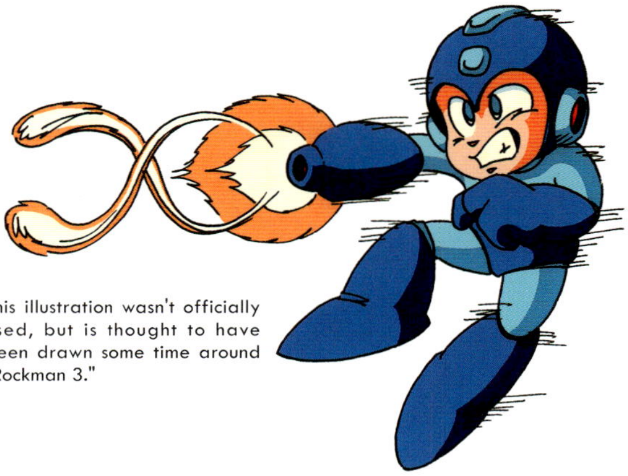

This illustration wasn't officially used, but is thought to have been drawn some time around "Rockman 3."

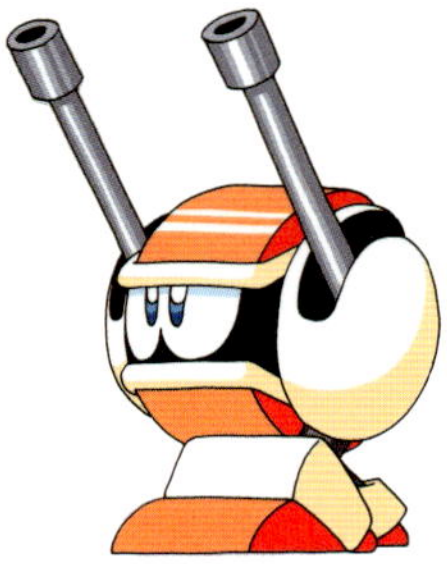

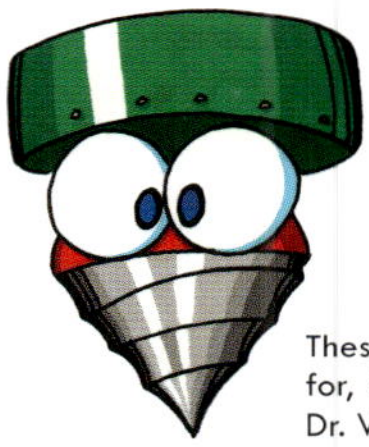

These characters were intended for, but not used in, "Mega Man: Dr. Wily's Revenge."

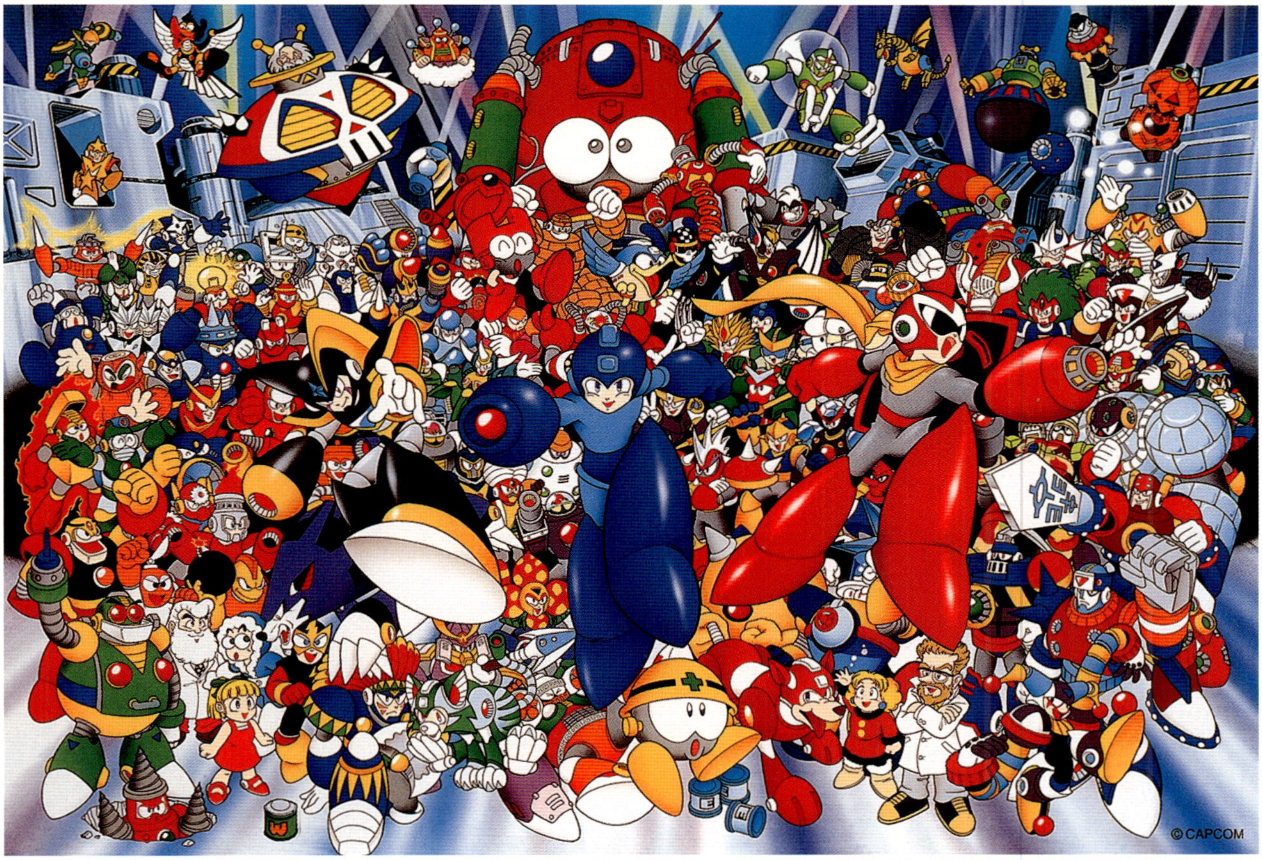

ILLUSTRATION FOR THE 10TH ANNIVERSARY JIGSAW PUZZLE

THE BIRTH OF MEGA MAN

This is a manga that was done by Keiji Inafune for the booklet "Rockman Character Collection," which was never available for retail purchase. The booklet was a special gift presented to everyone who participated in the boss character submissions for "Mega Man 4."

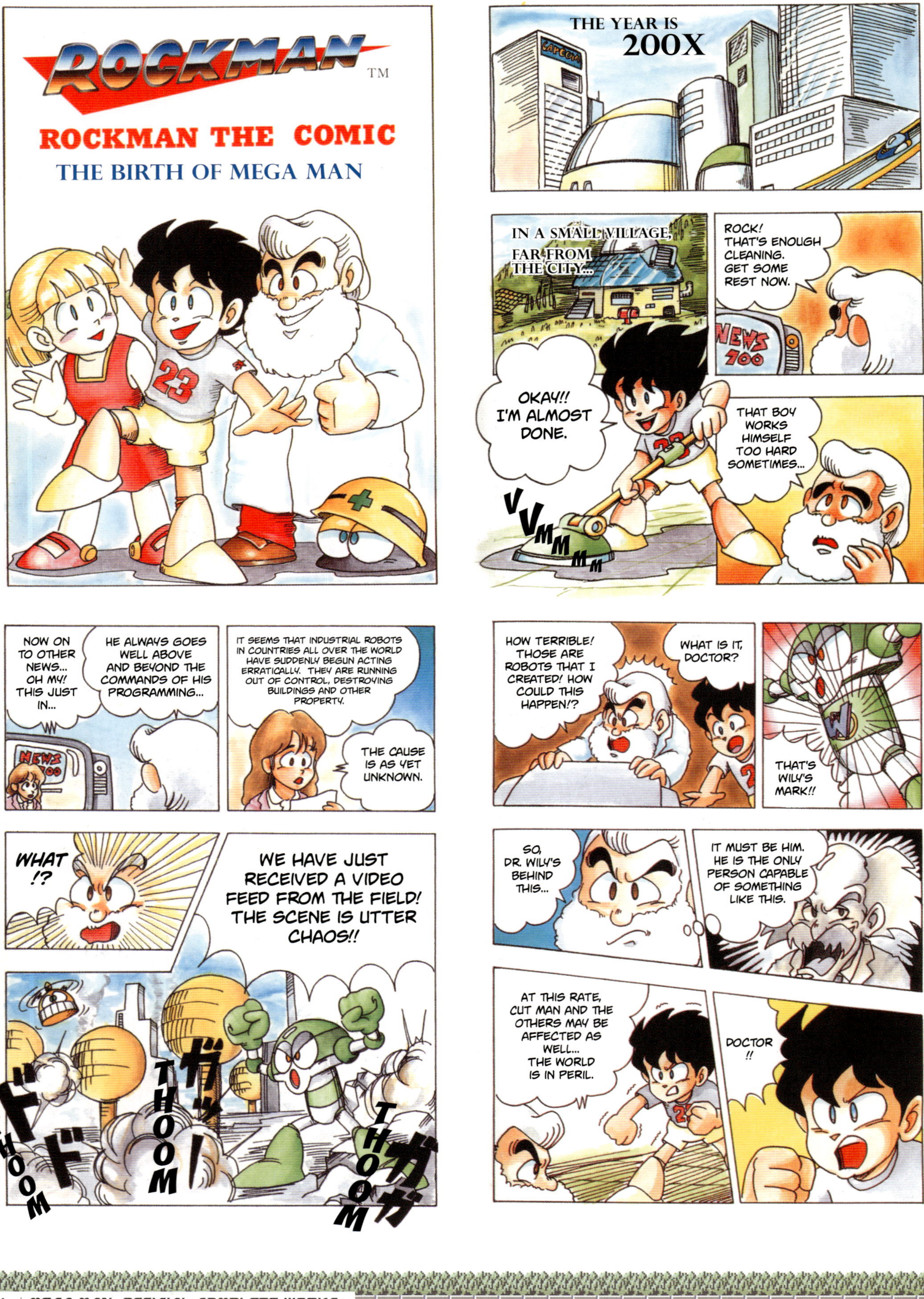

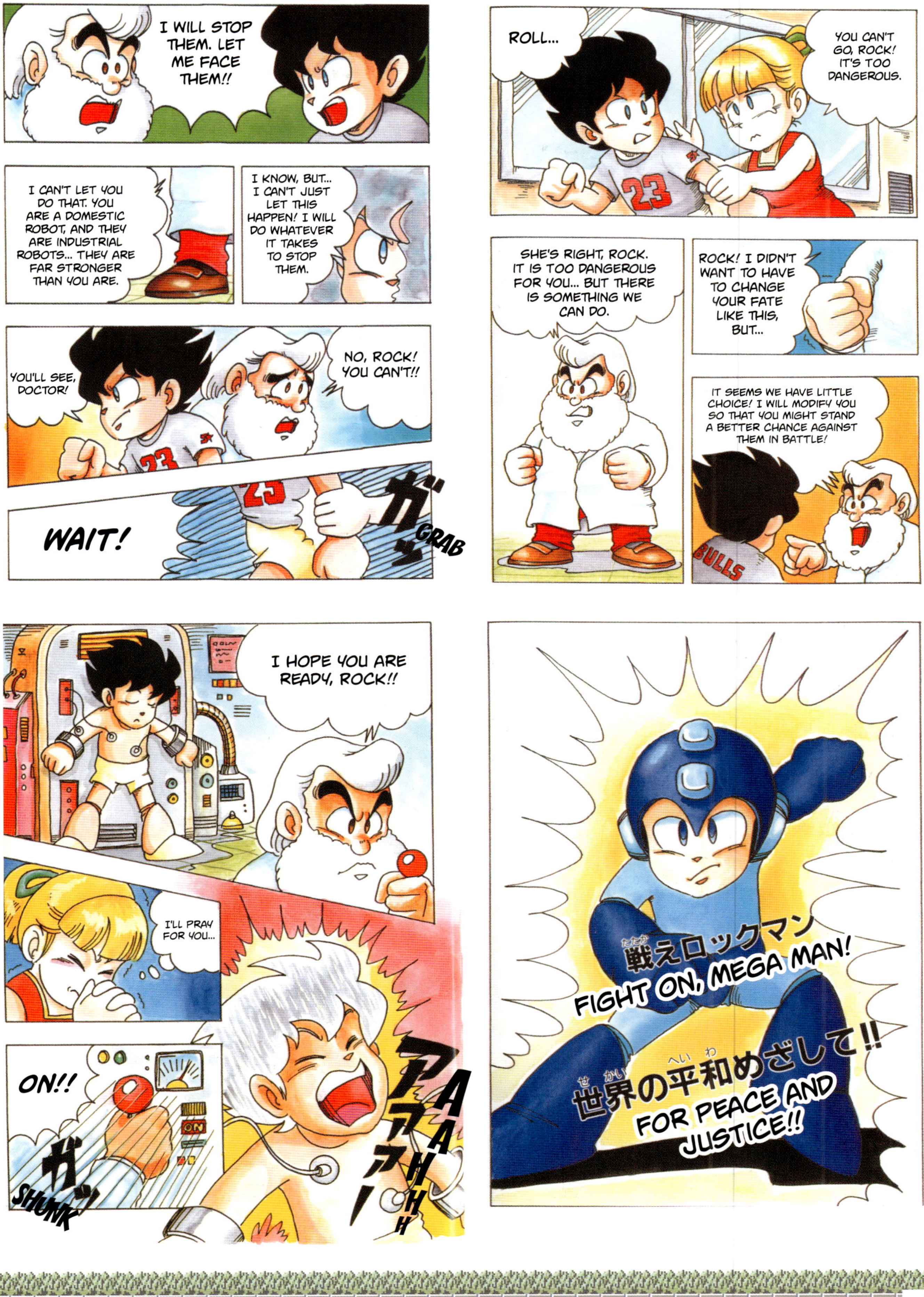
I WILL STOP THEM. LET ME FACE THEM!!
I CAN'T LET YOU DO THAT. YOU ARE A DOMESTIC ROBOT, AND THEY ARE INDUSTRIAL ROBOTS... THEY ARE FAR STRONGER THAN YOU ARE.
I KNOW, BUT... I CAN'T JUST LET THIS HAPPEN! I WILL DO WHATEVER IT TAKES TO STOP THEM.
NO, ROCK! YOU CAN'T!!
YOU'LL SEE, DOCTOR!
WAIT!
GRAB
ROLL...
YOU CAN'T GO, ROCK! IT'S TOO DANGEROUS.
SHE'S RIGHT, ROCK. IT IS TOO DANGEROUS FOR YOU... BUT THERE IS SOMETHING WE CAN DO.
ROCK! I DIDN'T WANT TO HAVE TO CHANGE YOUR FATE LIKE THIS, BUT...
IT SEEMS WE HAVE LITTLE CHOICE! I WILL MODIFY YOU SO THAT YOU MIGHT STAND A BETTER CHANCE AGAINST THEM IN BATTLE!
BULLS
I HOPE YOU ARE READY, ROCK!!
I'LL PRAY FOR YOU...
ON!!
ON
SHUNK
AAAHHHH
戦えロックマン
FIGHT ON, MEGA MAN!
世界の平和めざして!!
FOR PEACE AND JUSTICE!!

MEGA MAN 7

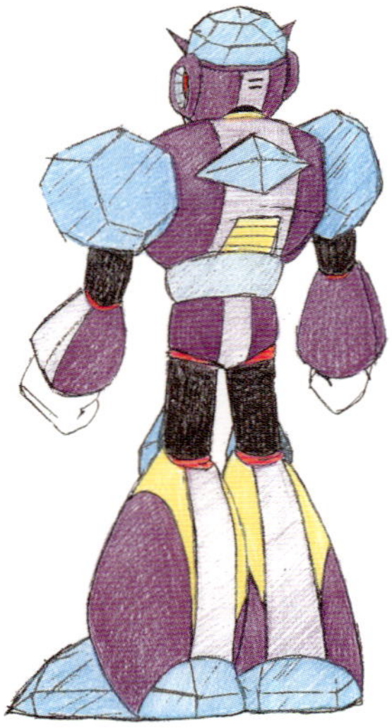

FREEZE MAN

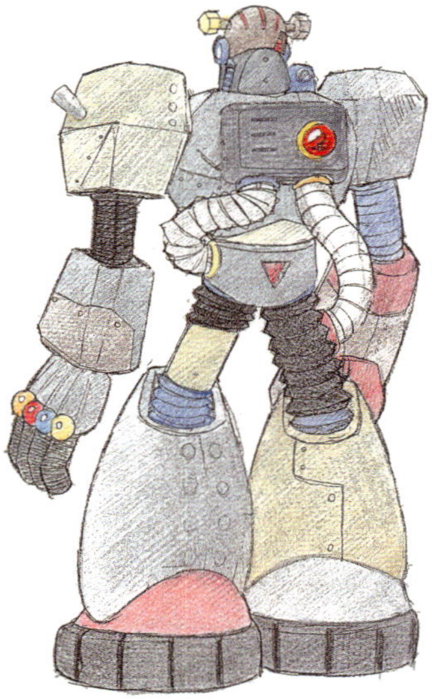

JUNK MAN

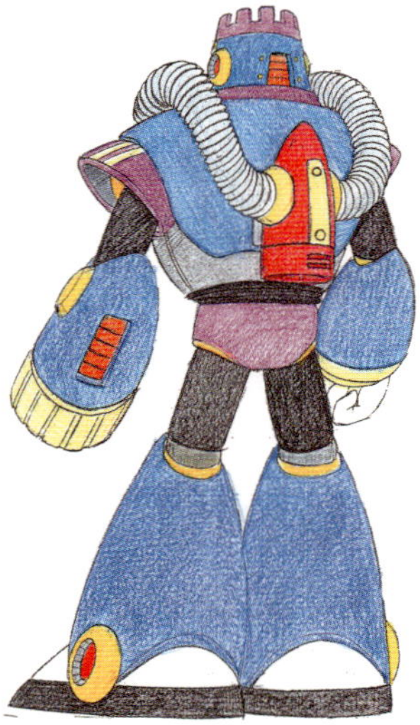

BURST MAN

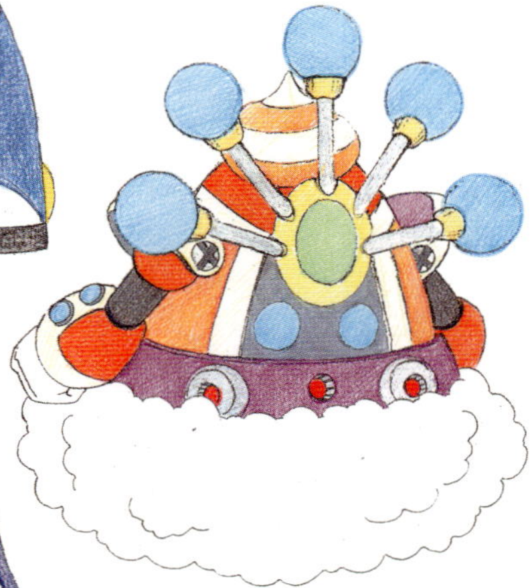

CLOUD MAN

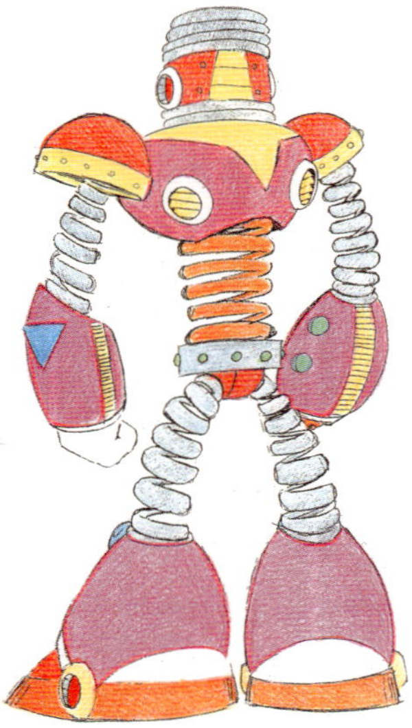

SPRING MAN

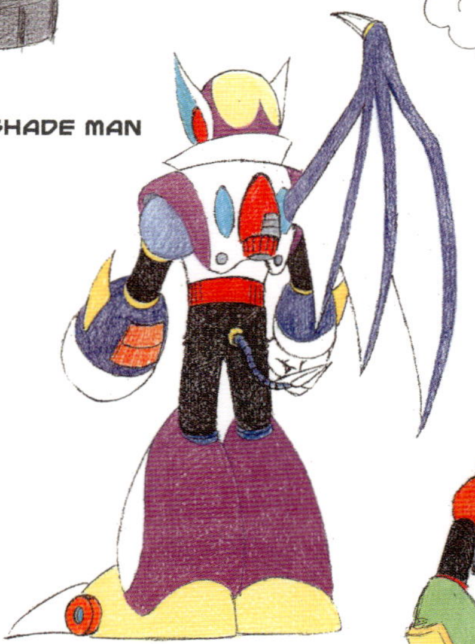

SHADE MAN

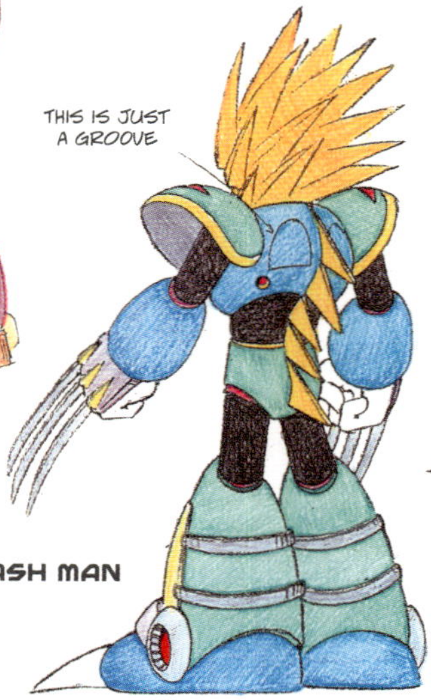

SLASH MAN

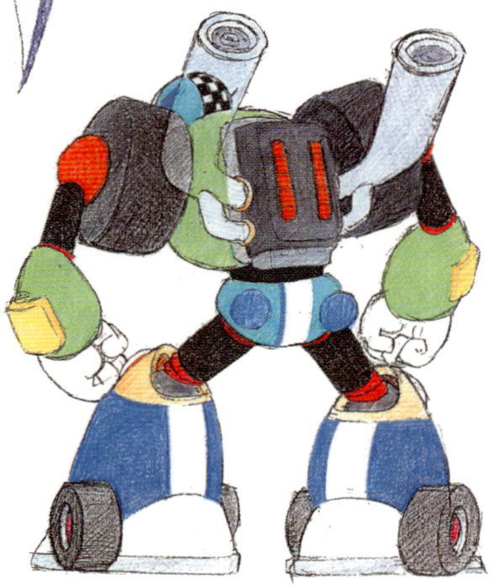

TURBO MAN

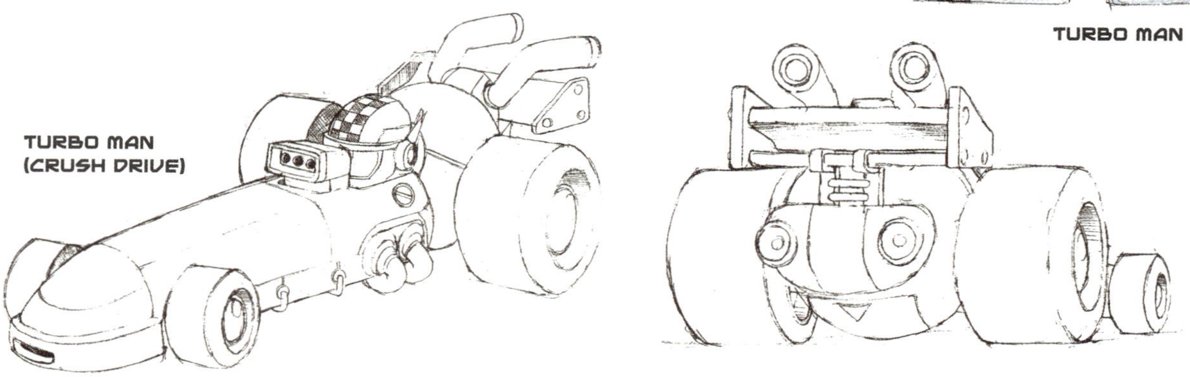

TURBO MAN (CRUSH DRIVE)

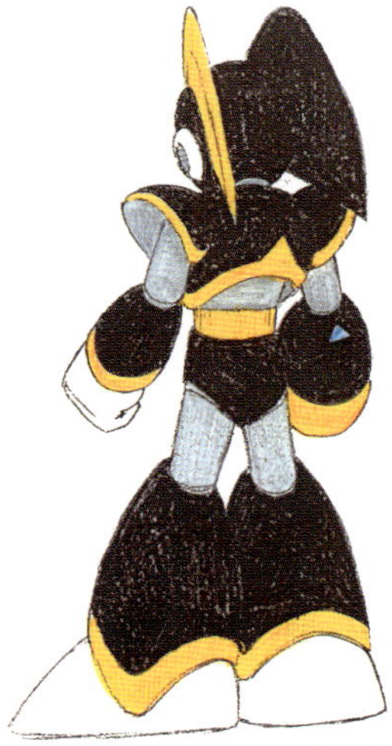

BASS

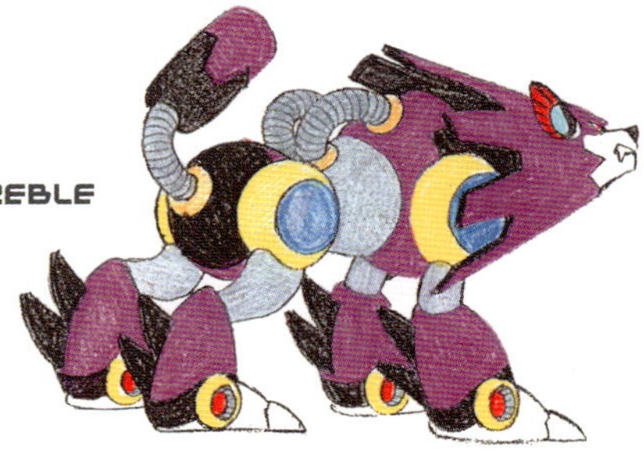

TREBLE

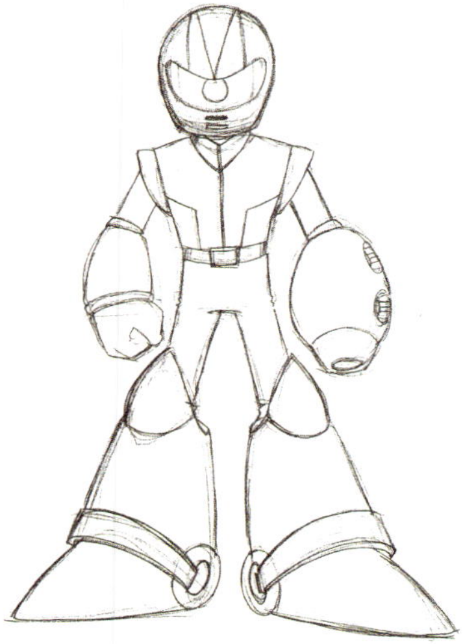

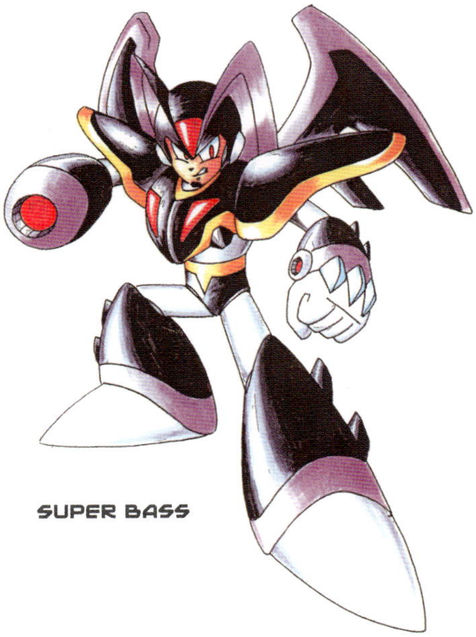

SUPER BASS

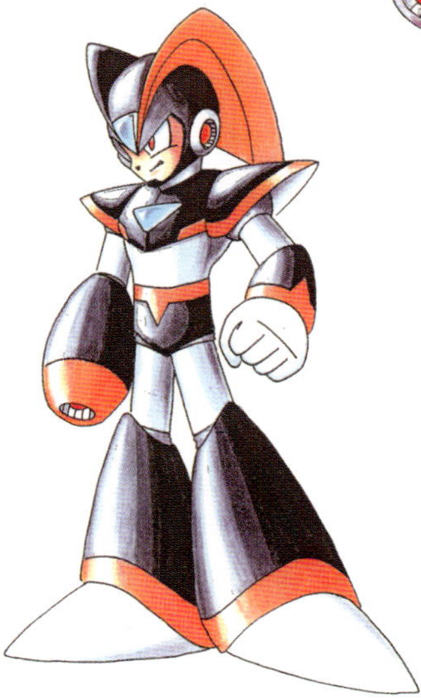

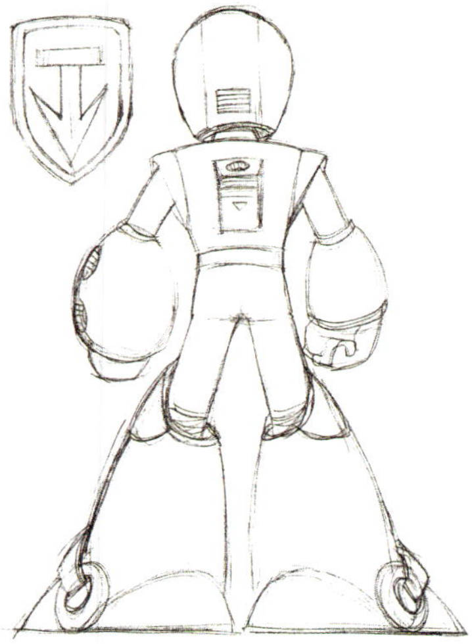

SNIPER JOE 01

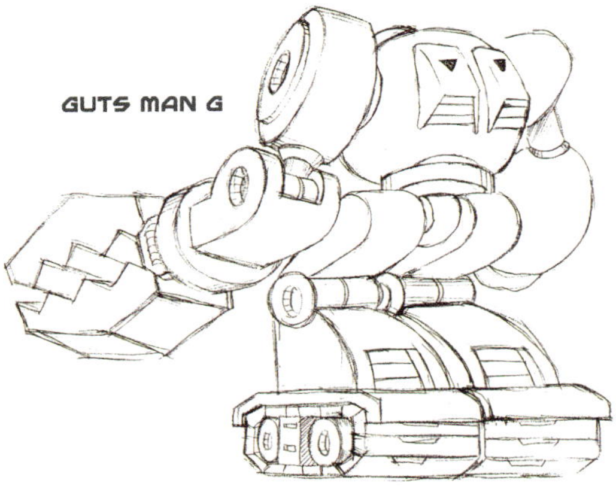

GUTS MAN G

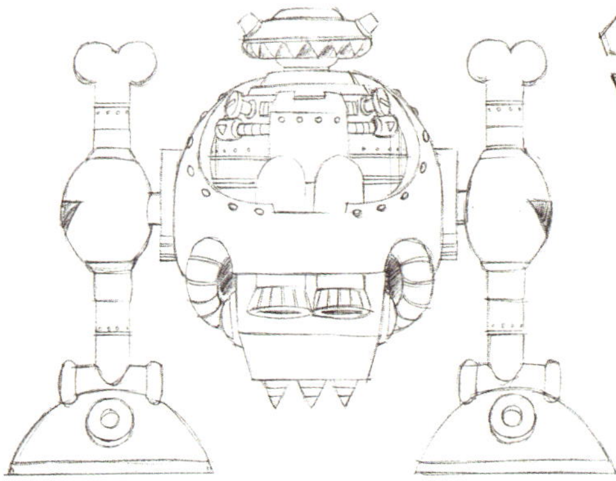

WILY MACHINE 7

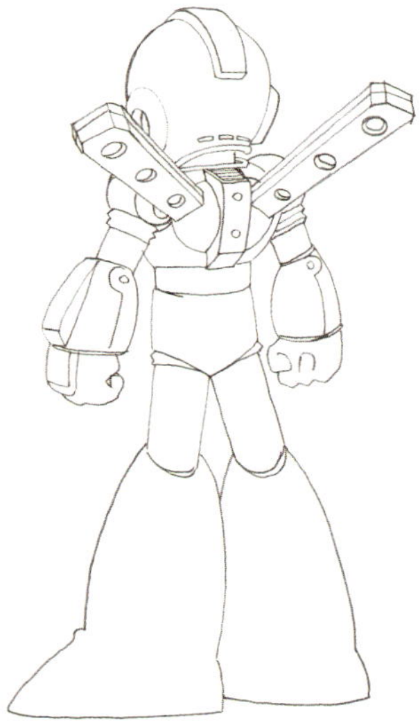

SUPER MEGA MAN

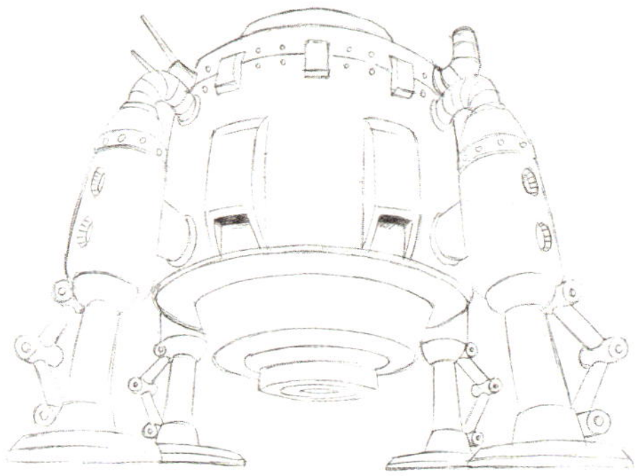

BIG EDDIE

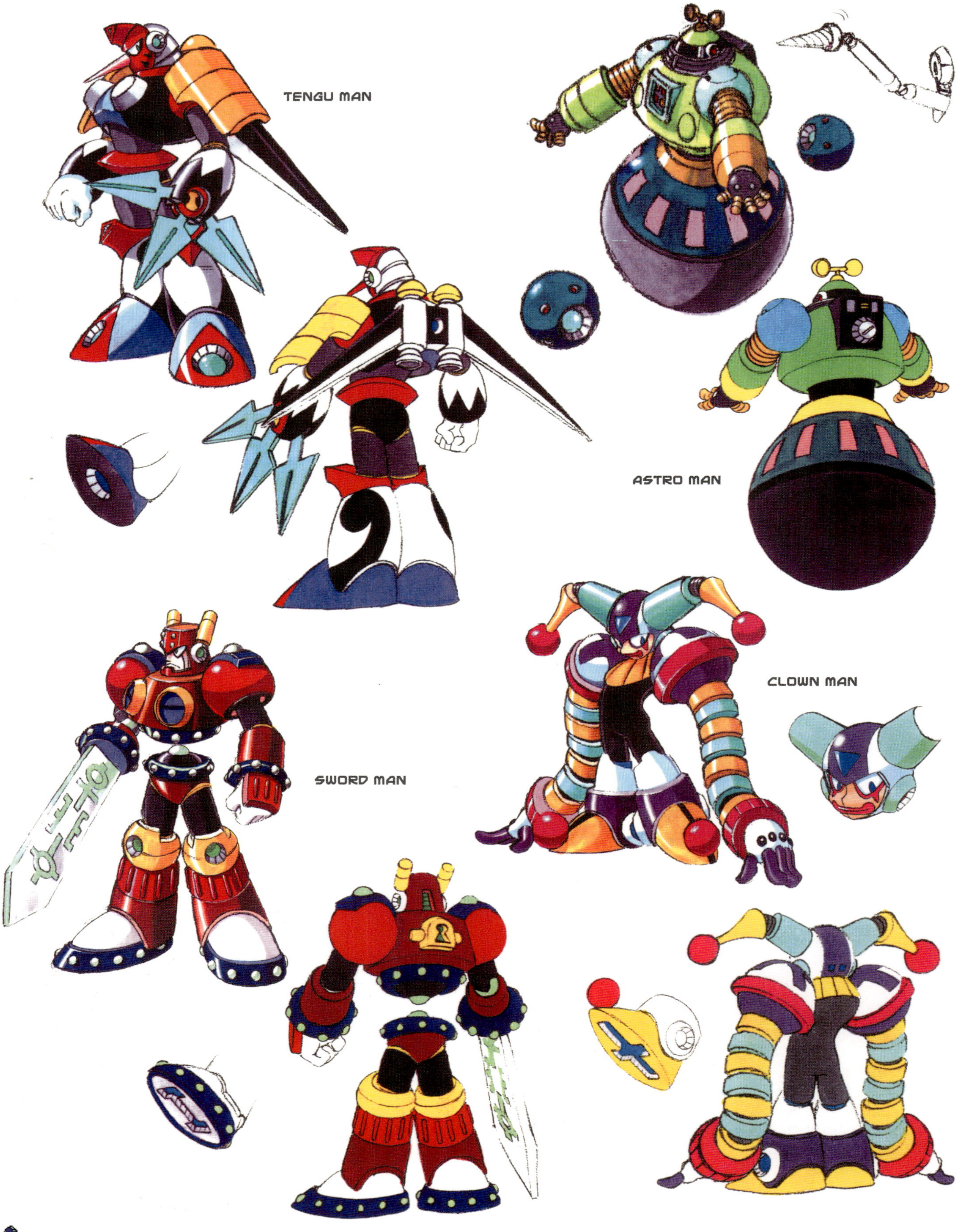
TENGU MAN
ASTRO MAN
CLOWN MAN
SWORD MAN

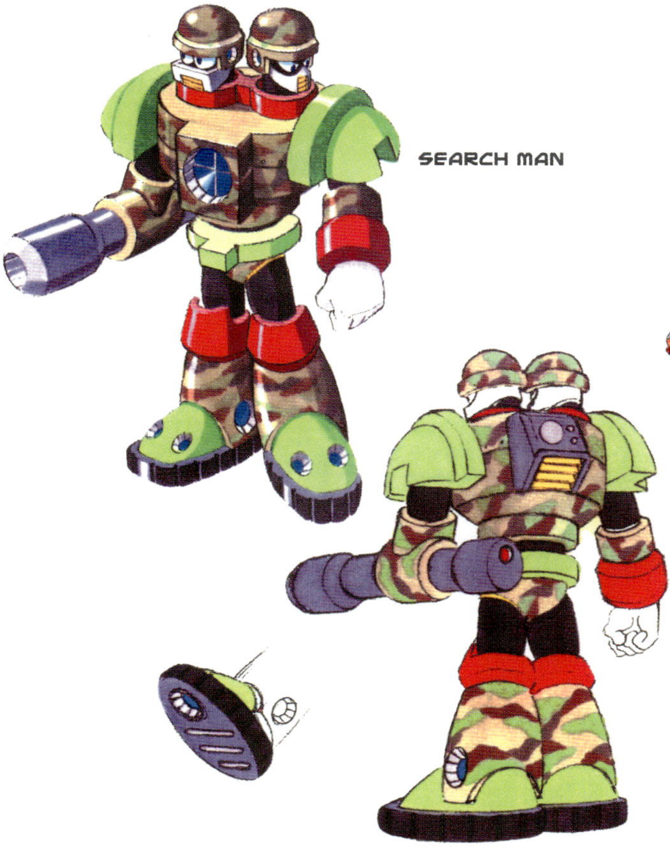

SEARCH MAN

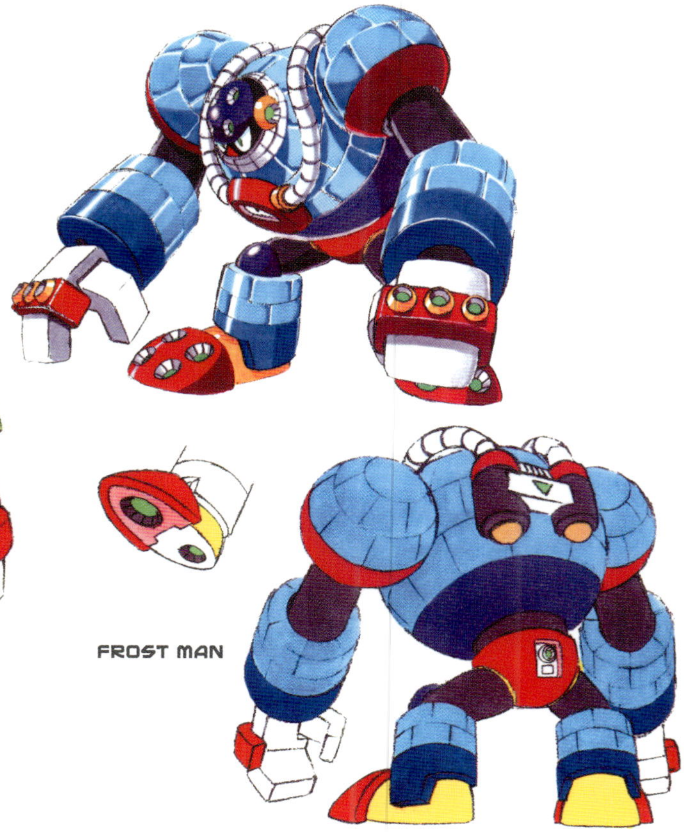

FROST MAN

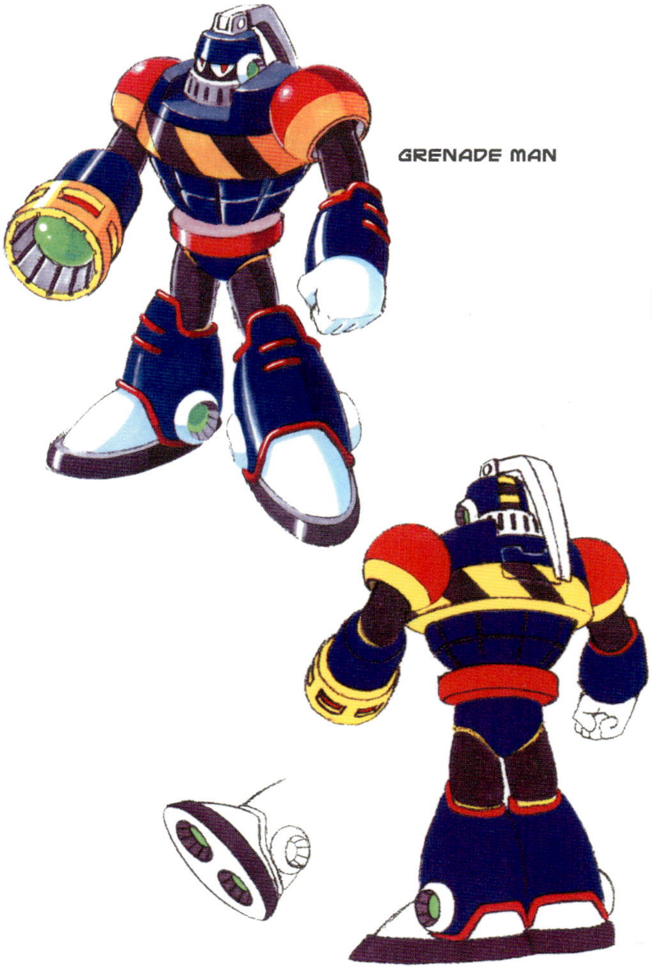

GRENADE MAN

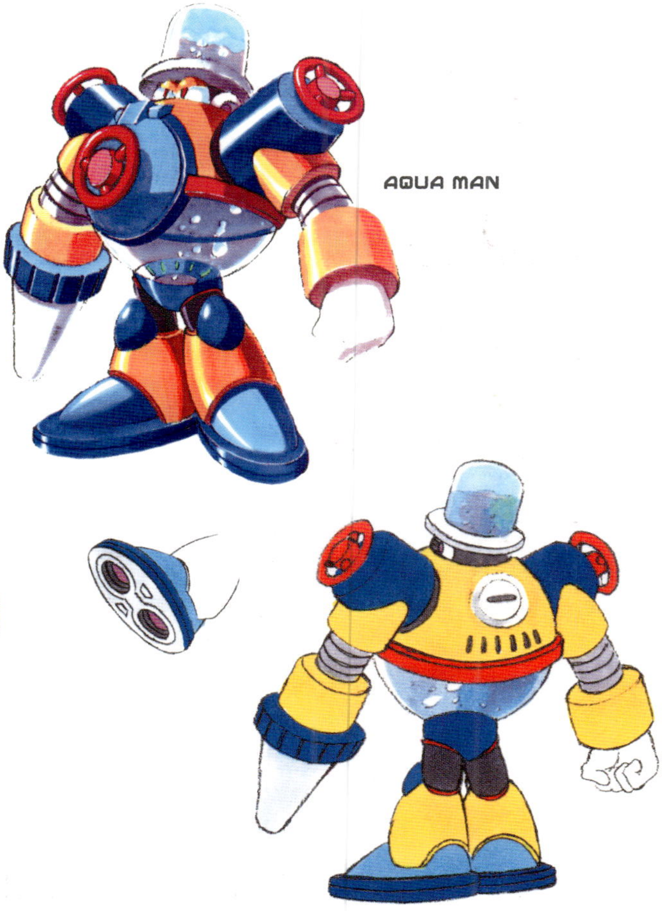

AQUA MAN

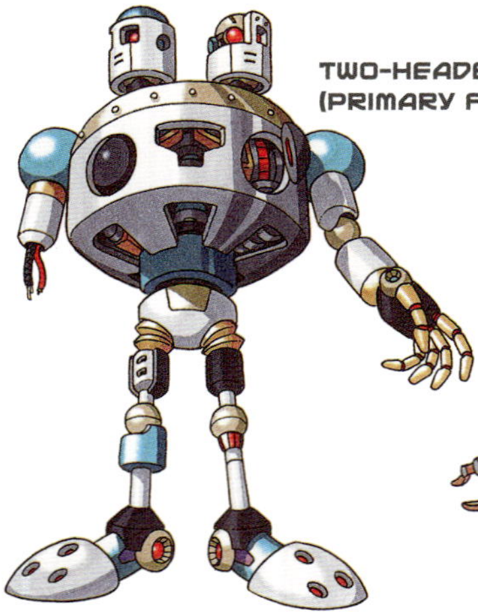

TWO-HEADED ROBOT
(PRIMARY FORM)

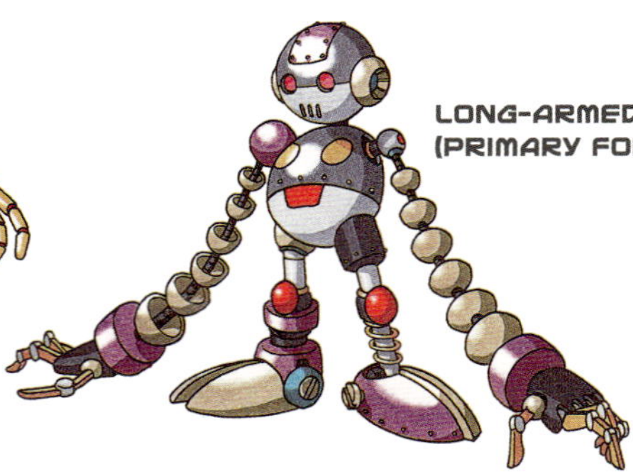

LONG-ARMED ROBOT
(PRIMARY FORM)

KATANA ROBOT
(PRIMARY FORM)

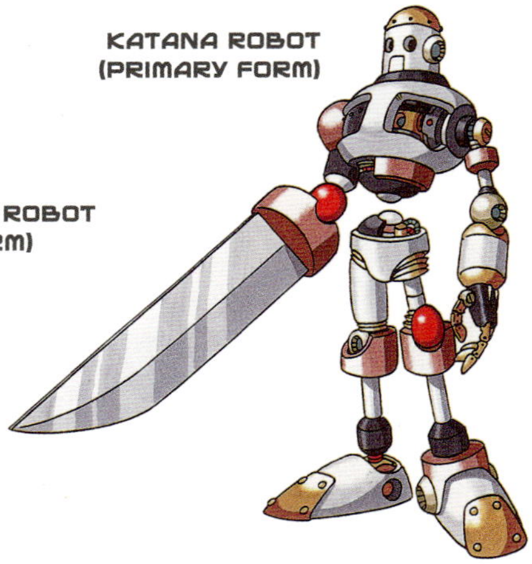

The boss character submission contest for "Mega Man 8" was run a little differently from the other ones. Capcom provided the basic forms seen above, and the public sent in ideas based on these forms. This method resulted in Sword Man, Clown Man, and Search Man. Tengu Man and Astro Man, to the right, were designed by Capcom first and published in magazines.

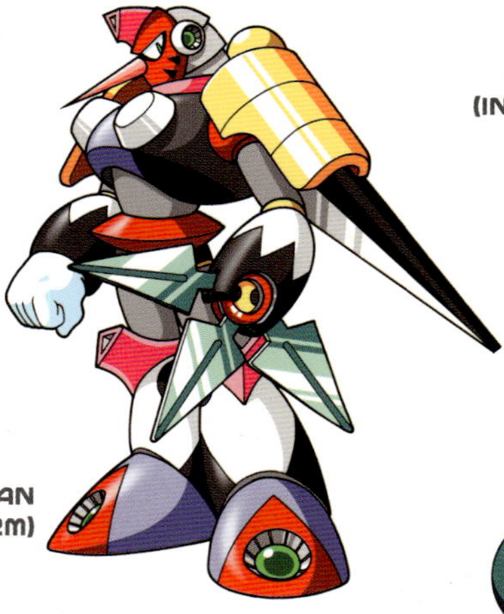

TENGU MAN
(INITIAL FORM)

ASTRO MAN
(INITIAL FORM)

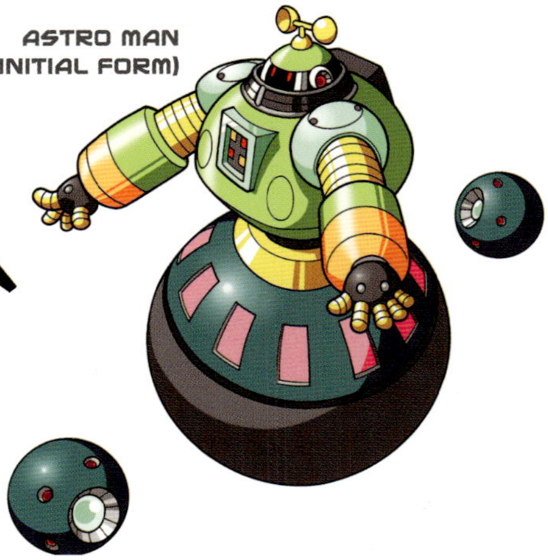

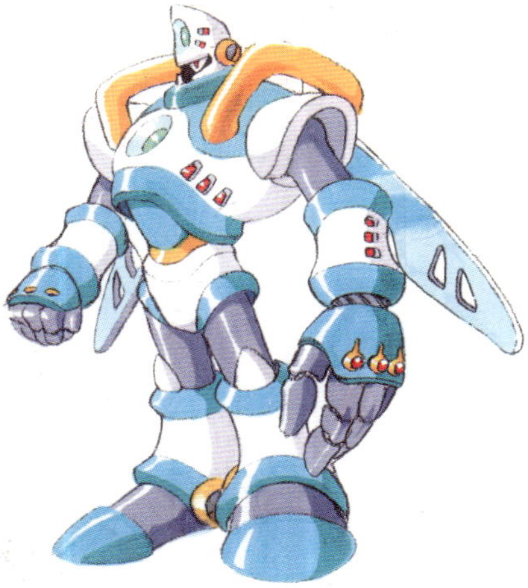

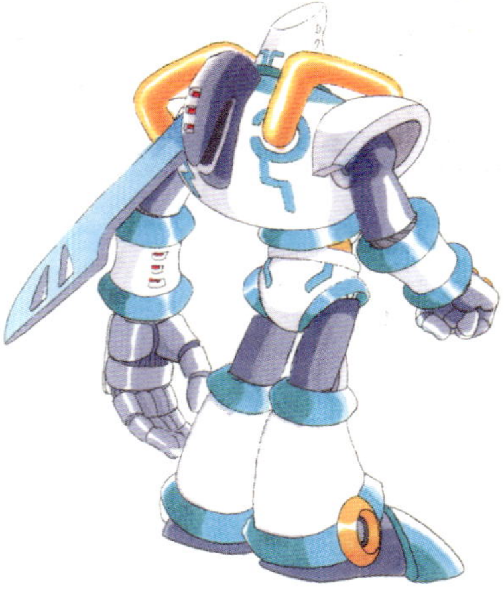

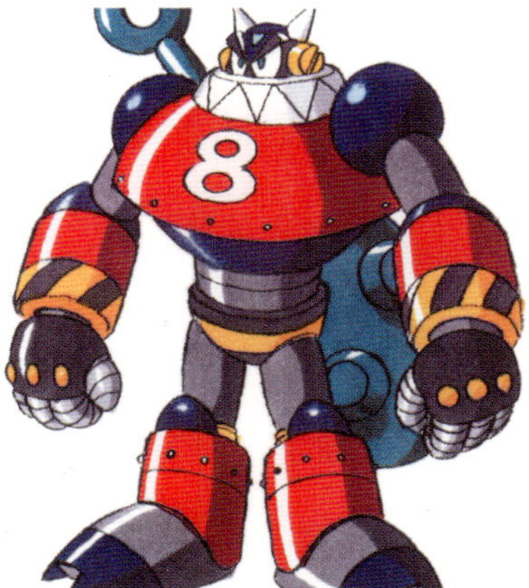

UNUSED
CHARACTER

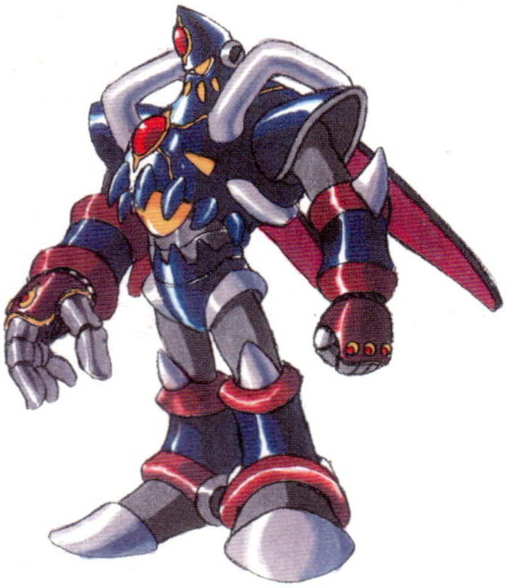

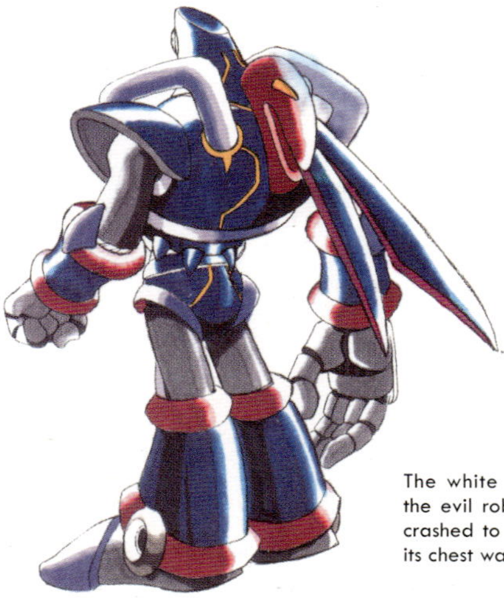

The white robot is Duo, and the black robot is the evil robot, in their original forms before they crashed to Earth. The robot with the giant "8" on its chest was never used in any of the games.

MINI CHARACTERS

Illustrations done for the labels of PlayStation and Sega Saturn versions.

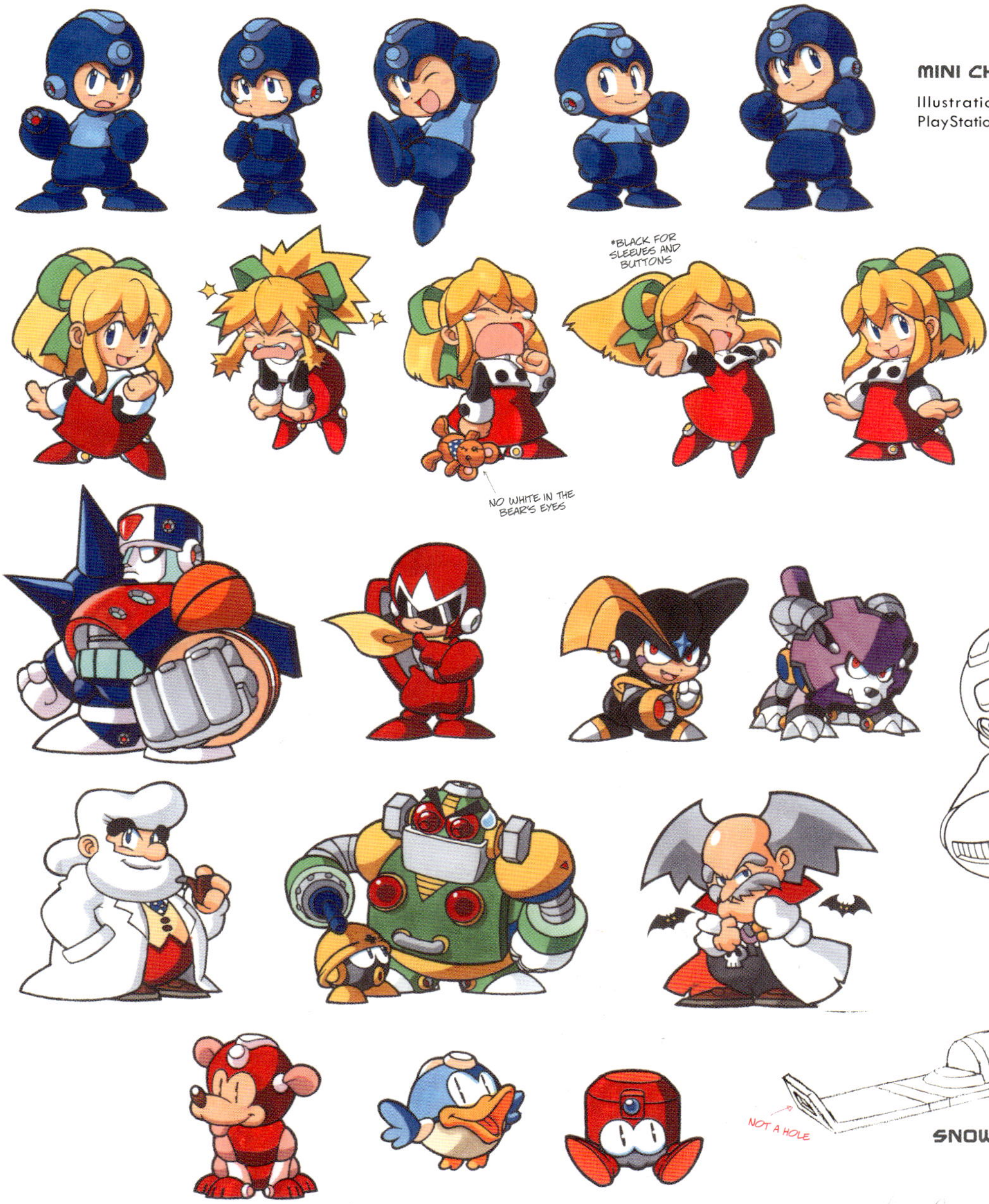

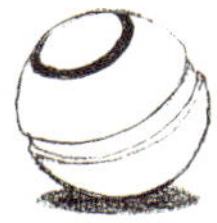

MEGA BALL

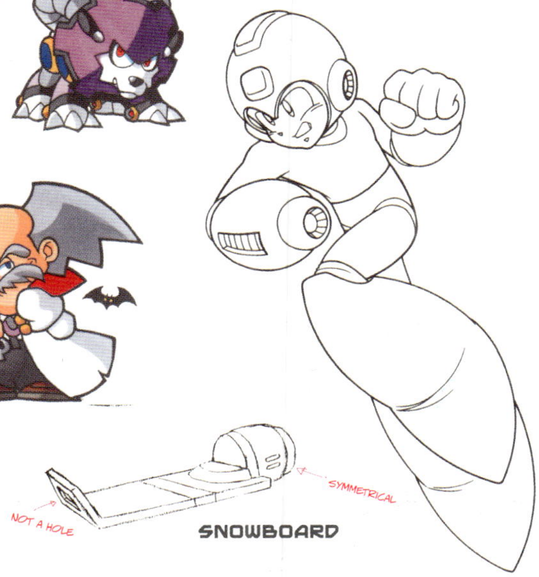

SNOWBOARD

ILLUSTRATION FOR TELEPHONE CARD (FAN CLUB GIFT)

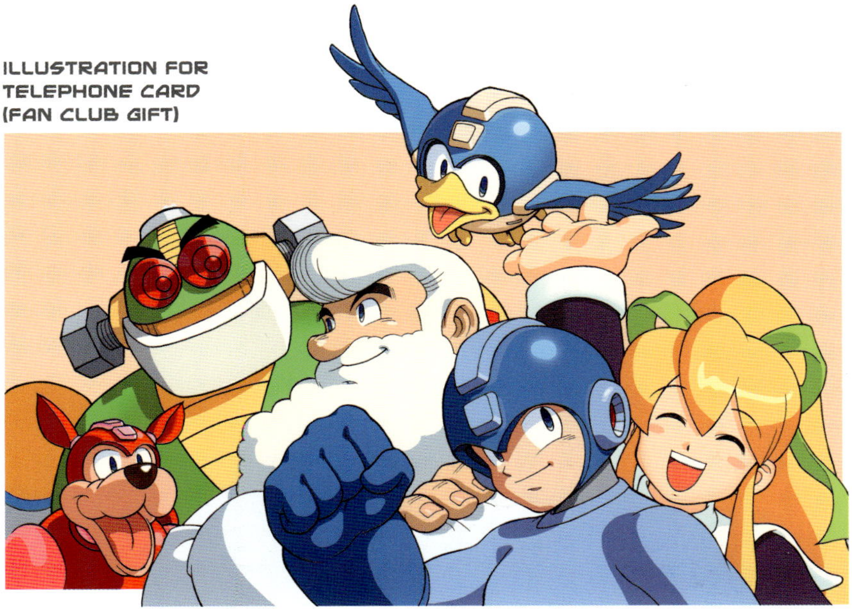

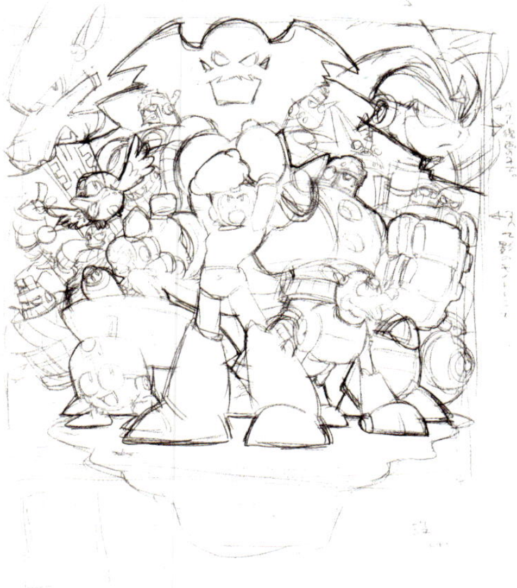

Early design for a main illustration. This one was rejected because Inafune said they should make the boss characters submitted by their users bigger so that they draw more attention.

"MEGA MAN 7" INSTRUCTIONAL COMICS

TEACH ME, DR. LIGHT!

MAKE A PLAN WHEN ENGAGING THE ENEMY

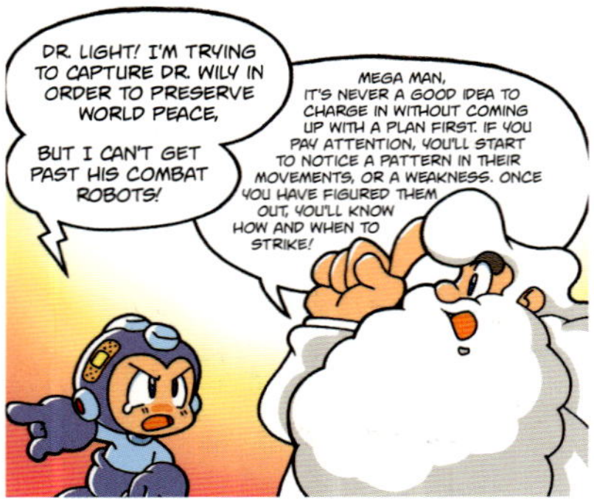

RUSH IS THERE FOR YOU

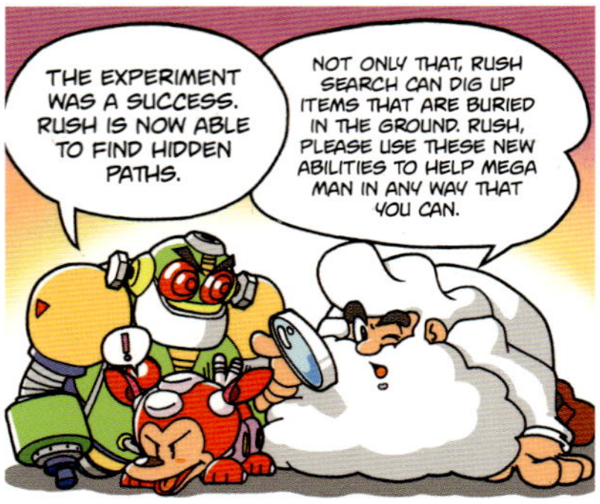

FIND THE R-U-S-H PLATES

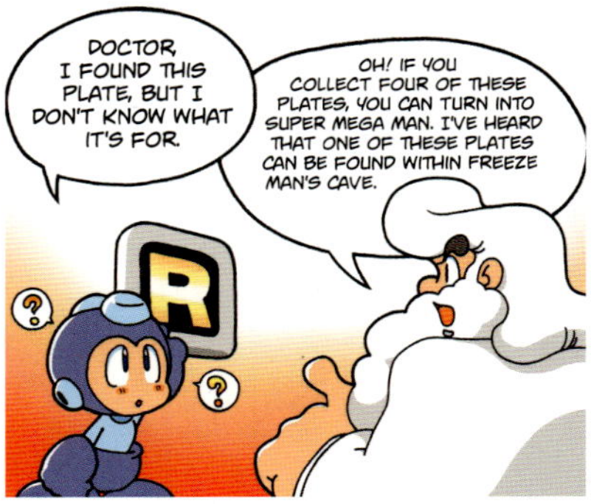

COLLECT LOTS OF BOLTS

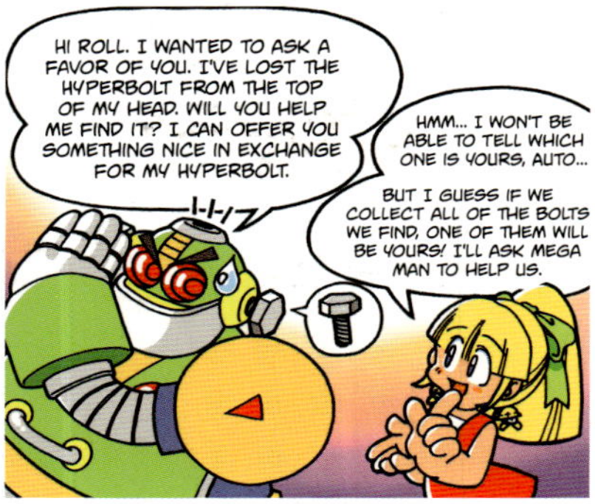

FIND HIDDEN PATHS

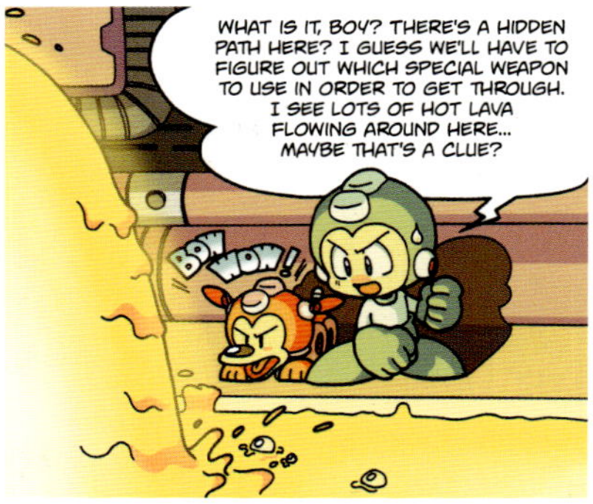

WHERE'S BEAT...?

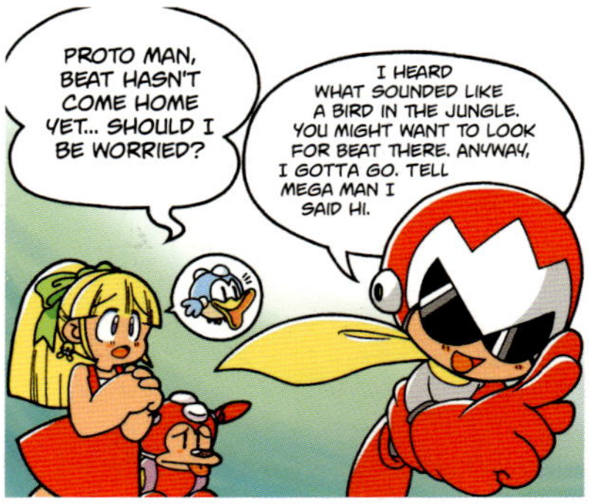

MEET UP WITH PROTO MAN

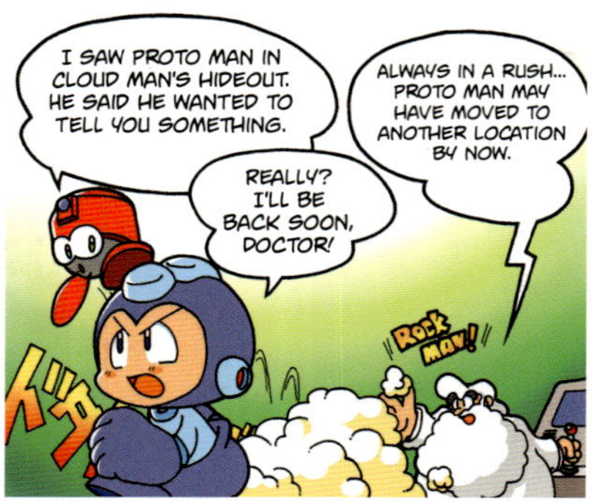

USE YOUR SPECIAL WEAPONS AGAINST ENEMIES

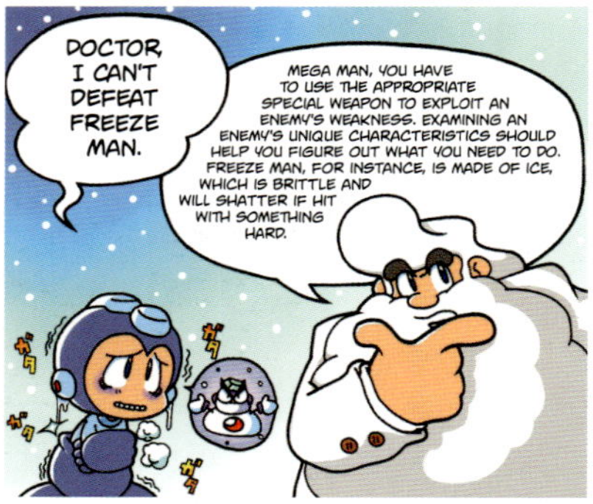

DON'T GIVE UP, MEGA MAN!!

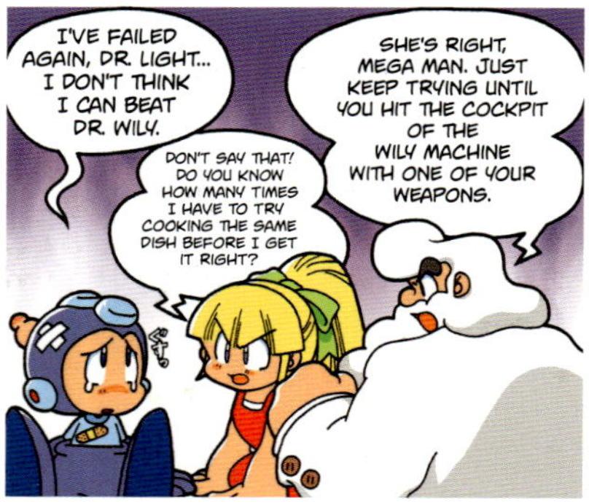

USE YOUR SPECIAL WEAPONS IN ALL SORTS OF PLACES

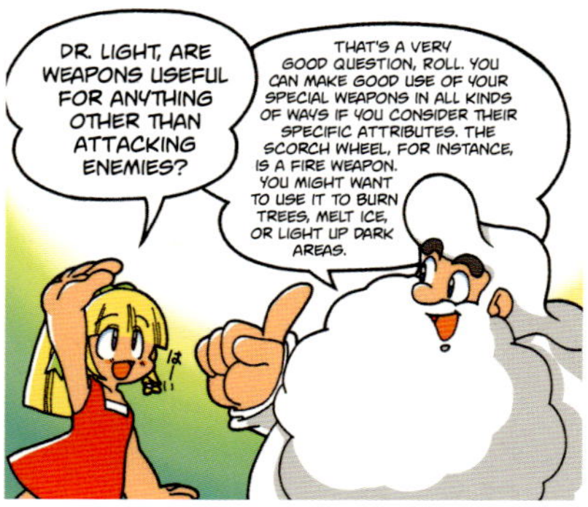

"MEGA MAN 8" INSTRUCTIONAL COMICS

PROFESSOR AUTO (?) EXPLAINS EVERYTHING YOU NEED TO KNOW!

WATCH FOR SIGNS

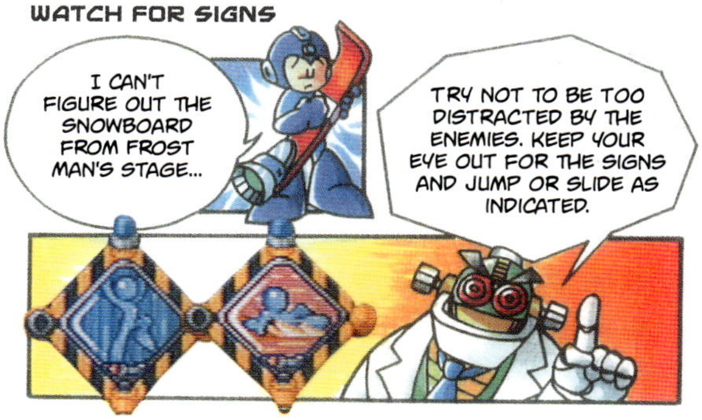

WHAT IS A "?" BOX

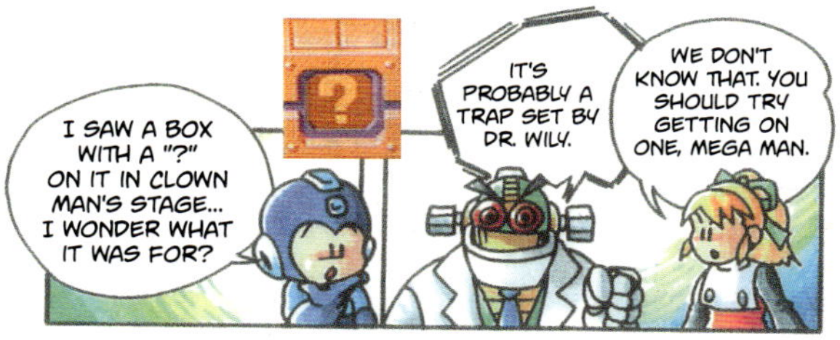

STEP ON THE SWITCHES

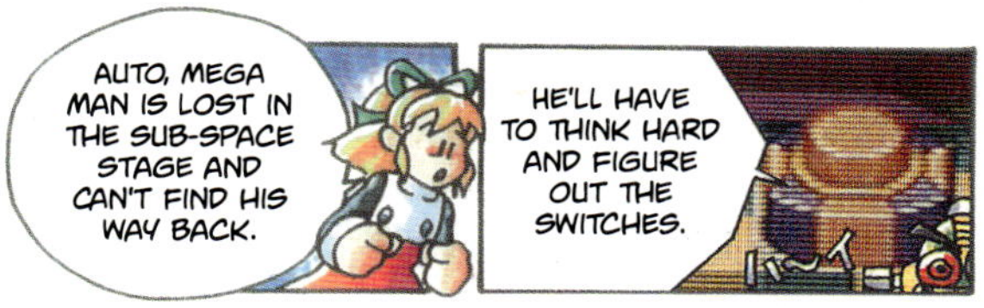

TRY SWINGING

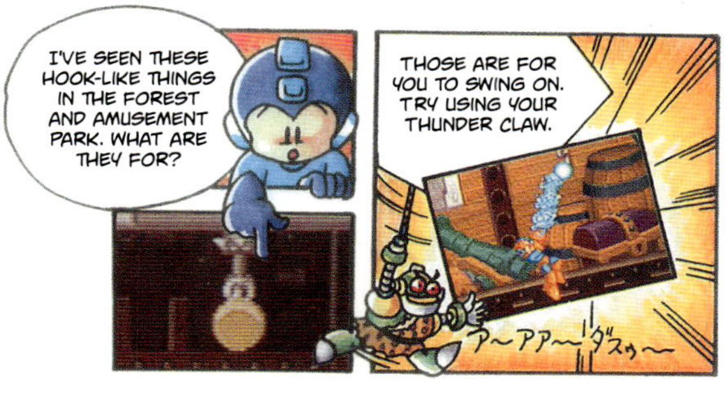

FIGURE OUT THE BOSS' WEAKNESS

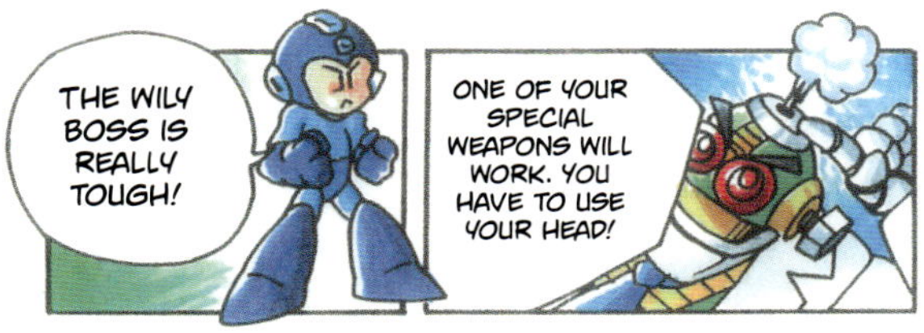

YOU CAN DESTROY IT

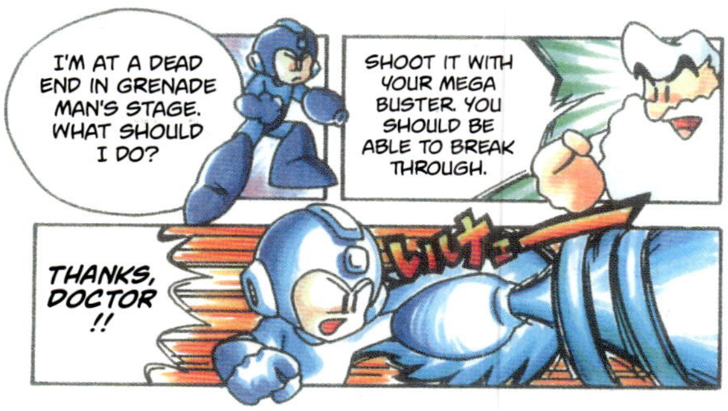

LOOK FOR HINTS

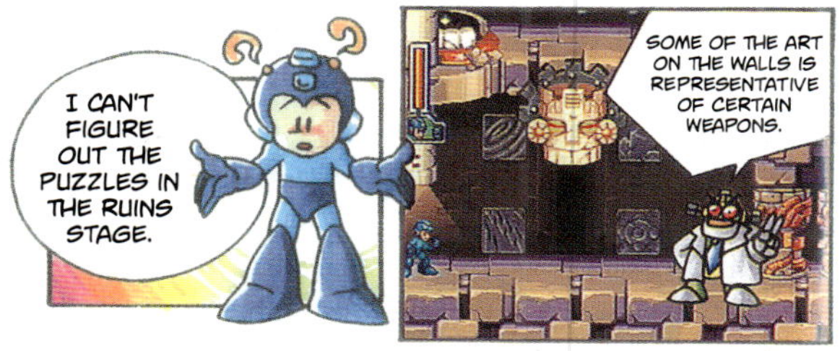

USE YOUR SPECIAL WEAPONS APPROPRIATELY!

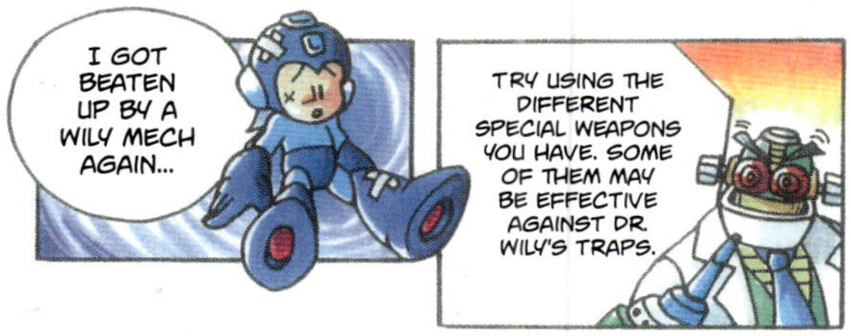

WHEN YOU'RE IN TROUBLE, CALL RUSH

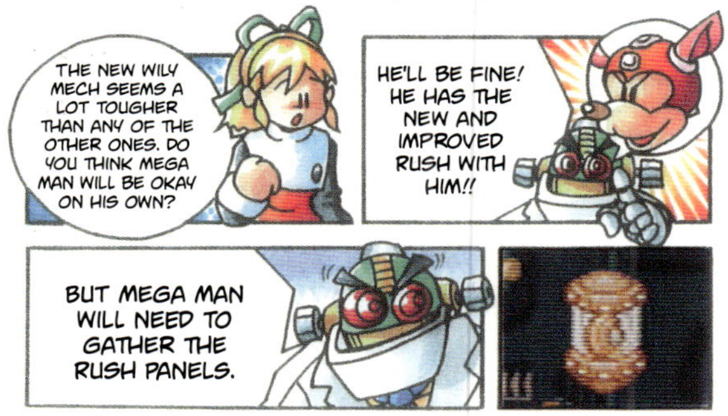

COLLECT BOLTS TO POWER UP

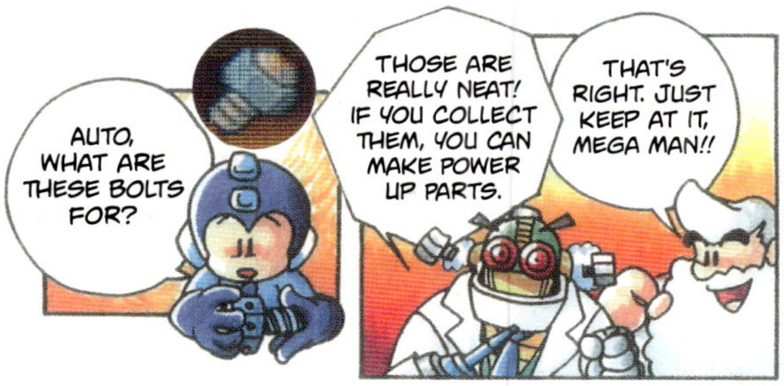

MEGA MAN & BASS

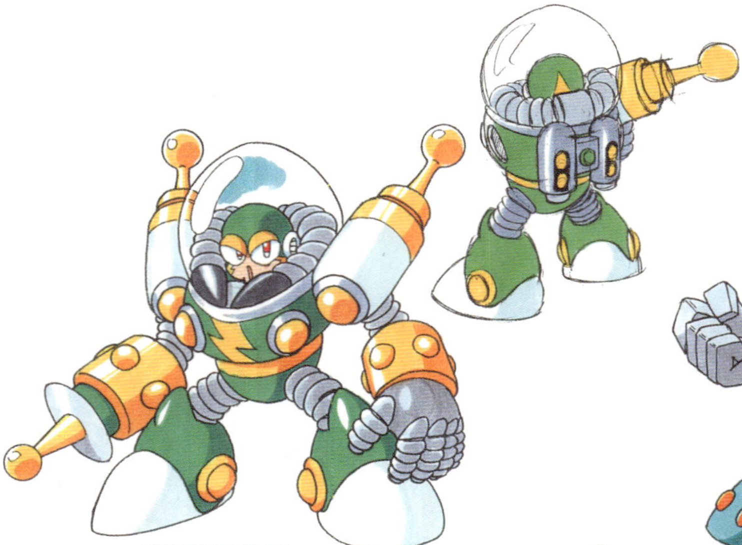

DYNAMO MAN

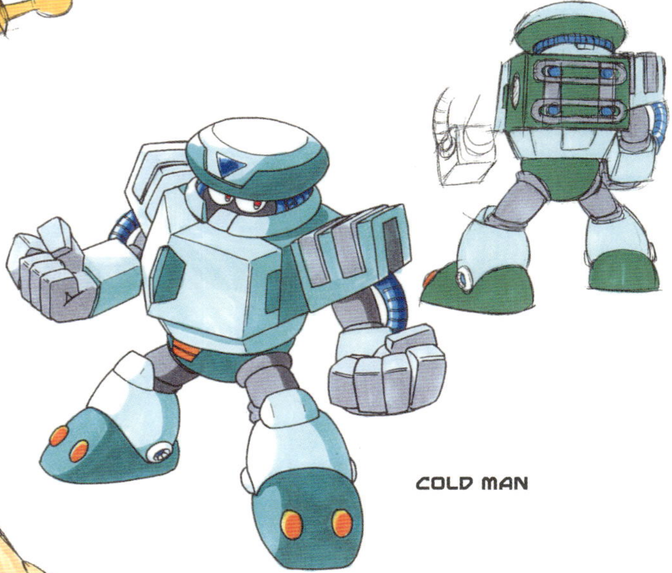

COLD MAN

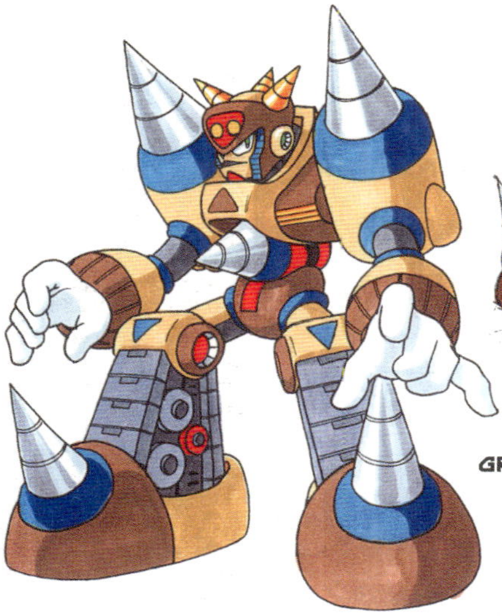

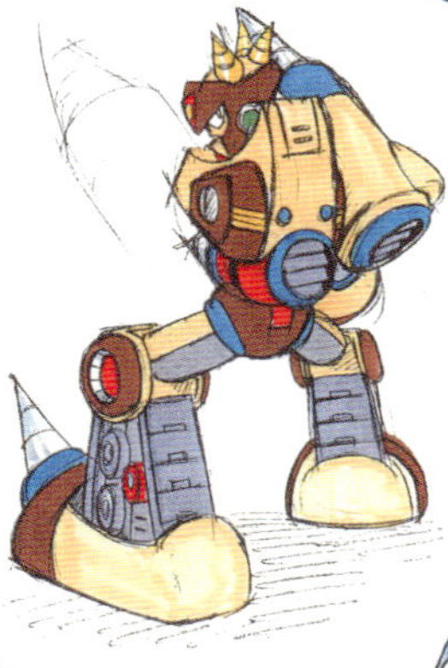

GROUND MAN

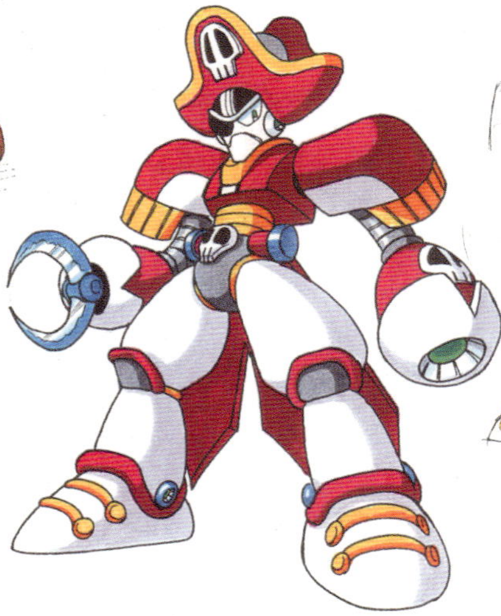

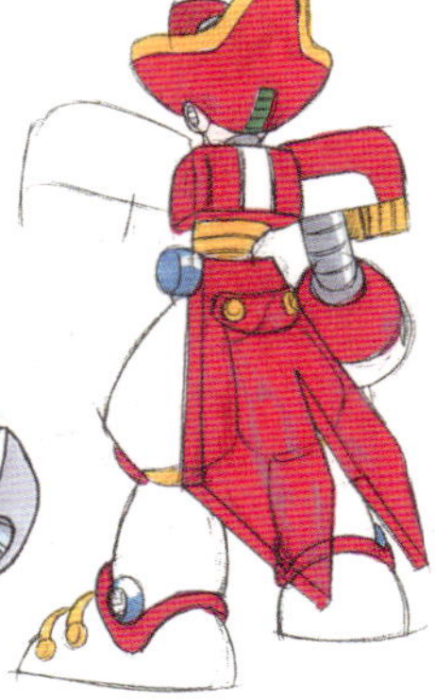

PIRATE MAN

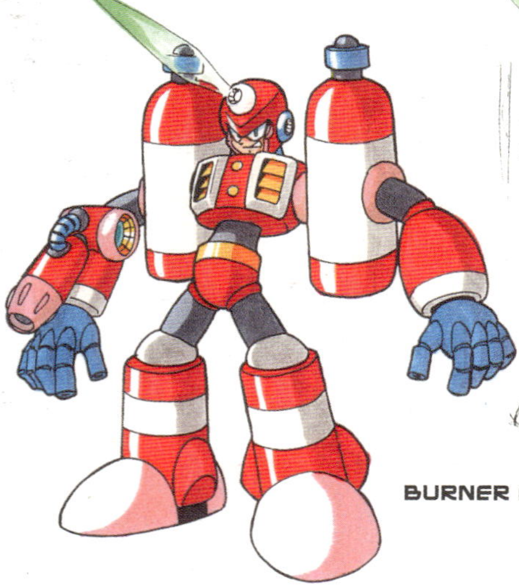

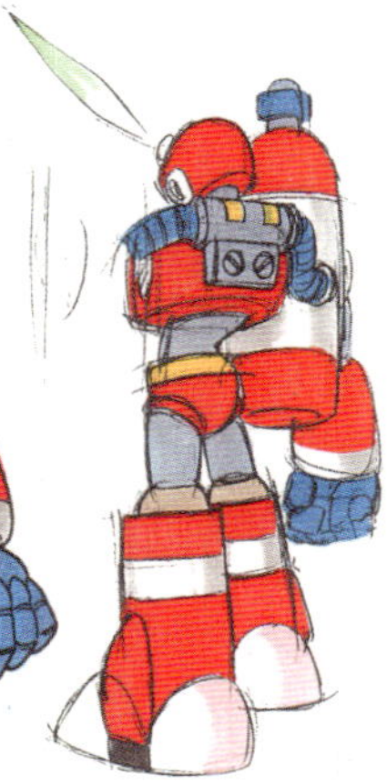

BURNER MAN

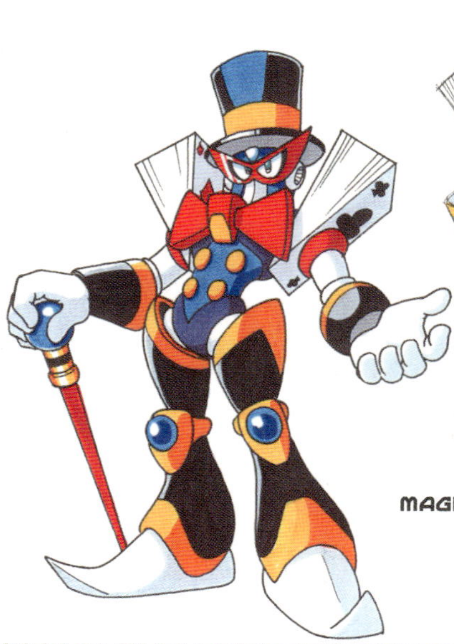

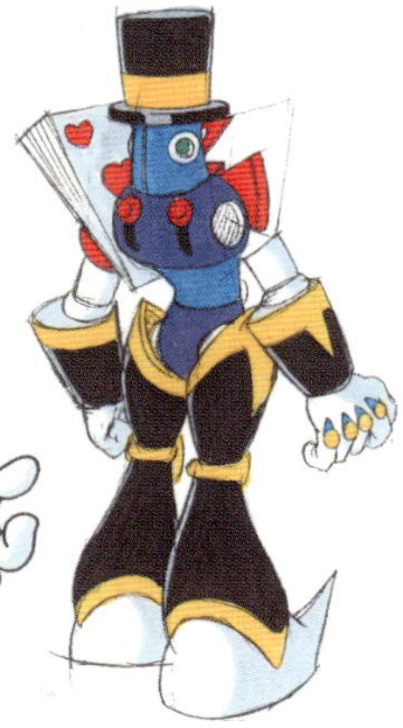

MAGIC MAN

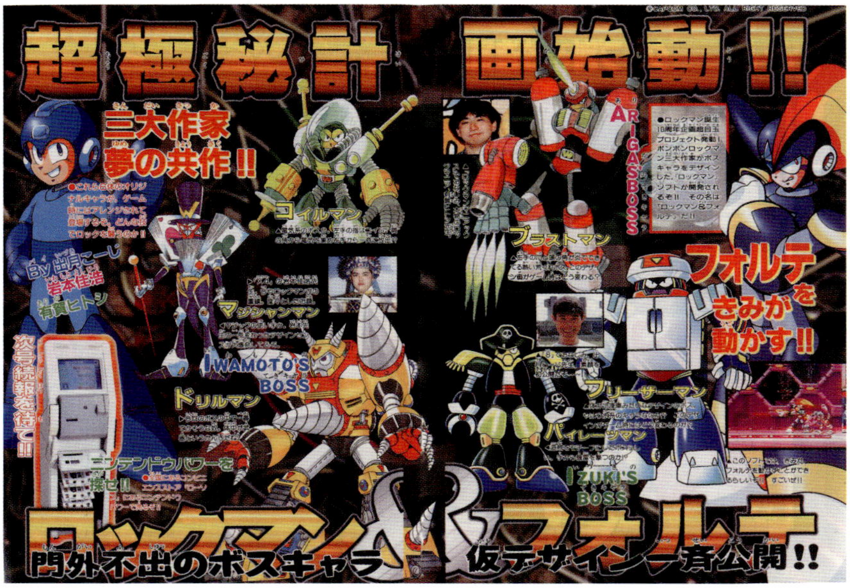

The teaser page from Kodansha's "BonBon Comics." Some of the bosses' names are different than they are in the final product.

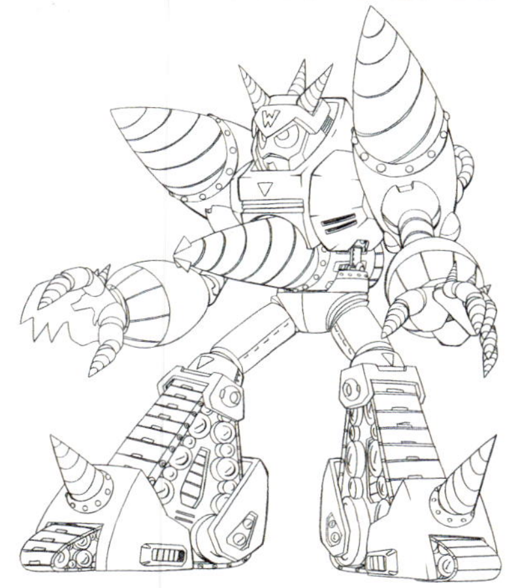

YOSHIHIRO IWAMOTO "DRILL MAN" CONCEPT ART

"All I was told was that the character should have a drill theme. I didn't even bother thinking up a name while I designed him. When I submitted his design, he was named Drill Man. I know there was already a Drill Man in '4.' (laughs)" (Iwamoto)

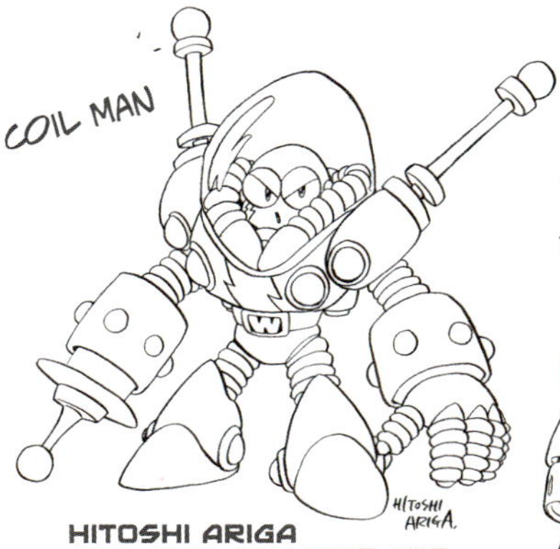

HITOSHI ARIGA COIL MAN CONCEPT ART

"With my specifications like 'the burner goes out when he dies,' and 'his canopy explodes when he dies,' I realize now that I probably ruined a lot of people's days with my annoyingly detailed depictions of my obnoxiously picky character concepts. (laughs)" (Ariga)

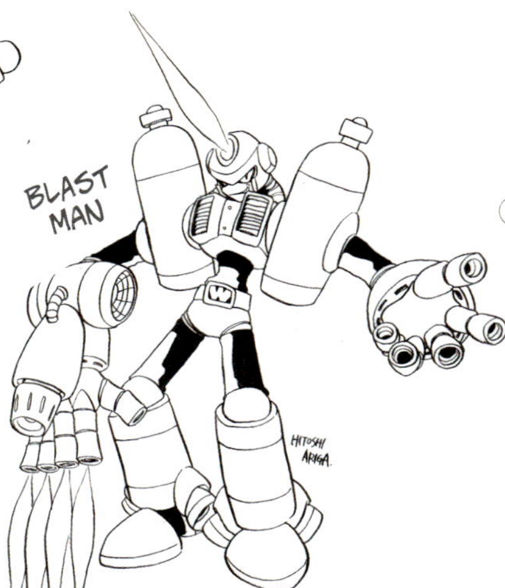

HITOSHI ARIGA BLAST MAN CONCEPT ART

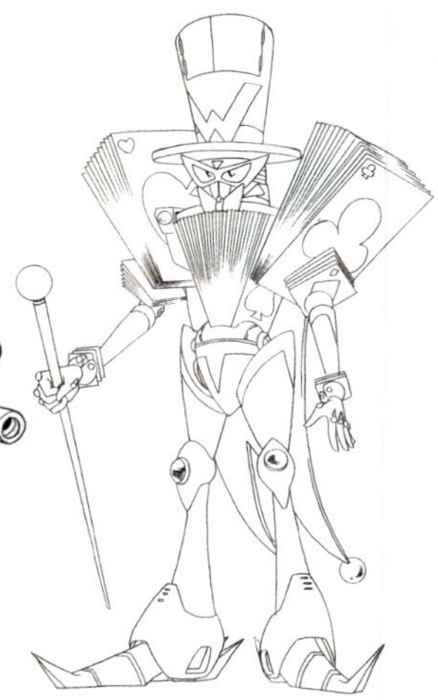

YOSHIHIRO IWAMOTO MAGICIAN MAN CONCEPT ART

"When I submitted my design to Capcom, I added a few last minute notes like, 'you could have doves fly out of his hat or something.'" (Iwamoto)

MEMORIES OF PIRATE MAN

"A pirate? A robot pirate? Well, you've all seen the result of that idea. I'm actually a little embarrassed that he turned out to be... well, a pirate... robot. I even seriously considered putting a parrot on his shoulder, but I managed to control myself. Still, now that I look back on it, I'm not sure it would have been such a bad idea." (Izuki)

MEMORIES OF "FREEZER MAN"

"Yeah, he's pretty much a fridge with legs! ... how embarrassing. When I tried to think of a freezer as an enemy, I saw a character whose chest would open up and perform an icy attack. I decided to make the torso square so that people would be able to easily identify it. I was so happy when I saw that they made him much better than I expected in the actual game." (Izuki)

"ROCKMAN & FORTE: CHALLENGERS FROM THE FUTURE" (WONDERSWAN)

Released by Bandai in 1999. Mega Man and Bass head to the dimension controlled by Rockman Shadow. The original boss characters for this project were: Dangan Man, Komusou Man, Aircon Man, Konro Man, Clock Man, and Compass Man. Compass Man and Rockman Shadow are friends.

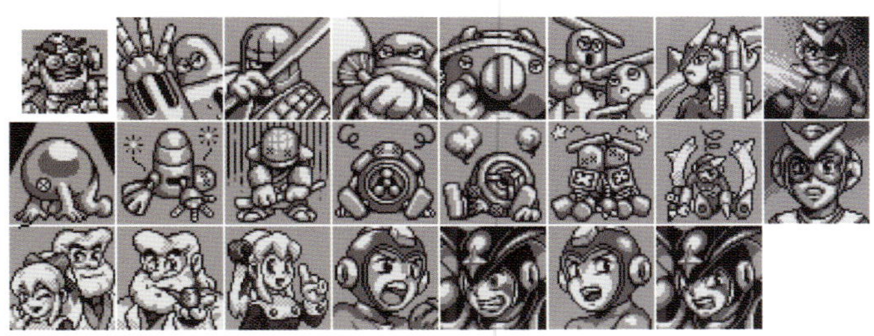

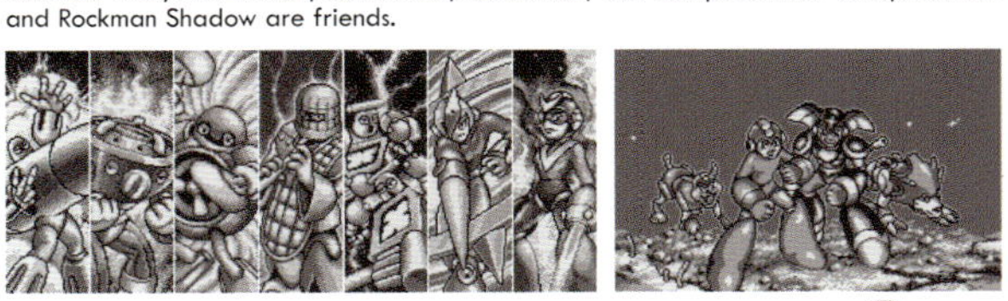

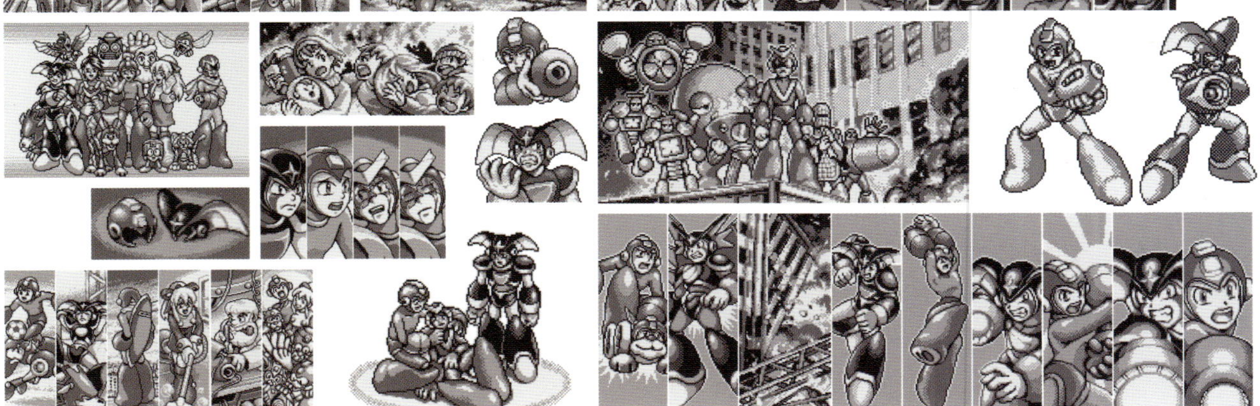

MEGA MAN: POWERED UP

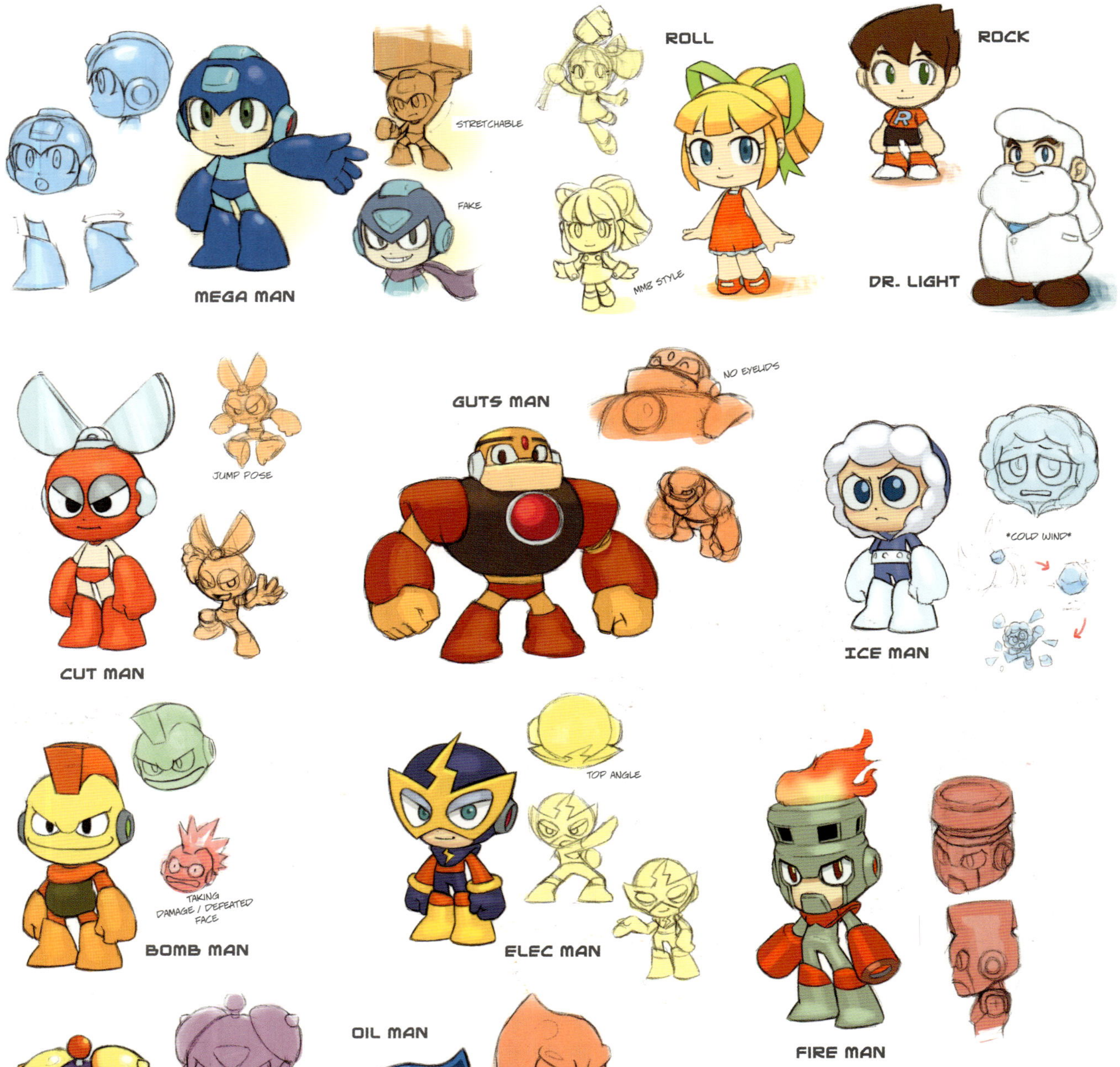

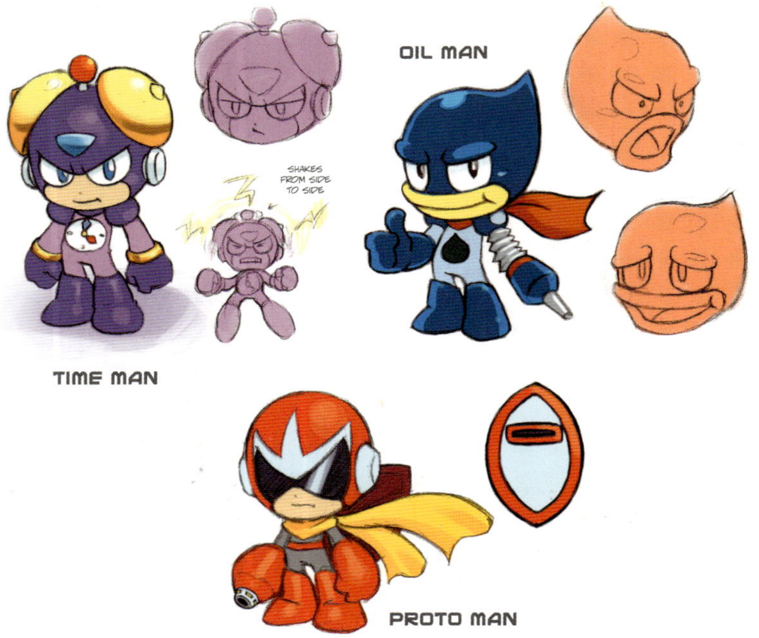

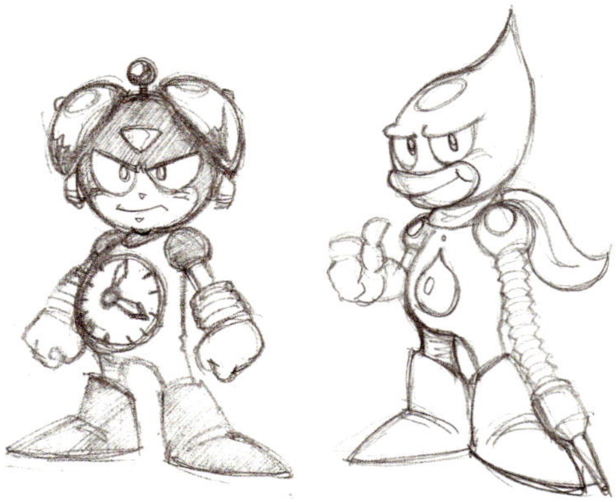

Inafune's rough sketches of Time Man and Oil Man.

DR. WILY

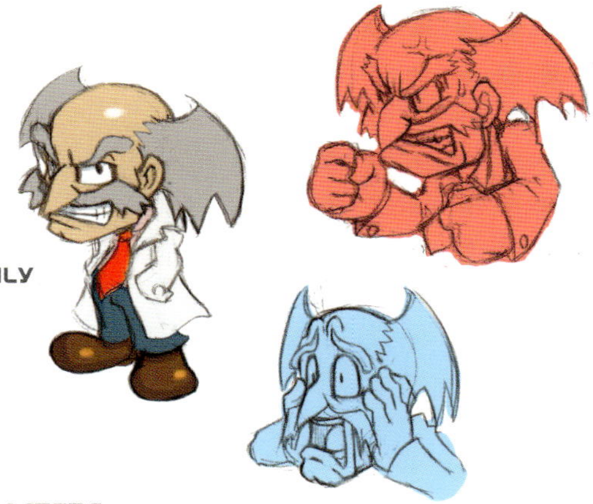

SNIPER JOE

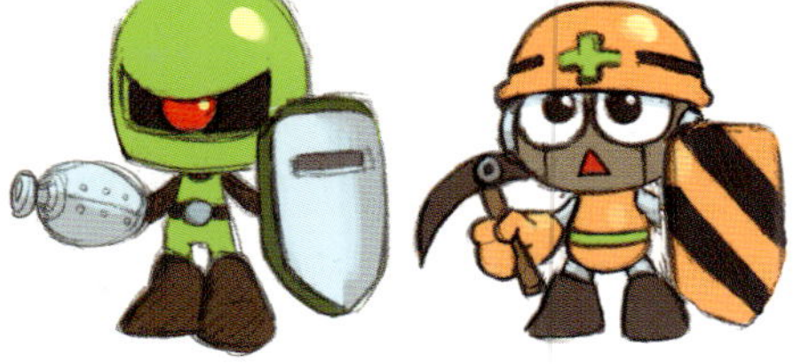

ENEMY CHARACTERS

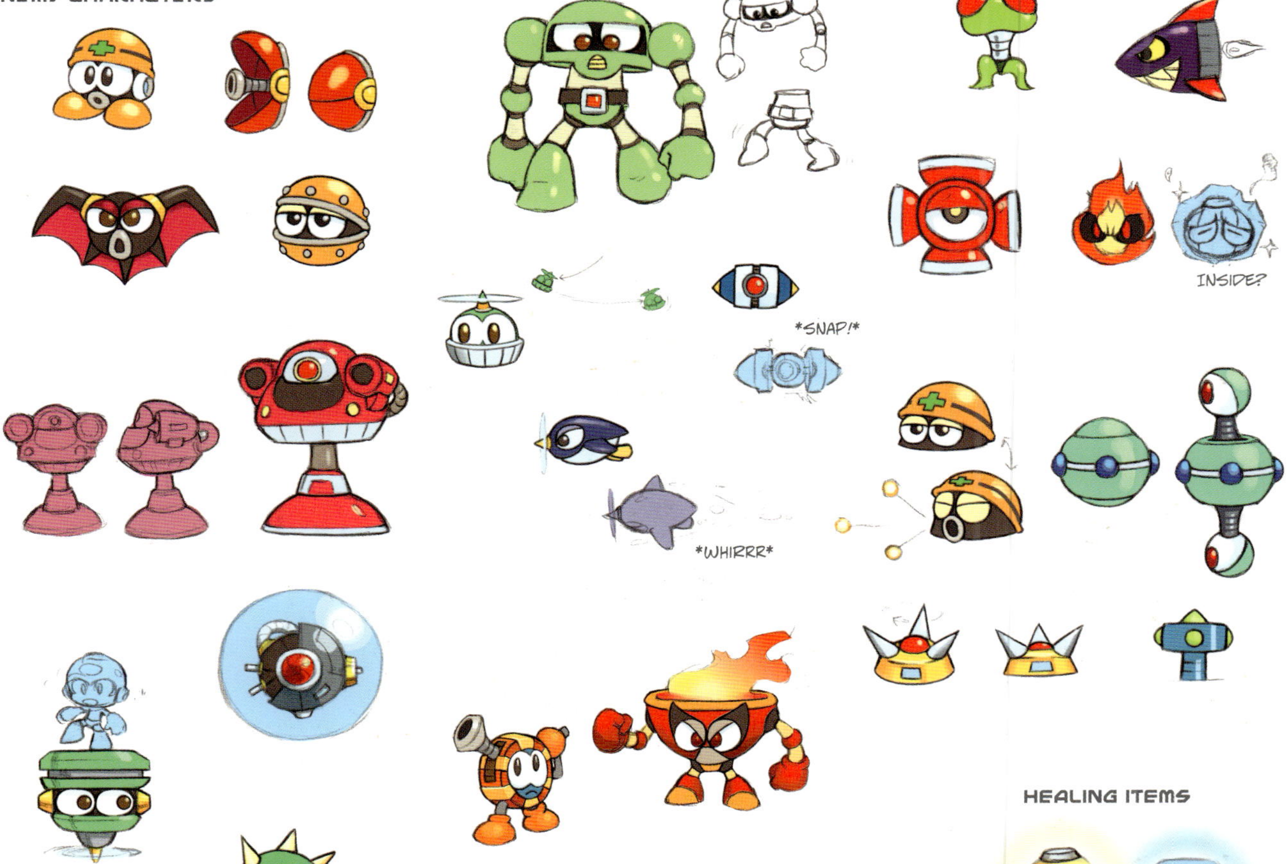

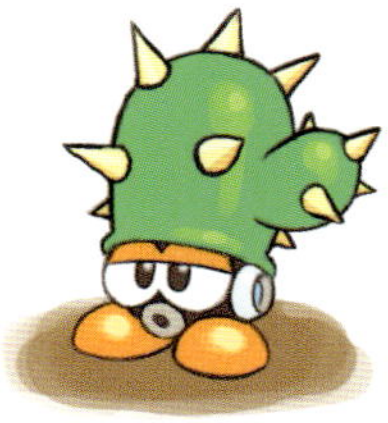

SABOTTOL

These Metalls were assigned to the desert regions. Unable to bear the heat, they decided to wear cacti on their heads to keep them cool. They don't have much in the way of work ethic, so they tend to wander off a lot.

HEALING ITEMS

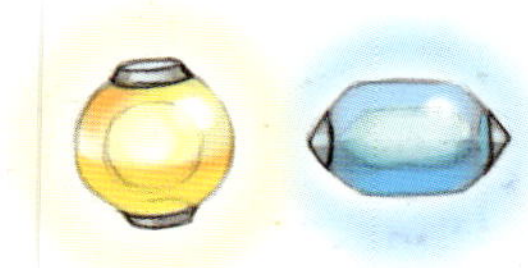

WILY MACHINE

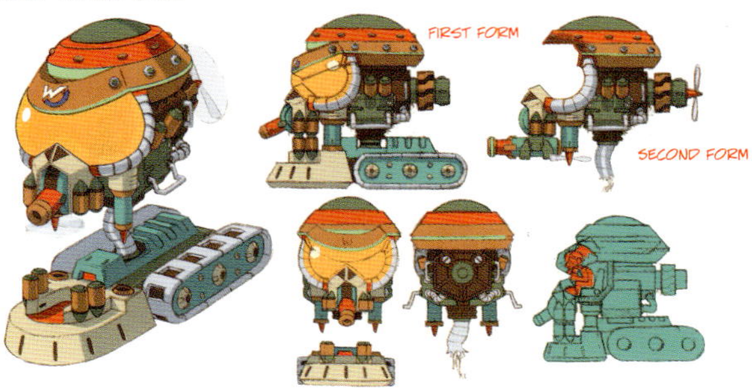

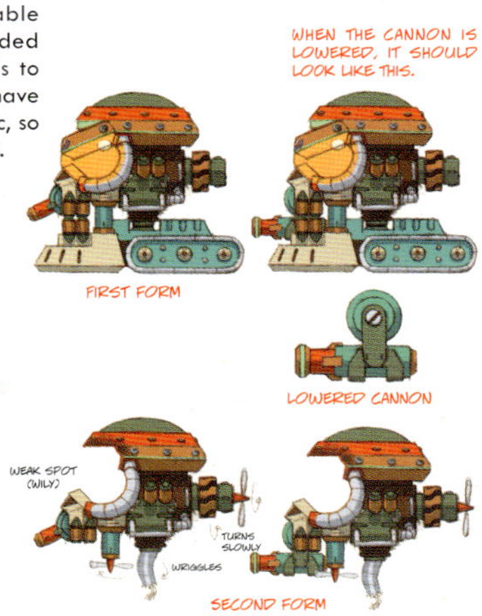

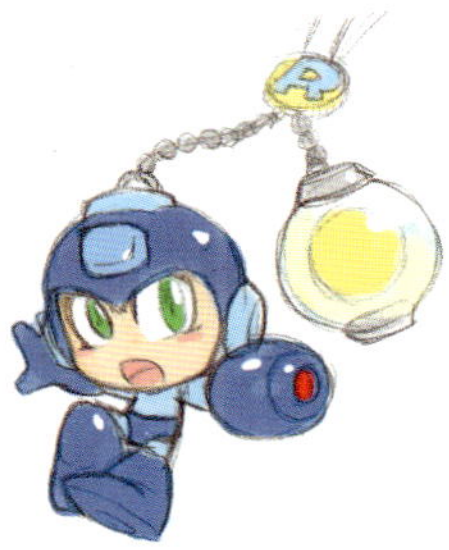

SPECIAL KEYHOLDER

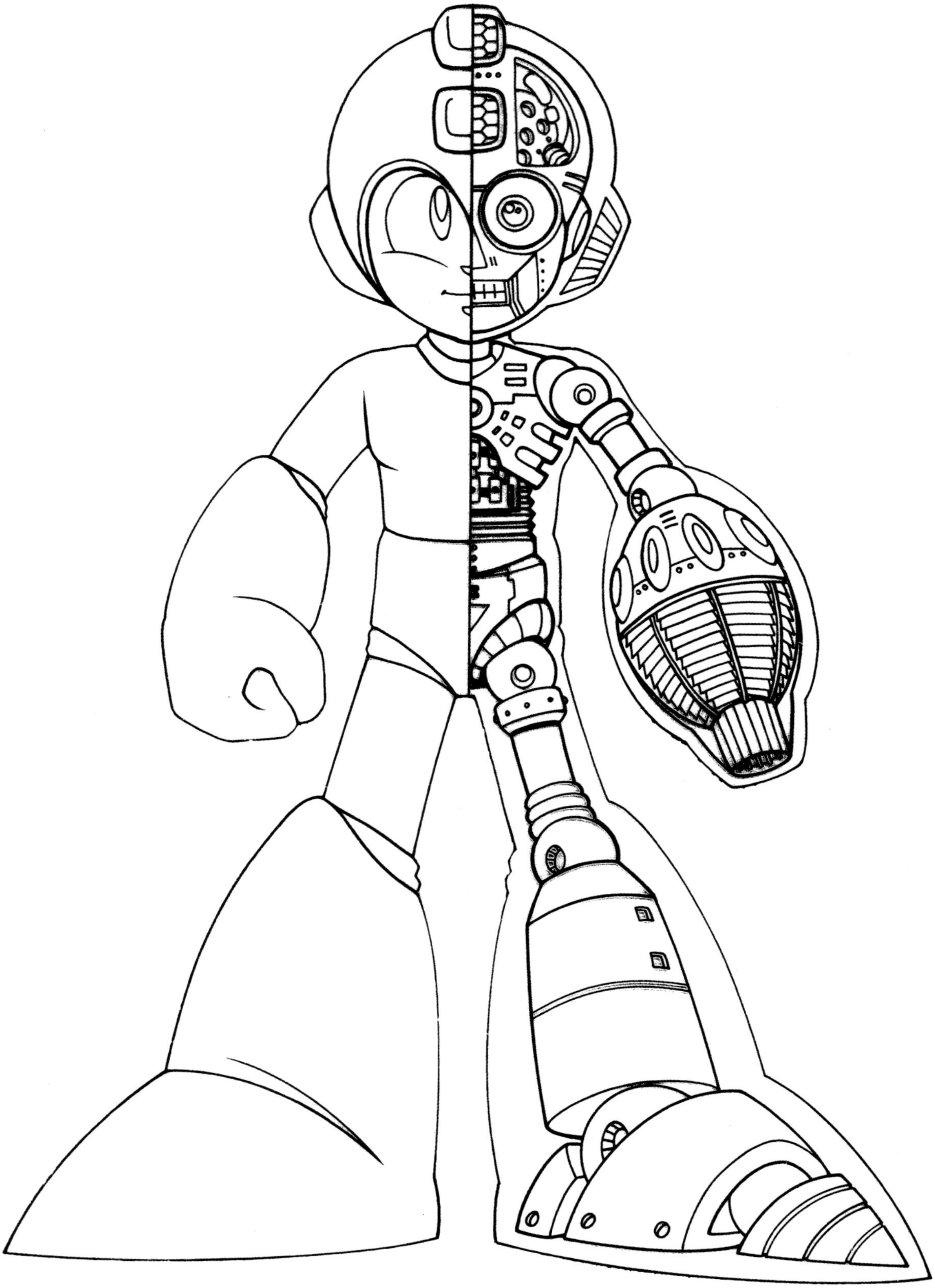

R20: ROCKMAN & ROCKMAN X OFFICIAL COMPLETE WORKS
(JAPANESE SOFTCOVER)

SPECIAL

スペシャル

To finish off this very special book, we have collected messages from the most important Mega Man series staff members, starting with Keiji Inafune. We even have a small strip by a special guest to top it all off.

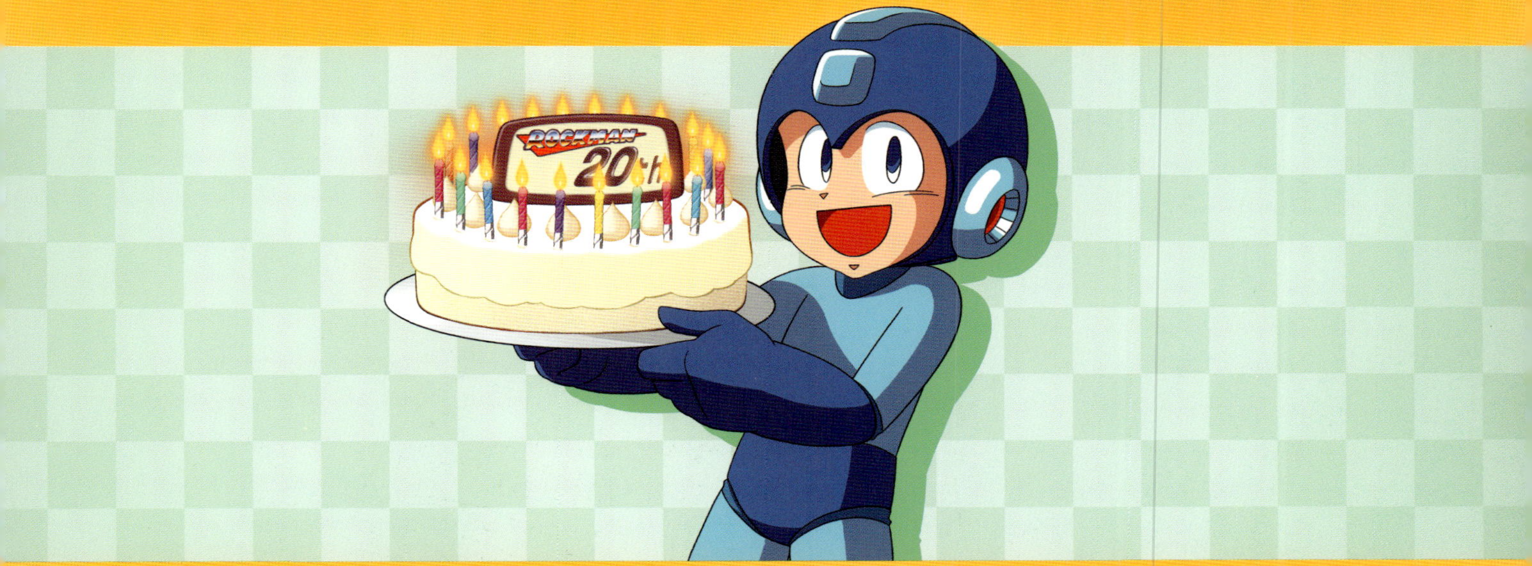

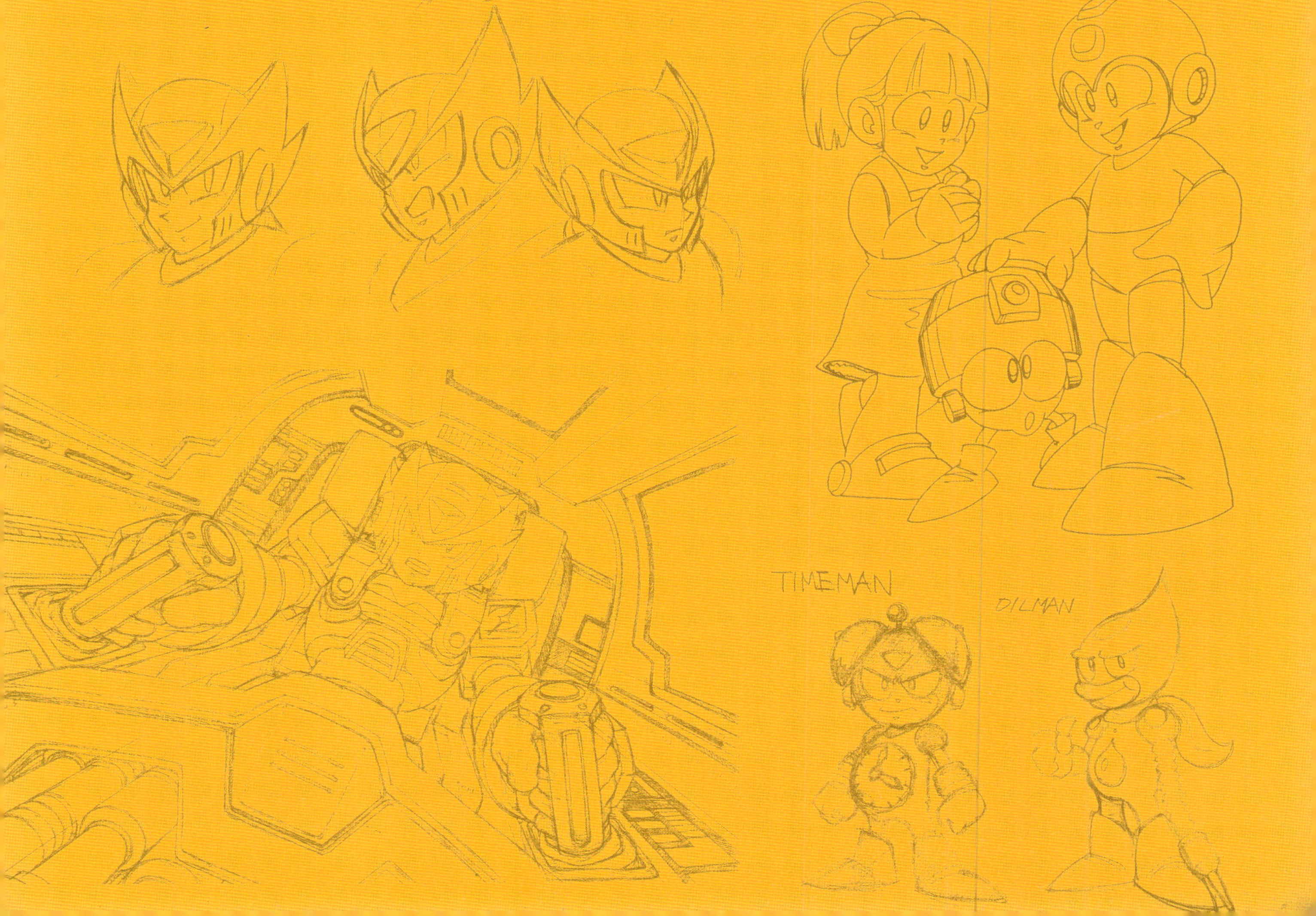

MESSAGE

Special messages from everyone who is involved in the Mega Man series, starting with the general producer, Keiji Inafune.

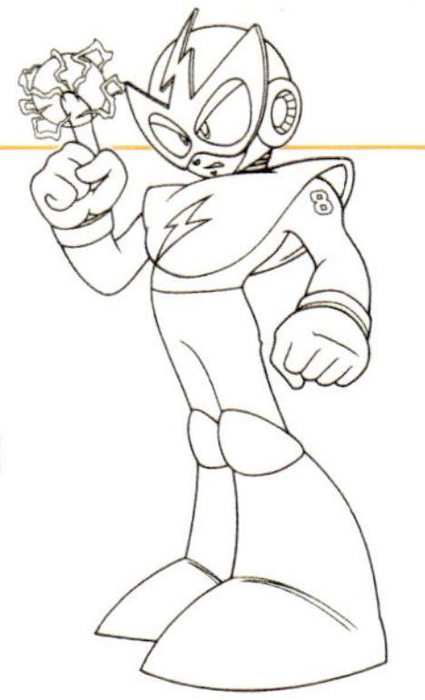

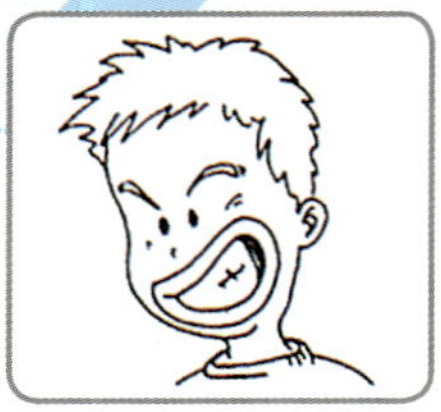

*Inafune self-portrait
(from the "Grand Rockman Exposition" Secret File)

稲船敬二 KEIJI INAFUNE

WE HOPE OUR FANS WILL HAVE PATIENCE AND LOOK FORWARD TO THE FUTURE WITH US.

THE FANS MADE US WHO WE ARE.

To be honest, when I first started drawing Mega Man, I wasn't giving any thought towards what the kids of the time (1987) might like. All of my early designs were based off of my childhood memories... the heroes and robots that I looked up to. I guess you could say that I was new to it all and didn't have the luxury of considering the feelings of our players, but the truth is I was simply self-centered while I was making the first game. All I was concerned about was what I thought was "cute" or "fun."

This mindset changed somewhere around Mega Man 3 and Mega Man 4. When I saw all of the postcards that came in for the boss character submissions, it really made me realize how important our players were to what we were doing.

So many fans attended our 20th anniversary event (the one held in Tokyo and Ikebukuro on November 18th, 2007)! It was so heartwarming to know that people still loved "the Mega Man of olde" in this day and age. This only made it more important to me that we stay loyal to our fans as we move forward with the series.

The company environment has changed a lot from the time we started working on Mega Man. Back in the day, the workplace didn't feel like a "company," but more like an "after school club." This sort of environment had both an upside and a downside.

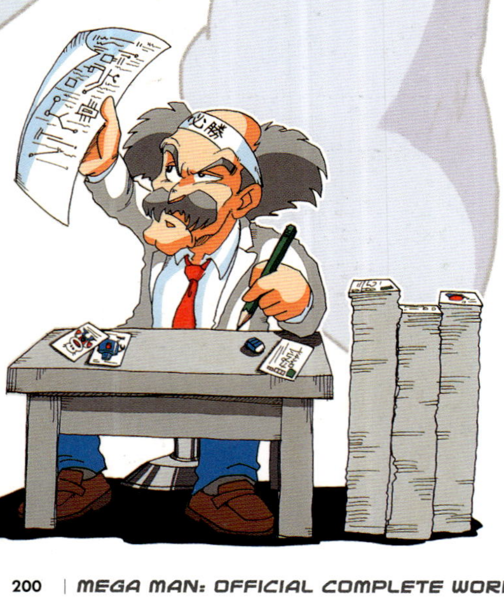

I HOPE FUTURE GENERATIONS INHERIT OUR OLD-SCHOOL IDEALS FOR GAME DESIGN.

For me personally, the perks of those days included the fact that I had more creative freedom with my work. The lack of time, money, and tools was not so great. Still, work was really fun. We weren't constantly worried about whether the game we were making would sell or not... it was all about the challenge of trying new things! That was the best feeling of all.

Don't get me wrong, though. It's not like I'm saying working at Capcom is boring or torturous... quite the contrary, actually. All of the things that make Capcom a great place to work haven't changed since day one. I do admit, though, that the "home away from home" vibe isn't as dominant as it used to be. As Capcom took shape as a company, I think it became more robotic in certain aspects, out of necessity.

Mega Man was a game all about robots, but the people working on it were the truest examples of humanity. It's interesting to think that you can manipulate such realistic human avatars in modern games, but the people and the processes behind the creation of the games have somehow become more mechanical. I understand that with large-scale games, there is a need for such mechanical precision and efficiency, but I do hope to bring back some of the "old style" game designing to this industry.

There are so many different formats for games now, including mobile games and electronically purchased games. In the face of these advancements, I feel it's more important than ever to create games that feel familiar and accessible.

Certain games, like Mega Man, have a very passionate and intense fanbase. I think that is really great, and I think such fans deserve to have games that are catered to their preferences. Certainly, massive games have their appeal, but classic games have their own unique charms as well. I'd like to bring old style games to our current players through the modern formats.

The people who have been around since the early age of Mega Man -- and those who can appreciate the games from that timeframe -- have faded away one by one over time. I'll keep doing what I can to keep the flavor of classic games alive while infusing it into future titles.

MEGA MAN WAS MADE BY FANS, FOR FANS.

If time would allow, I'd love to redo all of the Mega Man titles I've had a hand in so far. I guess that's my dream... to work on Mega Man in a relaxed atmosphere, without all of the stressing and rushing.

I'm very fortunate that there are so many people who love and want to work on Mega Man within Capcom. I think it would be awesome if I could gather them together in one place! We wouldn't let anyone who doesn't know or has never played Mega Man into our little club! (laughs) If that were possible, I think we'd have the greatest project ever on our hands.

The only problem with this idea is that we would probably end up with a "hobby" game. Such games are really well made, but you end up not being able to produce much in the way of quantity, and that results in higher prices. I think most people are familiar with toys that are like that. Still, I think it would be interesting to make a game like that.

I guess what I'm trying to say is that we, the creators, have all the same hopes and dreams that our players do, so I'd ask that our fans have patience with us while we crank out our next big thing. In the meantime, I hope they'll consider revisiting the old favorites listed in this book. (laughs)

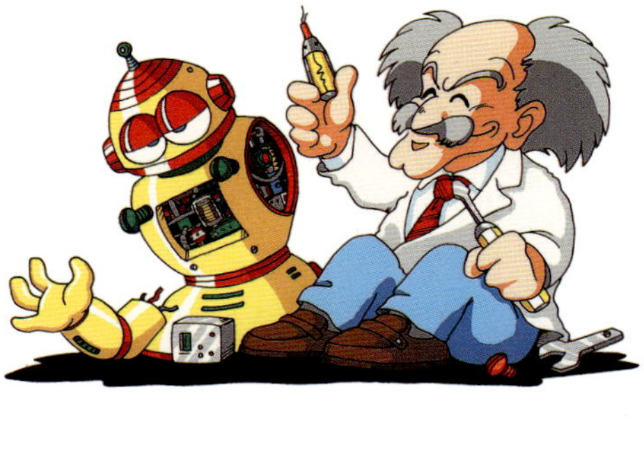

HAYATO KAJI

I feel like I've worked on at least half of everything that is Mega Man since joining Capcom, so I do have a lot of emotional attachment to the games. At first, I thought it was just some kids' game, but seeing the original fans continue to love the game even as adults really makes me realize just how epic this series is.

HARUKI SUETSUGU (SENSEI)

Whenever you are going through hard times and you feel like you might give in, just remember... you stood up to Sigma, one of the biggest, baddest bad guys ever, and you won. This is the message that I hope the players will take away with them, and keep with them forever.

TATSUYA YOSHIKAWA

I love Mega Man as much as, if not more than, any of the hardcore fans out there. If I ever get another opportunity to work on a Mega Man project, I'll be there without question. As long as someone out there continues to believe, I will too... so I hope the fans won't quit cheering us on any time soon.

RYUJI HIGURASHI

We always said Mega Man will be born in the year 20XX... and now, that time is closer than ever. Let's all do our part to protect our Earth so that we can hold our heads up high when we meet Mega Man for the first time, for real. We are all heroes, each and every one of us! I... don't think I'll be around to meet X (born 21XX), though.

SHINSUKE KOMAKI

I feel blessed to have had the opportunity to work on Mega Man, a character who's managed to attract a passionate and supportive fanbase, for over a decade after I joined Capcom. I hope my fellow fans and I will have the chance to continue supporting Mega Man for a good long while yet.

HIDEKI ISHIKAWA (ILLUSTRATOR)

Many of our Mega Man fans are all grown up and have children, who I hope are also Mega Man fans. Since we made it this far, I sincerely hope we will live to see grandchildren who are also Mega Man fans! I want us to have the opportunity to pass this passion on to a new generation of young people.

YOSHIHISA TSUDA (INTI CREATES CO. LTD.)

Thanks entirely to the warm support of the fans, the character Mega Man still exists today. No matter how much time passes, no matter what new formats might come along, as long as there are kids in the world who desire the fun of a video game and a hero role model, the spirit of Mega Man will live on forever.

SHO TSUGE (FORMERLY OF CAPCOM)

"And you as Mega Man X" ... this phrase is from the "X1" ending, and is my favorite thing out of all the work I have done. (laughs) I wonder what the players were feeling in that instant, as Mega Man X?

SHIGETO IKEHARA (MANGA ARTIST)

Mega Man has always reminded me of one of my favorite characters, Astro Boy. I really enjoyed drawing my Mega Man manga, and it also marked my first foray into the world of CG. I had so much trouble, though, because my machine was pretty much a piece of junk. The Mega Man manga is one of my most memorable projects, as the experience I got from it opened up all kinds of new potential in my work. I'll always keep it close to my heart.

YOSHIHIRO IWAMOTO (MANGA ARTIST)

My Mega Man X manga is a product of the support of so many people. I am just so grateful to the readers, the game and manga staff members, and to the whole Mega Man X series. Thank you all so much.

KOJI IZUKI (MANGA ARTIST)

I kind of fell into this whole thing, rushing in to try and pick up where the artists who came before me left off. As hard as I tried, I wasn't able to convey the total wonder and awesomeness that is Rock in my work. Instead, I feel like he taught me all kinds of things. Thanks, Rock! Truly, thank you so much.

YUSUKE MURATA SPECIAL GUEST

Seventeen years ago, when this manga artist was still in school, he sent in boss character submissions for Mega Man. Two of his submissions were actually used for Mega Man 4 and 5, and we came to know them as Dust Man and Crystal Man. Currently, he is working on Eyeshield 21 (originally by Riichiro Inagaki), a series that is running in Shueisha's "Shonen Jump" magazine.

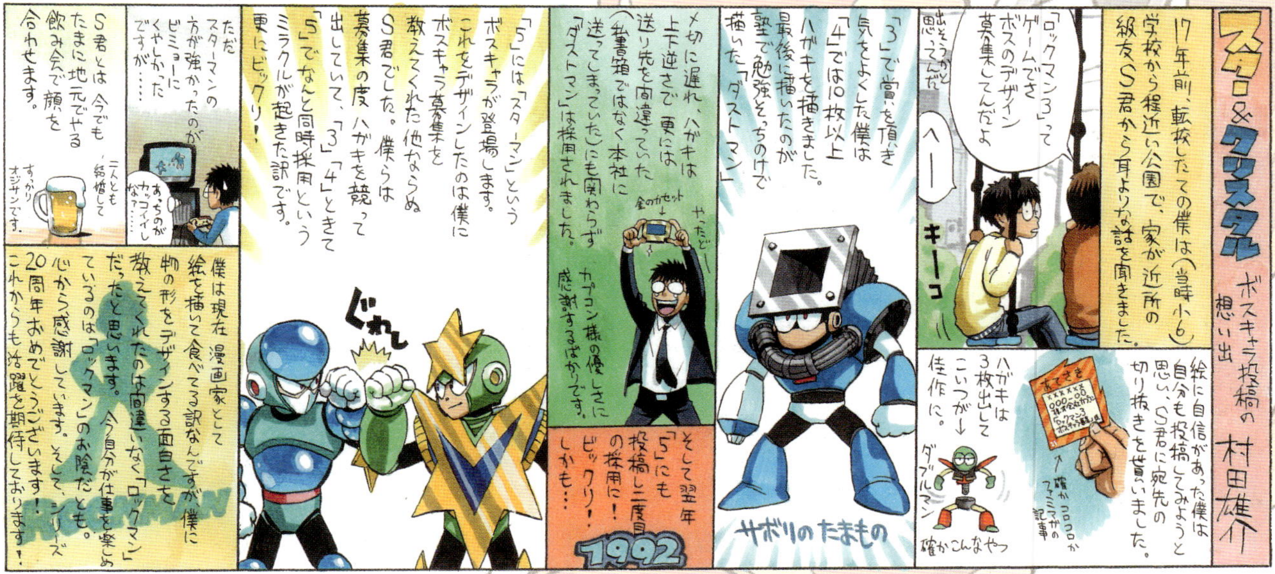

TRANSLATION:

STAR & CRYSTAL
YUSUKE MURATA

SEVENTEEN YEARS AGO, I WAS TRANSFERRED TO A NEW SCHOOL. I WAS IN 6TH GRADE AT THE TIME. ONE DAY, I WAS AT THE LOCAL PARK WHEN MY CLASSMATE "S" MENTIONED SOMETHING HE THOUGHT I MIGHT FIND INTERESTING.

THEY'RE ACCEPTING SUBMISSIONS FOR "MEGA MAN 3" BOSS CHARACTERS. I'M THINKING ABOUT SENDING SOMETHING IN.

COOL.

I LIKED TO DRAW, AND CONSIDERED MYSELF TO BE PRETTY GOOD. I DECIDED TO SEND SOMETHING IN, AND GOT THE CONTACT INFORMATION FROM S.

I SENT IN THREE SUBMISSIONS, AND THIS GUY WAS MY BEST CHARACTER: *DOUBLE MAN*

THEY GAVE ME AN AWARD FOR MY MEGA MAN 3 SUBMISSIONS, SO WHEN IT CAME TIME TO MAKE SUBMISSIONS FOR MEGA MAN 4, I SENT IN OVER TEN. THE LAST ONE I SENT IN WAS *DUST MAN*, A CHARACTER I DREW UP IN CLASS WHILE I WAS DOING MY BEST NOT TO LEARN ANYTHING.

I MISSED THE DEADLINE, DREW UPSIDE DOWN ON THE POSTCARD, AND SENT IT TO THE WRONG ADDRESS. (I ADDRESSED IT TO THE MAIN COMPANY ITSELF INSTEAD OF THE SPECIFIC DEPARTMENT.) CAPCOM NOT ONLY ACCEPTED MY SUBMISSION, BUT ACTUALLY USED MY IDEA IN THE GAME!

THE FOLLOWING YEAR, I SENT IN SUBMISSIONS FOR MEGA MAN 5, AND ANOTHER ONE OF MY SUBMISSIONS WAS USED! I COULDN'T BELIEVE IT! BUT THAT WASN'T ALL...

STAR MAN, ANOTHER ONE OF THE BOSS CHARACTERS IN MEGA MAN 5, WAS A DESIGN SUBMITTED BY NONE OTHER THAN MY OLD FRIEND S. WE HAD BEEN COMPETING WITH EACH OTHER EVERY TIME WITH THE NUMBER OF SUBMISSIONS WE SENT IN, AND WE FINALLY MADE IT INTO A GAME TOGETHER IN MEGA MAN 5. IT WAS A MIRACLE! THE SURPRISES JUST KEPT ON COMING.

BUT I WAS A LITTLE JEALOUS THAT STAR MAN LOOKED COOLER THAN MY GUY...

LOOK AT HIM...

I STILL MEET UP WITH S EVERY NOW AND THEN FOR A DRINK.

WE'RE BOTH MARRIED NOW.

YEP, WERE OFFICIALLY OLD GUYS.

DRAWING STUFF IS HOW I MAKE MY LIVING NOW, BUT I GIVE FULL CREDIT TO MEGA MAN FOR TEACHING ME THE JOY OF CREATING SOMETHING OUT OF NOTHING. I ALSO BELIEVE THAT MEGA MAN IS THE REASON WHY I ENJOY MY WORK SO MUCH. I AM GRATEFUL TO MEGA MAN, FROM THE BOTTOM OF MY HEART. CONGRATULATIONS ON YOUR 20 YEARS OF SUCCESS! I LOOK FORWARD TO SEEING WHAT YOU WILL ACCOMPLISH IN THE YEARS TO COME!

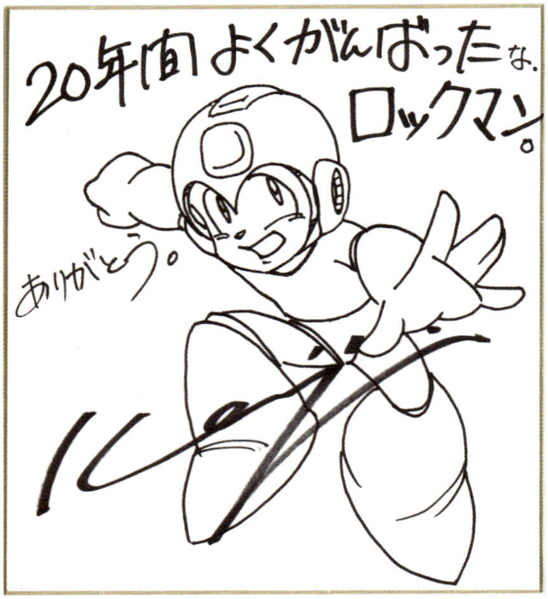

CAPCOM - KEIJI INAFUNE

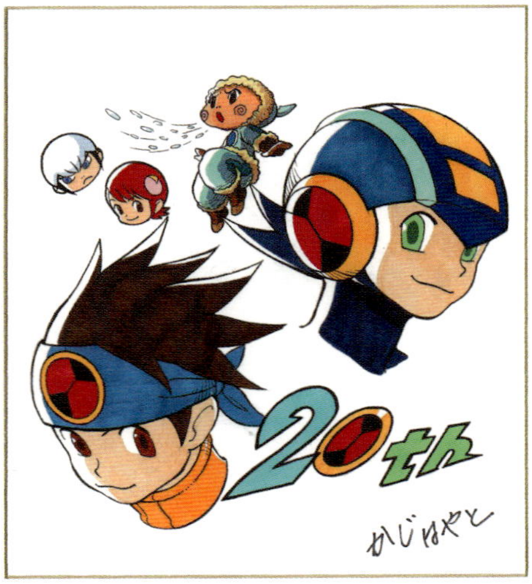

CAPCOM - HAYATO KAJI

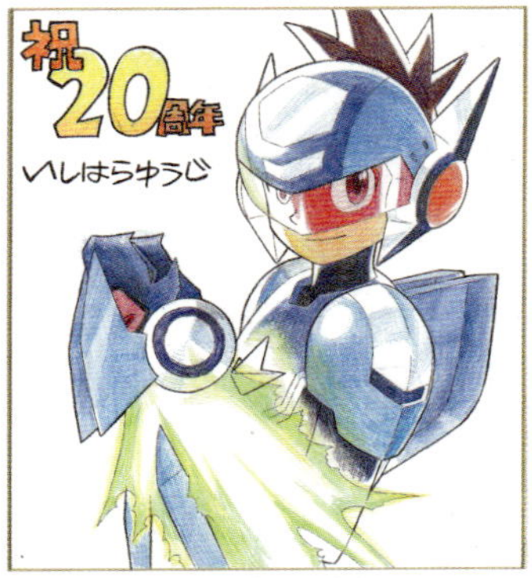

CAPCOM - YUJI ISHIHARA

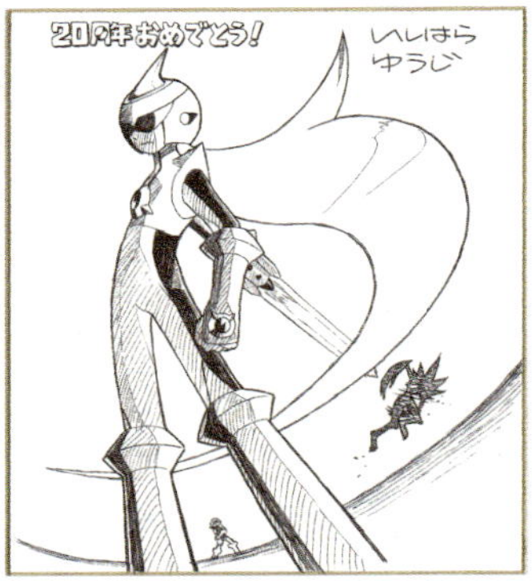

CAPCOM - YUJI ISHIHARA

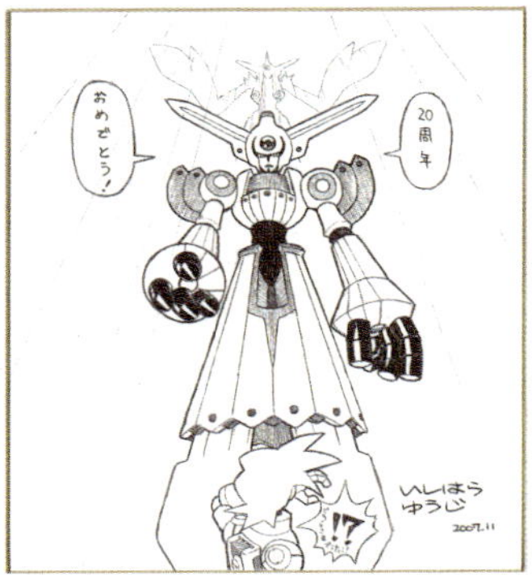

CAPCOM - YUJI ISHIHARA

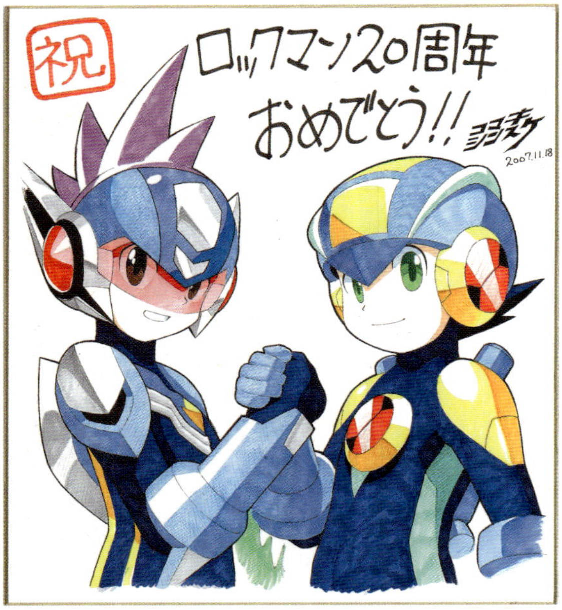

CAPCOM - SHINSUKE KOMAKI

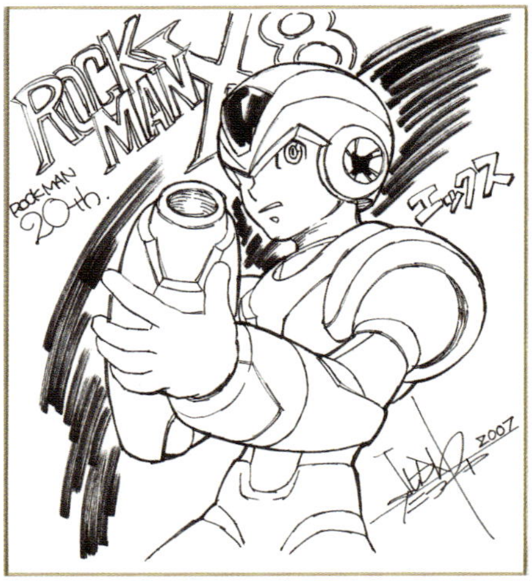

CAPCOM - TATSUYA YOSHIKAWA

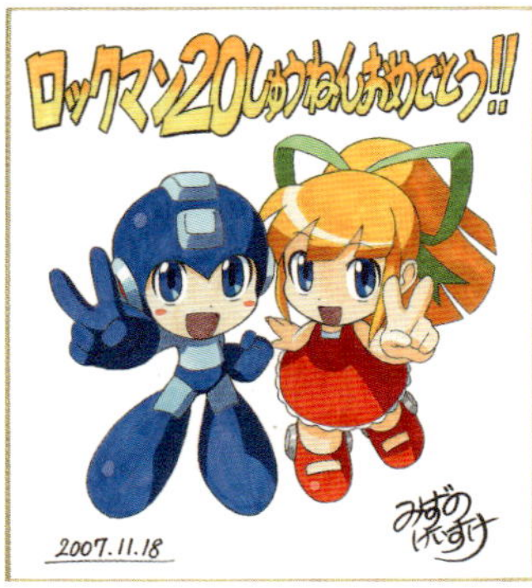

CAPCOM - KEISUKE MIZUNO

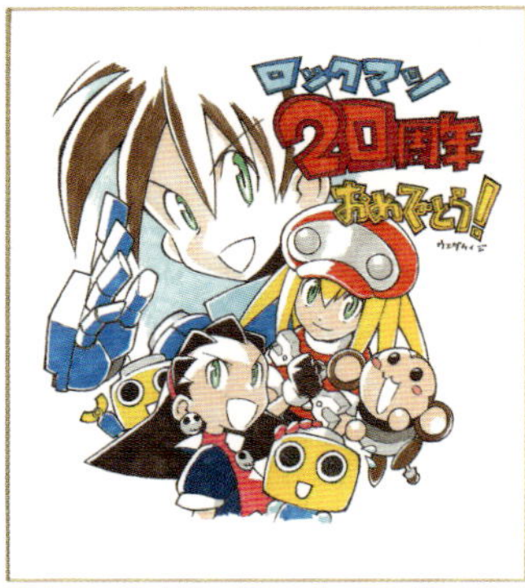

CAPCOM - KEIJI UEDA

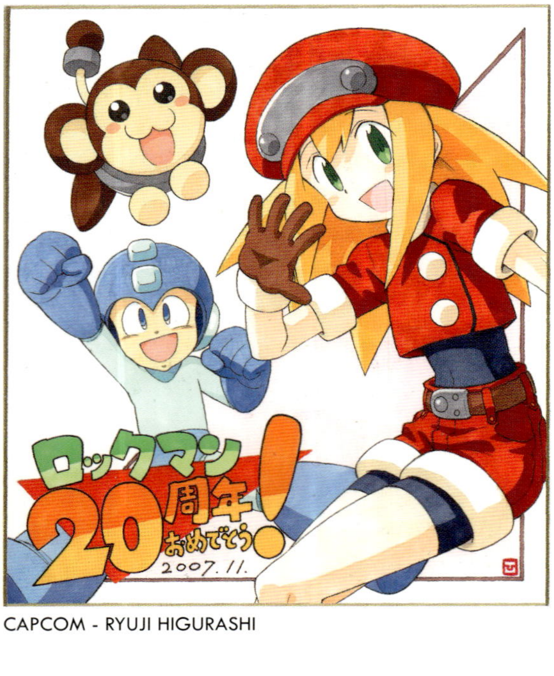

CAPCOM - RYUJI HIGURASHI

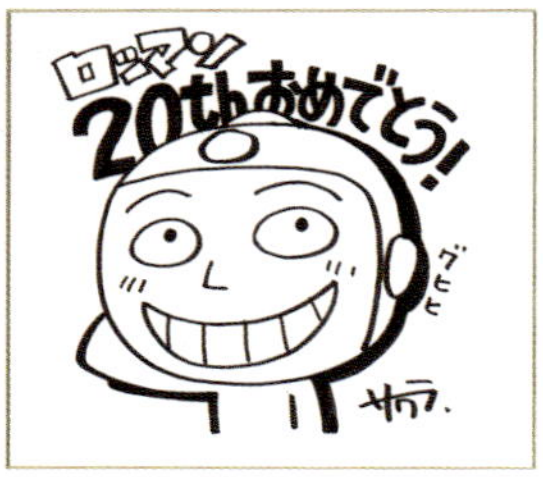

SAKURA

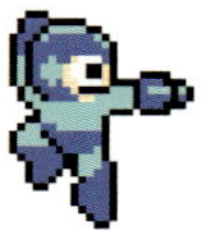

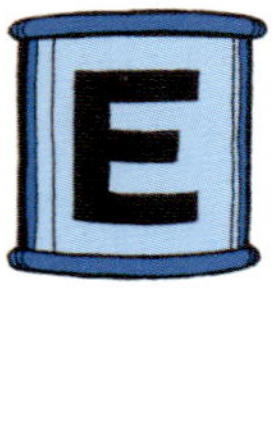

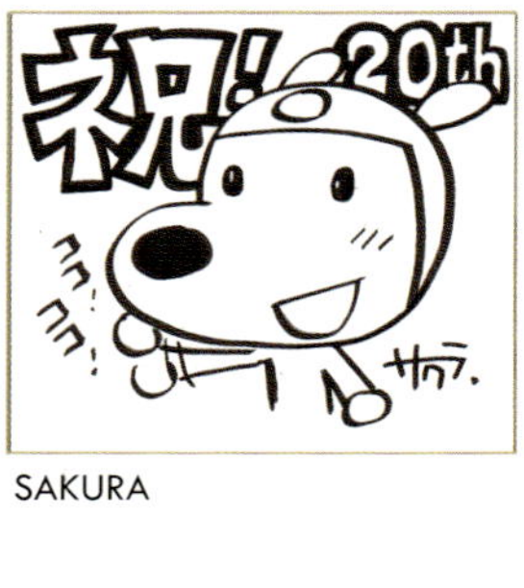

SAKURA

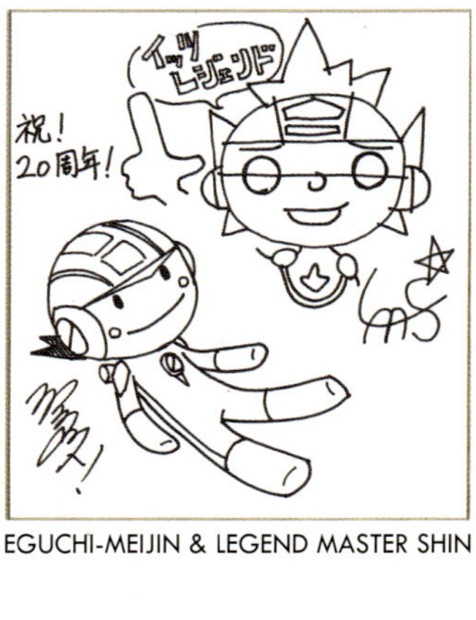

EGUCHI-MEIJIN & LEGEND MASTER SHIN

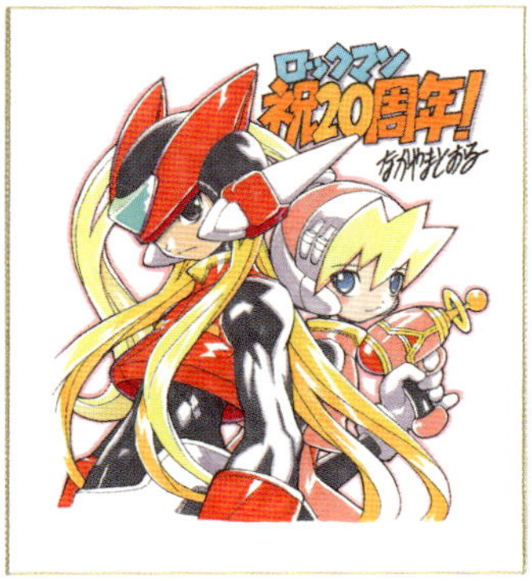

TORU NAKAYAMA

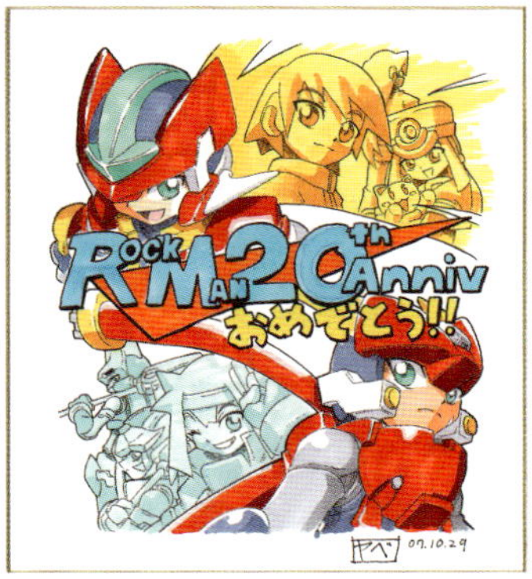

INTI CREATES - MAKOTO YABE

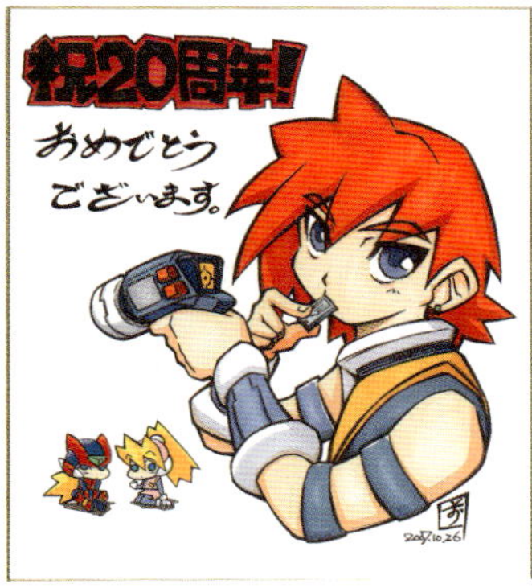

INTI CREATES - HIROKATSU MAEDA

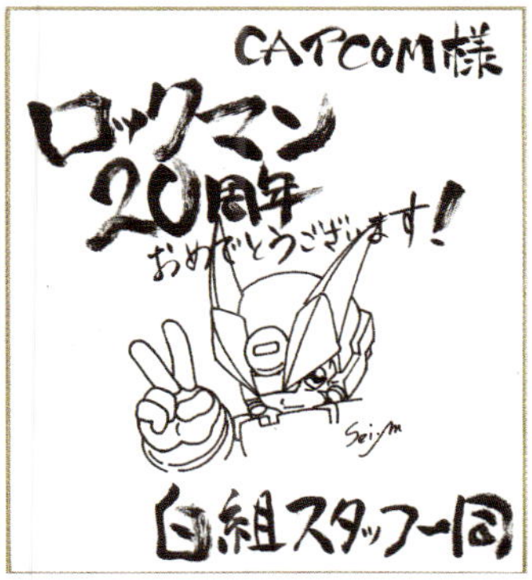

SHIROGUMI

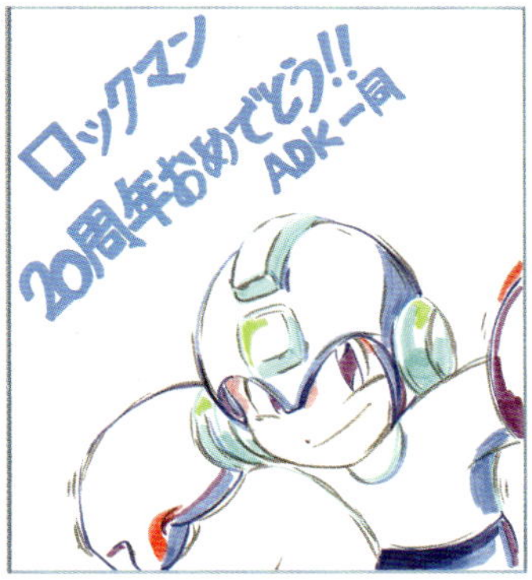

ADK

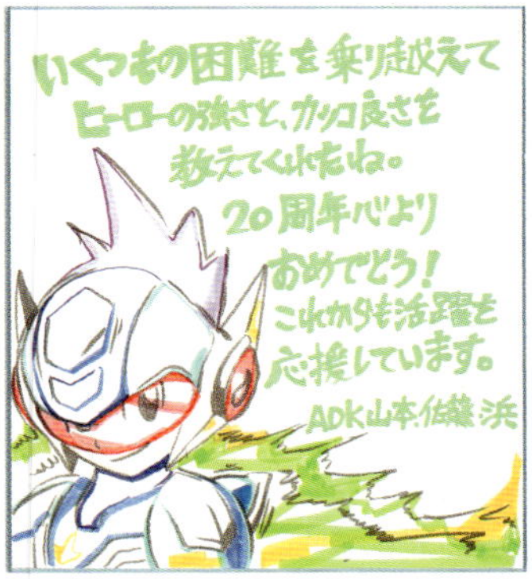

ADK

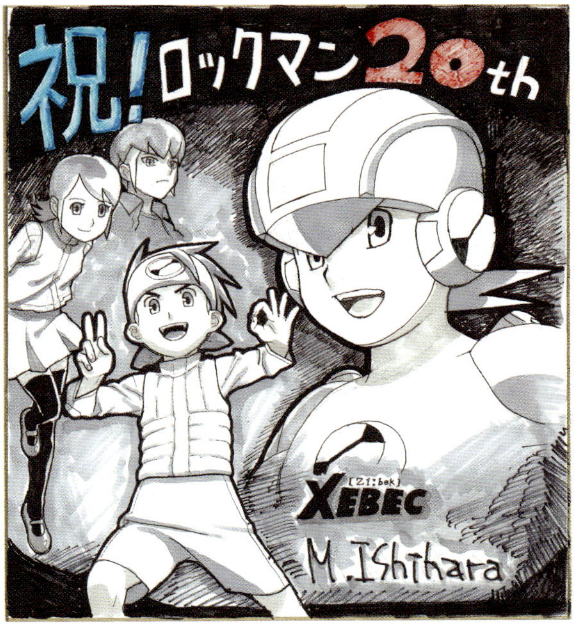

MITSURU ISHIHARA

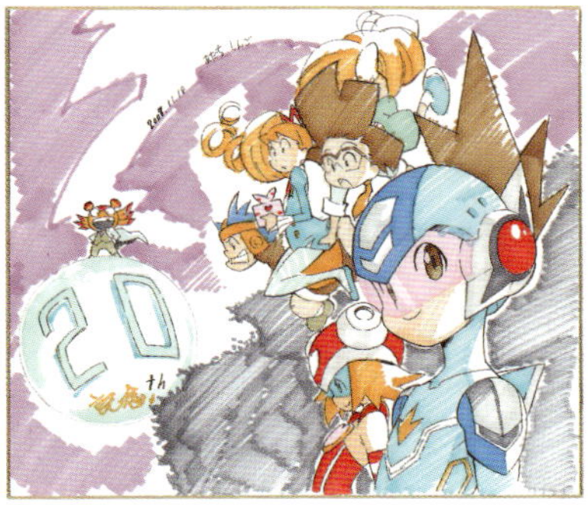
SHINGO ADACHI

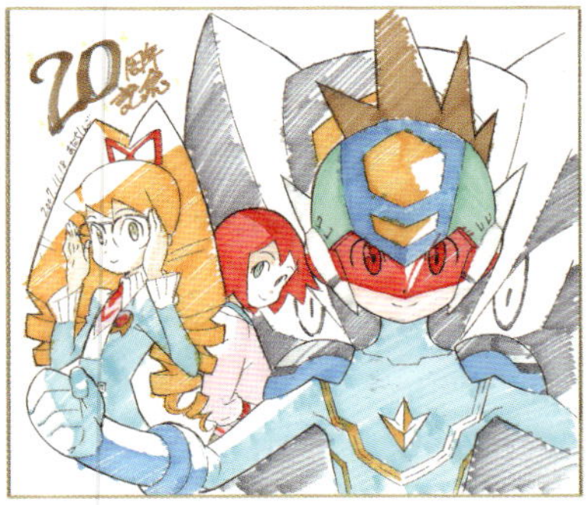
SHINGO ADACHI

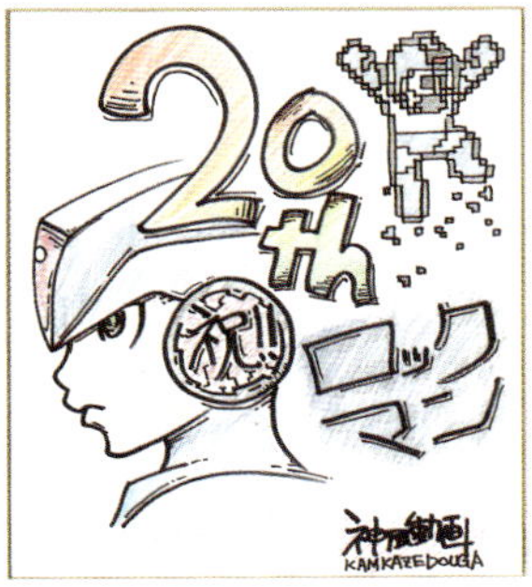

KAMIKAZE DOUGA

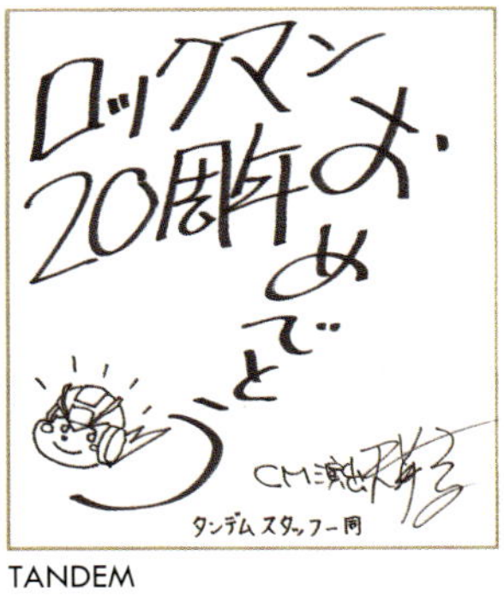

TANDEM

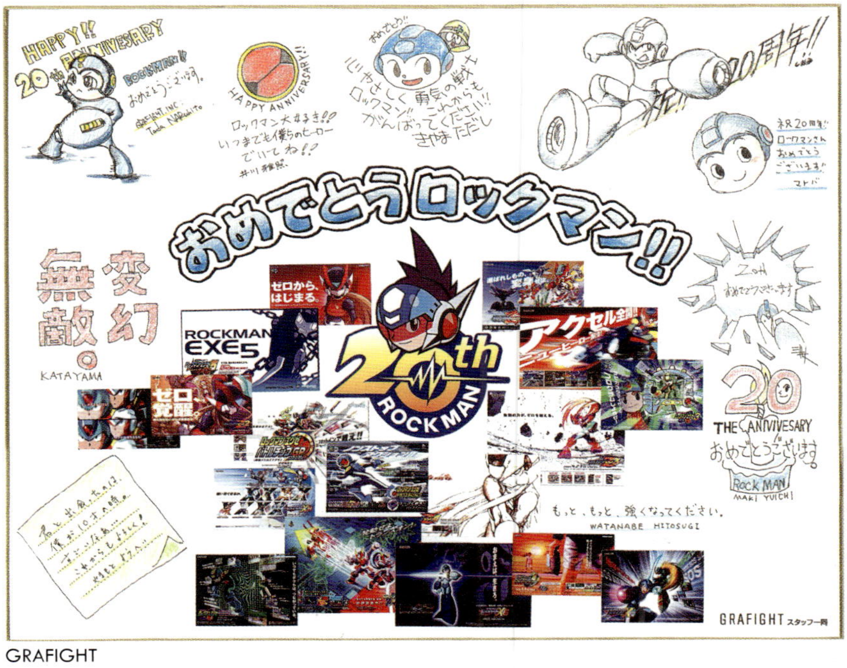

GRAFIGHT

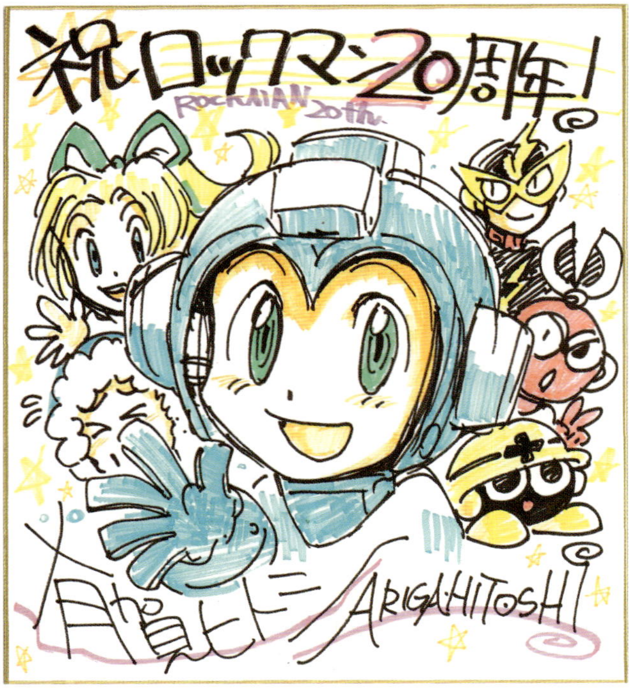

HITOSHI ARIGA

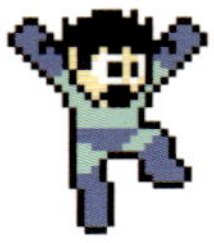

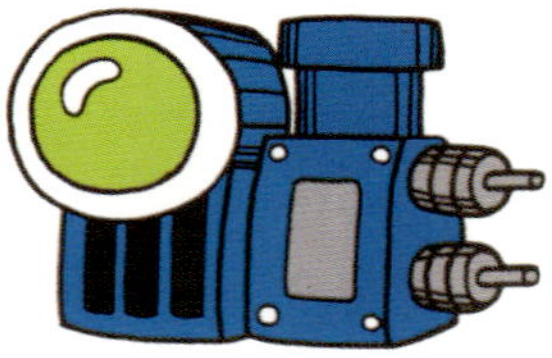

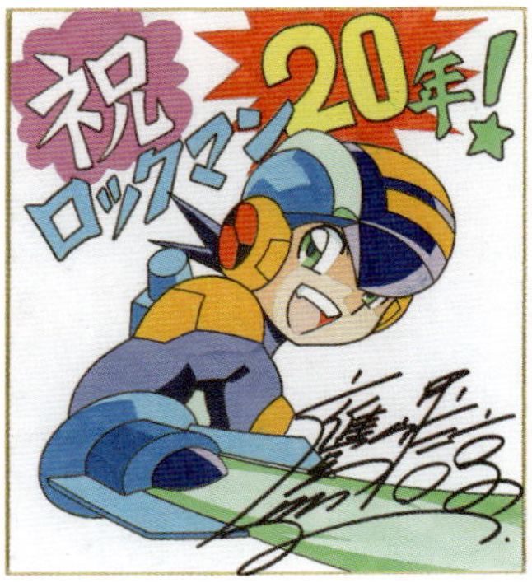

RYO TAKAMISAKI

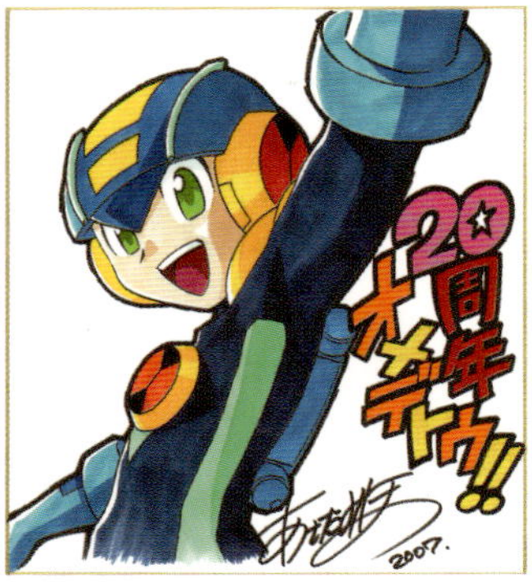

MIHO ASADA

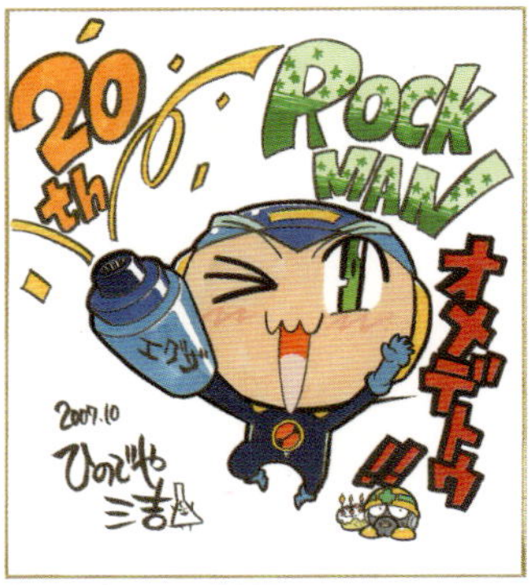

SANKICHI HINODEYA

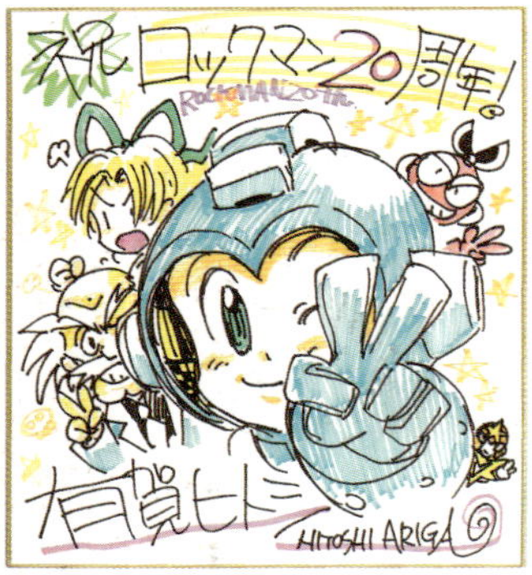

HITOSHI ARIGA

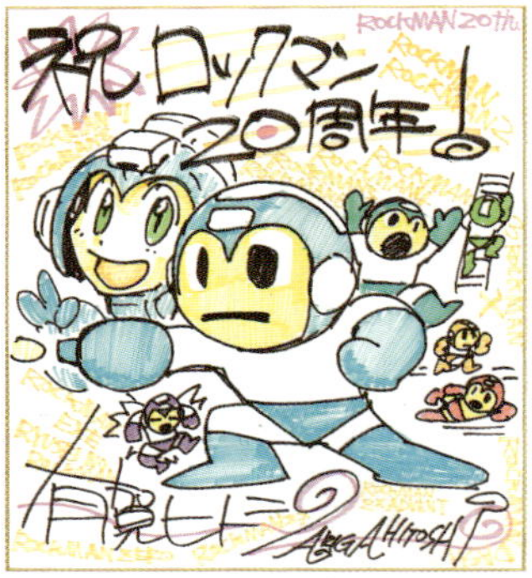

HITOSHI ARIGA

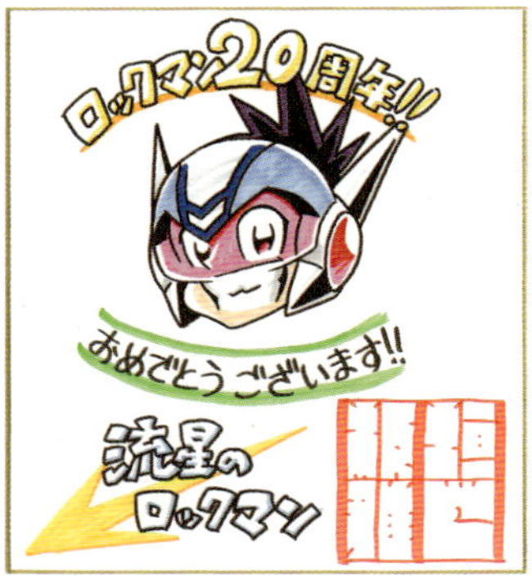

MASAYA ITAGAKI

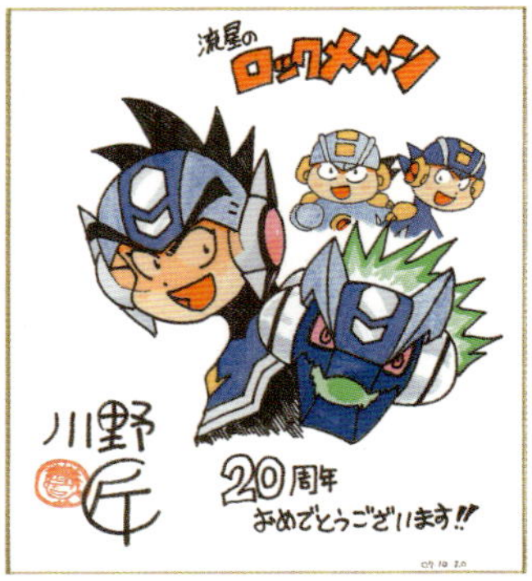

TAKUMI KAWANO

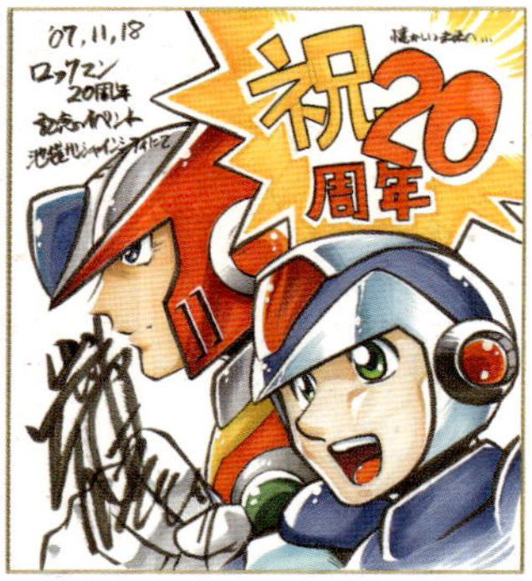

YOSHIHIRO IWAMOTO

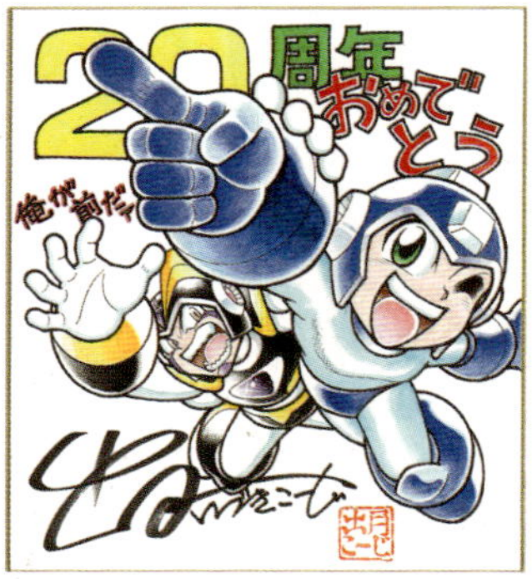

KOJI IZUKI

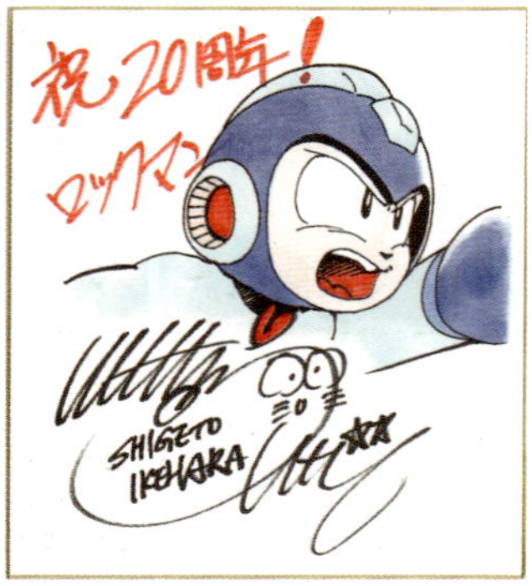

SHIGETO IKEHARA

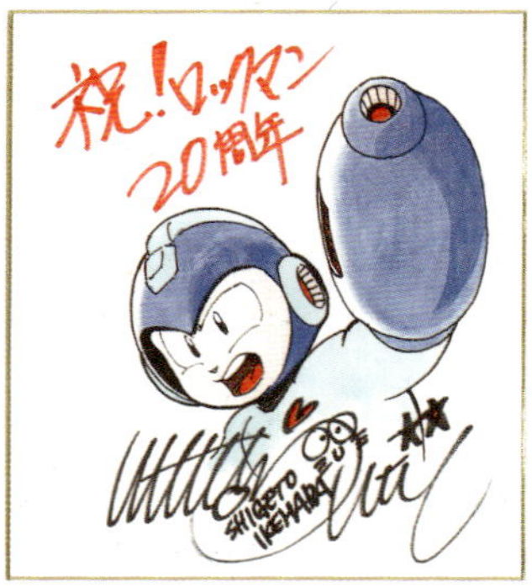

SHIGETO IKEHARA

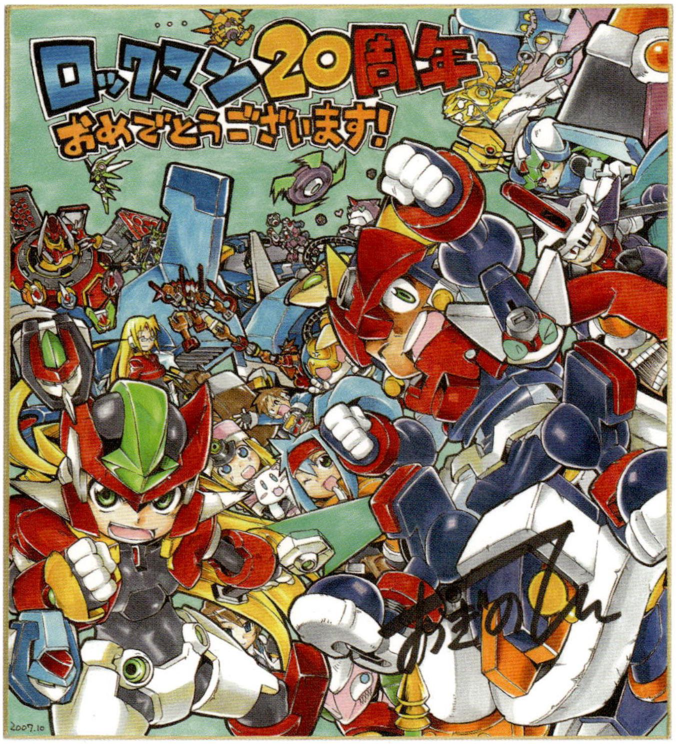

SHIN OGINO

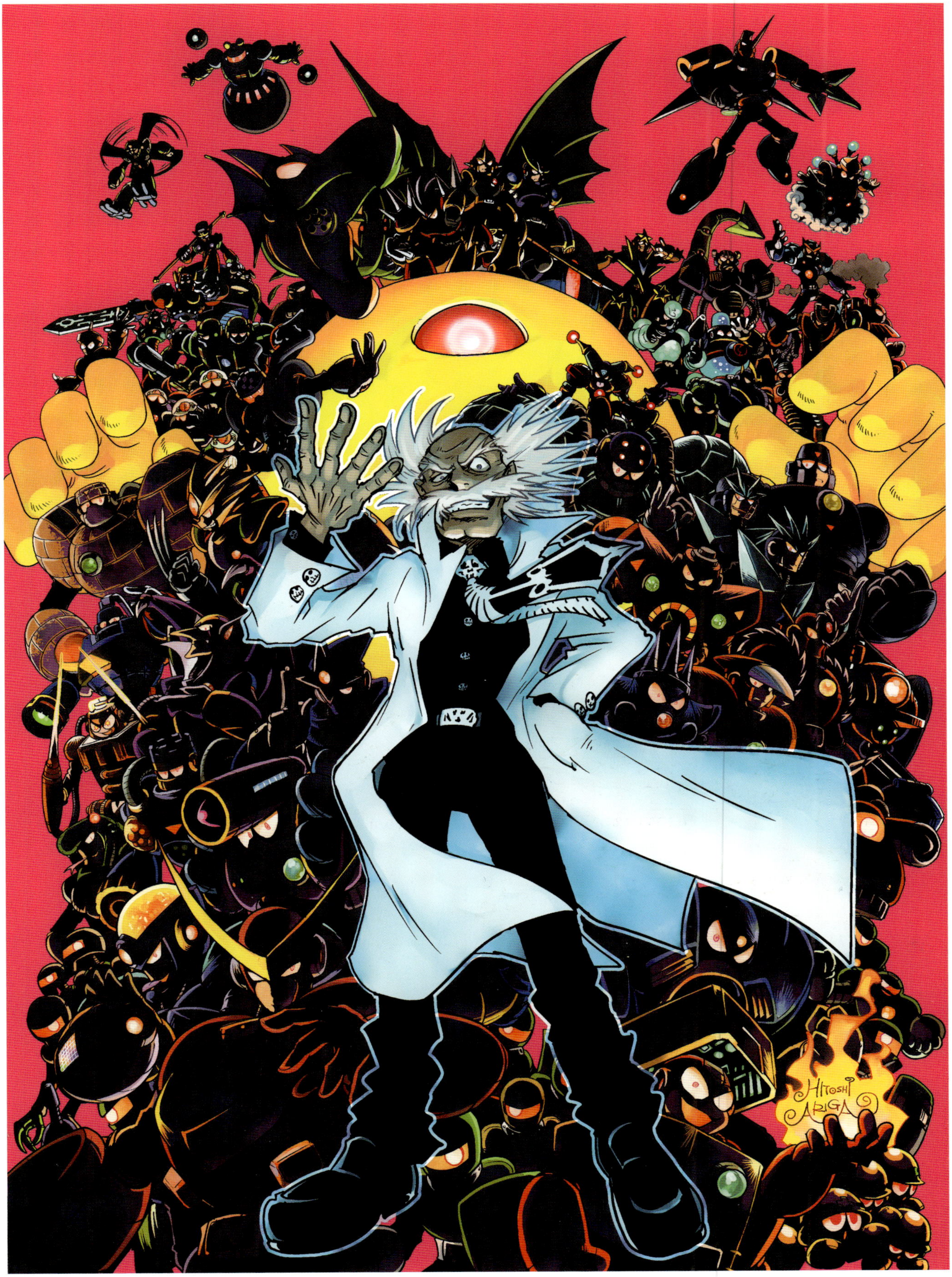

HITOSHI ARIGA (SUPERVISOR/MANGA ARTIST)

I feel so honored to have been brought in on this project. Working my way through this massive book has given me time to really feel the weight of 20 years' worth of memories. I am so grateful to everyone who took time out of their busy day to give me all of these priceless comments. As I was collecting and piecing together all of the sentiments of these people who had ties to Mega Man, I had so many laughs, nods of empathy, and tears. I had a real blast. It is my hope that this book will be enjoyed by new and old Mega Man fans alike, all over the world, for many years to come. You're the man, Mega Man!

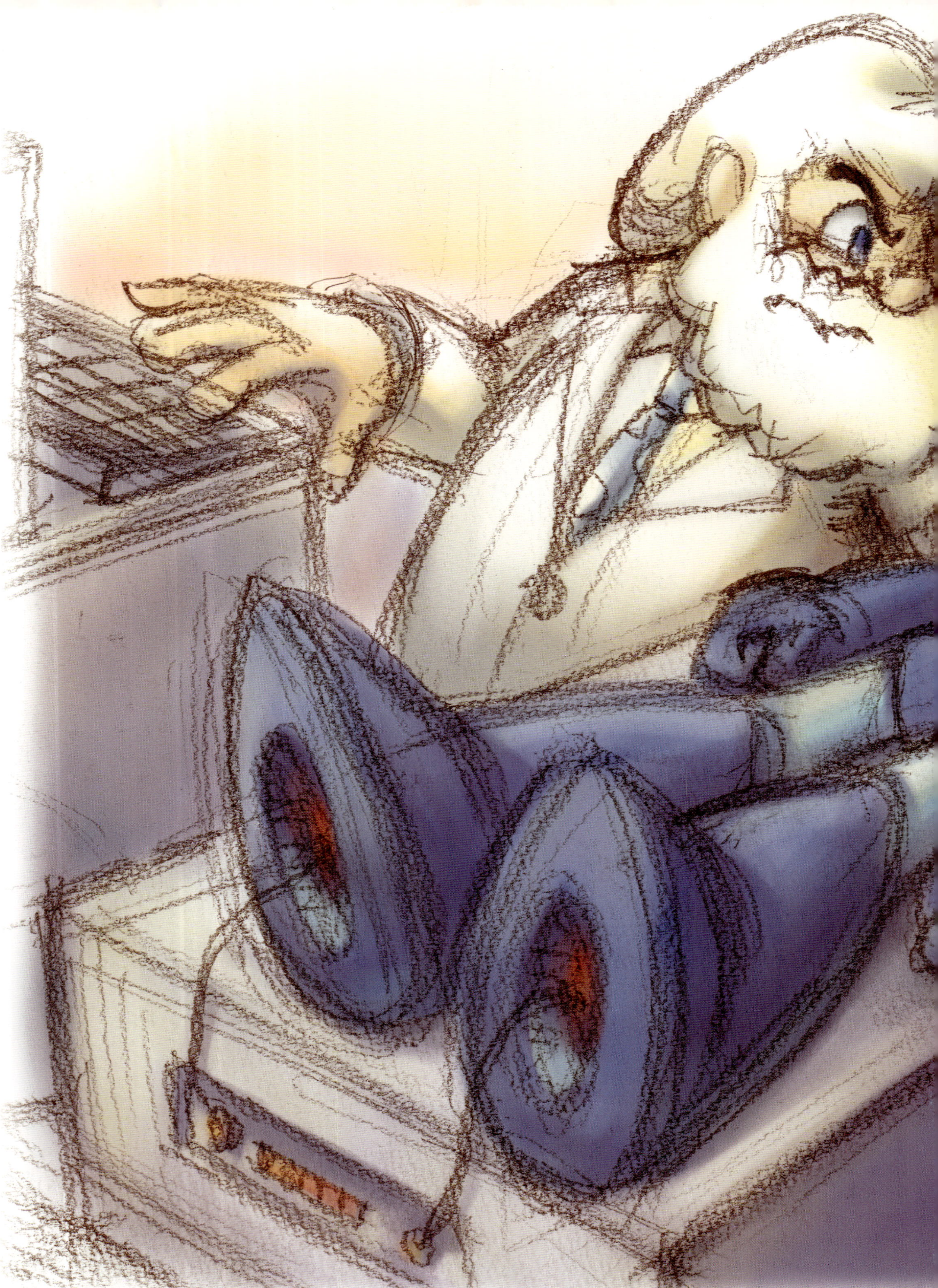

ILLUSTRATION: KEIJI INAFUNE

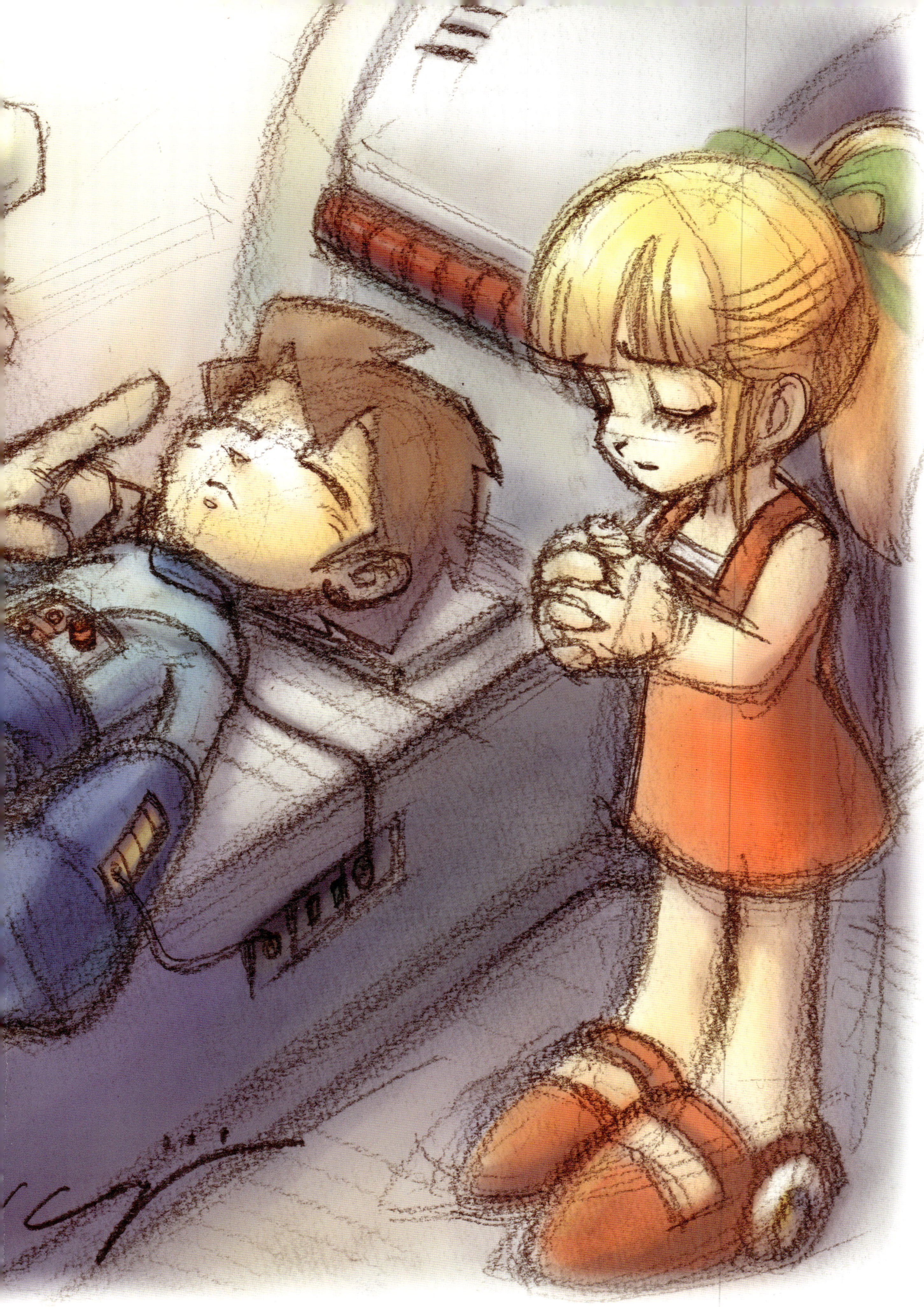

MEGA MAN
OFFICIAL COMPLETE WORKS
ロックマン オフィシャルコンプリートワークス

CREDITS - ENGLISH EDITION

ENGLISH TRANSLATION
M. KIRIE HAYASHI

LOCALIZATION AND EDITING
ASH PAULSEN

LAYOUT & DESIGN ADAPTATION
MATT MOYLAN

UDON STAFF

UDON CHIEF
ERIK KO

PROJECT MANAGER
JIM ZUBKAVICH

MANAGING EDITOR
MATT MOYLAN

EDITOR - JAPANESE PUBLICATIONS
M. KIRIE HAYASHI

MARKETING MANAGER
STACY KING

CAPCOM LICENSING

TOSHI TOKUMARU & TAKI ENOMOTO OF CAPCOM CO. LTD.
SEON KING, GERMAINE GIOIA, JOSH AUSTIN, MAYUMI RECKER,
STEVE LEE & FRANCIS MAO OF CAPCOM ENTERTAINMENT, INC.
MARC MOSTMAN OF MOST MANAGEMENT

SPECIAL THANKS TO

ALL CAPCOM STAFF
AND MEGA MAN FANS OF THE PAST, PRESENT, AND FUTURE

FIGHT, MEGA MAN!
FOR EVERLASTING PEACE!

CREDITS - JAPANESE EDITION

Editing & Publishing
株式会社カプコン

Executive Producer
稲船敬二

Editorial Supervision
有賀ヒトシ

Editor
北裏裕章

Coordinator
小林常二

Product Manager
大野哲也

Composition & Writing
株式会社ウェッジホールディングス
ブレインナビ事業部
小南英明 / 中西康哲

有賀ヒトシ

Design & DTP
有限会社ダイアートプランニング
小林歩 / 相星敬介

Supervision & Special Thanks

株式会社カプコン
加治勇人 / 北林達也 / 堀之内健 / 岡野正衛
小牧信介 / 末次治樹 / 日暮竜二 / 吉川達哉
片岩ゆり / 水野佳祐 / 佐藤真一 / 竹下博信

株式会社インティ・クリエイツ
津田祥寿 / 山田一法

石川ヒデキ / 柘植象 / 村田雄介
池原しげと / 岩本佳浩 / 出月こーじ

Published by UDON Entertainment Corp. PO Box 5002, RPO MAJOR MACKENZIE, Richmond Hill, Ontario, L4S 0B7, Canada

Printed by Suncolor Printing Co. Ltd.
E-Mail: suncolor@netvigator.com

First Printing: September 2009
ISBN-13: 978-1-897376-79-9
ISBN-10: 1-897376-79-0

Printed in Hong Kong

www.capcomcomics.com
www.udonentertainment.com